Richard Strauss

D0209685

149909

WILLI SCHUH

Richard Strauss: a chronicle of the early years 1864–1898

TRANSLATED BY MARY WHITTALL

780.92
S9122s

CAMBRIDGE UNIVERSITY PRESS
Cambridge
London New York New Rochelle
Melbourne Sydney

Alverno College
Library Media Center
Milwaukee, Wisconsin

Published by the Press Syndicate of the University of Cambridge
The Pitt Building, Trumpington Street, Cambridge CB2 1RP
32 East 57th Street, New York, NY 10022, USA
296 Beaconsfield Parade, Middle Park, Melbourne 3206, Australia

Originally published in German as *Richard Strauss: Jugend und frühe Meisterjahre. Lebenschronik 1864–1898* by Atlantis Musikbuch-Verlag Zürich/Freiburg i. Br. 1976 and © Atlantis Musikbuch-Verlag AG Zürich 1976

First published in English by Cambridge University Press 1982 as *Richard Strauss: a chronicle of the early years 1864–1898*
English translation © Cambridge University Press 1982

Printed in Great Britain at the University Press, Cambridge

Library of Congress catalogue card number: 81–12200

British Library Cataloguing in Publication Data

Schuh, Willi
Richard Strauss, a chronicle of the early years, 1864–1898
1. Strauss, Richard
2. Composers-Germany-Biography
I. Title II. Richard Strauss, Jugend und frühe Meisterjahre. *English*
780′.92′4 M4410.S93

ISBN 0 521 24104 9

Dem Andenken meiner geliebten Frau
Nelli Schuh-Keller (1901–1976)

Contents

Illustrations

Acknowledgments

All the photographs are from the Richard Strauss Archives, Garmisch, except for the following: p. 45, Dr Franz Trenner, Munich; p. 46, Universal Edition, Vienna; p. 54, Dr Willi Schuh, Zürich; pp. 38 and 394, Catalogue of the Richard Strauss Exhibition, Munich; p. 367, Karl Henckell, *Mein Lied*, Bard-Marquardt, Berlin, 1906.

Preface

> Why don't people see what is new in my works, how in them, as is found otherwise only in Beethoven, the human being visibly plays a part in the work . . .
>
> (Richard Strauss, 19 June 1949)

To begin with a personal note: the completion of this account of the life of Richard Strauss from 1864 to 1898 has been delayed for many years for a number of reasons. It was not the quantity of the material alone but also, and more significantly, professional burdens and recurrent bouts of illness, sometimes quite grave, which long hindered the exploration and processing of the documents, most of which are now in the Richard-Strauss-Archiv in Garmisch in Upper Bavaria, where they are in the devoted care of the composer's daughter-in-law, Frau Alice Strauss. It proved necessary, furthermore, to wait until some larger files of letters – especially letters to and from Strauss – became available. The more their number grew – there are now many tens of thousands – the more difficult became the imperative task of selecting material from them for direct quotation in this biography. I had always to bear in mind that a lot of Strauss's correspondence – that with his parents, Bülow, Thuille, Wüllner and others – had already been published, as well as two editions of the composer's recollections and reflections; on the other hand, familiar material could not be passed over altogether, but had to be included in its proper place in the chronicle. Nevertheless, whenever it seemed justified, precedence was given to previously unknown material. When no reference to a source is given in either the notes or the bibliography, the material quoted is housed in the Strauss Archives in Garmisch (either in the original or in a photo-copy).

My original intention was to discuss both the life and the work of Richard Strauss, but the present volume is confined to the life, and – so as not to overflow all bounds – particular attention is focused on those aspects of the life which are of significance in the development of the man and the artist. Priority was also given to documentation relating to periods and episodes in Strauss's life and career which have previously been overlooked or ignored.

The epigraph at the head of this preface is from the last comment that Strauss wrote on his work. It draws attention to the relationship between the life and the work which manifests itself quite openly at times, only indirectly at others, and at yet others only fragmentarily, but is in any event so important that there is no further need to justify a purely biographical study. Only when the circumstances of the composer's life, his experiences and his observations are known in full will it be possible to view the relationship of life and work more clearly. A chronicle of the life is the essential basis for answering questions as to when, where and how Strauss used 'personal experiences in conjunction with the free play of the imagination' (to the present author, 30 July 1946).

The compositions are discussed here only in their place in the chronology. The complexity of Strauss's scores – at least from *Don Juan* onwards – demands detailed critical analysis, such as is already to be found in Richard Specht's *Richard Strauss und sein Werk* (Vienna, 1921), in dissertations on individual works – pre-eminently and exemplarily Reinhard Gerlach's *Don Juan und Rosenkavalier, Studien zu Idee und Gestalt einer tonalen Evolution im Werk Richard Strauss'* (Bern, 1966) – and in Norman Del Mar's monumental *Richard Strauss, a critical commentary on his life and work* (3 volumes, London, 1962–72); the operas have been the subject of special studies by William Mann (London, 1964) and Anna Amalie Abert (Velber, 1972), and Alan Jefferson has published a monograph on the songs (London, 1971). Another book to be mentioned in this context is Ernst Krause's *Richard Strauss, Gestalt und Werk* (first edition Leipzig, 1955; subsequently numerous revised editions and translations into Czech, Russian, English and Rumanian).

Max Steinitzer's biography of Strauss (1911; seventeen editions by 1927) is an indispensable source for the period of his life covered in the present volume, and two other publications of the greatest value to me were Franz Trenner's selection *Richard Strauss, Dokumente seines Lebens und Schaffens* (Munich, 1954), and the memoirs of the composer's sister, Johanna von Rauchenberger-Strauss (*Richard-Strauss-Jahrbuch* 1959/60, Bonn, 1960).

The thematic catalogue begun by Erich H. Mueller von Asow and completed by Alfons Ott and Franz Trenner (3 volumes, 1955–74) gives exhaustive information about the individual works, and the bibliography edited by Oswald Ortner, Franz Grasberger and Günter Brosche lists nearly 3500 titles in its two volumes covering the years 1882 to 1964; readers will therefore find at the end of the present volume only a concise (but complete) list of the works up to 1898 (using the numbering of the Asow thematic catalogue) and a very brief bibliography including more recent publications and some of the more important sources drawn on in the text. Details of other sources are given in the notes. In the text and in the notes the Asow thematic catalogue is referred to as AV (*Asow-Verzeichnis*).

Most of the literature about Strauss is concerned primarily with his compositions, and in the nature of things new biographical material has been included only incidentally. The present chronicle of the life is intended to fill a gap in the literature, and places the accent on documentation, first and foremost on the composer's letters but also on his working notes, his drafts and scenarios, his diaries, memoirs and similar material. The narrative does not undertake any psychological or other forms of interpretation, but is content with the more modest role of commentary when it appears necessary for comprehension. Strauss's letters, especially those addressed to his parents and his sister, are so spontaneous, they reflect his reactions to events and impressions so immediately and frequently in such forthright language – while revealing the opposing poles in his nature, inherited from father and mother – that comment is often superfluous. Sometimes, however, notably in the case of the excerpts from his correspondence with Cosima Wagner, explanation and some evaluation seemed desirable.

It also seemed desirable to give as complete an account as possible of the many years of work Strauss devoted to his first opera. *Guntram*'s lack of success should not diminish the important role it played in the composer's development. The scenarios for other music dramas which he drafted during and following the time of his work on *Guntram*, the unsuccessful attempts to write a Volksoper about Till Eulenspiegel and an opera set in Schilda without Till, the plan to write a Singspiel (*Lila*, on a text by Goethe), which made considerable progress only to be abandoned – all these deserve to be described in some detail, for they demonstrate more clearly than has been done hitherto that, in spite of the rapid succession of symphonic tone poems, Strauss's doggedly pursued goal was the fulfilment of his artistic ideals in the lyric theatre.

The conducting engagements he was asked to carry out, especially in the second half of the 1890s, when he was in demand all over Germany and abroad as well, also enhanced his reputation as a composer. Together with his work at the Munich Court Opera, they also gave him the chance to champion the works of the composers he held most dear, above all Beethoven, Berlioz, Liszt and Wagner. While listing every single concert would involve too much wearisome repetition, it seemed important to include the programmes of some of the most outstanding of them, since the choice of items illustrates the single-mindedness with which Strauss followed his musical principles.

My work on this book has extended over many years. At all times I have had free access to the Strauss Archives in Garmisch, and I would like to express my heartfelt gratitude to the composer's son, Dr Franz Strauss, and even more to his wife, Frau Alice Strauss, who has made it one of the most important tasks of her life to arrange and add to the material in the archives, and has at all times been ready to give information and undertake useful research.

Dr Franz Trenner has taken a close interest in my work from the first and has been tireless in transmitting valuable information: to him too my sincere thanks. Dr Kurt Dorfmüller, Dr Karl Dachs and Dr Robert Münster have shown great kindness in assisting my access to the numerous Strauss documents in the Bavarian State Library in Munich, and I recall their help with gratitude, along with that of Dr Alfons Ott (former director of the City Music Library in Munich) and of Herr Gerhard Ohlhoff. I have pleasant memories too of the composer's sister, Frau Johanna von Rauchenberger-Strauss, with whom I had many an illuminating conversation about her brother's childhood.

Dr Martin Hürlimann, the founder and former director of Atlantis-Verlag, has fostered my work with the liveliest interest from the beginning, and Dr Daniel Bodmer, the proprietor and director of Atlantis Musikbuch-Verlag, has assisted it in its final stages with every conceivable kind of advice and practical help. I am particularly indebted to them both for their encouragement and also for their patience! My thanks also to Frau Marigna Gerig for the great understanding, interest and care with which she prepared the manuscript from tapes dictated by myself.

Finally it is with the deepest gratitude that I commemorate my dear wife, who bore the burden of the labour with me for decades, gave me the strength and was ready to make countless sacrifices. She saw the completion of the manuscript, but not the appearance of the published book, which I dedicate to her memory.

Willi Schuh
Zürich, 1976

Translator's acknowledgment

Excerpts from Richard Strauss and Romain Rolland: *Correspondence*, edited and translated by Rollo Myers (London, 1968), are used by permission of John Calder (Publishers) Ltd.

1

Family background and early childhood

Franz Strauss and the Wagner years in Munich

The year 1864, in the middle of which – on 11 June – Richard Strauss was born in Munich, was a historic one in the musical life of the city. The arrival there in May of Richard Wagner after the dramatic change of fortune which made him the favourite of King Ludwig II – who had just come to the throne at the age of eighteen – marked the beginning of those passionately fought battles that raged not only round the person of the composer but also round the new musical world set out in Wagner's works and theories. The distrust which the people of Munich felt for Wagner himself, for his influence on their idealistic and inexperienced young king, for his reputation as an 1848 revolutionary, but also for the whole conduct of his life, was reinforced by the resistance customarily met by all innovation. The 'artwork of the future' propagated by Wagner and by the assistants whom he summoned to Munich – above all by Hans von Bülow – ran headlong into the *genius loci*, the principal feature of which was stubborn tenacity blended with a propensity for self-satisfaction.

The most prominent figure in musical life in Munich at the time of Wagner's arrival was the sixty-one-year-old royal director of music, Generalmusikdirektor Franz Lachner (1803–90). As principal conductor and trainer of the Court Orchestra, which played for both the Court Opera and the subscription concerts of the Musical Academy, he was the founder of the excellent reputation enjoyed by those twin centres of musical gravity in the Bavarian capital, and he was also greatly admired as a composer, particularly for his songs and for the orchestral suites in which he paid tribute to the tradition of Bach and Handel. He it was 'who raised the Munich

Opera to the heights which made it the worthy exponent of the artistic ideals of a Richard Wagner' (Hans Wagner), but although the orchestra was solidly behind him he was unable to withstand the onslaught of the forces embodied in Wagner and Hans von Bülow. Thrust into the background, he applied for his pension; he was at first granted leave of absence, but retired permanently at the beginning of 1868. Hans von Bülow, who was appointed Hofkapellmeister in April 1867, enjoyed only a short but brilliant career in Munich. Its climaxes, the first performances of *Tristan und Isolde* (1865) and of *Die Meistersinger* (1868) and the concerts he conducted with the Musical Academy, served to draw the attention of the entire musical world not to Wagner alone but also to the extraordinary capabilities of the Munich orchestra. Bülow returned to Munich from time to time as guest conductor, but under Franz Wüllner, who, against Wagner's will, had conducted the first performances of *Das Rheingold* (1869) and *Die Walküre* (1870), and Hermann Levi, who initially shared the conducting of the Academy Concerts with Wüllner but directed them alone from 1870 to 1888, until his health compelled him to restrict his conducting to the opera house, the musical life of the Bavarian capital returned to calmer waters.

There were a number of excellent musicians in the Munich Court Orchestra. One of its outstanding members was the first horn Franz Strauss, Richard's father, who was with the orchestra for more than forty years, from 1847 to 1889.[1] His musical and personal authority was so great that he exercised a kind of moral leadership which it was not uncommon for him to put to use in opposition to a conductor's tempos or interpretations. The Musical Academy elected him 'controller' in 1854, he became professor at the Royal School of Music in 1871, and in May 1873 he was appointed 'Kammermusiker' (literally a 'musician of the chamber', a title conferred by the king in recognition of outstanding musical merit). In 1878 he and the bassoonist Christian Mayer were elected to the artistic committee of the Musical Academy. He quite frequently appeared as soloist in Academy Concerts and occasionally – when his asthma made horn-playing too difficult – played the viola in the orchestra and in the Mittermaier Quartet, which enjoyed a high reputation. He also conducted two amateur orchestras. He was rewarded for his services to musical life in Munich with the Ludwig Medal for Learning and Art in May 1879.

Richard's father, Franz Strauss

Richard's mother, Josephine Strauss-Pschorr

When Hans von Bülow was preparing the first performances of *Tristan* and *Die Meistersinger* with the Munich Court Orchestra, Franz Strauss was the active leader of the orchestra's opposition, which gave not only the conductor but Wagner himself many a bitter hour. When it came to playing, Strauss performed his duties with exactly the same conscientiousness and artistic perfection that he brought to the classical masterpieces. The man whom he so implacably opposed, Hans von Bülow, honoured him with the title 'the Joachim of the Waldhorn'. Wagner called him an 'intolerable blighter', who could be pardoned for everything as soon as he started to play. Bülow and his leading opponent in the orchestra never lost their mutual respect, since each acknowledged the other's integrity and musical ability. Although tempers flared at the end of rehearsals or performances, during which the horn-player was obedient to the 'whims' of Bülow's baton, according to Strauss's memoirs of Bülow 'the mixture of mutual admiration and conflicting artistic principles had the most extraordinary effect on the further course of the relationship between the two men'.[2] The opposing sides in the Wagnerian controversies that shook musical Munich to its core were not composed of anything so simple as a genius on one side and the ranks of Philistia on the other, but rather both sides were supported by the devout adherents of different musical creeds; nevertheless, personal elements undoubtedly increased the tensions. Bülow's acid sarcasm was met with Bavarian self-confidence and Bavarian bloody-mindedness. The unaccustomed technical and musical demands of Wagner's music must have helped to harden attitudes, since Bülow had not mastered the routine of a regular operatic conductor and 'with his endless rehearsals and his north German bite he gave the Munich orchestra, used only to the "bajuvarian" vulgarity of someone like old Franz Lachner, a bellyful of his beloved Wagner'. Richard Strauss's memoirs of his father contain a number of episodes in which Franz Strauss came into headlong collision with both Bülow and Wagner himself, which are as entertaining as they are characteristic of the men involved.[3]

Franz Strauss continued to regard Bülow with a certain, albeit grudging, respect, in spite of their practical differences, and even after Bülow had left Munich again, but his hostility towards Wagner was obdurate and unconditional. Horn-player and composer confronted each other for the last time in the summer of 1882, when

Strauss was taking part in the rehearsals of *Parsifal* in Bayreuth. (He did so only as a personal favour to Hermann Levi, who had shortly before launched Richard's career as a composer by giving his D minor Symphony its first performance at one of the Musical Academy's subscription concerts.) In a letter to his wife Franz Strauss gave vent once more to his abhorrence of the man he called 'the Mephistopheles of music':

> You can have no conception of the idolatry that surrounds this drunken ruffian. There is no ridding me now of my conviction that the man is ill with immeasurable megalomania and delirium, because he drinks so much, and strong liquor at that, that he is permanently intoxicated. Recently he was so tight at a rehearsal that he almost fell into the pit.

Even Wagner's death did not reconcile his old enemy to him. When Hermann Levi broke the news to the Munich Court Orchestra at a rehearsal in February 1883 and invited the players to stand as a mark of respect, obstinate to the last, Franz Strauss remained seated.

It was in this musical atmosphere laden with high tension that Richard Strauss was born. Although the most vehement of the confrontations with Bülow and Wagner took place before Richard was four years old, he must have been aware at an early age of the extra strains placed on his father's choleric temperament by the very high demands made by Wagner's music – not least on the first horn: Franz Strauss used to describe Wagner's horn parts as clarinet parts – and by fulfilling his professional obligations in spite of profound personal reluctance. It would be an exaggeration to say that Richard's childhood was overshadowed by the great musical controversies that were raging in his immediate proximity, yet throughout his early life the omnipresent subject of conversation in his home was the impossibility of reconciling classic-romantic music with Wagnerian 'non-music'. Later, when the influence of Alexander Ritter turned Richard into a fanatical apostle of Wagner, the irreconcilables became poles, and his own personality was able to develop in the field of tension between them.

The parents

Franz Strauss was forty-one years old when he married Josepha Pschorr, his second wife, on 29 August 1863. Josepha, born on 10 April 1838, was one of the five daughters of the much respected

Munich brewer Georg Pschorr the elder (1798–1867) and his wife Juliana, née Riegg (1809–62).[4] The marriage was registered in the parish office of the Frauenkirche, the Metropolitan Cathedral of Our Lady. Their daughter Johanna von Rauchenberger-Strauss recalled that Franz Strauss had 'courted Mother for seven years. He was a regular visitor to the Pschorr household, but could never muster the courage to propose to her because of the very modest circumstances – even for those days – which were all he could offer his wife on a salary of forty-two gulden a month.'[5]

It is possible that his origins were another reason why he held back for so long. Franz Strauss was born out of wedlock on 26 February 1822 in Parkstein, a small town in the Upper Palatinate in eastern Bavaria to a young couple, then both twenty-two years old: Urban Strauss, an usher in the local courthouse, and Maria Anna Kunigunda Walter, daughter of the tower-master Michael Walter (1771–1831) and his wife Elisabeth (née Strauss). At the time of the birth Urban Strauss was doing his military service in the Von Zandt infantry regiment; he was subsequently appointed 'foot constable' and went to live in Kirchenlamitz in Franconia. Although he continued his relationship with Kunigunda Walter – they had a daughter, Friederike Antonie, in October 1828 – he did not marry her. In 1832, by which date he had risen to the rank of a brigadier of constabulary, he married a Protestant, Friederike Grässel, in Rehau near the town of Hof. The couple had seven children who were brought up in their mother's faith. When Urban Strauss died on 10 April 1859 in Burgebrach near Bamberg, he held the post of usher in the royal Landgericht (higher district court). Kunigunda Walter died in 1870. Urban Strauss never seems to have paid much attention to the two children he had by her, although he acknowledged them and they bore his name. Franz was first put into the care of his uncle Johann Georg Walter (1813–98) in the house of his mother's parents in Parkstein and was later sent to another uncle, Franz Michael Walter (1802–74), who was tower-master in Nabburg. The duties of this office included keeping look-out from the church-tower and striking the hours at night as a sign of watchfulness, and also taking charge of the parish band and ensuring that it remained at full strength by training young musicians.

It was a family of assiduous musicians. Johann Georg, the eldest son of Franz Michael, became tower-master in Nabburg in his turn, and two other sons joined the Court Orchestra in Munich, where both were in time appointed Kammermusiker. Franz's mother Kunigunda played several instruments, and his uncle Johann Georg played not only the horn, his principal instrument, but also the violin, clarinet, trumpet, bagpipes, dulcimer and guitar. Franz was only five when he started to play the violin, but in the course of an exceptionally demanding apprenticeship he also learned clarinet, guitar and every single brass instrument. He was seven when he first played for the dancing at a village wedding and nine when he himself began to teach violin, clarinet, trumpet and trombone. While he was still at school he also had to share his uncle's watches at night in the tower; he kept himself awake by doing his Latin homework, for the priest taught him Latin in spite of his uncle's opposition. At twelve he demonstrated his talent as a singer: when a soprano who was due to appear in Regensburg fell ill, he took her place and sang the 'Grâce' aria from Meyerbeer's *Robert le Diable*. His uncle was a very thorough teacher but a hard taskmaster. 'There can't be many stalls in the choir at Nabburg where I didn't receive a box on the ears, for I wept many tears there', Franz Strauss recalled in later years. The boy had to go with his uncle's band to play for numerous events in the surrounding district; long treks on foot and a night's rest on a hard bench beside the stove in an inn were nothing uncommon.

These years of travail came to an end when Franz was fifteen, in 1837, when his uncle found him a post as guitarist in the service of Duke Max in Munich. Other members of the duke's orchestra included the zither virtuoso Johann Petzmayer and two of Franz's uncles, Joseph Michael Walter and Johann Georg Walter. The duke himself also played zither in his own orchestra. In this company of musicians Franz was encouraged by his uncle Joseph to continue to improve his practical and theoretical education. He gave concerts with his two uncles when the duke did not require their services. The trio visited towns large and small and their success was such that they extended their tours as far as places in Switzerland. It was during the years Franz spent in the service of Duke Max that he recognized that the horn was the instrument which meant most to him and on which he could become a virtuoso. He began to write for the instrument, and some of his compositions were printed, including a concerto for horn and orchestra (C minor, Op. 8), two concertos for horn and piano (D♭ major, Op. 7, and E♭ major, Op. 14), a Fantasy on Beethoven's *Sehnsuchtswalzer*, a 'Nocturno' and a Romance, *Les adieux*, for horn and piano. Richard Strauss and Hugo Rüdel published some concert studies and exercises for the horn after his death. He also composed a large number of dances and marches for amateur orchestra. In 1845, the year in which he was enrolled as a citizen of Munich, Franz Strauss made a concert tour of Bavarian towns with five other wind players. Two years later he joined the Bavarian Court Orchestra, which played for the Court Opera in Munich and, in addition to that, had voluntarily constituted itself as the 'Musical Academy', in which capacity it gave an annual series of concerts.

On 28 May 1851 Franz Strauss married Elisa Marie Seiff, the daughter of the bandmaster of the First Bavarian Regiment of Artillery, who was born on 19 October 1821. The first child of the marriage, Johann Franz, born on 19 June 1852, died of tuberculosis when he was barely ten months old. In the cholera epidemic of 1854 Franz Strauss lost not only his baby daughter Klara Franziska, also at the age of ten months, but ten days later, on 30 August, his wife as well.[6]

The severity of his early life in Nabburg, and also, one may suppose, the cruel blow of fate which robbed him of wife and children after so short a time, contributed to a hardening of Franz Strauss's character. Richard Strauss said in his memoir of his father that he had been embittered by a harsh youth; in his own home he was tyrannical and given to violent outbursts of rage, and it required all the tenderness and kindness of his gentle wife to preserve the unclouded harmony of the couple's relationship, although it was based on sincere mutual love and esteem. The true extent of the suffering caused to his sensitive mother was something that Strauss was no longer able to judge, he said. He did not write his memoirs until old age, and they contain two errors: he says that his father was the son of a tower-master, whereas in fact the uncle who brought him up was a tower-master and his father was a servant of the courts; and elsewhere he writes that his father was orphaned early, whereas Urban Strauss did not die until Franz Strauss was twenty-seven years old. What is true is the statement that he had no parental home.

In this context, there is an enlightening passage in the memoirs of Richard Strauss's sister Johanna, who retained an excellent memory into great old age (she died shortly before her ninety-ninth birthday, on 23 March 1966): 'He [Franz Strauss] had an extremely hard youth behind him, without a parental home. He was brought up by a very strict uncle who, however, gave him his earliest musical training. He never spoke to us about it.' As a result his children had to fall back on what they could glean from hearsay.

Richard Strauss's mother Josepha Pschorr (or Josephine as she was always called) was sixteen years younger than her husband. Richard wrote in a memoir of her:

> My mother had always had to take such care of her nerves that, although she had a talent for poetry, she was able to read very little and often had to pay for visits to the theatre or concerts with sleepless nights. A malicious or bad-tempered word never passed her lips and she was never happier than when she could spend summer afternoons in peaceful solitude, her embroidery in her hands, in the pretty garden of my uncle Georg Pschorr's villa, where we children too foregathered after school and usually spent the evenings out of doors or playing skittles.[7]

Georg Pschorr the younger, brewery owner and a leading figure in Munich's commercial world, was Josephine Strauss's brother. His villa was on Bayerstrasse, on the site where the family firm later erected their new brewery which was destroyed during the Second World War and rebuilt after the end of the war. Johanna had this to say about her mother:

> Our dear mother, although from a well-to-do middle-class family, was of a rare simplicity, modest and undemanding. She was the special pet of her father, the proprietor of the Pschorr brewery in Munich. The brewery was still in the city in those days, at 11 Neuhauser Strasse. When my parents married a small apartment was found for them in the neighbouring Altheimereck where, on 11 June of the following year, 1864, their first child, a son, was born.

The apartment, on the second floor of 2 Altheimereck, was actually in the rear portion of the brewery building, which occupied the full depth of the block: there was a passage through from the main gate on Neuhauser Strasse (a main thoroughfare in the very heart of Munich, now a pedestrian precinct) to Altheimereck, the narrow street behind. The ground floor of the brewery, as was and is customary in Munich, was given over to the sale and consumption of the Pschorr beers. It was destroyed in the Second World War but partly rebuilt afterwards: the beer-hall is still in business on

Neuhauser Strasse, but the rear part of the main building had to make way for an office block in 1963. The façade on this side, giving on to Altheimereck, had survived the wartime destruction and bore a handsome stone plaque with a commemorative relief by Karl Killer, dated 1910, above the two middle windows of the first floor. When the new building was put up, the stone plaque was removed to the Munich Stadtmuseum, and its place taken by a sober metal one.

Early childhood

Richard Strauss's birth is recorded in the baptismal register of the Frauenkirche under the date of 20 June 1864.[8] The day after the birth Franz Strauss had written to his father-in-law:

> My heart swells with a father's joy as I do myself the honour of informing you, my dear father-in-law, that yesterday (Saturday), at 6 o'clock in the morning, my dear good little wife bestowed on me the happiness of a boy, healthy, pretty and as round as a ball, and at the same time it gives me the greatest pleasure to tell you that mother and son are both very well.
>
> My dear little boy's birth took place quite quickly and easily. On Friday evening we were still at the Cellar [the private Pschorr *Bierkeller* on Bayerstrasse] and had not the least idea that my dear wife would give birth that very same night. It was therefore an extraordinary surprise for me when I came home, a little later than Josephine and Klara, to find that the preparations for the delivery were already in hand. And so my dear Josephine suffered all through the night, until 6 in the morning when she was freed from her travail and bore me a darling baby. You may be sure, my dear father-in-law, that our little boy has given us great happiness. I think my wife has already told you that Georg is to be godfather and that, according to her wishes, our small son is to receive the name Richard Georg . . . Your grateful son-in-law Strauss (12 June 1864)[9]

Since two of the other Pschorr sisters were settled in Munich (the eldest, Marie Moralt, was married to the principal cashier of the Court Theatre, and the second, Amalie, to the Auditor General, Anton Knözinger), and their brother Georg Pschorr the younger had two sons, Richard and his sister grew up in a large and close-knit family circle with numerous cousins, aunts and uncles. About a year after Richard was born the little Strauss family left the tiny apartment on Altheimereck and moved into a roomier, second-storey flat on Sonnenstrasse, on the corner of Schwanthalerstrasse. Here, Richard's only sister, Johanna, first saw the light on 9 June 1867. The house no longer stands. In 1869, when another flat became free in the Pschorr-Haus at 3 Neuhauser Strasse (on the third floor, on the left), the family at last found its permanent home.

Strauss himself left us very scanty reminiscences about his early childhood, and apart from the passage which has already been quoted he recorded only one other thing about his mother: 'My mother says of my earliest youth that I reacted to the sound of the horn with smiles and to that of the violin with floods of tears.' His sister's memories, written down in her old age, are more informative: they tell of harmless boyish pranks and paint a vivid picture of the brother she loved wholeheartedly. Since her reminiscences are the only source we have for the earliest years some passages may be quoted verbatim:

> Richard was a remarkably beautiful child, curly-headed, lively, with sparkling eyes, which could, however, take on a rapt, dreamy expression, as a photo of him as a small boy shows . . . He was an extremely lively child and so of course his urge to be always doing something led him into all kinds of mischief.

She tells us something about the relationship between their parents, too, as well as about the relations between parents and children:

> Our father was very strict and we had a holy respect for him. But his children made him so proud and happy, as he said in every letter to his wife, and he could not exhort her often enough to keep the closest watch on them and bring them up well. In view of the rigours of his own childhood he saw this as his prime duty, while Mother was kindness in human form and was only too ready to turn a blind eye. He wrote her one of his anxious letters on 25 July 1867, when Mama had already gone on holiday in the country with us children, ahead of him: 'Dear Josephine, I beseech you to keep a close watch on Richard, so that he doesn't become so naughty and disobedient, for that might drive me to distraction. Take care not to let him have too much to do with bad children. He may be as lively and as merry as can be, but he shall not be naughty. Keep a special watch on him when you are among strangers.'

[And in another letter of 17 May 1868:]

> 'I pray to God every day that He will not visit unhappiness upon us through our children. For the only thing that stands up to all the tests of life is a firm, wholesome upbringing based on a strict but loving foundation.'

Johanna and her brother were bound by the closest ties of affection:

> When his effervescent temperament provoked our father to take stern measures my tears quickly helped to calm him down and our ever-kind Mama was able to pour oil on the troubled waters . . . One of Richard's special pleasures was when Father had time to take him to hear the band play at the Changing of the Guard at midday on the Marienplatz. Our great-grandmother Pschorr had a house there, which later fell a sacrifice to the new City Hall. Enthralled, Richard used to listen to the band from the window of this house and then marched home with the marches ringing in his ears.

The great-grandmother mentioned here was Elisabeth Pschorr, née Blass, the wife of Joseph Pschorr who had been proprietor of the Hackerbräu brewery in Munich. When she died in 1874 she left her Pschorr grandchildren, including Richard's mother Josephine, 5000 gulden each, which enabled the Strausses to buy a Blüthner grand piano and take a holiday in Italy.

A letter from Franz to Josephine reveals that, though barely four years old, Richard did not simply enjoy the Changing of the Guard as a spectacle but relished the music too:

> Richard always comes with me to the Changing of the Guard, when I have the time, and takes great delight in the music. When we were making our way home yesterday he whistled the tune of the march the band had been playing and insisted that I should play him the whole march on the horn, but I couldn't, because I had paid no attention to it.

Some six months after that episode, in the autumn of 1868, Franz Strauss decided the time was ripe for Richard, now four and a half, to begin piano lessons. He entrusted him to August Tombo, a harpist in the Court Orchestra, with the subsidiary thought of helping his friend and colleague to supplement his income in this modest way. His mother watched over the fledgeling pianist in those early days, ready to help when necessary. Before long

Richard began to play the tunes in a book of operatic arrangements 'without any special prompting'. He was able to play a Mozart sonata to a visitor when he was only nine. His sister recalled:

> Richard made swift progress in playing the piano. Sight-reading presented him with no problems. His teacher played to him a great deal . . . and there was one trick that delighted Richard. His teacher played the bass part with his left hand, the top line with his right hand and the middle part with the tip of his long pointed nose.

In the autumn of 1870 Richard started to attend the Cathedral School, the Dom-Schule.

> He enjoyed it, everything went easily and aroused his interest, and he made a whole crowd of friends immediately. With his temperament he was soon the ringleader in his class, and Mama thought it wise to collect him from school every day. The little 'Fingergassl' [Finger Alley], now Maffeistrasse, incited the boys to all sorts of fun and games, especially in winter, when it was the ideal place for slides and snowball fights.

The repercussions of the Franco-Prussian War, which took place between Richard's sixth and seventh birthdays, can have made little impression on him. The Musical Academy's series of subscription concerts was interrupted – only one was given that year, on Christmas Day – and that will have lightened Franz Strauss's heavy load. It is possible that Richard's boyhood adventures are seen in a somewhat rosy light in his sister's memoirs, but there is no evidence to suggest that his spirit suffered the least oppression. Their father's exceptionally strongly developed sense of family was shared by their Pschorr relations. It was inherited by Richard Strauss and affected the whole conduct of his life. The role played by family and home in his thinking and feeling cannot be estimated too highly. Alfred Steinitzer, the brother of Richard's biographer Max Steinitzer, recounts that the most important date in the calendar of festivities bringing the large family together was the party that took place every year without fail after the Corpus Christi procession, when they assembled to drink bock beer and eat fried sausages in Uncle Pschorr's house on the Marienplatz.[10]

Franz Strauss bequeathed to his son not only his musical gifts but also a sense of duty, strength of will and the ability to work hard. 'The capacity to work hard and enjoy it is born in you, it's not only a matter of training', wrote Richard Strauss in old age. He also shared his father's combativeness, a 'spirit of opposition', and like him hated to waste an opportunity to exercise it. From his mother he inherited the soft and ready emotional responses which are so often displayed in his melodic writing and harmonic turns and are so often at odds with his paternal characteristics of sternness of purpose and obdurateness.

A few passages from the letters Franz Strauss wrote to his wife while Richard was still a child reveal that for all his stiffness Franz did not lack emotional depths. Shortly after Richard's birth he wrote:

> Not a quarter of an hour passes without me thinking of you and the baby and always I wish I could be with you . . . Life is only beautiful when one has a beloved wife at one's side, which I have, and a dear little boy as well, who gives us such great joy; and so my happiness is complete, if God grants us His grace and above all good health, which is what I pray for to Him every day.

Some years later, when he had left to go on holiday before his family, he wrote:

> I take unceasing pleasure in you all, my dears! Once again I realize that I cannot do without you for long, for I know no rest inwardly when I do not have you at my side. Nothing beautiful has half its value when I am deprived of you, so see that you come soon.

There is a postscript, however, in which paternal severity reveals itself again, though in a modified form: 'a little homily for Richard'. But it contains a characteristic rider: 'I would not want to live without you, and believe me, even if I am grumpy, you are everything to me.'

It was at this stage in his life that Franz Strauss received the honours and appointments which have already been listed. His positions as first horn in the Court Orchestra and professor at the School of Music kept him very busy, but he also gave private lessons, without accepting any fee, as both his daughter and his pupil Hermann Tuckermann bear witness. In addition he conducted the Harbni Orchestra, made up of members of the family and their friends, and from 1875 to 1896 he conducted the amateur Wilde Gung'l Orchestra, which he brought up to a very high standard and for which he also composed a large number of dances.* Richard's uncle Anton Knözinger was particularly fond of the domestic performance of chamber music; a string quartet used to meet in his house, made up of Franz Brückner, a leading orchestral violinist, Hans Schönchen, Franz Strauss (on the viola) and Knözinger himself. As Royal Auditor General, Anton Knözinger was later ennobled. Just how strongly the family bonds united Franz Strauss to the Pschorr family, doughty individualist as he was in every other respect, is shown by the fact that, like them, he joined Ignaz Döllinger's Old Catholic movement in the 1870s.

In spite of their modest circumstances, the Strausses regularly spent their summer holidays in the mountains. As Franz grew older he was increasingly troubled by asthma, which is a professional hazard for all brass players, and he sought relief for it in the mountain air. The family's favourite resorts were Doblach and, from 1872, Sillian in the Puster valley in Austria, which proved better for their mother's delicate nerves. In the summer of 1878 Richard wrote to his friend Ludwig Thuille that he was in Sillian playing Mendelssohn organ sonatas as well as trios and quartets and getting a great deal of fun out of it. His sister recalled:

> A love of nature was born in Richard on those holidays, which remained with him for the rest of his life. He had a great love for everything, mountains and forests, meadows and flowers, for all animals . . . Our parents gave us many wonderful things, especially unlimited freedom . . . On excursions and mountain walks, fishing, playing in the open air, we children were able to live without any restrictions. Sillian was the quintessence of bliss for us . . . In response to insistent pleas from Richard, the hotel keeper acquired a piano; he also used to play the village organ, a pleasure he was also able to indulge in when we paid short but happy holiday visits to Uncle Hörburger in Mindelheim. It was our greatest joy of all when we were able to go to Mindelheim at Easter, Whitsun and in the autumn, to visit Mother's favourite sister, Bertha, who was married to the district officer, Carl Hörburger. We always had wonderful happy times with our relations there. They lived in an old monastery. There was a corridor more than 50 metres long leading to the famous,

* The name 'Wilde Gung'l' is an allusion to another amateur orchestra, founded with similar objectives, by Joseph Gungl. According to Johanna von Rauchenberger-Strauss, the conceit was that the relation of the Wilde Gung'l to the original Gungl orchestra was that of the wild rose to the cultivated rose.

> beautiful baroque church, entering it in the choir, right beside the organ. Richard in particular was enthralled by that, the more so as the organ-builder and sacristan lived in the building on the same floor. His children were our friends. When Richard was allowed to play the organ from time to time, his friend pumped the bellows for him . . . Uncle Carl used to make music a lot, and enjoyed singing and playing with us children.

Carl Hörburger (1826–99) had married Bertha Pschorr when she was twenty-four, in 1864, the year of Richard's birth. Only two of their seven children survived infancy: Franz Carl Robert (1864–83) and Max Theodor (1870–1930). Franz and Josephine Strauss were their godparents. Carl Hörburger was the leading figure in the musical life of Mindelheim. In 1867 he took over the local male choral society, the Liederkranz, and Franz Strauss appeared as soloist at some of their concerts. Richard dedicated some of his early compositions to his Uncle Hörburger, such as the Grand Sonata no. 2 in C minor (o. Op. 60) of 1879. In 1879 Carl Hörburger was transferred to Staffelstein in Franconia, and Richard and his parents and sister often spent holidays there too. Hörburger retired in 1893 with the rank of Regierungsrat (approximately equivalent to Assistant Secretary in the British Civil Service). He spent his last years in Munich.

It is not completely certain when Richard began to play the violin. It was probably in 1872, that is, when he was eight years old. His father chose him an excellent violinist as teacher, Benno Walter, the leader of the Court Orchestra and Franz's first cousin, being the son of Johann Georg Walter; Richard addressed him as 'cousin'. From Johanna's memoirs we learn that playing the violin put a great strain on Richard and made him very nervous, so that he could never play or practise for more than half an hour at a time. The piano remained his principal instrument. In his own memoirs Strauss confesses to having been a bad pupil, since he took little pleasure in the practising he had to do. On the other hand he enjoyed sight-reading, as the best way of learning more and more music, and later he was good at playing on the piano from a full orchestral score. He never acquired a perfect technique, especially in the left hand. His friend Thuille, the 'pedagogue', teased him: 'I can tell exactly what Richard's fingering is from the next room.' He thought, however, that he was a good accompanist in vocal music, though rather free and never note-perfect; at all events, he was told that he had a good touch. He believed he was up to scratch in chamber music, but his fingers cried a halt when faced with the harder tasks of Chopin and Liszt.[11] These self-critical remarks do not refer to the beginner, of course, so much as to the teenager, whose piano tuition was in the hands of Carl Niest from 1875, when his parents bought the Blüthner.

With Richard's entry in 1874 into the Royal Grammar School, the Ludwigs-Gymnasium, which was in the Sendlinger Strasse in those days, a new chapter in his life began. Extra tuition made it possible for him to go straight into Form 2A in the Latin School (the lower school of the Ludwigs-Gymnasium). A 'confidential report' written at the end of his first year by his form-master Carl Welzhofer throws a sympathetic light on the master as well as on his favourite pupil:

> There can be few pupils in whom a sense of duty, talent and liveliness are united to the degree that they are in this boy. His enthusiasm is very great, he enjoys learning and finds it easy. He attends closely in class; nothing escapes him. And yet he is incapable of sitting still for a moment, he finds a bench a very tiresome object. Unclouded merriment and high spirits sparkle in his eyes day after day; candour and good nature are written on his face. His work is good, very good. No teacher could help but take to a boy like this, indeed it is almost difficult to conceal one's preference. Strauss is a promising musical talent.[12]

2

Boyhood

Richard began his first childish essays in composition shortly after entering the Dom-Schule. At the age of six and a half he wrote the Schneider-Polka ('Tailor polka') for piano (o. Op. 1) – consisting of an introduction and trio – which he was able to play himself, but 'he was not yet capable of writing it down. Papa had to do it for him. Mama added a note in pencil at the bottom: "Written down by Papa".' Johanna von Rauchenberger-Strauss suggests that the Schneider-Polka was the work referred to in a letter Richard wrote to his father, dated 13 June 1872, but that was in fact the Panzenburg-Polka, proudly numbered 'Opus 6' (o. Op. 10), which his father orchestrated and conducted at a rehearsal of the Harbni Orchestra. The letter in question was written when Franz was in Innsbruck on a concert tour.

> Dear, good Papa,
>
> I've already made away with your pig, we've slaughtered it already, it was very good, at least I found it very tasty. How did the Mozart Horn Concerto go, I held my thumbs [for luck] as tight as I could. I have promised Herr Niebler, August, my teacher and Theodor that I will copy my polka out for them, but I haven't had the time and secondly I haven't got any decent manuscript paper. Dear Papa, at the Cellar they call me Horneck and August Banzenburg. Lots of greetings from Mama, Hannerl [Johanna], Fanni, Herr and Frau Nagiller and last of all from your affectionate son Richard.

August Pschorr was a cousin, one of the sons of Georg Pschorr and his wife Johanna, née Fischerdick. Richard and he played chamber music together a great deal in the years that followed and the

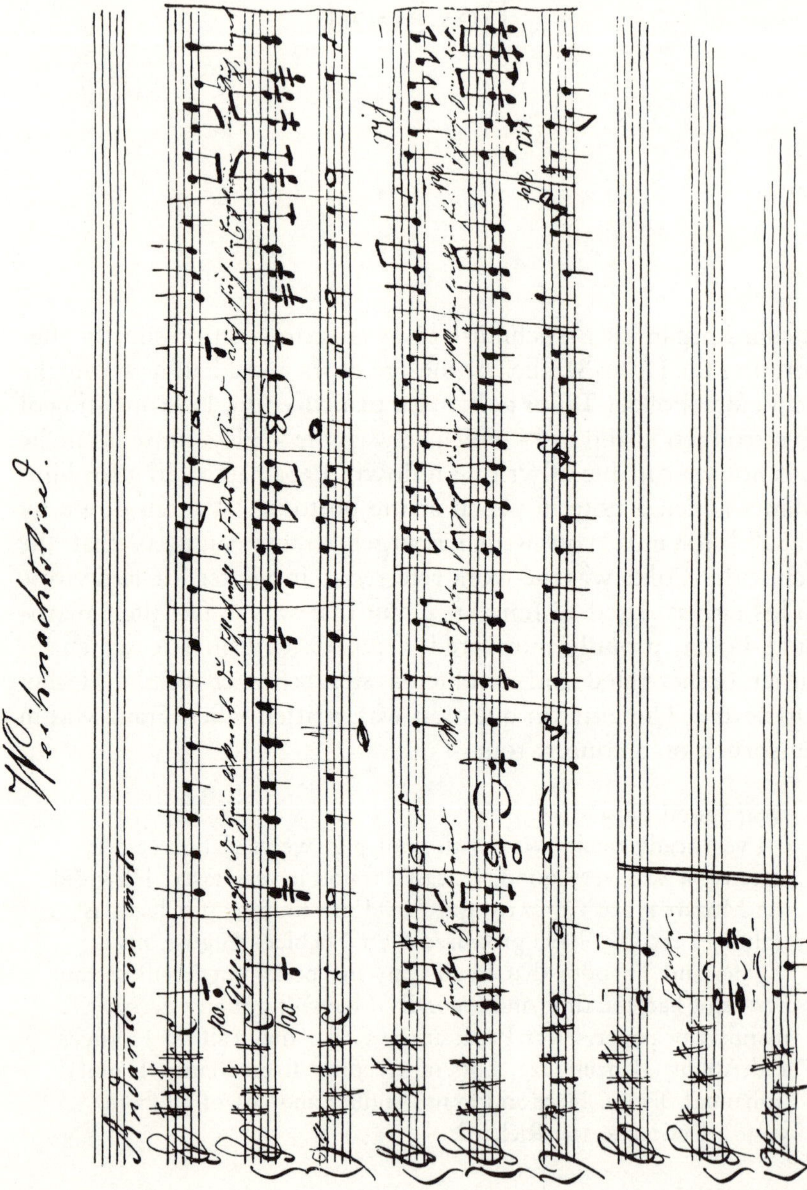

Weihnachtslied, the six-year-old's first song

Soldatenlied ('Soldiers' Song', o. Op. 48, 1878) was dedicated to him. Richard dedicated two small piano pieces (o. Op. 68) to another cousin, Georg, in 1880. Banzenburg (or Panzenburg) – literally 'Paunch Castle' – is the Bavarian name for a pile of empty beer barrels.[1]

The Harbni Orchestra was an amateur body, recruited from friends and relations; the name derived from the Bavarian dialect expression 'nie harb' ('herb' in standard German), meaning 'never bitter', 'never bad-tempered'. Franz Strauss composed a large number of dances and other pieces for it, as he did for the Wilde Gung'l. It met to play at Georg Pschorr's villa on Bayerstrasse. Franz Strauss wrote to his wife about the performance of the Panzenburg-Polka, in a letter dated 1 June 1872:

> There was a Harbni Orchestra rehearsal yesterday, at which we played Richard's polka. Those present were amazed and said they didn't believe it, but I assured them on my honour that it was all his own work, and I had only orchestrated it. It really is very nice and sounds quite good. He asked me first thing this morning if the gentlemen had liked it, and when I said they had his eyes shone.

Between these two polkas Richard had begun to try his hand at writing songs. He had special encouragement in this from his aunt Johanna, who herself used to sing in the family circle; most of these earliest songs were dedicated to her. Max Steinitzer knew them and listed them in his biography of Strauss. Unfortunately a number of them were lost during the Second World War, but even so a substantial corpus survives of songs dating from the years 1870–80, which not only illustrate the growth of the composer's emotional and technical capabilities, but also demonstrate great variety of forms and spheres of expression. The choice of texts is admittedly undiscriminating, but the settings range from simple, folk-like strophic songs to lyrical atmospheric pieces and to dramatic ballads. There are relatively few compositions from the months immediately preceding his move to the Latin School, but this is explained by the extra burden of work he had to do for the Widmer'sches Institut, the crammer's where he was sent to prepare for entry to the Ludwigs-Gymnasium. Even so, it was during this period that he attempted his first orchestral composition, an overture to a Singspiel, *Hochlands Treue* ('Highland Loyalty'; o. Op. 15).

At this stage in his development his experiments in composition were no more than equal in importance to his attendance at operas and concerts, for which his father used to prepare him in advance, his own playing on piano and violin, and also his growing appreciation of his father's performance on horn, violin and viola. Two études, for E♭ horn and E horn, written when he was nine, testify to his interest in the instrument his father played with such supreme mastery; it remained his own favourite instrument to his dying day. Johanna tells us that later, when Richard himself conducted the Munich Court Orchestra, he would, if possible, catch his father's eye after the satisfactory despatch of one of the more tricky horn solos in an opera or a concert. In his own memoir of his father, Richard Strauss wrote:

> Taking part in operas and concerts was always a solemn act for my father. He used to practise the difficult horn solos in the Beethoven symphonies, *Freischütz*, *Oberon*, *Midsummer Night's Dream* for weeks before a performance. But I still remember very clearly the profound impression it always made on the Munich audiences when he played the F major passage in the first movement of the *Eroica*, the solemn G♭ major passage in the Adagio of the Ninth: the performance could truly be called celebration.[2]

It was only natural that the children were familiar with all the famous horn solos from their earliest childhood. What Johanna says about Richard's first visits to the opera must be based on what her mother and Richard himself told her, since she was only four years old at the time, but there is no reason to doubt the authenticity of her account:

> Richard was about seven when our parents yielded to his passionate wish to go to the Court Theatre. Mother could not leave home with him early enough, for of course it was all immensely important for him and an experience of the very greatest significance. Even the theatre itself, the huge, high auditorium, the tiers, the boxes, the marvellous curtain with its painting by Guido Reni put Richard into a state of ecstasy such as he had never experienced before. The opera was Weber's *Freischütz*. The tuning of the orchestra caught his attention especially, because Father was there of course . . . Richard had already often played the overture as a piano duet, and he knew the arias very well too. He was almost trembling with excitement as he waited for the great moment when the curtain

> rose. When Samiel made his first appearance at the back of the stage, Richard squeezed Mother's hand and whispered anxiously: 'Is he going to do something to him?' The magnificent music – especially the Wolf's Glen – put him into an indescribable rapture . . .
>
> I think that *Die Zauberflöte* was the second opera Richard heard. He was especially delighted by Papageno. He was in a fever of impatience as he waited for the entrance of the serpent, Papageno with the padlock on his mouth and Pamina's arias. He had played it all on the piano beforehand, mostly as duets: the overture, the choruses, Sarastro's great aria and the great entrance of the Queen of the Night, which she made on the crescent moon.

These two first visits to the opera must have taken place in 1871.

Richard appeared with a group of other youngsters at two of the children's festivals put on at Carnival time in the Odeon, once as a Herald of Peace in the chorus from *Rienzi* and the second time as a Minnesänger from *Tannhäuser*. Steinitzer dates the group photographs of these occasions, which are reproduced in his biography, as 1870 and 1871, but a letter Richard wrote to his cousin Julie Hörburger, dated 15 February 1872 – the earliest of his letters to survive – tells us that the first of these performances did not take place until 1872.

> On Carnival Sunday I was a Herald of Peace at the children's festival in the Odeon, with August, Georg and six other boys. We had to sing three songs and I was the choir leader, we did it very well and got lots of applause.

The original of this letter is not available, however, and some doubt is cast on its date by the photograph of the group; Richard still looks very young, and it would be more consistent with a date of 1870 or 1871. There are only seven boys in the picture. The photograph of the group of Minnesänger is undoubtedly later in date. Steinitzer gives 23 February 1873 as the date of a performance of the Schneider-Polka, scored for small orchestra by Franz Strauss and conducted by Richard himself at a Carnival concert in the Odeon promoted by the Munich Philharmonic Association.

The first opera by Wagner that Richard heard was *Tannhäuser*. In his memoir of his father he wrote:

> As I gradually became familiar with the works of Richard

> Wagner, I can only remember that the thing in *Tannhäuser* that made the greatest impression on me was the transformation from the Venusberg to the Wartburg valley, and that I was completely at a loss in the first performances I heard of *Tristan* and *Siegfried*, although I was a passably well-educated musician by then, including three years of counterpoint with my excellent and kind-hearted teacher Wilhelm Meyer: I didn't understand a note. In short, my dramatic instincts responded earlier than my musical ones. Prejudice instilled by upbringing may well have had a strong influence on this.[3]

It was 1878 before he heard *Tristan* and *Siegfried*. His composition lessons with Friedrich Wilhelm Meyer had begun in 1875, with a grounding in harmonic theory, formal theory and contrapuntal technique, before going on to instrumentation. The lessons went on for five years, until 1880. Meyer was one of those who, while possessed of the most solid ability, do not know how to make anything of themselves. He bore the title of Hofkapellmeister and was Franz Lachner's deputy until the latter's retirement in 1868.* He normally conducted grand opera in the Court Theatre, but he had also directed Spohr's *Faust*; he conducted Wagner only when circumstances prevented the appearance of the scheduled conductor. In 1869, when Bülow was on leave of absence, he stood in for him at two Musical Academy concerts, and he succeeded him in the post of chief conductor when Bülow was dismissed in the autumn of the same year. (Hans Richter, who had been designated to succeed Bülow, withdrew after the performances of *Die Walküre*, which King Ludwig insisted on having staged against Wagner's will.) Meyer also acted as secretary to the Musical Academy until 1881. He retired in 1882. Johanna reports that Meyer and his wife loved Richard like a son, having no children of their own. The G major Serenade for orchestra (o. Op. 32), written in 1877 while Richard was still his pupil, is dedicated to Meyer 'in gratitude'. It is the first orchestral work that Richard Strauss scored himself, although the instrumentation probably owes something to his teacher's advice. At New Year 1879 Meyer gave Richard a first edition (1739) of Johann Mattheson's *Der vollkommene Capellmeister*. When he died in 1893 Richard wrote to his parents: 'I am

* The conducting establishment with the Munich Court Orchestra consisted of a chief conductor and a deputy, both with the rank and title of Hofkapellmeister, and a third, with the title of Musikdirektor. *Tr.*

profoundly sad at Kapellmeister Meyer's death. He was a simple man with a noble mind, and I shall always preserve affectionate and grateful memories of him; as Thuille once said very shrewdly, he did more for my development than he himself probably knew.' (10 June 1893)

Johanna's memoirs also recall the first concerts her brother attended after he had started at the Ludwigs-Gymnasium:

> Father used to give him some preliminary instruction in the various programmes. The first time he heard a Beethoven symphony he didn't understand it; he remained unmoved and even said he didn't care for it. Nor did he understand Beethoven's sonatas and quartets at that stage. In his piano lessons he preferred Chopin, Mendelssohn and Bach.

In fact Richard did not come to Bach, and in particular to Chopin, until some years after he had started going to concerts. The Pschorr family often met to make music together in the house of Uncle Georg and Aunt Johanna; at a children's concert on 19 March 1876 Richard performed Weber's *Invitation to the Dance.* A letter written to his father some two years later describes one such evening (the various children named, besides his sister, are their cousins):

> The Pschorrs came back on Saturday evening and I at once threw myself into organizing a concert at which the following were performed (it took place on Tuesday at the Pschorrs): Enghausen's C major Sonata, played by Robert, then the Tirolean folk song *Hans und Lise*, sung very prettily by Johanna, who was given a very pretty bouquet by Aunt Johanna, just like a proper singer, and very well accompanied by Robert; they both reaped great success. Then August played one of Mendelssohn Bartholdy's *Songs without Words* with – I am sorry to have to say – very little style or finesse; then August and I played *Ich wollt', meine Liebe ergösse sich*, also by M. B., in which we both pleased greatly. Then I played Weber's E♭ major Rondo to loud applause. Then the 'Toy' Symphony was given a most successful performance conducted and directed by *me* alone, but with everyone contributing their mites to its good conclusion and performing their parts very well. I was on the piano, August cuckoo and quail, Robert drum, Georg nightingale, Johanna *rattle*, Joseph triangle and cymbals. (31 July 1878)

Early concert-going

Richard wrote to his father about other concerts, given by conservatoire students as part of their annual examinations, which he heard during this same summer of 1878. His accounts reveal that his own musical studies made him a critical listener:

> In the last movement [of Beethoven's First Symphony] one of the violinists played B♭ instead of B♮ in the middle section, which put my teeth on edge. Next a Fräulein K. played the first movement of an A minor concerto by Schumann, which I didn't like very much, because it's not at all clear and the scoring is very thick, so that you hardly get to hear the piano. Next a Herr U. played the first and second movements of a beautiful bassoon concerto by Mozart, which set me thinking once again what an ungrateful solo instrument the bassoon is and made me laugh a lot at the gurgling noise it made. Next I heard two songs by Schubert, *Der Wegweiser* and *Die Post*, sung (very boringly *and* an hour too slowly) by Fräulein G. She has a pretty voice but an ugly mannerism of forcing some notes out. Then a Fräulein Ch. played the very, very long and boring first movement of a piano concerto in B♭ minor by Rubinstein. It begins very dramatically and ends very dramatically, but the bit in-between is *long* and very boring, and the piano keeps on growling about among the very lowest notes for quite a long time, which reminded me very, very vividly of *you know what*. The whole thing is not up to much. Next a Herr F. played a very pretty, tuneful Konzertstück for oboe by Rietz, which I liked very much, because it was simple and not tarted up and because the tunes were so pretty. Next Spohr's 8th Violin Concerto (Scena), played *very* well indeed by Herr S. I was quite delighted by the magnificent composition, just as I was the first time I heard it, especially when I heard my favourite bit [which he quotes]. The concerto has a quite unusual but very original character, due especially to the recitative and the main theme of the last movement.

In another letter he mentioned a Handel organ concerto, which delighted him by 'the wholesome, pithy stamp of every note of it', and he had this to say about Beethoven's Violin Concerto:

> This composition is, in my judgment, one of the most beautiful there is. The simplicity and noblesse, the melody, the magnificent modulations and *what* scoring; I was completely

Richard conducts his *Schneider-Polka* at a children's fancy-dress party in the Odeonssaal, 1873

Richard, aged about six

Richard and Johanna Strauss

> transported. [After three musical quotations]: That's spiritual riches: *geistreich* [intelligent] in the true meaning of the word; to be honest, when I heard it the first time it didn't really say anything to me, but yesterday I was quite carried away by this outstanding composition.

The fourteen-year-old also liked Chopin's F minor Piano Concerto:

> Chopin has a quite individual technique, he particularly likes particular chromatic passages, and the composition as a whole is very pretty; I particularly liked the dashing ending . . . of the first movement. In the last movement (6/8) the middle section has a most odd construction, which I found a bit disconcerting.

He was less enthusiastic about *Die Wallfahrt nach Kevlaar* by Engelbert Humperdinck, then a student at the Munich School of Music, finding it 'somewhat depressing':

> There's some obvious straining for effect, and the chorus and soloists alike sing their way through the long poem from beginning to end without any repetition or development; the chorus only had four-part songs to sing, but not what one usually thinks of as specifically choral writing; there isn't much melody to speak of, and the whole thing is not up to much. A symphonic movement (C minor, of course) by Philipp Wolfrum with some very pretty passages but frightfully thick, muddy scoring and *very* loud. All the players are puffing and scraping away together all the time, very bad scoring; an enormous brass section, making a heathenish din.

Elsewhere he writes:

> I've now played through the whole of Spohr's *Faust* and I find it just as interesting and magnificent a masterpiece; the whole tone of it is earnest and every character in it is individually drawn.

Immature as these expressions of opinion are, they already reveal a remarkable gift for comprehension, an ability to discriminate and a special interest in scoring, and not least the perfectly natural preferences of a boy of his age.

Ludwig Thuille

Of all the friends he made in his boyhood, Ludwig Thuille (1861–1907) was the one who had the most beneficial effect on Richard's development as an artist. The two met as early as 1872, when Richard was eight and Ludwig eleven. Richard's mother had heard about this gifted boy, who was being brought up in a monastic orphanage, from her friend Pauline Nagiller who lived in Innsbruck, where her husband Matthäus Nagiller (1815–74) was director of music. Richard's sister writes: 'Certain that this would be particularly nice for Richard . . . Mama invited our new friend to visit us in Munich . . . Father bestirred himself and got Ludwig into the School of Music, and Mama did her utmost to make him feel at home; he was treated like one of the family.'

From 1877 to 1879 Ludwig remained in Innsbruck to study with Joseph Pembaur the elder, and it is to that circumstance that we owe the voluminous correspondence that passed between the two boys.[4] It is concerned almost entirely with music: their opinions of concerts and operas, the work Richard happened to be doing at any particular moment, his study of theory and counterpoint, and of course his compositions. The correspondence has been much quoted, especially – to the (quite unnecessary) annoyance of Strauss in his old age – those passages which reveal the opinions he held of Wagner between the ages of thirteen and fifteen; at that stage Wagner's works did not engage him in the least and he enjoyed poking fun at them. On one occasion, after delivering a Philippic against the 'Meister', he sat down at the piano and played Isolde's 'Liebestod' in a parodic waltz-time.[5] The classical emphasis in his education and, especially, his father's hostility towards Wagner and all his works could not have failed to close the boy's mind for the time being. What he has to say in his youthful disrespect – above all the bumptious accounts, illustrated with musical examples, of performances he had seen of *Siegfried* and *Die Walküre* in 1878 – is often highly entertaining (and has often been quoted), but we should not forget that these are the opinions of a boy of fourteen, who is amusing himself by painting the 'horrors' of Wagner's music in lurid colours. He was a little less dismissive of *Lohengrin* in February 1879; he liked the plot and he admitted that, although taken as a whole the music bored him, it at least had some 'beautiful moments'.

Haydn, 'divine' Mozart and Beethoven command Strauss's love, as revealed in his letters to Thuille, but Spohr, Mendelssohn, Bach, and Graun's oratorio *Der Tod Jesu* also made an impression on him. Franz Lachner's E minor String Quartet inspired sympathy and respect. He enjoyed operas by Boieldieu, Auber, Lortzing and Marschner. He wrote enthusiastically about Clara Schumann's performance of Beethoven's G major Piano Concerto, which he heard in the autumn of 1879, and about the work itself:

> What grace, what beauty; then the wild Adagio, where the orchestra has all those wild phrases, which the piano counters as if soothingly, the orchestra ever quieter until at last it dies away in a murmur, then the light-hearted, joyful last movement to follow – it's quite enchanting and *what* instrumentat!!

Another letter expressed no less admiration for Mozart's piano concertos:

> At the moment I'm very diligently playing the Mozart piano concertos from our Mozart edition, and I can tell you it's wonderful, it's giving me enormous enjoyment. The abundance of the ideas, the harmonic richness, and yet the sense of proportion, the marvellous, lovely, tender, delightful ideas themselves, the delicate accompaniment. Yet one can't play anything like that any more! All you get now is drivel; either twittering or brash roaring and crashing or sheer musical nonsense. While Mozart, with few means, says everything a listener could desire to be refreshed and truly entertained and edified, the others use all the means at their disposal to say absolutely nothing, or hardly anything. The world is crazy! To blazes with it! But I've made a vow, when I appear at an important concert for the first time, where I shall be well and sensitively accompanied, I will play a Mozart concerto. (22 July 1879)

And in fact, when Strauss made his début as a pianist six years later, on 20 October 1885, at a symphony concert in Meiningen conducted by Hans von Bülow, he played Mozart's C minor Concerto, with his own cadenzas (unfortunately lost). Behind his enthusiastic words about Mozart it is as if we hear his father's voice.

To Richard, Ludwig, who dedicated his first string quartet to him in April 1878 as well as other things, was his 'dearest', his 'best', his 'handsomest', his 'splendidest'. Richard kept him au courant about his study of counterpoint with Friedrich Wilhelm Meyer, but also, more importantly, about the music he was writing for himself, independently of his lessons: songs; the G major Serenade for orchestra (o. Op. 32); the A major Piano Trio (o. Op. 37); the E major Piano Sonata (o. Op. 38); two numbers from Goethe's

Singspiel *Lila*: Almaide's aria and 'Auf aus der Ruh' for tenor solo, mixed choir and orchestra (he was to return to *Lila* in 1895); some gavottes – a dance form for which he had a special liking; the Variations for flute and piano (o. Op. 56) which he wrote for a schoolfriend; the Grand Sonata in C minor; the Romance in E♭ major for clarinet and orchestra (o. Op. 61); the now lost Wedding March with Church Scene; the A minor Overture (o. Op. 62) and others. Even so, there are some compositions from this period – October 1877 to July 1879 – which he does not mention, and he does not refer to numerous pieces which failed to get beyond various stages of sketching. The only exception is a brief mention of a string quartet movement (AV 211) which he began in July 1879 and abandoned in the forty-second bar. He also passed on pieces of his father's advice:

> With reference to learning about instrumental music the only good advice I can give you is not to learn it from a book, because, according to my Papa, that's the very worst thing to do. I advise you not to buy any book, since even my Papa knows only one, by Hector Berlioz, who himself scores with a trowel; instead ask Herr Pembaur to give you a table setting out the range and the best register of all the various instruments, and learn the rest, i.e. how to use and write for them, from the scores of the old, great masters. (31 December 1877)

On another occasion he passed on his father's advice to give up playing Chopin and pay more attention to the classical school. He responded gratefully to some critical comments Ludwig had made:

> With reference to the accompaniment of the 1st and last movements of my E major sonata [o. Op. 38] I do see the big mistake I've made there and in respect of the numerous bridge passages, and I will do my best in my 2nd sonata [in C minor, o. Op. 60] and my other things to shake off my old habit

> and produce a better-made accompaniment. I'm very grateful to you for drawing my attention to this, and if I'd noticed this glaring mistake earlier I'd never have had the nerve to let you set eyes on such a clumsy piece of work, let alone dedicate it to you as something equal to your sonata, which is of a much higher standard than mine. With reference to the 2nd section of the

Kinderconcert.

München d. 19. März 1876.

1. Vierhändiges Clavierstück.
   Johanna Strauss u. Joseph Pschorr.
2. Declamation.
   Bertha und Emilie Pracher.
3. Clavierpiece.
   Louise Halbreiter.
4. Duett.
   Emilie Halbreiter u. Jos. Pschorr.
5. Declamation.
   Pauline Oestner.
6. Serenade v. Haydn für Clavier und Violine.
   Emilie Oestner u. Rich. Strauss.
7. Declamation.
   Alexandra Hüther.
8. Duett: Gruss.
   Rob. u. Jos. Pschorr.
9. 2 Lieder v. Reinecke für Clavier, 1 Sopran u. Violine.
   1, Jos. Pschorr, Louise Halbreiter u. Mich. Strauss.
   2, Johaña Strauss, L. Halbreiter u. Richard Strauss.
10. Aufforderung zum Tanz v. K. M. v. Weber.
   Richard Strauss.

Anfang $\frac{1}{2}$ 4 Uhr.

Programme of a Pschorr family concert given by the children, Munich, 1876

1st movement I can tell you frankly that I didn't dare attempt a proper development and only wrote a short transition. (21 December 1878)

Composition is the principal topic in the letters of 1879 – the last which were written while Ludwig was still in Innsbruck. Two extracts give some idea of the enthusiasm and the capabilities the schoolboy enjoyed around the time of his fifteenth birthday:

I've got so much to do at present. 1. (for accursed school).
2. (I'm composing very busily).
(i) getting on with the scoring of my A minor overture.
(ii) I've re-written all three songs, this time without any special modulations, *ergo* to Papa's satisfaction.
(iii) I've composed 4 new piano pieces, including 2 gavottes, the second of which is very pretty and original.
(iv) I've written – wait for it – some variations for flute and piano [o. Op. 56] at the request of a chum.
(v) I'm now working on the last movement of the sonata [in C minor; o. Op. 60]; the 3 page long development section has come out all right, and so the rest won't take much longer. Besides that I'm going to give it a shortish, melodic A♭ major Adagio, from which I'll lead straight into a Scherzo. So you can see that I've had more than enough to do and still have.

Besides that I'm busy doing counterpoint exercises; I'm already up to 4-part fugue now, the pinnacle towards which all counterpoint aspires. (8 May 1879)

Papa is in the country, Mama and Hanna are at a spa, two hours away from Papa; *ergo* I am alone at home. I'm composing very busily. (1) I've written, perhaps I've already told you, a Romance in E♭ major for clarinet and orchestra [o. Op. 61], which I'm very pleased with; the theme that runs all the way through it produced a 6-part orchestral fugato after the first cantilena. (2) another new gavotte, No. IV in D major with a bagpipe tune (musette) as trio; gavotte form suits me extraordinarily well for shorter piano pieces; (3) I've written a comic wedding march with a church scene, for the wedding of my cousin Linda Moralt, for piano and toy instruments (cuckoo, quail, cymbals, triangle, drum, rattle, nightingale), which I shall perform on the wedding day with my band, Hanna and the 4 Pschorr boys; the whole thing is just a joke; (4) I've finished the A minor Overture at last; it makes a hellish din, I can tell you,

> but I think it'll be effective; further I've a quartet in my head which will shortly burst the vessel where it now reposes and manifest itself on manuscript paper [AV 211]. But first I must alter the Horn Variations in E♭ major that I composed last autumn and write them for *human* lungs and *human* lips; for they are almost unplayable as they are. (22 July 1879)

The Introduction, Theme and Variations for horn and piano (o. Op. 52), which Richard wrote in September 1878, was 'dedicated to his dear Papa for his name-day'.

There was no need for the exchange of letters to continue when Thuille returned to Munich in 1879 to finish his studies at the Royal School of Music with Joseph Rheinberger and Carl Bärmann. The two did not begin to write to each other again until 1884, when Richard went to Berlin for the winter. By that time, after doing brilliantly in his final examinations with his own piano concerto, Thuille had himself joined the staff of the School of Music in October 1883. In later life Strauss looked back on their friendship:

> Ludwig Thuille, the friend of my schooldays, during which his was probably the greatest influence on my development (through the exchange of ideas and through mutual competition) . . . showed a heartening talent for composition at an early age, was about two years ahead of me in development . . . A Violin Sonata [Op. 1], more mature than my own products of the same period, aroused my especial envy and competitiveness. Unfortunately the callow correspondence that passed between us in those days (airing empty-headed, impudent opinions about Richard Wagner, who was hardly known in those days, or at least not yet understood) still quite unnecessarily stalks the pages of biographical writing of all kinds (as the favourite nurture of our writers about music). As a pupil of Joseph Rheinberger, Thuille soon began to move in the direction of strict conservatism and shortly after graduating from the School of Music he became Rheinberger's successor as professor of counterpoint; before long, after Alexander Ritter's influence began to have its effect on me in 1885, he fell behind me, so that even my *Italy* [i.e. the symphonic fantasy *Aus Italien*] made the strict contrapuntalist shake his head and later he often asked me how I could justify the construction of this chord or the other, or how I would explain this or that polyphonic line. I would simply reply: 'I can't, I wrote it down because that's how it occurred to me.' So towards the end of the century we became

> less close than we had been – I only know that Thuille was disturbed by the *Taillefer* battle music [Op. 52]. I conducted his Romantic Overture [Op. 16] in Berlin, but I also followed the composition of his charming symphony and piano concerto (unpublished) with interest. His opera *Lobetanz*, with a libretto by Bierbaum, was a success in several German theatres and would still merit the attention of so-called theatre managements!

The precise date of this late memoir is unknown. Strauss also touched on their later relationship but forgot to mention his energetic championing of Thuille's opera *Theuerdank* in Munich in 1897 or his efforts to get *Gugeline* performed in Berlin in 1901–2. He himself frequently called on Joseph Rheinberger to show him his new compositions, up to the end of the 1880s, but after looking through *Don Juan* Rheinberger commented: '"It's a pity that you've got on to this false track, you've so much talent." So that was the end of that.'

Domestic music-making

Up to the time when Richard left school (1882) Franz Strauss had the most decisive influence on his development, both as performer and as composer. Playing with his father was always a rather heady kind of pleasure, because of his irascibility.

> He had an infallible sense for correct tempo. He reproached his chief Hermann Levi with never getting into the right tempo before the third bar of a piece. He was very strict about rhythm; how many times he bawled at me: 'You're hurrying like a Jew.' But I learned how to play well from him, all the countless times I had to accompany him in Mozart's beautiful horn concertos and Beethoven's horn sonata. He gave me a worthy preparation for the high school of performance and interpretation of the classical masterworks under Bülow.

Strauss also wrote that the fact that his father had brought him up strictly within the bounds of classical music until he was sixteen was the reason why in his old age his love and admiration for the classical composers had remained unclouded. The classics were the foundation of Strauss's whole oeuvre, not just of his juvenilia; nothing he wrote in his maturity denied them and in his last creative years he openly returned to his starting point.

Franz Strauss's strong personality, his style of playing, distinguished by meticulous phrasing and agogics, as much in the classics

Contrapuntal study: double canon, 1878/9

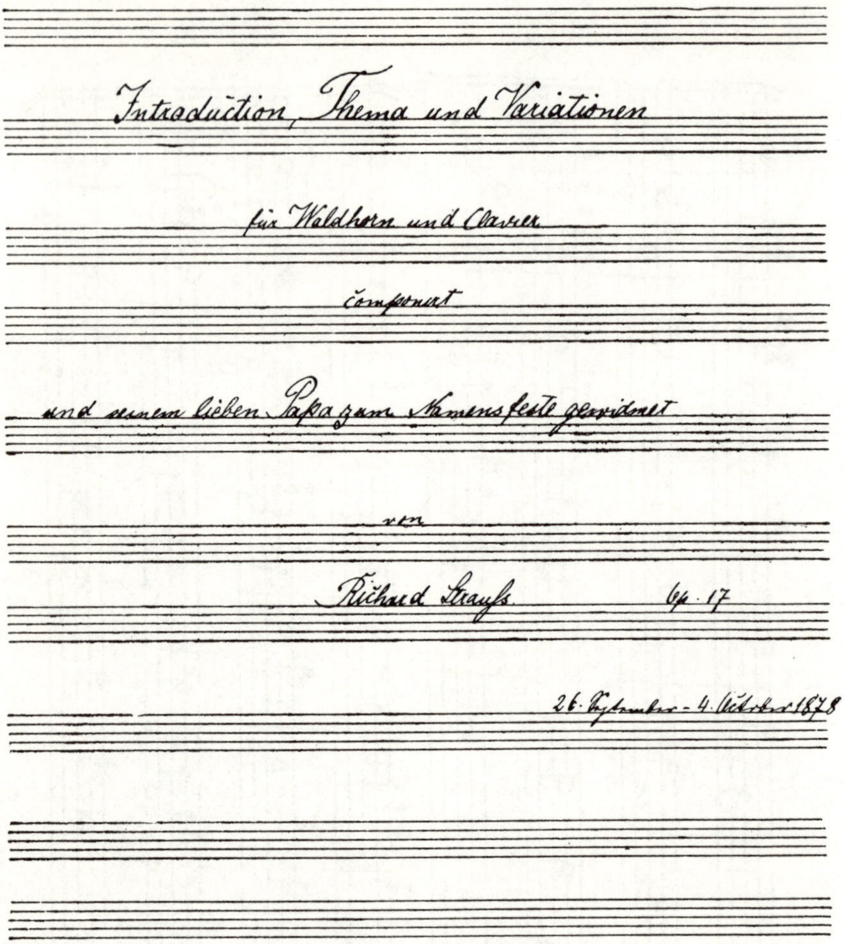
Introduction, Thema und Variationen
für Waldhorn und Clavier
componirt
und seinem lieben Papa zum Namensfeste gewidmet
von
Richard Strauß
Op. 17
26. September - 4. October 1878

Title page and theme of the Introduction, Theme and Variations for horn and piano 'Op. 17' (o. Op. 52), 1878

as in the Wagner he detested, made an impression on his son that was as indelible as that left by his sense of duty and his completely serious view of art. Hearing his father play and playing with him in their home provided the happiest conceivable complement to Richard's study of theory and reading of scores. From a very early age, too, he was able to take part in musical afternoons and evenings in the Pschorr family circle: as an attentive listener to begin with, but soon as one of the performers, when his own skill, at first on the piano and then on the violin, permitted it. After he had transferred from the Latin School to the Ludwigs-Gymnasium proper, he also

regularly visited the home of his cousin Carl Aschenbrenner, the son of a counsel in the Bavarian Supreme Court and one of his closest schoolfriends. Here, every other Sunday afternoon throughout the winter months and sometimes on weekdays as well, they played quartets. Richard and another cousin, Ludwig Knözinger (the son of the Auditor General and the dedicatee of one of Richard's most mature early works, the Romance in F major for cello and orchestra, o. Op. 75), took it in turns to play first and second violin, Carl Aschenbrenner played the cello and his father – an excellent violinist, who also played in the Wilde Gung'l – the viola.[6] In this way Richard became thoroughly familiar with the quartets of Haydn, Mozart, Schubert and Beethoven – up to the first of the Op. 59 quartets 'where the last movement at last put a check on our youthful enthusiasm', as Richard wrote in his memoirs. On the alternate Sundays Richard and Carl Aschenbrenner went to the house of a distant cousin, Carl Streicher, to play trios. The piano part was taken by Streicher's elder sister Marie, 'a truly musical pianist', who also sang Richard's songs, 'including the one about the kiss stolen on the stairs', one of three songs which Richard sent to Lotti Speyer some years later.

In old age Carl Aschenbrenner recalled the days when he used to play with Richard Strauss:

> When we were still at the Gymnasium we had a regular quartet, in which Strauss took it in turns with his cousin Ludwig Knözinger to play first violin. In those days we were very well-behaved and rarely departed, and then only slightly, from classicity. But it was always an especial pleasure to play a piano quartet, when Strauss would take the piano part. He was in his element then, when he could lead the ensemble from the piano, on which he was already a virtuoso. Frequently, when we had paused for a rest or after we had finished playing, Strauss would sit down at the piano and play us his latest composition or improvise freely. On those occasions we did sometimes get a glimpse of the later Strauss: his rhythms in particular betrayed his sly alter ego.

In addition to operas and symphony concerts, Richard regularly attended recitals by the Benno Walter Quartet and the Hans Bussmeyer Trio. During his schooldays he was also a keen theatre-goer and became well acquainted with the classics in particular, especially Shakespeare and Schiller.

At school nearly everything came easily to Richard, except for mathematics, which he detested, especially algebra and spherical trigonometry. He poured his heart out in one of his letters to his father, though not without blaming the teacher for explaining everything much too fast (25 July 1879). On the whole a benign spirit must have reigned at the Ludwigs-Gymnasium. His form-master's report when he was in the fourth form (1876–7) shows that his teachers continued to regard him with the same benevolence and understanding that we have seen in the report from his second year in the Latin School: 'A pupil of splendid gifts, proper disposition and good conduct; lively, keen, attentive, at times in rather too much of a hurry'. An episode narrated by his sister betrays a sense of humour as well:

> His school books were usually wrapped in shiny blue paper, but on one occasion when she hadn't any Mama used manuscript paper instead. He came home full of enthusiasm for this good idea: he had started to compose on the paper during a lesson. The French master was less enthusiastic when he noticed what Richard was doing and without any warning asked him a question. Richard was miles away and had no idea of the correct answer. As a punishment he was told to translate the following sentence into French: 'He must bring his "Kasimulia" [the teacher's teasing substitution for "musicalia"] and his charming, pretty sister with him', at which the whole class let out a howl of delight and cried 'Yes, he must, he must!' because Richard's friends were all my friends too.

Richard sketched part of his D minor Violin Concerto (Op. 8) while he was in his penultimate year at school (1880–1), and he also had opportunities to perform at school concerts. At the May Festival of 1879, for instance, he and his cousins Carl Aschenbrenner and Carl Streicher played Beethoven's Piano Trio Op. 11. On at least two occasions his own compositions were performed: a festive chorus with piano accompaniment (AV 169; lost) and, at an end-of-year concert (probably in 1881), a setting of a chorus from Sophocles' *Elektra* – the third stasimon, lines 1384–97 – for male-voice choir, clarinets, horns, trumpets, timpani and strings, which he had composed at the instigation of his Greek master, Professor Laroche. The manuscripts of both these works were kept in the library of the Ludwigs-Gymnasium and were destroyed by bombing in 1943, but the *Elektra* chorus survives in a piano reduction at least, which shows that it was simple in style (o. Op. 74). He was also allowed to play two piano pieces from his 'Op. 3' at the school's May Festival in 1882.

Franz Strauss was adamantly opposed to Richard's wish to leave the Gymnasium and go to the Munich School of Music instead, which led to frequent arguments. He was worried, indeed anxious, about his son's future and wanted him at all costs to have a good general education. Johanna recalled him saying 'Then you will be free to take advantage of every opportunity. Whether your talent will last has yet to be seen. Even good musicians find it hard to earn a crust. You'd be better off as a shoe-maker or a tailor.' In later years Richard was to remember his father's insistence on his staying at grammar school with gratitude. It was there that his abiding love for Greek antiquity was born, he wrote at the age of eighty-one to Professor Ernst Reisinger: *Elektra*, *Ariadne auf Naxos*, *Die ägyptische Helena*, *Daphne* and *Die Liebe der Danae* were all written in homage to the Greek genius. In his view the humanistic grammar school would discharge its obligation to give a complete intellectual and artistic education in full when it had added the serious study of music to the curriculum.[7]

In spite of all his school work, his study of music theory which continued until 1880, his domestic music-making and his composing, Richard did not neglect physical exercise, sport and rambling during his school days. From the age of twelve he was often to be found on Wednesdays and Saturdays at the athletics ground in Oberwiesenfeld. He went skating on the Kleinhesselohe Lake and swimming in the summer holidays. He also went for long mountain walks with his father or with other relations and friends. In a letter to Ludwig Thuille, written on 26 August 1879, he described a romantic walk he had taken in the region of the Kochel and Walchen Lakes, accompanied by rain and storm, which he had 'represented on the piano' the next day. In the summers of 1881–4 he went on longer excursions in Upper Bavaria and the Tirol with Josef Jenewein and his Pschorr cousins. Exercise and sport seem to have strengthened the boy, who was susceptible to illness. According to his sister, he often caught cold; he was particularly bad in the winter of 1877–8, when the doctor described him as 'rachitic'. Inflammation of the eyes and other minor complaints are also mentioned. In 1882 he founded a 'Monday Skittles Club' with ten of his cousins as the other members.

Early compositions

Writing to Friedrich von Hausegger in 1892, Strauss said that between 1872 and 1880 he composed more than at any other time, 'too much and too uncritically'. A look at the compositions of those years makes it possible to qualify that remark with more detail. He was already busy as a composer in the years between 1871 and 1876, but the period of greatest productivity began in 1877–8. By that time he had left the childhood stage of his development behind him, thanks in part to his lessons with Friedrich Wilhelm Meyer, but more importantly to his study of classical music and finally to his regular music-making with friends and relatives. He now had the confidence to work on his own, to a certain extent, and to try his hand at larger forms. Until about 1878 his compositions, with few exceptions, were written for private performance in the bosom of the Pschorr family. The course of his development corresponded very closely to the growth in his capacity to understand musical forms. The very earliest compositions were dances and songs, followed by small, still very primitive sonatinas and sonatas for the piano in the simplest, most classical idiom, a childishly naive piano fantasy (o. Op. 21), two songs for mixed choir, some numbers for a Singspiel, intended no doubt for a domestic performance (o. Op. 28), four unaccompanied settings from the Mass for mixed choir, written in connection with his composition lessons (o. Op. 31), and, after one previous attempt to write for orchestra (the overture to the Singspiel *Hochlands Treue*, o. Op. 15), a concert overture in B minor (o. Op. 30), written in 1876, 'scored with the help of Herr Kapellmeister Meyer' and 'dedicated to his dear Papa for his name-day', as was the G major Serenade of 1877 (o. Op. 32).

Many more pieces were started in this period but quickly laid aside, perhaps because they did not stand up to the composer's own scrutiny or the strictures of his father. A song, *Alphorn*, a setting in a folk-like manner of a poem by Justinus Kerner, has a part for the horn, written for his father, as well as piano accompaniment (o. Op. 29). The horn part is a difficult one, and Franz Strauss made some alterations to it. Richard had already written two études for the horn at the age of eight or nine (o. Op. 12), and in the September and October of 1878 he wrote – again for his father's name-day – a more ambitious work for horn and piano, the Introduction, Theme and Variations (o. Op. 52) which has been mentioned above. As Richard told Ludwig Thuille, the horn part of this work was so difficult that revising it was one of the many things he planned to do during the following summer, but it is doubtful whether he actually did it in the end.

Richard dedicated the great majority of his early songs to his aunt Johanna Pschorr, the remainder – insofar as they bear dedications at all – to his father or other relatives. While the childhood compositions make the most modest technical demands – the exceptional difficulty of the horn parts can be attributed to lack of experience –

two piano trios of 1877 and 1878 for the first time require greater skill from their performers. The first, in A major (o. Op. 37), was dedicated to Richard's uncle Anton Knözinger, the second, in D major (o. Op. 53), to his uncle Georg Pschorr. From around the time when Richard moved up from the Latin School into the upper school in the autumn of 1878, his composition became more consciously worked out and strictly controlled. His lessons in counterpoint played a decisive part. His desire to compete with Ludwig Thuille was strengthened in the autumn of 1879, when the latter entered the Munich School of Music. Increasingly Richard was now drawn to the orchestra. He was only thirteen when he wrote the four-part Serenade in G major (o. Op. 32). The fact that Father Strauss transcribed it for the Wilde Gung'l shows his opinion of it. When Munich was celebrating Strauss's centenary, the Wilde Gung'l, which still survives, again played the Serenade (on 9 June 1964) and revealed it as a graceful piece with a pleasing texture. During the summer and autumn of 1878 Richard worked on an orchestral overture in E major (o. Op. 51); in June 1879 a Romance in E♭ major for clarinet and orchestra, written for a school friend, was performed at the end-of-term concert (o. Op. 61); and in July 1879 he completed another overture (A minor, o. Op. 62), which he had started in the previous year. At the same time he did not neglect the exercises Meyer set him in counterpoint (fugues and double fugues) and in 1880, as a Christmas present for his father, he wrote a fugue for piano with four subjects (o. Op. 71). All the time he was also writing new songs and small piano pieces. He had a particular liking for variation form, and the Variations for flute and piano (o. Op. 56), mentioned in his letters to Thuille in the summer of 1879, demonstrate the strides he had made since the variation movements of some of the early sonatas. It may well have been at the suggestion of Friedrich Wilhelm Meyer that he experimented with four-part choral writing. The Seven Songs for vocal quartet or mixed choir (o. Op. 67; 1880) were dedicated, like many other juvenilia, to his father.

Richard still had more than a year at school in front of him when he first approached a publisher. Rather unwisely he offered one of his very earliest orchestral compositions as a specimen of his work, the Festive March in E♭ major written five years before, in 1876. The reason for this choice was probably the wish of the work's dedicatee, his uncle Georg Pschorr, who no doubt liked the idea of

Ludwig Thuille, 1881

Richard Strauss, drawing by Else Demelius-Schenkl, 1880

seeing it in print but was more concerned to give his nephew a treat. Not counting the Schneider-Polka, which had been reproduced in lithograph for friends and family, the Little Gavotte in F major (o. Op. 57) was the first work by Richard Strauss to appear in print. Probably composed in the first quarter of 1879, it was published in Munich in the same year, under the title *Aus alter Zeit* ('From bygone days'), in a 'Musical Picture Album' assembled by Lothar Meggendorfer (*Musikalisches Bilderbuch für das Pianoforte*, vol. 1, fasc. 1).

The Festive March that Richard hoped to see published was chosen by Father Strauss to open a concert of the Wilde Gung'l in March 1881. Franz Strauss had already performed one of his son's compositions in public, at a Wilde Gung'l concert on 29 May 1880. This was the Gavotte no. 4 in D major, written for piano originally and scored 16 July 1879 (o. Op. 59, no. 5), of which the *Süddeutsche Presse und Münchner Nachrichten* wrote as follows:

> A Gavotte on the programme was marked as a first performance and was given a favourable reception. After repeated calls, the president of the association led the composer on to the platform: it was the fourteen-year-old son of the conductor, Herr Strauss. He will at all events bring honour to his name: his indisputable talent and his great love of music are the guarantee of that.

In point of fact Richard was not fourteen but only a few days short of his sixteenth birthday. He was just fifteen when he wrote the gavotte, which has a trio section in the character of a pastoral musette. He was still not seventeen when he wrote to the Leipzig music publishers Breitkopf & Härtel as follows:

> At present I attend grammar school . . . but I shall devote myself completely to music and in particular to composition. I have studied counterpoint with Herr Kapellmeister F. W. Meyer . . . Herr Generalmusikdirektor Franz Lachner, who has kindly consented to look at my compositions from time to time, spoke very favourably of the March and of some of my other larger compositions. These include an as yet unpublished symphony for full orchestra, which is to be played at rehearsal in the near future by the Court Orchestra, at the express wish of His Excellency the General Intendant Herr von Perfall, and a string quartet, which is to receive its first public performance at the beginning of March by Herr Walter and his quartet; I shall wait to see what success it has and shall then perhaps take the liberty

of sending it to you for your kind consideration. (8 February 1881)

If Richard had not occasionally composed in school hours, he would hardly have had the time to write the works he mentions in the letter to Breitkopf & Härtel. He acquired the skill of composing away from the piano at an early stage: he sketched the A major Piano Trio, dedicated to his uncle Anton Knözinger, while ill in bed in December 1877, that is, when he was thirteen and a half. That was one of the pieces he had the chance to play to Franz Lachner, with Franz Brückner playing the violin. Early in the 1880s Richard made an arrangement for piano duet of Lachner's Nonet (AV 183). Franz Strauss also showed some of his son's compositions to Joseph Rheinberger, the composer and director of the Royal School of Music; as mentioned above, Richard continued to take his new pieces to Rheinberger for a number of years.

Breitkopf & Härtel at first declined the Festive March, but when Georg Pschorr undertook to pay the printing costs they published it after all, as Strauss's definitive Op. 1.

The large compositional forms became his principal interest from the early 1880s. He started the A major String Quartet Op. 2 in 1879, but did not complete it until 14 November 1880. He worked at the Cello Sonata Op. 6 over a relatively long period, 1880–3. He finally replaced the original finale, which he played through with Carl Aschenbrenner in 1883, with a completely new one. The most important work of this tempestuous period of rapid development is his first symphony (D minor, o. Op. 69), on which he worked from 12 March to 12 June 1880 – most of which period was school term-time. He wrote to his mother on 17 June: 'I'm getting on all right at school, the symphony is making jolly good progress, all 4 movements are finished now, I've scored the Scherzo completely and *almost* all the first movement.'

At the same time he was rehearsing his trio with his cousin Ludwig Aschenbrenner and playing quartets in the house of his uncle Anton Knözinger. In the same letter to his mother he wrote:

> Papa . . . is re-working my march for the Wilde Gung'l and told me this morning that if the Trio was in E♭ major instead of A major he would have been able to have the melody doubled by the trumpet. I nearly fainted and naturally (naturally?) protested in the most solemn terms against the very idea. Beautiful as the

trumpet is in the right place (in fanfares), it's hideous when it doubles a main melody.

He began to sketch his Violin Concerto Op. 8 in the autumn of 1880 and completed the work in 1882. A new and extensive piano sonata in B minor (Op. 5) was also begun in 1880 and finished 9 January 1881. The Five Piano Pieces Op. 3, yet another work started in 1880, were completed on 31 July 1881. He sent all these to Eugen Spitzweg, the director of Joseph Aibl Verlag, who published the majority of Strauss's early works with definitive opus numbers. (Richard had given opus numbers to his earliest compositions, but frequently altered them.) Spitzweg sent the Op. 3 pieces to his friend Hans von Bülow, who was not impressed. '*Do not care* for the piano pieces by Richard Strauss in the least . . . Lachner has the imagination of a Chopin by comparison. Fail to find any signs of youth in his invention. *Not a genius* in my most sincere belief, but at best a talent, with 60% aimed to shock.' Bülow had little more patience with the *Stimmungsbilder* Op. 9: 'Pity the piano writing is so clumsy, so much in need of practical improvements. Is it really so hard to learn the "proprieties" in this respect from Beethoven, Mendelssohn, Liszt, Raff?' The first of Strauss's pieces to please him was the Serenade for thirteen wind instruments Op. 7 published in November 1881; he liked it so much, indeed, that he added it to the repertory of the Meiningen Court Orchestra. Richard succeeded in interesting Franz Wüllner in the Serenade too, who gave it its first performance on 27 November 1882, in Dresden.

The first public performances

Richard's very earliest compositions were heard only in the family circle, but from 1881 onwards the almost bewildering number of works he produced in his last two years at grammar school attracted rapidly growing attention from the general public as well. The very first public performances – such as those of the Gavotte no. 4 and the Festive March Op. 1 by the Wilde Gung'l – were given in relative obscurity, but in the one month of March 1881 no fewer than four of Richard's works were heard in different Munich concert halls. On 14 March, in the first of a series of recitals in the Museumssaal, Benno Walter, Michael Steiger, Anton Thoms and Hans Wihan gave the première of the A major String Quartet Op. 2, completed in the previous November and dedicated to these players. The work was reviewed sympathetically in the *Münchner Neueste Nachrichten* on 20 March:

> It is proof of decided talent; it is characterized by natural sentiment and skill in handling the form. The themes of the first and last movements are not strikingly original; they remain within the stylistic frontiers laid down by Mozart and Haydn, while the development sections acknowledge the influence of Mendelssohn. The Scherzo is fresh in its invention, with a physiognomy of its own, not merely a reproduction of others, and the melodies of the elegiac Andante are filled with a warm emotion. Each movement was generously applauded and the young composer took two bows at the end at the insistence of an enthusiastic audience.

The cellist Ferdinand Böckmann, in whose home Richard was made welcome during his visit to Dresden in December 1883, found the quartet difficult, because of its rhythmic complexities, but he took an 'exceptional' liking to the first three movements.

> The beautiful second subject in the major is the making of the Scherzo and the marvellous heightening after the interpolation of the four bars in 3/4 time does the same for the Andante. I'm afraid the last movement does not appeal to me so much, the principal subject is too short and is made too restless by the way it always begins in the weak part of the bar, and then on the whole it is spun out for far too long.

Two days after the first performance of the quartet, on 16 March, Cornelia Meysenheim gave a recital in which she included three songs by Richard: *Waldesgesang* (o. Op. 55), *O schneller mein Ross* (AV 159) and *Die Lilien glühn in Düften* (AV 160). Ten days later the first performance of the Festive March Op. 1 by the Wilde Gung'l took place under Franz Strauss's direction in the Bürgerverein room in the Augsburger Hof hotel. The climax came on 30 March, when the D minor Symphony (o. Op. 69), written in the spring and early summer of 1880, received the honour of a first performance under Hermann Levi in the third of that year's season of Musical Academy subscription concerts in the Odeon. The work was announced in the programme as the 'Opus of a youth who has not yet completed his seventeenth year'. It was the first item in a programme that also included Brahms's *Variations on the 'St Antony' Chorale*, Mozart's concerto for three pianos (with Sophie Menter at the first piano), and *Wellington's Victory* by Beethoven. The symphony was applauded vigorously and Levi signalled its schoolboy composer to take a bow three times. It was an exciting occasion for the whole family, as Johanna recalled:

> My father would not hear of anyone but himself copying out the score and all the parts by hand, and of course he was playing in the orchestra. Father was naturally very nervous and worked-up, while Richard remained very calm and made no preparations. Mama and I were sitting in our usual subscription seats and Richard in his Sunday suit was standing, as he always did, behind the first pillar on the left, by where the artists came in. In my excitement I squeezed my thumbs tighter and tighter into my palms for luck, as if the success of the performance depended on my strength alone. Motionless and fearful I sat on the edge of my chair and with every bar the load on my spirit lifted, every note was as I knew it should be.
>
> It was an extraordinary success. The conductor Hermann Levi himself awarded the young composer the honour of his applause. Mother and I both felt as if a stone had been lifted from our hearts and my father may never have breathed such a sigh of relief after a concert as he could after this one. What it meant to him, to be playing in the orchestra in the first performance of a large-scale work by his own son, in the Odeon, the most distinguished venue of musical life in Munich, in front of an audience accustomed to the best, and professional critics who would judge the work by the severest standards, is something that nobody else can imagine with any ease. One of Richard's school friends, Max Steinitzer, who years later wrote the first biography of my brother, says that the boys in his class did not notice any change in him after the publicity he had had; and he behaved at school and in lessons just exactly as he had before. In spite of his triumph we did not have any great celebration at home. My parents wisely restrained themselves in praising him.

In Franz Strauss's manuscript copy of the D minor Symphony the headings of the movements were altered from what they were in his son's original autograph – no doubt as the result of the experience gained in performance of the work:

Original	*Copy*
First movement:	
Introduction: Andante / Allegro vivace	Andante maestoso/Allegro vivace

Second movement:	
Adagio ma non troppo	Andante
Third movement:	
Scherzo/Trio	Scherzo: molto allegro, leggero/Trio
Fourth movement:	
Allegro con brio	Finale: Allegro maestoso

In spite of his parents' self-restraint, Richard's triumph did not go altogether unmarked. His relatives and friends presented him with his very first laurel wreath after Cornelia Meysenheim's recital. It was small, no bigger than a plate, and there was a blue ribbon attached with an inscription in gold letters: 'Presented on the most memorable day of your life, 16 March 1881.' His sister cherished it all her life and recalled that 'he also received a gold signet ring with a black oval stone with his monogram R. S., which he always wore until he gave it to his grandson Richard on his eighteenth birthday [1 November 1945]'.

The critics gave the symphony a benevolent reception. The *Münchner Neueste Nachrichten* reported on 3 April:

> The third of the Musical Academy's subscription concerts included one new work, a symphony in D minor by Richard Strauss. The recent performance of his String Quartet had already drawn our attention to the significant talent possessed by this still very young composer. The symphony, too, shows considerable competence in the treatment of the form as well as remarkable skill in orchestration. It must be said that the work cannot lay any claim to true originality, but it demonstrates throughout a fertile musical imagination, to which composition comes easily.

The D minor Symphony was not heard again until 5 January 1893, when the Wilde Gung'l played it under Franz Strauss in the Museumssaal. Richard had given the amateur orchestra exclusive performance rights. After the first performance in 1881, Father Strauss asked Hermann Levi how he could thank him; Levi promptly seized his chance to ask the great horn-player to take part in the first performances of *Parsifal* at the Bayreuth Festival in the following year. He was only too well aware of Strauss's hostility towards Wagner, so this was taking him at his word with a vengeance. Strauss had no option but to consent. When he went to

Bayreuth in the following summer, he even took Richard with him. So it was that Richard heard *Parsifal*, but it seems to have made little impression on him – at all events not a positive one. This was the last occasion on which Richard Wagner and his old opponent crossed swords. In the letter to his wife which was quoted near the beginning of the first chapter of this book, Franz Strauss's animosity seems to boil over in virulent hatred.

By 1879 Richard had heard all Wagner's later works – *Tristan*, *Die Meistersinger*, the complete *Ring* – in Munich. His account of his first reaction to *Tristan* and *Siegfried* – how he understood not a note, although he was 'a passably well-educated musician by then' – has already been quoted in part. He goes on to say:

> Prejudice instilled by upbringing may well have had a strong influence on this. At any rate, it was only after I had disobeyed my father and studied the score of *Tristan* that I succeeded in penetrating that miraculous work (and later the *Ring* too), and I still remember how, when I was about seventeen, I feverishly devoured the pages of the score of *Tristan*, until my enthusiasm reached a pitch of intoxication which was dashed only when I went once again to a live performance, in the hope of reinforcing the impressions that my eye and inner ear had received from the page. Renewed disappointment and doubt, renewed resort to the score – until I realized that it was the discrepancy between a mediocre performance and the great composer's intentions, which I had read aright in the unsullied pages of the score, that prevented the work from sounding in the theatre as I had heard it inwardly . . . After that, (in spite of my old uncle's warning words about the 'swindler of Bayreuth') I became a *complete Wagnerian*.

Although several years passed from the time when the boy first began to sneak a look at the score of *Tristan* to his complete commitment to Wagner, yet while he was still in his last year at school, according to Max Steinitzer, he gradually began to slip pacifying remarks into his conversations with his father: 'But remember, the overall effect of the thing is different, you sit in the middle of the orchestra, playing your part on the horn' was typical. As for Richard's compositions, it was still to be a very long time before they began to show the slightest trace of his coming to terms with Wagner.

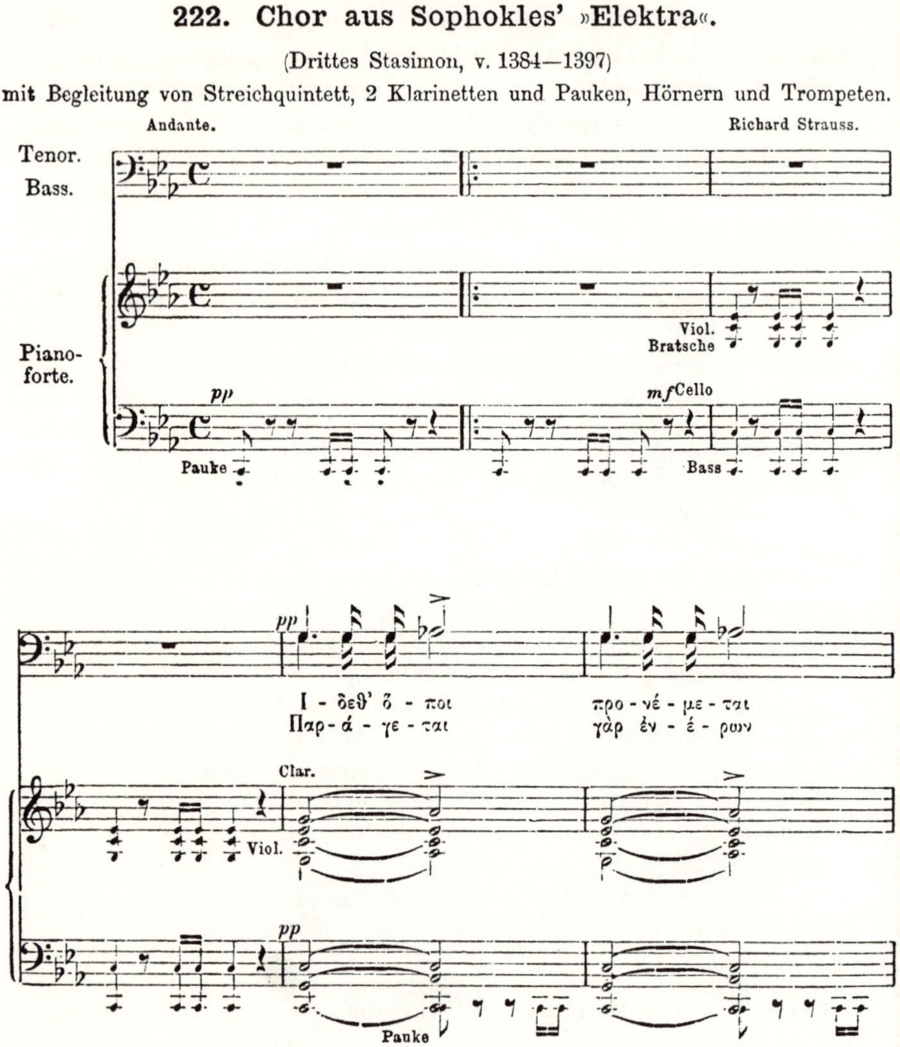

Chorus from Sophocles' *Elektra*, *c*1881

The last year at school

Although composition and performance made great demands on Richard's energies and time, his school work remained on the whole good, or at least satisfactory. He had the following report at the end of his penultimate year: 'Keen, tries hard, but is in too much of a hurry, lacks the capacity to reflect; in spite of his pronounced preference and gift for music he has not been negligent in any subject except mathematics'.

In his last year at school (1881–2), in spite of the demands of his work, Richard continued to compose as prolifically as before: he began or planned several larger works, including the D minor Violin Concerto Op. 8, the *Stimmungsbilder* Op. 9 for piano, and the Horn Concerto Op. 11. At the annual May Festival in the Great Hall of the Museum, when the pupils of the Ludwigs-Gymnasium recited poems or performed on musical instruments, on 16 May 1882 Richard played two piano pieces from his 'Opus 3'. Since he frequently changed the opus numbers he gave his early works, it cannot be established with any certainty which pieces these were: they may have been from the set of five sketches he wrote in 1879, o. Op. 59, or the Two Piano Pieces, o. Op. 68. The programme for this concert has survived, but it does not make clear whether or not Richard also accompanied his cousin Carl Aschenbrenner, in an Adagio and Rondo by a composer identified only as Werner, or other performers in works for solo vocalists, clarinet and chorus.

Karl Klindworth gave an encouraging reception to three of Richard's compositions in May 1882:

> So far as the form of the pieces is concerned, there is little to find fault with, but I could wish for content of greater significance before the young composer embarks on a public career. Even so, I liked the Violin Concerto best, and I should be delighted if it turned out to be effective and viable enough to banish Bruch's G minor from our concert halls.

But Strauss's concerto has never become very popular, unlike the Bruch which is still often heard.

Richard's final school report, dated 5 August 1882 and signed by Commissioner von Pessl of the Ministry of Education and the headmaster of the Ludwigs-Gymnasium, Erich Kurz, has the following comments:

Religious knowledge	–
Latin	good
Greek	good
German	nearly good
French	nearly good
Mathematics and Physics	middling
History	very good
Gymnastics	exempted

The report concludes with the general remark that:

> Despite the fact that he has also distinguished himself in his musical pursuits, he has nevertheless worked hard at his language studies with good results, and has displayed a mature understanding in exposition of the classics. His historical knowledge is also very creditable. His conduct has been irreproachable throughout.

First concert tour and university

On leaving school Richard first took a holiday in the Puster valley in the Tirol and in the Dolomites. On his return home, now freed from the considerable burden of his school work, he was at last able to devote himself fully to composition. He finished his Violin Concerto, which was given its first performance on 5 December of the same year in the old Bösendorfer rooms in the Herrengasse in Vienna, during Richard's first concert tour. The concerto was in fact performed with a piano accompaniment, played by the composer himself, instead of an orchestra. He wrote home:

> The concert yesterday went well, the hall was reasonably full thanks to the complimentary tickets, my violin concerto was very well received; applause after the first F major trill, applause after each movement, two bows at the end. Otherwise Walter and Menter took only one bow after each item, both played wonderfully, I at least didn't make a mess of the accompaniment. (6 December 1882)

The violinist in the concerto was his cousin Benno Walter; the other works in the programme for piano solo were played by Eugenie Menter, sister of the better-known pianist Sophie Menter.

During his short stay in Vienna Richard went to a performance of *La traviata*. Wilhelm Jahn, who was in charge of the concerts of the Gesellschaft der Musikfreunde in the 1882–3 season, made his box at the opera available to Strauss and his companions. Richard was very blasé in his comments on Vienna: '. . . just an ordinary city like Munich, only the houses are bigger, more palaces than inhabitants. The girls aren't any prettier than they are in Munich.' (6 December 1882)

He paid courtesy calls on Hans Richter, the conductor of the Vienna Court Opera and the Philharmonic concerts, and Wilhelm Jahn, but failed to find Ludwig Speidel or Eduard Hanslick at home. He persuaded Max Kalbeck of the *Wiener Allgemeine Zeitung* to publish an article about his concerto and himself before the concert took place. He went to a concert of the Vienna Philharmonic and was astonished to hear hissing after the Adagio of Brahms's Orchestral Serenade in D major.

Two months after the Vienna concert, on 8 February 1883, Benno Walter played Richard's concerto at one of his recitals in Munich, with Richard again accompanying on the piano, and with Eugenie Menter on the piano in the other items. It was to be another thirteen years before Strauss's Violin Concerto was at last performed in its orchestral version, at a concert of the Liszt-Verein in Leipzig in 1896, conducted by Strauss and with Alfred Krasselt as soloist. A few days before the concert in Vienna in December 1882, the Serenade in E♭ major for thirteen wind instruments (Op. 7, 1881) had received its first performance at a matinée of the Dresden Tonkünstlerverein under Franz Wüllner.

In accordance with his father's wishes, Richard attended Munich University for the winter semester of 1882–3. As he recorded in autobiographical notes, he went to lecture courses on the history of philosophy, aesthetics, cultural history and Shakespeare, but stuck it out for only a year. 'Listening to the drone of a professorial voice for three quarters of an hour at a time made my musical ear so tired that I soon opted for the acquisition of that kind of knowledge through reading and making my own choice of teachers!' Even in those days, long before Alexander Ritter initiated him in the philosophy of Schopenhauer, he had occasional discussions about the subject with Arthur Seidl.[8]

Marking time

Strauss's further education benefited far more from his experiences as an active member of the Wilde Gung'l, the amateur orchestra conducted by his father, which was very popular with Munich audiences. He played with the first violins, at the third desk to begin with and later at the first, until September 1885, with a break between October 1883 and April 1884, when he was in Berlin. It gave the young violinist the chance to learn about orchestras and orchestral music from the inside. It seems likely that on occasion he was also allowed to conduct at a rehearsal in his father's place. In the years that he was in the orchestra they gave public performances of works by Bach, Haydn, Mozart, Beethoven, Weber, Schubert,

Hummel, Gade, Auber, Boieldieu, Reissiger, Kretschmer, Verdi (the Triumph March from *Aida*) and dance numbers by Johann Strauss. Carl Aschenbrenner recalled some of the Wilde Gung'l rehearsals in the days when Richard was a member:

> Quite apart from his sunny nature and over-flowing high spirits, which won him the friendship of all who knew him, he often came into the most severe – though good-humoured – conflict with his father. The latter attached the greatest importance to orderly tuning, and there was nothing he hated more than that one player should still be plucking at a string after he had raised his baton to start. But our friend Richard was almost always still plucking or stroking his E string, which was almost never in tune. Every time it happened his father was beside himself at his undutiful son's musical transgression. But the way Richard was unable to control his laughter made all of us laugh too, and in the end pacified his scolding father as well.

In the first six months of 1883, besides some songs and piano pieces for his uncle Knözinger, Richard wrote an (unpublished) Romance in F major for cello and orchestra (o. Op. 75), which he finished on 27 June. The work was given a number of public performances, in Aachen, Freiberg, Baden and elsewhere, by Hans Wihan, the principal cellist of the Munich Court Orchestra and founder, in 1892, after he had left Munich for Prague, of the celebrated Czech String Quartet.[9] Wihan was married to the Dresden-born pianist Dora Weis, who was to play an important role in Richard's life. He also gave the first public performance of Richard's Cello Sonata Op. 6, on 8 December 1883 in Nuremberg with Hildegard von Königsthal at the piano. This sonata quickly became one of Strauss's most frequently performed works. While he was still writing it, Father Strauss wrote to his wife: 'Richard ought not to work too fast and too much at his sonata, and he ought to be rather more critical while he is working, because not everything that just happens to come into one's head is worth writing down.' Richard eventually replaced the sonata's original finale with a completely new movement. He wrote a verse by Grillparzer on the manuscript as motto:

> Tonkunst, die vielberedte
> sie ist zugleich die Stumme.
> Das einzelne verschweigend
> gibt sie das Weltalls Summe.

('Music, the eloquent, is at the same time dumb. Keeping silent about one individual thing, she gives us the sum of the universe.')

During the summer of 1883 Richard spent a holiday in the little spa of Heilbrunn midway between Bad Tölz and the Kochelsee in Upper Bavaria. Here he made the acquaintance of the Speyer family from Frankfurt. The father of the family, Dr Otto Speyer, was a lawyer but he was the son of Wilhelm Speyer, a composer of lieder who was well-known in his day. Richard quickly made friends with the two daughters and, in particular, conceived a sentimental regard for Lotti. Photographs were exchanged and later he sent her three songs, one of them dedicated to her 'in the most profound respect': this was *Rote Rosen*, a setting of a poem by Carl Stieler (o. Op. 76, 11 September 1883). He wrote to her:

> I take the liberty of dedicating it to you as a little memento of those delightful days in Heilbrunn, but I sincerely beseech you to regard it as written specially for you alone, my dear Fräulein, a little verse for your album with my music a mere addition below the lines, and in no way intended for even the smallest audience, while you may do whatever you please with the other two songs.
>
> I implore you not to be cross with me for *Rote Rosen*; because of the delightful memories that it holds *for me*, I could not resist the impulse to set it to music for you, although I am afraid that the text does not really lend itself to composition and so the result is not particularly felicitous. Nevertheless, the little poem, which I found quite by chance in Paul Heyse's *Münchner Dichterbuch*, has given me enormous pleasure. To a certain extent it applies so fittingly to you, and the ending to me, that at the first reading I was thrown into utter confusion; however, as I say, only *to a certain extent*: you may judge for yourself how far. (19 October 1883)[10]

His plea that she should not sing the song even in the most restricted company is a sign of a growth in self-criticism. Lotti wrote in reply:

> I want to say first of all that it is a long time since anything gave me so much pleasure as receiving your song and your letter. My most sincere thanks for everything! It was my very secret wish that you would dedicate a little song to me, and now it has been so beautifully granted. *Rote Rosen* is very beautiful, there is no question of 'being cross with you'; but the comparison you draw with the text is far too flattering to me. I am very glad that you still think of me and have not forgotten me, but the text of *Rote Rosen* has inspired your artistic imagination to conjure up

something a little different. Be that as it may, you have given me great pleasure with it, and I have certainly not forgotten your promise, since September I have run often enough to our letter box, to see if anything had come for me from Munich. (11 November 1883)

The music Richard was writing at this time was still of two distinct kinds, for domestic and public performance. The *Variations on a Theme of Cesare Negri* for string quartet (AV 174), which he finished on 30 September 1883 and dedicated to his cousin August Pschorr for his twenty-first birthday, belonged to the first category, for example. He took the theme from a modern edition, by Oscar Chilesotti, of fifteen dances by Negri, which had originally appeared in Milan in 1602 under the title *Le gratie d'Amore.* But he was simultaneously working on his concerto for horn with orchestral or piano accompaniment (E♭ major, Op. 11) and on a new symphony (F minor, Op. 12). Another work that he completed was a Concert Overture in C minor (o. Op. 80), which was given its first performance at a Musical Academy concert in the Odeon in Munich on 28 November 1883. Once again, as with the D minor Symphony eighteen months before, the conductor was Hermann Levi. The overture, which Richard originally designated as 'Opus 10', then as 'Opus 4', was never published, but it was performed several times in 1884, in Augsburg under August Schletterer, in Berlin under Robert Radecke, in Innsbruck under Joseph Pembaur and in Dresden under Ernst von Schuch, and in 1886 Strauss himself conducted it in Meiningen. It had occasional airings even later. Both the public and the critics liked it. The *Münchner Neueste Nachrichten* found in it

new proof of the originality of the young composer's talent. Obviously influenced by the *Coriolan* Overture, the work seizes the listener's attention by its fiery, energetic, forward impulse, and the composer had the skill to make the principal theme interesting by the alternation of duple and triple rhythms. The work is well constructed (only the short fugal section seems unmotivated) and it is very effective – if perhaps a little heavily scored in places. It was warmly received.

The overture was dedicated to Hermann Levi. It was probably also in 1883 that Richard composed a *Song without Words* in E♭ major (o. Op. 79). He intended it to be an orchestral piece, but it appears that he abandoned it after writing the particello.

Concert Overture in C minor, 1883 (copyist's hand)

3

The Berlin winter, 1883–4

Richard's successes as a composer made it easier for Father Strauss to give way to his urgent pleading to be allowed to spend the winter of 1883–4 in Berlin. He was now nineteen years old: the trip would give him the opportunity to experience the musical life of a metropolis, to establish worthwhile connections, to play his compositions to influential people and to learn how to comport himself in the 'big world'. Richard took advantage of everything that was offered him with all his native energy and exuberance. He stayed in Munich only until his C minor Concert Overture had been performed, and then set off in the first week in December. His first halt was in Leipzig. His letters to his parents reveal the intensity of his interest in attending every concert and opera performance he could, and the single-minded diligence with which he called on the conductors and composers to whom he had been given letters of introduction. The compositions he played on the piano to these gentlemen included the Concert Overture and the completed movements of the new symphony in F minor; he finished the Finale of this work on 6 December, but was still working on the Adagio after his arrival in Berlin. He played the overture to Carl Reinecke, the conductor of the Gewandhaus concerts, and parts of the symphony to the composer Heinrich von Herzogenberg and his wife Elisabeth.

Richard spent longer in Dresden, which he found an agreeable change after 'grubby and uninteresting' Leipzig – not least because of the warm welcome he received in the home of Herr and Frau Weis, the parents-in-law of the cellist Hans Wihan. 'Frau Wihan's parents are extraordinarily kind, I feel quite at home' he wrote to his parents on 12 December. In the same letter he described the impres-

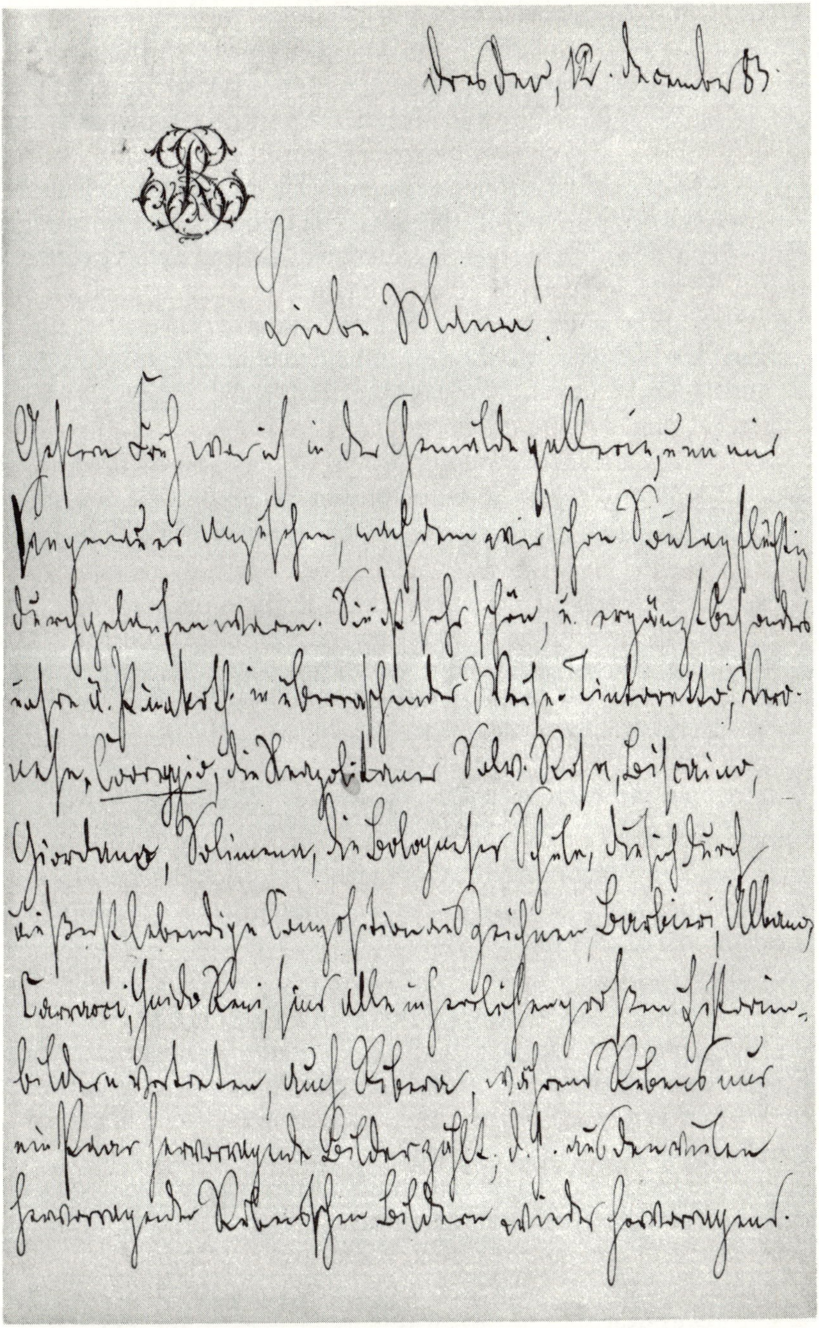

Dresden, 12. November 83.

Liebe Mama!

Gestern früh war ich in der Gemäldegallerie, um nur Einzelnes anzusehen, nachdem wir schon Sonntag flüchtig durchgelaufen waren. Die ist sehr schön, u. ergänzt besonders sehr d. Berliner in überraschender Weise. Tintoretto, Veronese, Correggio, die Neapolitaner [illegible] Giordano, Solimena, die bolognesische Schule, die sich durch [illegible]

Letter to his mother from Dresden, 12 November 1883

sions a visit to the Dresden Gemäldegalerie had made on him. It was the first of the innumerable visits he was to make, throughout his life, to the art galleries in every town his travels took him to, if he could possibly find the time. Neither a superficial glance at the contents, nor a selection of the gallery's most celebrated treasures satisfied him: he always made a systematic inspection of everything that was to be seen, and in this way he built up a very thorough knowledge of different schools and styles, assisted by his excellent memory which enabled him to relate comparable works. He became familiar with all the works by great masters in every gallery in Europe – and was equally well-informed about the subjects they depicted. The musical associations of Raphael's *Sistine Madonna*, which he pointed out to the present author when he was eighty-four years old, are already found in this letter to his parents describing the 'sublime impression' it made on him when he first saw it:

> The form is soft, the conception full and splendid, and the mass is perfect: the way the white halo gradually loses itself in the blue of the sky, until it becomes a little denser in the heads of the cherubs, which I needed my opera-glasses to see properly: that is marvellous. The picture, and the overall impression it made on me, reminds me very vividly of the *pp* G major passage in the introduction to the *Consecration of the House*, the gentleness, softness and conciliatoriness accompanying the splendour of the design and the conception. (12 December 1883)

On his first visit to Italy two and a half years later, in April 1886, he was even more deeply touched by another Raphael, the *Saint Cecilia* in the Pinacoteca in Bologna: 'Contemplating this magnificent work of art, tears came into my eyes' he wrote to his family.

While in Dresden he received some pressing advice about his composition from his father. After expressing his pleasure at the good reception Richard was meeting with in musical circles, Franz Strauss wrote: 'Halt! In your next compositions pay more attention to the quartet and less to the wind. The string quartet is always the most important thing!' (16 December 1883)

Richard remained in Dresden until 21 December. As the sons of the Weis family went down with measles, he moved to the home of Ferdinand Böckmann, the principal cellist of the Court Orchestra, whose wife Helene, then thirty-one years old, looked after the young composer with as much solicitude as Herr and Frau Weis. When she was ninety, Frau Böckmann wrote a brief memoir of the visit, including a comic incident which Strauss himself related to the Dresden orchestra in 1932 and again in a letter to the Böckmanns' great-grandson, Kurt Wilhelm, in 1945. Helene Böckmann's version was as follows:

> He practised conducting with one of my large wooden knitting needles, modelling himself on our celebrated von Schuch; my husband was in the middle of long and demanding rehearsals of Wagner at the time – he took the needle away from him with the words: 'My dear Richard, do just stop that! I've had Schuch fumbling about under my nose for three hours today, and I've had enough of it!'
>
> I had to close the grand piano several times, too, because of the way he used to rage away on it.

He was practising his cello sonata, which he and Böckmann played on 19 December at a 'practice evening' of the Dresden Tonkünstlerverein, held in the Drei Raben.

> Well, my sonata was a great success, it got colossal applause, I was congratulated from all sides and there wasn't a single dissenting voice. Böckmann, who played quite beautifully, was blissfully happy with it and he likes the sonata very much, he's going to play it again, at a trio soirée, or at one of their concerts of new compositions. Grützmacher, Lauterbach and Scholtz all came just to hear the sonata and expressed themselves very complimentarily. (To his parents, from Berlin, 22 December 1883)

Oscar Franz, the principal horn in the Dresden Court Orchestra, confirmed the sonata's success in a letter to Franz Strauss:

> Your son's wonderful sonata had a magnificent reception from the Tonkünstlerverein, and it is indeed a splendid work, full of original feeling, and everything flows so wholesomely in it. Your son is fundamentally wholesome by nature, and I hope it will be many a long day before he is sicklied o'er with the pale cast of thought. I rejoice from the bottom of my heart and take the greatest pleasure in your son's success. (20 December 1883)

Of all the works from this period in Strauss's creative life, the Cello Sonata is the one that is still heard most often.

Another acquaintance Richard made in Dresden was that of Franz Wüllner, who was at that time principal conductor of the Court Orchestra and director of the Dresden Conservatory. When he became the principal conductor of the Gürzenich Concerts in Cologne in 1884 he proved himself one of Strauss's most energetic champions: he gave the first performance in Germany of the F minor Symphony and invited Strauss to conduct *Wandrers Sturmlied* himself; *Till Eulenspiegel* (1895) and *Don Quixote* (1898) received their first performances in Cologne under his baton, and he was one of the first to add *Also sprach Zarathustra* and *Ein Heldenleben* to his repertory.

On 21 December Richard arrived in Berlin. He stopped first at the home of Fritz Fischerdick, a brother of his aunt Johanna Pschorr, and then moved into a modest but conveniently situated room at Leipziger Strasse 96/III, where he remained for the rest of his three months' stay. The introductions that he had brought with him, from Hermann Levi among others, the outstanding reputation his father enjoyed among other musicians, the interest that had been aroused by public performances of some of his compositions and – not least – Richard's winning nature combined to open the doors of Berlin's cultural circles to the newcomer. The ease with which the young composer – which is how he now thought of himself as a matter of course – took to the life of the metropolis, throwing himself into the pleasures of society, while not neglecting the opportunity to broaden his horizons in the opera house and concert hall as well as at musical evenings in private houses – such as those of the painters Anton von Werner, Carl Becker, Emil Teschendorff and Ludwig Knaus – speaks for the excellence of his upbringing. The intendant of the Prussian royal theatres, Botho von Hülsen, gave him a free pass to all performances at the opera and the playhouse. Sardou's *Fedora* made a great impression on him, indeed, he pronounced Sardou to be 'the greatest dramatist (not dramatic poet) since Shakespeare', since he was the first person since Shakespeare who understood how 'to intensify conflict and human passions to such a pitch that the audience almost loses its powers of sight and hearing'.

> The play excited me enormously, I was still trembling in every fibre three hours later and I got some relief by writing down there and then a tremendous introduction to my new piano variations with fugue in A minor [o. Op. 81]. I've been burning the candle at both ends a bit, and the excitement did me good and was very refreshing . . . I've recovered my appetite for work and I've had several new ideas. (To Johanna, 5 March 1884)

Othello and *Macbeth* were the only other plays to have a comparable effect on him. At the opera he heard *Le domino noir* – he found Auber's music 'undemanding . . . but very refined and melodious' – *Le maçon* and *Die Zauberflöte*; he was very critical of the performance of this last in a letter to his sister. He heard Hans von Bülow playing the piano and wrote about it in terms of the greatest admiration: phrasing, touch and execution in Raff's 'dreadfully insipid C minor Concerto' were 'phenomenal'; he characterized a C minor symphony by Xaver Scharwenka as 'a pianist's symphony'.

For all the excitement of being in Berlin, Richard remained a critical listener and faithfully reported his impressions of works and interpreters – Eugen d'Albert, for instance, whom he thought 'really phenomenal' – and of performances to his father and Ludwig Thuille. He wrote to Thuille about the Joachim Quartet: 'It's the finest quartet in existence – that has ever existed, I think. The sheer beauty of the sound, the purity, the ensemble, the wonderful nuances, everything you could possibly ask for is there. For good measure, all four of them play Strads.' (13 January 1884). In the same letter he was, on the other hand, very critical of the Philharmonic Orchestra under Wüllner; he found the woodwinds and horns, in particular, wretched by comparison with the Dresden orchestra.

He heard several performances of Brahms's Third Symphony. After the first hearing he wrote to Thuille that he did not understand it yet, and to his father he wrote:

> My head is still spinning [three days later] from its lack of clarity and I frankly confess that I haven't understood it yet, but it's scored so wretchedly and unclearly that there were only two coherent four-bar ideas you could get hold of in the first and last movements, in the middle sections, and while the movement that replaces the Scherzo is very pretty and interesting, the Adagio [*recte*, the Andante] is really bleak and lacking in ideas. Of course, you can't say so here, because Joachim etc. rave about Brahms. (6 January 1884)

Three or four weeks later he formed a more positive opinion, after hearing a second performance and then, 'with great enjoyment', a third at one of Wüllner's concerts. He was now convinced that the symphony was 'really very beautiful' and that his father would like it too. He confessed that he had liked it better at each hearing and was now virtually enthusiastic about it:

> The form and structure are clear, the working-out is capital, it has delightful themes and a drive and energy that are almost Beethovenian. After a capitally energetic movement, with the most magnificent invention, there's an Andante . . . which amazes you by its simplicity. Then comes the best thing of all: a delightful Allegretto, in 3/4; the only word for it is unique, and you can tell it came to Brahms all in one piece; there's a delightful horn solo in it which is remarkable in mood, first challenging and defiant, then rippling away mysteriously, then climbing vigorously up again. It ends *pp*, the violins *con sordini*, with a melting together of all the themes in the whole symphony. This symphony (F major) is one of the most beautiful, the most original and the freshest things Brahms has ever written. The orchestra played very dashingly and he conducted capitally. He was also the soloist in his D minor Concerto and played it with great beauty and drive. The concerto is not as fresh and original as the symphony, but it's still very beautiful and interesting. (1 February 1884)

He wrote to Thuille in much the same spirit:

> Brahms's No. 3, not only his finest symphony, but probably the most important that has ever been written . . . A colossally fresh and dashing first movement in 6/4 opens the symphony, then there's a C major Andante, without any very deep emotion but very pretty, then comes the most delightful little minuet I've heard for a long time, a teeny little thing in C minor, but it's all of a piece and the ideas are wonderfully pretty; a very dashing last movement, with just a hint of the daemonic, brings the work to its close: I can't yet bring myself to care much for the finale, which rather runs away into the sand, but it's a capital piece all the same. As well as that Brahms played his D minor Concerto, which is another very interesting piece. I'm beginning to get very attached to Brahms as a whole, he's always interesting and very often really beautiful as well. (8 March 1884)

Another letter to Thuille, about the Fourth Symphony, was equally enthusiastic. Richard's admiration for Brahms was only strengthened by a concert under Bülow in Munich in November 1884, and in the following year, when he went to Meiningen, the fire was fuelled again by what he later called 'the suggestive influence of Bülow'. He wrote to Otto Lessmann:

> Herr von Bülow has done Munich yet another great service, in breaking the ground for our great master Brahms at last. Until

now the Munich public, from lack of understanding of course, has never warmed to Brahms. Bülow's Brahms evening has broken the ice . . . The Tragic Overture, the B♭ major Variations and the magnificent Third Symphony were all given a marvellous performance, likewise the B♭ major Concerto, in which Herr von Bülow's playing was what I can only call incomparable. (21 November 1884)

Then, in next to no time, Richard's passion for Brahms was swept away, never to return, by the 'tempestuous' influence of Alexander Ritter, high priest of an exclusive cult of Wagner and Liszt, who took the view that Brahms should be studied until such time as the student realized that there was nothing in him. Even towards the end of his life Strauss wrote to the present author, referring to Brahms's symphonies as 'badly scored piano sonatas', though he always excepted the *'St Antony' Chorale Variations* from the general condemnation.

While he was in Berlin Richard also enjoyed performances of the classical masters and, among other things, Mendelssohn's 'delightful overture' to *Die Heimkehr aus der Fremde*, Felix Weingartner's Serenade for Strings in F major Op. 6, Berlioz's *Benvenuto Cellini* overture and Spohr's Double Quartet in E minor. Of this last he wrote:

. . . drenched in agreeable sounds, it's a delightful work, bursting with harmonic refinement and made even better by the extremely subtle combination of the two quartets, and Spohr has poured all the sweetness of his most beautiful melodies over it, which enchanted me so much that I almost entirely forgot a slight rhythmic monotony in the first movement, which was rather obtrusive after the Beethoven F minor [Op. 95]. (To his mother, 19 February 1884)

He also thought that Spohr's C minor Symphony had deserved its airing, although it was already rather dated. A Mass by Albert Becker was 'a very fine piece of craftsmanship and interestingly scored' but 'too chromatic and too long and boring', and an eight-part *Stabat Mater* by Franz Wüllner made a much better impression on him. He found it impossible to like Berlioz's *King Lear* or *Roman Carnival* overtures.

Richard was received kindly by the musicians Philipp and Xaver Scharwenka, by Karl Klindworth and Heinrich Hofmann, and by the writers Richard Voss, Julius Rodenberg, Julius Wolff, Rudolf

Lindau and Friedrich Spielhagen. He met younger musicians in Berlin, too. Robert Radecke was particularly well-disposed towards him: he performed the C minor Concert Overture while Richard was still in Berlin, on 21 March, and he also expressed an interest in the F minor Symphony, which was completed on 25 January. Richard had several opportunities to give private performances of his Cello Sonata, partnered on different occasions by Robert Hausmann and the history painter Anton von Werner; in this way it was heard by Radecke and Joachim as well as by Hermann Levi's cousin Martin. Shortly before Richard left Berlin, the sonata had a public performance too, which earned it 'unqualified praise' from the *Fremdenblatt*, which had torn the Concert Overture to shreds. The Wind Serenade Op. 7 was also played twice during his stay in Berlin; the first performance was given by the orchestra of the Konzerthaus concerts under Benjamin Bilse, who gave it three more airings. Whether this was done deliberately, to steal a march on Bülow and the Meiningen orchestra, who were to give the other performance, is something that must now remain a mystery; Richard suspected that such was the case and was both angry and anxious as to the possible reaction of Bülow and his agent Hermann Wolff. He was not satisfied by Bilse's interpretation: 'Much too slow, I thought they were all going to sleep, and then the players' intonation was completely out.' The Meiningen orchestra played the Serenade in Berlin on 27 February, but the performance was directed by Franz Mannstädt, not Bülow.

One event of the greatest importance was making Bülow's personal acquaintance. Remembering his father's clashes with the man who had been Wagner's principal champion, Richard looked forward to the encounter with some apprehension, but after the introduction had been effected by Hugo Bock he was able to write home:

> He was very amiable, very well-disposed and very witty and told me to come to the rehearsal on Wednesday, so that I could hear him conduct my Serenade himself. He lavished unusual praise on it and afterwards invited all the players to give me a round of applause, and himself joined in. In the evening he sat in the audience during the concert, which was conducted by Mannstädt, stood up after the Serenade and turned round to applaud and beckon, but he couldn't see me, because I was actually in the front row. However, I didn't go up on the platform. (29 February 1884)

Richard wanted to play Bülow the Concert Overture and the F minor Symphony, but Bülow refused, as he had to practise the piano in preparation for a concert tour. 'Moreover he talked about you with the most colossal respect, you were the most refined musician, the most beautiful tone, magnificent phrasing and execution: "I learned a lot from him", he told me, "do write and tell him so."' When it came to telling his father what he thought of Bülow as conductor, he showed some critical discrimination:

> He conducts capitally, everything by heart, rehearsals and performances, and he has the whole score in his head, right down to the smallest details, as I've been able to see for myself. His interpretation of Beethoven is very subtle in part, but in part it's very recherché and nuanced and unspontaneous.

Before long, however, Strauss was won over completely to Bülow's interpretation of Beethoven. In Meiningen he marked his scores of all nine of the symphonies in exact accordance with Bülow's interpretations, and these remained the basis of his own throughout his life.[1] On the occasion of the performance of his Serenade, Richard also got to know a colleague of his father, Gustav Leinhos (1836–1906) the first horn of the Meiningen orchestra, who played a part in negotiating Strauss's appointment as Bülow's successor in Meiningen and soon established a friendly relationship with the young conductor.

The powerful impression made on Richard by the violin playing of Joseph Joachim is conveyed most forcefully in a letter he wrote to his sister:

> In the evening I heard Joachim, the greatest artistic pleasure I've yet experienced in quartet playing. The ensemble is magnificent, the purity of intonation and figuration, the clarity, the wonderful interpretation, the colossal calm of the adagio playing, the way Joachim subordinates himself when he has nothing special to say, he's just the top line, not the *primarius*, and then the colossal technique, a style of playing completely devoid of any kind of impropriety, a magnificent, noble tone, I was in the seventh heaven. De Ahna (second violin) is also excellent, ditto Wirth (viola) and Hausmann. They're all as good as each other, each of them knows exactly where he ought to take the lead, and yet it's all contained within the framework of harmonious quartet playing; it's an artistic pleasure which is enough reason in itself for Papa to come to Berlin.

1. Beethoven B♭ major Quartet Op. 18, the Adagio of which they played captivatingly (they always play with such a wonderful sense of rhythm and yet it's never rigidly metronomic).
2. Herzogenberg G major Quartet, very attractive, but it imitates Brahms (whom Herzogenberg greatly reveres) too much in the recherché turns and ideas. The Minuet is very fine.

They ended with Schubert's magnificent C major Quintet, which was also played incomparably. It was a wonderful evening. (1 January 1884)

Richard again assiduously visited galleries and exhibitions in Berlin and wrote at length about the *Christ before Pilate* of the Hungarian artist Mihály Munkácsy, a gigantic canvas that was causing a great stir at the time. He was upset by the preponderance of pictures of battle scenes in the Nationalgalerie. He received an introduction into the society of artists as well as musicians. In a memoir he wrote as late as 19 June 1949 he recalled an evening of quartets at the home of the hospitable history painter Carl Becker, when he played second violin and Anton von Werner cello. He made the acquaintance of Adolf von Menzel on that occasion, 'but the prickly little scratch-brush had no words to waste on a nineteen-year-old'. At a dinner-party given by Anton von Werner he met Alfred Pringsheim, professor of mathematics at Munich University, and his wife (née Dohm) – the future parents-in-law of Thomas Mann. Emil Teschendorff, a pupil of Karl von Piloty, was another artist in whose home Richard took part in playing quartets and quintets, in which he played second viola. He also met the genre painter Ludwig Knaus, the painter and illustrator Paul Thumann and the sculptor Gustav Eberlein during this first visit to Berlin.

His letters to his parents, to his sister Hanna and to Ludwig Thuille provide a detailed and faithful account of that winter, covering not only his musical experiences and impressions but also his social life and personal encounters. Although he neglected no aspect of music-making, was punctilious in paying calls, made many useful contacts – among others, with Otto Lessmann, the editor of the *Allgemeine Musikzeitung*, and with the publishers Bote & Bock although without any immediate benefit[2] – he enjoyed the freedom of social life in Berlin to the full. At the Fischerdicks he took part in rehearsals of some comic quartets, and he went to a number of balls – a subscription ball at the Opera House, one at the house of the banker Gerson von Bleichröder, another given by Radecke and several others — where he danced 'till his legs gave way' and enjoyed himself royally. It was in the house of a family which had originally come to Berlin from Munich, that of the wholesale coffee dealer Hermann Klose, that he learned to play Skat, the game that became an indispensable form of relaxation to him in later life. But he still found the time to finish the F minor Symphony Op. 12, of which the Adagio had been left till last. He told Thuille that he had thought of a very appealing 'coda melody' for it, with a 'delightful story' attached to it, which he would tell him when he got back to Munich (13 January 1884). Unfortunately we do not know the story. It was also in Berlin that he finished the cycle of six piano pieces (*Stimmungsbilder* Op. 9), which had also been started in Munich, and wrote seven of the variations in the set of variations and fugue in A minor for piano, later entitled Fourteen Improvisations and Fugue (o. Op. 81) and dedicated to Hans von Bülow. (Only the fugue was ever published and the rest of the work has been lost.) He also made a reduction for piano duet of the C minor Concert Overture, but came to the conclusion that he had now advanced beyond the D minor Symphony: he no longer wished it to be performed, he told his father. After reeling off a list of all his compositional activities in a letter to Thuille, he wrote:

> You see that in spite of never getting up before 11 (I seldom get to bed before 1.30, very often it's 3 or 4, and it was 7 after the Artists' Ball) and spending every evening in society or at the theatre or a concert, and paying calls most days or writing letters, I have not been idle, and I hope that by the time I return to Munich you will have decided on the tempo and key of the Adagio [of Thuille's symphony].

There's no mistaking the sly dig in the last clause.

Father Strauss kept up the flow of advice and admonition in his letters to Richard. It was a role he sustained faithfully up to the time of the *Symphonia Domestica*, although he must have realized long before that that his advice was not always heeded. The following is just one example of what he wrote to his son during his stay in Berlin: 'When you are doing something new, make sure that it is melodious and not too heavy, and that it's pianistic. Increasingly, it's my experience that only melodious music makes a lasting impression on musicians and amateurs, and melody is the most viable element in music.' (11 February 1884) He also responded to Richard's enthusiasm for Sardou:

> In art . . . truth is the principal determining factor. There is no art which does not rest on deep, inner truth. External stimuli may excite the audience but they will not give an inner spiritual quality. In art the world of the sensibilities is the primary factor, the critical element must, if it is to be true art, take the second place. This is the only thing that enables art to bestow the inner spiritual quality. All the head has to do is put things in the right order, but where both factors complement each other, a true work of art can be created. (8 March 1884)

It was of course only natural that in his social life, the visits and the balls (at one of which he also volunteered to be 'an angel of peace in a Greek tunic' in one of the *tableaux vivants* which were so popular in those days), beautiful women and girls should make an impression on the nineteen-year-old boy, and that he too should make an impression on some of them. This is something else that he wrote about frankly in his letters. The girl who attracted him most was the youngest daughter of the writer Friedrich Spielhagen, a 'wonderfully pretty, eighteen-year-old bluestocking with a delightful figure, perfectly beautiful throat and face, shining grey eyes', with whom he was able to converse about Schopenhauer, the naive and the sentimental in art, and other interesting topics, and 'might almost have fallen in love'.

> She really [is] the most beautiful, piquant and clever girl I've seen for a long time . . . I'm frightfully bored with the usual herd that you meet at balls, that at a pinch you can talk to about the German theatre and – if they've money and you're desperate – you can marry. But with her you can go on talking all evening without running out of subjects, and she really is devilishly pretty, so even chattering gives 'Him' pleasure. We talk about 'French plays, Spinoza, the existence of a Higher Being', then we poke fun at the other people there – in short, it was delightful, and I shall not waste the invitation to call on her. (24 February 1884)

He was equally taken with a young singer, Fräulein Pollak, whom he heard as Susanna in *Figaro*: 'She's Hungarian but intelligent and delightfully kind, modest, unassuming and good-natured, and in addition she's wonderfully pretty.' Fräulein Schwarz, of the

Court Theatre, whom he heard singing lieder by Schubert and Brahms, had invited him to show her some of his songs, 'which I shall certainly do, since she lives with Fräulein Pollak'. He commanded the songs to be sent from Munich by special delivery.

In his late autobiographical writings, Strauss recalled yet another infatuation as briefly as he mentioned his friendship with Fräulein Spielhagen, and with as little significance attached to it. This time it was a married woman, the beautiful and much younger wife of Reinhold Begas (1831–1911), a sculptor who was much admired in his day.[3] Richard wrote to his parents that he had 'spent many agreeable evenings chatting with the amiable lady'. Elsewhere he wrote '. . . Reinhold Begas, with whose beautiful wife Grethe I had tea almost twice a week. Reinhold used to come home from cards at about 7.30.' There are frequent references to his visits to Frau Begas in the letters to his parents and sister, the first in a long letter he wrote to Hanna on 1 January, in which he also told her about the music he had been hearing and playing in private houses:

> Last night (New Year's Eve), besides my invitation to the Kloses . . . I had one from the beautiful Frau Begas from 10 o'clock onwards. A wonderfully beautiful woman, who is very fond of flirting, expects it of you indeed, and will take pleasure in a compliment even if it's not quite as refined as it might be, she and her husband, who's a very important artist, were very kind, went into raptures over my compositions and especially were quite ecstatic about my *playing*, at 1.30 a.m. I was playing two Beethoven Adagios.

On 11 January Richard told his father that 'on Tuesday I spent a delightful evening with Frau Begas (unfortunately her husband wasn't there!)', which is perhaps a little ambiguous, especially when it is read in conjunction with a letter he wrote to Thuille two days later, saying that he had been 'received in the most delightful manner by the beautiful Frau Begas – I will give you fuller details when I see you'. In another letter to his friend, of 8 March, he referred to 'Begas, whose beautiful wife has locked me deep in her heart'. He appears to have written rapturously to Helene Böckmann in Dresden as well, since she teases him about it in her replies.

It would be a mistake, however, to read more into the affair than adolescent raptures on Richard's part and coquetry on that of the young woman. The image of a harmless flirtation is filled out and confirmed by the statement in Helene Böckmann's memoirs that Richard told her 'he had composed some lovely songs at the feet of the beautiful Frau B., with the manuscript paper resting on her knees'. Exactly which songs he composed in those circumstances is unknown, but one of the surviving *billets doux* that Richard received from her can be quoted in illustration:

> Dear little great Strauss!
>
> Are you still in Berlin? I was really quite ill and could see no one. Now I am a little better. Can you dine with us at 5 o'clock, quite informally and absolutely alone? (We're in mourning.) Hoping to receive your acceptance on the enclosed card, I am your aged and probably long-forgotten foster-mama, Gret Begas.

A letter she sent him three months after his departure from Berlin, in which she addresses him as 'My dear little Strauss', suggests that she was not very happy. 'Things are not always up to much with me. My life is the same as always.' And in 1887 her cousin Carl Heine included a message from her in a letter to Richard, conveying the best wishes of his 'I hope not-yet-forgotten foster-mama Gret B. to her dear foster-son'.

Franz Strauss's reaction to his son's tales of his social encounters in Berlin is so characteristic of him that it deserves to be quoted:

> It gives me great pleasure to hear that you are moving in such good social circles, it will be of extraordinary benefit to you in your general development; nothing else gives such refinement to the mind and the sensibilities as association with cultivated men and women of refinement and nice feeling. What is an artist without a refined mind and warm sensibility? . . . Don't give offence, your tongue is liable to run away with you, so think before you speak. (10 January 1884)

Berlin itself, the capital of an empire where horse-drawn trams were still adequate to meet the needs of public transport, and the opportunity to rub shoulders with 'lots of prominent people' made an indelible impression on Richard. At a subscription ball at the Opera House, which he sought and obtained his parents' permission to attend, he even saw Emperor Wilhelm, by then well into his eighties. In one of his letters to his parents he wrote 'the social life here is marvellous, we've just no idea at home', and he poured out much more of his enthusiasm to his sister. He wrote to Lotti Speyer, too, with a summary of his impressions:

> Berlin hospitality is phenomenal, and in consequence I have an invitation of one kind or another almost every evening, then that means more calls and return calls, when I have a free evening I rush to a concert or the theatre, then sometimes I really do have to do some work, and so the days and weeks here just fly past . . . I like it very much here in Berlin, the city is very beautiful, immensely bustling and with a lot of amusements to offer. I've already heard a lot of new and beautiful music at concerts and some famous artists, led by Joachim, the king of all violinists, Brahms, d'Albert . . .

After recounting his own successes as a composer, he went on:

> But now I really must tell you something more about Berlin society, which suits me down to the ground, as some very kind introductions have given me the entrée into charming circles.

Then he told her about all the people he had met, not forgetting the delightful Fräulein Spielhagen, the Bleichröder daughters and Grete Begas. (8 February 1884)

Strauss felt at ease in the informal and stimulating atmosphere of Berlin even on his first visit, and the city was never to lose its appeal for him. He was quick to recognize that the complacency prevalent in Munich at the time was a potential threat to any artist, as he told Thuille: 'I'm sorry you're not here. Until I knew about your appointment [as tutor in piano and theory at the Munich School of Music], I was counting on your coming with me. For the lethargic air of Munich is your artistic death.' (8 March 1884)

The stay in Berlin came to an end in the last week in March. Strauss left for home on 29 March, a few days after the performance of the Concert Overture (on 21 March) and the Cello Sonata (on 25 March). He spent Holy Week in Staffelstein with the Hörburgers, and in April he resumed his place in the Wilde Gung'l Orchestra. He composed some songs in May and on 16 May he finished the A minor Improvisations and Fugue intended for Bülow, who never played them, however. A more ambitious composition, *Wandrers Sturmlied* (on a text by Goethe) for chorus and orchestra, Op. 14, was also written in 1884, though it was not performed until 1887, when Strauss conducted it in Cologne.

Eugen Spitzweg

Richard's attempts to establish a business relationship with a publisher in Berlin had been without success, but he now found in Eugen Spitzweg a publisher who not only offered encouragement but was also prepared to take risks. Spitzweg's father Edmund Spitzweg had taken over the music publishing firm of Joseph Aibl when the Aibl family died out, and Eugen (who possessed 'an artistic rather than a commercial temperament' according to Max Steinitzer) and his brother Otto were its directors from their father's death in 1884 until 1904, when they were bought out by Universal Edition of Vienna. Altogether thirty of Strauss's works appeared under the Aibl imprint: Opp. 2, 3, 5–14, 16, 18–21, 23–30, 32, 34–7. Since Spitzweg was also a friend of Bülow, he consulted him as to whether he should publish Richard's work. To begin with, as has already been mentioned, Bülow's reports on works like the Piano Pieces Op. 3 were not very favourable. The fact that Spitzweg published the Piano Pieces, in spite of Bülow, and so many of the subsequent works testifies to his independent judgment, but it also owed something to his friendship with Richard. He first sent him a fee in July 1884, for the Horn Concerto Op. 11, which was to receive its first performance by Gustav Leinhos and the Meiningen orchestra under Bülow, but he made something of a joke of it.

> Dear Herr Strauss,
>
> Your shabby publisher unfortunately cannot afford to pay you a fee for your Horn Concerto, in view of the material success he has had with your works so far. However, since I want him to be the first to pay you a fee, I have advanced him the sum you have asked for, and told him to act as if it was from *him* – of course, when publishers are hammering at your door, he will expect you to remember that he was not block-headed or broad-headed, nor was he goat-legged.

('Broad-headed' [breitköpfig] and 'goat-legged' [bockbeinig] are allusions to the rival firms of Breitkopf & Härtel and Bote & Bock.)

When Spitzweg sent Bülow the Wind Serenade, he liked it so much that he suggested that Richard should write another piece for wind ensemble, and even drew up an outline of the form it should take, which Spitzweg forwarded to Strauss. Strauss wrote to Bülow:

> As a result of the suggestion you were kind enough to make, I have recently been working on a suite for thirteen wind

> instruments. Unfortunately the scheme you drew up for it came too late for me to be able to follow it in its entirety. I did not receive it from Herr Spitzweg until after I had already sketched the first movement (Prelude) and the second (Romance), and now only the last two movements (Gavotte and Introduction and Fugue) are in conformity with your kind advice. (9 August 1884)[4]

Strauss's conducting début

When the B♭ major Suite for thirteen wind instruments was published (by Fürstner in 1911) it was given the opus number 4, which had originally been reserved for the Concert Overture. Bülow was asked to look over the first three movements, but did not reply. Then, on 22 October 1884 Strauss learned from Spitzweg that the Meiningen orchestra was going to perform the work at a matinée concert in the Odeonssaal in Munich, and that he himself was to conduct it. (Rheinberger's *Wallenstein* Symphony was also on the programme.) Bülow informed Richard on 25 October that he could rely on the players having spent some time on the suite before they began their tour, so that 'it will give you more pleasure than trouble to direct the work personally, according to your own interpretation, on the morning of 18 November in Munich'. Richard was aghast, as he had never conducted in public before. There was no question, however, of his rehearsing the work with the orchestra in person. Bülow declared bluntly: 'There won't be any rehearsals. The orchestra has no time for that on tour.'

We have Strauss's own account of the momentous occasion:

> I went to fetch Bülow from his hotel: he was in an abominably bad mood. As we were going up the stairs in the Odeon he was fulminating against Munich, which had cast Wagner and him out, against old Perfall, called the Odeon a cross between a church and a stock exchange, in short, he was as delightfully unbearable as only he could be, when he was furious about something. The matinée ran its course. I conducted my piece through something of a haze; all I can remember now is that I didn't make a complete mess of it, but I simply couldn't say what it was actually like otherwise. Bülow didn't listen to my début at all, he was storming round and round the instrument room, chain-smoking. Just as I got back in there, my father came in by another door, deeply moved, to express his thanks to Bülow. That was what Bülow had been waiting for. He

> pounced on my father like a ravening lion. 'You have nothing to thank me for,' he yelled, 'I haven't forgotten the way you treated me, here in this god-forsaken city. I did what I did today because your son has talent, not for your sweet sake.' Without another word my father left the room, whence all others had fled as soon as they saw Bülow erupt. Of course the effect of this scene was to completely ruin my début for me, but all of a sudden Bülow was in the best of tempers. He later made amends for the affront he gave my father on that occasion, and my father did not harbour resentment against his son's benefactor.[5]

In spite of everything, Strauss's conducting début must have made a good impression, otherwise Bülow would not have summoned the son of his old enemy to join him in Meiningen the following year.

New compositions and performances

The growing success he was enjoying with his chamber and orchestral works did not prevent Strauss from continuing to write occasional pieces for his cousins and the Wilde Gung'l. For the Pschorrs he wrote a Festive March in D major for piano quartet (AV 178) and he wrote another work with the same title and in the same key for the orchestra (o. Op. 84). He revised the latter in 1888, altering the brass parts to bring them into line with the tonalities then customary and adding cinelli to the percussion. The first version of the orchestral Festive March was written towards the end of 1884 or the beginning of 1885. Richard also wrote a song for male-voice choir, *Schwäbische Erbschaft* (o. Op. 83), probably for a competition; it failed to win a prize and lay forgotten until it was rediscovered in 1950.

Bülow, who permitted Richard to accompany him to Augsburg on the next stage of the tour after the Munich matinée, suggested that he should send his Suite to Brahms and ask for his opinion, and promised that he too would write to Brahms, in support of Richard's request. Richard lost no time and wrote to Brahms the day after the Odeon concert, saying he would count himself 'more than fortunate' if Brahms would write him a few lines about the Suite (19 November 1884). The score was still in the keeping of the Meiningen orchestra, so Richard asked the horn-player Gustav Leinhos to see that it reached Brahms. How Leinhos accomplished this mission is revealed in a postcard he sent Strauss from Pressburg on 21 November: 'Herr Dr Brahms has the score. He had had your letter. I impounded his overcoat yesterday evening in the concert hall and insinuated the score into the pocket . . . Brahms showed great interest in you and I sang your praises without stint.' Leinhos wrote again on 15 December: 'When he gave me back your Suite he spoke very highly of your work, though he had looked in vain for the spring of melody which ought to be overflowing at your age.'

Richard began a work on a larger scale in the months following his return home from Berlin: the Piano Quartet in C minor Op. 13, which, like *Wandrers Sturmlied*, shows the influence of Brahms. On 3 October 1884 the Berlin Tonkünstlerverein announced a competition for a piano quartet with a prize of 300 marks. The judges were Heinrich Dorn from Berlin, Joseph Rheinberger from Munich and Franz Wüllner from Cologne. Wüllner wanted to put Richard's entry, submitted under the epigraph 'Die Tonkunst, die vielberedte', in first place; Rheinberger wanted to put it second, and Dorn eighth, but in the end Strauss's work was given the prize. It was given its first performance in Weimar on 8 December 1885, by Strauss himself with members of the Halir Quartet, and was played in Meiningen on 6 January 1886 – again from manuscript, like the first performance – by Strauss, Leopold Müller, August Funk and Robert Wendel. Another performance, at the first chamber-music matinée of the Allgemeiner Deutscher Musikverein festival in Cologne, on 30 March 1887, earned the work considerable acclaim, but Richard's duties in Munich prevented him from being present on that occasion. After the award he had written to Wüllner:

> While it's not proper for me to say 'thank you' for the fact that my C minor Quartet won the prize, all the same I would not want to delay telling you how greatly honoured and happy your verdict has made me. Not the least of my pleasures was learning from the reports published in Munich that you recognized the creator of the F minor Symphony in the composer of the C minor Quartet. The Berlin award will spur me on to make new, serious efforts and to give my artistic accomplishment ever new depth. (13 January 1886)

He had more first performances in the new year of 1885. On 8 January the Wilde Gung'l, directed by Father Strauss, played the Festival March in D major for orchestra o. Op. 84 at one of their public concerts, and on 13 January the F minor Symphony had its German première at a Gürzenich concert in Cologne under Franz

Wüllner (the world première had been given in New York on 13 December 1884 under Theodor Thomas, at a concert of the New York Philharmonic Society). After attending a rehearsal in Cologne, Richard wrote to his parents:

> So the symphony was rehearsed on Saturday. It's immensely difficult but sounds colossal. I was almost moved by the first movement. You should have seen them in my Scherzo, coming cropper after cropper, it was hilarious. The Adagio sounds magical, and the Finale is just as good. I hope the Gürzenich audience will like it as much tomorrow as its infatuated composer did on Saturday. Papa will open his eyes wide when he hears how modern the symphony sounds, and perhaps there's just a little bit too much counterpoint in it, but in compensation for that everything surges and pulsates so that it's a joy to hear it. (12 January 1885)

The critics were amazed by the work:

> One can hardly believe one's eyes [*sic*] when one hears in this symphony by a twenty-year-old a wealth of modulation which recalls the leading orchestral composers and does not appear, pre-eminently, as felicitous imitation but, for the most part, as original invention. It is precisely the quality of originality in the whole that leads us wholeheartedly to acknowledge the young composer's talent.

Strauss wrote to Franz Wüllner on 23 February: 'I'm still drawing nourishment from my success in Cologne, which is probably the handsomest and most important I have had to date.'

Yet another première took place on 4 March 1885: Gustav Leinhos gave the first performance of the Horn Concerto Op. 11 at a concert in Meiningen. Strauss himself could not be present, but his uncle Carl Hörburger made the fifty-mile journey from Staffelstein to Meiningen specially and wrote to him about the occasion. Bülow conducted the concerto 'obviously with great commitment and interest'. When Hörburger spoke to him afterwards and happened to say that he thought the ending a little too abrupt, Bülow retorted: '"Why? I don't think so, after the horn passages and the final C" (and he sang it to me) "I think the ending is rather good, what do you want an orchestral postlude for as well?"' The Horn Concerto had already been published in August 1884, with a dedication to Oscar Franz, of the Dresden orchestra. However, the manuscript copy of Strauss's own arrangement of the concerto for horn and piano bears a dedication to his father: the change of dedication in the published score was in all probability made on Franz Strauss's advice.

Family distress

The joy his successes gave the young composer was interrupted in April 1885 by an event which caused sorrow and deep distress to the whole family. His mother Josephine Strauss, then forty-seven years old, had to enter a nursing home on 14 April to receive treatment for a nervous disorder. The stay, which was to be only the first of many, lasted two months; in November of the same year she returned to the nursing home for a further five weeks. After an interval of over eight years she had to resume treatment, and between 1894 and 1909 she spent periods in institutions which varied in length from one to ten and a half months.

In his memoirs Strauss recalled his father's outbursts of rage: making music with him was always a pleasure spiced with apprehension. In the home he was 'very vehement, short-tempered, tyrannical', and it required all the docility and kindness the gentle Josephine possessed to sustain tranquillity in the couple's relationship, rooted though it was in sincere love and esteem. 'How much suffering this may have caused my mother with her very sensitive nerves is something which it is impossible for me to judge after all this time.' Richard's sister Johanna speaks of her mother's 'rare simplicity and modesty' and says that she had been 'her father's pet'. Of her own father Johanna says that he was very strict with Richard and that both children had a 'holy respect' for him, whereas their mother was 'kindness in human shape', and used to intervene in the disputes between father and son in the role of mediator and peace-maker. It must therefore have been a terrible shock to her husband and children when the delicacy of her nerves combined with the effects of the climacteric to induce a nervous illness requiring medical treatment. The treatment itself had deleterious consequences: according to Johanna, her mother – who had become obsessed by the idea that her family were persecuting her – was given an overdose of morphine to calm her, which brought on an attack of raving insanity. Her removal to the nursing home alleviated her disorder, but in the long term recurrences necessitating further committals could not be prevented.

At the time of the first attack Hanna was away visiting the Rhineland with relatives, while her father and brother remained at home. To this circumstance we owe an exchange of letters which give us a particularly penetrating view of the effect that the event had on the life and spirit of the family. Four days after his wife's committal Franz Strauss wrote to Hanna:

> Unite your prayers with ours for a speedy recovery by your dear, good, kind Mama, so that we shall soon have her back with us and will be able to make her happy by our boundless love for her, for I know that the love of her dear ones and of the Pschorrs is her highest happiness . . . Do not worry about me, God will help me to bear everything patiently. Richard is very affectionate and good to me and does not spare himself in showing me every attention. (18 April 1885)

Five days later, on 23 April, it was Richard who wrote to his sister, with news of a perceptible improvement in their mother's condition: 'She is often fully lucid now for half an hour at a time, she's read your cards, we take her sweets and flowers which it gives her joy to receive.' The nurse in charge had assured them that she would be cured, though she could not give any idea of how long it would take. He wrote again on 26 April:

> My optimism and spirits seem to be slipping gradually, there's a limit to everything, I'm afraid, and when I pull myself together as best I can and comfort Papa, it's a waste of time trying to distract him – that's the sad thing – he's becoming more and more unsociable, I think he feels that he's doing dear Mama a moral wrong of some kind if he allows himself to be distracted and doesn't sit all day brooding on our misfortune. Even though I'm forever preaching to him that on the contrary it's his duty to keep himself strong and fit by diverting and dispersing the dark thoughts for the sake of Mama and Hanna and me, it doesn't have any effect and so I'm often at a complete loss to understand what has happened to the moral strength that a man should possess more of than a woman. I hope you're in no doubt that I do everything possible to demonstrate my loyalty and devotion to Papa, I do the best I can to work off some part of the immense debt I owe him in these circumstances, and I hope my resolution will hold out until you come home. I'm sorry, I don't mean that as a reproach; the only thought that gives me any consolation in this situation is that you at least are recruiting

> your strength . . . The doctors have given us an assurance that Mama's illness will be completely cured.

Indeed, by 7 May he was able to write and tell her that he had been to see their mother again and found her 'very happy and contented, perfectly lucid and rational, only a little excited and restless. The most remarkable thing is that she knows full well that all the dark thoughts she had were pure nonsense and she remembers all of them in minutest detail.'

In the letter he sent to Hanna on 26 April, Richard had also made a veiled allusion to the first serious love of his life, an attachment which was to last for a number of years:

> At present I'm not in the very best of spirits and hope to be better disposed and brighter again in a few days' time perhaps.
>
> Your friend Dora [Wihan] is going to Reichenhall on Saturday next for four weeks, with her mother, who is arriving on Thursday. Hans is going to Russia at the beginning of May.

Three days later (on 29 April), replying to a question Hanna must have asked him about his low spirits, Richard wrote: 'I'm afraid you can't share the thing that is oppressing me, even if you came home early', which she had offered to do.

It does not appear to have occurred to Hanna to see any connection between his reference to his low spirits and the mention of Dora Wihan's imminent departure in the next sentence. But there can be no doubt that the two things were connected: Richard had fallen passionately in love with the wife of his friend the cellist Hans Wihan. She was a young, attractive woman and a very gifted pianist, five years younger than her husband and four years older than Richard, who had known her since 1883 at the latest. Hans Wihan was a member of the quartet who had played godparents to Richard's A major Quartet Op. 2 in March 1881. Richard must have known him from the date of his joining the Court Orchestra in 1880 and the two had soon become friends. Wihan proved himself a vigorous champion of Richard's Cello Sonata Op. 6, of which he had given the first performance, and the Romance for Cello o. Op. 75. On 21 February 1884, when Richard was in Berlin, Hanna wrote to tell him that Hans and Dora had played the Romance from the Sonata 'very beautifully'. The only letters from Wihan to Richard that survive date from the few months in the winter of 1883–4, when Richard was staying in Dresden with Dora's parents and then in Berlin. Two of these letters (dated 16 January and 8 February 1884) illustrate how energetically he had taken up his young friend's works, and contain some good advice. (He had presumably been reading the letters Richard sent home to his parents.)

> I'm following your letters with great interest of course, and am always delighted by your successes, which I hope you won't let go to your head too much, because just as you like to talk a lot of nonsense and say things that will please people, but it's all only talk, so other people like to do exactly the same to you; sort out the corn from the chaff therefore, and forget the rest.

There is no doubt that this counsel was not purely gratuitous; it reveals insight into Richard's impulsiveness and his occasionally fallible understanding of human nature.

Richard's letter to Hanna mentioning his low spirits can also be interpreted as a reference to the tensions that already existed between the Wihans – tensions of which Richard was aware and which grew so much worse in the following twelve months that the couple were legally separated in 1887. So when Richard tells Hanna that perhaps he will be better disposed and brighter again in a few days' time and then immediately goes on to tell her that Dora is going away with her mother while Hans leaves for Russia, it is reasonable to speculate that the prospect of the couple's temporary separation is what promises to bring Richard some relief. It is even possible that he hoped to remain in touch with the woman he loved by letter. It was not to be expected that his feelings would remain hidden from those close to him for long: early in the following year, after Richard had told his father about purely social encounters he had had with some actresses in Meiningen whose company amused him, Franz Strauss replied in a tone of some concern:

> It's very agreeable of course to converse with cultivated, respectable and witty women, but a young artist, who belongs after all to the public, must make it his first concern that his reputation does not suffer from it . . . Don't forget how people here have talked about you in connection with Dora W.
> (9 January 1886)

Richard originally dedicated the third of the *Stimmungsbilder* for piano Op. 9 to Dora, as 'Second Album Leaf'.

The beginning of this relationship has been recounted here, because it fell in the period between Richard's return from Berlin and his departure for Meiningen. The way it developed in the years that followed will be described in a later chapter, with the aid of the few documents that survive.

4

Meiningen, 1885–6

The invitation to go to Meiningen came as a complete surprise, offering an escape from the depressing atmosphere at home, which persisted in spite of the hopes of his mother's recovery, and from the emotional pressures of his love for Dora Wihan. Using Spitzweg as an intermediary, Bülow, who was to go on tour in Russia and in western Europe in the coming winter, enquired whether 'Richard II' would be interested in conducting the Meiningen orchestra in his absence 'gratis and interimistic, in the interests of his education – as a practitioner'. He would be replacing Franz Mannstädt (1852–1932) who was leaving to take up a post in Berlin.* Naturally Richard jumped at the chance, for although he was gaining a reputation as a composer the time had come for him to earn his own living. Unlike his friend Ludwig Thuille he had not the least desire to teach and, indeed, his private musical education would probably have disqualified him if he had applied for a post, and so the prospect of conducting seemed like the answer to his prayers. He wrote Bülow a rapturous letter of thanks, emphasizing what a privilege he would count it to be able to conduct not only the Meiningen Choral Society but perhaps also sectional rehearsals of the Court Orchestra itself:

> Since I have no practical experience behind me yet in this field, the good fortune of beginning my conducting career in this post would be so great that I hardly dare even to hope for it. When I think of the permanent benefit it would be for my musical education to attend all your rehearsals and so have the chance to study your interpretation of our symphonic masterpieces in the closest possible detail, I am at a loss for words. (26 May 1885)

* Weingartner, Nicodé, Mahler and Zumpe were all interested in the vacancy. 'We're swamped with applicants', Bülow wrote to his wife (5 May 1885).

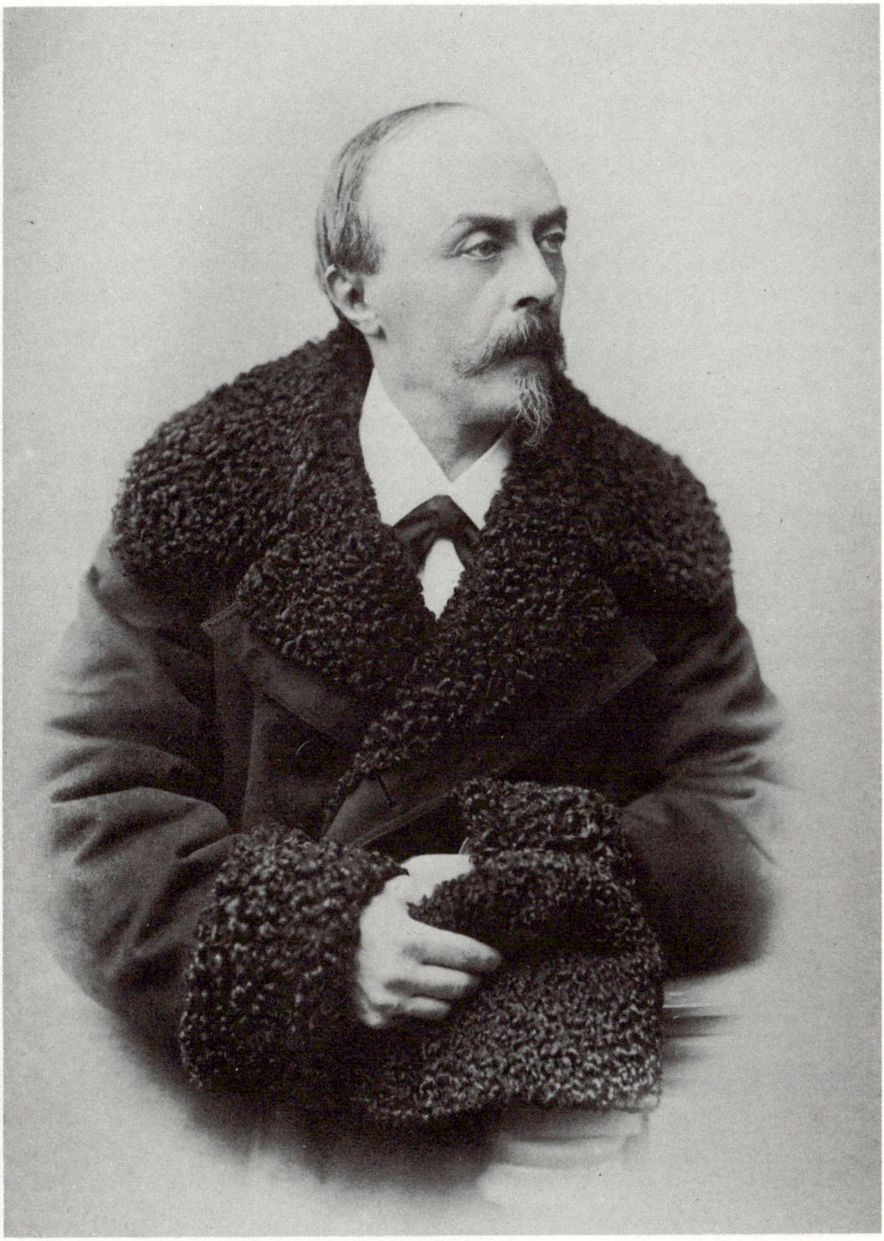

Hans von Bülow

Richard Strauss, Munich, 1888

For the time being Bülow left it to Spitzweg and Gustav Leinhos to conduct the negotiations with Richard, but there was an unavoidable delay, as the Duke of Meiningen, whose consent had to be obtained, was in England. From a letter Leinhos wrote to Richard on 31 May 1885 we learn that Bülow had asked him whether he thought the older men in the orchestra would be willing to work with Strauss; Leinhos had told him that Richard was 'popular and highly esteemed' and so they would place themselves under his direction 'with pleasure'. In the same letter he told Richard the terms and duties of his employment:

> He [Bülow] envisages your post as non-stipendiary to begin with, but you would nevertheless have to bind yourself from 1 October to 15 April next year. He would take most of the rehearsals himself in the month of October, in preparation for the tour, but he thinks that would be the best thing for you too, and give you the chance to get to know him and the orchestra.

On the other hand Strauss would be expected to conduct the Choral Society without any assistance or guidance. The society consisted of eighty ladies from the best social circles who had been given an excellent training by Franz Mannstädt and were augmented for concerts by fifty male voices, recruited among teachers, officials and various musical societies.

> Herr von Bülow will also hand over to you the direction of the subscription concerts in the Court Theatre, and would be very willing for you to introduce some of your own compositions into the programmes if you wished. There will be a tour of Holland and Belgium in November, during which period the preparation of an oratorio will be [assigned] to you. In December H. v. B. goes to Petersburg to conduct a series of concerts, in March he will be touring with us again, and your concerts will take place here in the intervening period.

Leinhos also mentioned the title and the fee, 1500 marks, that Richard would receive. There had been no fewer than twelve good applicants for the post, so it would be as well if Richard sent his acceptance to Bülow, who was in Frankfurt, without delay. Bülow would then recommend the duke to confirm his appointment.

Bülow, for his part, advised Strauss to come to Frankfurt, there to make the acquaintance of the duke's sister Princess Marie of Meiningen, a very good pianist (she was the pupil of Kirchner,

Ehlert and Bülow himself), and to make a 'conquest' of her, since she would have some say in the matter. Another reason for going to Frankfurt was that he would be able to attend Bülow's piano course at the Raff Conservatory, in which he held forth variously on Bach, Handel, Mozart, Beethoven and Raff. Bülow was a particular champion of Joachim Raff, who was also the teacher of Alexander Ritter. In 1885 Strauss arranged two of the marches from Raff's incidental music to *Bernhard von Weimar* for piano duet (AV 184) – doubtless to please Bülow.

Richard lost no time in following Bülow's advice. In Frankfurt he first took a room in the Hotel du Nord, and then moved to lodgings in Altgasse 33/III. He began attending Bülow's course on 9 June and the very next day he played his Improvisations and Fugue to Princess Marie in Bülow's presence. A letter to his father tells us of the new acquaintances he made on his arrival in Frankfurt: the conductor Fritz Steinbach, the composer Anton Urspruch and a distant relative on the staff of the Raff Conservatory, Max Fleisch. Frankfurt's largest music shop had laid in a stock of all Strauss's works that were available in print and displayed them. Richard did not omit to tell his father that Bülow had asked after him. He had been for a drive in the country outside Frankfurt with Frau von Bülow and some other acquaintances. He also took some steps to promote his own works during his stay in Frankfurt: he played his Symphony to the conductor Karl Müller and his String Quartet was rehearsed before a private audience, while the spa orchestra gave two performances of his C minor Overture. He wrote enthusiastically about Bülow's course to his father: 'I go to the Conservatory every day, and I'm rapidly coming to the conclusion that Bülow is not only our greatest piano teacher but also the greatest executant musician in the world.' (19 June 1885) He took part in a concert held to raise money for a memorial to Raff and signed a petition in aid of the same cause.

He wrote Ludwig Thuille a long letter about how much he was enjoying his stay in Frankfurt:

> I have the chance to admire him [Bülow] every day. I wish you were here, you would enjoy the classes in the Raff Conservatory too. Unfortunately the majority of students are women, who either don't understand him at all or misunderstand him. There are a lot of musicians, some in their 40s or 50s, that I'd like to see at the course. He has so much to teach!

The princess, in his view, was no beauty, but she was very amiable and intelligent. After playing her the Variations, 'which went tolerably well', however, he had almost had a nervous collapse. Bülow's first words had been:

> 'By Jove! Here's a dangerous rival.' He was very complimentary about the Variations, so I reminded him that they were dedicated to him. He said to me later: 'It's a good thing the princess has been impressed by your piano playing, since you will have to play duets with her in Meiningen.'

He also told Thuille about some of his visits to the opera and theatre in Frankfurt:

> I'm having a right royal time here, I've survived a performance of *Walküre*, seen a new opera by Massenet, *Hérodiade*, which is very charming in places, especially the ballet music, but doesn't amount to anything and has a rotten text. The thing that I've enjoyed most was Bülow playing part of the last movement of the C minor Sonata Op. 111, which made me realize how wonderfully beautiful the movement is. On Saturday I went (with Bülow) to see Heyse's latest tragedy, *Don Juans Ende*, which is really capital and has once again given me a great respect for Heyse. (15 June 1885)

Bülow had written to Duke Georg, recommending 'the uncommonly talented young man' in the warmest terms, and requesting permission to conclude an arrangement with him. Strauss's only failing was his youth, he wrote:

> Twenty-two years old [in fact Richard had only just celebrated his twenty-first birthday] but everything about him commends him to the respect of the orchestra, which has already learned to esteem him as a composer. Yesterday he played a new work, a set of variations, to the Princess, with which Her Highness was greatly pleased. At the same time he presented his credentials as a competent duet partner for Her Highness. (11 June 1885)[1]

On 18 June Richard received a formal confirmation of his appointment, issued by the office of the marshal of the court of Saxe-Meiningen, assuring him that His Highness the Duke was graciously pleased to confer on him the position of a conductor of the orchestra of the ducal court for the season 1 October 1885 to 15 April 1886, with the title of Hofmusikdirektor and a remuneration of a total of 1500 marks to be paid in twice-monthly instalments.

> The said Herr Strauss will undertake to observe at all times and without question all directives of the intendancy of the Ducal Court Orchestra with regard to performances, public concerts and concerts at court, and to the necessary rehearsals. In particular he will be obliged to act as the representative of the intendancy whenever the intendant, Hans Freiherr von Bülow, requires it.

The duke received Richard at the Rheinischer Hof hotel during a brief visit to Munich. The appointment was gazetted on 9 July and Richard wrote from Feldafing to thank Bülow two days later. He did not omit to say how much he had gained from Bülow's course at the Raff Conservatory:

> In particular what you had to say about the performance of Bach and Beethoven opened many new vistas to me and I hope to be able to profit sufficiently from all your suggestions concerning the Mozart concerto, for the first movement of which I've already drafted a cadenza, to satisfy you with my account of it. (11 July 1885)

Bülow had invited Strauss to play Mozart's C minor Concerto at one of the Meiningen concerts. The performance took place under Bülow's direction on 20 October 1885. The concert was a triple début for Strauss, who had taken up his post on 1 October, since he also conducted his own F minor Symphony. He acquitted himself so well in all three roles, as soloist, composer and conductor, that Bülow wrote to Eugen Spitzweg the very same day: 'Strauss: *homme d'or.* Symphony *capital.* His playing – like his conducting début – downright breathtaking. If *he* wants to, he can step into my shoes tomorrow, with H. H.'s consent.' Even three years later he recommended Spitzweg to publish Strauss's cadenza to the C minor Concerto, but Spitzweg's courage failed him. Bülow had already written to Hermann Wolff, the Berlin agent, on 17 September, describing the F minor Symphony as 'really very important, original, formally mature' and Richard as a born conductor:

> He is developing into an excellent musician in every way: elastic, eager to learn, his tact as ready as his beat is steady [*taktfest und taktvoll*], in short a 'first-rate' talent. N.B. As yet he has never conducted – nor has he ever played the piano in public – but he's going to make a success of the Mozart Concerto as of everything else the first time he tries. Fine career in front of him.

Meiningen, the seat of the reigning dukes of Saxe-Meiningen, enjoyed an excellent reputation at that date, which owed much to the tours made by its theatre company and orchestra far beyond the tiny duchy's frontiers. Duke Georg II was deeply interested in both the theatre and the orchestra, for which he had succeeded in engaging Bülow as principal conductor, and though he took a more active role in the management of the theatre he was always fully informed about the orchestra's affairs. His express approval was required for all concerts and public rehearsals, as well as for the content of the programmes and the engagement of guest soloists.[2]

The letters Strauss wrote to his parents at the time gives us an excellent account of his activities there. The players gave him a friendly welcome and he threw himself eagerly into his new work. He at once began rehearsing Mozart's Requiem with the ladies of the Choral Society, and after only one week was able to write home boasting of his achievements:

> Frau von Bülow was absolutely enchanted by the capital way I acquitted myself with the sixty ladies at the first rehearsal of the Choral Society; well, after all, one doesn't reach the ripe old age of twenty-one without learning something! The choir is better than I thought it would be, and there are some pretty faces in it. (8 October 1885)

Eager to learn all he could, he attended Bülow's orchestral rehearsals and also the rehearsals and concerts of chamber music. He devised programmes for those and took part in some as pianist. (A letter he wrote to Bülow on 13 December 1885 contains his suggestions for four chamber-music soirées due to take place in the following month.)

The personal relationship with Bülow, in whose home he was always a welcome guest, became very important to Strauss. When Bülow was away on tour his wife Marie kept him informed of what Strauss was doing and how he was coping. On one occasion she wrote:

> Our wee Strauss keeps up his frenetic rehearsing. Three hours yesterday morning on his symphony alone. At the end applause from the orchestra – which he received sceptically and yearns for criticism. Very sensible. Once again the choral rehearsal went very well. I sang so energetically and enthusiastically that

> Strauss paid me the charming compliment of asking me to step out and listen in some of the difficult passages, so that he could find out how the others manage without my assistance.
> (13 October 1885)

A few days later:

> The thing that will chiefly interest you is to hear that wee Strauss demonstrated an astonishingly quick wit and talent. (In the concert with the blind Princess of Hessen.) He has made a definitive conquest of the princess. She said to me: 'This is certainly something very different from that Mannstädt fellow.'
> (15 October 1885)

Four weeks after that:

> He [Strauss] went to the Casino Ball here on Monday and danced till he dropped. It goes without saying that he has made some conquests, of course the slyboots won't breathe a word about them, but he has not yet been conquered to the point of an engagement. Tell the Bear [Brahms] this from me (I am delighted that you find him an agreeable travelling companion) and that for the time being his place has been usurped [in the hearts of the ladies of Meiningen].

Later in the same letter:

> Yesterday Strauss brought me a song-cycle he has written with the intention of singing it to me, but he had to confine himself to playing it, while I followed the score, my sore throat worried him. Then I was 'critical', i.e. I did not simply praise it, but I also said which bits I didn't care for, which bits struck me as not having been really felt. The young man went away well pleased.
> (11 November 1885)

The cycle in question was the Eight Songs Op. 10 after poems by the Tirolean poet Hermann von Gilm, composed between August and November 1885. There were originally nine songs, but *Wer hat's gethan?* was omitted when the work was published in 1887; it is now impossible to know whether the composer decided this of his own accord, at the suggestion of the publisher or in response to Marie von Bülow's criticism.[3]

From Munich Father Strauss replied to his son's letters with the usual fund of advice:

> Don't forget, my dear Richard, what I have often told you, to

> make the last notes in a figure clear and not to dash them off in too much of a hurry; it's something you can do perfectly well, if you only take your time and devote a little more care to the bass line . . . Always be pleasant to the ladies, don't single one out for more praise than the others, that would be the surest way to create bad feeling. Don't let any musical errors pass and be as polite as possible in correcting them, and don't let yourself be disarmed by a pretty face. Impartiality is the first and most estimable virtue of the conductor. Pay *no* attention to any gossip of the kind that ladies love to indulge in, preserve an absolute neutrality. (9 October 1885)

Richard, however, no longer took such lectures altogether seriously: 'Papa amuses me capitally with his affectionate admonitions.' (12 October 1885) He began conducting the orchestra by the second week in October – five hours one day, three the next; at first he found it extremely tiring, primarily because of the abundance of physical and emotional energy he put into it. He jumped in off the deep end, with Brahms's Violin Concerto and A major Serenade, and he also began taking the orchestra through his own F minor Symphony and the Wind Suite. He wrote to Hermann Levi:

> Herr von Bülow is kindness itself to me, and I like my new career very much. Bülow has been away since last Monday and I have been wielding the baton, rehearsing my symphony, which is to be performed next Sunday, the 18th, in a concert in which I shall play the Mozart C minor Concerto. Brahms is coming here on Saturday the 17th, to rehearse his new Fourth Symphony with our orchestra for the first time . . . You can imagine how thrilled I am to be meeting him personally, especially as he has promised to be here by the day of my symphony at the very latest.
>
> Apart from my symphony and my suite for wind, I have also rehearsed the Brahms Violin Concerto and his A major Serenade Op. 16 this week, yesterday the blind Prince Alexander of Hessen, who is here at the moment, and Konzertmeister Fleischhauer played Bach's Concerto for two violins and string orchestra, in the presence of Their Highnesses. Then Their Highnesses asked for the *Holländer* Overture, and I, with unexampled impudence, never having set eyes on the score before, conducted a brisk and breezy performance of it at sight; it went very well. Bülow played it through just once only the other day. Their Highnesses were mightily impressed by my impudence. (10 October 1885)

Strauss told this tale again in the account of his days in Meiningen that he included in his memoir of Hans von Bülow, and also wrote home about it: 'Papa knows that the *Holländer* Overture is difficult, with all those tempo changes, especially for someone like me who only knows it superficially! Well anyway, I conducted very dashingly, it went superbly, and thus I scored my first conducting success – and with a piece by Wagner.' (14 October 1885)

Richard had a rehearsal every morning, which gave him 'enormous fun'. It meant that he could play through whatever compositions he felt like, old and new:

> With rehearsals every day I am becoming adept at conducting, I have a very good sense of tempo and I've already conducted at sight a few times, Schubert's B minor, the *Manfred* Overture, without having looked at the score first, and I've got the tempos and all the modifications spot on, to the great delight of Ritter, who is a charming and very cultivated man, of whom I'm seeing a great deal. (To his father, 20 December 1885)

He continued to worship Brahms in Meiningen. After meeting him and receiving a message to pass on to his father, he wrote to Franz about the Fourth Symphony, which the Meiningen orchestra had prepared for its first performance. It was

> beyond all question a gigantic work, with a grandeur in its conception and invention, genius in its treatment of forms, periodic structure, of outstanding vigour and strength, new and original and yet authentic Brahms from A to Z, in a word it enriches our music – it's hard to put into words all the magnificent things this work contains, you can only listen to it over and over again with reverence and admiration. (24 October 1885)

Another time, after telling his father that he liked the Brahms symphony better and better, 'equally, I'm quite delighted by the magnificent Violin Concerto, which can hold its own with Beethoven's, especially in the first movement, for grandeur and beauty'. He was baffled by the obscurantism of someone like Benno Walter, who 'so disgracefully fails to recognize the quality of a work which, with Beethoven's, belongs to the most beautiful (for a player, of course, who is an outstanding violinist and, even more, musician) and the most grateful in the whole literature for the violin'.

(28 October 1885) He wrote to Franz Wüllner, too, about Brahms and the Fourth Symphony:

> You can well imagine what a feast it has been for me, with Brahms here. The new symphony is one of the grandest creations in the whole field of orchestral music, it yields nothing to the other three symphonies, it's completely new and original and yet it's authentic Brahms from beginning to end. I don't think I could wish you anything better than that you should make the personal acquaintance of the work as soon as you can, description is impossible, it can only be admired.
> (31 October 1885)

He also told his father that Brahms had spoken to him about his own symphony: 'What he said to me . . . was very interesting and I shall not forget it; but in general he praised it to Bülow.' He prudently omitted to tell his father *what* Brahms had said to him, but it went into his memoir of Bülow. Never one to waste words, Brahms said:

> 'Quite charming', but added some advice worth taking to heart: 'Young man, take a close look at Schubert's dances and practise inventing simple eight-bar melodies.' It is chiefly thanks to Johannes Brahms that since then I have never disdained to incorporate a popular melody in my works (however low may be the opinion of such tunes in the higher academic reaches of criticism nowadays). Another of the great master's reproofs: 'There's too much thematic trifling in your symphony; all that piling-up of a large number of themes on a triad, with only rhythmic contrast between them, has no value whatever', has remained clearly etched on my memory. That was when I realized that counterpoint is only justified when there is a poetic necessity forcing two or more themes to unite for a time. The most illuminating example of that kind of poetic counterpoint is to be found in Act III of *Tristan*.

Strauss took Brahms's criticism to heart at the time, but it was only later, after his final conversion to Wagner, that he began to use 'poetic counterpoint' in his works.

To his father he confessed there was a little too much counterpoint in his un-Haydnish and un-Mendelssohnish symphony. The critical reception was in part very kind to the work: 'If he adds some practical experience to his talent and to what he has already achieved, the world will be able to look for a great symphonist in this young composer.' But elsewhere the same review had it that the first movement recalled Brahms and the Finale had 'brilliance but not genius'. Richard was entertained by this review and by another which described his Piano Quartet as 'unlikeable', and added his own comment: 'Whatever a critical muttonhead like that and the great general public dislike the first time they hear it, is always something good or at least undoubtedly original.'

Strauss appears to have become aware of the weakness of his symphony as he worked on it in rehearsal; that at least is the conclusion to be drawn from a letter to the management of the Leipzig Gewandhaus Orchestra, in which he reminded them that they had agreed to play the work in rehearsal and then decide whether to give it a public performance or not. He went on:

> The chief purpose of this letter is to ask you not to make up your minds on the strength of the first impression gained at a first run-through, since, because of its great difficulty and somewhat dense orchestration and its rich, somewhat too rich, contrapuntal work, the symphony makes a thoroughly unclear, confused, indeed perhaps even ugly impression in the first few rehearsals. (2 April 1887)

He very much wanted to conduct the symphony in Leipzig himself, but it was October 1887 before the wish was granted. He never lost his ability to view his works with critical objectivity.

Before the Meiningen concert took place he wrote to his parents that he was going to play and conduct from memory. 'But you don't need to worry on that account, or to think of me with deep emotions in your hearts. I'm very contented and cheerful and not the least trace of excitement', which may not have been strictly true but was intended to reassure his parents. He had practised the Mozart concerto diligently all summer. During the concert itself, after the first movement, Bülow encouraged his young friend with the words: 'If you weren't something better, you could become a pianist if you wanted to.' Richard commented in his memoir of Bülow: 'Even if I did not take the compliment as something I had fully deserved, it nevertheless increased my self-confidence enough to allow me to give more freely of myself in the last two movements.'

His sister Hanna had hoped to obtain her parents' permission to go to Meiningen for Richard's concert, but in vain. She wrote to her beloved brother on 7 October:

Just think, I've had a magnificent idea, but to my utmost sorrow it is not coming to fruition. I wanted, and I still want, to come and visit you, and in particular to do it when it would coincide with your first great début, but although I keep dropping hints as broad as a barn door Papa takes absolutely no notice and so my wonderful plan comes to nothing. Wouldn't it have been splendid? I'm always with you in spirit and I'd already thought out everything magnificently . . .

For today farewell and receive the warmest hugs and 1000 kisses from your faithful sister Hanna.

There are numerous letters which bear witness to how close the brother and sister were. That Christmas Richard sent her the material for her first ball-dress. 'When I wear the dress you gave me, I shall be exactly twice as happy and pleased', she wrote. In January she sent a progress report: 'Two dress-makers are sitting in the room with me at the moment and have nearly finished my first ball-dress . . . I shall be entering the room at exactly 7 o'clock on Saturday evening.' Six days later:

The ball-dress from you is ready at last and it is quite delightful. The pale blue goes quite charmingly with the lace and I shall create a sensation with it. I shall probably wear it to the Franconian Ball for the first time. As a consolation I can assure you that I have not danced with any officers. (19 January 1886) I wore the beautiful ball-dress you gave me to the Franconian Ball and I was telling you the strictest truth when I said that I should enjoy myself even more when I was wearing it. You would stare if you saw how many dancing partners your dear sister has. I wasn't able to sit down for one moment. (29 January 1886)

Though Hanna stayed away, Ludwig Thuille and Count Seilern, a family friend and music-lover, came to Meiningen for Richard's concert. Seilern must have given the family a rather extravagant description of Richard's conducting, for Franz Strauss wrote to his son:

It is ugly to make those serpentine gestures when conducting, especially for a bean-pole like you. It's already not pleasant to look at in Bülow, and his is a small, graceful figure. Fieriness in conducting lies somewhere else altogether . . . The conductor's left hand has nothing to do but turn the pages of the score, and when there is no score in front of him it should remain still. The conductor encourages his players to greater feeling by the way he uses his baton and by his eyes . . . Please, my dear Richard, follow my advice and get rid of these silly habits. You don't need them.

Franz appears also to have learned more than Richard had told him about Brahms's opinion of the F minor Symphony from Thuille and the Count, for we find in the same letter:

> I was delighted at the advice Brahms gave you about the use of counterpoint in your things. My dear son, I beseech you to take this truly good advice to heart.
>
> I have been very worried by the fact that in all your more recent things you have paid more attention to contrapuntal affectations than to natural, wholesome invention and execution. Craftsmanship should not be discernible. And where it predominates then it is only craftsmanship and not art at all. In art it is often the case that the truly magical, the truly divine lies in the unconscious. That is how it is and nothing will change it . . .
>
> The first, and I would say the only, duty of music is to beat at the world of the emotions and for that reason no other art arouses such enthusiasm in the recipient; if it surrenders the divinity which through this dwells within it then it surrenders its most beautiful, its most sacred attributes and sinks to hair-splitting. Clarity and simplicity are compatible with nobility and greatness, or, to be even more accurate: clarity and simplicity are essential to greatness!
>
> Convey to Herr Brahms my warmest thanks for his honest and excellent opinion and my sincerest good wishes.
>
> As for you, with a loving father's heart I ask you to follow that advice. You have enough talent for something better than affectation. (26 October 1885)

Richard's answer betrays some annoyance: 'Who told Papa that I have developed silly habits when I conduct, I'm not a clown, and who told him so precisely the advice Brahms gave me, I didn't write to tell him the details.' Early in November, however, he had the satisfaction of writing to Hanna:

> Now, pay attention! Following Seilern's gratuitous remarks I took a firm hold on myself when conducting and conducted relatively calmly, with the result that Bülow noticed. He said he thought I hadn't conducted as elastically as at the concert, and when I told him that I had intentionally taken a firm hold on

myself, following Seilern's counsel, he said, Bally rubbish, I wasn't to take any notice of that, I had conducted very nicely, etc. So there!

It would seem that the young conductor's spontaneous, sweeping gestures had provoked mirth in some observers; that, at least, is the conclusion to be drawn from a description – published in the Copenhagen newspaper *Politika* and reprinted in *Isaria*, the Sunday supplement of the Munich *Süddeutsche Presse* – which shows that in some circles in Munich an opportunity to goad Bülow was always welcome:

> Dr Hans von Bülow perambulated about the rostrum and surveyed the auditorium. A pale, long-haired youth [Strauss] is to conduct the overture. He looks as though for the last fortnight he has eaten nought but new-born lambs and drunk nought but Karlsbad water. The duke and his wife enter the little ducal box and the orchestra strikes up. Herr von Bülow works away at Swedish drill, swinging the upper part of his body vigorously to and fro, and the long-haired youth seems from his gestures to be seasick.

Among the acquaintances Strauss made in Meiningen were the pianist and piano-teacher Marie Jaëll, Brahms's publisher Fritz Simrock, the art-historian Henry Thode (who married Bülow's daughter Daniela in 1886), Professor Erich Schmidt, curator of the Goethe Archives, and the singing-teacher Emilie Merian-Genast (whose sister was married to Joachim Raff). He started to compose a scherzo for piano and orchestra (*Burleske* o. Op. 85), read a great deal, borrowing books from Marie von Bülow, improved his French, played the piano (practising, among other things, his own Improvisations and Fugue o. Op. 81, the piano part in his Piano Quartet Op. 13, and Bach's *Well-Tempered Clavier*) and also regularly took an hour's walk.

On evenings when there was no music, Richard generally went to the theatre. At that date the Meiningen company was in the van of theatrical art in Germany. For Georg II (who had made a morganatic marriage with the actress Ellen Franz and ennobled her as Freifrau von Heldburg) the style of historical verisimilitude in stage design which was later decried as 'Meiningerei' was only an external frame, within which he worked to develop a disciplined style of ensemble acting, with the help of the actor and director Ludwig

Chronegk, whom he had won over to his reforming ideas. In seeking out and delineating the unique character of each individual drama, special value was placed on inner unity, and the 'authenticity' of sets and costumes – which had a counterpart in the history painting of the day – in no way led to neglect of the poetic essence of the drama. The company concentrated its efforts primarily on the dramas of Shakespeare and the German classics, but comedy had its fair share of the repertory. Guest appearances by famous actors added variety, which was particularly welcome to Strauss.

He received some of his formative theatrical impressions in Meiningen, which were to be supplemented later, most significantly in Berlin by the work of Otto Brahm and Max Reinhardt. In his 1909 memoir of Bülow, Strauss wrote:

> During this particular winter the famous Meiningen Theatre Company did not go away on tour, and naturally I was there every night for the splendid performances. When I took my leave of the duke and his wife [in April 1886], Frau von Heldburg, who had always been slightly jealous of Bülow and the orchestra's fame, bade me a gracious farewell with the words: 'His Highness the Duke and I are very sorry to lose you so soon (I sketched my first, flattered bow), you have been the best *claqueur* we have had in the theatre for a long time.'

In his old age, in the late memoir he wrote of his early life, he still remembered the duke's 'magnificent' productions of the classics; their special distinguishing feature had been

> the direction of the crowd scenes, in which every move was plotted with the greatest care, and the stylistic verisimilitude of the staging. I shall never forget the first act and the Coronation act in Schiller's *Jungfrau von Orleans*, the entrance of the cuirassiers in *Wallenstein* and *Julius Caesar*. An example of how the duke worked: one New Year's Eve [1885] the rehearsal went on until 9 o'clock, 10, at last it struck midnight, the duke stood up, everyone breathed a sigh of relief. The duke: 'I wish the company a very good New Year, the rehearsal may continue!' There was no 8-hour day then.

Strauss, who had taken lodgings with the overseer of the ducal gardens, also found time to take part in the social life of Meiningen. Princess Marie, to whom, and to a blind Fräulein von Bardenstein, he gave piano lessons, invited him to a *thé dansant*, where he had the honour of dancing the 45-minute-long cotillion with her. ('Prrr! She was very nice and jolly', he wrote home.) It was not an isolated occasion, and in the winter he danced the 'Française' with the princess on the ice without skates, which illustrates the degree to which he was accepted in court circles. His word for the time he spent giving the princess her piano lessons, however, was 'sour'.

Of incomparably greater importance to him were the opportunities, in the second half of October, to see Brahms frequently, and to mix with the leading players of the Court Orchestra – the clarinettist Richard Mühlfeld, who stimulated Brahms to write his chamber-music works for the clarinet, the first oboe Anton Kirchhoff, the leader Friedhold Fleischhauer and the first horn Gustav Leinhos – and also with actors and some 'jolly good actresses', which, as we have already seen, aroused his father's anxiety. Richard's reply shows that he was no longer content to be tied to the parental apron-strings.

> You cannot reproach me if I express my joy at finding in this town of Meiningen, which has been accursed by the god Amor, the oasis of a few jolly actresses. You surely do not want that cheerful fellow you used to know, your son Richard, to return to Munich a philistine.

After his father had reminded him of an unfavourable review of the F minor Symphony and exhorted him to be more economical in his use of brass and to pay attention to other people's advice rather than cogitate alone too much, because all such excesses were an evil and true greatness lay only in clarity and simplicity, Richard, whose self-confidence had been strengthened by his successes in Meiningen and elsewhere, replied:

> If a financial newspaper takes it upon itself to make idle comments on the symphony, so be it; but it's just as well that I myself am probably the person who knows best how I should compose, and that I do not need to be told how by a muttonhead like that, who, if he could do what I can do, would be able to write symphonies of his own, instead of crying down the symphonies of others. You've long known that prattle like that has no effect on me.

By the end of this letter he had calmed down, and added: 'It simply isn't true that I pay no attention to your advice, but you must pay less attention to the public and the critics, neither of whom understands anything.' He got on well with the members of the orchestra, but he had a lot of fault to find with their tuning. Bülow, 'like all pianists, of course, hasn't a good ear for it at all'.

A serious difference arose between Bülow and Brahms in the November. Brahms, having previously agreed that his friend and champion should conduct the first performance in Frankfurt of his Fourth Symphony, did it himself. There can be no doubt that he did not intend an affront to Bülow, but had simply forgotten his promise or else yielded without thinking to the persuasion of someone in Frankfurt. He was quick to recognize his 'stupidity', as he wrote to Bülow, and their cordial relations were restored.

While Bülow was in St Petersburg he learned from Strauss that the wish he had expressed to Princess Marie, that the orchestra's strings could be augmented for the performance of Brahms's Fourth planned for the duke's birthday, had not been fulfilled. A letter which had been supposed lost – it is absent from the Bülow–Strauss correspondence published in 1954 in the *Richard-Strauss-Jahrbuch*, but turned up in 1973 – records Bülow's view of the episode as 'a new personal fiasco'. (To Strauss, 30 March 1886)[4]

Bülow had long planned to leave his post in Meiningen. His resignation meant that from December 1885 Richard was the sole conductor of the orchestra. Luck and his own merits placed him in a position in which his talent and his enthusiasm stood him in good stead. On 13 January 1886 he wrote to Franz Wüllner, who had conducted the first German performance of the F minor Symphony in Cologne exactly a year earlier: 'Herr von Bülow's departure means that I can direct and manage things here exactly as I like, and the daily rehearsals with this excellent orchestra suit me down to the ground.' He described his work-load in the following three months in a letter of condolence that he sent to Dr Otto Speyer, whose daughter Helene – Lotti's sister – had died.

> I have so much work to do here that I don't know if I'm on my head or my heels. Herr von Bülow's departure means that the whole of the artistic direction of the Court Orchestra lies on my shoulders, and some of the administrative burden too. Konzertmeister Fleischhauer has been ill for months and it is left to me alone to see to the chamber-music soirées, the choral society, the princess's lessons, festivities at court, composing new works and preparing them for publication (proof correction etc.) [all these things] make such demands on me that I can

> hardly find the time for correspondence of the most essential nature, official and professional. (30 March 1886)

The Choral Society, in particular, was a constant source of vexation and extra work because of poor attendances at rehearsals.

The works of which Strauss composed the whole or at least the greater part during the months in Meiningen are the Op. 10 songs already mentioned, which are among his best-known; the *Burleske* o. Op. 85, a scherzo for piano and orchestra begun in November 1885; and, at the duke's suggestion, a new setting of the bardic song in Klopstock's *Hermannsschlacht* (*Der Bardengesang* AV 181). Strauss recalled that Bülow rejected the *Burleske* with some heat as 'unpianistic and with too wide a stretch for him (he had small hands, with a span of barely an octave)'. He said to Strauss: 'A different position for the hands in every bar – do you think that I'm going to sit down for four weeks to learn a crossgrained piece like that?' Bülow's eventual opinion of the piece was mixed. To Brahms he wrote: 'Strauss's *Burleske* decidedly has some genius in it, but in other respects it's horrifying' (11 January 1891). And to Eugen Spitzweg: 'Ever since he has turned into an exclusive Bayroutrider* and a decided Brahms-Thersites – he has only my most impersonal sympathy, that is, when he produces a beautiful work of art. That category does not include the *Burleske*, if truth be told.' (14 January 1891) After the first performance, given at the twenty-seventh festival of the Allgemeiner Deutscher Musikverein at Eisenach on 21 June 1890 by Eugen d'Albert (to whom the piece was dedicated and at whose request Strauss had made some cuts and simplifications in the piano part), Bülow wrote to his wife: 'D'Albert admirable in Strauss's piece, which is as interesting as it is, for the most part, ugly, but he made it seem more beautiful and almost graceful.' Strauss did not have the *Burleske* printed until 1890, when he needed the money badly, and he wrote to Alexander Ritter: 'It really goes against the grain to publish now a work which I have left far behind me and can no longer defend with the fullest conviction.' In recent years the *Burleske* has become a favourite with pianists.

In his memoir of Bülow and in his autobiographical memoir of his early life, Strauss recounted a series of interesting and entertain-

* *Baireitknecht.* As so often with Bülow, it's impossible to render in translation all he packs into one biting word. *Baireit* = Bayreuth (perhaps the Prussian gentleman mocking Franconian pronunciation); *Knecht* = labourer, menial, serf etc.; *Reitknecht* = a groom, mounted attendant. *Tr.*

ing episodes from his Meiningen period, including a performance, conducted by the composer, of Brahms's Academic Festival Overture (a favourite of the duke's), in which Bülow played the cymbals and Strauss himself the big drum and, both of them lacking experience in counting rests (Bülow kept on asking the trumpets which letter in the score they had reached), there were more wrong entries in the percussion than on any other occasion he could remember.

At the invitation of Hermann Levi, Strauss went to Munich to conduct his F minor Symphony at a Musical Academy concert on 25 November 1885. In Meiningen he performed two of the works he had rehearsed with the Choral Society, Brahms's *Schicksalslied* and Mozart's Requiem, from which he trimmed some of 'Sussmayer's dreadfully muddy instrumentation'. The choir, as he told his father, sang cleanly and accurately, so he was satisfied, as he told Bülow. He had opened the concert with Gluck's overture to *Iphigenia in Aulis*, with Wagner's concert ending, which he thought stylistically appropriate. With the orchestra, apart from the standard classical and romantic repertory, he tried out works by Lachner, Rheinberger, Rubinstein, Liszt and Tchaikovsky – 'a crazy suite, which could well be called "Journey to Siberia" . . . but very jolly' – as well as Bülow's *Nirwana*, and on 23 February 1886 he conducted the F major Symphony which his friend Ludwig Thuille had finished a short time before. It was 'a very beautiful, attractively scored piece and with its lively temper, genial Minuet and profound Adagio it will make a great impression on the public'. He wrote to tell Thuille about the performance and the audience's reception of the work:

> My most cordial, sincere congratulations on the great success your capital work achieved here yesterday. The performance went off very well, the orchestra played outstandingly, with such delight, love and precision that you would have been beside yourself with joy. The public received it gratefully, and His Highness spoke very favourably of the last three movements, the first movement bored the duke because he couldn't follow it, actually the first movement is rather disproportionately long, and really only a musician can appreciate the first movement's great virtues. The Adagio was much liked, also the last two movements. All the players have been speaking very warmly about the work, one of them said that he thought it would make its mark in the musical world. You already know my opinion,

> so I only need to congratulate you once more and convey especially warm greetings from Ritter. (24 February 1886)

Thuille's reply shows that he was moved by Richard's opinion and advocacy of his work:

> You can well imagine how profoundly pleased I have been by your frequent reports on my modest work. They have demonstrated your true friendship to me once again, and I thank you from my heart for the good will and what I have no doubt were the great pains you took in studying and rehearsing it.

Strauss also wrote to his parents on the day after the performance of Thuille's symphony, to tell them about the concert – the soloist in some songs by Brahms, Amalie Joachim, was 'a marvellous singer, with no trace of anything *passé*, in spite of her forty-seven years, the voice is still big and beautiful, technique superb, execution outstanding' – and also to tell them that he had finished the *Burleske* and was planning a new work, a Rhapsody in C♯ minor for piano and orchestra. In fact he wrote only forty-one pages and then abandoned it (AV 213). He gave a run-through of *Der Bardengesang* on 19 February: it 'pleased His Highness very much'. His father urged him to write more songs for his aunt Johanna Pschorr, to whom he had dedicated almost all the songs he had written as a boy; Richard replied that he could not promise his aunt any songs until he had found some nice texts: 'Sitting down and composing songs in cold blood, as I used to, is something I can't do any more.' (January 1886)

After his Russian tour, Bülow returned to Meiningen for a concert at the end of January. At one of his rehearsals Richard, 'to Bülow's great amusement', played with the second violins in Tchaikovsky's Suite no. 3. In the concert itself, on 29 January, he played the cymbals in *Nirwana*, an orchestral piece Bülow had written originally as the overture to *Ein Leben im Tode*, a play about suicide by his old schoolfriend Carl Ritter. Richard found the piece 'frightfully atmospheric and interesting, a bit savage'; it gave excellent expression to the sense of weariness with life. After the concert he was enthusiastic: '*Nirwana* went very well indeed . . . it's a magnificent piece and proves that Bülow might have been a great composer too, just as he's the greatest pianist and conductor.' But he was far more profoundly stirred by Bülow's interpretation of the

Eroica, the only one of Beethoven's symphonies, except the Ninth, that he had not yet heard him conduct:

> Although our band admittedly lacks the brilliance of the Munich orchestra, although the acoustics are bad in our hall, although there was a little lapse in the violins in the finale, it was a performance such as I shall never hear a second time. In the Funeral March there was a spirit and a soul in every note that I would never have believed an orchestra could possibly achieve, and the finale: of the finale I can say that the full light of Beethoven's sun shone on me for the first time in my life; Beethoven himself, if he'd heard it, would have said 'Only now do I understand the greatness of my music.' I was so moved that after the last movement I cried like a child in the instrument room; I was alone with Bülow there and he put his arms round me and gave me a kiss that I shall never forget as long as I live. (To his father, 31 January 1886)

Strauss also included an account of this concert in a letter he wrote to Hermann Levi, thanking him for the performance of his F minor Symphony with the Musical Academy in the previous November. As well as conducting the *Eroica* and *Nirwana*, Bülow had been the soloist in Rubinstein's Third Concerto and a Rhapsody by Liszt; the concert had made an unforgettable impression on Strauss, he wrote.

> Apart from accompanying the piano concertos, which went off very well, thank God, but during which I sweated blood, I also had to conduct Rheinberger's overture to *The Taming of the Shrew*, which, if you happen not to know it, I can heartily recommend in the dearth of good concert overtures; it's an attractive and grateful piece. The whole concert was an immense triumph for Bülow, but it did not lead to His Highness inviting our maestro to stay and take up the intendancy again, which I believe would have met with no very great resistance from Bülow.

He also told Levi about the cutback of the orchestra, about the three-year contract (at 2000 marks a year) which the duke had offered him, and about the decision he had made, with Bülow's approval, to return instead to Munich, where there would be a vacancy at the Court Opera in August. He had already written to the intendant, Freiherr von Perfall, and now he told Levi:

> As you have always shown the greatest kindness in assisting me

> in my artistic career, I take the liberty of informing you of this move and of adding the respectful request that you will not withdraw your gratifying benevolence and kind protection in this matter and in the eventuality of my obtaining the Munich post.

After describing his various musical activities he went on:

> . . . and there's also a court ball from time to time, or a dance at the princess's, as well as the Prater three times a week, recently Ibsen's *Doll's House* with Ramlo as guest star, yesterday Heyse's *Ehrenschulden*, and so there's no fear of my getting bored when I'm off-duty. The people at the theatre also provide my social intercourse, for there's no question of mingling with the philistines of Meiningen over their beer; it might just be possible with the officers, but they're very exclusive. (6 February 1886)

(Once he wrote to his parents: 'Life is very jolly here in the little nest. After all, you only live once!')

It is hardly surprising that Father Strauss's reaction to the unusual enthusiasm expressed by his son after the performance of the *Eroica* was to attribute it in part to Richard's adherence to Bülow, which would have predisposed him to be carried away. It is equally unsurprising that he did not waste the opportunity to address fresh admonitions to the budding composer:

> Let this eternally youthful work of genius be your paradigm, bear it always in mind, for the greatness of a work lies only in sublime simplicity. You have only to think of the ancient Greeks! It isn't necessary to copy your paradigm, but your ideas can be directed towards its great, clear simplicity. (2 February 1886)

After the termination of Bülow's appointment, the future of the Meiningen orchestra became uncertain, as Strauss's letter to Levi indicates. In the middle of December he had written home:

> It looks as though everything here will soon be breaking up, after the business arrangement that the *art-loving* duke made with Bülow comes to an end, it's all the same to me, I'm still making the most of my opportunities, try out whatever I like, I've had a chance to savour Bülow, achieved everything I wanted, and when there's nothing more to be done here [I shall] depart consoled, with my wishes fulfilled.

He had no need to be worried about his next step.[5] He received what amounted to an offer from the intendant of the Munich opera, Carl von Perfall, before December was out, to which he had replied without committing himself, while referring to the uncertainty of the position in Meiningen:

> Unfortunately there is a prospect that the Court Orchestra here will be reduced at the end of the season to those members who have long-term contracts. In that eventuality I shall have the great pleasure of being at Your Excellency's disposal. If the orchestra stays together next winter, however, then I owe it to Herr von Bülow, whom I have to thank for so much and who has placed his trust in me, to remain here.

He promised to inform Perfall as soon as the situation was clarified. (27 December 1885)

Bülow, who was then in St Petersburg, advised him to sit it out in Meiningen for the time being and see how things developed. If the orchestra was not cut back,

> then it seems to me your baton would be hard put to it to find an opportunity elsewhere to perform its function with greater artistic renown or satisfaction. If patriotism and homesickness for your family call you back to Munich – well and good – that's your affair. But . . . in your position I would provisionally refuse [Perfall's offer]. You are one of those exceptional musicians who have no need to work their way up from the ranks, who have what it takes to assume at once a post of higher command. *Pas de zèle* – put off the decision. Do not be in a hurry to expose yourself to the (in your case admittedly not very grave) danger of turning into a philistine, a yahoo, a *swell* on the banks of the Isar. Wait for the invalidization of H. L. [Levi] to reach its crescendo and then – in good time – take his place without first climbing every rung of the bureaucratic ladder. (23 December 1885)

Richard set foot on the ladder in the end, but he gained some artistic advantages from the experience. The moment of decision came after Bülow's concert in January, when the Marshal of the Court informed Richard that the orchestra was definitely to be reduced to thirty-nine members and offered him a three-year contract and a salary of 2000 marks a year. According to Richard, this extremely modest sum was offered him because he was, after all, 'in comfortable circumstances' (to August Steyl, 19 February 1886). The decisive factors which led him to reject the offer were the reduction of the orchestra and 'His Highness's growing loss of interest'. Bülow, too, now advised him to take the Munich post. On 1 February Richard wrote a letter of acceptance to Freiherr von Perfall, although he would have preferred to go elsewhere because, as he told Bülow, he wanted 'to get to know the world somewhere else besides Munich'. The intendancy of the Royal Bavarian Court Theatre put his name forward to King Ludwig II on 17 February; on 3 April he learned that the king had approved his appointment, and on 16 April he received a contract for three years, 1 August 1886 to 31 July 1889, with the entitlement, after those three years, to pension rights and the prospect of a permanent appointment and advancement from the rank of Musikdirektor to that of Hofkapellmeister. His salary in the first year would be 2200 marks, and 2400 marks in the second and third years.

For the present, concerts in Meiningen continued under Richard's direction. The *Berliner Tageblatt* published a muck-raking report that Strauss was 'glad, as a consequence of disharmony with the orchestra, to have an honourable excuse to escape from the situation here, which is becoming uncomfortable'. With the express approval of the duke, the office of the Marshal of the Court lost no time in issuing a notice correcting the report. The duke remained well-disposed towards Richard and wrote him a very friendly letter accepting the dedication 'in respect and gratitude' of the Piano Quartet:

> Your dedication of this beautiful and original Quartet will give me special pleasure. Let me take this opportunity to say how very sorry I am to see you depart, and to confess that your achievements here have *thoroughly* cured me of my previous erroneous belief that your youth made you unfitted as yet to be the sole director of my orchestra. (24 March 1886)

The letter was followed by the award of the Cross of Merit for Art and Learning, Richard's letter of thanks for which survives (31 March 1886). On 29 May he applied to the intendancy of the Court Theatre in Munich for permission to wear the decoration, which had given rise to another paternal admonition:

> Don't forget, my dear son, to remain simple, true and modest, this I beg you with a fearful heart. It is not that I doubt your good sense, but it has been my experience that good fortune makes its recipients arrogant and ungrateful. I do not expect this

> in your case, however, because it is not characteristic of our family, neither immodesty nor ingratitude, and you are certainly the true son of your parents, only I think a few words of warning will do no harm. (4 April 1886)

The second chamber-music recital organized by Richard took place on 5 March. In addition to Beethoven's Cello Sonata Op. 5 no. 1 and Brahms's Horn Trio, the programme included four of Strauss's songs from his Op. 10 set: *Zueignung*, *Nichts*, *Die Georgine* and *Allerseelen*. (These were still as yet unpublished.) In a concert on 18 March, he conducted the Choral Society in Bach's cantata *Gottes Zeit ist die allerbeste Zeit,* Brahms's *Gesang der Parzen* and Mendelssohn's *Walpurgisnacht*, which he thought 'not easy but beautiful'. The concert was a great success. Richard and the soloists were called back three times on to the platform, the duke and his guests, the Prince and Princess of Altenburg, continued to applaud to the end, and the Choral Society presented Richard with a laurel wreath as a farewell gift. There was another chamber-music soirée a week later, with a 'very attractive' Clarinet Sonata by Théodore Gouvy, Robert Volkmann's D minor Trio and Beethoven's Quintet for Piano and Wind.

Richard's mother and sister were present at his last orchestral concert, on 2 April. As well as Brahms's Fourth Symphony and '*St Antony*' *Chorale Variations* – both conducted by the composer – the programme included songs by Wagner and the Prelude and 'Liebestod' from *Tristan.* Richard conducted these last as Bülow would have done – 'as far as possible, of course', as he wrote to his mentor.

He took his leave from the orchestra on 5 April, and from the ladies of the Choral Society at a rehearsal on the same day. The ladies gave him a letter of thanks and a casket decorated with views of Meiningen. The speech he made to the orchestra was reported in the *Allgemeine Deutsche Musikzeitung* of 9 April by Alexander Ritter; it ended with the words: 'Gentlemen, let us all, those remaining and those departing, vow to make the best we can of the talents our master gave us. We will send a telegram to him conveying the expression of that vow and our profound respects, and that done – let us part.'[6] In a letter to his father Richard described the occasion as 'very solemn and edifying'. Konzertmeister Fleischhauer made a speech, a *Tusch* was blown in Richard's honour and *Nirwana* was played in Bülow's. Now all that kept Richard in Meiningen was the last of the chamber-music soirées he had organized, which comprised works by Saint-Saëns, Beethoven, Schubert and some of Richard's own piano music. He wrote to tell Bülow that he had gone through his *Burleske* with the orchestra, and had found it 'inhumanly difficult':

> The accompaniment, I suppose, is somewhat overloaded and the piano part too detailed. I shall cut out some of the orchestral writing, then, given an outstanding (!) pianist and a first-rate (!) conductor, perhaps the whole thing will turn out not to be the unalloyed nonsense that I really took it for after the first rehearsal. After the first run-through I was totally discouraged and I've begun without delay to remodel the C minor Rhapsody for piano and orchestra (with harp) which I've just started.
> (7 April 1886)

In February 1886, when it was already known that Richard was to leave Meiningen and Fritz Steinbach's appointment to replace him was imminent, Dr Wilhelm Langhans wrote in the *Neue Zeitschrift für Musik*:

> In Richard Strauss we possess a warrior from whom, in view of his youth, we may expect more brilliant victories of the sort he has already won with his witty and prismatic F minor Symphony, with the performance of which in a symphony concert of the Royal Orchestra [in Berlin, in December 1885] Robert Radecke has done another service to the progress which has been so long anathematized here.

In other words, even Richard's 'classicist' F minor Symphony was regarded as 'progressive'.

Richard had received the foundations of his 'classical education' from his father, and he always took pains to emphasize the precise nature of what he owed to Bülow; for instance, in his memoir of Bülow, written in 1909:

> In October 1885 I began, in my new post, an apprenticeship which could not imaginably have been more interesting, more impressive or – more entertaining. Every morning, from nine till twelve, there took place those remarkable rehearsals such as only Bülow could conduct. The image of the works he rehearsed (all from memory) on those occasions is lodged immovably in my soul. In particular the way he dipped deep into the poetic content of the works of Beethoven and Wagner was absolutely convincing. There was never a trace of wilfulness, everything

> was a compelling necessity, imposed by the form and content of the work itself; his irresistible personality, always governed by the strictest artistic discipline and fidelity to the spirit and – the letter of the work (the two are more nearly identical than is commonly acknowledged), brought the works through painstaking rehearsals to a purity of execution which, for me, still represents the peak of perfection in the performance of orchestral works. I must not forget the grace with which he wielded his baton, the delightful manner in which he used to rehearse – instruction often taking the form of an epigram . . . He was the wittiest compère who ever lurked in the guise of a schoolmaster of genius. As pedagogue, his pedantry could be incontestable, and his axiom 'You have only to learn to read the score of a Beethoven symphony *exactly*, and you will already have the interpretation too' would adorn the gates of any college even today.

Strauss appears to have forgotten, by the time he wrote that, how critical he had been of Bülow's performance of *Don Juan* in 1890. On that occasion he told his father that Bülow 'really has no understanding any longer for poetic music, he has lost the thread', but that opinion must be seen in the context of Strauss's conversion to Wagner, while Bülow had increasingly come to reject him. The gratitude that Strauss felt towards Bülow is expressed in the first paragraph of his memoir:

> Anyone who ever heard him playing Beethoven or conducting Wagner, who ever attended his piano classes or witnessed him taking an orchestral rehearsal, must regard him as the paragon of all the shining virtues of the interpretative musician, and his moving sympathy for me, his influence on the development of my artistic abilities were – apart from the friendship with Alexander Ritter which, to the sorrow of my good father, made a Wagnerian of me – the most critical factors determining my career. Apart from what I owe to my father – the 'Joachim of the Waldhorn' as Bülow called him – such understanding of the art of interpretation as I can call my own I owe to my father's implacable enemy, Hans von Bülow.[7]

The friendship with Alexander Ritter

In his appreciation of Bülow, Strauss names his third mentor: Alexander Ritter. Ritter (1833–96), composer and violinist, was a school-mate and lifelong friend of Bülow, who recruited him as a member of the Meiningen orchestra in 1882. He also worked for music publishers as an arranger and had an interest in a music shop in Würzburg.[8] Strauss first mentions him in a letter he wrote to his parents on 8 October 1885, a few days after his arrival in Meiningen: 'A. Ritter will arrive in Munich tomorrow, will Papa be playing in his opera?' This was the one-acter *Der faule Hans*, which received its première at the Munich Court Opera on 15 October 1885. On 12 October Richard asked his father to tell Ritter about his, Richard's, activities in Meiningen: '[He] is personally a very agreeable, cultivated man, his daughters are pillars of the [Choral] Society.' In mid-December he referred to an evening he had spent with the Ritter family: 'Very agreeable, I sang them my songs, which were much appreciated.' The performance of his opera in Munich and, probably, too, the reduction of the Meiningen orchestra influenced Ritter to accept an invitation to join the Munich orchestra, although in the end he had to be content with the position of a viola-player and not of violinist as was first envisaged (and with a salary, therefore, of 1200 instead of 1500 marks).

Ritter had taken this decision before Richard received the first overtures from Perfall, and the fact that Ritter would be in Munich may have been one of the reasons why Richard finally accepted the Munich post. He had become closely attached to Ritter from his very first weeks in Meiningen; the violinist, thirty-one years his senior, had received him like a father, and Richard even spent Christmas Eve with the family that year. Richard made only passing references to Ritter in his letters to his parents, but the likely explanation for that is that he recognized that his father would not be pleased to hear of the influence that was being exercised upon him by so fanatical an admirer of Wagner and Liszt. In other contexts he was always ready to emphasize the importance of his debt to Ritter. In an autobiographical outline which he wrote in 1898 at the request of James Huneker, the American writer on music, Strauss referred to the strictly classical education he had received, growing up with Haydn, Mozart, Beethoven, and to how, at the time of meeting Ritter, he had advanced, by way of Mendelssohn, Chopin and Schumann, as far as Brahms. It was Ritter, through years of patient instruction, who had revealed to him the importance of Wagner and Liszt in the history of music, and who had thus turned him into a 'musician of the future'. The understanding of these two great composers imparted by

Ritter had set him on the right path. Ritter had also introduced him to the philosophy of Schopenhauer. He was exceptionally widely read in classical and modern philosophy and, in general, was a man of great and wide culture. His influence on Strauss had had an impact something like a whirlwind. He had urged him to follow the examples of Berlioz, Liszt and Wagner in developing the expressive, the poetic in music.[9]

Strauss gave a photograph of Ritter to Arthur M. Abell, the American writer who lived in Weimar in the 1890s, saying 'Here you see how the man looked to whom I owe more than to any other human being, living or dead. Ritter's advice marked the turning-point in my career.'[10]

In other autobiographical writing, Strauss described his becoming acquainted with Ritter as 'the most important event of that winter in Meiningen'.

> He was the son of that noble woman Julie Ritter, who supported Richard Wagner for years, and the husband of Franziska, née Wagner, the composer's niece. He invited me to his house, and there I found an intellectual and spiritual stimulus which had a decisive effect on my future development. My education had left me with some remaining prejudices against the works of Wagner and, in particular, of Liszt, and I hardly knew Wagner's writings at all. Ritter introduced me to them and to Schopenhauer, patiently explaining until I both knew and understood them, he demonstrated to me that the path onwards from Beethoven 'the musician of expression' (*Musik als Ausdruck* [Music as Expression] by Friedrich von Hausegger, as opposed to *Vom musikalisch Schönen* [The Beautiful in Music] by Hanslick) led via Liszt, who, like Wagner, had rightly recognized that sonata form had been extended to its utmost limits with Beethoven. With Anton Bruckner, the 'stammering Cyclops', the form actually bursts, especially in his finales – and with Beethoven's epigones, particularly Brahms, it had become an empty vessel in which there was plenty of room for Hanslick's flowery phrases, the invention of which required not too much imagination and little personal creative ability. Hence the great amounts of empty figuration in Brahms and Bruckner, especially in transition passages.
>
> New ideas must seek out new forms for themselves: the basic principle adopted by Liszt in his symphonic works, in which the poetic idea really did act simultaneously as the structural

element, became from then onwards the guideline for my own symphonic works.

In the above passage from the late memoir 'Aus meinen Jugend- und Lehrjahren', Strauss telescoped the beginning of his friendship with Ritter in Meiningen and everything that he subsequently learned from him in the years of his first engagement in Munich. The course of his relationship with Bülow, Brahms and Ritter demonstrates how strongly personal influences and first impressions could work upon the young Strauss, and how quickly they could be overthrown by contrary influences and impressions. While Bülow's conservatism continued to become more entrenched after understandable personal reasons made him turn away from Wagner, Strauss was won for Wagner once and for all by Ritter. He had, after all, devoured the score of *Tristan* in secret at the age of sixteen, and there can be little doubt that he would have come to Wagner in time unaided, but the single-mindedness with which he devoted himself to Wagner from his mid-twenties onwards must be attributed first and foremost to Ritter's influence and to his fanatical, even bigoted, adherence to Wagner and Liszt. For a time, too, Strauss was infected by Ritter's pronounced anti-semitism, an attitude which was nourished by the frequently tense relationship between his father and Hermann Levi.

Richard left Meiningen on 10 April 1886. The six months he had spent there, first under Bülow and then conducting the orchestra on his own, in rehearsal and before the public, determined his career as a conductor. In old age he declared that he had had two lives, one at his desk composing and one on the rostrum conducting; the importance of the second should not be underestimated. It assured him an independence that he would have gained only decades later, when he became famous, if he had been solely a composer. In Meiningen he served his apprenticeship in his 'primary profession', that of conductor, which he was to practise for many years in permanent positions and in guest appearances. His composing was, so to speak, a sideline. In his first term as a conductor at the Munich Court Opera, ranking third, the demands that were made on him were not enough to satisfy his energy or his ambition.

Italy

Richard was to take up his appointment in Munich on 1 August, so he had four months in which to fulfil his long-held wish to visit Italy. After travelling home to Munich via Staffelstein, he set out again on 17 April in the company of the two sons of the Bavarian ambassador to Rome. The journey followed a conventional tourist's route, via Bologna to Florence and on to Rome, which he left for short excursions to Naples and Capri early in May; on the return journey he stopped briefly in Florence again. He described his impressions at length in letters to his parents. In Bologna he was moved to tears by Raphael's *Saint Cecilia*, while a performance of *Aida* wrung from him the verdict 'dreadful, Redskin music'. In Rome, where he stayed at the Hotel Minerva, he 'wallowed in works of art', as well as enjoying the magnificent natural beauty, the views over the Campagna and the mountains from the Lateran Hill, and the hours he spent scrambling about ruins. He was amazed by what he found in St Peter's,

> where it was purest Corso, the whole fashionable world surged to and fro, more beautiful women in one spot than I have ever clapped eyes on before. All these people strolled up and down in St Peter's during the Miserere, chatting and laughing as if they were walking round the Chinesischer Turm [the pagoda in a public park in Munich]. (22 April 1886)

He was also impressed by the elegance of the women, the hundreds of smart private carriages to be seen everywhere in the streets between the Corso and St Peter's. But, he wrote, 'I've already vowed not to go to the theatre again, I don't think I shall ever become a convert to Italian music, it's such trash. Even the *Barber of Seville* could only be enjoyed if the performance was outstanding.' He hardly modified this attitude towards Italian opera for the rest of his life; the only exception he would make was for Verdi's *Falstaff*, which he admired as one of the greatest works of art in the whole operatic repertory.

One unhappy experience was having his Gsell-Fels guide-book stolen, which he had to replace with a Baedeker. He paid a number of duty-visits, to Count Arco and Count Seilern among others, and made one new acquaintance that meant a lot to him: that of the painter Franz von Lenbach. 'I'm thrilled to have Lenbach's acquaintance', he wrote to his father, 'he's a true artist, as well as being very witty in conversation and genial company.' (27 April 1886) Father Strauss's replies to these enthusiastic outpourings included the usual admonishments. He was glad to hear that Rome was making such a powerful impression on Richard, because he was sure it would have a beneficial influence on his music and encourage him to think more about the expansiveness and breadth desirable in overall design. He commended Michelangelo as the best possible model, since 'for grandeur of conception he remains the most important of all'. There is a note of impudence in Richard's answer to this, betraying that his father's advice no longer made any very deep impression on him: 'For all Michelangelo's grandeur, Papa would open his eyes wide if I tried to introduce foreshortenings and dislocations like his into my music. Raphael is the true ideal.' And he confesses candidly: 'I do not understand Michelangelo well enough.'

He went down to Naples at the end of April, where he was greatly struck by the Pompeian murals in the museum, but here again nature made as strong an impression on him as art. He visited Pozzuoli, the lake of Averno and the Sibylline grotto and, after an eight-hour crossing on a choppy sea, Capri, Anacapri, the Blue Grotto and Monte Solaro, which he ascended on a donkey. (5–6 May 1886) He also climbed Vesuvius, naturally. 'The whole cone . . . with steam coming out of every fissure and the most wonderful play of colours, is extremely interesting, while we were up there Vesuvius erupted violently, threw hundreds of stones in the air with a great roaring noise; capital!' (10 May 1886)

Another boat-trip took him from Sorrento to Castellanum and Pompeii and then to Salerno. On the return journey the following day the boat called in at Amalfi and then sailed on back to Sorrento in a violent storm. Richard's account of this adventure is thoroughly characteristic of him; after describing the waves, two storeys high, that they encountered after rounding the promontory, he goes on:

> It was quite wonderful, and then there was the wonderful sunset with the storm in the distance, Capri black in front of us with its colossal pinnacles and cliffs, the sea flashing under the oars as if it was electric, although there was no moonlight, in short, this marvellous voyage will be one of my best memories, in spite of making me feel rather uncomfortable for nearly three hours, although I wasn't seasick. (5 May 1886)

His reaction to the theft of his suitcase, containing clothes and other items, was equally typical: 'Well, it might have been worse, there's no need to let it spoil our good temper.'

He returned to Rome on 10 May. He called on Lenbach again and (for the first time) 'heard Verdi's Requiem in a really tolerable performance: thoroughly Italian, music and performance very theatrical, but not bad. There are some very attractive and original things in the Requiem, I actually stayed till the end.'

Venice was also on his itinerary, but an outbreak of cholera there made him change his plans. After some 'wonderful days' (as he told Bülow) on Lake Como, he crossed back over the St Gotthard and made for Munich via the Lake of Lucerne and the Rigi. In the same letter to Bülow, written after his return, he wrote: 'Back at home, sitting at my desk again, I was nevertheless very content to be there, for the one pleasure that persists, of which I shall never tire, is the work to which I have dedicated myself entirely.' (23 June 1886) It was a sentiment to which he held throughout his life. The beauty of nature was necessary to him and gave him great enjoyment; it could inspire him – witness his plans for a symphonic triptych on a very large scale, although the *Alpensinfonie* was the only part of it actually realized. But he gained his deepest satisfaction, time and again, from the work he did sitting at his desk: from composition. On his return to Munich from Italy on this occasion, admittedly, work of another kind was waiting for him: the study of operatic scores and the practice of a career as a conductor in the opera house. His urge to compose was as little weakened by his holiday in Italy as it had been by the demands his multitudinous duties had made on him in Meiningen. There, while conducting the orchestra every day in rehearsals and concerts, directing the Choral Society, playing the piano as soloist and in chamber music, he still found time to write the Improvisations and Fugue (o. Op. 81) and the *Burleske*; now, for the first time, nature was his inspiration. The impressions he had received in Italy took shape in the 'symphonic fantasy' to which he gave the name *Aus Italien* (Op. 16), and significantly it fell to the orchestra to reflect them.

5

At the Munich Opera, 1886–9

Strauss had sketched his symphonic fantasy while still in Italy, before his return to Munich at the end of May 1886. He began the full score on 22 July and finished it on 12 September, a few days before his début as conductor in the opera house in the city of his birth. In the letter he wrote to Bülow on 23 June he depicted his Italian experiences and spoke of the effect that Rome, in particular, had had on his musical imagination. 'I've never fully believed in the idea that natural beauty acts as a stimulus, but in the ruins of Rome I learned better, the ideas just simply come, in flocks.' (While he was still in Rome he had told his mother, in a letter dated 11 May, how much he was composing.)

He also informed Bülow, in the same letter, of the first works he would be required to direct on taking up his duties at the Court Opera: Cherubini's *Les deux journées* (known as *Der Wasserträger* – The Water Carrier – in German theatres) and Boieldieu's *Jean de Paris*. In fact he made his début on 1 October with *Jean de Paris*, but instead of *Les deux journées* the second opera he conducted was Mozart's *Così fan tutte* (on 12 November), a work for which he felt the greatest affection and which he championed throughout his life, at a time when it was by no means as highly esteemed as it is today. It was not until towards the end of the 1886–7 season that he took over *Les deux journées*, conducting it for the first time on 13 May. Before that he had conducted Rheinberger's *Des Thürmers Töchterlein*, taking it over from Levi at short notice without a single rehearsal, two works by Auber (*Le domino noir* and *La part du diable*), Delibes's *Le roi l'a dit* – a work he esteemed, Nicolai's *Die lustigen Weiber von Windsor* and Goldmark's *Die Königin von Saba*. After *Les deux journées*, he still had Lortzing's *Die beiden Schützen*, which again he took over from Levi, and Verdi's *Il trovatore* to tackle before the season ended.[1]

An invitation to conduct his own F minor Symphony in one of the Museum Concerts series in Frankfurt on 7 January 1887 brought a welcome break from the opera house. The *Kleine Presse* hailed him as a 'genius': 'Already a master despite his youth, he knows that he must wear his mastery with modesty, for its springs are not voluntary but imperative.'

In the 1888–9 season he repeated some of the operas from his first season, as well as Weber's *Der Freischütz* and Peter Cornelius's *Der Barbier von Bagdad*, both taken over from Levi. In January and February 1889, additionally, he was in the pit for Donizetti's *La favorita* and Verdi's *Un ballo in maschera*. In old age, looking back on his first term at the Munich opera in 'Aus meinen Jugend- und Lehrjahren', Strauss confessed soberly:

> I was not a particularly good third conductor. Although I was adept at taking over at short notice – even in the first few months I took over one of Rheinberger's operas – my lack of the 'routine', in which many less talented colleagues were vastly superior to me, my idiosyncratic insistence on 'my own tempos', on occasion often hindered the smooth dispatch of operas in the approved manner. The result, more than once, was what we call a 'Schmiss', when singers and orchestra get out of time with each other, the more so because the operas I had to conduct in those days did not interest me sufficiently to study them properly, and really required much more careful preparation than I gave them – work which I found much too boring in the case of operas like *Nachtlager* and *Martha*.

His memory is at fault here: it was not until his second term that he conducted Conradin Kreutzer's *Das Nachtlager von Granada* and Flotow's *Martha* at the Munich opera (on 14 January 1896 and 9 March 1895 respectively, for the first time).

In Meiningen Strauss had been able to do more or less as he liked in rehearsals with the orchestra, but in Munich he had to fall in with the daily routine of the opera house and, first of all, reconcile himself to the quite different conditions governing operatic conducting. Once, during a performance of Lortzing's *Zar und Zimmermann*, when he beat *alla breve* at a point where the orchestra was accustomed to a crotchet, there was a 'Schmiss' which forced him to stop and start again. 'He was beside himself when he came home, saying they'd let him down and he'd had to call a halt', his sister recalled; honesty compelled her to admit that Richard's headstrong temperament in those days had not yet discovered the virtues of prudence and conventional diplomacy; 'he had to run wild first'. A memoir by one of Johanna's friends, Lily Sertorius, with whom Richard often played duets, suggests that his mind sometimes wandered while he was conducting. She was once sitting in the front row of the stalls at a performance of an opera by Lortzing, when she suddenly noticed Richard check his beat and lower his head. 'Then – a jerk – and he went on conducting as if nothing had happened. The orchestra had calmly gone on playing and the audience noticed nothing.' When Lily later asked him, in some concern, whether he had felt ill, Richard had laughed and replied: 'Oh, no, it was only that a tune suddenly occurred to me. The orchestra can still do it without me.'[2]

Strauss was not only exposed to the control and criticism of his superiors, the other, senior conductors, the singers, and an orchestra used to the ways of Hermann Levi and Franz Fischer (who was 'conducting-mad'; Strauss called him a 'real malefactor in the pit'), he was also under the particularly watchful eye of his father. Franz Strauss, who celebrated forty years with the Court Orchestra on 1 June 1887, 'still sat at his desk in 1889, with the difficult horn part in *Così fan tutte* in front of him, not nearly as worried by the ticklish solos of "Per pietà" as by the fear that his son would choose to conduct at excessively modern (i.e. excessively fast) tempos'.[3]

Strauss's tempos and his interpretations were found disconcerting; in a letter to Bülow he described the consternation he caused by a few 'perfectly harmless nuances' in the overture to Nicolai's *Lustige Weiber*, which everyone present seemed to regard as complete novelties. One piece of advice from a colleague, which he was glad to take to heart and observe for the rest of his life, came from the heroic tenor Heinrich Vogl, who asked him not to conduct with 'too long an arm', in the interests of fluidity.

The intendant of the Munich opera, Perfall, was anxious to preserve the tradition laid down by Franz Lachner to the very letter. Perfall was himself a composer in the mould of Mendelssohn but lacking any spark of colour, so from the first he was disposed to regard the pupil of Bülow with distrust. The smallest ritenuto in a classical opera led to arguments and admonitions that could not help but harm Richard's self-confidence. He soon felt frustrated by his very position as third in the conducting hierarchy, and when Perfall asked him to take the rehearsals for what was to be the first performance anywhere of Wagner's early opera *Die Feen* in the spring of 1888, but refused to allow him to conduct the première itself, disappointment turned to fury. He had just returned from a holiday in Italy and he poured out his heart to Bülow:

> When Levi went on three months' sick leave in March, I was entrusted in his place with the preparation of Wagner's *Feen*, which was scheduled to be ready by now and in fact is. By not so much as a word was it ever hinted to me that if Levi was not back in time I should *not* conduct the work. I've been immensely conscientious and I've rehearsed that work really well. Now Levi's leave has been extended to 15 August and today Perfall reveals to me that he has transferred the direction of *Feen* to my superior in rank (Hofkapellmeister) and seniority (in art!!) Fischer. Imagine it! *Final* rehearsals start tomorrow, the performance is fixed for the 29th [August]; I'd placed colossal hopes on the work, as the first one which I've rehearsed from scratch – it was my chance to show at last what I can really do; all that's gone by the board, thanks to the disgraceful malice of Fischer (who calmly stood by while I took all the rehearsals) and the spineless insolence of that scoundrel Perfall . . .
>
> [Perfall said that] he couldn't discredit the work in advance by letting it be conducted by a Musikdirektor. In addition to that, Fischer, he said, was my superior in routine, which is the most important thing in the theatre. Can you believe your ears? And yet there was no fuss a few weeks ago, when I conducted Zöllner's *Faust* (which is very difficult and had been rehearsed by Levi in an extraordinarily slipshod way) with one little rehearsal, and *Freischütz* (which I've never done before) *without* a rehearsal of any kind. Further, he said that talent was neither here nor there, in this matter as in everything else, seniority was what counted. Then he can't abide my Bülowish conducting, so I had to listen to the usual abuse of you, your school has got to be rooted out once and for all, and so on and so forth. Then he lectured me about my presumption in making such claims at my age. It's all more than I can stand, as you will appreciate. I've now at last realized that this is not the soil to nourish a musical life which is to give any kind of joy. I'm not capable, on my own, of pulling the cart out of the mud that everything here is stuck in. The whole place is a waste land, a swamp, a beery swamp. (17 June 1888)

The vehemence with which Strauss expresses himself here is understandable in the circumstances, and his wish to leave Munich is hardly surprising. In the same letter he asked Bülow's advice. 'Unfortunately I have to admit that I do not have the means to give up the post here, badly paid as it is, without something to take its place.' Marie von Bülow and Eugen Spitzweg both wrote to counsel patience, that is, that he should carry on until his contract ran out in August 1889. But this dispute was not the first occasion on which Richard had expressed the desire to leave Munich. Already in May 1887 he had asked Bülow whether Hanover, where the intendant, Hans von Bronsart, was a friend of Bülow's, might not be a better place for him, but the gist of Bülow's advice then was that the Bavarians were preferable to the Hanoverians and that he should exercise patience – a virtue of which the young Strauss possessed very small stocks.

A letter he wrote to Otto Lessmann, the editor of the *Allgemeine Musikzeitung*, depicts his impressions of *Die Feen* at a time when he was still in charge of the rehearsals:

> I have been given the task of rehearsing *Die Feen* . . . which I find extremely interesting and full of capital things. The opera is very dashing, has colossal drive, the Wagner of *Holländer* and *Rienzi* already expresses himself in it to a quite significant extent, while there are also some extremely individual features (especially in the ensembles), which reveal the Beethoven enthusiast, the Wagner of the C major symphony. (5 May 1888)

Another letter, written on his twenty-fourth birthday to his uncle Carl Hörburger, also refers to *Die Feen*: 'The opera Wagner wrote when he was twenty contains some splendid stuff, the ghost of Beethoven haunts the finales, elsewhere you can detect Weber and Marschner too, and Wagner's lion's paw is already quite strong, especially in the more dramatic scenes.' (11 June 1888)[4]

To begin with, he had been more guarded, indeed – as he had written to Bülow in March – the public performance of *Die Feen* struck him as 'sheer profanation' because, he argued:

> If the work fails, which admittedly I don't think it will do, then we've certainly not done the master a favour; if it succeeds, on the other hand, that will be even worse, because it will prove that the general public is not yet ripe for Wagner's major works. Wagner is present in *Die Feen* all right, but he's still wearing baby's bootees, Herculean though they are. (25 March 1888)

Richard's conversion to Wagnerian music drama was completed under the influence of Alexander Ritter during his first term as a conductor at the Munich opera. The letter to Carl Hörburger which has just been quoted also contains a passage about a rehearsal of *Tristan* under Martucci, which he had heard early in June in Bologna, and reveals the feelings with which he now heard and saw Wagner performed:

> Orchestra was excellent, except not soft enough, singers excellent in some cases, but production and acting very middling. To the Italians *Tristan* was just another opera (or a concert with backcloths), as it might be by Bellini, the idea of drama intended by Wagner is as much a closed book to the Bolognese as it is to most Germans. On the credit side there is one remarkable thing: I have never been made so acutely aware of how much marvellous bel canto there is in *Tristan* as I was in Bologna. Whether this was due to the language, or merely to the singers' magnificent legato and their vocal skill, which makes every single word clear and comprehensible, the fact remains that the whole of this *Tristan* was the most magnificent bel canto opera, the very one that Herr Hanslick and his boon companions are always sighing for in vain.

Certainly the memory of the Bologna *Tristan* influenced Strauss's own interpretation of the work, which he conducted for the first time in January 1892 in Weimar. He had already been deeply impressed by two performances of it that he had heard in Bayreuth in August 1886, conducted by Felix Mottl, but he was still at a loss with *Parsifal*.

Alexander Ritter's influence strengthened daily. They met almost every evening at Leibenfrost's wine parlour, sometimes joined by Father Strauss, though he did not see eye to eye on artistic questions with the fanatical, partisan adherent of Liszt and Wagner. On the other hand it is likely that there was considerable agreement between the two of them on the subject of musical life in Munich in general and Hermann Levi in particular, who, now a sick man, ran the opera on a slack rein and had, moreover, not kept his promise to find Ritter a place among the violins in the Court Orchestra. The anti-semitism of both Ritter and Franz Strauss was, as has already been mentioned, largely conditioned by their fraught relationship with Hermann Levi. It was inevitable that it should rub off on Richard as well in these years. Levi was sincerely well-disposed towards his 'young friend' and remained in touch with him from the time when he conducted the first performances of Richard's D minor Symphony and his C minor Concert Overture; Richard first got to know Mahler's First Symphony by playing it as a piano duet with Levi. This relationship was clouded in time, and Ritter and Franz Strauss were largely responsible. When Richard sent Bülow a detailed report of a performance of Beethoven's Ninth Symphony under Levi and called it 'the most demeaning, the most abominable' account of a piece of music he had ever heard (26 December 1887), there can be no doubt that his judgment was affected by the negative attitude towards Levi expressed by his father and Ritter, although another factor will certainly have been his own view of Beethoven which, moulded by Bülow, differed considerably from Levi's. Franz Strauss could not forgive Levi for, as he put it, 'never getting into the right tempo before the third bar of a piece', and he made no bones about sticking to his own tempo in preference to Levi's. When he and Richard were playing together at home, and he had occasion to shout at his son 'You're hurrying like a Jew', it was of course Levi that he had in mind. When Franz Strauss was pensioned off at very short notice in June 1889, it naturally made the personal relationship between Richard and Levi very tense indeed.

That Strauss also turned his back on Brahms – an 'object of revulsion' to Ritter, according to Max Steinitzer – was again due in some measure to the strictures of the follower of Liszt and Wagner. Steinitzer, who was close to Strauss in these years in Munich, undoubtedly puts things in the correct light when he writes in his biography of his old schoolfriend:

> The very facts of his marriage to a niece of Wagner and his acquaintance with Liszt in the Weimar days placed Ritter, with all the incandescence of his temperament, in the progressive camp, and the burden of his teaching to Strauss was all too often: 'Burn what thou hast worshipped!' Besides Brahms, the established romantics of the concert hall, Mendelssohn and Schumann, and their 'puerilities' fared particularly badly at his hands; at times he sounded more like a tub-thumping party man than a musician weighing composers' merits and demerits. He was not altogether free of that degree of egocentrism in the New German school which made its members try to do everything anew for themselves, to disclaim the wealth of forms piled up

over centuries of subtle and discriminating work by the Italian, French and German masters.

Strauss's chief reason for admiring Ritter as a composer was that he was the only one known to him who had 'grasped the relationship of the musician and the writer in drama in the same way as Wagner'. Others, by contrast, 'completely misunderstanding the essence of the drama of the future, imitate the dazzling externals of Wagner the musician, while their feet still stand firmly on the soil of old-style opera' (from his diary). In a late memoir entitled 'Meine Freunde und Förderer', in which he recalled some of the people who had helped and encouraged him (and which has not been published), Strauss wrote:

> Let me add here that the true importance of Alexander Ritter in the history of music, as a bold pioneer in the aftermath of Wagner, has yet to be recognized. Ritter's songs are new in their treatment of language and in the origination of the melody in the word, in a manner for which Wagner's creation of vocal form was the model.
>
> Ritter's gift of musical invention is inferior to that of his contemporary Peter Cornelius, and he shares some of the technical weaknesses of Berlioz . . . What can be said to be derived from Wagner [in my work], without imitating him, I owe from the first to Ritter's teaching and his songs, and to his two one-act operas.

Leaving Leibenfrost's at about 7.30, Strauss often accompanied Ritter to his home,

> where 'Sträussle', as they called me, was always invited to share their modest supper, and where, after the meal, the topics of our conversation were reminiscences of Wagner and Liszt, the gospel of Schopenhauer, Ritter's new works, songs and operas, among which the score of *Wem die Krone?* came in for its share of critical and constructive interest. We made music too, among other things I once played Liszt's *Faust* Symphony from the score.

During these three years in Munich his relationship with Ritter and his family was the only thing that gave Strauss pleasure. 'What splendid, notable, dear people they are!' he wrote to Bülow. Again, after the fracas over *Die Feen*, he told Marie von Bülow that Ritter was his only solace. It was Ritter who introduced Strauss to

Schopenhauer, though it would be wrong to imagine that this took the form of an objective explication of his philosophy. For all his wide reading, Ritter was not the man for that. As he grew older he became more and more steeped in religio-mystical Schwärmerei and he had always been prone to regard music from ethical standpoints – which harmed rather than benefited his own artistry. Strauss, for his part, did not possess what it would have taken to get thoroughly and comprehensively to grips with Schopenhauer. As we shall see, he made a serious attempt to do so in the early 1890s and also formulated a tentative critique on the basis of his own fundamentally different view of life, but in doing so he confined himself to a few quite specific aspects that touched him personally. At Christmas 1889 his parents gave him an edition of Schopenhauer, undoubtedly at his express wish, but Tolstoy and Dostoyevsky continued to attract him more powerfully than philosophy, and Ibsen, some of whose plays he had seen in the theatre by now, was another of his favourite authors.

Strauss's position as third conductor at the Munich Court Opera did not allow him to develop his abilities to the full; it is true that he acquired more and more of the 'routine' that was so highly valued in the theatre, but – apart from *Così fan tutte* and one or two other operas – he was not given the kind of work worthy of the full application of his energies. He gained some compensation from the requests from orchestras outside Munich for permission to perform his works, with occasional invitations to conduct them in person. The most notable of these events was a performance of his F minor Symphony by the Gewandhaus orchestra in Leipzig.

He had already conducted the F minor Symphony himself in Meiningen (18 October 1885); the first performance of it in Germany had been conducted by Wüllner in the previous January, and there were other performances under Hermann Levi in Munich (25 November 1885), Radecke in Berlin (22 December 1885), Nicodé in Dresden (19 February 1886), Bülow in Hamburg (17 January 1887) and Bremen (18 January 1888), and Volkland in Basel (3 February 1889). Strauss conducted it himself in Frankfurt (7 January 1887), Leipzig (17 October 1887) and Cologne (in June 1889); it was a particularly great success on this last occasion. In Frankfurt he had received the personal congratulations of Clara Schumann, and in the following April an honorarium was paid him of 15 marks! When he conducted *Aus Italien* in Frankfurt two years later (8 April 1889) he received another honorarium, this time of 30 marks. Bülow continued to follow the progress of his pupil and protégé with sympathetic interest; Strauss heard him conduct the F minor Symphony in Hamburg in January 1887, and while he was there took the opportunity to hear *Carmen*, also under Bülow. He wrote to his father about it: 'Bülow's direction is simple; it is direction *par excellence*.' (12 January 1887) In old age he still spoke of that performance with the greatest admiration. Bülow had a particular sympathy for the F minor Symphony. He had written to Hermann Wolff the day before Strauss conducted it in Meiningen, describing it as 'truly significant, original, formally rich', and adding the comment that Strauss was a born conductor. (17 October 1885) After a performance in Bremen he wrote to his wife that the audience, otherwise a very cool one, had received the symphony with a warmth that had increased movement by movement. He told Hans von Bronsart that it was immensely difficult but 'colossal' and that he still greatly preferred it to Strauss's recent symphonic poems. (22 January 1890) Strauss wrote to his father about Bülow's performance of the symphony in Hamburg:

> Symphony found favour yesterday and went very well. Bülow conducted very affectionately without a score, but was within a hair's breadth of letting it fall apart in the last movement – at the end of the first section at the bit for timps: but they were all together again on the E at the fermata. I was called for after the Scherzo and last movement. (18 January 1887)

The performance of the symphony in Leipzig was an important occasion for Strauss. He had offered the work to the management of the Gewandhaus concerts on 25 September 1886, and wrote again to enquire about the prospects of a performance on 2 April 1887. In a third letter, of 17 June 1887, he acknowledged the orchestra's agreement to perform the work during the following season.[5] They gave it on 17 October 1887. Strauss wrote to Bülow to report a resounding success, clouded only by some journalistic sniping, 'which doesn't matter'. While in Leipzig he met Gustav Mahler, whose adaptation of Weber's *Die drei Pintos* aroused his lively interest, and he recommended it strongly to Bülow. Bülow was less enchanted by it: 'The whole thing, *per Bacco*, is an infamous, out-moded concoction.' (27 March 1888) Mahler struck Strauss as 'a highly intelligent musician and conductor, who understands the art of tempo modification and subscribes to some splendid views altogether, especially on Wagner's tempos (by contrast with the accredited Wagner conductors of our day)'. (To Bülow, 29 October 1887)

He would gladly have relinquished one conducting duty that fell to him in Munich, but he had no option but to undertake the direction of a ladies' choral society which enjoyed the patronage of Baroness von Perfall, the intendant's wife. It was a far greater satisfaction to be invited by Count Antonio Freschi to go to Milan to conduct two symphony concerts, which proved to be his first successes, as both conductor and composer, outside Germany. The concerts took place on 8 and 11 December 1887, and the same programme was performed at both: Weber's overture to *Euryanthe*, Strauss's F minor Symphony, Beethoven's *Leonore* Overture no. 1, Glinka's *Kamarinskaya* and Wagner's prelude to *Meistersinger*. Six rehearsals gave Strauss the opportunity to do an astonishing amount with the orchestra, which he described to Bülow as 'very willing and very capable' – the secret of his success with them was sectional rehearsals. 'I believe I conducted the concert very much in your spirit, I took very great pains, at least.' (26 December 1887) The orchestra enjoyed working under him so much that they presented him with 'a silver baton with an inscription', which pleased him all the more because he was 'far from spoiled by recognition and benevolence in my beloved home town'. The euphoria of his stay in Milan spilled over into his letters to his father: 'Today's rehearsal went capitally and everyone is in raptures over my symphony.' After the first concert: 'I am the lion of the hour. Everyone in raptures, concert went excellently and a great success, especially the symphony . . . everyone delighted by my compositions and my conducting.' After the second concert: 'Even greater success today . . . Scherzo encored. I took four calls after the symphony.' He made himself understood in rehearsals by the use of French and his few scraps of Italian, and there was a clarinettist able to double as interpreter. He also took the opportunity of his stay in Milan to call on Ricordi's, to enquire about tempos in Verdi's *Otello*.

Wandrers Sturmlied, which Strauss conducted at the invitation of Franz Wüllner at a subscription concert in Cologne on 8 March 1887, was far less of a popular success than the F minor Symphony.

Aus Italien

Only a few weeks after his return from Milan Richard was asked whether he would be able to conduct a symphony concert in Berlin, in which the soloist would be Carl Halir, the leader of the Berlin Philharmonic Orchestra, a member of the Joachim Quartet and first violin in a quartet of his own. The soloist was to have been Joseph Joachim, but he had injured his finger. Strauss confirmed his availability, but the agent Hermann Wolff engaged Gustav Kogel instead. Strauss was hurt by this, all the more because he had recently had several opportunities to conduct: on 10 January 1888 he had directed the F minor Symphony in Mannheim, and in Berlin, at a concert of Bülow's on 23 January, he had conducted his symphonic fantasy *Aus Italien* (which had already had its first performance by then, in Munich), and repeated it two days later at a 'popular' concert (a matinée, at reduced prices, at which the Berlin Philharmonic Orchestra repeated the programme of a symphony concert given a day or two before). Of course he lost no time in writing to his father about the first concert in Berlin:

> Well, my success was really capital, I had to take a bow at the end of *each* movement (*two* after the third) and at the end I was called back twice, by Berlin standards a colossal success for a new work, especially such a daring one. The Philharmonic Orchestra is the most intelligent, capital, alert orchestra I know. They catch hold of a conductor's every nuance, their comprehension is colossal, and technically they're outstanding. I don't believe I shall ever hear my fantasy more beautifully played, everything came over, and these people have such expression when they play, a freshness, a youthful ardour and they played the fantasy with great enthusiasm and love. Bülow was charming, greatly delighted, like various other people . . . he liked the last movement best: the difference between North German intelligence and South German philistinism! The first time they read through the finale the orchestra burst out laughing, people have a sense of humour here . . . It's glorious here, the whole concert was heavenly: *Leonore* under Bülow a *revelation, Meistersinger* prelude encored, glorious, magnificent!!! (24 January 1888)

Bülow was in two minds about the Italian fantasy, which was dedicated to him. He was admittedly depressed by circumstances in

Hamburg when he wrote to Alexander Ritter, critically and with reservations, after seeing the score:

> Is age making such a reactionary of me? The author is a genius, but I find he has gone to the utmost limit of what is musically possible (within the bounds of beauty), and has often, indeed, gone beyond the limit, without any really pressing need for it. A wonderful, enviable mistake, the prodigality of the ideas, the abundance of associations, only . . . well, I look forward to its performance. What I deplore more than anything are the colossal difficulties for the performers. (30 December 1887)

The two performances of the pioneering symphonic fantasy in Berlin had been preceded by three others, all conducted by Strauss himself. He gave the first performance with the Court Orchestra in Munich on 2 March 1887, another at a Gürzenich Concert in Cologne on 8 January 1888 and the third on 18 January at a Museum Concert in Frankfurt. The turmoil caused by the Munich première can be judged from the recollections of Richard's sister Johanna:

> It was quite an occasion, and I cannot begin to describe my father's anxiety and excitement. He was practising the difficult, audacious solos for the horn at home long before the day. Both the players and the critics were full of doubts about the work before the performance. The first three movements were received with applause, but there was less applause after the last movement, indeed signs of disapproval and derisory whistles came from various quarters.

Johanna goes on to assert that the press turned against the work and that Oskar Merz, in particular, the critic of the *Münchner Neueste Nachrichten*, was hostile towards Richard and expressed his opinion without mincing his words, but her memory is at fault; on the whole the review was benign:

> Everything about the planning and realization of the work shows that the young composer has become better acquainted with modern music and now wishes to reflect the impressions it has made on him in an individual manner. It is not surprising that on his first sortie into the realm of programme music he has not yet altogether succeeded in reaching the goal he has set himself, but let there be no mistake about it: he reveals a rich and fertile imagination and a very unusual sense of original musical coloration.

The first movement ('Auf der Campagna') was the one Munich's leading paper picked out as the most successful.

Writing to Ernst von Schuch to offer him the work, Strauss said:

> The performance of the work, from the manuscript, at the Musical Academy Concert here was under my own direction (1 [*sic*] March 1887), the work was well received, although there was some dissent among the so-called orthodox musicians, on the grounds of various new and unfamiliar aspects of the form and the content. (27 August 1887)

In a letter to Karl Wolff, the writer on music (1848–1912), Strauss wrote about the kind of misunderstanding his symphonic fantasy encountered. The letter supplements his own analysis of the work (see below), and sheds important light on his attitude to its 'programme'.

> With the horrifying lack of judgment and understanding typical of a large proportion of today's pen-pushers, many of them, like a large proportion of the general public, have allowed some of the external features of my work, which may be dazzling but are *of purely secondary importance*, to deceive them as to its real *content*, indeed to overlook it altogether. It consists of *sensations evoked by* the sight of the wonderful natural beauties of Rome and Naples, *not descriptions of* them – in one review I read 'a musical Baedeker of Southern Italy'.
>
> It really is ridiculous to suggest that a present-day composer, whose tutors have been the classics, especially late Beethoven, as well as Wagner and Liszt, would write a work three-quarters of an hour in length in order to show off with the kind of piquant tone painting and brilliant instrumentation that almost every advanced composition student still at a conservatory can write nowadays. *Expression* is our art, and a piece of music which has nothing truly poetic to convey to me – content that is, of course, which can be properly represented *only in music*, a content that words may be able to *suggest but only suggest* – a piece like that in my view is anything you care to call it – but not music.

These words, written when he was twenty-three, constitute the credo to which Strauss held fast all his life, and which provides the key to his symphonic poems and his stage works alike.

Bülow, to whom Strauss represented *Aus Italien* as the 'first step on the road towards independence', accepted the dedication of the fantasy 'with the same enthusiasm' that he was 'accustomed as a rule to display when refusing such marks of distinction'. He recommended Spitzweg to publish the work, which Spitzweg duly did.

Strauss told Lotti Speyer that he was proud of the work, half of which had been hissed at its first performance. It was 'fairly new and revolutionary' and the last movement, 'Neapolitanisches Volksleben', had provoked great opposition, or at the very least much shaking of heads, among the fuddy-duddies old and young:

> Of course I found it all tremendous fun: 'eine Hetz' as they say in Vienna. Some of them applauded furiously, some of them hissed vigorously, in the end the applause won. The opposition have pronounced me half-crazy, talk about going astray and all that kind of rubbish. I felt immensely proud: the first work to have met with the opposition of the multitude; that proves it must be of some significance.

He went on to tell Lotti that he was now working on an orchestral piece to be called *Macbeth*, 'which is of course very wild in character, and on a violin sonata. I also wrote heaps of songs last winter, eight of which have been published by Aibl, while another eleven are in the press at this very moment.' (23 June 1887) The last sentence is a reference to settings of poems by Adolf von Schack, which were published as Op. 17 (D. Rahter, Leipzig) and Op. 19 (Joseph Aibl).

The eagerness with which Strauss greeted everything new, and his dismissal now of Brahms, is well illustrated by a letter to the Dresden composer Jean Louis Nicodé, whose Symphonic Variations he had heard on his visit to Dresden in December 1883 and praised to his father as an 'interesting and talented piece', and with whom he had struck up a correspondence. After a performance of Nicodé's orchestral fantasy *Die Jagd nach dem Glück* (composed in 1882) at a Munich Academy concert, Strauss wrote: 'For myself, I greatly enjoyed your work, with its attractive, piquant invention and its immensely witty, spicy instrumentation . . . After the Brahms D major Symphony, which, after all, is really badly and aridly scored, the resplendent sound of your up-to-the-minute orchestra was a great solace.' (14 December 1888)[6]

During these three years in Munich Strauss found himself and made the decisive breakthrough to a 'music of expression' in which his personality was able to unfurl to the full, while at the same time giving a clear definition to forms that were unmistakably his own and developing a musical style that bore his own distinctive stamp. To a correspondent in Milan, Consul Emil Struth, he described himself as 'dug in' at his desk, where he felt very happy (17 January 1888). The music he wrote up to the point of his departure from Meiningen is not without individual traits in which, with hindsight, one can detect signs of a personal language and occasional (usually very temporary) divergences from the paths of convention, but it is on the whole an echo of the music of the classico-romantic tradition in which he had been reared. The early songs, the chamber music and the orchestral works up to and including the F minor Symphony could reckon on a favourable reception because they are distinguished by the technical proficiency and assurance which he had acquired young and bear witness to uncommon formal gifts. In some cases there is no mistaking one particular model, in others there is a blend of influences; no sooner has the hint of one appeared than it vanishes again. The 'classical line', of which he used later to speak, predominates. Reminiscences of Mendelssohn and Spohr, more rarely of Schubert and Schumann, occasionally of Chopin and of lesser composers from Strauss's immediate musical environment – such as Franz Lachner and Joseph Rheinberger – serve perhaps to lend colour or suggest a particular technical procedure, but their importance is never more than secondary. The influence of Brahms is more palpable in works like the C minor Piano Quartet (Op. 13) and the choral piece *Wandrers Sturmlied* (Op. 14), and it is also present in the *Burleske*, although Strauss's more mobile, nervous temperament already breaks through unmistakably in the quirky piano part, while the rhythmic piquancy occasionally foreshadows *Till Eulenspiegel* and some of the melodic shapes look forward to *Der Rosenkavalier*.

The symphonic fantasy *Aus Italien* is the turning-point in Strauss's creative life. For the first time personal experience – the impressions received on his first holiday in Italy – demanded musical expression, but for the first time, too, Strauss adopted Liszt's fundamental principle that new ideas must be expressed in new forms. He was not yet capable of carrying the principle through to its conclusion. In his late memoir of his early life he wrote 'The first timid experiment was made in the suite *Aus Italien*, by means of rearranging the movements and, as in the third movement ('Sorrento'), the individual sections of the movements themselves.' The analysis of the work which he wrote in 1889 for the *Allgemeine Musikzeitung* – the only one of its kind by him that we possess – gives at least some clues as to how he regarded the relationship of the poetic idea and the musical layout:

1. *Auf der Campagna*: Andante 4/4 (G major). This prelude, which reproduces the mood experienced by the composer at the sight of the broad extent of the Roman Campagna bathed in sunlight, as seen from the Villa d'Este at Tivoli, is based on three principal themes [quoted: first theme; subsidiary theme; coda theme].

2. *In Roms Ruinen*: Allegro con brio (6/4, 3/2) C major. Fantastic images of vanished glory, feelings of melancholy and grief amid the brilliant sunshine of the present.

The following themes correspond to the three basic moods identified in the heading: [five themes quoted: main theme; subsidiary section of the main theme; second subsidiary section of the main theme; first and second coda motives – middle theme]. The formal structure of the movement is that of a great symphonic first movement.

3. *Am Strande von Sorrent*: Andantino (A major 3/8). This movement essays the representation in tone painting of the tender music of nature, which the inner ear hears in the rustling of the wind in the leaves, in bird song and in all the delicate voices of nature, in the distant murmur of the sea, whence a solitary song reaches to the beach: [quotation of the A minor episode] and the contrasting of it with the sensations experienced by the human listener, which are expressed in the melodic elements of the movement. The interplay in the separation and partial union of these contrasts constitutes the spiritual content of this mood-picture.

4. *Neapolitanisches Volksleben* (Allegro molto 2/4). The principal theme is a well-known Neapolitan folk song [quoted] and in addition a tarantella which the composer heard in Sorrento is used in the coda: [quotations: tarantella and middle themes]. After a few noisy introductory bars, the statement of the principal theme by the violas and cellos launches this crazy orchestral fantasy, which attempts to depict the colourful bustle of Naples in a hilarious jumble of themes; the tarantella, at first heard only at a distance, gradually asserts itself towards the end

of the movement, and provides the conclusion for this humoresque. A few reminiscences of the first movement may express nostalgia for the peace of the Campagna.

After his Italian fantasy, which lies somewhere between a suite and a symphonic poem, Strauss composed one last piece of chamber music in 1887, the Sonata in E♭ major for violin and piano Op. 18, dedicated to his friend and cousin Robert Pschorr; he had written two movements by August 1887 and completed the finale on 1 November. Various influences were once again at work, notably in the Andante, which bears the heading 'Improvisation' and is a 'song without words' with a dramatic middle section, while the thematic material and the development of the outer movements already display some of the impetus and driving energy which were to be the hallmarks of the symphonic poems. The freedom of the chromatic modulations and the occasional signs of an orchestral approach are other features that separate the Violin Sonata from all Strauss's previous chamber music. Rather it looks forward to what was to come – in fact the main theme of the finale directly anticipates the stormy opening of *Don Juan*. Even so, Strauss was soon to reckon the sonata among the products of a period he had outgrown. Its first public performance was given on 3 October 1888 in Elberfeld by Robert Heckmann and Julius Buths.

In the field of chamber music, Strauss wrote only one string quartet, one cello sonata, one piano sonata (in B minor, Op. 5, 1880–1), one piano quartet and only this one violin sonata. He started a sonata for horn and piano (o. Op. 86A), intending it to be a silver wedding present for his parents, but by the time of the anniversary (29 August 1888) he had completed only the slow movement, a C major Andante in 2/4 time, and he never finished the work.

He also completed a substantial number of songs between 1885 and the spring of 1888. The seventeen published as Opp. 15, 17 and 19 were all settings of poems by Count von Schack, with the exception of one by Michelangelo. Some of them, such as the early *Ständchen, Lob des Leidens, Breit' über mein Haupt dein schwarzes Haar, Wie sollten wir geheim sie halten* and others, are still among the songs by Strauss which are most often performed nowadays. Few of them are notably Straussian in character; their significance in his development as a composer of lieder lies in the painstaking treatment of the declamation and in the richer and more characterful working of the piano accompaniment, compared with the first published collection of songs, the Op. 10 set. His next collection, *Schlichte Weisen* Op. 21, was dedicated to his sister and consisted of settings of poems by Felix Dahn. This group may well have been inspired by Alexander Ritter's *Schlichte Weisen*, his Op. 2, written many years earlier; the title means 'plain – or unadorned – melodies'. This collection, composed in the summer of 1887, again includes some established favourites, such as *All mein Gedanken* and *Du meines Herzens Krönelein*. Four more Dahn settings, *Mädchenblumen* Op. 22, completed early in 1888, are completely different in character. Strauss told Eugen Spitzweg that they were 'very complicated' and experimental, and that he did not expect them to be a success with the public – as proved and still proves to be the case. In 1890 Strauss sent them to the Berlin publisher Adolph Fürstner, who had begun to take an interest in him. 'Out of sheer bravado' he asked for a fee of 800 marks for these 'extremely ungrateful songs' and, when he refused to lower his demand, Fürstner actually paid that amount. Until then he had had to be content with very modest fees: Spitzweg had paid him only 200 marks for the five songs of Op. 15, and 500 marks for *Aus Italien*. Originally Spitzweg had been unwilling to pay anything at all for *Aus Italien*, since engraving it already involved him in a loss.

To oblige a friend Strauss wrote anonymously the incidental music for a production in Munich of Shakespeare's *Romeo and Juliet* (o. Op. 86). Requiring only small forces (female chorus, woodwind, harp and triangle), it consisted of four numbers – 'Moresca', 'Tra-la song' (which was not used), 'Epithalamium' and 'Funeral Music' – and was first performed on 23 October 1887.[7] He also wrote again for the Wilde Gung'l. In 1888 he revised the D major Festive March o. Op. 84 which he had originally composed for the orchestra in the winter of 1884–5 and which had been performed on 8 January 1885. The new version was played in 1888, though the exact date can no longer be established. He wrote another Festive March (in C major, o. Op. 87) for the Wilde Gung'l, to celebrate its twenty-fifth anniversary; the first performance was conducted by Franz Strauss on 1 February 1889, in the ballroom of the Centralsäle in Munich.

Macbeth (I)

It seems probable that Strauss began to think about a one-movement symphonic poem, based for the first and last time in his career on a play, Shakespeare's *Macbeth*, soon after he had finished *Aus Italien*, by the spring of 1887 at the latest. On 11 January 1888 he wrote about the work to Carl Hörburger as one in which he had 'set out upon a completely new path', towards which the Italian fantasy had served as a bridge. The first version of the work, which has never been published, ended with a triumphal march celebrating Macduff, which Hans von Bülow rightly criticized: 'It is quite in order for an *Egmont* overture to end with a march celebrating the triumph of Egmont, but a symphonic poem called *Macbeth* cannot end with the triumph of Macduff.' Strauss took the objection to heart, and admitted that the work needed 'to be reworked before it corresponded to the correct stylistic principles of the authentic programme-music composer', as he recounted in his memoir of his early life. The path on which he set out in *Macbeth* aroused the misgivings both of Father Strauss and of Bülow, who was appalled by the amount of dissonance. Richard replied as follows to his father's objections:

> *Macbeth* belongs with *Don Juan* in my development, it will be published for the benefit of those who are interested in my development, and I don't give a toss for the others. 'The enemies' will have damned little time for *Macbeth*, and that's perhaps a very good thing, as not every professor at a university or an academy is capable of reading a complicated score like this . . . There's no question of ignoring my debt of gratitude to Spitzweg, as he still has the option of publishing *Macbeth*, I won't give him *Tod und Verklärung* until *Macbeth* has appeared. As for Bülow, his sensitive ears are a burden he must bear, and I really cannot concern myself with his fads any more. Boom! (31 December 1889)

As Spitzweg hesitated to print *Macbeth*, Strauss had been thinking of offering it to Peters Verlag, who had expressed an interest, but in the end it appeared under Spitzweg's Joseph Aibl imprint.

The first public performance of *Macbeth* did not take place until October 1890, when Strauss directed it himself at a concert in Weimar, but he had had the opportunity to hear and assess it during 1889, when he ran through it with the orchestra in Mannheim at a rehearsal in January at which he also directed his symphony, and in Meiningen, when he heard Fritz Steinbach rehearse it; on both these occasions what was played was in all probability the revised version. In a lengthy letter following the Weimar performance, Franz Strauss implored his son to resist his inclination to experiment:

> The greatest music can be written without experimentation, with great and noble ideas simply attired, without grand instrumental brilliance, and then it is understood at all times and by all people. All the great artists in every age have achieved their most magnificent work with the simplest means, you have only to think of Greek sculpture and the great . . . Italian painters of the Middle Ages. (17 October 1890)

And – 'with a heavy heart', since he knew he was wasting his time – he advised Richard to go through *Macbeth* once again with great care, discarding the 'rolls of excess instrumental fat' and giving the horns – as always his special concern – a better chance to detect what it was that he really meant to say. Although Richard was by then virtually impervious to paternal objurations, he did rework *Macbeth* once more, but probably on the strength of what he had realized while rehearsing and performing it with the Weimar orchestra, and not to please his father.

The revision of the instrumentation, which Strauss began that November, took him until 4 March 1891, five months after the first performance. A letter to the work's dedicatee, Alexander Ritter, makes it clear that he did no more than retouch the scoring; he had, he wrote, 'no more fault to find with the structure and the whole idea', but he was still not satisfied with the instrumentation. 'In many places too many inner parts prevent the principal themes from standing out as clearly as I would wish, and I've already more or less made up my mind to rework the whole piece completely.' He also mentioned the revision in a letter to his sister and wrote a fuller report about it to Ludwig Thuille, in a letter of mid-November 1890. A performance of *Macbeth* in Berlin on 29 February 1892 finally proved to the composer that his labours, spread out over four years, had been worthwhile. He was equally pleased with the work and with its performance. Once again he wrote to Ritter:

> Just think of it: *Macbeth* had a *great* success both at the final rehearsal and at the performance and really seems to have made a deep impression. The orchestra played wonderfully, the piece

> sounded fabulous and what with the clarity of the new version – there's no longer a single theme that doesn't 'stand out' – and the powerful way in which it steadily intensifies right though to the end, it gave me tremendous pleasure.

He wrote in similar terms to his parents, laying particular stress on the effectiveness of the bass trumpet: 'It's the only possible bridge and intermediary between trumpets and trombones and softens the brass colossally.' (1 March 1892) Bülow, too, now expressed a positive attitude towards the work, clapping Strauss on the shoulder after the performance with the words 'it *is* a good piece after all'. He wrote to Eugen Spitzweg about the work and the performance:

> Tidings of great joy. True, one should not praise the public rehearsal before the concert – but *Macbeth*'s success this morning was *colossal*! The audience roared for Strauss four times. The sound of the work, too, was – overwhelming. The composer has never had a reception like this in Berlin before. A surprise for all of us and grounds for mutual congratulations. Go hang yourself for not having been here! There may well yet become an optimist of your old friend Nanusch. (PS.) Air full of dynamite, I mean electricity. (28 February 1892)

He also wrote to his wife after the public rehearsal in similar vein, while he had already told Strauss that he had been won over by the work he had previously found fault with:

> Anyway, it gives me great pleasure to assure you that the revised version of your *Macbeth* has made a great impression on me, in spite of all its acerbities and the monstrosities of its material. I sympathize – as one of the species musician – far more with this opus than with its predecessor *T[od] und V[erklärung]*, I find more logic and genius in it. (1 February 1892)

Strauss had written two more symphonic poems before *Macbeth* was finally cast in its definitive form, so it has the opus number 23. The composer called it a 'tone poem', and it was in this one-movement piece that he finally worked out the expressive form that met his needs, as well as his own highly expressive musical language. By contrast with that of Liszt in his symphonic poems, the musical language of Strauss's tone poems is based on a luxuriant orchestral polyphony which made the expansion of the individual sections of the orchestra ever more imperative. The primary purpose of the enlargement of the orchestra, in *Macbeth* and its successors, was not to increase the volume of sound, as some people have always believed, but to enhance the differentiation possible to the orchestra. In *Don Juan* the essential characteristics of orchestral music are exhibited in new formal developments which correspond to the 'pre-existing poetic model': the energy of thematic development, the expressive intensity of harmony, the saturated colour of orchestral sound with solo lines picked out against the background, and also the power of the formal coherence of opposing zones of expression. Nothing in these early tone poems is stereotyped. A fresh, powerful breeze blows through them from a mind and spirit receptively open to life. Realism is blended with a high-spirited idealism.

'Music as expression'

The score of *Don Juan* is prefaced by some quotations from Nikolaus Lenau's play of the same name, but there is only a loose connection between them and the structure and content of the tone poem. The earliest thematic ideas date from May 1888; Strauss wrote them down in the cloister-garth of Sant'Antonio in Padua, while on his second visit to Italy. Mozart's *Don Giovanni* does not appear to have played any part in the choice of subject, to which Strauss was to return a few years later (1892) when he thought seriously of writing an opera on it. It was suggested to him by his reading of Lenau's unfinished verse drama, as well as by a play by Paul Heyse, *Don Juans Ende*, which had made a powerful impression on him when he and Bülow had seen it together in Frankfurt, as long ago as July 1885. He finished the score of the tone poem on 30 September 1888. While he was working on it he wrote a letter to Bülow, which acknowledges the value of some suggestions the latter had made but is notable primarily for its thorough and insistent explanation of the new path along which Strauss was now determined to go.

> For the time being *Macbeth* lies contentedly buried in my desk, while the dissonances will see if they can eat each other up. *Don Juan* will perhaps go to keep him company soon. In days to come perhaps there may bloom on both their graves that menseful little flower whose quiet poesy I am struggling to learn to like in double woodwind. Seriously: I make you a firm promise that double woodwind will be there in my future

works! I will also take the greatest conceivable pains to limit the great technical difficulties. But as to whether I envisage the possibility of turning round on the path on which my logical development from the F minor Symphony has brought me – on that subject I can as yet say nothing definite. It seems to me that the only way in which a *self-reliant forward* development of our instrumental music is possible for some while is in carrying on from the Beethoven of the *Coriolanus*, *Egmont* and *Leonore III* overtures, of *Les adieux*, from late Beethoven in general, all of whose works in my opinion could hardly have come into being without a pre-existing poetic model. If I should prove to lack the artistic strength and gifts to achieve something worthwhile along this path, then it's probably better to leave it at the great nine and their four celebrated successors; I don't see why, before we've even tested our strength, found out whether we're capable of self-reliant creation and perhaps advancing art by one little step, why we should persuade ourselves that we're epigones and dispose ourselves in advance to take up the position of epigones; if it all comes to nothing – well: I still think it's better to follow one's true artistic conviction and to have said something wrong up a blind alley than something superfluous while keeping to the old, well-trodden high road.

Let me get just one more thing off my chest, which may help to explain my standpoint to you exactly: perhaps I shall succeed in saying in a letter what I have not been able to say face to face. From the F minor Symphony onwards I have found myself trapped in a steadily growing antithesis between the musical-cum-poetic content that I have wanted to communicate and the form of the ternary sonata movement which we have inherited from the classics. In Beethoven the musico-poetic content generally fitted exactly into that very '*sonata form*' which evolved in his hands to utmost perfection and is the exhaustive expression of what he felt and wanted to say. Yet even with him there are works (the last movement of the last A♭ major Sonata, the adagio of the A minor Quartet) where he was forced to create a new form for a new content. But the 'form' which was absolutely fitting for the highest and most sublime kind of content in Beethoven has been used for the last sixty years now as a 'formula', regarded (but I emphatically deny it) as inseparable from our instrumental music, and 'purely musical' content ('musical' in the strictest and soberest meaning of the word) has simply to adapt itself, by force if necessary, to fit the formula, or, worse, the formula has been filled in and filled out with contents unworthy of it.

Now, if one wants to create a work of art, the mood and structure of which are of a piece and which is to make a vivid impression on the listener, then the author must also have had a vivid image of what he wanted to say before his inner eye. This is only possible as a consequence of fertilization by a poetic idea, whether appended to the work as a programme or not. In my opinion it is a purely artistic process to create a new form to correspond to each new poetic model; making the form a beautiful one, complete and perfect in itself, is of course very difficult, but that makes it all the more stimulating. Making music according to the rules of pure Hanslickian form is in any case no longer possible, from now onwards there will be no more beautiful but aimless phrase-making, during which the minds of both the composer and the listeners are a complete blank, and no more symphonies (Brahms excepted of course), which always remind me of an immense garment, made to fit a Hercules, which a skinny tailor has tried on in the hope that he will cut a fine figure in it.

The precise expression of my artistic ideas and feelings and stylistically the most self-reliant of all my works to date, the one in which I was most conscious of my intentions, is *Macbeth*.

Perhaps a newer work by me, one with a less brutal or gruesome content than *Macbeth*, will reconcile you to the path that I have now set out along.

If not, then please pardon and forget this feeble and perhaps incoherent attempt 'not to remain unheard' by you at least.
(24 August 188)

But Bülow's conservatism, becoming steadily more pronounced as he grew older, was impervious to such attempts at explanation, even when garnished with loaded references to *Die Meistersinger*. His comment in the margin of Strauss's letter shows that he was less inclined to play Hans Sachs to Strauss's Stolzing than to dampen his ardour with the pragmatism of Goethe's Mephisto: 'Theory can be grey or green, but practice is making beautiful, melodious music.'

A letter Strauss wrote a few months later to the composer and conductor Jan Levoslav Bella (1843–1936),[8] who had been commended to him by Hans Wihan, shows how filled he was with the new musical ideas he was exploring and how strong was his need to communicate them to others. After congratulating Bella on an 'outstanding leading article' and a stylish performance of Liszt's *Prometheus*, he went on:

Our great concert-giving institutions are still wallowing in their troughs, complacently grunting their way through endless repeat performances of *Judas Maccabeus*, *Elijah*, *Paradise and the Peri*, and under a hypocritical mask of venerating the classics they get away with artistic murder, by performing symphonies by Mozart and Beethoven in a manner that makes every true venerator of the classics turn away with a shudder, not out of indolence but for reasons that lie in the depths of his heart.

How few present-day musicians, roaming about in the noble framework of the four-movement formula, have fully understood the essential nature of our glorious musical heritage. Our 'music as expression', not Hanslick's 'resounding form'. (2 December 1888)

Here – and elsewhere – Strauss was emulating Alexander Ritter, both in the emphasis of his rejection and in the fanaticism of his credo. A second letter to Bella, written to thank him for an article about *Wandrers Sturmlied*, includes another attempt to define his position, and although it dates from some time later, after he had moved to Weimar, it is not inappropriate to quote it here:

The practitioners of music here are divided into two groups, those to whom music is 'expression', which they use as a language every bit as precise as the language of words, but to express things beyond the capacity of words; and those to whom music is 'resounding form', that is, they provide the work they want to compose (calmly and unthinkingly utilizing a classical form which is no longer form but formula) with some general underlying mood or other, and develop such themes as arise according to a totally exterior musical logic which, now that I acknowledge only a poetic logic, I cannot even understand.

Programme music: real music!

Absolute music: can be written with the aid of a certain routine and craftsmanship by any only moderately musical person.

The first: – art!

The second: – craft!

Remarkably enough, present-day music took No. 2 as its starting-point and was made fully conscious of its true destiny only by Wagner and Liszt.

We present-day musicians therefore still begin with No. 2, until we come to realize that it is not music at all, and that the fundamental condition of a musical work is 'the most precise

> expression of a musical idea' which has to create its own form, every new idea its own new form. (13 March 1890)

Later we shall be able to observe the extent to which Strauss held to these principles throughout his life and how far he eventually admitted modifications. For the moment we will anticipate his future attitude only by quoting a statement made in 1905 to Romain Rolland and two passages written much later. Rolland had raised an objection to the 'programme' of the *Symphonia Domestica* that had been published in music guides. Strauss replied:

> You may well be right about the programme of the *Domestica*, moreover you are in complete agreement on the matter with Mahler, who utterly condemns programmes as such. But (1) I never provided a programme to accompany the *S. Domestica*, (2) you yourself, I think, have a false conception of the purpose of such a programme.
>
> For me the poetic programme is nothing more then the initial cause which shapes the forms, in which I then give expression and purely musical development to my feelings; not, as you suppose, merely a *musical description* of certain events in real life. That, after all, would be completely contrary to the spirit of music. But if the music is not to seep away in pure wilfulness, it needs certain boundaries to define the form, and a programme serves as a canal-bank. Even for the listener an analytical programme of that kind should be no more than a guide. Whoever is interested should use it. Whoever really understands how to listen to music probably has no need of it. (5 July 1905)

He was to express himself in a very similar fashion in his memoir 'Aus meinen Jugend- und Lehrjahren', which probably dates from the late 1930s, though the exact date is unknown: 'A poetic programme can well be the stimulus to the creation of new forms, but where the music does not develop logically out of itself it becomes "literary" music.' Finally, in a reflection 'on the melodic idea' of about the same period or perhaps slightly later, he wrote:

> Our learned musical theorists – I will name the two principal ones: Friedrich von Hausegger ('music as expression') and Eduard Hanslick ('music as sounding moving form') – laid down formulations which have been regarded ever since as irreconcilable antitheses. That is wrong. They are the two ways of creating musical form and each complements the other.[9]

The letter to Bülow, to which he received no answer, and the 'supplements' to it addressed to Bella testify that it was the increasingly urgent necessity of expression, of individualization of the instrumental parts, which transformed Strauss's music from within and led to new forms appropriate to the 'poetic idea'. Berlioz and Liszt were among his predecessors, but the stimulus and example of Wagner's orchestral language were incomparably stronger. Because to begin with Strauss formed his own musical language in symphonic works, he did not remain long in danger of becoming a Wagnerian epigone – though his first stage-work, *Guntram*, in which the predominant texture is an expressly Wagnerian one, the 'resplendent organ-peal of quadruple horns', shows that he skirted it. But even in the earliest tone poems, Wagner's harmonic innovations and his polyphonic orchestral writing undergo further development and transformation, above all in respect of psychological differentiation. Greater flexibility of harmony and rhythm, expressive colouring of the orchestral sound – alternately lightened and made denser in the service of powerful climaxes – burst upon the listener as the characteristics of his style, an orchestral style par excellence.

The influence Alexander Ritter had upon Strauss, undeniable and by no means entirely beneficial as it was, should not be overestimated. Ritter helped him towards self-knowledge and hastened the process of freeing himself from the restraints of formal stereotypes, but his role in developing Strauss's orchestral language was only an indirect one, in that he introduced him to the work and the ideas of Wagner and Liszt. Strauss was by far Ritter's superior in musical powers and he had already outstripped his mentor and friend in *Macbeth* and *Don Juan*. It is Ritter's songs which represent him at his best and most individual as a composer, and they came nearer than anything else he wrote to exercising an influence on Strauss's own song-writing at a certain phase: their attraction for Strauss lay in the exemplary declamation, the original treatment of dissonance, and the tendency of a cantabile line to turn suddenly into a kind of urgent recitative at a significant point in the text in many of the songs. Ritter's liking for dissonances in the relationship between the vocal part and the piano accompaniment was another feature that was bound to capture Strauss's interest. At all events he paid Ritter's lieder – many of them not written until the 1890s – a great deal of attention and carefully collected them.

A visit to Bayreuth in the summer of 1888, where he heard *Die Meistersinger* under Hans Richter and *Parsifal* under Felix Mottl, helped to deepen his knowledge and understanding of Wagner. He was also invited to a soirée at Wahnfried. He went to Bayreuth again in 1889, this time as a musical assistant. 'The last *Tristan* was glorious', he wrote home, 'and *Meistersinger* yesterday was magnificent. *Parsifal* and another *Meistersinger* still to come, then it's over, then the usual theatrical rubbish begins again.' (15 August 1889)

During the three years of his first term at the Munich opera, Strauss's plans for an opera of his own matured, encouraged by Ritter. He took the germ of the idea, as he told Arthur Seidl, 'from a small and unremarkable reference in a feuilleton article in the *Neue Freie Presse* [of Vienna] to the existence of secret, artistic-cum-religious orders, which were founded in Austria to combat the worldliness of Minnesang'. He originally thought of giving the drama the Dostoyevskian title of 'Guilt and Atonement',* but he soon changed that to the name of the opera's principal character, Guntram. It was Ritter, again, who encouraged him to write his own text, as a true Wagnerian should. Letters from Strauss to Ritter and Marie von Bülow show that he began to work on the text early in 1888. He finished a first complete scenario, with which he was 'very satisfied' and which Ritter liked too, in March. He at once started to work it into a complete text for a three-act tragic opera, which he described as 'created entirely by myself, wholly personal and original', but was forced to break off the work; various references in his correspondence reveal that he also made numerous revisions to the scenario. Only in November 1888 was he able to start again on the libretto, which then took him until well into 1890: he finished the second act in May, and the third in October. By then he had moved to Weimar, and we shall return to the opera at a later stage in this chronicle.

First acquaintance with Pauline de Ahna

Although Strauss led a quiet life in Munich, apart from his work at the Court Opera, he kept up to date with musical and other artistic events in the city during these three years, though with mounting distaste. Verdi's *Otello*, rehearsed and directed by Levi, was one

* *Schuld und Sühne*, the title given in German to the novel known to the Anglophone world as *Crime and Punishment*. *Tr.*

work which profoundly impressed him. He wrote to Emil Struth about the production: 'Levi had taken great pains, Vogl was outstanding, especially dramatically, ditto Gura, chorus and orchestra unsurpassable'. (30 April 1888) He also took pupils, including the tenor Heinrich Zeller, whom he coached in Wagnerian roles, and the composer Hermann Bischoff. Zeller made his stage début in Weimar as Lohengrin, on 20 November 1888, in a guest performance which was simultaneously an audition. When Strauss went to Weimar in 1889, Zeller was already there as a member of the company, and he created the title role in *Guntram* in 1894. Hermann Bischoff, too, went to Weimar when Strauss did, and worked there as a co-repetiteur. It is not certain whether Strauss also gave lessons to a pupil of Ludwig Thuille, the charming Comtesse Montgelas, who later entered a convent. At all events he took a lively interest as she grew into an enthusiastic Wagnerian, turning completely daft about the music of the future, or so he told Dora Wihan. With Thuille she studied songs by Jensen, Peter Cornelius's *Weihnachtslieder* and, above all, the songs of Liszt.

In the summer of 1887, in Feldafing, Strauss made the acquaintance of Pauline de Ahna, the daughter of Major-General Adolf de Ahna, who had a post in the War Ministry, and his wife Maria, née Huber. The general was a protestant, his wife a catholic. Pauline, who was born in Ingolstadt on 4 February 1863, studied singing at the Munich School of Music, and also took lessons with Max Steinitzer, Strauss's future biographer, who, however, could make little progress with her education and handed her on to his friend.

> I complain to Strauss, who is on a visit to his uncle Pschorr, that I am having musical difficulties with a very pretty, charming young lady, who lives across the road, almost opposite; I urge him to stand in for me with her occasionally. I assure him that the family are wild about his works and would certainly be glad to receive him. Strauss agrees, everyone is thrilled, and after the very first lesson with Pauline Strauss tells me: 'She is much more talented then you think, we have only got to bring her gifts out.'[10]

Strauss himself, in 1947, erected a 'little memorial to his beloved wife', as Pauline became in 1894, before he himself departed from 'the ruins of his artistic existence'. It begins:

> I met Pauline in 1887, or thereabouts, in Feldafing, where I was

> paying one of my frequent visits to the beautiful villa of my dear aunt Johanna Pschorr . . . Pauline's father, the worthy General de Ahna, had a fine baritone and enough musical ability to teach himself the duet (Sachs/Walther) from the third act of *Meistersinger*. Pauline had already spent some months studying at the Munich School of Music, and with the courage of a complete amateur had naively stormed her way through the aria from *Freischütz* at an examination-recital in the Odeon, to the thunderous applause of her military admirers! As her father did not care for the ways things were done in the Odeonsplatz, he handed her to me for tuition, and I suggested that she should also take lessons in acting from Franziska Ritter . . . Pauline had dramatic talent, which benefited from the good grounding she received from Alexander Ritter's excellent wife. In Munich I coached Pauline in the roles of Agathe, Elsa and Gounod's Marguérite, and when I went to Weimar as Kapellmeister in 1889, Pauline followed me as my pupil.[11]

For technical vocal training Pauline went to Emilie Herzog and later, in Weimar, where she was engaged to sing the youthful dramatic soprano roles, to Rosa von Milde and Emilie Merian-Genast.

Approaches from Weimar

Strauss's urgent wish to exchange the tedious routine of a third conductor for a position better suited to his abilities when his Munich contract expired on 31 July 1889 was granted. Hans Bronsart had been friendly with Hans von Bülow since the period that both had spent in Weimar with Liszt in the 1850s; in 1865 he succeeded Bülow as conductor of the Gesellschaft der Musikfreunde and he was intendant of the opera in Hanover from 1877 to 1879, when Bülow was principal conductor there.[12] Their friendship survived the temporary ill-feeling accompanying the circumstances in which Bülow was ousted from that post. Bronsart became intendant in Weimar in 1887. His interest in Strauss was due above all to Bülow's advocacy of his protégé, but also owed something to the recommendation of the director of music at Weimar, Eduard Lassen.[13] Bronsart first wrote to Strauss, expressing the wish to meet him, on 25 August 1888. Formal negotiations did not begin until January 1889, and were concluded on 7 March in conversation between Bronsart and Strauss. One of the letters Strauss wrote to his future intendant during the negotiations contains an outline of his own recent experience and his hopes for the future:[14]

> After being engaged three years ago, without any knowledge of the theatre and without any of the routine essential to every aspect of it, as a *third* conductor (Hofmusikdirektor) in this swamp of antiquated, 50-year-old traditions (for the great years which the Munich Court Theatre experienced under the direction of Richard Wagner and Hans von Bülow are obliterated as if they had never been), and as the colleague of conductors whose sole ambition was to bring off, with the help of their routine, what they called a *smooth* performance, wherein everything that cannot be presented *con molto espressione* is whipped through at a brisk Mendelssohnian quick-march tempo – I very soon recognized, to my great distress, that I had made a fundamental miscalculation in the extent of the influence I had hoped to exercise here.
>
> Fresh from the school of Bülow, I came here primarily as a new broom to institute some good, *expressive* orchestral playing, in which I was, however, only partly successful and then only after fighting every inch of the way; the reason for this was my position as *No. 3*, which meant that I lacked all authority, and not only could *not* reckon on the backing of my chief, [but] could also be sure of the inveterate opposition of my two colleagues, who simply follow other principles, such as are more comfortable for all concerned.
>
> If, for instance, I had rehearsed the orchestra in an opera, in the style I considered suitable, for which admittedly *only a tradition that is derived, if possible, from the composer himself* can be the criterion, three weeks later, when the opera was to be performed again after an interval during which perhaps only my two colleagues had conducted their operas, I inevitably discovered that the whole style of execution that I had rehearsed with the orchestra had been completely forgotten and blotted from their minds.
>
> These experiences have convinced me that, if I am to obtain that influence which will set a new standard for the orchestra, I must insist in Weimar on a full and varied share of the work (enough to bring me into intimate association with the whole company), on coordination with Lassen and also on the title and rank of a Hofkapellmeister.
>
> With members of the orchestra and the company in the theatre, it is not the artistic authority but the authority of the

> *rank* that counts first and foremost, and it is through the plenipotency of the rank alone that artistic influence can be acquired. Having said all this, it is probably unnecessary for me to expatiate to you, honoured Herr Generalintendant, on the importance that directing the concerts will have for me in moulding the orchestral playing . . .
>
> To revert to the unimportant subject of myself, as far as concerns the theatre, of which I knew virtually nothing before I took up my present position, the experiences I have had here, some of them very painful (especially with producers), and my careful study of Wagner's writings and dramas have forced me to recognize how urgent the need is for reforms in this sphere too. An expressive style of delivery, beautiful enunciation of the words, acting which is at least approximately suitable to the sense and situations, have become almost completely foreign to singers, whose *strength* nowadays seems to consist almost entirely in showing off their brilliant vocal equipment. And it's so much more difficult to have any effect on singers than on an orchestra! Here, the unconditional, strict authority of a *first* conductor is almost the only thing that carries any weight. (1 March 1889)

In spite of these arguments, Richard failed to obtain the rank he wanted. The principal difficulties in settling the terms of his contract concerned the salary he asked for; the sum was reasonable enough from his point of view, since he could not and did not expect his parents – with whom he had been able to live in Munich – to continue to assist him financially if he took up a post elsewhere. By February 1889, however, he was already prepared to accept the post at Weimar, in spite of the meagre salary, hoping that he would be able to earn enough to reach a modest standard of living by taking additional work. His negotiations with Bronsart had to be conducted in secret at first, as it was not until 12 March 1889 that the Grand Duke of Weimar gave his intendant official leave to approach Strauss. The terms of the contract were agreed on 30 March. It was to date from 1 August, as Strauss's Munich contract did not expire until 31 July, and he was to take up his duties on 1 September, to enable him to take part in the Bayreuth Festival of 1889. He was confirmed in the appointment – as Kapellmeister, not *Hof*-kapellmeister as he had wished – only when he had been in the grand ducal service nearly a year. The decree, dated 20 June 1890 and signed by Carl Alexander, Grand Duke of Saxe-Weimar-Eisenach, refers to his being appointed 'in recognition of his outstanding achievements and in the expectation that he will continue to Serve Us with the same unswerving zeal'.

At 2100 marks the salary offered was actually less than he was already earning in Munich. On 1 January 1890 it was raised to 3000 marks, but there was no further rise when his appointment was confirmed, or later. Understandably, this low salary made Strauss increasingly resentful, especially as the reputation of the Weimar opera was greatly enhanced by his devoted hard work. A further disappointment was the refusal to award him the title of Hofkapellmeister. The enthusiasm he felt at the prospect of working in a new and more promising environment persisted throughout the first year but then gradually waned and was replaced by an ever stronger dissatisfaction with the restrictions of his position and the growing resistance to his fanatical cult of Wagner and Liszt.

During the last year of his Munich appointment there were some events to compensate Richard for his continuing disappointment in the theatre. The happy memories of himself that he had left behind in Meiningen led to his being invited back to conduct his symphonic fantasy *Aus Italien*, which Fritz Steinbach had rehearsed with the orchestra. While he was there, Eugen d'Albert showed him his F major Symphony, which Strauss found to be 'a work of quite significant talent'; he especially liked the 'immensely atmospheric Adagio'. (To Bülow, 30 December 1888) *Aus Italien* was performed in the first few weeks of 1889 in Frankfurt and Cologne. 'The fantasy will go brilliantly [in Frankfurt] . . . orchestra very contented and kind.' (17 January 1889) In the same month, in Mannheim, there was a chamber concert at which the Piano Quartet and the Violin Sonata were performed (14 January). While he was there he took the Mannheim orchestra in a rehearsal of the F minor Symphony on 11 January; '*Macbeth* is technically difficult even for the violins and especially for the trumpets, but didn't sound anything like as dreadful as on the piano'; the players were 'extremely startled and taken aback by the bound' from the earlier work to the later. (17 January 1889) On 1 February, in Munich, the first performance of the Festive March in C major was given, to celebrate the twenty-fifth anniversary of the Wilde Gung'l.

Another enjoyable event was a trip to Berlin in March 1889, in the company of Ritter and Thuille, in order to hear Bülow conduct Beethoven's Ninth Symphony. 'A glorious concert yesterday, Bülow conducted like a god, orchestra played like angels, every one. The *Tannhäuser* Overture brought the house down, Bülow was called back ten times etc. etc.' (To Franz Strauss, 5 March 1889)

During this period of his life, too, Strauss deepened what was to be a close and lifelong friendship with Friedrich Rösch, whom he had known since their schooldays at the Ludwigs-Gymnasium. Their personal relationship was also to be a professional partnership and alliance in the struggle for composers' copyrights.[15] Strauss recalled his friend in an unpublished memoir:

> Rösch was two years ahead of me at the Gymnasium, and went on to university at the Maximilianeum. He studied law and music and had an agreeable talent for composition, to which his songs and two very witty oratorios (*St Antony of Padua*, after Wilhelm Busch, written for the Akademischer Gesangverein) testify. He had conducting talent, shown at its best in Petersburg with the generous support of his noble wife, Marie Ritter, herself a loyal admirer of Hans von Bülow. Rösch had already followed my early efforts at school with interest, became an increasingly close friend of mine during the years 1883–9, and with Alexander Ritter made up the trio (L. Thuille and Arthur Seidl occasionally joined us) which met every evening from 6 to 7 at Leibenfrost's wine parlour (Promenadeplatz) to exchange noble ideas and listen to the teachings of the Lisztian Ritter.

A charming Russian girl, Sonja von Schéhafzoff, was another member of Richard and Johanna Strauss's circle of friends. She had been a piano pupil of Bülow and Richard probably first met her at Bülow's course in Frankfurt in July 1885. The few surviving letters to Strauss reveal little about their friendship, but it continued after his move to Weimar. When he went there early in March 1889 to discuss the terms of his appointment with Bronsart, he was accompanied by Sonja, who hoped to secure from Bronsart, a committee member, an invitation to give a solo recital at a meeting of the Allgemeiner Deutscher Musikverein.

In March 1889 Strauss met Cosima Wagner. Of all the acquaintanceships of this period of his life, this one was to have the most important consequences for his immediate future. The association with Bayreuth was strengthened during his stay there in July and the first half of August. Thanks to a recommendation from Hans von Bülow to Julius Kniese, Cosima's musical adviser, he took part in the festival as a musical assistant with particular responsibility for rehearsing the choir of voices from the middle height in the Grail scenes in *Parsifal*. The conductors at that year's festival were Hermann Levi, Felix Mottl and Hans Richter, and other assistants, besides Strauss, included Carl Armbruster, Otto Gieseker, Engelbert Humperdinck, Oskar Merz, Hugo Röhr, Heinrich Schwartz and Arthur Smolian. Including the time he spent listening in at rehearsals he steeped himself in the art of his adored master for eight hours a day without experiencing 'the least nervous exhaustion', as he told Ritter. 'I attribute this to the strict concentration on one master and one style; it's the mixture of a lot of different things that one usually has to gobble down that is so dreadfully tiring.'

The ardour with which he threw himself into his work in Bayreuth is reflected in his letters home. Proudly and delightedly he recounted that Cosima had taken an interest in him and invited him to dine at Wahnfried – 'I'm in great favour with Frau Wagner, I'm the only one besides Levi and Mottl who plays in the piano rehearsals' – and that the whole Wagner family showed him every mark of distinction. Felix Mottl and Hans Richter also treated him with great kindness; but he had as little to do as he could with the other conductor, Hermann Levi, since he resented the curt manner in which his father had been given notice in June that he was to be pensioned off from the Munich orchestra. He had a stream of visitors during his weeks in Bayreuth that summer: Sonja von Schéhafzoff, Thuille, his pupil Heinrich Zeller, Pauline de Ahna and her father, Friedrich Rösch and Alexander Ritter. After the festival was over Cosima went through *Tannhäuser* and *Lohengrin* with him – the first Wagner scores he was to rehearse in Weimar.

It was in Bayreuth, in the house of Wagner's biographer Glasenapp, that Strauss got to know Bruckner's Seventh Symphony, probably his first encounter with any of Bruckner's music at all. He had been in Berlin at the time of the Munich première of the Seventh, on 10 March 1884. According to Max Auer, August Göllerich tried to win Strauss and Ritter for Bruckner. Strauss and Göllerich played the Adagio of the symphony on the piano together, to the astonishment of all present. 'Ritter was breathless with excitement as he turned the pages for them, and was completely won for Bruckner. Strauss thought the first movement "lacked a climax"! He described the second subject as "totally academic".'[16] Strauss was never to take to Bruckner. He was inclined to dismiss his symphonies out of hand, although he quite often performed some of them.[17] He would probably have echoed the verdict of Cosima Wagner, who wrote to him once:

> I also heard some movements from symphonies by Bruckner. He's a good soul, and I would make him my court composer and commission a cantata, a festival mass or a Te Deum from him once a year, in the confidence that it would be a first-rate composition. Being trumpeted as a genius makes a simpleton of him. (26 March 1890)

Before going to Bayreuth Strauss had attended a session of the Allgemeiner Deutscher Musikverein in Wiesbaden, where his future intendant Hans von Bronsart, as a member of the committee, had invited him to conduct a concert that included *Aus Italien* and Brahms's D minor Piano Concerto. Strauss's reaction against Brahms had been strengthening in direct proportion to the growth of his admiration for Wagner and Liszt. In Wiesbaden – whither he was accompanied by Ludwig Thuille, whose Sextet was also to be performed there – he dared to replace Brahms's German Requiem with Liszt's *Héroïde funèbre.* Cosima Wagner was greatly impressed by this 'brilliant exploit' when he told her about it in Bayreuth. It was in Wiesbaden that he heard from his sister of Levi's 'despicable behaviour' – although Perfall was principally to blame – over their father's pensioning. Without any previous warning to soften the blow, Franz Strauss had received his notice through the medium of a letter pinned to the orchestral notice board. Richard wrote to him from Wiesbaden:

> Now dear Papa, use your retirement to take a good rest and look after your health and strength, so that we shall have you with us in good health as our loving and beloved father for a long time to come. I wish you that with all my heart! The prospect of leaving home this time [to go to Weimar] has become very hard for me, harder than you may have realized – think of me with the old love and affection. (19 June 1889)

Hanna wrote to him two days later:

> You wrote so fondly and beautifully that it moved me to tears and made me think about your leaving us again . . . Papa has got over this shabby act easily. The first evening I was rather apprehensive and I was afraid that Papa's exaggerated jollity was only a front and might make him feel even worse inside, but

he's really cheerful, praise be, and now, in fact, is receiving congratulations from all sides.

The expiry of his Munich contract on 31 July 1889 found Strauss looking forward with great expectations – too great, as it turned out – to his new job in Weimar, although he had heard rumours by then of the orchestra's lack of discipline. 'Well, if it's true, I shall just have to go in there like the wrath of God', he wrote to his father from Bayreuth. (4 July 1889) His confidence was strengthened by the assurances he had from several members of the orchestra that they would welcome a stricter régime. And since even Eduard Lassen, who gave Strauss the impression of having exhausted all his energy and let everything slide, admitted that there was much room for improvement, while Bronsart was looking forward to his arrival with great good will, Strauss understandably threw caution to the winds and formed the highest hopes. Even in his second season in Weimar he was still able to tell Alexander Ritter: 'My ultra-progressive artistic views have not yet met with any resistance, nor with any positive response either – but they let me do what I like.'

The three years in Munich which brought the conductor so much disappointment and even humiliation were extremely fruitful ones for the composer. The first of the 'tone poems' (the term Strauss preferred for his orchestral works up to *Ein Heldenleben*), in which he worked through to the emergence of his own personal style, date from this period. After the transitional work, the symphonic fantasy *Aus Italien*, and the one-movement *Macbeth* – which did not receive its definitive form until 1891 – came the first great conception, *Don Juan*, and the larger part of *Tod und Verklärung*. Strauss did not actually finish the score of this new tone poem – which he appears to have kept a secret for some time – until 18 November 1889, in Weimar, but he had already finished the particello before he left Munich. He was so busy during his first few weeks in Weimar that – as we discover from a letter to his parents – it was the middle of October before he could get back to work on the orchestration of it. If the years in Munich were a decisive period in his development as a composer, the years in Weimar were to be of equal moment for his career as a conductor. He threw himself into his new tasks in the opera house and the concert hall with an incomparable ardour.

Dora Wihan-Weis

Before following Strauss to Weimar, it is time for us to pay some attention to a relationship of the greatest consequence for his emotional life: his love, in early manhood, for Dora Wihan. There is very little direct evidence of it, and therefore all the greater room for speculation. The early stages and the tensions that already existed in the Wihan marriage have already been mentioned. A number of letters refer to relations between the Strauss family, the Wihans and Dora's parents in Dresden, as well as to Dora's friendship with Hanna. When Richard first met Dora in 1883 she was twenty-three and he nineteen. During his visit to Berlin in the winter of 1883–4 her name occurs more than once in the letters he received from both her husband and his sister. In one of his letters, about his plans to perform Richard's Romance for Cello on a concert tour, Hans wrote:

> The day before yesterday we went to the Charity Ball, which took the form of a fashionable redoute this year. My wife went as Domino and greatly enjoyed herself; with Frau Hirth she carried on a flirtation with P...... for about half an hour, and even persuaded him that she would meet him at the Propyläen on Saturday at 6.30.

The number of dots suggests Ernst von Possart, or even perhaps Perfall. The letter ends with the words: 'Cordial greetings from my wife and a friendly clasp of the hand from your old friend Hans.' (4 February 1884) A letter from Hanna from the same time ends '10,000 greetings and kisses from your Hanna and Dora'; Dora's name is in her own handwriting. Hanna had sent her brother a photograph of herself and her friend in December. He did not like the picture in the least but wrote to his mother: 'The photograph of Frau Wihan and Hanna is good, but I don't understand why the former is pulling such a despairing face and the latter such an ironic one.' (26 December 1883) A few weeks later Hanna wrote to Richard that Dora would have liked to go to Dresden (to her parents, that is) with Hans, but he had not allowed her to, and so she was annoyed. (21 January 1884) Even these few lines contain a hint of marital discord. In the sad period which Richard had to spend alone with his father in the spring of 1885, while his mother was ill and Hanna was away, Dora's name appears several times in the letters exchanged by brother and sister. On 14 April Richard wrote:

> I saw your friend Dora yesterday and conveyed your greetings to her, but I cannot say that I am as pleased with her condition as I am, relatively, with Mama's. In our household the care of the sick is excellent (I have nothing but praise for Papa and myself), but at the Wihans it is as bad as ever. Frau Wihan will probably have to go to Bad Reichenhall, where her husband, out of jealousy, will not let her go alone.

Two days later he wrote again: 'Frau Wihan is not especially well, I went there today; she has had your card and sends you her love.' Another two days later: 'I sent half of your beautiful roses to Frau Schreiber and half to Dora Wihan, who is still not particularly well.' It was 26 April before he was able to report: 'Your friend Dora is going to Reichenhall on Saturday next for four weeks, with her mother, who is arriving on Thursday. Hans is going to Russia at the beginning of May.' He was clearly well informed, although he tried to conceal his personal feelings by the consistent and careful use of formulas like 'your friend Dora', 'Frau Wihan' or 'Dora Wihan'.

The relationship of the Wihans approached a crisis in June 1885, after Hans's return from Russia. This time it was Richard who was away, attending Bülow's piano course at the Raff Conservatory in Frankfurt, but receiving news from home which implied that the Wihans were on the verge of separating. It was Father Strauss who wrote: 'Hanna has had a letter from Dresden, from Dora. She is quite well. Her dear? husband joined her again in Dresden for a week, to her horror.' (13 June 1885) Richard replied: 'The news of Dora Wihan took me very much by surprise, but I was not amazed by it, I've seen it coming for a long time.' (19 June 1885) He wrote to Hanna the next day in the same vein: 'The news about Dora W. has taken me by surprise, but it did not come as a shock.' (20 June 1885) Whether he was really taken by surprise or had already heard from Dora herself before his family knew is uncertain.

At the beginning of April 1886 Strauss returned to Munich from Meiningen, signed his contract to join the Court Opera as third conductor, and on 17 April set out for Italy. After short stops in Bologna and Florence he arrived in Rome on 26 April, and took a room in the Hotel Minerva, near the Pantheon. A day after his arrival, after having heard from Hanna that Dora was in Rome, he wrote: 'I've seen nothing of Dora Wihan, I didn't know she was here.' Really? It is very improbable that he had been out of touch with Dora during the preceding weeks and days, and equally improbable that neither of them knew of the other's plans to travel to Italy. It is nevertheless quite likely that after the break-up of her marriage Dora decided to conduct herself with particular discretion; she may even have left Munich and gone to stay with her parents in Dresden, and so her contact with Richard may have been broken for a while. Whether they met in Rome on this occasion is a question that, like many others concerning their relationship, must remain unanswered.

Only one letter from Richard to Dora survives, which proves that she left Munich for good in or before 1887. A year before her death (31 January 1938) she gave the letter to a friend, the singing-coach Ida Schuberth-Koch. It was published for the first time in the *Richard-Strauss-Jahrbuch* 1959–60, with a commentary by Ernst Krause, in whose possession it now is. Krause makes one mistake, in stating that Dora was two years older than Richard, when the difference in their ages was in fact four years. His assumption that only one letter survives from Dora to Richard is fortunately also wrong: there are three, which will be quoted in full below.

There is not a shred of evidence to support any suggestion that the intimacy which established itself between Richard and Dora was a cause of the break-up of the Wihan marriage. On the other hand there can hardly be the slightest doubt that Richard was passionately in love with his 'only one', as he called her in the inscription he wrote on a photograph of himself, or that his courtship made a deep impression on a woman who was already greatly disappointed in her marriage, and led to a close relationship which endured for years.

After a journey to America, Dora took a post as lady's companion and piano teacher in Lixoúrion (Lixouri) on the island of Kefallinía off the west coast of Greece. She and Richard corresponded regularly during the years she spent there. The destruction of his letters – there must have been a very great number of them – immediately after her death, in accordance with instructions she gave her sister, is probably the most serious loss of Strauss correspondence, for they would have given us important insights into his emotional life during these years, of a kind which is to be found nowhere else in his letters, where he was always very discreet about his inner feelings. It is wholly to Dora's credit that she treated these intimate letters, from which she would not be separated until the very last, as her most personal possession and that by her strict instructions to destroy them after her death she prevented their profanation and inevitable publication either in the lifetime or after the death of her former lover and his wife. For his part, Strauss, who normally carefully preserved all letters, whether important or not, destroyed hers. That three survived is probably due either to oversight or accident. They are valuable because they show Dora's character in the very best light. Unfortunately they date from a relatively late phase, and the familiar 'Du' appears only in the earliest, which was written after Richard's arrival in Weimar, about six months after the only surviving letter from him to her. In the two others she uses the polite 'Sie': their relationship must have passed a decisive turning-point during the winter and spring of 1889–90. Whether the long separation caused the young man's ardour to cool, while the image of his distant beloved began to fade in the light of his association with Pauline de Ahna, whom he saw virtually every day, remains uncertain. Dora herself, who followed the rapid rise of the successful young conductor and composer from afar, may have convinced herself of the necessity of giving him up, and perhaps she had never seriously entertained the idea of eventually marrying him, which would certainly have met with considerable obstacles.

The full text of Richard's only letter to her is as follows (he calls her 'Du'):

Munich, 9 April 89

My dear, good Dora,

Where shall I begin today? With the sorrow your letter gave me, with my thanks for your good wishes on my name-day, what's new, what's happened – ? In short, I don't know. The fact is that your letter, putting off the prospect of seeing you, my sweet Dora, again for the foreseeable future, has upset and distressed me deeply. God, what wooden expressions those are for what I really feel. Do you want me to console you? How, pray? I can't quote 'Meister, 's ist nicht so gefährlich'* at you, or say that time heals all wounds, because it is precisely 'time' which is dealing the wounds, heavens, I'm even cracking jokes about it – in one word, it's abhorrent!!!!

So you think you will be able to pay me a call *sometime* in years to come, in that case let me commend to you a song (as yet unperformed) by one Richard Strauss: *Geduld* [Patience] Op. 10, A♭ minor. Apropos, have you received the piano score

* *Die Meistersinger*, Act III, Scene 4.

of the Italian fantasy, if it gives you a little consolation, I shall be glad! To tell you now that things are *going well* with me is really a mockery, and yet it's true, Rich. Str. the artist is in the pink, now that the Munich Hofmusikdirektor is departed out of him, after three years of breathing the miasmas of that swamp, some fresh air is doing him a lot of good. It will of course be very hard for me to leave Munich and my family and two friends like Ritter and Thuille, to whom I've become more attached than you could easily imagine, but I must go, because my whole future depends on it, and on not being laid low by Munich swamp fever. With Ritter's help I am at least now well provided with a solid philosophy of life and art, I have firm ground under my feet after a lot of floundering, and now I can even dare to take up the cudgels on my own account against the Jews and the Philistines. Imagine, I've even joined the Lisztians now, in short, a more progressive standpoint than the one I now hold is hardly conceivable. And yet, with the clarity that has come to me, I feel so well – but it's impossible to write about things like this. There's nothing for it, you will have to come and see me; would you know me when you saw me?

Now I will answer your questions. I'm going to Bayreuth as an assistant, piano rehearsals and so on. Recently I made Frau Wagner's acquaintance, she took a great interest in me, I even had the honour of going to *Freischütz* with her. How that came about is a very funny story! The good Levi fell into a pit he had dug for my feet, which was very comical! How did I get on in Berlin? More blissfully than you could begin to imagine. *Ritter, Thuille and I* under the motto

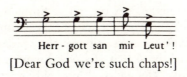

[Dear God we're such chaps!]

The Ninth was indescribably wonderful, the *Tannhäuser* overture simply the most fabulous thing, I still start to tremble when I think of what it sounded like! Bülow conducted like a god, simply, although otherwise his behaviour – leathery St Johannes was also there – was rather too like Hans Wurst, but on the other hand immensely touching! 'Two souls there dwell, alas, within his breast!' Poor devil! My God, I've got so much to tell you! And you won't come!!! By the time you do I shall have forgotten everything.

If you think this is all madness, yet there is method in it! Good Lord! I must have caught quotitis! (Thuille's latest joke, born of the Berlin spirit.) Bülow is safe and sound in America – to earn money! Where am I going? Now, if you promise not to tell a soul, by word of mouth or by letter, because it must remain a deadly secret – *Weimar!* To work with Lassen and under Bronsart as intendant! What a capital exchange for Munich! Weimar, the town of the future, the place where Liszt worked for so long! I have the *highest* hopes! Bronsart is a capital fellow, a man of honour from tip to toe (just like Perfall), and very progressive (just like Perfall), while Lassen is old and tired and looking forward to being relieved of some of his burden (just like Fischer). My pupil Zeller has also been engaged there as heroic tenor from next September, one of the first operas I shall conduct there will be Ritter's *Der faule Hans* with Zeller in the title role, and his newest one-act opera *Wem die Krone*! In short, I think everything will be capital. Bronsart is in addition on the committee of the Musikverein and a few days ago he asked me if, in case Nikisch can't get away from Leipzig, which is very likely, I would conduct not just my Italian fantasy but also the first two concerts at this year's general meeting at Wiesbaden on 27 and 28 June: including Berlioz's *L'enfance du Christ*! Isn't that capital? Oh, yes, Strauss the artist is doing very well! But may no happiness be complete?!

On the way back from Berlin I stopped in Meiningen. Steinbach had already rehearsed my *Macbeth*, so I got them to play it for me four times; it sounds horrid, but I think it impresses thinking people, even in its present state. At the moment I'm arranging it for piano duet and hope to publish it this spring. In the text of my opera I've finished (at any rate, until the next revision) the first act and the second act as far as the end of the big love-scene. Ritter is very pleased with it.

I've also finished the sketch of a new tone poem (probable title: *Tod und Verklärung*) and shall probably start the full score after Easter.

Apropos! If you've read the Wagner books I sent you, please be so good as to send them back, as I now want to have them all bound! Dostoyevsky, *nicht wahr*?!!!

One other thing! If you knew *how* I read your letters, you would not write about 'distractions par une comtesse', who is in fact a charming creature, is completely daft about the 'music of the future', and is one of the few great admirers your own Richard has! That reminds me of a delightful quote from

Wagner! In one of his letters to Uhlig he holds up Ritter's sister Emilie as a model and says 'Women are our comfort, for every woman comes into the world as a human being, while every man is born a philistine, and it's a long time before he works his way up to human being, if he ever does!!' Yes indeed, why not! Besides, I'm winning a 'truly' good 'human being' for '*our*' art, which is, however, worlds away from what people nowadays think of as 'music'!

Well, now I must thank you cordially for your fond wishes for my name-day, you good, constant creature; I would only add from the bottom of my heart that I hope I shall never see fulfilled any wishes of mine which run counter to yours – only you really mustn't leave me alone for so long – my God, I have hoped for two years, only to close the book of my hopes at the end of that term with the words 'It just isn't possible.' Oh dear, I don't want to become sentimental, but if my new orchestral piece contains more dissonances than your little ears can stand, you will have no right to complain!

Farewell now, stay fond of me and this time don't make me wait so long for an answer.

Your old constant R.

The complaints about the length of their separation stand out in strong contrast to the confession that 'Strauss the artist is doing very well'. He had written *Aus Italien*, *Macbeth* and *Don Juan*, which, thanks to the clarity that had come to him, assured him that his advance along the 'new path' was in the right direction, he was making progress with the text of *Guntram*, and the new post in Weimar, which was to allow him to escape from 'the miasmas of the Munich swamp', was his, although he promised himself too much from it. The 'distractions par une comtesse' is a reference to Thuille's pupil, the Comtesse Montgelas, and not to Pauline de Ahna. The letter also shows that Richard sent Dora copies not only of his compositions but also of books he wanted her to read by Wagner and Dostoyevsky. It casts a spotlight on his attitude to Bülow at this particular date: while he still revered him as a conductor of Wagner and Beethoven, he was irritated by what he considered his clownish behaviour and by his ever more pronounced liking for 'leathery St Johannes' (Brahms!). It was on the day following that concert in Berlin (on 4 March 1889) that an event occurred which Strauss described in the memoir of Bülow that he wrote twenty years later:

Bülow had performed the *Tannhäuser* Overture in the imperious and rousing fashion that was uniquely his in my experience, without receiving a single word of praise from Ritter, the friend of his youth and schooldays, who had heard the overture with him in Dresden in the forties under Wagner himself, and whose opinion he always respected. They met on the hotel stairs the next morning. Bülow came straight out with 'How was the *Tannhäuser* Overture yesterday?' And the old mule answered 'Oh, it was superlative. It brought back to me very vividly the days when we both worshipped an ideal to which *I* have remained true.' Whereupon Bülow fell on his friend's neck, burst into tears and rushed to his room without saying a word in reply.

When Richard wrote 'I have hoped for two years, only to close the book of my hopes at the end of that term with the words "It just isn't possible"', it remains open whether he already anticipated having to relinquish his hopes altogether in the end. It is not altogether clear what he meant by the reference to the song *Geduld*, that is, to the poem by Hermann von Gilm of which it is a setting. He wrote the song on 29 August 1885, just a few weeks after the rupture of the Wihan marriage had become known publicly. In the text the poet replies to the beloved's insistence that he should be patient with an urgent expostulation that time will not stand still for them, and that his love will not endure the passing of his life's springtime.[18]

The first of Dora's three surviving letters was sent to Weimar, where Richard had taken up his new job on 8 September 1889.

Lixouri, 15 October 1889

My dear, good Richard,

It is not my fault that I haven't written to you for so long, I asked Hanna for your new address weeks ago; she sent it to me only yesterday (is it right, or do you want your full title on it, if so please write and tell me what it is!) and now my very first act must be to thank you very warmly for your dear fond wishes for my birthday. You want to know which birthday it is? Oh, do not ask, it is dreadful how old I have grown here: the 29th! Isn't that awful? But in this country, where Methuselahs are nothing rare, it's regarded as the prime of life and so this will probably not be the last year to see me on Crusoe's island, as you would like, dearest Richard! The south seems to be my destiny and I may well live out my useless life here. You know,

I'm far too stupid, far too much the yokel now to show myself in decent society in Germany, you will have such a surprise; so this will be the best place for me for the time being. I shall come back (like nuns when they take the veil!!!) just once more, not to confirm the old saying: Ματαιότης ματαιοτῆτων, τὰ πάντα ματαιότης!* but on the contrary, to enjoy myself to my heart's content just once more and be happy if it's possible! But after that it will be time for the old hag to disappear from the scene. Do you understand, my old friend, *how much* that makes me look forward to my journey in the spring? Where will you be in the summer, for if I remember rightly, doesn't the theatre in Weimar close then? Well, friendly fate will bring us together somewhere, especially if we take 'chance' by the arm to help it along, isn't that so? If you didn't go to Milan until the spring, it would be by no means impossible for me to meet you there and then travel on with you. I would like so dreadfully to go to Venice for a few days, tell me, Richard, would you go there with me? I've promised myself that little detour as a reward for sticking it out in my exile for nearly three years! One other question: is it true, as one sometimes reads in the papers, that there will be performances at Bayreuth again next year? That would make me very happy, for you wouldn't believe how I berate myself for a fool for having missed so many opportunities to go to B. when I had the chance. And who knows whether you won't already be wielding the conductor's baton there by then! Your friendship with Frau Wagner has planted all sorts of fine plans and hopes for you in my heart, and they are not at all rash, for – well, I don't want to make you vainer than you've already grown with all the homage you receive, my old friend, and if that displeases you, console yourself with the very true words of Goethe: 'Friends reveal to one another more clearly than anything else the one thing that they do not say to one another.' Or write?!

Have you finished scoring your new tone poem, *Tod und Verklärung*? You told me you expected to have done it by the middle of October; and what is *Guntram* doing? How do you feel in your new position? Hanna writes about it in glowing terms, I can easily believe that it was a delightful time for you both. I had so very much hoped that Hanna would go on to Dresden from Weimar, but unfortunately the invitation reached her too late by an oversight, I was very sorry because it was such a good opportunity. Isn't the Grützmacher with whom

* 'Vanity of vanities, all is vanity!' Dora uses modern Greek cursive script.

> you're lodging a brother of the Dresden one? And also a cellist? Is it a nice place to live? Alas, it's such an impossibly long time, 15 or 16 years, since I was in Weimar that I can't visualize it at all clearly any more, and yet I would so like to be able to imagine everything really accurately and clearly; perhaps I shall get there myself after all, although people will in any case find that very '*shocking*'! I don't know if you are another of those men who don't like long letters, in any case I won't bore you with my epistle any longer! Farewell, my old, beloved friend, and accept another thousand deeply felt greetings from your
>
> Dora

After two years apart, their relationship was as close as ever. If one takes into consideration the reticence usual in letters at that time, Dora's proposal to meet him in Italy and spend several days in Venice with him is a very clear pointer to the intimacy of the relationship, but also demonstrates that, alone in life as she was, Dora was not the prisoner of prejudice. Nothing came of the attractive plan. The sentence 'If you don't go to Milan until the spring . . .' implies that there was a prospect of Richard's making a return visit there as guest conductor, which did not come to fruition – perhaps because of his commitments in Weimar. The second of Dora's surviving letters shows that by April 1890 there could no longer be any question of their meeting in Italy during the summer break, which Richard spent in Marquartstein. It is idle to speculate whether the impossibility was not altogether unwelcome to Richard in the spring, that is, at the busiest time of the year in the theatre; but it cannot be ruled out that his feelings were already changing as a result of his relationship with Pauline de Ahna, who was in Weimar as his pupil. In the face of Strauss's pronounced reticence in the matter of his emotions and the absence of confidential outpourings to a third person, we can again only ponder possibilities. Father Strauss courted his wife for seven years before asking for her hand. It is not inconceivable that Richard – whose extremely modest salary hardly permitted him to marry, by the standards of the day – was also prepared to wait for years before confessing his love to Pauline.

A letter of Hanna's written a year after Dora's from Lixoúrion, can perhaps be read as a confirmation of this supposition. From Ritter Hanna gathered that Pauline now looked on herself as 'already quite the prima donna' and behaved herself accordingly;

Richard was to be admired for the patience with which he bore her whims and caprices. Not too much importance should be attached to the occasional quarrels between Richard and Pauline during the Weimar years, although Richard was once driven to write her a letter terminating their friendly relations; if Pauline's combative temperament is borne in mind, the recurrent friction does not constitute an argument against the supposition that Strauss's feelings may already have begun to change during the winter of 1889–90.

There is another possible reason why Strauss and Dora did not meet in Italy. The second of the surviving letters from Dora, written on 25 April 1890 in her hometown of Dresden, implies that none of her plans for the spring were realized, and that she did not even go to Weimar. The letter gives a reason, but leaves open the question whether, torn between her undoubted desire to see Richard again and the realization that it would be wiser to avoid doing so, Dora finally gave way to the second consideration.

Dresden, 25 April 1890

Dear Richard,

Your kind note was waiting for me on our return from Halle and Leipzig. I am *eternally* sorry that on this occasion I shall almost certainly have to forego the pleasure of visiting Weimar and – which is of far greater significance – seeing you; but unfortunately Mesdames Jacovato are with me and not only do they take up all my time, now they are already talking of the return journey! And so once again the pleasure with which I have looked forward to something has been in vain, but what can I do?

According to what Hanna tells me, they do not expect you in Munich until July, I shall have left Europe again long before then, and so I must look forward to other years!

With a thousand cordial greetings, always your old

Dora Weis

She no longer uses the intimate 'Du' of old. Something of significance, originating with Strauss, must have passed between them in the interval since the letter of the previous October. The affectionate tone is still present, though muted, in the closing formula.* Signing herself as 'old' seems to have a deliberately double meaning: she is his 'old friend', but, at thirty, now counts herself an 'old woman' and wishes to remind him of the difference in their ages.

* 'Cordial' [herzlich] is a conventional word compared to the 'innig' of the earlier letter. *Tr.*

The signature 'Dora Weis' shows that she had reverted to the use of her maiden name.

She returned to Germany the following year. Hanna wrote to her brother on 14 November 1890: 'I have had some very good news from Dora. She is coming back to Germany for ever in the spring, to live with her parents, and she has already made a rendez-vous with me in Bayreuth. If everything works out as planned, it would be marvellous.' (In the same letter Hanna tells Richard that Lieutenant Rauchenberger is courting her determinedly. She married him in Munich on 8 July 1895.)

Dora did indeed return from Greece in 1891. Richard, who was again working at the Bayreuth festival as a repetiteur and musical assistant, arranged for a ticket to be reserved for her, and wrote to Hanna from Bayreuth: 'I have not yet been able to get a ticket for Dora for 27 or 30 August, at the moment the only one reserved is the one for the first performance. So if you don't hear anything further, Dora will have to come on the 19th.' (12 July 1891) Whether Dora did in fact attend the festival that year and see him again is unknown. Since Pauline de Ahna took part in the festival, alternating with Elisa Wiborg in the role of Elisabeth in *Tannhäuser* as well as singing one of the solo Flower Maidens in *Parsifal* (the third in the first group), if Dora did go she can hardly have remained unaware of the friendly relationship between the soprano and her teacher.

The last of the three surviving letters from Dora is dated almost two years later. It was again written from Dresden, where she had returned to live with her parents and to work as a teacher of piano. We do not know whether it was addressed directly to Cairo, where Richard was at the time, or whether it reached him by a roundabout route.

Dresden, 10 March 1893

My dear friend,

Will you be very, very surprised, if a sign of life from me surfaces after such a long time? The reason that presses the pen into my hand is a remarkable one, or rather it is no reason at all, but only an impulse, but why shouldn't one follow an impulse once in a while, even at the risk of being laughed out of court? (Mirth is very good in convalescence, incidentally!) External circumstances: house arrest, sorting out old things, and the letters you sent me at Lixouri came to hand. Inner condition:

> recognizing the truth of the old saying that the greatest human happiness is the power of memory. Do not be afraid, dear friend, I am certainly not going to become sentimental, but the outcome was that I had to write you a few words, even though it is only a friendly greeting despatched to the far south to tell you *how glad* I am that you are now fully recovered. Are you very angry with me now, at this unexpected invasion of your retreat from the world? Then punish me and never reply to
>
> Your old
> (now truly *old*)
> Dora

It is hard to imagine a more conciliatory epilogue. Once again there is the word-play with 'old' at the end, which this time is certainly not accidental. It seems to have some bearing on the now irrevocable resignation – whether the decision had been taken on one side or both. This last letter – we do not know if it ever received a reply – allows us to surmise that Richard meant hardly less to Dora than she to him. It sympathetically completes the picture of a warm-hearted and sensitive woman. The few, but important surviving pieces of evidence leave no doubt that she was worthy of Richard's love.[19]

Dora remained on friendly terms with Hanna. In December 1898, by which time Richard was in Berlin, it emerges from a letter from his father that Dora was in Munich on a visit, and heard a performance of *Till Eulenspiegel* with Hanna. The last encounter between Strauss and Dora Weis of which we have any knowledge took place in January 1911, during the turbulent days of the première of *Der Rosenkavalier*. Hanna, who was in Dresden for the occasion, saw her old friend several times and also arranged a meeting between her and her brother and his wife. She does not seem to have been deterred by the thought that this would embarrass Richard and annoy Pauline; it is conceivable, indeed, that, as she was never able to establish a truly warm relationship with her sister-in-law and would probably rather have seen Dora in the role, she did not feel inclined to consider their feelings. Later Strauss wrote to her:

> Since you yourself ask me about Pauline, it gives me the chance to tell you that she was very put out in Dresden by the fact that you were always in the company of your friend D. W., whose constant presence even in the most intimate family circle was

> bound to be burdensome to Pauline. Since you obviously had no consideration for her, you have no reason to be surprised that Pauline, who is very sensitive in these matters, proved somewhat withdrawn. At all events, it was not her intention that you should notice her mood, but it is very difficult for her to disguise her feelings when something has upset her. She has probably already forgotten the matter: so there is no need for you to refer to it again. (3 March 1911)

Strauss does not distance himself from Dora here, but takes his wife's part.

6

The first years in Weimar, 1889–92

It was a sign of the great sympathy and equally great expectations with which Hans von Bronsart looked forward to having Strauss working in Weimar that he placed no difficulties in the way of his new Kapellmeister's not taking up his duties until 8 September, although his contract ran from 1 August 1889. The ardour with which Strauss threw himself into his work on arrival in the small residency of the Grand Dukes of Saxe-Weimar-Eisenach was a matter for comment by all those who witnessed it. Weimar was to Strauss above all the place where Liszt had spent some of the most important and productive years of his life; it was encircled for him by a nimbus, and although he was soon forced to realize that actual circumstances did not warrant his reverence, his disillusion if anything strengthened his fanatical determination to overcome the difficulties and win Weimar over to his artistic plans, in which Wagner and Liszt occupied the prime positions. Although Eduard Lassen, as Hofkapellmeister, was Strauss's superior in rank, he welcomed his young colleague and readily acknowledged his artistic superiority. He was now in his sixtieth year and content to hand over almost the whole of the German repertory to Strauss, reserving for himself only *Fidelio*, *Der fliegende Holländer*, *Die Meistersinger* and the *Ring*, as well as the four subscription concerts which were given annually in the theatre, although in the event these last also fell to Strauss to conduct. The fact that Lassen borrowed a small sum of money from Strauss, which he did not repay until after the latter had returned to Munich, put him under a certain obligation to his assistant which affected their professional collaboration. Their relationship was friendly, and they usually ate their midday meal together at the Hotel Erbprinz, where the chief topic of their conversations was Wagner, a subject on which they did not see eye to eye. In his book *Talks with Great Composers* (which is full of mistakes and should be consulted only with the greatest caution) Arthur M. Abell writes of his surprise at Lassen's vigorous applause after a performance of *Don Juan*, which he claims to have heard Strauss conduct at a Weimar subscription concert in October 1890. Lassen explained:

> I am not applauding *Don Juan*, I am applauding Strauss. He is a great conductor. He is only twenty-six years old and I am sixty; I have been conducting the Weimar Orchestra for twenty-nine years and Strauss has only been here one year, but he produces greater effects with the musicians than I ever have been able to achieve. Strauss is a genius and I am only a talent.

In its essentials, we can accept that this is an accurate statement of Lassen's attitude towards Strauss. At around the same date Abell, whose 'talks' arose from his asking a number of famous composers about 'their intellectual, psychic and spiritual experiences while composing and . . . the soul forces within [them] when they felt the creative urge', had some conversations with Strauss about immortality and inspiration. According to Abell, Strauss said that the 'descriptive text' accompanying *Tod und Verklärung*, which depicts the hero's death struggle and the triumphant opening of the gates of heaven, contained his own credo and, when asked if he believed in immortality, he replied 'I certainly do, and I am convinced that there is a great deal of truth in Alexander Ritter's conception of it' (he was referring to the poem which prefaces the score of *Tod und Verklärung*, which Ritter wrote after the tone poem had been completed). Strauss went on: 'Swedenborg . . . claimed that he could actually look into heaven and that he found it a glorified earth, where we carry on and perfect the work we start here. I believe that.' Even if Strauss really did express himself in that form, the reader should not attach too much weight to these remarks, which may very well be coloured by the speaker's adapting himself momentarily to the expectations of his listener. However, one statement of Strauss's which Abell reports is undoubtedly correct: in their conversations Strauss emphasized the importance of Alexander Ritter's influence in directing his ideas and said that it was Ritter who had drawn his attention to Kant's treatise on Swedenborg. Referring to the 'visitations' which Swedenborg had described in *Hell and Heaven*, Strauss said, according to Abell, 'I know from my own inspirational experiences when composing that those higher visitations are sudden and fleeting.'

Strauss described Weimar in a letter to Eugen Spitzweg as a 'delightfully situated town'; he had no criticisms to make of it: pure Elysium! He saw before him the prospect of 'the most beautiful free time for work' (24 October 1889). The work he had to do admittedly consisted of conducting, not composition. He had already succeeded in securing the engagement of his pupil, the tenor Heinrich Zeller, in spite of the opinion, expressed when Zeller made a guest appearance in the previous spring, that his voice was 'pleasant, but too small for a heroic tenor'. He made his début as a permanent member of the company in September, singing Erik in *Der fliegende Holländer*. Strauss was able to employ another pupil, Hermann Bischoff, in the theatre as a co-repetiteur, and of course Pauline de Ahna also followed her teacher to Weimar. Without too much difficulty he succeeded in arousing the Weimar orchestra, which possessed only six first violins and had rather too many members approaching retirement age, from a state of lethargy and quickly brought about a marked improvement in their standards by the example of his own enthusiasm. After only a few weeks he was able to write home: 'The orchestra is delighted with me . . . My two orchestral rehearsals went excellently, all the members very willing and agreeable. Br[onsart] introduced me with a very charming speech, in short, everything is as right as can be.' (21 September 1889) For the symphony concerts Strauss was able to augment the orchestra with players from the Weimar School of Music.

The operas Bronsart expected Strauss to conduct in the 1889–90 season included three works each by Mozart, Weber and Lortzing, two by Wagner (*Tannhäuser* and *Lohengrin*), *Iphigenia in Aulis*, *Fidelio*, Nicolai's *Die lustigen Weiber von Windsor*, Marschner's *Hans Heiling*, Auber's *La muette de Portici*, *Le prophète* and *L'Africaine* by Meyerbeer (whom Strauss detested), Bellini's *Norma*, Flotow's *Stradella*, Maillart's *Les dragons de Villars* and *Der Meisterdieb* by Eugen Lindner (1858–1915), who was a teacher of singing at the Weimar School of Music. Strauss had not conducted the great majority of these works before.

Apart from his musical activities, some of Strauss's time during the first few weeks in Weimar was taken up with receiving visits from Friedrich Rösch and Sonja von Schéhafzoff, who was also a close friend of Alexander Ritter's niece Marie. Nevertheless, as a true apostle of Wagner and Bayreuth, he devoted all his energies to his first major undertaking: the rehearsals of *Lohengrin*, which he intended to perform in the authentic Bayreuth style. He set to work straightaway in rehearsals to tidy up the singers' performances, following guide-lines that Cosima Wagner had given him in the previous August. His ambition was to eliminate everything which had 'insinuated itself as tradition, i.e. as bad habits and incorrectness'. He conducted his first public performance of the opera as early as the first week in October, with only two small cuts (which Strauss qualified as 'provisional'): in the chorus 'Von Gott ist er gesandt' and in the C♯ minor ensemble in Act III. He was able to inform his father that Bronsart, Lassen and every member of the company showed him so much good will that he was thoroughly happy with his new post. (2 October 1889: still early days!) He also wrote to Cosima Wagner, to tell her that he had been able to give the work two five-hour orchestral rehearsals, one *Arrangierprobe* (a rehearsal to plot stage-movement), and a series of rehearsals with the piano for the soloists and the chorus: a total amount of rehearsal that was quite unprecedented in Weimar! The first performance had 'an immense public success', though he had his own reservations about it: he gained the greatest satisfaction from the orchestra's contribution, and from his success in imposing the slower tempos stipulated by Frau Wagner. On the other hand, although he had lectured the singers at length in rehearsal on the subject of good style, 'that is, the most meticulous accuracy', and although they had the best of intentions to follow his wishes, in the performance itself they had simply fallen back into their old bad habits. Lohengrin (Zeller), Telramund (Franz Schwarz) and Ortrud (Louise Tibelti) had offended least in this respect. The worst aspect of the performance had been the staging, and Bronsart had agreed with him that the production would have to be overhauled completely in a series of the most thorough rehearsals. (To Cosima Wagner, 9 October 1889)[1]

In her reply to this letter Cosima asked Strauss to pay the greatest attention to clear enunciation: 'In Munich, for example, in addition to not being able to hear a note, one cannot understand a word', in spite of Fischer's diligence in his own special field – a remark which she evidently added in full knowledge of Strauss's negative attitude towards his former colleague. (12 October 1889) Cosima's assurances of her 'most earnest interest' gave Strauss the most powerful encouragement, since they nourished his hopes and his ambition of being invited to conduct at Bayreuth one day.

Strauss's contentment during his early days in Weimar is expressed in his letters to his family, while to Eugen Spitzweg he wrote:

> I feel very happy here. Herr von Bronsart is the most delightful intendant imaginable, Lassen the most charming of colleagues and, like Bronsart, a sensitive artist; the orchestra is good and has taken me to its heart, and the singers too have been as cooperative as you could imagine. Moreover there are some excellent musicians in the orchestra and among the singers, so that I have found the most profitable occupation here, in spite of the small scale of operations . . . In addition I have the most beautiful free time for work and it will not be long before I have finished the score of my new orchestral tone poem *Tod und Verklärung*. My libretto has also made great progress, so everything is as right as can be. (24 October 1899)

Tod und Verklärung (I)

It is a proof of Strauss's capacity for hard work that, as well as his work in the theatre and for his subscription concerts – the programme for his first (21 October 1889) included Beethoven's *King Stephen* Overture, Lalo's *Symphonie espagnole* (with Carl Halir as soloist), Bülow's *Nirwana* and Liszt's *Die Ideale* – he still had time to write the full score of *Tod und Verklärung*, which he had sketched before leaving Munich, and additionally to keep on with the text of *Guntram*, which gave him a great deal of trouble.

He finished orchestrating the tone poem *Tod und Verklärung*, which he had conceived in Munich in the winter of 1888–9, on 18 November 1889, when he had been in Weimar just over two months. In an unpublished note on the work Strauss draws attention to an unusual formal characteristic: '*Tod und Verklärung* makes the main theme its point of culmination, and does not state it until the middle', that is, at the point where the 'Ideal' motive breaks through *fortissimo*, five bars after letter T in the score.

Even today, one still comes across the claim that *Tod und Verklärung*, as an expression of the most personal experience, is connected with an illness so severe that Strauss's life was threatened. That this is not the case is established by the recognition that the tone poem had long been finished and had been performed before Strauss was admitted to the Sophienhaus hospital in Weimar in May 1891, seriously ill with pneumonia. In 1895 Strauss wrote about the work in a long letter addressed to Friedrich von Hausegger, who had asked a number of composers and writers for information about their creative processes:

> It was about six years ago [i.e. 1888] when the idea occurred to me to represent the death of a person who had striven for the highest ideal goals, therefore very possibly an artist, in a tone poem. The sick man lies in bed asleep, breathing heavily and irregularly; agreeable dreams charm a smile on to his features in spite of his suffering; his sleep becomes lighter; he wakens; once again he is racked by terrible pain, his limbs shake with fever – as the attack draws to a close and the pain subsides he reflects on his past life, his childhood passes before him, his youth with its striving, its passions, and then, while the pain resumes, the fruit of his path through life appears to him, the idea, the Ideal which he has tried to realize, to represent in his art, but which he has been unable to perfect, because it was not for any human being to perfect it. The hour of death approaches, the soul leaves the body, in order to find perfected in the most glorious form in the eternal cosmos that which he could not fulfil here on earth.

Strauss also emphasized in the letter to Hausegger that no actual experience lay behind the work. At that date he had not himself come through a serious illness, nor had he ever been at a deathbed; he could not remember having read anything that had directly inspired it either. Perhaps it was his imagination that had discovered the material for the piece, which had become celebrated in particular for its realistic expression and graphic representation. If that was so, then an extraordinary cerebral process must have taken place. Whereas an ordinary person needed to have actually experienced something if it was to stick in his mind, for the artist it took only some quite insignificant stimulus – something said by a friend, or read in a book – which was developed internally, unconsciously, for years and then suddenly, as if placed under a magnifying glass, presented itself to the eye in a dimension which bore no relationship whatever to the often very slight initial stimulus. Artistic creation, Strauss concluded, was composed of many hundreds of contributory elements.[2]

He had originally regarded 'Death and Transfiguration' as a

provisional title but decided in the end to keep it, as he was not attracted by Alexander Ritter's suggestion of calling the work 'Seraphic Fantasy' and providing it with a motto from the last scene of Goethe's *Faust*:

> Das ist mächtig anzuschauen,
> Doch zu düster ist der Ort,
> Schüttelt uns mit Schreck und Grauen . . .
> Steigt hinan zu höherem Kreise . . .
> Die zur Seligkeit entfaltet.

> ('This is powerful to behold, but the place is too sombre, [it] shakes us with fear and horror . . .' 'Rise up to a higher level, you who unfold into bliss'.)

Ritter then wrote a poem, which Strauss copied into the autograph of the score.[3] This poem was also printed in the programme at the first two performances (given in Eisenach on 21 June 1890 and in Weimar on 12 January 1891). It was only on publication that Ritter composed the poem ('In der ärmlich kleinen Kammer') which is printed in the engraved score and is too anchored in realistic description to do justice to the simple idea underlying the work or to the ideals which inform it. Strauss dedicated the work to his 'dear friend Friedrich Rösch'. Some forty years later he wrote to Wilhelm Bopp:

> *Tod und Verkl.* is purely a product of the imagination – it is not based on any kind of personal experience (my illness was two years later). It was an idea just like any other, probably ultimately the musical need – after *Macbeth* (begins and ends in D minor), *Don Juan* (begins and ends in E minor) – to write a piece that begins in C minor and finishes in C major! Qui le sait? (9 February 1931)[4]

The first performance of *Tod und Verklärung* and the way the work was received will be described later, since the earlier tone poem, *Don Juan*, must take precedence.

Strauss also continued to teach in Weimar, though not as much as previously. He gave priority to Pauline de Ahna (who had arrived there on 7 October, having made her first contact with the Weimar Court Opera on 11 August) and to Heinrich Zeller, and was tireless in coaching them in new roles. He also recommended his two protégés to Cosima Wagner, who promised to look after them during a stay in Bayreuth 'like my own chicks'. Somewhat later he acquired some new pupils: Amelia Passi, a Frau von Barby and the charming Fräulein von Graba; initially there may have been some justification for Hanna's suspicion that this last was a 'little flame' of Richard's, but he appears gradually to have become rather disappointed in her, for he wrote to his sister in June 1892:

> I am growing a little tired even of Fräulein Graba, she has, on closer inspection, except for being young and pretty, much in common with Aunt Adelheid [a sister of their mother's]; there's also her North German hoity-toity-ness, her eternal fault-finding, instead of applying herself to her true vocation, which is to look pretty, or else acquiring some *real* culture, also the impossibility for her of becoming really enthusiastic about anything, instead eternal rationalism – you see, my child, once again I am dominated overwhelmingly by what is perhaps my worst characteristic, the craving for variety.

In the same letter he also complains to her about being already thoroughly sick of Schopenhauer and wanting 'really to get away from here soon'. Pauline de Ahna, 'in spite of all her crotchets', was still the only one to show any true attachment to him. As early as March 1890 he arranged an audition for Pauline in Kassel, where she was offered a five-year contract. She declined it, however, as she did not want to tie herself down for so long and had hopes of making her début in Weimar before long – which she in fact did on 22 May 1890, as Pamina.

Richard also took a vigorous interest in the Richard-Wagner-Verein, and was instrumental in founding a full branch of the association in place of what had merely been local representation. He was also admitted to Weimar polite society. At the houses of Baroness von Meyendorff, a friend of Liszt who had been born Princess Gorchakov, and of Emilie Genast, the singer and singing teacher with whom Pauline de Ahna studied, he played his *Don Juan* on the piano before its orchestral première had taken place. He also made the acquaintance of Paul Zhukovsky (1845–1912), an intimate of Wahnfried and the designer of the sets and costumes for the 1882 production of *Parsifal* in Bayreuth. He spent many of his evenings, mostly in the company of Eduard Lassen, at the 'Künstlerheim', which he depicted to his father as 'a frivolous means of passing the time, with a charming bar in an old smithy'. An artists' ball was held there in December, in imitation of the Paris Universal Exhibition, which Richard attended as a blackamoor sweet-seller; it was for this occasion that he composed, on 7 December 1889, his Scherzo-Quartet for male voices on a text he had found on a box of matches made in Sweden: 'Ůtan svafvel och fosfor' (o. Op. 88).

The première of *Don Juan*

A few days before completing (on 18 November 1889) the score of *Tod und Verklärung*, which he had begun soon after Easter, Strauss began rehearsing his *Don Juan*, which was to receive its première in Weimar at Bronsart's special request. In view of the weakness of the Weimar strings, Strauss would have preferred the first performance to be given in a town rejoicing in a larger orchestra, but did not wish to disappoint his intendant. After sectional rehearsals on 7 November he wrote to his father to express his delight at the progress he had made in instrumentation.

> It all sounds capital and comes over resplendently, although it's dreadfully difficult. I felt really sorry for the poor horns and trumpets. They blew till they were blue in the face, it's such a strenuous business for them . . . The sound was wonderful, with an immense glow and sumptuousness, the whole affair will make an incredible impression here.
>
> The sound was especially beautiful in the G major oboe passage with double basses in four parts, divided cellos and violas, all with mutes, and the horns all with mutes, it sounded quite magical, likewise the tricky passage with harp bisbigliando and viola ponticelli . . . A good thing that as a whole the piece is not really *difficile*; it's only very hard and demanding, but fifty notes one way or the other won't really make any difference . . . The rehearsal yesterday was a success in *my* eyes, since I saw that I had made further progress in sureness in my writing for orchestra. The orchestra seemed to be enjoying the whole affair, in spite of their understandable amazement at such novelties.

Realizing that this description was not calculated to make his father's bosom swell with joy, Richard added:

> On Tuesday I spent two hours rehearsing the Pastoral Symphony, but this Beethoven fellow is devilishly hard, since he is so immensely *difficile*. I very much hope that it will go well [it was to be played in the same concert with the *Don Juan* première], although whenever I come to

I always have to think of my incomparable Papa, whom nobody else can touch in playing things like that.

Richard lost no time in writing to his father again after the first rehearsal with the whole orchestra:

[It] went excellently, the piece sounded wonderful; Lassen was quite beside himself, and declared that it would be another ten years before another piece like this was written. The orchestra wheezed and panted, but did their part capitally. A splendid joke: after *Don Juan*, one of the horn-players sat there bathed in sweat, completely out of breath, and sighed 'Dear God! What sin have we committed, for You to send us this rod for our backs (that's me)! And we shan't be rid of it so easily.' We all laughed till we cried. The horns in particular played as if death had no sting for them. (10 November 1889)

Lassen's comment concealed his antipathy for the work. Strauss was only too easily inclined to take apparently approving remarks at their face value.

He had little to say about the first performance on 11 November, at the second subscription concert of the season, when he next wrote home: 'Well, *Don Juan* was a magnificent success, the piece sounded magical and went excellently and unleashed a storm of applause fairly unprecedented for Weimar.'

Predictably his father did not stint his advice, wishing that in future Richard would be more frugal and provident in his writing for brass, 'less intent on outward glitter and more on content', since colour was 'always only a means to an end'. He appears also to have lamented the absence of beautiful sound in the piece, since Richard wrote to Hanna: 'Let Papa come [to the performance in Berlin] and hear for himself how deficient *Don Juan* is in "beautiful sound".' In the same letter he expressed his opinion of audience reactions: 'If I was now on the same level as present-day audiences, within five years *Don Juan* and *Macbeth* would be as dead as ditchwater. So wait and see. Things will take their peaceful, natural and, for the last hundred years, *good* course.' (16 January 1890)

Hans von Bülow, who had come to Weimar for the première, wrote to his wife:

Strauss is enormously popular here. His *Don Juan* has had a

> quite unprecedented success. Went to see him at 9 o'clock this morning with Spitzweg, to hear his new symphonic poem, *Tod und Verklärung* – which has inspired me with greater confidence than ever in his development. Very significant and enjoyable too, in spite of all kinds of dross. (13 November 1889)

He wrote to her again the next day, saying how happy he had been to be able to give Strauss his hearty encouragement as both conductor and composer. Strauss himself, his enthusiasm for Bülow's piano-playing revived by hearing him in Beethoven, Hummel, Mozart, Raff and Liszt, wrote to his father: 'I had to play *Tod und Verklärung* to him, and he was very taken with it, especially (alas) with its melodious passages, which he said he was *too old* now to do without.'

Bülow was unable to muster as much sympathy for *Don Juan*. He conducted it in Berlin himself, at the seventh Philharmonic Concert of the season, on 31 January 1890, three weeks after it had been performed in Dresden under Adolph Hagen. It was only moderately successful in Dresden: Bülow wrote to his wife of a 'failure', which did not deter him from conducting it in Berlin, while Strauss described the performance to his parents as a 'decent success'. In Berlin, too, Strauss found that although Bülow was up to the technical demands made by the piece he did not do justice to the work's expressive content. Two letters he wrote home about the Berlin performance, which he attended in the company of Rösch and Sonja von Schéhafzoff, refer to this state of affairs and also illustrate that Strauss had now distanced himself from Bülow and was ready to criticize him. After the general (public) rehearsal he wrote that Bülow had 'no inkling of the piece, but the orchestra gave a very decent account of themselves'. He conducted *Don Juan* himself, four days after Bülow's performance, at one of the Philharmonic Orchestra's 'popular' concerts, and wrote to tell his parents the next day of the attention he had attracted, of the respectful notices in the press, and of Bülow's kindness and affability, but went on:

> What more do you want, dear Richard, you will ask? Well, this is my answer: What use to me is success based on *misunderstanding*? Bülow has a total misconception of my work, in tempos, in everything, no inkling of the poetic content, and he treated it like any other piece of melodious music rejoicing in subtle instrumentation and interesting combinations and

> harmonies, no question but he approached it with great diligence, the greatest application and with a holy fear of failure (which he can't take any more, as he's become awfully vain), put the rehearsals mainly into the hands of his abominable Jewish entourage of wolves [Hermann Wolff], oxen [Siegfried Ochs] and cooks [Friedrich E. Koch], and introduced the public to a very interesting piece of music, but it was not my *Don Juan*. Bülow really has no understanding any longer for poetic music, he has lost the thread . . . You will understand that this totally misconceived performance by Bülow (for there's very little you can tell him, he is very touchy, he never even enquired about the precise content of *Don Juan*) caused me nothing but anger and vexation, if I tell you that I am not desperate for success, and have no wish to owe my fame as a composer to misunderstanding, when I see that my communication to the public *could not be understood.* I want to serve my art honourably and I am not afraid of a lack of success, so long as I can be sure that what I have to communicate has reached the public forum *correctly and accurately*. Success on any other footing is indifferent, indeed, unwelcome to me. (Weimar, 5 February 1890)

'With the exception of Sonja von Schéhafzoff and my dear, excellent Rösch' (who, like Alexander Ritter, encouraged Strauss's anti-semitism), his stay in Berlin had been an ordeal to him, he told his family. He maintained a close friendly relationship with Rösch throughout his years in Weimar. Early in 1892 he did his best to secure his friend's engagement as assistant conductor at the Karlsruhe opera, but although he enlisted Felix Mottl's support Rösch did not obtain the post, as he lacked the necessary operatic experience.

After the experience of Bülow's interpretation of *Don Juan*, Strauss considered it doubly important to make sure that the leader of the Philharmonic Orchestra and the principal wind players fully understood the programme and his expressive intention in key passages before conducting it himself at the popular concert:

> I had . . . the tremendous pleasure of seeing the excellent Philharmonic Orchestra following my tempos, modifications, *all* my intentions exactly, *without* rehearsal, with the result that the performance created a colossal furore, and Lessmann, Eichberg and large numbers of people expressed their astonishment, and that only now did they understand *Don Juan*, that it was a

> modern work etc. etc. I took the piece a good third faster, Bülow beat crotchets nearly all the time, where I wanted passion he had generalized emotion, the one passage (beginning of the great final climax) where I start more broadly he took so fast in rehearsal that the wind players could hardly get it out (and I pleaded with him about it), but the expression of so many small but essential details was exactly the opposite of what it should have been. (To his parents, 5 February 1890)

It is surprising that Bülow got the tempos wrong, because Strauss had sent him precise metronome speeds for *Don Juan* at his express wish (letter of 15 January 1890). However, he qualified the information with the remark 'Where they [the metronome speeds] are not in accord with your interpretation, I implore you simply to overrule them', which, while it demonstrates the respect he still had for Bülow, was unwise of him, to say the least. As in the case of his other symphonic poems, he emphatically refused to provide a thematic analysis of the work to be printed in the programme notes, perhaps because of the experiences that must have resulted from the analysis he wrote of *Aus Italien*. Instead he asked for the lines by Lenau that preface the score to be included in the programme, 'with all the expressive dashes', and he repeated this request to Franz Wüllner, when the latter conducted *Don Juan* in Cologne on 3 February 1891. In years to come, however, Strauss ceased to attach any weight to programmatic notes or analyses.

Strauss was undoubtedly influenced in his harsh opinion of Bülow's interpretation of *Don Juan* by Rösch and Sonja von Schéhafzoff, but the critical attitude he now adopted towards his former tutor did not cause him to forget how much he owed Bülow personally and artistically. Bülow became so incensed by Strauss's conversion to Wagnerianism that Father Strauss, warned by Spitzweg, advised Richard not to go to Berlin for the performance of *Tod und Verklärung*: 'Avoid conflict with him, after all it is no disgrace for you if you placidly accept an affront from him.' Bülow was also put out by Richard's good standing at Bayreuth, Franz Strauss warned. (5 February 1891) Nevertheless, Richard went to Berlin and conducted *Tod und Verklärung* there on 23 February. Writing to his father on the same day, all he said about Bülow was that he was 'a complete reactionary' and that he had always been one in his heart of hearts, according to Cosima Wagner; 'in those days the powerful personalities of a Wagner and a Liszt, and the chance of a good set-to, drew him into the "music of the future" camp, but really – – – !' For us, this is an allegation that invites scepticism.

In the spring of 1892 Strauss wrote to his father again after another concert in Berlin:

> The performance of the Ninth and the *Eroica* was wonderful, although, as I became aware on this occasion, Bülow is beginning to show his age in the fact that he has started to make Beethoven just a little more comfortable, he has diminished just a little the full brusqueness and harshness his performances of Beethoven used to have, he no longer forces a *molto cresc.* or a *p subito* to the very edge, nor does he always extract the utmost *ffo* from the orchestra any more, which used to be his strong point; the Scherzis [*sic*] are no longer as taut and energetic in tempo as they used to be; nevertheless, there still remained so much of the old glory that there was much to enjoy and much to learn. The last movement of the Ninth has never seemed more magnificent or more natural . . . Miracle the first movement of the Ninth and *Eroica*. The Adagios of both symphonies were not so beautifully uniform in tempo as in the past, and he didn't really mediate enough between contrasting tempos, especially in the Funeral March, but the reason for that may perhaps have been his nervousness.

And he added that Bülow had had a 'colossal' reception and was very pleased with his brilliant farewell:

> In himself he was charming! One morning he came to my room when I was still in bed and began to talk with great emotion about you, my dear Papa: he said he was troubled in his conscience and was very sorry for the injustice he had done you, when he offended you so greatly in Munich. He virtually asked my pardon on your behalf, and asked me how I thought you would take it if he visited you . . . in Munich. I replied, correctly I think, that you would take it very well, because one can't reject a confession and an apology for an injustice.

Before Bülow arrived in Munich, Franz Strauss had gone to Bad Aibling for the cure, so they did not meet on that occasion. It was not until 3 June 1892 that Bülow was able to pay a call on his old enemy and set the seal on their reconciliation.

The performances of *Don Juan* strengthened Strauss's conviction that he was on the right path artistically and spurred him on. At that period his goals did not lie so much in his own composition as in his determination to see Wagner and Liszt firmly established at the heart of the standard repertory, both in the opera house and in the concert hall. The programmes he proposed to Bronsart for his first three subscription concerts consisted, apart from three works by Beethoven, exclusively of works by Wagner (the *Faust* Overture and the *Siegfried Idyll*), Liszt (*Die Ideale*, *Festklänge*, *Orpheus*), Berlioz (*Symphonie fantastique*), Bülow (*Nirwana*), songs by Ritter and Lalo's *Symphonie espagnole*. That Bronsart's reaction was to raise his hands over his head and smite them together is all the more understandable because already in that October Eduard Lassen had conducted a staged performance of Liszt's *Saint Elisabeth*. Strauss had to consent to some alterations in his programmes. Nevertheless, at the end of the year he was able to write to his uncle Carl Hörburger: 'I had four very good concerts which, in spite of insanely modern programmes: Liszt, Wagner, Berlioz, Bülow, Richard Strauss and admittedly one or even two works by Beethoven in three of the concerts and Schubert's C major Symphony in the last, were very well attended and much applauded.' (29 December 1889)[5]

He still had to contend with the urgent expostulations of his horrified father, who persisted in invoking the names of Mozart, Haydn, Spohr and others. He attempted to justify himself by pointing out that Mozart's operas and Haydn's string quartets were permanently in the repertory, and he was just beginning to study Gluck's *Iphigenia in Aulis* (while Lassen took on *Iphigenia in Tauris*). After the second subscription concert Strauss had the first sign of disapproval from Bronsart, who described his interpretation of the Pastoral Symphony as a little too 'Bülowish'. A rather more serious difference between them was caused by Strauss's fanatical adherence to Bayreuth, whereas Bronsart was 'rather heated in his personal attitude towards Frau Wagner'. (To Franz Strauss, 15 November 1889) Since Strauss, at that date, was intent on acting entirely in accordance with the spirit of Wahnfried, that is, of Cosima Wagner, and on thus earning her approval, the initially cordial relationship with Bronsart was soon subjected to ever-increasing strains and pressures. Strauss was able to devote himself to his duties as conductor all the more single-mindedly, because he temporarily ceased composing after finishing *Tod und Verklärung* in mid-November. (He resumed work on the text of *Guntram*, but, as he confessed to his father, his brow was wet with nervous perspiration while he kneaded away at it; he would get the better of it in the end, though.) His performance of Schubert's Great C major Symphony exemplified his energetic approach to all conducting. The prestissimo at which he took the finale 'had the orchestra half out of their seats'. His zeal was noticed by Grand Duke Carl Alexander, who in December 1889 ordered his young Kapellmeister to be given a salary increase of 900 marks.

He had plenty of work to do in the opera pit; the first very important event for him was the revival of *Lohengrin* on 5 October 1889. The rehearsals he insisted on for this had turned 'half the theatre upside down'. *Lohengrin*, with *Tristan*, was one of the works of Wagner he loved most. Two days after a performance attended by Cosima Wagner, Richard wrote to his sister to tell her how impressed she had been:

> The *Lohengrin* was a *brilliant* success. Colossal praise from Frau W., who was quite enchanted and said that only in Karlsruhe (among all opera houses) had she been so profoundly impressed as the day before yesterday by my *Lohengrin*. All the tempos wonderful, the modulations of them [had] been sensitive and unobtrusive, there was great breadth in the performance, the orchestra [had] been finely shaded and discreet . . . In short, she was full of praise, quite moved and even kissed me, she herself began to applaud after the prelude, and in fact I have never conducted so well in my life as I did the day before yesterday . . .

He also had news of Pauline de Ahna, who made a good impression on Frau Wagner in an audition in which she sang Elisabeth from *Tannhäuser*; as a result she had been invited to go to Bayreuth the following summer, with the chance of being offered the parts of the Shepherd Boy in *Tannhäuser* and an esquire and a Flower Maiden in *Parsifal*. Furthermore, Strauss wrote, he had played Frau Wagner his *Don Juan* twice, as well as lieder by himself and by Ritter, half of *Figaro* and, at her special request, Bülow's *Nirwana*, of which she held a very high opinion:

> She was altogether of the most delightful amiability and discussed a large number of intimate matters with me in the most charming manner, I was frightfully interested in her perfectly correct judgment of Bülow, of whom we talked a great deal . . . She has completely finished with Levi and is waiting for the first good opportunity to get rid of him in some adroit

> way . . . She mentioned Papa several times in the most amiable fashion, how wonderfully he played, she regarded his opposition in the most just of lights, she understands very well, she says, how difficult it was in those days for the gentlemen of the Munich orchestra to be fair about something so completely new, those difficult and demanding works and the whole business of Wagner and Bülow, who had come there as declared enemies. In short, she swept me off my feet and I am completely enchanted by her amiability, by all that she stands for and by her profound understanding. In general I have achieved one of the biggest and most important successes of my whole artistic career to date and I am very happy. (21 February 1890)

The one-hundredth performance of *Lohengrin* at Weimar was approaching. This was an event of especial importance to Strauss, as he regarded it as an opportunity to celebrate the memory of the first Weimar performance, the work's première under Liszt, and he was anxious to have the worn-out, inadequate sets and costumes replaced by something worthy of the occasion. If the intendancy would not meet his request, he declared his own readiness to put up 1000 marks – a very substantial sum for him in those days, which he could raise only by asking his father to lend it to him. Lassen was of one mind with Strauss in this matter: 'It would be the greatest disgrace to Weimar, if *Lohengrin* was not newly dressed for the jubilee.' The producer Fritz Brandt, Strauss wrote to his father, intended to speak to the duke in person and inform him of Strauss's determination

> to pay the 1000 marks out of my, that is *your*, pocket (of course I shall soon pay it back to you; I just haven't got it at the moment), and ask him if my gift will be accepted . . . If he will not accept my gift, then I've done my best and have nothing to reproach myself with; I will not conduct *Lohengrin* in such a state, nor can I possibly remain in a theatre which behaves so disgracefully towards an artist from whose works it has been drawing the greatest profits for nearly forty years *without paying a single royalty*. (4 April 1891)

In the end the duke himself paid the sum required for the jubilee performance, which was given on 11 May 1891.

Strauss took care to maintain his contact with Cosima Wagner, and often reiterated the expression of his devotion and gratitude for the instructions on performance that she had given him during the summer of 1889 in Bayreuth. 'Today, as yet, I can only use words to clothe what I enjoyed, experienced and learned in Bayreuth; but it is my most ardent wish to have the chance eventually to prove my sincere and loyal devotion to the Bayreuth cause through action.' (9 October 1889) It was in the concert hall that he had his first opportunities for action, in performances of Wagner's *Faust* Overture, *Siegfried Idyll* and *Huldigungsmarsch* on 9 December. When Cosima suggested that he should apply for the conductorship of the Frankfurt Museum Concerts, which was due to become vacant on the retirement of Carl Müller, he declined on the grounds that they would not give him enough scope to promote the Bayreuth cause. (19 January 1890) An official approach from the president of the Museums-Gesellschaft in Frankfurt, Dr Fritz Sieger, received a reply in the same spirit:

> I have no intention at present of leaving the theatre, the more so as in Weimar I occupy a post which, although modest, suits me so thoroughly. In this modest post I can nevertheless do more than I should be able to do in an institution of such a different character, even so admirable a one as the Frankfurt Museum Concerts, for the cause of Bayreuth, to which I am devoted body and soul.
>
> I shall be true to that cause, even in the face of the temptation offered by such a brilliant position. Another reason is that you yourself have taken the precaution of bolting the door to any dreams I might have of establishing a Liszt cult at the Museum, so I must decline the direction of Schumann, Mendelssohn and Brahms's symphonies, and prefer to stay with Wagner, Liszt and even Berlioz, and remain in my little Weimar. (7 July 1890)

Instead of himself, he recommended Felix Weingartner, Engelbert Humperdinck and 'with special urgency' Fritz Rösch, whose lack of experience was offset by his great talent for conducting and who was 'perhaps the *most significant musician* in Germany at present'. Later in the same year he received a discreet enquiry from Felix Mottl, asking if he would care to become his assistant at Karlsruhe (1 December 1890), but although by then Strauss had experienced a few disappointments in Weimar he decided doggedly to stay there for the time being.

His overriding ambition was to champion Wagner's works in the theatre. He wrote Cosima a scathing account of a performance of *Tannhäuser* in Dresden under Ernst von Schuch: Schuch was immensely competent, the orchestra wonderful and showed a masterly discretion, but the superficiality of the conducting, which gave no sign that the conductor possessed either temperamental affinity or readiness to immerse himself in the work, had made Strauss recoil in horror. In the title-role, Heinrich Gudehus had struck him as 'dreadful, downright abhorrent': 'It would be hard to find another example of such amateurishness in the portrayal of this difficult part.' Deportment, make-up and comprehension (or rather non-comprehension) had been so banal, trivial and characterless that Strauss was at a loss for words. 'Pfui for such a man, who for years enjoyed the good fortune of singing at Bayreuth and was able or willing to learn so little there.' (19 January 1890)

The operas of Alexander Ritter

Among the personal and artistic relationships that were important to Strauss during his years in Weimar, alongside his old friendship with Ludwig Thuille and his new one with Cosima Wagner, he continued to cherish that with Alexander Ritter. Straightaway in the first season Strauss succeeded in staging Ritter's two comic one-act operas, which indicates, incidentally, that he must have had a substantial influence on programme-planning. On hearing the news, Bülow wrote to Bronsart: 'Strauss has more vitality [than I], he encourages even *over-idle Hans.*' (22 January 1890)

Der faule Hans ('Idle Hans'), with a text by Ritter himself, based on a story by Felix Dahn, had had its first performance in Munich in October 1885, and had subsequently been staged by a number of other theatres. When it was given in Dresden under Ernst von Schuch, the invitation to Ritter, who had wished to be present at rehearsals in order to have some influence on them, was sent at too short notice for him to be able to do so, which led Strauss to launch an unjustifiably violent attack on Schuch in a newspaper article. Strauss had followed the writing of the new opera, *Wem die Krone?* ('Whose is the crown?'), again on the composer's own libretto, 'with sympathy and encouragement'. The autograph score was sent to him in instalments, so that he could start rehearsing it in Weimar as soon as possible (it did not appear in print until January 1891, under Spitzweg's Joseph Aibl imprint). As late as 19 March he was still waiting 'on tenterhooks' for the complete opera: he was afraid of not being able to rehearse it properly. During rehearsals he wrote to his father that *Wem die Krone?* was 'damnably difficult for the singers, who are simply not in the least used to anything so new'. (30 April 1890) When he at last had the whole work in his hands he expressed his joy with as much delight as later when he had Humperdinck's *Hänsel und Gretel* in front of him. He wrote to Ritter:

> Well now: my heartiest, sincerest, warmest congratulations on your Heinz [the principal character], he is a splendid creation and you can be really proud of your work: the build-up to the climax is tremendous, the whole thing is magnificently felt; I lack the words to describe the impression that the complete Heinz has made on me today; I can only tell you that he moved me in the very depths of my being.

This is a tone such as Strauss seldom strikes in his correspondence. Its sincerity is demonstrated by his persistence in championing Ritter's operas to the very end of his life. Over and over again he tried (in vain) to persuade conductors of their merits and they were even included in his 'artistic testament', the proposals for the resuscitation of German opera that he entrusted to Karl Böhm after the German collapse in 1945.

Der faule Hans and *Wem die Krone?* were performed in Weimar under Strauss's direction as a double bill on 8 June 1890. The part of Hans was sung by Strauss's pupil Heinrich Zeller, that of Heinz by Hans Giessen, Richildis in *Wem die Krone?* by Agnes Denis and the Queen in *Der faule Hans* by Pauline de Ahna.

Strauss threw himself into the preparation of both works with ardour; he thought *Wem die Krone?* quite wonderful. To Hanna he wrote:

> I flay the orchestra and singers without mercy, but in spite of that I have the great pleasure of seeing the whole company immensely interested in both these impudent works and really enthusiastic about them; I hope I shall succeed in satisfying Ritter to some extent, then I would be fearfully happy, if I can only give him a little joy. Things like this make it really worth the trouble of driving myself all winter, ploughing through the standard repertory, [Lortzing's] *Waffenschmied* etc., sometimes it gets me down. (24 May 1890)[6]

The two one-acters remained in the repertory until February 1892, with a total of eight performances. As a result of the production in Weimar, which brought many of Strauss's and Ritter's friends to see it, other opera houses took up one or both of the works. *Der faule Hans* was given in Riga, Karlsruhe (on the strength of Strauss's own recommendation to Mottl), Dresden, Prague and Frankfurt, *Wem die Krone?* in Leipzig and Brunswick. They were not fated to become permanently established in the repertory, in spite of Strauss's indefatigable efforts on their behalf. Against the claims of Ritter's son-in-law Siegmund von Hausegger of 'tumultuous success, constantly reaffirmed at every performance', we must set the comment in Pauline de Ahna's diary after a performance on 17 October 1891, in which she sang the Queen, that *Der faule Hans* met with little enthusiasm from the audience. At all events Ritter himself, as we learn from a letter to his brother Carl as well as from other sources, looked on the performances in Weimar as the pinnacle of his composing career.

One outcome of Strauss's intensive preoccupation with Ritter's two operas was the attempt to write a short essay about them, which he intended to publish in the Weimar newspaper, though it is not known whether it in fact appeared there or not. All that survives are a few introductory remarks and a cursory outline of the rest. The introduction starts with the assertion that it was essential that Wagner's artistic achievement should serve as the basis of a school, for it stood isolated at present 'like a gigantic colossus of pure ore on the swampy ground of the German theatre'. It was no good his being imitated by people whose feet still stood on the soil of Meyerbeerian opera and who – with the exception of Ritter –

> in the matter of dramatic structure, in the matter of correct treatment of the German language in musical declamation, in the matter of assurance in the expression of a poetic idea, of dramatic material, have not yet learned the smallest lesson from Wagner . . .
>
> Only when enough works of that nature have come into being for a repertory to be built from them (in addition to Wagner and the classical masterpieces of earlier opera, the works of Beethoven and Mozart, Gluck and Weber) . . . have we made sure of preserving Wagner's artistic achievement. For only then will we have the guarantee of the creation of the correct style in which Wagner's works should be performed and thus the guarantee of Wagner's artistic achievement surviving for us or, to express it better, arriving at its full effectiveness.

The outline for the main part of the essay takes the following form:

> I. The above as introduction (then raise Ritter).
> II. Next the chief principle of Wagnerian drama from Wagner's *Opera and Drama*, its precise application to Ritter, who, as a true pupil of Wagner, goes his own way, like Liszt, the only real pupil of Beethoven, in the field of programme music.
> III. Closer examination of Ritter's two operas. Emphasis on the national element etc. Biographical information about Ritter. Ritter as lieder composer, little known because of his individual character.
> IV. Conclusion:
> Ritter, the only composer I know who has understood the relationship of the composer to the poet in drama in Wagner's sense, whereas others, totally mistaking the essence of the drama of the future, imitate the dazzling externals of Wagner the composer, while they still stand foursquare on the ground of earlier opera.

(The last remark was a reference to works like Chabrier's *Gwendoline*.) Strauss added some further notes to section II, taking up some of the ideas in *Opera and Drama* and mentioning the 'impossibility of bringing real drama into existence on the basis of absolute music':

> In conclusion, the moral to be derived from the introduction, when the repertory has been sufficiently enriched by Ritter's operas for us 'to be able to dispense with opera' with the exception of the old classical masterpieces (naturally, model translations of *Don Giovanni, Figaro* etc.). Then we shall have a 'German' theatre.

The ideas outlined in this sketch were probably inspired by Ritter's own to some extent. The growing vogue for Italian *verismo* opera (Mascagni, Leoncavallo), which Strauss regarded with contempt, must have spurred on his efforts to establish a German repertory over the next few years. The ideas he expressed about Ritter's one-acters were of course guiding principles in the creation of his own first opera *Guntram*. Throughout the years in Weimar he took a great interest in every new German opera, and (in addition to *Wem die Krone?*) gave there the first performances of Eugen Lindner's *Der Meisterdieb*, Hans Sommer's *Loreley*, Engelbert Humperdinck's *Hänsel und Gretel* and Felix Mottl's *Fürst und Sänger*. He also seized every opportunity he could to hear new operas in other towns. As early as April 1889 he went to Würzburg to hear Cyrill Kistler's opera *Till Eulenspiegel*, the text of which he thought was 'frightful' and the music amateurish, though he admitted that it showed 'talent and temperament'. It is possible that even then Kistler's opera gave him the idea of treating the same subject in a totally different form, but for a long time his slow progress on *Guntram* stood in the way of any other project. When he heard another opera by Kistler, *Kunihild*, with a text by Ferdinand von Sporck, in Halle in December 1893, he expressed himself no less critically in a letter home. The following year he sent Kistler a copy of the newly published vocal score of *Guntram*.

Rehearsing Hans Sommer's *Loreley*[7] was a depressing business because 'the thing is so badly scored'. (To his father, 28 May 1892) After the première on 12 June he wrote to his sister:

> It was a gigantic slog, but it went capitally and was well received. Sommer was called to take a bow after the love duet and several times at the end, after the fourth act I too was applauded so much that I had to take a bow. Frau Stavenhagen was quite outstanding, the orchestra excellent. General satisfaction all round, although the opera, mainly because of its impossible text, will never survive. Sommer, I'm afraid, will never grasp that nowadays one can't just haul Loreleis out of the romantic attic; he is very pleased; and I'm glad that we have once again done a little honour to a German composer who isn't a Jew. (14 June 1892)

Once again we are reminded of how susceptible Strauss still was at that date to the anti-semitism of his father and Alexander Ritter, and of his fervent nationalism. In his last season at Weimar, on 15 October 1893, he gave the first performance of yet another German opera: the three-act music drama *Hagbart und Signe* by Richard Metzdorf (1844–1919), the son of the horn virtuoso Gustav Metzdorf. Strauss summed it up as 'Kapellmeister's music'.

Strauss had included one of Alexander Ritter's songs, *Sternen Ewig*, in the programme of his first concert in Weimar in October 1889, and he was keen to promote his friend's instrumental works as well. In the second subscription concert of the 1891–2 season, on 23 November, he conducted an overture, which he described to his father as 'very beautiful and vital' and quite excellently written for orchestra, apart from having 'now and then rather too much brass'. (24 November 1891) Three weeks after the première of the double bill of Ritter's operas in June 1890, in a letter to Dr Fritz Sieger, the president of the Museums-Gesellschaft in Frankfurt, he warmly recommended two other works by Ritter, *Olafs Hochzeitsreigen* (Op. 22), which he was himself to conduct on several occasions, and *Sursum corda!*, a 'Sturm und Drang fantasy' for large orchestra (Op. 23). Strauss himself conducted *Sursum corda!* for the first time during his second term in Munich, at a Musical Academy concert on 6 March 1896. On the following day he saw Ritter for the last time: he died on 12 April.

In February 1891 Strauss told his father that he planned to orchestrate one of Ritter's songs for Frau Stavenhagen to sing (*Nun hält Frau Minne Liebeswacht*, no. 8 of Ritter's early song cycle *Liebesnächte* Op. 4). Whether the performance took place at that time is unknown, but Strauss did orchestrate the song. The autograph bears a much later date – Munich, 18 January 1898 – but the answer is probably that Strauss orchestrated the song in 1891 and made a fair copy of it for the Ritter family in 1898, so that the date applies to the dedication. The dedication ('Sträusschen to his dear Ritters') was not addressed to Alexander and his wife Franziska, as stated in Mueller von Asow's thematic catalogue – both were dead by then, Franziska having died in 1895 – but to their surviving daughters, Else, Julie and Hertha.

Strauss's championing of Ritter's operas met with the approval of Cosima Wagner. When Ritter revisited Weimar for one of the later performances of his one-acters, Strauss was able to show him hanging in his room the double portrait of themselves, painted by Leopold von Kalckreuth in 1890. The portrait is based on a study, which is considerably less successful; Leopold von Kalckreuth (1855–1928), at that date professor at the Weimar School of Art, 'threw it on to the canvas in one hour' one day when Strauss and Ritter visited his studio. The double portrait shows Strauss wearing his hair very thick on top of his head, as in the photographs taken of him in May 1890 (see pp. 199 and 220). His father commented on the photograph that was sent to him that he liked it, only 'I'm not happy about the tuft of hair, it's so thick that it diminishes the face. The expression is rather serious, but the picture as a whole conveys a mood.' (6 October 1890)

When Ritter came to Weimar yet again for a performance of his

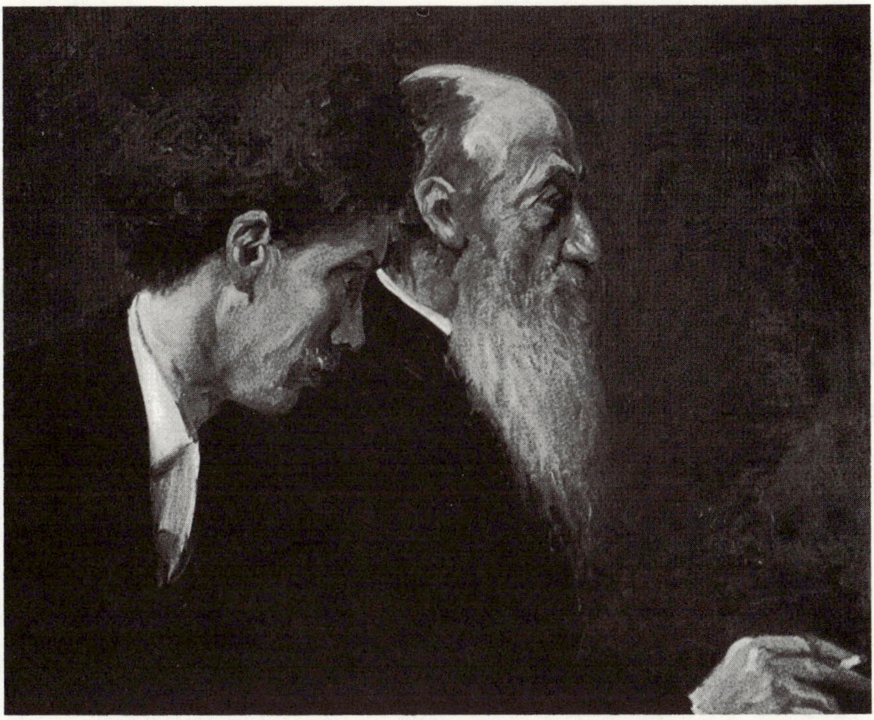

Richard Strauss and Alexander Ritter, painting by Leopold von Kalckreuth, Weimar, 1890

two comic operas, Richard wrote to Hanna about the pleasure it gave him to confide in his old friend:

> It's happy days with me at present, as at last, in my wonderful Ritter, I again have a friend with me to whom I can unbosom myself in complete confidence and with whom I know I am completely at one! I can't tell you all how much good it does me to talk everything over with him in the thick of the chaos that reigns in the theatre here. Aah! It's like a breath of fresh air! (20 February 1892)

At that date Kistner of Leipzig was preparing to publish the vocal score of *Der faule Hans*. Since no piano reduction of the overture existed, Strauss did it as a favour to Ritter.

Cosima Wagner, sketch by Franz von Lenbach

Strauss and Bronsart

Strauss was as determined to set high standards for the staging of Wagner's works as he was for their musical performance, being guided in both spheres by Cosima. He regarded it as vitally important for the work he wanted to do with regard to Wagner that he should have the last word in matters of production, and this was bound to affect his relationship with the intendant. Bronsart wrote to him on 8 July 1890 that there could be no question of the producer being subordinate to the conductor: the latter could give advice, but not orders. It would not be right for Weimar to become an affiliate of Bayreuth:

> Some modification of your ultra-radical views would be altogether desirable, and although I hope that, with more experience, the forces which drive you to overhasty overthrow will settle into a harmonious equilibrium, yet I am obliged to say, in some alarm, that ever since you assumed your office I have, in fact, seen you advance further and further along that path.

He hoped that sooner or later Strauss's essentially sound artistic nature would rid itself of the whole, long-discredited gallimaufry of its own accord, and he invoked the names of Goethe and Liszt to remind Strauss that greater men than he had willingly adapted themselves to the temper of Weimar in the past. He went on to express his belief that the cult of Wagner which had been forced upon Strauss was essentially alien to his nature, and he had some harsh words to say about Cosima Wagner:

> Every good musician who had a close association with Wagner has a better and more reliable knowledge of [the performance of his works] than the Meister's unmusical widow. But above all, everyone who knew Wagner at all well knows how liable the Meister himself was to change his mind about a host of things – staging, tempos, etc. – and you yourself, my dear Strauss, sometimes select tempos (let me remind you of the end of the *Tannhäuser* Overture among many other instances) which notoriously contradict Wagner's known intentions, in other words, to use your own argument, which cannot be reconciled with correct performance style.

Bronsart moved on to animadvert on Strauss's lack of self-control:

> You must learn to control yourself at least enough, even when you are excited, to stop using at every moment turns of phrase which you would condemn severely in the mouth of another person. You *must* learn to respect individualities in your dealings with *your* artists at least enough, even though they are working under your general direction, to acknowledge their entitlement to a certain degree of independent artistic judgment, and you must not call it 'style-less' every time that somebody feels differently from you about a matter. Finally, you must learn to control yourself enough not to lose sight altogether of our respective positions, however worked-up you may be.
>
> If you will take to heart what I am here saying to you truly from the heart and in fatherly sincerity, you will do yourself the best possible service and forestall bitter experiences which might otherwise have a crippling and destructive effect on all your activities, wearing you out spiritually and physically before your time, while you will also preserve for the good of us all an artistic ability more promising than any I have ever dared to dream of . . .
>
> If your temperament – whether innately or by upbringing is immaterial – is so immoderate that you cannot control it then you have no future in circumstances which rest on subordination.

The fact that Bronsart concluded his letter, a minor masterpiece in its mixture of encouragement, exhortation and warning, by describing the path that Strauss had set out upon with *Aus Italien* and *Don Juan* as dangerous and fateful, must have struck Strauss with particular force as he was now unshakeably convinced that he had left epigonism behind and had found the only way in which – as he had told Bülow nearly two years before – 'self-reliant forward development of our instrumental music is possible'.

Only a week earlier he had written to Bronsart, to thank him 'for the truly noble attitude you have shown towards my artistic endeavours, for the friendly goodwill and fatherly indulgence you have evinced towards my hot-blooded eccentricities (always kindly bearing in mind the good intentions from which they spring)'. (1 July 1890) So Bronsart's letter must have hit him like a cold shower. At all events he seems to have expressed a belief that Bronsart was out of sympathy with him, as the intendant wrote to him again on 5 August.

> There is no question of my being out of sympathy with you; on the contrary, the goodwill and sympathy which I have felt towards you from the first have increased rather than diminished in the course of our association. I spoke in my letters of a serious alarm that fills me since recognizing that the extreme artistic opinions you have made your own, even if you have adopted them from an alien source, have taken deeper root than I believed before we knew each other.

It was Strauss's official position that was in doubt, not his, Bronsart's, attitude towards him.

In spite of the inevitable tensions, Strauss's positive commitment to his work in Weimar was not at first seriously affected. Soon afterwards he wrote to Franz Wüllner: 'Things are very well indeed with me, the exceptionally favourable and delightful circumstances in Weimar suit me down to the ground and I feel thoroughly at ease there.' (23 August 1890)

The relationship between Strauss and Bronsart had begun to come under strain with the preparation of *Tannhäuser* in the previous March. Strauss had rehearsed the work from scratch, and done it with only two cuts, one stanza of Tannhäuser's song in praise of Venus in the first act, and a small cut in the entrance of the Thuringian nobility in the second act. His rehearsal schedule was exceptionally arduous, and he sought Cosima Wagner's advice on all manner of questions concerning the production. For example:

> Act II, duet: Is it right, at the words, 'Fern von hier, in weiten, weiten Landen, Dichtes Vergessen hat zwischen heut' und gestern sich gesenkt', if Tannhäuser gazes earnestly at Elisabeth's face, looks away only at 'all mein Erinnern' and does not move at all until 'Euch zu begrüssen', where a slight gesture of humility and devotion is perhaps appropriate? (3 March 1890)

He wrote to her after the performance on 27 March that he had looked forward to it 'really somewhat despairingly', since he thought the sets for the first and in particular the third act a complete failure and that reasonable dispositions on the stage were therefore hardly possible. Now that the première had taken place he could report that, 'except for the idiocies in the staging and the frightful performance by the Elisabeth', the performance had delivered more than the rehearsals had promised. In particular, he had been amazed by the Tannhäuser of his pupil Heinrich Zeller, with only six months' experience of the stage behind him. 'And so I have advanced our cause just a little way after all', he wrote. (3 April 1890) Cosima Wagner's close interest in his performances of Wagner – she had enlarged to him on her view of *Tannhäuser* during a visit to Weimar in the previous February – meant more to Strauss at that time even than the news he received of performances of his own works, such as one of the F minor Symphony in Amsterdam in February 1890.

Since Strauss often showed a lack of patience and moderation in working with singers, whom he measured by Bayreuth standards, the intendant's alarm and concern are understandable. It was Strauss's ambition to usher in a new golden era in Weimar's musical history. He undoubtedly succeeded up to a point, for the eyes of the German musical world increasingly turned towards the town where this young artist who was already making a name for himself as a composer was conducting operas and concerts which were far above the usual provincial standard in respect both of their choice of repertory and of the impetuous manner of their interpretation.

Bronsart's admonitory letter of 8 July was followed before the summer was out by two more, written in the fatherly tone which still marked his sympathy for the young firebrand but more expressly critical both of Strauss's insubordination and of his interpretation of the classics and Wagner alike. The first letter, that of 5 August, reiterates that it is alarm, not lack of sympathy with Strauss, which urges him to renew his warnings. Citing his own development, as 'the older and more experienced', he emphasizes that Strauss's official position is the chief issue. The 'fanatical cult of Bayreuth' was leading him to excesses. It was essential for him to acquire a certain degree of objectivity; as an example, Bronsart deplored the liberties he took in the matter of tempo:

> You out-Wagner Wagner – not to mention Beethoven! Franz Liszt used to direct a Beethoven symphony freely, God knows, and not *à la Capellmeister-Metronome*, but the style was still Beethoven's and never became as free and fantastic as when he played Weber or Chopin. But you, my dear Strauss, often conduct Wagner himself in such a manner that I don't understand why you don't introduce other instruments, other harmonies etc. *ad Beliebitum.** The fact that I and, I'm sure, every other musician find these 'metrical revisions' rather

* '*ad Beliebitum*' combines *ad libitum* with its German equivalent: *nach Belieben. Tr.*

> interesting is one thing: a musician of your gifts can never do anything boringly. But there is a sense in which this attitude of 'car tel est mon plaisir' must cause concern.

At the end of August Bronsart addressed another 'very serious and urgent admonition' to his assistant conductor, asking him first to make more effort to control his nervous excitement at least while in the exercise of his official duties and secondly to adapt his artistic endeavours 'completely and unconditionally' to his, Bronsart's views:

> Neither, I fear, will be easy for you; but it is essential, if you want to keep your post and use it to exercise a beneficent influence. The expressions of your extreme tendencies would cause me no alarm as to your future – I regard them as no more than the symptoms of a certain Sturm und Drang phase which natures of genius customarily go through in order to work off a certain excess of vigour, and from which you will emerge in time with a harmonious equilibrium restored, if you are fundamentally sound – but they do represent a danger to the sphere of influence you enjoy in your position.

Wagner, Bronsart went on, was now given his due by former opponents, while the blind enthusiasm of the past had calmed down to a reasonable level. Strauss's fanaticism belonged to a point of view that had been overthrown, one that was now 'truly forbidden'. But there was no reasoning with fanaticism, it consumed itself or it destroyed its man – and Bronsart reminded Strauss of the fate of Bülow. The letter closed with the advice that his 'assistant' should not work against him: Strauss must learn self-control. Strauss received this letter immediately before the beginning of his second season in Weimar.

On 2 October Strauss wrote to his father, saying that Bronsart was 'still very decent, and I think we shall get on all right together. For my part, at least, everything shall be done so that we do get on all right together.' There is ample evidence to show that Bronsart was still well-disposed towards Strauss, including the fact that they remained on good terms socially: Strauss spent New Year's Eve 1891 in the intendant's house. Bronsart's letters confirm the composer's own perceptive confessions that at that time he 'forfeited a certain amount of sympathy through youthful recklessness and immoderation'. The years in Weimar were in fact, as Bronsart said,

Strauss's (relatively late) Sturm und Drang period. In the circumspect letters that he wrote to his parents, one must often read between the lines to get at the truth of this.

Berlioz

A friendship ripened between Strauss and Siegfried Wagner, who visited Weimar for *Tannhäuser*. They came to call each other 'Du', an intimacy in the use of which Strauss was always very sparing. They met in Frankfurt early in March, when Siegfried showed Richard his contrapuntal exercises and asked for his opinion of them, and in the following November Strauss gave Ludwig Thuille a detailed account of a conversation in Weimar in which Siegfried had taken part:

> It was a great pleasure to have Siegfried here. He's a really likeable fellow, of refined upbringing and with his head, his heart and his mouth all in the right place. There was an argument with Lassen and Giessen about Berlioz, for whom they both have an excessive enthusiasm, and without any help from me he defined the true relationship between the Frenchman and Wagner–Liszt in exactly the right terms – against the silly claim that Berlioz invented modern orchestral technique and that Wagner then made use of it, he argued very rightly that the chief element distinguishing modern orchestral writing from Beethoven's does not lie in the augmentation of the means but in the augmented expressive capacity of the instruments separately, in their individualization, and this was first brought about with very modest means indeed by Weber, and Wagner goes on from there. No instrument in the whole of Berlioz speaks such a distinct human language as the clarinet in the *Freischütz* Overture and the bassoon in the finale of Act III of *Freischütz*. And *Holländer*, *Tannhäuser* and *Lohengrin* were written without knowledge of Berlioz's scores. And the augmented means of the *Ring* orchestra are not the consequence of the longing for unfamiliar, more refined sounds *as such*, but of the insistent need for new expression. (19 November 1890)

Thuille and Strauss held completely opposed opinions about Berlioz's *Grande Messe des Morts*. Strauss expressed his to Cosima Wagner:

> I think it is the richest creation of this unique genius and the most important work in the field of church music except the

> *Missa Solemnis* and [Liszt's] Gran Mass. The wealth of ideas of genius, which one is accustomed to, after all, in this original artist, is combined here with a profundity of emotion of which I know few examples in Berlioz's works. At the side of a gigantic work like that, a German Requiem by that canting, abstemious Temperance-Leaguer Brahms looks puny indeed! (26 November 1889)

He wrote to his sister in exactly the same vein, citing the *Symphonie fantastique* as well, which interested him more for its curiosity value and for its 'bizarre' musical ideas. (24 November 1889) For his part, Thuille maintained to Strauss: 'I tell you, there never was such drivel.' (4 April 1890)

Cosima's view of Berlioz was more selective. She wrote to Strauss: 'I have been through a formal breach and a reconciliation with Berlioz. The first happened with the Requiem, the monstrosity of which truly horrified me. I owe the reconciliation to *Béatrice et Bénédict*, a refined work, which, gracefully enhanced by Mottl's recitative, was outstandingly well rehearsed by Jahn.' (26 March 1890) *Béatrice et Bénédict* remained one of Strauss's favourite works, even late in life. In another letter to him Cosima Wagner acknowledged Berlioz to be 'one of the most significant personalities in the history of art':

> And even in the Requiem, which so repelled me, there are details of the very greatest style . . . He throws up problem after problem, and even if his edifice leans like the Tower of Pisa, and one can take no pleasure in the grotesque and absurd – and, alas, trivial – elements, yet one contemplates it as if it was one of the damned from Dante's Hell, with a mixture of horror and sympathy.

She had loved his *King Lear* Overture when she was young and an oboe theme from the introduction to it had remained fixed in her memory as particularly beautiful. She especially commended *Les nuits d'été* to Strauss. (21 May 1890)

Strauss heard *Les Troyens* under Mottl in Karlsruhe in December 1890. In a letter to his father he was very critical of the work's dramatic structure – 'a mixture of stupefying nonsense and spine-tingling genius, the frantic struggles of a musician of genius to find the most profound, emotional expression, combined with absolute blindness for the stage and dramatic construction' – but he was enthusiastic about the music, especially Dido's love-scene, in which Berlioz had 'written music of such fabulous beauty and magical sound' that Strauss 'forgot the entire nonsense on the stage'. In his view the 'nonsensical principle of opera' (as defined by Wagner) was taken to the furthest extreme in *Les Troyens* but he had found the performance 'immensely instructive' and the 'fabulous orchestral refinement' so interesting that it was hard for him to think of another occasion on which he had been stirred by such a jumble of emotions. The whole work deserved unquestionably to be performed, 'so long as we go on playing opera, and not Wagner and Ritter alone'. (9 December 1890)

Franz Liszt

The performance of Liszt's *Saint Elisabeth* under Lassen's direction, a few weeks after his arrival in Weimar, made a deep impression on Strauss, and he frequently referred to her father's works in his correspondence with Cosima Wagner. In his view, the best way to win Liszt the acclaim he deserved would be to give a concert made up exclusively of his music, and he in fact put this idea into practice, in a concert which took the listeners 'from Heaven above, through the world to Hell'. Liszt, 'surely the most many-sided and various of all symphonists from the aspect of musical expression', needed to be illuminated from all sides, he emphasized.

> Therefore, I think, the indescribably beautiful and fine A major Concerto benefited greatly from having the contrasts within it expressed separately, in *Orpheus*, on the one hand, and in *Totentanz* and the *Inferno*, on the other hand, where they are presented so monumentally and drastically that even the most cracked philistine skulls could not remain in any doubt about their plain meaning. As the corner posts of the programme, additionally, the Heaven of the real, true conqueror of the world opposing – I am tempted to say – the Heaven of dogma! (To Cosima Wagner, 15 August 1890)

After performing the *Faust* Symphony, Strauss wrote to Thuille:

> Hearing Liszt's works come to life in sound, I was once again made vividly aware that Liszt is the only symphonist, the one who had to come after Beethoven and represents a gigantic advance upon him. Everything else is drivel, pure and simple. And even the several-movement form, which he otherwise used

only in *Dante*, is so necessary to this piece, so essentially *different and new* from Beethovenian form. The dramatic action *per se* does not take place until the 'Mephisto' movement, which is really the 'symphonic poem', the two great characters Faust and Gretchen are so complex that it simply wasn't possible to include their representation as well as the dramatic development in one movement. So the exposition consists of the two greatest character pieces that have ever been written (there is a certain development, as well, in the 'Faust' movement) and the dramatic complication takes place in the 'Mephisto'. Then the linking of the three movements, by the anticipation of 'Mephisto' in the first movement, the introduction of the Faust motive in 'Gretchen', is so masterly that you're simply lost in admiration, and the dazzling invention, the precision in the poetico-musical expression, the assurance of the instrumentation, it simply beats everything! Oh well, perhaps my enthusiasm is making me talk utter nonsense; at all events, it was glorious! . . .

I worked up such energy and passion and rhythm that the theatre shook and then I swayed about and stormed so much in 'Mephisto' that it gave me the father and mother of a stitch in my side. It went away at the Eternal Feminine. (19 November 1890)

Two years later, after a concert in Leipzig at which he conducted *Die Ideale* and *Mazeppa*, Strauss wrote to Cosima Wagner:

I feel so completely at one with the symphonic poems, at least, and they correspond to my nature so completely that I really believe that, without ever having known the great master, I am capable of expressing the poetic content of his works in a mode that at least 'corresponds' (according to A[lexander] R[itter]). (14 March 1892)

His letters to Alexander Ritter were also full of the deep impressions Liszt's music made on him during these years, but they have been lost, and only some passages quoted in Steinitzer's biography survive: 'The lofty flight of the ideas and the deep inner emotion of the "Purgatorio" (in the *Dante* Symphony) – the *Bénédiction*, a glorious, sublime piece – *Mazeppa*, a glorious piece.' *Saint Elisabeth* is 'beautiful and deeply felt': 'so little handicraft and so much poetry, so little counterpoint and so much music'. The first section of *Die Hunnenschlacht* is 'grandiose', the *Mephisto Waltz* has 'an impudence that really only a genius can afford to indulge in – it has red blood and life'.

But even if the 'fundamental principle' of Liszt's symphonic works, 'in which the poetic idea was also in fact simultaneously the structural element', was an inspiration and an example to Strauss, there can be no question of stylistic dependence. Steinitzer hits the nail on the head with his observation that the polyphonic element in the conception of Strauss's symphonic poems justifies the assumption that he was more often inclined to look on Liszt 'as a model directly contrary to his own creative intention'. Steinitzer quotes in this context a letter Strauss wrote to his uncle Carl Hörburger which illustrates that, even before he went to Weimar, he consciously kept a distance between his own methods of working and Liszt's procedures. He was working, he wrote, at a kind of symphonic poem (i.e. *Macbeth*) 'but not after Liszt'. (11 January 1888)

During his years in Berlin, Strauss included Liszt's symphonic poems, one by one, in the programmes, alongside works by Beethoven and himself. On the occasion of the Liszt centenary in 1911, the editor of the *Allgemeine Musikzeitung*, Paul Schwer, circulated a questionnaire among a large number of musicians. Strauss's reply to the question 'Wherein do you think the decisive significance of Franz Liszt lies for the development of German music?' was 'Franz Liszt was the first creative genius of the nineteenth century, before Richard Wagner, *to understand Beethoven correctly*.' (*Allgemeine Musikzeitung*, no. 42, 20 October 1911)

In his letters to Cosima Wagner Strauss constantly refers to the contrast between the attitude to art upheld by and practised at Bayreuth, which he took as his ideal, and what was customary in other theatres throughout the country. Conditions in Weimar soon began to oppress him, and the higher he raised his sights the greater his disillusion became:

> There is need for the true pursuit of art at least for two months in the year [i.e. at the Bayreuth Festivals], for what we 'accomplish' in our court theatres amounts with few exceptions (e.g. the fortunate Mottl [at Karlsruhe]) to nothing more than attempts so modest that one's whole courage simply goes overboard – apart from that the 'German people' – but forgive me, is there such a thing? I think that now there's only a German public and that's pitiable enough – so let's at least speak of a German people, even if it no longer exists, so, the German

people needs 'once a year' a reminder, in letters of fire, that it could have a German art, if it 'wanted'. (5 January 1890)*

Strauss's attacks on works like Gounod's *Faust* – the success of which in Germany he calls 'one of the greatest blots of shame' – and especially on Mascagni's *Cavalleria rusticana* – 'a pot-pourri of the very worst, crass operatic effects' – are characteristic of his belief in the unqualified superiority of German art, in which he had been encouraged by Cosima Wagner, as well as by Alexander Ritter. Cosima wrote to Strauss that she had fled from the second act of Hermann Goetz's *Der Widerspenstigen Zähmung* ('The Taming of the Shrew') 'for its false goodfellowship and shrieking beer-hall joviality were really more than we [!] could bear'. (26 March 1890) This remark demonstrates the lofty attitude the chatelaine of Bayreuth took even to a lot of German post-Wagnerian music (such as Anton Bruckner's). At that date her opinions had some influence on Strauss.

Emmanuel Chabrier

Cosima's authoritarian attitude is shown at its most glaring in the 'case' of Emmanuel Chabrier, which should be aired here, because Strauss was one of those to whom she addressed her extreme disapprobation and because he too added his voice to hers. The music of Chabrier had been taken up by Mottl and some other German conductors: indeed his operas *Gwendoline* and *Le roi malgré lui* enjoyed a far greater success in Germany than in France, where later composers such as Debussy, Ravel and Poulenc were the first to appreciate him. (Stravinsky, too, admired his *opéras comiques*.) The world première of *Gwendoline* was actually given in Karlsruhe on 30 May 1889, under Mottl's direction and with Pauline Mailhac in the title role, and it was performed in Dresden, Leipzig, Munich (under Levi), Stuttgart and Düsseldorf within the next eighteen months. *Le roi malgré lui*, which had its German première on 2 March 1890, again under Mottl in Karlsruhe, was also heard in several other German houses (Dresden, Munich, Cologne) in a short space of time. At first Cosima Wagner was quite gracious about *Gwendoline*. After attending the première in Karlsruhe she wrote to Strauss:

* This passage (it begins 'Not tut . . .') employs a vocabulary rich with Wagnerian associations as well as explicit quotations from Wagner's dramatic texts, notably *Die Meistersinger*. *Tr.*

Chabrier's *Gwendoline* . . . seemed to me to be one of those bad works with some talent in them, it has something of everything in it – I avoid using the word eclectic – recalls Gounod, Meyerbeer, but in particular the symphonic poems and ends up in an apparently inevitable Tristanish vein. I'm quite sure, however, that the composer's next products will be significantly better because, for all the borrowings, there were distinct signs of originality and even spontaneity. The text [by Catulle Mendès] was simply disgraceful and such a Jewish mish-mash that the naive trickery of the plot of *Fra Diavolo* the next evening seemed a work of genius by comparison. In my opinion Auber was the last *French* composer, though even he knew little enough of the noble school of the eighteenth century, and nobody there now knows anything of it at all. (12 October 1889)

Chabrier was one of Wagner's most ardent admirers, and in July 1889 he was invited to Wahnfried with other French visitors to the festival. During the course of the evening, in ecstasies at the honour, he played the prelude to *Gwendoline* – and *España*. The vision of Chabrier – who has been aptly described as the 'archetype of a "bonhomme" from the Auvergne, an original mixture of shirt-sleeved provincial and quick-witted boulevardier, of stolid bourgeois and waggish clown'[8] – sitting at Wagner's piano and thumping out *España* to Wagner's widow is not without its funny side. Mottl did his best to prepare Cosima for *Le roi malgré lui*, of which Ravel commented that it had 'changed the direction of French harmony'; he told her that it contained 'among other things, some grossness, which might be made tasteful with different sauces. In spite of that there is no mistaking a vigorous talent.' (22 January 1890) After the première on 2 March, which Chabrier attended, Mottl wrote to her in more positively favourable terms:

The opera undoubtedly benefits from being seen in the theatre! And I really enjoyed the second performance (yesterday), which went very well indeed. Chabrier was given a magnificent, demonstrative reception, which made him very happy . . . One thing is certain: the man has a very great deal of talent, and when one contemplates the miserable musical incompetents we have in Germany, someone like him looks quite good by comparison! (6 March 1890)[9]

Cosima must have pricked up her ears at the last sentence in particular. But having seen a performance of *Le roi malgré lui* under Ernst von Schuch in Dresden on 26 April, she wrote to Mottl:

> The whole thing is simply rubbish from A to Z! It's beyond the help of God or gleeman. No! The grossness, the absence of any kind of thought! Offenbach, Meyerbeer and Gounod with Berlioz-like japes in the scoring. Why Chabrier ever came to Bayreuth will surely remain a mystery. As Countess Wolkenstein and I were leaving we said to each other that one good thing had come of it, that we would never listen to another note of Chabrier. If *Gwendoline* is bad, this is abominable! He can't even write a bearable dance-tune. In the first act I was horrified, in the second act furious, in the third so depressed that I lost all notion of why I was enduring such misery. The performance was good. Scheidemantel sang the king, and the orchestra under Schuch was very lively and graceful. But no interpretation in the world can disguise this lowest form of café-chantant triviality for one moment. It forces itself upon one in a bestial manner.

After writing that, to Strauss she could only say:

> Have I written to you about the *Roi malgré lui* by Chabrier in Dresden? I cannot possibly describe the impression it made on me, and have managed to do so only in an explosion of rage to Mottl; a thing like that should not be performed, it is simply horrifying and I cannot speak about it calmly. (21 May 1890)

Gwendoline was given in Munich on 20 November 1890 at the Court Opera under Hermann Levi, with Milka Ternina in the title role. Cosima, in spite of her earlier resolve, saw a performance and was able by then to write more calmly about this work of Chabrier's at least: 'I found Munich in an uproar over *Gwendoline*, which – after [Massenet's] gruesome *Manon* – I found not quite so bad, though still bad enough, as when I heard it in Karlsruhe.' (To Strauss, 6 December 1890)

Three years later Friedrich Rösch was every bit as dismissive of Chabrier, again in a letter to Strauss:

> I heard *Gwendoline* for the first time recently, and not long before that a concert piece by Chabrier: *La sulamite*. The way these Wagner-yea-ners [Wagner-Janer] go to work with the most external of Wagnerian means, displaying hollow, platitudinous, blind powerlessness, without having a single grain of the

> Meister's *spirit* to bless themselves with, is so stupid it's downright funny! I used to find it distasteful, or even disgusting. But recently, as I say, almost the only thing I could do was laugh at it. (20 April 1893)

Of course Chabrier is not in the same class as Wagner. But the incapacity to understand phenomena from a different musical sphere is revealed with alarming clarity in such utterances.

It is not certain whether Strauss heard *Le roi malgré lui*, but he went to a performance of *Gwendoline* in Leipzig in 1890. He expressed his opinion (undoubtedly influenced by Cosima Wagner's) in letters to his parents and Alexander Ritter:

> [We] had little joy of it, however. It was fairly obvious that Chabrier has studied Wagner's scores a great deal, but *without knowing German*, and without that one's understanding of Wagner can be only superficial. And that was what ensued: a bad and boring libretto, set to music of the utmost refinement, all in the style of *Tristan*, without distinction, whether it was suitable or not. Musically it has a lot of talent, wonderfully orchestrated, but in its externals imitation Wagner. (To his father, 16 February 1890)

> The spirit of the German language is the only means whereby Wagner may be grasped entirely. He always has the right expression, for the most simple things as for the most complex. [Chabrier, on the other hand, seemed to think it enough] to appropriate from the outside the most difficult features of the style of *Tristan*, regardless of whether it is suitable or not. He lavishes the most over-excited harmonies and over-refined instrumentation on the simplest episodes – until one begins to feel nauseated. (To Ritter, 21 February 1890)

Accurate observation mingles in these passages with a failure to recognize the typically French elements as well as the personal elements in Chabrier's music; it is by no means true that he applied 'the style of *Tristan* without distinction', although the looming presence of Wagner in *Gwendoline* and *Briséis* alienated the composer himself from his own works from time to time.

A few years later, when Strauss had freed himself from the overriding influences of Ritter and Cosima Wagner, he developed a more positive view of Chabrier. One of the first premières he put on at the Berlin Court Opera was a staged performance of the fragment *Briséis*, in January 1899; Chabrier, who died in 1894, completed only the first act, and that had received only a concert performance in Paris. Before the première in Berlin Strauss wrote to his parents: 'Next week the first performance of Chabrier's *Briséis* (only one act), very free, highly seasoned French music: it'll sound charming but won't be much of a success.' (29 December 1898) On the day of the première itself he wrote again: 'One act of very refined, delightfully scored music.' (14 January 1899) And in the following April he said to Romain Rolland: 'C'est moi qui ai donné la *Briséis* de Chabrier qui m'a fait beaucoup de plaisir.'[10] In 1902 and 1903 he included Chabrier's *Joyeuse marche* in the programmes of modern works that he played with the Berlin Tonkünstler-Orchester. He also took an interest in Alfred Bruneau's opera *L'ouragan* (1897–1900, with a libretto by Zola) while in Berlin, but the lack of a German translation prevented its being staged.

The correspondence with Cosima Wagner

The correspondence between Strauss and Cosima Wagner came to have very great importance during his years in Weimar.[11] Not only did she lend a sympathetic and understanding ear to his complaints about the 'wretchedness' of his situation in Weimar and the limited opportunities he had to put his artistic ideals into practice, but her comments also stimulated him to think more deeply about himself and about the intellectual and emotional foundations of his compositions. After he had played *Don Juan* to her, she wrote:

> Both the ear and the emotional responses require the form to be delineated first, that is the form and the melody irrespective of the effect that the actions and modulations in which they are involved have on them.
>
> It seemed to me, in your *Don Juan*, that you were more interested in the presentation of your characters than in the way your characters had spoken to you. I call that the play of intelligence against the emotions.
>
> It's very difficult to express oneself about these things and everything I say to you on the subject seems very foolish to me, because inadequate. Perhaps an analogy will help: as I imagine things, form comes into being for the artist as the statue did for Pygmalion, and the movement comes from the passionate sympathy aroused by the statue with the blessing of beauty.
>
> Your very choice of subject shows the dominance of the intelligence. I am sure you had no sympathy with Lenau's Don

Juan, who surrenders himself out of the excess of boredom, but the conception caught your interest and gave you a lot of ideas which you have shaped with astonishing assurance.

My advice is, do not follow the lists of your imagination any further, but surrender to what pleases your heart, whether it is the glow of the setting sun, the whisper of the waves, the hero facing his end, or the revelation of truth by virgin innocence. For our art is what leads us back to the eternal motives and teaches us to perceive and recognize them through all the deceptions of appearances. (6 March 1890)

Other remarks from her on the subject of intellect and emotion elicited this reply from Strauss:

It is my belief (speaking generally) that in the case of a broad and generously disposed artistic nature the unconscious and the instincts, which together form the fundamental basis of every true and intensive productive urge, whether in the creative or the interpretative artist, will always be more powerful than the intellect, however highly developed the latter may be.

Your significance, dearest lady, for us small people is to remind us of the gigantic task we have if we are but to gain an approximate understanding of the stage to which our art has advanced thanks to the Meister's works and writings, which were so far in advance of their time; such understanding will prevent us from blithely sowing our seed all over again, in sheer stupidity (like the worthy Brahms), in ground that has long borne magnificent flowers.

Geniuses like Mozart, Haydn and Schubert were able to create with complete spontaneity, they had no precursors or models to follow in the art, which they founded for themselves (Bach was almost unknown to them). The glorious unconscious was able to unfurl totally uninfluenced by the intellect; nowadays, however, we have to assimilate the short but gigantic development of total art in order to reach but the stage to which it has advanced, and we have to cudgel our brains to do it. Wherever the heart beats strongly, it will always keep on burning in the intellect. Forgive me if I have contradicted you here, but be assured that nonetheless I shall take your kindly advice 'to heart'; if the heart is sound, then I believe the intellect, whose growth in my case is incidentally still very stunted, will be unable to harm it. (3 March 1890)

(In this context there is no call to comment on Strauss's view of the history of music.) Three weeks later he returned to the same subject:

> I think I have understood [you] correctly and I look forward to producing evidence next time we meet, in the form of my third symphonic work, which was finished last November and bears the provisional title of *Tod und Verklärung*, that I have perhaps already made a significant advance, even in the choice of *subject*. It's very difficult to say how far the artist is responsible (directly, of course) for his subject, since it forces itself upon him with irresistible necessity, and the question that primarily concerns the artist is 'how' he is to give it form, and the answer determines the yardstick that is to be used for his work of art. The 'higher responsibility' of which Schopenhauer speaks so beautifully at the end of the first book of his *Ethics*, *On the Freedom of the Will*, has some application here too.
>
> I feel as though all this has been perhaps clumsily expressed, I still find it frightfully difficult to use language on these topics. (22 March 1890)

(Strauss refers to *Tod und Verklärung* as his 'third' symphonic work; the others were *Macbeth* and *Don Juan*, so he did not admit *Aus Italien* to the same category.)

Cosima Wagner's personal concern for her young friend at this time is revealed in a remark she makes in one letter about Franz Strauss, Wagner's old enemy:

> The fact that you are the son of an artist who found it very hard to follow us is a source of great consolation to me, and of illumination too. To me it proves that his heart was with us after all, and only birth, habit, upbringing, circumstances and all those other daytime phantoms came between us. There is hardly anything on which my thoughts dwell more contentedly than on this silent weaving of fate in defiance of all human prejudices. (15 April 1890)

Cosima suggested that he might consider writing a symphonic poem on the subject of a poem, *Der Tänzer unserer lieben Frau* ('Our Lady's Dancer') from Wilhelm Hertz's *Das Spielmannsbuch*,[12] but Strauss did not follow it up. At this period, in what free time he had after fulfilling his conducting duties in Weimar, he was busy with the text of *Guntram*. There was a pause in his symphonic writing after *Tod und Verklärung*: the considerable detour which he made, drawing up and starting to put into execution the detailed plans for a new opera on the subject of Till Eulenspiegel, was a necessary stage for him to go through before he returned to the symphonic poem after several years with *Till Eulenspiegels lustige Streiche* (1895). He did follow Cosima's advice in October 1890 and read Gustav Freytag's *Bilder der deutschen Vergangenheit* and the dialogues of Heinrich von Stein, Siegfried Wagner's tutor.

Naturally enough, Strauss's letters to Cosima frequently refer to his dealings with Bronsart. Even the letter of 22 March 1890 quoted above describes a disagreement that took place between them during a rehearsal of *Tannhäuser*:

> When I told him that these courtiers' antics and the greeting of the guests by the Landgrave and Elisabeth simply lacked style, he grew bitterly angry and told me that he knew more about court ceremonial than I and that I was not to meddle in the matter etc.

On another occasion he described Bronsart, undoubtedly with some justice, as 'a progressive of thirty years ago', against whom he would have many a hard fight to wage yet. Not long afterwards he complained that the intendant lacked 'the necessary energy and enthusiasm for *our* cause'. 'Our' cause: that is, Wagner and Liszt. Richard fought for Liszt in the concert hall with the same dedication as for Wagner in the theatre, where, after *Lohengrin* and *Tannhäuser*, he prepared to launch *Rienzi*, although Bronsart declared that he could see nothing more in the work than a 'galvanized corpse'. During the preparations for the production, Richard once more requested and received advice from Cosima, on the subject of cuts among other matters. Cosima wanted to go significantly further than Strauss had in mind, partly for dramaturgical considerations, and partly because she regarded it as impossible to find a soprano capable of negotiating the coloratura in the Act V duet. Strauss also undertook the 'post-instrumentation' of two numbers in Act I (the Introduction and the Trio) and of the Act II finale. When Cosima had occasion to look at the work again, in November 1892, Strauss wrote from Brindisi to the librarian of the Weimar Court Theatre, asking him to send her those sections of the opera. In the season before the Weimar production, *Rienzi* was staged in Karlsruhe, and here, too, to Mottl's regret, Cosima 'sacrificed a number of musical features for the good of the drama. (But in return restored a large passage which isn't even in the score any more: Act III, "Klaget

Jungfrauen, weinet".)' (Cosima Wagner to Strauss, 21 May 1890)

While Strauss was deriving the 'fullest enjoyment' from the rehearsals of *Rienzi*, he wrote to Thuille that one important aspect of the production would be to prove by the style of the performance, which would have to be twice as intensive and free, that even this early work had nothing to do with 'opera' but was authentic, unadulterated, though young Wagner. He had to admit that the finale of Act II could equally well be Meyerbeer or Wagner, depending on how it was performed. (19 November 1890)

Thuille had been working, at Strauss's request, on a piano duet version of *Don Juan*, which was dedicated to him:

> Today I spent six hours poring over the score of *Don Juan*, trying, in the sweat of my brow, to transform your 'fermenting dragon's venom' into the 'milk of human kindness', as is fit for the piano. It's going very slowly, the transition to the second subject (with the 'tedium' motive) was especially hard, and it still doesn't sound right, since the motives and their rhythmic *staffage* always coincide in the same place. (4 April 1890)

Later Thuille was to do the piano score of *Macbeth* as well, as a favour to his friend.

Pauline de Ahna in Weimar

Urged on by Pauline de Ahna's former teacher Franziska Ritter (Alexander's wife), Strauss persuaded Bronsart to give his pupil and protégée her first chance on the stage before his first season in Weimar was out. On 22 May 1890 Pauline sang Pamina in *Die Zauberflöte*, with the posters cautiously billing it as her 'first theatrical essay'. In fact she was so successful that she was promptly given a five-year contract at the Weimar Court Theatre from 1 July, though on extremely modest terms: an annual salary of 1200 marks. Strauss asked Eugen Spitzweg to get a mention of her début inserted in the *Münchner Theater-Anzeiger*, saying 'that my pupil, Fräulein de Ahna, making her début here as Pamina on 22 May, scored a great success (the wonderful voice, excellent technique and the beautiful and assured dramatic talent aroused great, well-earned public interest)'. To Hanna he wrote:

> Fräulein de Ahna had a tremendous success and sang capitally, as well as acting and moving on the stage with a boldness and assurance that amazed everybody. The voice blended

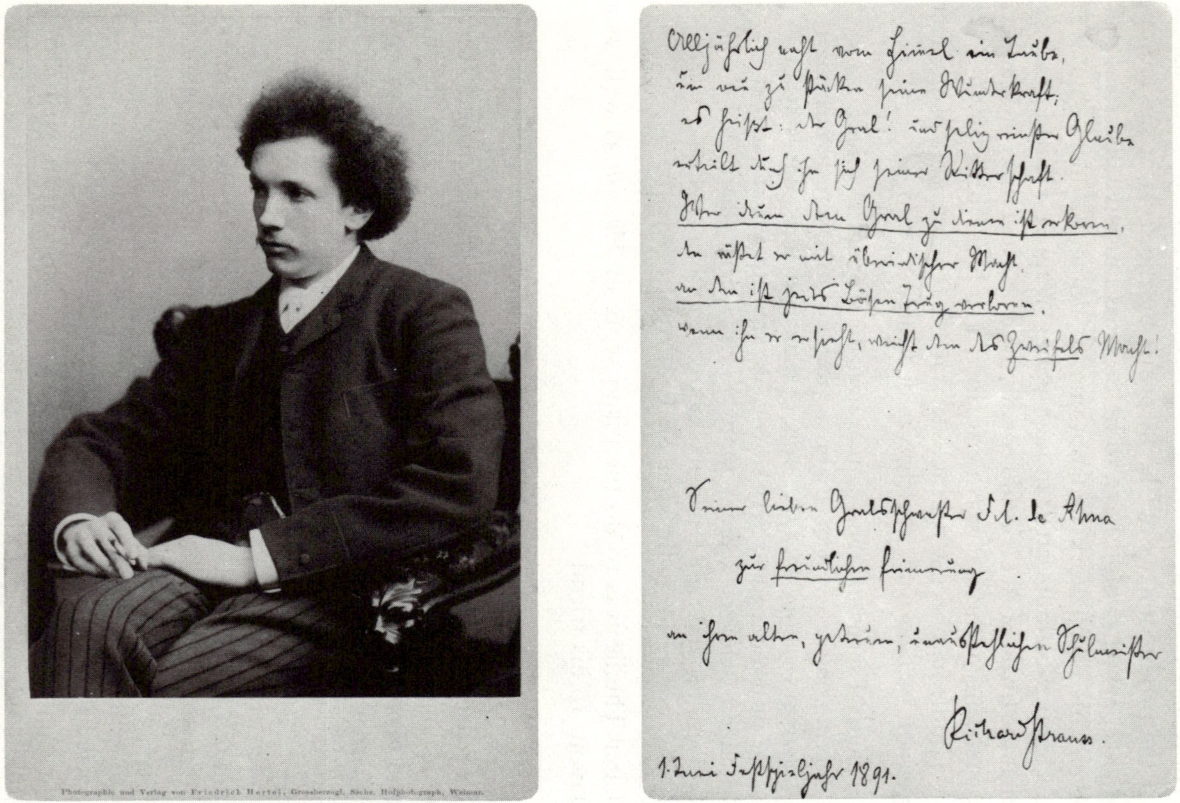

Richard Strauss, photograph taken in Weimar 1890, with an inscription to Pauline de Ahna on the back, dated 1 June 1891

Pauline de Ahna as Elisabeth, Bayreuth, 1891

> wonderfully with the orchestra, in short, her success exceeded all expectations. Such a shame that Frau Ritter wasn't here, she would have had enormous pleasure from the fruits of all the hard work she had in teaching her. (24 May 1890)

In the 1890–1 season Pauline sang Pamina again, Anna in Marschner's *Hans Heiling*, Eva in *Meistersinger*, Elvira in *Don Giovanni*, Elsa in *Lohengrin* and Elisabeth in *Tannhäuser*. In the fourth subscription concert of the season (26 January 1891) she sang Clärchen's songs from Beethoven's music for *Egmont* and Isolde's 'Liebestod'. She also appeared in Delibes's *Le roi l'a dit* – 'without reaping any applause' – and, standing in at short notice, as the solo Messenger of Peace in *Rienzi*. Although the generally favourable reception strengthened her self-confidence, Pauline was not unself-critical. Of her Elvira, for instance, she noted in her diary: 'Too dainty and much too fluting, too lovable and German in expression and acting – not a Spanish woman thirsting for revenge.' (5 April 1891) On 17 February 1892, on the other hand, she wrote: 'Conceived much too dramatically.' Her position in the Weimar ensemble was confirmed by her Elsa. After one performance Richard wrote home:

> The performance . . . of Elsa was simply fabulous, in particular magnificently acted, she had so sunk herself into the role, was completely absorbed in it, her mime was simply breath-taking. Frau Ritter ought to have been here, she would have marvelled at the Paulinchen she used to know.
>
> She scored an enormous success; the Grand Duke himself said to her he'd never seen such an Elsa, she had usurped Rosa von Milde in his esteem! You couldn't ask for more! (14 February 1891)

Pauline was again a success when she made a guest appearance as Elsa in Karlsruhe in May 1891 under Mottl's direction. Strauss had coached her in the part so thoroughly that he was able to assure her after an 'excellent rehearsal this morning, where you did your bit really outstandingly' that she could set her mind at rest, she knew the part perfectly. (6 February 1891)

During the following season Pauline sang, among other parts, roles in *Mignon* (in a guest appearance at Eisenach in 1892, as well as in Weimar), Ritter's *Der faule Hans* (the Queen), *Der Freischütz* (Agathe), *Fidelio* (Leonore), Cherubini's *Les deux journées* (Constance), *Don Giovanni* (Donna Anna as well as Elvira – she noted in her diary on 11 December 1892 'well sung but sugary'), *Figaro* (the Countess), *Die Walküre* (Fricka), *Werther* (Charlotte), August Enna's *Die Hexe*, *Tannhäuser* (adding Venus to her repertory) and Felix Mottl's *Fürst und Sänger*. Eduard Lassen, no doubt correctly, found her not sufficiently heroic in *Fidelio*, but her teacher Emilie Merian-Genast wrote to General de Ahna after a rehearsal:

> The role is so difficult, it makes such absorbing demands on the singer's physical and emotional resources that it is impossible for Pauline to do justice to herself when she is performing it for the first time, but the rehearsal was bound to tell me whether everything with which my pupil has given us such pleasure in the drawing room, the tone and beauty of the voice, the power and depth of emotional expression and the interpretative ability, was combined with the assurance of expression which is essential on the stage. Your dear daughter fulfilled all my expectations in that respect, time will take care of what she as yet lacks: experience and further study. I regard Pauline as one of the most gifted and artistically sensitive singers of recent years and she is now on the way to reinforce her talent with the professional training without which nobody can have a great and successful career. (17 April 1892)

She made more appearances at concerts in Weimar, at court and in private salons. Strauss did not tire in his efforts to obtain engagements for her elsewhere; he wrote, for instance, to Gustav Kogel, the conductor of the Frankfurt Museum Concerts, who was planning to perform *Macbeth*:

> Should you ever need a young, interesting . . . soprano, let me urgently recommend my pupil Pauline de Ahna . . . Fräulein de Ahna (who sang Elisabeth at Bayreuth two [*recte* one] years ago) has a very beautiful voice and her singing of Isolde's 'Liebestod' and songs by Liszt and Strauss would certainly meet with your approval. (11 October 1892)

Cosima Wagner had heard Pauline as Saint Elisabeth in Liszt's oratorio in 1890, on the strength of which she decided to try her at Bayreuth in 1891 as a Flower Maiden and the Shepherd Boy in *Tannhäuser*. She wrote to Strauss, asking 'Will you take on the Shepherd with her, in the way we have agreed the part should be sung? The training must be there, but absolutely imperceptible.' She also asked him to coach Pauline in the roles of one of the Flower Maidens and one of the esquires in *Parsifal*. (12 August 1890) Strauss had presented his pupil at Wahnfried in June 1890. 'Wahnfried is giving Paulinchen a quite remarkable impression of herself, it is quite outside her previous experience', he wrote to Hanna. (18 June 1890) In 1891 and again in 1894, Pauline sang Elisabeth in *Tannhäuser* at Bayreuth, alternating with Elisa Wiborg in the part, and in the same two festivals she also sang one of the solo Flower Maidens. Her Bayreuth début was well reviewed in the *Münchner Neueste Nachrichten*: 'The youthful singer acts with the most graceful poetry, and her singing is nobly expressive, especially in the third act.' But she did not seem to have quite all the grandeur and brilliance desirable.

Shortly after one of Strauss's attempts to obtain a guest appearance for Pauline, this time in Kassel (10 March 1891), there was a crisis in their relationship, apparently because the pupil decided to assert her own independence. At the end of March Pauline sang the Angel Gabriel in Lassen's music for *Faust* and at one point – it emerges from the diary which she and her mother took turns in writing – she came in a bar too soon. Possibly she paid more attention to Lassen's advice than Strauss liked. At all events, he wrote her the following letter:

> Most respected Fräulein,
> By all appearances you are now so set on going your own way that my presence and the influence it inevitably exercises could only seem a burden to you; I regret therefore that I must gratefully decline your kind invitation both today and in the future, and I remain with best wishes, yours most sincerely, Richard Strauss. (2 April 1891)

A crisis of a different kind arose in January 1892, and this time Strauss was to blame. He described the situation to his father, explaining that he had had to turn down offers of guest conducting engagements in Berlin, Leipzig and Heidelberg, because he had to stay at his post in Weimar, which had become a hotbed of intrigue after he had been foolish enough to advise Pauline de Ahna to resign; he had hoped, by this, to trump the 'Stavenhagen–Lassen clique' which was riding high at that time, after Bronsart had decided not to cast Pauline as Elisabeth in a revival of *Tannhäuser*, for fear that Frau Stavenhagen (Agnes Denis) would leave.

> Unfortunately I, and Brandt too, overestimated the Grand Duke's regard for Fräulein de Ahna, things blew up in our

> faces last Sunday, and Bronsart, without a word of warning, engaged a first-rate, ultra-dramatic singer (a kind of Ternina, mezzo-soprano). Now that Fräulein de Ahna has withdrawn her resignation, with which Bronsart is in agreement so far, and the matter is to that extent repaired, the prospects are almost good, because the new singer will hardly ever collide with Fräulein de Ahna, and Bronsart, with the accomplished fact of having three sopranos on his hands all of a sudden, spoke to one of them of not renewing Stavenhagen's contract from next year. (21 January 1892)

Father Strauss's response to this tale was to ask, with good reason, 'Why will you always try to go head first through a brick wall?' Again a disagreement arose between Richard and Pauline; having learned of it from General de Ahna, Franz Strauss wrote to his son to express his deep regret and the sincere hope that they would soon be reconciled:

> So, dear Richard, do it to please me and put things straight again . . . Fräulein de Ahna seems to be rather given to over-exciting herself, and a man of good breeding can always allow some latitude to a lady of that kind, without lowering himself. Also I am sure she is the singer who will come closest to realizing your intentions.

On this occasion also peace was restored.

The fact that Pauline was not invited to sing at Bayreuth in 1892 was one of the reasons for the abrupt deterioration in Strauss's relations with Wahnfried in March of that year. On 13 March 1893 Pauline de Ahna's contract with the Weimar Court Theatre was renewed on better terms.

Strauss's illness in May 1891

We shall come to Pauline's performances in Engelbert Humperdinck's *Hänsel und Gretel* and in Strauss's first opera *Guntram* later. Her favourite role was and remained Elsa in *Lohengrin*. The opportunity to take part in the Bayreuth Festival in 1891 was of major importance for her career. Strauss, too, took part in the festival again that year, but only as repetiteur, coaching the soloists, and as musical assistant. Cosima would not allow him to conduct in the theatre because he had fallen ill with pneumonia in May – for six days he had lain in hospital in danger of his life.

He went to convalesce in the house of his uncle Georg Pschorr in Feldafing for three weeks. While there he still vainly nurtured the hope – according to Pauline – of being allowed to conduct *Parsifal* and *Tannhäuser* at Bayreuth. He wrote to Cosima, in the hope of assuring her of his recovery: 'From that day forth my convalescence has proceeded apace in the seven-league boots with which Friend Ritter so kindly shod me in his verses.' (6 June 1891) He also told her of his good resolutions – to give up smoking cigarettes for the time being and to alter his way of life completely – and signed himself 'dying of longing for Bayreuth'. After he was out of danger Cosima had written to Houston Stewart Chamberlain: 'When I see you I shall tell you all about this remarkable man [Strauss], who for strength and sureness in our art has no rival. He is not quite as great as [Heinrich von] Stein, but it would have been a great blow to me to have lost him.' (24 May 1891)

It gave Strauss particular pleasure when Cosima and her daughter Eva came to visit him in Feldafing, where she also met her husband's one-time bitter foe, Franz Strauss. The old enmity was forgotten: Cosima Wagner strolled around the garden on Father Strauss's arm.

Strauss wrote to her again from Feldafing on 12 June. He was pining for redemption in the purgatory of convalescence, he felt like Merlin, who looked on the hedge of flowering white-thorn as the walls of a tower in which he was incarcerated. 'The beautiful green trees around my uncle's garden look like prison walls to me and the most beautiful panorama of mountains and the most glorious view seem to mock me as I think of the view from the Festival Hill.' This time he signed himself 'most tractable and most in need of instruction'. On 20 June, when he had had to give up hope of being in Bayreuth in time for the start of rehearsals, he wrote to her again, beginning the letter: '9 o'clock in the morning, in Bayreuth at this moment the first rehearsal for *Tannhäuser* is starting: while my fingers tremble with impatience I must sit here and send you a medical report. Isn't that frightful?' The doctor had said his lungs were in excellent condition, only he was anaemic and undernourished; nevertheless he had permission to go to Bayreuth on 1 July. After the consultation he had taken up Cornelius's *Der Cid* to help his recovery; it had pleased him enormously in the greater part of Act I, and throughout the whole of Act II: 'What a pity that the librettist totally bungled the third act and the listener is denied the tragic ending which he thinks inevitable after the way the first two acts develop.'

The impatience with which he looked forward to recovery is also given words in a letter he wrote to Alexander Ritter while he was still in hospital:

> I am to relax mentally now, am I? Dear uncle Ritter, if I am to do so, you will have to instruct me how yourself when I come to Munich, or Feldafing as the case may be. How am I supposed to banish my thoughts, which performed half acts of *Tristan* entirely from memory in the very first days of my convalescence?

Ritter visited Strauss in Feldafing on the eve of his birthday (11 June), bearing a gift from Cosima, who celebrated the occasion with Pauline and Zeller in Bayreuth. *Tristan* was uppermost in Strauss's thoughts. With *Rienzi* already in hand, his principal ambition now was to present *Tristan* for the first time in Weimar, in spite of the inadequate forces at his disposal. He wrote to his uncle Carl Hörburger from Feldafing, saying that his illness had done him the world of good and he was fitter and fresher than ever before. When he at last got to Bayreuth (where he met Romain Rolland for the first time) he wrote to his parents, assuring them too that he was perfectly well and healthy, but in spite of that Frau Wagner absolutely refused to allow him to conduct that year:

> She says she would be so worried and would not be easy in her mind listening to a note conducted by me. She says the doctors have written to her that I need to be spared as much as possible and suchlike nonsense and that is why she is so fearfully worried. Although I'm not conducting, I'm treated like M[ottl] and L[evi], eat luncheon and dinner with the Wagner family, and am cared for and watched over like a small child. I must console myself with the thought of next year. (7 July 1891)

There is no reason to doubt the sincerity of Cosima's concern for Strauss's health, but she may also have been influenced by considerations of Levi's and Mottl's position. This seems the more probable because in the following year she again opposed Strauss's wish to conduct, which unleashed a serious crisis, in view of the letter she had written to him on 25 August 1891, asking whether he would not like to move to Bayreuth and become her 'personal

Kapellmeister'. But we shall return to that crisis, which was documented in their correspondence.

Strauss spent Christmas Eve 1891 at Wahnfried as Cosima's guest, and they had a long discussion about the question of who should conduct what at the 1892 festival. Strauss told his sister that Mottl had been very charming and declared himself ready to step down in favour of Strauss, for whatever works Strauss wanted; Richter and Levi, however, had insisted on the letter of their contracts. (28 December 1891)

It was also on the occasion of the Christmas visit that Frau Wagner persuaded Strauss to write an article about his impressions of *Tannhäuser*, which had been presented at Bayreuth for the first time in 1891, in the Paris version. The article was published in *Bayreuther Blätter* in 1892 (15:4), under the rubric 'a letter from a German conductor'. After writing a draft version of it, Strauss wrote to his father on 3 January 1892 that he didn't know whether it was any use or not; as yet it was 'infernally crude', to which his father replied:

> As for the article . . . I beg you most sincerely, avoid all forms of crudeness. There is no point in being crude, you only do more harm than good. Surely the purpose of your article is to create a favourable attitude towards Bayreuth, but the way you have set about it you will only achieve the opposite. If you do it that way you will cause offence in every quarter, only make yourself more enemies than before, harm the cause you want to assist.

Strauss listened to this good advice. The finished product was still far from bland, but the accent was on the positive achievements of the Bayreuth production:

> If I survey my memories of last year's production of *Tannhäuser* at Bayreuth as a whole, I find that in all of them the common characteristic of the indelible impression which it made upon me is the *absolute stylistic perfection* of the execution of the score of *Tannhäuser*. This rare *agreement between the dramatic and the musical aspects*, achievable only on the basis of the *strictest observance of the Meister's wishes*, ruled out in advance the possibility of any form of arbitrary interpretation, from any source whatever, and by the act of restraining arbitrary interpretation (always coupled with lack of understanding), it bestowed on the whole performance the *high dignity* and the *gripping simplicity* which ought to be the ultimate goal of every truly artistic presentation.

Tristan in Weimar

Secret study of the score as a schoolboy, repeated hearings of the work in Munich in youth and in his first three-year term on the music staff of the Court Opera, meant that Strauss knew *Tristan und Isolde* intimately, and had already established his view of it when he assisted in the rehearsals of the work in Bayreuth in 1889. As a result, greatly though he admired Mottl's interpretation, he was still capable of some critical reservations about it, as he told his father: 'Mottl conducted *Tristan* very beautifully except for some excessively fast tempos, which, extraordinarily enough, were the wish of Frau Wagner.' (12 July 1889)

In May 1891, while convalescing at Feldafing, he went through the score working out in the minutest detail the dynamic nuances that would be necessary in performance in a theatre where, unlike Bayreuth, the pit was neither sunken nor covered, having regard to the right total effect of the work as *drama*. While he was so engaged he wrote to Arthur Seidl, whom he had persuaded to talk about *Tristan* to the branch of the Wagner-Verein which he had founded in Weimar: 'Dying is probably not so bad, but I would like to conduct *Tristan* first.'

The work placed quite unusual demands on the Weimar company. With Fritz Brandt as the producer, Strauss threw himself into the task of preparation with the utmost energy and irrepressible enthusiasm. Letters to his father and to Cosima Wagner plot the course of the production, not the least remarkable feature of which was that it was to be done without cuts. He wrote to Franz Strauss on 5 October 1891:

> Yesterday I rehearsed *Tristan* [Act] I with the whole orchestra for the first time, it's going very well already and even though the rehearsals are very painstaking and precise, with all the details being worked out in the most meticulous manner, the orchestra almost seem to enjoy it. How times change! My nuances are proving to be capital, there is no point now where the singer is swamped.

And on 17 October he wrote to Frau Wagner:

> The opposite of what I feared in Bayreuth has come to pass. Instead of being thoroughly dissatisfied, I am delighted by the least good, or good-intentioned, thing that we bring off

artistically. What really made me ill last winter was an immense longing for the ideal in dramatic presentation; that was what made me press the administrators of the theatre here more and more, in the hope of reaching simply that which I believe I can more or less reach. But in Bayreuth this summer that ideal was realized so wonderfully and gloriously that I have found again the right yardstick by which to measure the very different world of ordinary theatres and, luxuriating in the memory of the festival, I am tolerably contented with my profession, conducting *Zauberflöte* while being obliged not to have conducted *Tannhäuser* [in Bayreuth] yet.

The fact that, notwithstanding, I shall conduct *Tristan* here does not seem to me to embody any contradiction with what I have just said, for the way in which I have approached *Tristan* for Weimar – rightly, I believe – will make it a '*Tristan* in dramatic vocal score', which it has never entered my head to compare with Bayreuth, where *Tristan* is performed in its original form. Perhaps you will laugh me out of court, dearest lady, but since you have given me leave to tell you everything that occupies me you will not scold your 'Expression' for writing something silly. Truly: as a result of my thorough-going revision of the nuances of the orchestral score, the complete relinquishment of every massed effect, the meticulous working out of all the technical details, which even the orchestra enjoyed doing, the orchestral writing has acquired something intimate, like chamber music, and the absence of the score's attractions gives it a unique attraction. Perhaps you think it all sounds like the private amusement of a poor hack of a Kapellmeister, but the good artistic endeavour in it has given me so many moments of happiness, which I am sure you will not begrudge me.

The première took place in Weimar on 17 January 1892; Strauss wrote to Bayreuth again a few days beforehand:

The *Tristan* rehearsals have given me the greatest pleasure up till now, since all the people concerned have applied themselves to realizing their colossal tasks as well as possible with the utmost diligence and true dedication, and the results we have achieved so far are really (relatively speaking of course) remarkable. Zeller is excellent, I would never have believed that Frau Naumann would still be capable of stirring her old theatrical jog-trot into a respectable little gallop, Bucha's Marke is really very exciting, Brangäne and Kurwenal likewise do their very best. We have had gigantic *Arrangierproben*, Weimar has never seen the like

> before and the whole town is talking of them. For the first time I have been able to see the great gifts Fritz Brandt has for direction, and what colossal energy he possesses. What he has achieved compels my greatest respect and admiration, even though we've had some first-class rows, since he lacks something of the sense of simplicity in execution that I have learned in Bayreuth. The drastic expression he wants seems to me to be thoroughly mistaken, especially in the interpretation of Isolde (the ironic parts in Act I). In this respect Brandt goes much further than I ever did in my wildest days; and now I am tamer than I used to be. We have managed to come to an agreement in most cases, and where I have not been able to prevail with my view and he is mistaken, in my opinion, nevertheless everything he does stems from a truthful and honest sensitivity, so that one can accept it, even if it is flawed. At all events, I am more than happy to have him here, and if I am not always allowed to be right in the end, I remind myself that I too have an obstinate, swollen head which is happy when it gets its own way. (12 January 1892)

Cosima replied to her 'dear Expression' on 22 January:

> Well, how was it? I am very interested indeed! I can very easily imagine your differences with Brandt and I am grateful to you for insisting on the Bayreuth principle of simplicity. If Brandt knew that originally in Karlsruhe an Isolde was wanted who would be a young girl who did not yet know love, his conception would probably be different. The danger now, when we perceive nothing but unreason in the German theatre, is that we shall apply only reason to art, and the whole daemonium will be completely destroyed. Yet this daemonium – if it exists at all – needs nothing but education. You should hold the Ludwigs-Gymnasium in high honour, I cannot repeat it often enough. A sure sense of proportion is attained through the capacity for methodical thought, which our friend lacks, for all his other gifts, and you may rejoice that you possess it.

Strauss wrote accounts of the first performance to both his father and to Cosima. He wrote home on 21 January 1892:

> The performance of *Tristan* was wonderful; the orchestra of the greatest refinement and elasticity, the staging done by Brandt as beautifully as it could be without any money, and all the singers excellent . . . In spite of some things on which I disagreed with him, Brandt proved himself a superb producer, the performance

> was thoroughly unified and aroused the greatest enthusiasm. Brandt and I took a call after the first act, and after the third, and I look back on our great deed with the greatest satisfaction: the Weimar première of *Tristan*, without a cut and using the resident forces.

The corresponding letter to Cosima is dated 23 January:

> The great event actually did take place last Sunday without mishap: the Weimar première of *Tristan*, using the resident forces and without a cut. Within the limitations of the means at our disposal, it was an excellent performance of this glorious work and it aroused a tempest of enthusiasm among the audience and the artists, it was as if the wonderful work raised every one of those taking part to a height far above his normal capabilities. I was really pleased with the orchestra; they played with exceptional finesse, very free and elastic, so that my *alla breve* could respond as I wished to every modification on the singer's part . . . Brandt laboured under a few dramaturgical errors, which I couldn't talk him out of and which I'll tell you about by word of mouth, but in spite of them he worked wonders. With each single singer he read the part through at least a dozen times, explaining it, demonstrating how it should be played, and proving himself an outstanding artist. In general, almost all the poetic intentions were clearly represented on the stage, the best proof of that being the enthusiasm of the audience, the presentation had an overall unity, the sets very happily contrived, in short, for Weimar it was quite superb and I am more than happy.
>
> Now I've conducted *Tristan* for the first time, and it was the most wonderful day of my life!

Strauss paid so much attention to the dynamic nuances of the score in order to ensure the greatest possible degree of audibility of the text wherever it is essential to the understanding of the drama – above all in the first act. The singer was not to be degraded 'to a mere mouth-opener'. Experience taught him later that 'no restraining of the orchestral volume in the great polyphonic symphonies of the second act of *Tristan* and the third of *Siegfried* can transmit to the listener the enjoyment of the poet's words'.[13]

The *Tristan* prelude enjoyed a privileged place in Strauss's concert-hall repertory throughout his career. The American conductor Sidney S. Bloch, who played under his direction for several years as a violinist with the Berlin Opera orchestra, summed up the impression his performance left on all who ever heard it: 'I have never before or since heard the Prelude to *Tristan and Isolde* as interpreted by him: he attained the highest conceivable tension. He made it an absolutely new work of art.'[14] The source of Strauss's interpretation can be traced. In the letter Cosima Wagner wrote to him on 22 January 1892, enquiring about the Weimar première, she asked: 'Have you heard the prelude of *Tristan und Isolde* under the direction of Herr von Bülow? And if not, could you hear it? You will learn later why I ask the question and make the request.' Strauss replied: 'I do not know [Bülow's] conducting of the *Tristan* prelude, and unfortunately I do not at present foresee an opportunity to hear it, but if one comes along, I shall certainly do as you wish.' (14 March 1892) It is not hard to guess what lay behind Cosima's last sentence. It must have been a reference to Bülow's interpretation of the prelude. If her wish had been solely that Richard Strauss, as a disciple of Wagner, should make himself acquainted with Bülow's interpretation so that he could adopt it as a model, she would certainly have formulated the sentence differently. *Tristan* was conducted at Bayreuth at that date by Felix Mottl, and we know that his interpretation of the prelude (which is preserved in the markings in the Peters edition of the score) was fundamentally different from that of Bülow, who had, however, conducted the very first performance of the work under Wagner's supervision. Was it Cosima's intention to warn the young Strauss against Bülow's interpretation? At all events, whatever her wishes may have been, Strauss made Bülow's interpretation his own. One of his blue notebooks contains the entry, not previously published: 'My performance of the *Tristan* prelude (ebb and flow) is yet another thing that I owe to teaching given me by Bülow by word of mouth.' It is not certain when this teaching was imparted, but it had probably already happened before the Weimar première of 1892, for on 18 February 1891 Hermann Levi, who must have heard a performance of the *Tristan* prelude in Weimar wrote to Strauss: 'Your *Tristan* prelude gave me great joy yesterday. I have not heard it so beautifully played since 1871 (under Wagner), for extraordinarily enough this is the one piece that Mottl has never been really successful in.' Mottl's tempo markings – 'Do not hurry!' 'Never hurry! If anything, broader!' 'Remain *a tempo*!' 'Slow down very gradually' – are completely incompatible with the Bülow–Strauss conception of 'ebb and flow', embodied in a powerful surge in the tempo and a flowing re-establishment of the pace (which is to be associated with Wagner's marking 'gradually holding back slightly in pace' – 'Allmählich im Zeitmass etwas zurückhaltend'). The difference was discussed illuminatingly by Alexander Berrsche in a review originally published in 1936:

> Strauss conducted the *Tristan* prelude in the grand manner of one drawing in and letting out a single breath, which is said to go back to Hans von Bülow. In the past I had doubts about this interpretation, but today I cannot reiterate them with quite all my former confidence. There is a marking in Wagner's score which gives one pause for thought, at the least, if one reads it carefully. This is the instruction 'belebend' ['getting livelier'] half a bar before the onset of A major, or more precisely, the exact point at which it ceases to apply. All conductors except Strauss (but including Mottl and Fischer) have always slowed the tempo again as early as the middle of the first bar in A major. But according to Wagner's marking the music should not begin to slow until the beginning of the second bar. Strauss is the only one to observe that exactly and the effect is stupefying, downright revolutionary. Correctly played, the one and a half bars are revealed as belonging to a totally different expressive type from the one to which we are accustomed, as describing exactly the same shape in miniature that Strauss's interpretation does over the whole piece. There is something particularly compelling about this realization, because it does not rest on an analogy but arises out of the direct organic evidence and can be grasped, so to speak, physiognomically. The proof of it is to be found in the different interpretation of earlier great conductors. They were too good musicians not to have recognized the symptomatic and decisive character of this apparently very small difference in interpretation. They departed from Wagner's marking because they sensed the consequences to which following it exactly would lead: to Strauss's interpretation, of which they were afraid.[15]

Mottl conducted *Tristan* at Bayreuth. Was his interpretation inspired by Cosima Wagner and recommended to other conductors by her?

A review of the Weimar *Tristan* which appeared in the Leipzig weekly *Musikalisches Wochenblatt* (28 January 1892) mentions that there were no fewer than seventeen rehearsals with the orchestra, and remarks:

> If many aspects of the performance revealed an astonishing increase in artistic capabilities, thanks are owing to the invigorating, inspiring influence of our brilliant conductor Richard Strauss, who devoted countless rehearsals to instructing the artists in the essence of their roles and who was really the soul of this excellent performance. He began by modifying the dynamic markings in a score intended for performance by a covered orchestra sufficiently for the singers' audibility not to suffer in a theatre with an open pit.

Macbeth (II)

The concerts he conducted in Weimar gave Strauss the chance to promote his own works, as well as Wagner's and Liszt's. He had performed *Aus Italien* in Weimar before taking up his official post there (30 April 1888). After *Don Juan* (11 November 1889), which though not to everyone's taste, was soon launched on a triumphal career through the world's concert halls and was conducted by its composer himself in Berlin and Frankfurt in the following year, it was the turn of *Macbeth* to receive its first performance in Weimar (13 October 1890). The tone poem was of course inspired by Shakespeare's play, but Strauss did not provide a programme; in the score the first subject (D minor) is marked 'Macbeth' and the second subject (A major) 'Lady Macbeth', though there is an additional reference to the text here:

> Hie thee hither,
> That I may pour my spirits in thine ear;
> And chastise with the valour of my tongue
> All that impedes thee from the golden round,
> Which fate and metaphysical aid doth seem
> To have thee crowned withal.

Strauss's intention of putting *Macbeth* in the same concert as Beethoven's *Eroica* dismayed his father, who urged him to reconsider so foolhardy an enterprise. Strauss's reply was addressed to his mother the day after the performance took place: the advice had unfortunately arrived too late, the programme had already been printed, and 'anyway, the risk paid off and I enjoyed yesterday's concert devilishly, as I've seldom enjoyed anything else'. Bronsart,

Lassen and a few others had looked taken aback, but remarkably enough the whole orchestra had been genuinely enthusiastic. 'There were just a few people there who recognized that behind the dissonances something other than sheer joy in dissonance for its own sake was at work, namely an idea.' (To Alexander Ritter, 19 October 1890)

We have already seen that Strauss revised the score after this first performance, acting as much on his own second thoughts as on his father's advice. As early as 10 October he told his father that he had already revised the scoring of four pages, but then in a letter of 14 October he wrote that though he had enjoyed the performance there were some things in the thematic working which might be clearer and that he was thinking of rescoring some passages. On 23 October he told Spitzweg that he considered the form and content of the work perfectly successful, but that he was now going to rescore it, and repeated this, in almost exactly the same words, in another letter written on the same day to Franz Wüllner. By 6 November he was able to tell his sister: 'I've already rescored almost thirty pages of *Macbeth*, a task which I'm thoroughly enjoying; as there wasn't enough brass in it I am adding a part for bass trumpet, which is rendering capital service.' He tried out a new seating arrangement for the orchestra at the end of September 1890, but it proved to need far more room than they had, so, as he told his father, he would have to press for more space before he could think of the new arrangement. He included a sketch to show what he had in mind. (2 October 1890) He was still at his desk, 'diligently rescoring *Macbeth*', in the middle of November. (To Thuille, 19 November 1890) The definitive version of the score, which Strauss dedicated to his 'greatly honoured and dear friend Alexander Ritter', was not completed until 4 March 1891.

Iphigenia in Tauris

It was at this time that Eduard Lassen, 'flown with wine', volunteered to let Strauss conduct *Das Rheingold* and *Siegfried* in his place (they were not performed at all in the end), and in return to conduct Strauss's new version of *Iphigenia in Tauris*. In the event it was 1900 before this was performed in Weimar, however, when Strauss had long since moved to Berlin.

Strauss had finished this new adaptation of Gluck's opera 'for the

German stage' in short score in September 1890. He wrote about it to the publisher Adolph Fürstner a few months later:

> Taking Richard Wagner's version of Gluck's *Iphigenia in Aulis* as my model, I have completed a revision of the same composer's *Iphigenia in Tauris*, which I hope to see performed here next season. My revision consists of a completely new translation, actually a new text in parts (with some elements taken from Goethe's play), especially in the first act, in which the order of the scenes has been entirely changed, and the last act, for which I have composed a new ending, as well as changes in the scoring, to bring it into line with modern requirements at least to some extent, etc., etc. My only purpose in writing now is to enquire whether you might be interested in publishing this version, which has given new life to a beautiful work? I am sure we would be able to agree on terms, and I am ready and willing to send you the score, the piano score and the libretto for your inspection, if you were interested. (18 April 1891)

Fürstner agreed to publish the new edition, though it was 1895 before it appeared. Strauss also sent a copy of it to Cosima Wagner for her approval, which it received. She sent him a 'wonderful letter', saying how she had gone through his *Iphigenia* with Julius Kniese and how highly she esteemed it. (Strauss to his father, 15 October 1891) Max Steinitzer convincingly demonstrated that Strauss's decision to retain the verse-metre of the original text in his translation, while abandoning rhyme, was as problematical as his re-arrangement of the scenes in three acts instead of four, and as his new ending.[16] The Weimar Court Theatre, as has been said, did not venture on presenting it until 9 June 1900, long after Strauss's departure. It was conducted by Rudolf Krzyzanowski and aroused little interest then or since. Only a few other theatres – including the Zürich Municipal Theatre – have ever staged it.

Tod und Verklärung (II)

Tod und Verklärung, by contrast, was a great success. The first performance was conducted by Strauss at a meeting of the Allgemeiner Deutscher Musikverein in Eisenach, on 21 June 1890. After a rehearsal he wrote to his sister: '"Death and Transfiguration" has dealt death to everything else, the players were flattened and flabbergasted, it made a remarkable impression.' (18 June 1890) He conducted it in Weimar on 12 January 1891, at the third subscription concert of the season, in a programme in which Mozart's 'Jupiter' Symphony was the principal item. After the first performance in Berlin (23 February 1891), again conducted by the composer, Bülow did not say a single word about it to Strauss, 'for he simply didn't understand it and was *that* honest, at least', Strauss wrote to Hanna; in every other respect he had been very friendly, 'he has become very *calm*'. (24 February 1891) The repeat performance at the Berlin Philharmonic's popular concert (24 February) was attended by Cosima Wagner, who told Strauss that he was 'by far the most talented of them all', a remark by which she avoided committing herself to an opinion on the work itself. Her praise of his technique hides a negative response to the work's intellectual and spiritual content. Strauss appears not to have noticed, since he wrote to Hanna that Cosima Wagner had been completely won over by the performance; previously she had not thought much of him as a composer, but now, or so he had been told by Klindworth, she was 'quite astonished by the colossal technique etc.' (25 February 1891) On the occasion of another performance which she heard in Würzburg in March 1894, Cosima wrote to Prince Ernst zu Hohenlohe-Langenberg, complaining of the contorted aridity of the ideas and the sovereign command of the technical means, a combination which distressed her. She added that Strauss had conducted the piece himself and had produced quite astonishing results from the players, who were students from the local conservatory.[17]

Hans Richter took up the cause of Strauss's earliest tone poems with dedication. When he conducted the first Viennese performance of *Tod und Verklärung* on 15 January 1895, Eduard Hanslick wrote a remarkably prophetic review, which included the sentence: 'The nature of [Strauss's] talent is really such as to point him in the direction of music drama.'[18]

Strauss wrote to Eugen Spitzweg about printing the score:

> I am rather embarrassed as to what to ask you for *Tod und Verklärung*; since the work is the latest and most mature thing I have written, and since I do not expect to compose anything more for a while, as I am turning my back on absolute music altogether, in order to seek my salvation in drama, therefore I should like a tidy little sum for it, which I need on my damn small salary, but, since it's you, only half what I would ask another publisher for.

> Take your time to think over what you might be able to offer me for it, perhaps we could come to some arrangement whereby you pay me in instalments spread over three or four years; that way it will last me longer.
>
> I can't and won't ask you straight out for a particular sum, since I don't know how our shares stand, and the confounded thing about my business is that one can never be sure that it won't take ten years for something to start showing a profit and I really wouldn't want to do you any injury. (19 November 1890)

Spitzweg paid him 1600 marks. Strauss was right in his prediction that *Tod und Verklärung* would be his last symphonic work for quite a long time; five and a half years passed before he finished *Till Eulenspiegel* – and that had originally been planned as an opera. Strauss did not return to any of his earlier works while he was in Weimar, with one exception: when the tragedy *Zriny* was staged to celebrate the centenary of its writer, the romantic poet and playwright Theodor Körner (1791–1813), the performance was preceded by Strauss's Concert Overture in C minor.

Differences with Cosima Wagner

The first crisis in Strauss's relations with Wahnfried, which has already been mentioned, broke in March 1892. It began with Strauss expressing his annoyance at the fact that Pauline de Ahna and Heinrich Zeller had not been asked back to Bayreuth for the 1892 festival; the 'disgraceful' Max Alvary was to sing, yet Zeller was to be 'barred from the interpretation of a great role on the grounds of lack of voice', while the identical deficiency did not prevent Elisa Wiborg's engagement. That Fräulein de Ahna, 'of whose great gifts I grow continually more convinced, in spite of everything', was not to attend the festival, although she was 'vocally adequate', while 'that miserable ham-actor' Alvary, in spite of his boundless and indisputable lack of talent, was once again to be awarded the undeserved honour of appearing at Bayreuth, because he had 'at least a little bit of voice', was incomprehensible to Strauss.

> Forgive me, dearest lady, for speaking my mind like this, but I feel that I must not conceal from you any of the foolish thoughts and ideas I have concerning our holy cause, even at the risk of making you seriously angry with me, as last summer . . . In my

> opinion the strong and weak points of the two Elisabeths we had last year exactly complement each other, so that you cannot very well invite one and exclude the other; if a new Elisabeth appears, who really is better than Wiborg and de Ahna, then drop *both*, naturally, but if that is not the case then you need have no qualms about allowing both of them to sing the part again. Exactly the same applies to Zeller and Winkelmann. I must confess that it *hurts me personally* (that is really neither here nor there, but since I am making a clean breast of things for once, I ought to mention everything, if I cannot be completely honest I am not worthy to work for the exalted and glorious cause or to possess the happiness of your approval) to be asked to assist in the direction of the festival at the very moment when I am so cruelly disowned by you, most honoured, gracious lady, in the persons of two of my closest artistic protégés, with whom the object of all my pains has really been to train them *solely for Bayreuth.* (14 March 1892)

He went on to remind her of the precise occasion in the previous summer, in the Hofgarten in Bayreuth, when she had told him she would have both Elisabeths back, and he also complained about his situation in Weimar:

> If I did not occasionally get away as I did recently to Berlin and two days ago to Leipzig, in order to refresh myself, I should be in a really sad way and it is often very hard for me to stick it out. It is at times like these that I summon up my glorious memories of Bayreuth and reflect that salvation is to be found somewhere after all.

He had more or less finished his libretto, he wrote, and was getting down to writing the music, following Ritter's advice. He also told her of the 'glorious impression' Bülow had made on him with his interpretation of the great *Leonore* Overture and Berlioz's *Béatrice et Benédict* Overture and *Harold en Italie*. This was also the letter in which he replied with a cautious negative to her enquiry as to whether he had ever heard Bülow conduct the *Tristan* prelude.

Having received an answer from Cosima to this letter of 14 March, he wrote again on 28 March, objecting to some of her arguments: 'You write that . . . if you now invited Zeller to sing Tannhäuser, *it would look* as if you thought he was *the* Tannhäuser. Does it follow that Alvary is *the* Tristan? Is Winkelmann *the* Tannhäuser?' She had also told him that she had decided he should take the rehearsals for Hans Richter's *Meistersinger* performances, and that she was thinking of letting him conduct the last two; Strauss was bitterly disappointed and declared that he was not prepared to take the rehearsals, and then to be given two performances only after 'the great Hans Richter has had the pleasure of ruining again all that I have built up in those rehearsals':

> Not from wounded vanity, I'm a stranger to that, but because I know very well that I shall not achieve anything if I am 'squeezed in' as a stop-gap. I'm a newcomer in Bayreuth and need time and a chance to make myself at home in the work entrusted to me slowly and in collaboration with all the people involved [Strauss had not yet conducted *Die Meistersinger*]; preparing a work for somebody else is beyond me, my nature's not pliable enough for that.

He asked her to forgo his assistance, 'for I am not cut out for the role of a plodding rehearsal-taker, as played by the rank and file of repetiteurs'. He felt it was unnecessary to assure her of his devotion to the Bayreuth cause, he would give everything he possessed to help it, but he would have to occupy a position there where he would be able to accomplish something worthwhile. He was nobody's 'stand-in', he wrote, but an obstinate mule. He begged her, if she seriously regarded him as a fit person to conduct at the Bayreuth festival, to declare the same publicly and to entrust him with one of the works officially, with all the rights and obligations entailed. His demand seems justified, not least by the *Tristan* which he had conducted in Weimar in the previous January, to loud critical acclaim. Cosima's reply is not known, but there is another letter from Strauss in which he confesses abjectly that an evil demon must have guided his pen in his last letter. Cosima's reproaches, to the effect that personal ambition, vanity and a sense that he had been passed over had spoken from the letter, touched him to the quick and he now declared himself ready to serve the Bayreuth cause 'as a lamp-cleaner or orchestral attendant' if need be. Whatever Cosima wanted him to do at Bayreuth he would try to do superlatively well, but if Richter was to conduct the dress rehearsal and most of the public performances, then he would 'really and truly not' be able to do his best; Richter was his complete opposite; if it were Mottl it would be a quite different matter. Then he asked if it was at all possible for him to have *Tristan* or *Tannhäuser* all to himself, as works where he would be able to stand on his own feet. In that case, he would be happy to take rehearsals for *Meistersinger*, without expecting to conduct any of the performances. A letter he wrote on 18 April indicates that Cosima offered him *Tristan* in response to this plea but she then appears to have withdrawn the offer and once more to have offered him only the last two performances of *Meistersinger*. In despair Strauss refused, for he could not possibly take on responsibility for those performances on the heels of Richter, with whom he had 'not one artistic point of contact'. He was faced with the most difficult choice he had ever had to make in his short life, and for that reason he had turned to his friend Ritter, whose reply he enclosed for Cosima to read. If Richter agreed, he would accept the first two performances of *Meistersinger*, otherwise he asked her to relieve him of any artistic participation in that year's festival at all. (15 May 1892) This time we have Cosima's reply, beginning 'My dear friend': Richter was going to be in London during the rehearsals, and in Vienna on the date of the last two performances, and for that reason the offer she had already made was the only one she could make. Furthermore, she had started working on *Tannhäuser* with Mottl the year before, and she could not begin again at the beginning *now*, and there would be hardly any rehearsals for *Tristan*. The only possibility was a complete re-arrangement of everything, in view of Levi's illness. 'It is possible that we will need a second conductor for *Parsifal*. In that case I would ask Mottl to take on *Parsifal*, *Tannhäuser*, the rehearsals and the last two performances of *Meistersinger*, and give *Tristan* to you.' She also came to Richter's defence and reminded Strauss – in a manner characteristic of her way of referring to Wagner as if he was a supernatural being – that 'it is written of him: "My Hans Richter, doer of the impossible, much tested, who answers for everything"'. And she went on to assure him of her belief that

> each of us here does his best, and should Richter spoil your intentions then I assure you that Others have befouled Mine before now; and should you be vilified, then all I can do is offer my comradeship once again, and so long as I continue to work you too shall continue to conduct here, even though your reputation has been torn to shreds.

Mottl had been more severely criticized for his direction of *Parsifal* than almost any other conductor in history, yet he had continued to conduct the work and would do so again:

In every human being there is a daemon and if yours urges you to leave me then my only wish is that you will do it in good heart, knowing that I shall mourn it deeply but hope that you will feel the better for it, and shall stay your friend and shall once again have perceived that things do not lie in our power and that our best will has but little significance against circumstances . . . Constantly, C. Wagner.

As PS. one further observation, that you have, I think, too monumental a view of things here. I regard a good rehearsal as already in itself a gain for art. It is what I like to call the living aspect, with which there is necessarily also some fouling.

I am worried lest I have been not cordial enough in my letter. But it is now late at night and the day always brings something. Use your knowledge of me to fill in what is lacking. (18 May 1892)

Strauss conveyed his assent in a telegram, as she had asked him to do, and she wrote again two days later:

I believe that this is the right way to do things, my dear Expression, and hope to God that you will not regret it . . . Now let us look forward to a right joyful reunion . . . Receive my greetings, dear, good Expression. You have caused me distress, but who does not and I am glad to bear it when it comes from you . . . Fare you well, greet your good inner self from me; with that I know that I shall always walk in harmony. Most constantly, C. Wagner. (20 May 1892)

It was Cosima Wagner's little joke to address Strauss, the champion of 'music as expression', as 'Expression' and even 'Deep Violet Expression'.

We find a somewhat distorted echo of Strauss's dispute with Frau Wagner in his letters to his parents and sister. There is, for instance, the long letter (in which he also wrote in considerable detail about Bülow's performance of the *Eroica* in Berlin, which had lacked the old 'brusqueness and harshness') written when he was under the impression that she wanted him to conduct *Tristan*:

At present acrimonious controversy between Wahnfried and me. Frau Wagner actually wanted to foist Richter's *Meistersinger* rehearsals and two performances on me. I wrote back very acrimoniously that I wouldn't think of such a thing and in those circumstances I wouldn't go to Bayreuth. That brought a great wailing from Frau Wagner in a letter lamenting my disloyalty.

> Thereupon mighty arguments on my part, why and wherefore and insisting on having a work all to myself. I was infernally vehement and actually won my point. Frau Wagner yielded and will talk to Mottl (only now!) about his letting me have *Tristan*. The whole correspondence was very amusing. Frau Wagner's letters at first full of refusals and reproaches, then offering a few loopholes and finally giving in, I shall have whatever I wish and a grand reconciliation. Frau W's last letter ended thus, word for word: 'I am old, you are young. I will very gladly understand your youth, only it cannot guide my age and its decisions.' How about that? Well, we shall see! (7 April 1892)

Franz Strauss's response to this report throws both his dislike for Bayreuth and also the anti-semitism fuelled by his tense relations with Levi into sharp relief. Writing jointly to Hanna and Richard in Weimar, he said:

> On the matter of conducting at Bayreuth, I could have wished that after his controversy with Frau Wagner Richard would stay away from Bayreuth altogether this year, because accusing him, the loyalest of the loyal, of disloyalty is a bit thick. It looks as though only slaves are wanted in Bayreuth. In my opinion she'd better take Jews, there are enough of them about. My experience has always been that the person who is over-eager to offer his friendship is not valued and I wish with all my heart that Richard does not suffer a sad experience. The first signs of it are already beginning to show. Of course I don't know what his relationship with Bayreuth is at the moment and whether he has already had offers from there, but in my mind's eye I foresee some unpleasantnesses still ahead for him. It would make me very sorry on his account. He really ought to let the Jews get on with it. As I see it, everything points to a greater interest in making money than in purely artistic matters, how else could they prefer a comedian like Alvary again? The whole business looks to me like a kind of Jewry in 'Aryan' clothing.

In the years to come, Father Strauss's prognosis would be shown to have some truth in it. Richard had already put his sister in the picture about the whole business in February: 'I'm not going to make myself available just to take the *Meistersinger* rehearsals for that lazy blighter Richter.' The same letter contains further biting criticism of the tenor Max Alvary, who was very popular with the general public at the time but whose engagement at Bayreuth was a sore point with Strauss. He was undoubtedly right in seeing it as a concession to the public, motivated by a wish to benefit from Alvary's drawing power. He had heard Alvary in Munich as well as at Bayreuth, and now, after the tenor had given some guest performances in Weimar, he gave full rein to his rage:

> I have never seen anything more impudent, disgraceful, untalented and untrue than this Tannhäuser. It was pure knockabout farce, which is of course exactly what the public likes better than anything.
>
> The Grand Duke, at all events, did not care for Alvary; he spoke to me on the subject yesterday, at a soirée at Frau Krousta's, and expressed himself really very perceptively and gratifyingly about my *Tristan* and Zeller and Naumann. The Hereditary Grand Duke, too, who spoke to me the other day when he was riding in the street and expressed his appreciation of the performances of *Tannhäuser*, said he did not like Alvary. (11 February 1892)

The altercation between Cosima Wagner and Strauss was highly characteristic of both of them. Only a short time after it had reached its conclusion, however, Strauss fell ill again, which put an abrupt end to all his Bayreuth plans. From 5 to 10 June a bout of pleurisy kept him in bed in Weimar. He got up sooner than he should have done, in order to conduct Hans Sommer's *Loreley* on 12 June. As he told the Weimar composer Eugen Lindner on 14 June, he found the work 'insanely difficult', but he had to bring it off with five orchestral rehearsals. His health worsened; after a short stay in Schwarzburg he went to Munich where a severe attack of bronchitis forced him to go to Reichenhall for the cure in mid-July, where Pauline de Ahna with her parents and her sister Mädi followed him. Since it was found that the pneumonia of the previous year was not, as had been thought, completely cured, Strauss was obliged to obey his doctors and go south for the winter, as will be narrated in due course.

It was a bitter blow to him to be forced to miss Bayreuth, and he lamented it without restraint in his letters to Frau Wagner. After he had got over the initial shock of the illness, he wrote, he fell to reflecting on his plight. It must be a punishment from heaven for having given her so much trouble during the winter over the matter of what he was to conduct:

> Two performances of *Meistersinger* were not enough for me, I wanted to play the lion too, and now? I am not conducting a note, I do not hear a note, I devote myself to the curing of his

> eminence my health and sit here in Reichenhall, surrounded by Berlin Jews, taking saline baths and drinking whey . . . Ah, dear lady, if I could tell you what is in my heart . . . (14 July 1892)

A week later he was 'despairing and deeply dejected', because at that hour, 8 o'clock in the evening, the festival guests would soon be re-entering the theatre for the third act of *Parsifal*, the first performance for four years.

After hearing of the illness, Bronsart wrote to say he hoped Strauss would return in the autumn fully restored to health 'to wield your victorious baton again, though perhaps *un poco moderato*'. He turned down Strauss's request for an increase in salary and a widening of the scope of his activity, however, since, quite apart from the inroads granting the latter would make in the territory of Lassen, the older and higher-ranking conductor, Strauss had already enlarged his field himself to an unprecedented extent by his own insistent demands. Bronsart exhorted him to come to an arrangement with Lassen:

> Look here, my dear Sträusschen, if the two of you would only agree to look on yourselves as opposing poles, which are nonetheless striving towards the same centre, it would make me as happy as only in my wildest dreams. But if you set up a centrifugal force instead of a centripetal one, then I in the middle get pulled hither and thither and come off very badly indeed. (June 1892)

Bronsart's reference in the same letter to 'Lassen's perhaps somewhat exaggerated calm and objectivity' may nonetheless be interpreted as a concession to Strauss, but his wish to be promoted to the rank of Hofkapellmeister continued to be refused.

Strauss and Bülow: the last years

Alexander Ritter's idolization of Wagner and contempt for Brahms exercised a strong influence on Strauss, and the necessarily harmful effect that this had on his relations with Bülow was only made worse by an article Ritter published in the *Allgemeine Musikzeitung* (6 March 1891) entitled 'Vom Spanisch-Schönen' ('On the Spanish Style of Beauty'), in which Ritter adopted an unambiguously acrimonious attitude towards Bülow's reverence for Brahms and his defection from Wagner and Liszt. Many of Bülow's letters to his wife and his old friend Eugen Spitzweg express the ambivalence of his feelings towards Strauss, such as the declaration to Spitzweg that 'ever since he has turned into an exclusive Bayroutrider and a decided Brahms-Thersites – he has only my most impersonal sympathy, that is, when he produces a beautiful work of art'. (14 January 1891)

It is understandable that Bülow should regard Strauss's all too obvious dependence on Wahnfried and on Ritter with disapproval. But the direction that Strauss was taking as a composer in his symphonic poems also aroused his disquiet, though it did not prevent him taking up his works, and, after initial mistrust of the 'witches' cauldron bubblings' of *Macbeth*, allowing himself to be powerfully affected when Strauss conducted the final version of the work at one of Bülow's Philharmonic Concerts in Berlin on 29 February 1892. Even before the performance, during rehearsals he wrote to his wife: 'You know – *Macbeth* – is mad and benumbing for the most part, but *in summo gradu* it's a work of *genius*' (27 February 1892); and after the public rehearsal he wrote to Spitzweg: 'Tidings of great joy . . . Macbeth's success this morning was *colossal*. The audience roared for Strauss four times. The sound of the work, too, was – overwhelming.' (28 February) After Strauss's illness and recovery in May 1891 he wrote to Spitzweg: 'Thank God Strauss is safe! That one has a great future before him, he deserves to live.' And another letter to the publisher shows that Bülow fully recognized Strauss's significance, notwithstanding the conservatism of his own taste. 'Your "Brahms" [i.e. Strauss] towers over your other composers in point of musical training and of imaginative genius – like Munich Railway Station over the one at Ingolstadt.' (The other composers on Spitzweg's list included Alexander Ritter.) Before the Berlin performance of *Macbeth*, Strauss, conscious of his debt of gratitude, wrote a deeply emotional letter to Bülow to thank him for the 'affectionate and kindly attitude' demonstrated by his promoting *Macbeth*:

> I greet this new proof of your benevolence towards me with all the greater joy because your reaction to the change that has taken place in my artistic philosophy since the time when I still had the honour of being directly under your tutelage has necessarily, in these last few years, aroused in me the belief, to my great and sincere distress, that you were no longer so well-disposed towards me personally as once.

He voiced a suspicion that 'base machinations' such as had operated against Bülow himself in Berlin might have had a part in this, and assured Bülow that 'nothing, nothing on this earth ever was or will be capable of slaying or even diminishing my unbounded love, respect and profoundest gratitude'. (30 January 1892) Bülow's answer expressed his sincere pleasure at discovering 'that you believe it worthwhile not to sacrifice our *personal* relations from the Meiningen days to the *objective* difference that has separated us these two years'. He would not budge, he said, from the standpoint of his present artistic opinions and principles, which it had cost him a 'hard, painful and *laborious*' struggle to achieve. 'I shall continue to represent the "Spanish Style of Beauty" without wishing to be, on that account, blind, deaf, unjust towards your shibboleth – pardon me, I do not remember exactly how your friend A. R. [Ritter] phrased it.' In any event, he wrote, he was glad to be able to tell Strauss that the revised version of *Macbeth* had greatly impressed him 'in spite of all its acerbities and the monstrosities of the material', and that he sympathized ' – as one of the species musician – far more with this opus than with its predecessor *T. und V.*', as he found more logic and genius in it. He also congratulated Strauss on his latest exploit as a conductor – the Weimar production of *Tristan*. He signed himself 'Your old admirer who sincerely holds you in high esteem'. (1 February 1892)

The improvement in their relations may have influenced Strauss's decision to go to Berlin again 'in spite of shortage of money' to hear Bülow conduct the Philharmonic in Beethoven's *Eroica* and Choral Symphonies (with Zeller among the soloists) in concerts held on 4 and 5 April. 'Who knows how much longer one will be able to hear something like this, one must stand up and be counted.' (To his father, 24 March 1892) When Bülow heard of Strauss's illness in June 1892 he wrote to him: 'Volcanic natures like your own "worthy" self require somatic revolutions like this from time to time in order to gather new strength for unusual evolutions.' (25 June 1892)

Bülow also remained friendly disposed towards Alexander Ritter, at least to the extent of asking Strauss to convey his good wishes. Less than a year before his death he wrote to Spitzweg:

> Always the most profound good wishes for Strauss, whether near or far [Strauss was in the south]. Would to God I could again become capable of following his development with lively

> sympathy. After *him* [Brahms] by far the most personal, richest personality! All honour to you for having really discovered it, having been the first to recognize it! May God guard his *physis*, then all will be well with his *psyche*. (2 April 1893)

Bülow was already gravely ill and on the point of leaving for Egypt when Strauss called on him for the last time, in Hamburg on 20 January 1894. A few days later Strauss and other friends took their leave of Bülow on the Anhalt Station as he passed through Berlin. Bülow died in Cairo on 12 February. Strauss had written to his family about the last meeting in Hamburg:

> I called on Bülow twice, he showed himself the second time and sat with us for an hour. He is very despondent and weak, but I don't know but what Egypt, where he is off to in ten days time, won't restore him to health. It is a fairy tale that he's become addicted to morphine. Normally he won't see anybody and I was very pleased by the distinction, he was very winning and gave the impression only of a man totally destroyed by pain! (22 January 1894)

A letter written by Bülow's daughter Daniela Thode in reply to a letter of condolence from Strauss confirms the affection with which Bülow thought of the younger man to the very last:

> I must express the thanks of my stricken heart for your words. May God reward you for your feelings for him who no longer suffers among us, whose innocent, great soul is in blissful peace, who loved you and took pleasure in all that you did. When I saw him in Trieste on 2 February he told me about your visit, about your Italian Symphony and how glad he was that you had dedicated it to him, and asked me about your opera. (February 1894)

Strauss was to honour the memory of Bülow for the rest of his life. He wrote the 'Erinnerungen an Hans von Bülow' in 1909 for the Vienna paper *Neue freie Presse*, in which he called him 'the model of all the illuminating virtues of the interpretative artist'. Even in the last years of his life he would still talk about encounters with Bülow as if they had taken place only a short while before, so fresh were they in his memory. The controversy that arose in connection with a concert in Bülow's memory in Hamburg later in February 1894 will be described later.

The daily round in Weimar

The restraints of life in Weimar and the resistance which not only his exclusive cult of Wagner and Liszt but also his 'all too subjective' interpretations of Beethoven met with from his intendant, who was not in fact inherently hostile towards the New German school, led time and time again to tensions which made Strauss discontented and overwrought, but also prompted him to relieve his feelings in ill-considered outbursts about the theatre's 'day-to-day trash'. In spite of all their differences of opinion, Bronsart remained well-disposed towards him, and from time to time Strauss acknowledged as much. For instance, he wrote to his mother on 31 October 1891 that he once more owed Bronsart an apology, for, setting aside his blinkeredness, he was an excellent fellow; Brandt's support '*in puncto* Wagner' would help him to make his peace with Bronsart. But usually such concessions and good resolutions were unable to stand up for long to the daily round in Weimar. He told his sister on 8 June 1892 that he would like to get away from there soon – 'otherwise one becomes so settled' – and that he had decided to submit a memorandum to Bronsart before the theatre closed for the summer holiday, in which he would request (1) a salary increase of 100 marks a month, (2) the transfer to him of the direction of *Fidelio*, *Der fliegende Holländer*, *Saint Elisabeth*, the *Ring*, Cornelius's *Der Cid* and *Les Troyens*, on the grounds that 'Lassen probably won't attach too much weight to these works as they don't involve Giessen [the Weimar opera's resident heroic tenor]!!!!', (3) new sets for *Lohengrin*, which had been approved the year before, (4) an official decision about his edition of *Iphigenia in Tauris*, which he had given to Bronsart in the previous November.

> From Bronsart's answer to these four things I shall be able to see how far I can reckon on his cooperation altogether. I've been here three years now and I'm still the second wheel beside that old scheming fool L [Lassen], who always makes the whole theatre dance to Giessen's tune; I'm getting thoroughly fed up with these unwholesome conditions. I shan't react at all to Bronsart's answer, whatever form it takes, even if it's a flat refusal, but shall look round for something else as soon as possible according to how things turn out!

Strauss made several attempts to leave Weimar for some other sphere of activity but none succeeded. Nothing came of his hopes for Karlsruhe (after Mottl's departure) or, later, for Hamburg. He turned down offers that were made him from Schwerin and Mannheim as the terms were not good enough. Occasional visits to Bayreuth, where he was exhorted to stick things out, if anything increased his growing tenseness and dissatisfaction.

His work in the theatre, where he made the utmost demands on himself and on his colleagues, took up so much of his time and energy that he composed only a small number of minor pieces during the first four years in Weimar. Most of these were occasional pieces, such as the quartet for male-voice choir, setting the text on a Swedish match-box, composed for a concert in aid of a Weimar artists' charity, in competition with Eduard Lassen, Hans Sommer and Eugen Lindner. Another was the Fanfare (o. Op. 88A) which he wrote for a gala performance of Wilhelm Iffland's play *Die Jäger*, given in the Weimar Court Theatre on 7 May 1891. The score of the Fanfare was first uncovered in 1972 by Strauss's biographer Ernst Krause, who published an article about it, reproducing two pages of the manuscript, in *Die Opernwelt*, 1 January 1973. A short introductory flourish prefaces a *largo* middle section for solo string players, which flows along evenly, to be followed, in marked contrast, by an *allegro vivace* finale quoting the 'Freude, schöner Götterfunken' theme from Beethoven's Ninth. In a letter to his sister of 24 April 1891 Strauss said that much against his will he had got to conduct Liszt's *Goethe* March and music for the epilogue at the gala performance of *Die Jäger*. At a rehearsal he had conducted a Beethoven Adagio at the end and the Grand Duke had been delighted by it. On 28 April he wrote to ask his father for some Mozart symphonies, which he needed for entr'actes at the gala performance: it is not clear whether they were used for this purpose or not, nor are there any accounts of the performance of the Fanfare. In the event Strauss cannot have conducted at the gala, as he was in hospital with pneumonia, and his life was actually in danger from 6 to 8 May.

In December 1891 Strauss wrote the two songs *Frühlingsgedränge* and *O wärst du mein*, settings of poems by Nikolaus Lenau, which he dedicated to Heinrich Zeller (Op. 26). The second song, in particular, goes beyond the range of the purely conventional occasional works of this period in Strauss's creative life, to tackle, in a concentrated form, harmonic problems that had preoccupied him since the composition of *Don Juan*, *Macbeth* and *Tod und Verklärung*. With its chromatic shifts and, especially, its alternation between F♯ minor (the tonic) and B♭/A♯ minor, *O wärst du mein* shows Strauss experimenting with new harmonic possibilities such as he was to explore more fully after his return to Munich and, to some extent, still in his early years in Berlin.

For the Golden Wedding anniversary of Grand Duke Carl Alexander and Grand Duchess Sophie, a Dutch princess, Strauss wrote four orchestral movements (o. Op. 89) to accompany *tableaux vivants*, a then fashionable genre. He finished them on 21 August 1892, while he was on holiday in Marquartstein, and they were performed in Weimar on 8 October. Strauss published the first of them on its own in 1930, with the title *Kampf und Sieg* and with a short preface in which he erroneously gave the date of composition as 1894. The Four Songs Op. 27 were composed during his last year in Weimar, as a wedding gift for Pauline.

His principal concern throughout his years in Weimar was his work on the text of *Guntram* and the initial stages of the composition of the music. At the same time, however, he considered subjects for other operas. In March 1892 he sketched the scenario for a *Don Juan* and in letters to his parents dating from the early summer of 1893 he mentions his ideas for an opera about Till Eulenspiegel. We shall return to those projects in due course.

Strauss's declaration later in life that he wrote little music in Weimar, apart from *Guntram* and a few good songs (Opp. 26 and 27), because what time he could spare from his fiancée was devoted to playing cards, might give the impression that the five years were an idyll, but nothing could be further from the truth. He was kept extremely busy as a conductor. In addition to the subscription concerts, which he conducted single-handed, there were chamber-music recitals which required his services from time to time, although from 1890 onwards the position of Court Pianist was held by Bernhard Stavenhagen (1862–1914), who also occasionally conducted and composed (two piano concertos, among other works). It does not seem particularly necessary to enumerate all the operas which Strauss directed in Weimar, whether after rehearsing them from the first or taking them over from Lassen, or to give a complete list of all the works he performed at subscription concerts. In the latter case, it is sufficient to illustrate the basic drift of his programme planning by some examples. Even if his letters to his parents did not tell us, the programmes would be enough to demonstrate how stubbornly he championed those composers who had become central to his artistic creed: Wagner, Liszt and Berlioz. Haydn, Mozart and Beethoven are joined by Gluck and Cherubini and a few of the romantics – primarily Schubert, Weber and Mendelssohn. Schumann's symphonies had no appeal for Strauss. In a letter to Ritter he went so far as to describe the inclusion of Schumann's Third Symphony in a Weimar concert as a concession. (1 May 1890) The rhythmic and metrical uniformity, and probably Schumann's instrumentation as well, seem to have been the barriers to his appreciation. Other composers whose works he conducted in Weimar include Lalo, Rheinberger, Nicodé, Bülow (*Nirwana*), Raff, Humperdinck (*Die Wallfahrt nach Kevlaar*), Gade and Draeseke, and he also found room for songs by Alexander Ritter, himself and others. The readiness of Bronsart and Lassen to give Strauss his head to quite a large extent – something he was rarely able to bring himself to admit – was probably partly due to the reputation that Strauss was winning far beyond Weimar with his consistent and committedly 'progressive' outlook. The repeated invitations he received to conduct concerts of the Leipzig Liszt-Verein will have made a particularly strong impression in Weimar, where they were conscious of their Lisztian obligations, and there can be no doubt of Bronsart's goodwill, even though he treated his second conductor's one-sided programme planning with more forbearance than the latter was capable of appreciating in his fanatical zeal, which grew more obstinate the longer he remained in Weimar. In his old age Strauss took a fairer view of the period:

> I alienated the sympathies of many with my youthful impetuosity and extravagances, so that when Possart offered me a second contract in Munich as First Kapellmeister (in place of Hermann Levi, whose health was poor), there were some who were not sorry to see me and Pauline go.[19]

It was Strauss's interpretation of Beethoven that most disturbed Bronsart. Father Strauss, too, in his letters repeatedly warned his son of the dangers of taking 'too modern' a view of Beethoven – in vain, naturally. He had as little success, as we have already seen, with his attempt to dissuade him from playing *Macbeth* and the *Eroica* in the same concert. While Strauss defended his view in his letters, his extremely intense and impetuous approach to the classics seems to have aroused a far more positive response from his players, as well as from the audiences, than it did from Bronsart and

Lassen. His own capacity for enthusiasm, at least, appears frequently to have been infectious. But even in his first season, in the autumn of 1889, Bronsart complained that his interpretation of the 'Pastoral' Symphony was rather too 'Bülowish' and both their attitudes subsequently hardened. One should bear in mind that Bronsart was no layman, but a professional musician and a composer, some of whose works enjoyed considerable success.

Guest conductor

Strauss's self-confidence in his direction of the Weimar concerts was bolstered by an ever-growing number of invitations to appear as a guest elsewhere, though, with the exception of the Leipzig Liszt concerts mentioned above, the majority of those invitations were to conduct his own tone poems. His performance of *Don Juan* in Berlin in January 1890 has already been mentioned; shortly afterwards, in February – that is, still during his first season in Weimar, and straight after conducting Mozart's *Don Giovanni* there for the first time in his life, delighting with all his heart in the 'wonders and felicities' of the score – he went to conduct *Don Juan* again, at one of the Museum Concerts in Frankfurt. There he paid daily calls on the art historian Henry Thode, son-in-law of Cosima Wagner and Hans von Bülow, and at that time director of the Städelsches Institut. Daniela Thode gave Strauss a portrait of her grandfather Liszt at the age of twenty-one, inscribed 'à Loulou' (her own pet-name in the family). Other friends whom he saw in Frankfurt included Siegfried Wagner, Sonja von Schéhafzoff, Engelbert Humperdinck and the cellist Hugo Becker, deriving all the greater pleasure from their company because of the 'antediluvian artistic conditions' that prevailed in the city for the most part, in his view.

Through the good offices of Friedrich Rösch, Bülow came to Weimar, where he played Beethoven's and Liszt's E♭ major concertos on 15 February 1890. In the same concert he also conducted Brahms's Academic and Tragic Overtures, which was less to Strauss's taste. Strauss in turn was invited to Berlin, where he conducted *Tod und Verklärung* with the Philharmonic Orchestra on 24 February 1891, and again at the customary 'popular' repeat concert, which was attended by Cosima Wagner and her son. He wrote to his sister:

> *Tod und Verklärung* was a great success today; I was

> tumultuously received at both concerts and took two calls at the end of each, to the most vociferous applause; I took care to wait a very long time before coming out again each time. A few very timid cat-calls doubled the energy of the applauders; the performance was pretty good, but I thought the one [in Weimar] was better, you could see that the Philharmonic Orchestra, which is so proficient in every other respect, does not play very much modern music; the harps were bad and my handful of string players cut more of a dash then Bülow's fourteen first violins. (25 February 1891)

In the first quarter of 1892 Strauss again fulfilled a number of guest engagements, for instance in Cologne, where the respected music critic Otto Neitzel called him the most outstanding living composer, as he proudly told his father, in Mainz (*Aus Italien*) and in Berlin, at Bülow's invitation, where he conducted *Macbeth*. That performance has already been discussed, but it is pertinent here to quote from Strauss's 1909 memoir of Bülow:

> It was a long time since I'd looked at the piece myself and (always a bit negligent in this respect and relying on my tolerable facility in score-reading) I had not even studied the score before the rehearsal, so that I presented the worthy gentlemen of the Philharmonic with the spectacle of a composer with his nose stuck fast in the pages of his own score. This enraged the conscientious Bülow, and he scolded me mightily afterwards: 'The score in your head, not your head in the score, that's the proper way to do things' (cutting short my excuses) 'even when you wrote the thing yourself.'

The Liszt-Verein in Leipzig asked him back on several occasions to conduct not only Liszt's works but his own as well, *Tod und Verklärung* in March 1892, for instance. He also visited smaller towns such as Heidelberg to conduct his own works, and sometimes attended performances of his tone poems by other conductors: for instance he went to Dresden in January 1890 to hear Adolf Hagen direct what was only the second performance of *Don Juan*, two months after its première in Weimar. He was greatly impressed by the Dresden orchestra on that occasion; it was, he wrote, indisputably 'the best at the moment, all the wind players [are] ideal and have a *pp* that's simply fabulous'. (To his father, 11 January 1890) In March 1890 he went to Berlin to hear a performance of his *Wandrers Sturmlied*, which had been very well rehearsed by Siegfried Ochs. In

January 1891 a telegram arrived offering him a two-year engagement to direct the New York Symphony Concerts; he refused, in spite of the very tempting fee of 30,000 marks, as he rightly felt he was not yet ready for that sort of thing and his work in Weimar still held greater interest for him. The Munich opera, too, where he had returned to conduct one performance of Boieldieu's *Jean de Paris* and four of Auber's *La part du diable* after his departure for Weimar, asked him back to direct two performances of *Così fan tutte* (22 December 1891 and 5 January 1892) – though this admittedly was a matter of standing in for Hermann Levi.

These frequent trips outside the duchy show that Weimar allowed him quite a lot of freedom and respected him as a composer, not just as the Grand Ducal Kapellmeister. The fact that he was able to present his three tone poems in his first two concert seasons in Weimar supports this assumption. He also played an enthusiastic part in organizing song recitals for the Wagner-Verein in Weimar, the membership of which quickly rose to ninety-five, including the Grand Duke.

The number of his engagements sometimes put a considerable strain on him, as a letter to his father on the eve of one of his Leipzig concerts shows:

> Several exhausting days lie behind me. Tuesday evening *Tristan*, then left for here [Leipzig, some 60 miles] at 11.30 at night, Wednesday took the first rehearsal for the Liszt-Verein concert from 10 to 2.30, back to Weimar in the evening. Yesterday, Thursday, evening conducted *Lohengrin* in Eisenach, returned here at 1 a.m., today the second rehearsal, from 10 till 1 and from 3 to 6, tomorrow principal rehearsal at 10, concert in the evening, programme: Liszt, *Die Ideale*, Schubert–Liszt: *Wanderer Fantasy* (Siloti), *Mazeppa*, piano solos, *Tod und Verklärung*. (12 March 1892)

Since the members of the Gewandhaus Orchestra were forbidden to take part in the Liszt-Verein concerts, Strauss had to use the band of the 134th Regiment, augmented to eighty players, who showed themselves 'willing to make colossal sacrifices, immensely inspired' by his conducting talents. 'I was born to fight battles like this!' After the concert he wrote:

> The whole affair in Leipzig was a sensational success . . . and my interpretation made the greatest impression. *Tod und Verklärung*

> didn't go really well until the repeat on Wednesday, after all technically and in its polyphonic style it was even newer for the orchestra than Liszt. On Wednesday, when I arrived for the rehearsal, the orchestra received me with a *Tusch*; young enthusiasts accompanied me to the station and cheered as the train pulled out, one even kissed my hand. In short, my fame is advancing by leaps and bounds. (18 March 1892)

Nonetheless, his father continued to offer advice, not only to the conductor on the matter of programmes and interpretations, but also to the composer. After the première of *Don Juan* he had expressed his hope that performing it would have taught his son to be more sparing and circumspect with the brass in future, and to pay more attention to the inner content and less to external glitter. (14 November 1889) After hearing a performance in Munich he said that on the whole he liked the work, 'aside from the fact that he was an adherent of the classics'. He found that it had 'independence, overall breadth, invention, no uncertain groping in the dark', it did not lack form, it had fire and dash, was dazzlingly orchestrated, said – in one respect – exactly what it intended, but he was inclined to think that it had been thought out a little bit too much and invention should have been allowed a freer hand. He also objected that the work was 'fearfully difficult'. (4 March 1891) *Macbeth*, as we have already seen, moved him to even greater demurrings and an appeal to the example of Greek sculpture and medieval Italian painting.

Franz Strauss did not pass any comment on *Tod und Verklärung* until he had heard it performed in Munich under Levi (12 December 1892), and this time his verdict was largely positive. He confessed that it had made a great impression on him, especially in the simple passages, where the life of the soul had been given the greatest prominence. There was too much polyphony in the scoring, by contrast, in the violent struggle with death, and the themes tended to get submerged as a result, which made it very difficult for the listener, for if it was hard for a professional musician like himself to follow, it must be much worse for a layman. The beginning and the close made a great emotional impact, such as he could not imagine done in any other way.

In the case of the symphonic poems, Franz Strauss's observations concerned scores that had been completed and performed, but – as we shall see – he was able to follow the slow progress of *Guntram*, as first the text and then the music came into being, always exhorting his son to greater simplicity, to melodiousness and to economical, transparent, instrumental textures.

Although the symphonic poems were received with occasional expressions of disapproval, as Strauss himself noticed, they were already being hailed with delight by young musicians and music lovers. The young conductor Leo Blech, for instance, then twenty-two years old, who was later to enjoy a distinguished career, working at Strauss's side at the Berlin opera, where he was able to remain until 1939 in spite of his 'non-Aryan' origins, wrote to Strauss:

> I have now heard your work *Tod und Verklärung* several times. I wish I could tell you how your work has gripped, delighted, stirred me. In short, it has allowed me to savour all the sensations that a human being can know when he hears the genius of another speaking to him. Each time that I have heard your work I have absorbed such a quantity of exaltation that I can no longer help myself and I come to you with this store of youthful enthusiasm, in order to lay it at your feet and beg you: 'Accept it!' I discern in your work the most beautiful expression of all that is ideal, true and noble and if you knew me better you would be able to understand how a person who strives for 'truth' as I do has no alternative but to honour and love you. (22 March 1893)

A 'Don Juan' opera

In March 1892, in Berlin, Strauss got to know John Henry Mackay, a writer of his own age, whose novel *Die Anarchisten* had caused a stir when it was published in the previous year, because of its socialist tendencies.[20] Strauss set four of Mackay's poems to music: two, *Heimliche Aufforderung* and *Morgen!* went into the book of songs that he gave Pauline on their wedding day (Op. 27, nos 3 and 4); they are among his best-known songs. The other settings came a few years later: *Verführung* for voice and orchestra (Op. 33, no. 1) in 1896, and *In der Campagna* (Op. 41, no. 2), which has a piano accompaniment, in 1899. Strauss told his father about the meeting:

> In Berlin I made an engaging new acquaintance, the Scottish poet John Mackay, a great anarchist and the biographer of the Berlin philosopher Max Stirner, the most significant antagonist of Schopenhauer and Christianity, the exponent of absolute egoism and author of *Der Einzige und sein Eigentum*. Withal,

Stirner died in Berlin of starvation, sacrificing himself for his family and relations. Theory and practice! (7 April 1892)

The impression that *Die Anarchisten* made on Strauss can be judged from a story told by Arthur Seidl in his book *Straussiana*: three hours before the curtain was due to go up on the first performance of *Guntram* in Weimar, he and Strauss were having a passionate discussion about the book.

Mackay urged him to read Stirner's *Der Einzige und sein Eigentum* (The Individual and his Property),[21] which purveys an uncompromising solipsism, centred on the ego as the only reality. Strauss did not finish the book, but it inspired him with extravagantly high-flown ideas for an opera on the subject of Don Juan, on lines that it is hard to conceive of him bringing off in musical reality in the 1890s.

It is of interest to reproduce here Strauss's two draft scenarios for the plot of this *Don Juan* and passages he copied from Stirner's book, because they afford an insight into his thinking at that period about the meaning of sexual love – a question to which he was to return in Egypt, when he started to read Schopenhauer again and was casting around for new dramatic ideas.

Don Juan

Act I. Don Juan in the full heat of sensuality, proponent of absolute and unrestrained egoism (Stirner?), in pursuit of beautiful women, is involuntarily drawn to a woman sixteen years his senior, who is in the grip of a frantic passion for him; when he approaches her, he is seized by an insuperable diffidence, draws back and hastens after other women; among them a beautiful but utterly depraved creature (Y), who also was seduced in earliest youth, luxuriates only in sensuality and has never experienced true love. This love gradually awakens in her through her passion for Don Juan.

Act I finale. X discovers – perhaps from A, whose philosophy of life makes him the complete antagonist of Don Juan's egoism, a 'pessimist' (Schopenhauer, Christ) – that Don Juan *is her son.* But her passion for him has already grown to such horrifying madness that she yearns nonetheless for union with him.

Act II. Don Juan succumbs to his mother's blandishments and is united with her. Afterwards, in the frenzy of passion and as though in order to intensify her love to a state of the highest madness, she confesses to him that she is his mother. Discerning his own reflection in this appalling perversion (after he has strangled his mother), he comes to acknowledge the fearful guilt of individuation and in his extreme horror at himself thinks of suicide, but recognizes – perhaps thanks to Y who prevents him (?) – that death would be not the punishment for which he yearns but a release, and resolves to remain alive for the sake of the fearful penance he imposes on himself: never again to touch a woman; the penance of continuing renunciation, when his uncontrollable natural instinct urges satisfaction.

Act III. Don Juan as penitent, caught in the most appalling struggle with his most frightful urges (recognizes true love in Y's sacrifice), is slain by officers pursuing him on account of the murder of his mother (among them perhaps A, who loved Don Juan's mother without requital and wishes to avenge her death). Don Juan pleads for his life, as he wants to live in order to do penance, and sustains death, which *releases* him from his torments, as the cruellest punishment.

Weimar, March 1892

The idea of a self-imposed penance anticipates the final version of the ending of *Guntram*, which Strauss wrote that November in Athens and which led to a disagreement with Alexander Ritter. The 'pessimist' A (= Alexander) clearly takes Ritter as a model. The following excerpts copied from Stirner's *Der Einzige und sein Eigentum*, as well as a second outline for the plot of the opera, date from the same month as the first draft.

How little man is able to control! He has to allow the sun to run its course, the sea to drive the waves, the mountains to tower up to heaven. And so he is powerless before the uncontrollable! Can he avoid the impression that he is powerless against the gigantic world? p. 96 [of the 1845 edition of Stirner's book]
How beggarly small is our portion, aye, as good as nothing! All has been taken from us etc. Happy *unrestraint* of the desiring man, how unmercifully you have been laid upon the altar of *restraint*! p. 100
If I cherish *you* because I love you, because my heart finds nurture in you, my need assuagement, *this is not for the sake of a higher being whose sacred body you are*, not because I discern in you a ghost, i.e. a spirit that manifests itself in you, but from egoistic desire: you yourself with *your* being are dear to me, for your

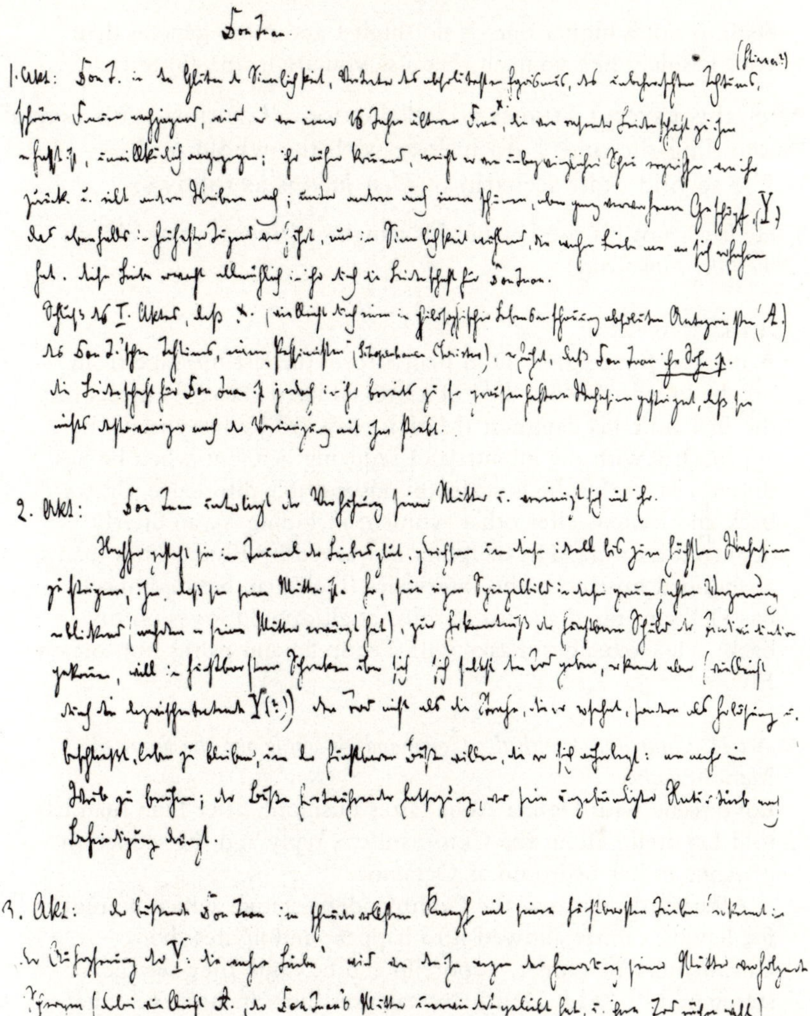

Draft scenario for an opera, *Don Juan*, Weimar, March 1892

being is not a higher one, is not higher and more general than you, is solely like yourself, because you are it. (p. 45) Stirner.

After this excerpt Strauss added the note: 'Contrast with Lenau: "wounding the one, I am in love with the whole sex".'

The second draft scenario of *Don Juan* is as follows:

He loves not his mother but his daughter (sixteen years old, *in the fullest innocence*).

Act I: Masked ball
A masked figure gives Don Juan a rose, the last message from one he loved who has died of a broken heart. Here he meets for the first time his daughter (Maria), ensnared by her charms he approaches with the intention of seducing her, but when he has drawn near to her he is seized by insuperable diffidence, draws back and hastens after other women, including Y, an utterly depraved creature. His daughter is warned by Elvira, Don Juan's abandoned mistress, who intervenes (Don Juan beside himself, has Hell conspired against me, to set all my old loves on my back). He exchanges masks with Leporello and palms him off on Elvira.

Act II: Churchyard with the Commander's statue and the grave of Maria's mother
Love scene with Donna Anna (after Pushkin), after Don Juan has told Leporello about the Commander's reply and the seduction of Anna in her bedroom as Octavio.

Afterwards abuse of the Commander's statue, which he mocks for having calmly allowed it to happen, and invites the Commander to supper. Leporello and he think they see the statue nod its head. Don Juan reassures himself, however, that what with the moonlight and his excitement it was a mere delusion; as the pair are about to leave the churchyard, Maria approaches, late, to see her mother's grave for the first time. Here scene with Maria's murder, after he has recognized her as his daughter. At the end of Act II perhaps Y.

Act I: end of the masked ball
Don Juan strikes down a rival and jumps out of the window, and escapes unharmed.

Marie Ritter sent him Molière's *Dom Juan* and Pushkin's *The Stone Guest* as further reading on the subject. But the mention of

Pushkin's name in the second sketch shows that Strauss was already acquainted with the latter, though it may only have been through what Marie Ritter had already told him. Strauss quickly abandoned the Don Juan plan, like a number of others, as we shall see. With the scene in the churchyard he would have been too close to Mozart for comfort.

1892: year of crisis

The year 1892 was a fateful one for Strauss. His grave illness in May forced him to spend the winter in a warmer climate, following medical advice. Thanks to the generosity of his uncle Georg Pschorr, who gave him 5000 marks, he was able to plan a stay in Egypt, preceded by a visit to Greece and rounded off by a few weeks in Sicily. Strauss himself recognized that a long holiday was necessary, not only for the sake of his physical health, but also to give himself time to relax and to take stock of his position. He had now been in Weimar nearly three years and he was nervous and overwrought. His state of mind is revealed in a letter he wrote while convalescing in Schwarzburg in June 1892 to Eugen Lindner.[22] Some derogatory remarks attributed to Strauss had come to Lindner's ears, in connection with the revival that summer of his opera *Der Meisterdieb*, which Strauss had already conducted in his first season in Weimar. In his letter Strauss tried to mollify Lindner, saying his words had been misunderstood and maliciously twisted, and he used the opportunity to try and explain his character to his colleague. We need not concern ourselves here with the advice he offered Lindner for the composition of an opera *Das stählerne Schloss* (apparently either not written or at least not performed), which consisted mainly of recommending him to keep it simple and take pains; but the character study Strauss paints of his own nature as one 'that presents itself transparently and frankly' is of great interest:

> I really believed, up until now, that there could be hardly any remaining doubts as to my true artistic convictions, even if I do happen to have studied, as a curiosity, Max Stirner's philosophy of egoism. I believed at least that I had always applied my ethical principles in practice to the best of my ability. You should not forget, my dear Lindner, that this honest application often meets with the most remarkable obstacles, even in my own breast, which put all my good intentions at risk and, with the help of my distinctly overwrought nerves, often encourage the most

extraordinary blossoming of paradox or, if you want it in plain language, *nonsense*. One of those obstacles is a devil of opposition, who means well but has three powerful enemies in the world, and he goes crazy at the sight of them; those three enemies are *hypocrisy*, the *impudence of dilettantes* and *philistinism*.

When I meet with hypocrisy, for instance, if someone always has the religion of love on his lips and is himself the crassest of egoists, with no consideration for the best and most self-sacrificing of friends, when the exaltation of his own person is at stake –

When I hear that impudent, uninformed laymen judge our most sublime works of art as if their creators were no better than they –

And as for philistinism with its hired aesthetic sense and its traditions – if I collide with these three devils then it may very well come to pass that I utter things which, taken out of context, sound quite extraordinary.

As I see to my joy, my dear friend, that really you have confidence in me, please be good enough, the next time you hear of something crazy originating from me, to make a few enquiries as to whether one of the above-mentioned three devils was lurking in the vicinity!

However, I really must put up a serious defence of myself against the charge of intolerance; I do not believe that there are many people who make a more honest and sincere attempt to do justice to everything that is beautiful, or that at least *is produced by serious artistic endeavour*, and to *exercise and express* that judgment, as long as I find myself in the company of *honest, truthful* artistic understanding. In other circumstances it can perhaps come to pass that, if somebody holds up Mozart's *Don Giovanni* to me as a more formally perfect, profounder work of art than *Tristan*, I may declare Mozart's *Don Giovanni* to be utter trash, or, if somebody praises *L'amico Fritz* to me, I may reply that *Der Trompeter* is a very respectable work of art in a decent German sort of way.[23] That can happen, and has happened to me in the heat of battle! But it has nothing whatever to do with my serious, settled view of art. You think that I undervalue Lortzing etc. Truly and honestly, No, and thrice No! If from time to time my nerves are not as taut in the third act of *Der Wildschütz* as in the third act of *Tristan*, where they *must* be drawn as taut as they will go, even if the whole man is really already done for, then I can't help it. My willingness is never wanting, not even in *Das Nachtlager* [by Kreutzer], but I'm only human, and if neither the performers nor the audiences show as much interest in these venerable old warhorses as they do in *Lohengrin*, devil take it, there's nothing I can do about it. What incomparable pains I took with Mozart's *Entführung*, and what a barely mediocre performance it was in the end! (14 June 1892)

This self-analysis reveals Strauss's ability 'to be aware of himself in a number of different personifications and to face up to the intrigues conducted by any one part of his divided ego'.[24] During his stay in Greece and Egypt he went on with the exploration of his own personality and an advance towards self-knowledge in more favourable external circumstances. The principal evidence of this is to be found in the notes he made after reading Schopenhauer's *The World as Will and Idea*, but there is also some in the scenarios for new operas which he sketched in those months, though none of them came to anything.

A few days after Strauss wrote to Lindner, Pauline de Ahna received a copy of the vocal score of Liszt's oratorio *Saint Elisabeth* inscribed: 'To his kind and selfless Samaritan, this beautiful gospel of pure loving-kindness is dedicated, in sincerely grateful memory of 17–18 June 1892, by a teacher and a patient who cannot ever repay her.' (From Munich, 20 June 1892) His condition worsened during the three days of 'bottomless boredom' which he spent in Schwarzburg, so that, although he was hardly fit to travel, he had to go on to Munich, where he was laid low by a bad attack of bronchitis. While still in Schwarzburg he had written to Hanna that there was only one cure for him, namely 'to forget my illness in a great deal of work'. (17 June 1892) Confined to his room in the family home, he worked on *Guntram*. It was the middle of July before he could go to Reichenhall to convalesce. Disappointments multiplied during this summer. The memorandum he had sent to Bronsart early in June, the contents of which we know from his letter to Hanna, met with a firm refusal. He gave vent to his disappointment and anger in a letter to Hans von Bülow: now that there was no chance of his going to Bayreuth, he wrote, he glared in fury at the four walls of his room, having a further cause of rage in his dear intendant, with whom he was now so much at loggerheads (Bronsart having turned down his really not unjustified request for an improvement in his terms of employment for reasons that would have been more appropriate if addressed to a junior clerk) that he would probably waste no time in shaking the hallowed dust of Weimar and its traditions from his feet and tell Herr Bronsart to find himself a nice biddable mediocrity, who would not so subjectify *his* Beethoven. (30 June 1892) His other great disappointment – as indicated in the same letter – was that there was no question of his conducting anything at Bayreuth that year. He wrote to tell Cosima Wagner on 21 July that he was 'despairing and deeply dejected'. In the middle of August, however, Pauline de Ahna received an unexpected and urgent summons to stand in as Elisabeth in *Tannhäuser* at the festival, in the form of a telegram from Strauss. Although she replied the very same day in a telegram sent directly to Bayreuth, accepting the invitation, she then received an answer from Adolf von Gross, Cosima's business adviser: 'Kind acceptance unfortunately arrived too late, sincere regrets, Gross.' Deeply offended, Pauline jumped to the conclusion that the whole manoeuvre had been a feint; rightly or not is something that cannot now be ascertained. At all events the incident helped to weaken the already slightly shaken trust in Wahnfried.

After Reichenhall, Strauss also spent some of the summer with Ludwig Thuille in Marquartstein. Another subject to which he devoted some attention was a fairy-tale plot for an opera, on which Alexander Ritter made some critical comments in a letter. It is possible, however, that Strauss did not intend the material for himself, but for Ritter or Thuille. Ritter's observations give only a rather vague impression of what the scenario was like:

> I think the first act is quite excellent. It is a short, concise, yet very clear and very dramatic exposition. I would find it a pleasure to write. The other two acts, however, are extremely colourless, and they seem to me misconceived in every respect. The fact that on one occasion Hans runs away from Gertraud and this makes her very sad is nowhere near strong enough a motive to teach Heini compassion. But then, after he has once been taught it, to have Gertraud deserting Hans in turn is dramatically quite pointless.
>
> The second act ought to demonstrate the horrifying misery brought about by the magic spell on all sides. Hans is in the grip of melancholia, will not work any more, the forge is going to rack and ruin. One section of the village populace thinks that Hans and Gertraud are bewitched, another suspects that Hans and Gertraud have committed some serious crime and are now a

prey to the pangs of conscience. Both of them are avoided, as if they were lepers or outlaws, and in their own home they find no comfort but only mutual lovelessness, despair. Only thus would the awakening of Heini's compassion make emotional sense.

Then I think it fundamentally wrong to attempt to explain the magic spell psychologically, on the basis of traits in the couple's characters. As soon as we abandon the whole naive credulity of fairy tales, we pull the carpet out from under the whole tale. (10 August 1892)

The last objection illustrates the fundamental difference between the approaches of Strauss, with his interest in psychological motivation, and Ritter, whose taste was for the popular and the naive.

At the end of September Strauss had to go back to Weimar, to resume his unsatisfactory duties. His discontent will not have been greatly assuaged by the award, early in October, on the occasion of the Grand Ducal couple's Golden Wedding, of the Knight's Cross, Second Class, of the Grand Ducal House Order of Vigilance or the White Falcon, or by the commemorative gold medal issued after the festivities, with a picture of the duke and duchess and a letter of thanks. These favours from the court will at best have reconciled him somewhat to the task of rehearsing the music he had written during the summer to accompany the *tableaux vivants*, a dubious manifestation of the taste of the times, that formed part of the programme of entertainment drawn up for the Golden Wedding celebrations. The performance was given on 8 October and repeated on 16 and 17 October. Lassen had already written the music for one of the *tableaux* ('The Reconciliation of the Admirals'), which meant that as soon as he got back to Weimar Strauss had to write a new piece: 'The Treaty between Orange and Marquis Spinola, 1609'. (We learn this from an unpublished letter to Franz Strauss, dated 28 September 1892, which confirms the second of the present author's hypotheses, summarized by Mueller von Asow in his note on o. Op. 89, AV p. 1218.) The most important outcome of the celebrations, as far as Strauss was concerned, was the installation of electric lighting in the theatre, though it was only provisional to begin with. Even so, the accounts of the festivities which he sent to his family were quite enthusiastic, although the letters of these last few weeks in Weimar also contain such statements as 'the rubbishy theatre is becoming steadily more distasteful to me and Lassen's megalomania will probably reach its peak this winter' and

> The affair with Lassen is approaching its climax, he won't be able to go on like this much longer, as he is on very bad terms with Bronsart, to whom Brandt and I have enthusiastically attached ourselves. [!] I believe that Bronsart has already spoken to the Grand Duke about the possible departure of Lassen, who increasingly does what he wants, which is something Bronsart cannot endure.

Once again, however, Strauss's assessment of the situation was wrong: Lassen continued to occupy his post in Weimar until 1895.

Numerous letters of this time testify to the difficulty Strauss had in lasting out in Weimar before his departure for the south. Cosima Wagner, too, wrote to an acquaintance about a meeting her son Siegfried had had with him at a performance of *Das Rheingold* in Munich, at which Siegfried – whose relationship with Strauss was still close at that time – had 'restored his equilibrium'. Before he left for Greece, Strauss wrote to Cosima to take his leave, stressing how important it was for him to see more of the world:

> To throw off just once everything that from one's youth has hung about one as fetters – though they were necessary fetters no doubt, an in part beneficial constraint, intended to guide one in one's inexperience on to the right path – to subject everything that one learned and absorbed in youth to critical examination, in complete isolation, so as to discover its true value and usefulness for later life, to immerse oneself in the contemplation of alien and great cultures and in that way, far from the Philistines' comfortless Germany, to prepare oneself for independent maturity, seems to me a most desirable purpose, quite apart from the anxiety about my health, and so I launch myself upon this journey with real enthusiasm. That I long to spend at least a few hours, before I take this important step, in our glorious Bayreuth, on the last rock on which German culture has taken refuge, and to kiss your hand, most honoured and gracious lady, you can well imagine! (20 October 1892)

He does not appear to have gone to Bayreuth, however, but there was probably a brief encounter in Munich before he left. The Grand Duke gave Strauss a farewell audience and was 'frightfully decent and kind'. His last engagement was a Liszt-Verein concert in Leipzig.

7

Guntram and the Egyptian winter, 1892–3

Strauss had been working on the text of his first opera since the summer of 1887. The numerous interruptions it had suffered were not all to be laid at the door of his work on the three symphonic poems, or his conducting duties. It was the task itself, the creation of an opera libretto, which, for all the eagerness with which he returned to it each time, imposed the need for periods of rest during which to mull over the unfamiliar problems set by dramatic form and the writing of verse. During the winter of 1891–2 he made himself better acquainted with the milieu in which the action of *Guntram* is set by reading Alwin Schultz's *Das höfische Leben zur Zeit der Minnesänger*. Excerpts copied from the book are to be found among his papers. From the first his intention was to write, not a 'historical opera', but a work close to the sphere of *Tannhäuser* and *Lohengrin*, and the ambition was undoubtedly strengthened by his intensive preoccupation with both works when he directed them in Weimar. The influences of Schopenhauer, Nietzsche, Stirner and Mackay, too, can be picked out in *Guntram*. Originally Strauss wanted to avoid using the designation 'opera' and call his work 'Guntram in three actions', but in the end he had to abandon that idea, principally at the urging of Eugen Spitzweg. The eventual title was '*Guntram*, In Three Acts, Poem and Music by Richard Strauss'.

The earliest mention of the plan to write an opera is in a letter to Marie von Bülow dated 26 August 1887; it was six years before the score was finished, on 5 September 1893. Written in spurts, a first complete version of the text was finished in Weimar on 17 March 1892 (there is little that can be ascertained today about earlier, provisional treatments). This version, now lost, came into the possession of Wilhelm Klatte, who furnished the following account of it:[1]

> Guntram slays the young duke, who has poured scorn on his song in praise of human nobility and loving-kindness, and believes that in so doing he has removed the scourge from his country, which groans under tyranny. But in his prison cell (Act III) he recognizes that the innermost motive for his deed was his love for the unhappy wife of the cruel prince. He fails to quiet his conscience by railing against the dead tyrant: 'Thou remainest unmoved by fervid pleading, the call of compassion falls strangely on thine ear, thou hast not heard the commandment of love proclaimed to thee in ecstatic song: thou hadst to fall that thousands might live!'
>
> The inner conflict is intensified from without by the entrance of the Duchess Freihild; her heart has long been his, and she wishes to free him from prison. How to resolve the conflict?
>
> In the first version the scene between Guntram and Freihild makes up the whole of the third act. The fiery embrace of the beloved reveals his guilt to Guntram. He tears himself from her arms and unburdens his soul by confessing that he has acted contrary to the injunctions of the brotherhood of which he is a member, an order of men dedicated to God, and he is now unworthy to bear either the knightly sword or the singer's harp. For ever outcast, he will, he *must* devote his life henceforth to solitary penance, mindful of his broken vows. 'I will go on pilgrimage to the Holy Land, to strengthen myself with fervent prayer at the Saviour's Sepulchre for the heavy age of solitude, where the soul shrinks in contemplation of the divine, I will raise myself up to the grace of the Everlasting.'
>
> He tells Freihild to assume the high duties of a mother of the poor and protector of the weak; she relinquishes him and Guntram departs to begin his penance.[2]

Alexander Ritter approved heartily of this ending: the manuscript bears in his hand the comment 'Quite wonderful, superb!' In a later version – partly in order to relieve the principal singer of some of his immense burden – Friedhold, a representative of the brotherhood, also made an appearance in the third act, to summon Guntram to appear before a tribunal of the order. In the final version, as the leader of the 'warriors of love', Friedhold also appears in the first scene of Act I. Strauss introduces yet another figure into the third act as well, the Fool, who is devoted to Freihild, and enters to announce the death of the old duke and the people's rejoicing at Freihild's accession to the throne. The '*Guntram* Chronicle' in the following pages traces the course of Strauss's decision to change the ending again, with Guntram refusing to stand trial before the brotherhood and instead electing to do a penance of his own choice. The ending continued to exercise the composer, Ritter, Friedrich Rösch and Ludwig Thuille intensely, and it did not reach its final form until Strauss was well into the composition of the music of the first act, which he started in February 1892.

Strauss was under no illusions about the deficiencies of the text of *Guntram*. Even in his old age, in 1945, he wrote to Joseph Gregor: 'Certainly the text is no masterpiece (even the language leaves something to be desired), but it provided the 'prentice Wagnerian, sloughing his skin in the process of gaining independence, with the opportunity to write a great deal of fresh, tuneful, sappy music.'[3] It was for the sake of the music that between 1934 and 1939 he produced a greatly cut, but in other respects unchanged version which was first performed in Weimar on 29 October 1940, forty-six years after the première of the original version.

Since the genesis of the opera was spread out over such an exceptionally long period, the reader may welcome the following chronological survey, consisting of quotations from the composer's correspondence. It is justified, not so much by the measure of what Strauss achieved in his first opera, which follows too closely in Wagner's footsteps for its own good, but by the work's significance in the composer's development during these six years. The chronicle does not aim to be exhaustive but does include some quotations which are trivial in themselves, and some which repeat the same substance in almost the same words addressed to different people, in order to draw attention to the periods of most intensive activity.

Guntram chronicle

The reader will find a synopsis of the plot in Appendix 1. Except where otherwise stated, all the excerpts are from letters written by Richard Strauss. As recipient he is identified as R.S. Where neither author nor recipient is named, the letter is one from Strauss to his parents. Where the place is not named, the letter should be understood as being sent from the writer's normal residence at the time.

26 August 1887, to Marie von Bülow
. . . and furthermore I'm working on the draft of the text of an original opera.

10 September 1887, Alexander Ritter to R.S.
I'm immensely pleased to hear about your draft. You won't credit how lively an interest I take in this work of yours. Keep it up – *it must be*!

11 September 1887, to Hans von Bülow
. . . and I'm working on the fabrication of – wait for it – the text of a three-act tragic opera, all my own work and completely original!!

25 March 1888, to Hans von Bülow
I've finished a first complete draft of the plot of my opera, and I'm pleased with it. Ritter actually likes it very much indeed.

14 April 1888, to Franz Wüllner
. . . working on the text of an original opera, the first draft of which I've already finished.

30 April 1888, to Emil Struth
. . . libretto, of which the first draft is now complete.

6 September 1888
. . . written out the first draft of my libretto, which, I think, will be very good. The draft is good, as long as turning it into verse doesn't present any insuperable difficulties!

9 April 1889, to Dora Weis
In the text of my opera I have finished (that is, until the next revision) the first act and the second act as far as the end of the big love scene. Ritter is very pleased with it.

24 October 1889, to Eugen Spitzweg
My libretto has also made great progress.

28 November 1889
Today I've started work on my libretto again and I knead away at it until my brow is wet with nervous perspiration, but I'll get the better of it in the end.

30 April 1890
I'm working very diligently on my libretto, and hope to finish the second act by the end of this week.

27 September 1890, to Hanna
I've got to the end of my libretto for now, provisionally.

2 October 1890
. . . have written a fair copy of my second act.

6 October 1890, Franz Strauss to R.S.
I was delighted to learn from your letter that you've finished your libretto. Do please have a copy made soon and send me either the original or the copy, I would dearly like to become better acquainted with the whole thing, for I'm afraid that it's much too long.

14 October 1890
I haven't quite finished writing the fair copy of my libretto, as soon as I have, I'll send it to you at once.

25 October 1890, to Hanna
Today the libretto will be finished.

6 November 1890, to Hanna
I'm delighted by your enthusiastic verdict on my opera. That it meets with Papa's approval too is capital. I beseech him to let me know his criticisms of it as soon as possible. I almost believe now myself that *Guntram* will come to something; up till now I've always been doubtful, because whereas I'm completely sure of my opinions where my music is concerned and know exactly what it's worth, faced with my first work of poetry I'm completely unsure.

10 November 1890
What did Ritter say about my libretto? Did he find much fault with it?

14 November 1890, Hanna to R.S.
Ritter is still poring over the libretto, he seems to take the critic's task very seriously.

19 November 1890, to Eugen Spitzweg
. . . I am turning my back on absolute music altogether, to seek my salvation in drama.

19 November 1890, to Ludwig Thuille
Have you read my libretto? What have you got to say about it?

21 November 1890, Franz Strauss to R.S.
What struck me, as I read your text for the first time, is that in my opinion they shouldn't be minnesingers. It ought to be a kind of secret society with aims to improve the world – like Freemasons and so on – which sends its members out on missions, choosing young, enthusiastic members for the purpose,

who are skilled in singing and oratory and have been given the task of setting the world a conspicuous example by their model behaviour and not letting themselves be led astray by sensual desires, which is exactly how Guntram is presented. I also think the cause of Guntram's killing the duke is too slight, that the servant refuses him entry into the room is a good enough reason for killing the servant but not for G. to kill the duke.

Then Guntram is allowed to go without being called to account for this deed, which I don't rightly understand. Also I find the scene with the mystic temptress superfluous, it smacks too much of Frau Venus. Why drag in supernatural beings at all, when it's not necessary, it only holds up the action. You must take great care not to get into the atmosphere of *Parsifal* or *Tannhäuser*. Ritter also said that he thought that the words are often not significant enough, probably because you have not read very much poetry. By and large I liked the plot, especially the last scene. But I think it's a bit too long, there are too many words in the monologues, and above all you must drop the references to the church and the priesthood altogether, they're quite unnecessary and would only make you a lot of enemies.

14 February 1891
I wrote a new draft of the first act of my opera on my way to Cologne, and now, I think, it will really come to something. But it's turned out completely different! I thought of a good first scene as an exposition and Minna [the mystic temptress] has gone altogether.

24 April 1891, to Hanna
I've used every free hour to work on the libretto, and the draft of the second act was more or less finished yesterday.

2 October 1891
. . . already begun to do some more work on the third act of *Guntram*.

12 October 1891, to Eugen Spitzweg
. . . libretto fabrication . . .

1 December 1891
Act I of *Guntram* finished.

28 December 1891
Yesterday I read my libretto to Brandt, who was greatly taken with it.

3 January 1892
Whenever the mood is right now, I shall work at the second act, which is the weakest at present.

8 February 1892
I've been working very conscientiously on Act II of my libretto, it's going very slowly; if a thing's worth doing, it's worth taking time over.

11 February 1892
I'm working conscientiously on Act II of *Guntram*; at present it's coming on quite nicely again, but its progress is by fits and starts.

20 February 1892
On Wednesday I read [Alexander Ritter] my libretto, which he liked so much, and thought so nearly complete, that he advised me to start writing the music at once. That was capitally encouraging, of course, and now even I am beginning to *believe* in *Guntram*. Ha! I'm curious to find out how I shall take to composing again after the two-year break.

24 February 1892
If I were not in Berlin I would celebrate your birthday [Franz Strauss's seventieth] on the 26th by beginning to compose my *Guntram*; I know you will be pleased!

29 February 1892, Franz Strauss to R.S.
I was overjoyed to hear that you are on the point of starting to compose the music of your opera, and don't forget that you must make the stage your centre of gravity and not the pit, and don't go thinking that if something sounds melodious it is necessarily commonplace. What did Wagner make his name with, after all? With *Tannhäuser* and *Lohengrin*, where the melody alone is the predominant element. *When you have so desired*, you have shown, every time, that you do not want for noble melodies, so why deliberately avoid them!

7 March 1892, to Hanna
The libretto is as good as finished and now I'm frightfully pleased with it, I've even composed the end and the beginning already!

14 March 1892, to Cosima Wagner
As it happens, I've more or less finished my libretto, and on Ritter's advice I've already made a start on the music.

[17 March 1892: manuscript of the first complete version of the text finished.]

17 March 1892, to Eugen Spitzweg
For the last two weeks I've been in the grip of enthusiasm as I've been getting set to start composing my opera.

18 March 1892
Yesterday I finally completed my libretto.

24 March 1892
I've now composed the short prelude to *Guntram*, which depicts the brotherhood and establishes the first Guntram theme. You'll marvel at what simple and tuneful music it is. The fact is, I've done all the roaring I want to do in every conceivable symphonic poem, and now I'm becoming frightfully simple.

7 April 1892
The prelude to *Guntram* is finished . . . May I ask you and the Ritter family to read the text of *Guntram* quickly and send it back to me *as soon as possible.*

10 April 1892, to Hanna
In one happy evening, the day before yesterday, I composed the whole of the first scene of *Guntram* at one go (I'd taken the precaution of copying it for my own use) and now I'm stuck. I must have my text back *at once.*

10 April 1892, Hanna to R.S.
It's very different now and shorter than it was and altogether much more original and new.

24 April 1892, Franz Strauss to R.S. and Hanna
I really quite liked Richard's libretto, only I think that some of the monologues are somewhat too long and cannot be made interesting musically for so long, and there will be boring passages for the listener. Also I think the scene for Guntram and the duchess is somewhat too long, and he calls her name aloud rather too often. The vision in the cell – the apparition of the murdered duke – is something else that I think ought not to be there, because that sort of thing has been overdone. There's no need for ghostly apparitions, it can all happen in his fevered imagination. Also I would avoid the words 'priest' and 'prince', there are other expressions you can use instead for both of them . . . I'm very much looking forward to the music of *Guntram* and am very keen to know what style it is in. I can't say too

often: Melody! Clarity! Simplicity! Emotional depth! Only what comes from the heart will reach to other hearts!

2 May 1892, to Alexander Ritter
[The music] will be enormously simple, very melodious, only cantilenas for the singer; for my own text the music just flows from my hand . . . The more rehearsals there are for *Loreley* [Hans Sommer's opera], the simpler *Guntram* becomes.

8 June 1892, to Hanna
. . . trying in vain to breathe some fresh life into the ending of the first act of *Guntram*, which seems to have something wrong with it wherever I look.

[26 June 1892: short score of Act I finished in Munich.]

30 June 1892, to Hans von Bülow
. . . out of boredom [during convalescence] I'm composing Act II of my opera (the first is already finished).

16 October 1892, to Hanna
. . . have composed the duke's big scene and Freihild's aria, and I expect to bring the second act of *Guntram* with me to Munich in a very healthy state.

[18 October 1892: short score of Act II finished in Weimar.]

19 October 1892
Guntram Act II finished.

29 October 1892, to Engelbert Humperdinck
Two acts of my *Guntram* are now ready.

16 November 1892, Franz Strauss to R.S.
Don't be in too much of a hurry with your opera, and don't neglect the melodious element, and bear in mind that it was really *Tannhäuser* and *Lohengrin* which made Wagner famous, where he was still content with closed melodies, and you certainly do not lack melodic invention. Of course you will turn your nose up at my opinion, but do not disregard my plea altogether, there is no one who wishes you better than your father, whose heart and mind are in the right place.

17 November 1892
. . . already working slowly at revising the text of Act III of my *Guntram* . . . Also I've already concocted a new subject for an opera.

19 November 1892 (Athens), to Engelbert Humperdinck
Meanwhile I'm working on Act III of *Guntram*.

19 November 1892 (Athens)
After dinner the scene between Guntram and Freihild. The essentials of Act III are now established.

23 November 1892 (Athens) [R.S.'s diary]
Finished Act III of the poem of *Guntram*.

23 November 1892 (Athens), to Eugen Spitzweg
. . . have a lot of time to spare, and therefore I'm already well into my third act, the text of which I've revised and which I'll begin to compose in Cairo.

24 November 1892 (Athens) [diary]
Wrote fair copy of Act III.

25 November 1892 (Athens)
. . . working on the completion of my third act.

25 November 1892, Else Ritter to R.S.
I got Rösch to explain the new idea for the end of *Guntram* more fully, and I think it's excellent.

25 November 1892 (Athens)
Yesterday I made the enclosed fair copy of the third act; I believe it's a *success*! . . . Read it yourselves, then give it to Ritter, and when he has read it, be sure that he gives it *to you*, and then *you* should give it to Rösch. But when it's been copied please send my manuscript back to me at once!

1 December 1892 (Cairo) [diary]
Began Act III [short score].

5 December 1892 (Cairo)
. . . working hard and have already composed Act III, scene 1; please send my manuscript back soon.

8 December 1892 (Cairo)
I'm composing busily.

11 December 1892 (Cairo)
. . . in addition to that I'm now so caught up in composing the third act, of which I've already done up to Friedhold's entrance, that I'd really prefer not to interrupt it. The love scene has a colossal drive and has turned out capitally, it's still a long way from classical Greek simplicity (well! one has to digest all these things a little bit first), there's rather too strong a whiff of 'cockchafer' music [a favourite expression of Franz Strauss, to denote over-busy music] in it but – dashing! It's all *alla breve* and

very often semibreves; the tempo is insanely fast almost throughout, *sempre accellerando*! Now the Simon-pure, rhyming-pure brother is about to enter, and the pace drops to *moderato*!

13 December 1892 (Cairo) [diary]
Began scene 2.

14 December 1892 (Cairo)
The composition is going ahead very quickly, I'm already well into the Friedhold scene and hope to have finished the third act before I go up the Nile at the beginning of January. While I'm on the Nile . . . I shall make a start on scoring Act I.

[The plan to sail up the Nile had to be abandoned.]

19 December 1892 (Cairo), to Arthur Seidl
By the time this letter is in your hands, Act III of *Guntram* (the text of which has been *substantially* rewritten) will be finished.

19 December 1892 (Cairo), to Alexander Ritter
[R.S. thanks Ritter for sending the Miserere intonations; he doesn't know if he will be able to use them. (He didn't.)]

24 December 1892 (Cairo) [diary]
Christmas Eve, *Guntram* finished.

[At the bottom of the short score]
Cairo. Christmas 1892, 24 Dec. 3 p.m. Deo Gratia (and to Saint Wagner). Duration 57 min.

24 December 1892, Franz Strauss to R.S.
[Ritter] at once began to talk about the changes to your Act III of *Guntram* and is quite in despair over the new version and requested me to write and ask you to stop composing for the time being, he will be writing to you in full about it. We had a long talk about it, during which he represented to me that the fine, noble integrity of the character of Guntram has been destroyed.

He said: the resistance that wells up in Guntram towards the brotherhood destroys the unity of the idea that underlies the plot. As the sinning party, it is not for him to punish himself, instead he must return to the brotherhood in penitence and thus expiate his crime. He asked me to tell you he wishes that you would for God's sake return to the first idea, which was so fine.

I must confess that I too was greatly affronted by the way

Guntram, for no reason, turns so vehemently against the brotherhood, which is in no way to blame for his crime. The entrance of the Fool, where he describes the *battle* and the death of the duke, is very distracting. The Fool has no business to be in the third act at all, in my view. I think Guntram ought to say a few words renouncing love and then return to the brotherhood; it must all be made credible to the audience and that will only happen if Guntram humbly submits to the punishment meted out to him. Ritter has asked me to send him the text again. I will write to Rösch today to ask him to send it back to me, and will send it on to Ritter.

27 December 1892, Friedrich Rösch to R.S. [Summary]
[Rösch expresses his firm conviction that the present version of the third act is] probably the only *possible* way of bringing the action to a *reasonably satisfactory conclusion.* It's true that Freihild now comes off even worse than before, but on the other hand the delineation of Guntram is now very much sharper, clearer and better characterized, and above all we are now enlightened, in broad outline at least, about the nature of the mysterious brotherhood. And of course the music will tell us a lot more, I expect. [He advises Strauss to look at the language again with great care and to eliminate at least the most stilted of the genitival constructions. The third act still had a number of things that were incomprehensible, incorrect and even badly written, unlike the second act where such things were not to be found, or only in isolation.] The simplest and most natural is also the most audacious! [Rösch also objects to the way that Guntram fell back into a realm of ideas to which he had subscribed at best only at an earlier stage, as a 'warrior of love', as one of the brothers, i.e. as a dogmatist. The idea of 'becoming like God', and of 'wishing to bring salvation' is in essence absolutely altruistic, that is, anti-egoistic.] It can only be born where at least two, where a large number, a mass, an association exists in a brotherhood. A single person in isolation, left completely to himself, will not conceive of such ideas . . . 'Released by love from the power of Minne'* is a monstrous notion, for every love is at once ideal and real. Or have you now finally come round to professing Ritter's 'heavenly love'? [That is 'sentimental languishing' and completely out of place in this context; after the change that has taken place in Guntram such sentimentalities are uncharacteristic of him. A number of things remain which are] absolutely

* That is, by a 'higher' love from a 'lower'. *Tr.*

irreconcilable with Guntram's decision to be his own judge . . . Away with dogmatism, where it is uncalled for . . .

The lines 'Mich straft kein Bund, / Das Gesetz – nur die That!' [No brotherhood punishes me, / the law – only the deed!] are not as clear and comprehensible as their vitally important meaning makes it essential that they should be (quite apart from the grammatical construction, which leaves it very uncertain that 'Gesetz' is supposed to be a nominative and 'die That' the dependent accusative). A statement as important as this one must be immediately comprehensible; if not it is useless. Perhaps it should be something on these lines (but not in the least like this): [Rösch then offers a more expansive version, which would allow Strauss to cut certain other lines.]

29 December 1892 (Cairo) [diary]
Began scoring first act.

2 January 1893, Franz Strauss to R.S.
Ritter, who called on us a few days ago, said that he has started a long letter to you but hasn't finished it yet, because he hasn't had the time.

7 January 1893 (Cairo)
I was afraid that Uncle Ritter wouldn't approve of the new version of Act III, and I'm sorry, but I can't do anything about it. The present dénouement is the only course that makes the most of the material to any extent and Guntram must be like *this* and not contritely return to the fold. In any case all the music has been written now and it is only in *this* form that Act III has the right intensification in the development of Guntram's character. The first was much too pallid!

13 January 1893, Franz Strauss to R.S.
Ritter has already told me that he has written to you about the last act of *Guntram*. I think it best if you wait to discuss it with him until you have come home.

17 January 1893 (Cairo), to Hanna
I'm working very conscientiously at the instrumentation of *Guntram*, which is giving me enormous fun and will be very refined and dainty. No inner parts in the harmony, on principle, it's all tunes – Rösch will enjoy the polyphony. He has written me a very interesting letter, at last the first one of the three to have a sensible word to say. Thuille really ought to write too. And what is Uncle Ritter doing? He hasn't answered my letter yet.

17 January 1893, Alexander Ritter to R.S. [Excerpts and summary of part of the twelve-page letter.]
The impression I had and still have after reading your new third act [is] one of the most *profoundly painful* things that I have experienced in the whole of the last decade of my life . . . By the form you have given your third act you have thoroughly ruined your work, because: 1. The work has now been robbed of any kind of *tragedy*. 2. It is now bereft of the essential minimum amount of artistic unity. 3. The character of the hero has been transmogrified into a hazily patched together, psychologically quite impossible characterlessness. 4. The tendency of the work is now eminently *immoral*, making a mockery of every ethical principle. [Ritter then adduces individual details in support of his four points and continues:] Weighing all this, I have no hesitation in addressing the following urgent, imploring entreaty to you from a full heart: My dear friend! Come to your senses! Do not ruin your work, which is so very fine in the first two acts, beyond repair! Take this new third act – even if the music has already been written – and throw it, lock, stock and barrel, into the fire! Having done that, for your inner purgation read a chapter from the Gospels or from Schopenhauer's *Ethics* or Wagner's *Religion and Art*. Then set to and make a new third act according to the earlier draft, but restore Guntram's heroic deed of self-mastery, let him humbly submit himself to the judgment of the brotherhood. And when you have done that, let a Magnificat be sung. Oh, if only God would lift up your soul to this resolution! . . . From the depths of my soul I embrace you compassionately, your old friend, A. Ritter.

21 January 1893 (Luxor), to Eugen Spitzweg
The [composition] sketch of *Guntram* was completely finished before I left Cairo and for the last three weeks I have been scoring the first act, thirty pages of which have already been spattered with highly neat and dainty little notes. It will be a very elegant little score. If all goes well, the whole opera may be finished by next Christmas!

25 January 1893 (Luxor)
. . . from 10 till 1 I work: the scoring of the first act is proceeding slowly but surely forwards . . . I hope to finish scoring the first act here. In Sicily it will be the turn of the second and by Christmas, I think, it will all be finished.

27 January 1893 (Luxor), to Engelbert Humperdinck
The sketch of *Guntram* is completely finished; I'm already

diligently scoring the first act; it will be a neat little score and everything should be ready by Christmas. In between times I study Schopenhauer and am moving – in spite of all inertia – nicely *forwards*. Whoever will now engage me as Kapellmeister can give the first performance of *Guntram*! How they will fight for the privilege! Oh well, even if they don't, *I* like it!

30 January 1893, Ludwig Thuille to R.S.
Unfortunately I haven't seen the revised version of *Guntram* . . . but it sounds *very* plausible, in fact the *only* thing possible.

1 February 1893
. . . working very conscientiously: Guntram's monologue is ready, I've already written fifty-six pages (some double) of the full score, I think the first act will be finished by the beginning of March and the only thing that has disturbed my calm was a letter two days ago from Ritter, which was very kind and friendly but expressed a truly moving horror at the alleged changes to my third act. He begs me so imploringly to change the third act and beseeches me, for the sake of my soul's salvation, to extinguish the infamous tendencies, that for love of my old, dear, true friend I almost would do it.

But alas, only almost! For I really don't know exactly what Ritter wants. I have changed nothing in the tendency of *Guntram*, it always took this shape, only now, for the first time, the conception I have long sensed is fully revealed in broad daylight. Obviously up till now Ritter has always read something into *Guntram* that was quite different from what I intended from the very first; besides, I can't find anything in the least un-Christian or immoral in the tendency – if *Guntram* even has such a thing. Ah well, more about that when we can talk about it. My immediate problem is what on earth I am to say in my letter to Ritter, because explanation in writing is extremely difficult and long-winded. For the time being the third act can lie in peace and I shall hardly get as far as scoring it while I am still on my travels. Perhaps the music will clear up some of the misunderstanding.

Ritter warns me against all kinds of demons and influences (Stirner, Nietzsche and others unnamed), which exist only in his imagination, alas; while I am composing I read only Wagner, Schopenhauer and Goethe, so I keep really the very best of company, but in the end there is no one who can forbid me to look at the world through my own eyes from time to time, even if they do not always see straight. In the end it is only what one has seen *oneself* that has any real significance. I am really very sorry that my dear good Ritter has got into such a state about it, and I'm really in something of a quandary as to how I can uphold my convictions, which I am not prepared to renounce, without hurting him.

3 February 1893 (Luxor), to Alexander Ritter

. . . until then I will read your letter over and over again and see if I can *change* my *Guntram* as you wish. For to be frank – now I must ask you for friendship as well as frankness – following your advice amounts to completely overthrowing the whole figure of Guntram, as I have envisaged it for four years . . . I now perceive the difference between our two conceptions of Guntram very clearly in your desire to have him return to the brotherhood and submit contritely to their punishment, an action which from the very first has been alien to my Guntram, or rather, to my conception of the brotherhood itself and of Guntram. You will remember that in the very first version Guntram returns to the brotherhood, after his confession of guilt he is *cursed by the brotherhood*, and only then, finding himself between the brotherhood which casts him out and Freihild who offers him her love, did he make the decision voluntarily to renounce Freihild. I only mention this to elucidate my conception of the brotherhood, vague as it was at the time. In the second version the brotherhood itself has no bearing on the matter at all, and after renouncing Freihild Guntram goes in search of solitude without mentioning the brotherhood in any way that sheds light on his relationship to it or to its aims. Naturally this version was also highly unsatisfactory, and in trying to improve it the only question was whether to throw the brotherhood out of the drama altogether . . .

Now I'll try to shed some light on the character of Guntram, as I see him now, as I hope that I have represented him, and as I have always conceived him, even if only as an ideal. Don't say now: Sträusschen, you're constructing this after the event, you're persuading yourself of it under the pernicious influences that have unconsciously been working on you! (Incidentally, I really have only a nodding acquaintance with all those influences: I didn't get to the end when I was reading Stirner and I believe that I don't overestimate him, at the very least. I've never read Nietzsche's *Beyond Good and Evil*; for the last four months I've studied only Wagner, Goethe and Schopenhauer, and the last, I hope, will provide me with what I would like to say in order to disarm your complaints about the unartistic, un-Christian and immoral tendency of *Guntram*.) . . .

Guntram is the product of an order that has taken upon itself the task of uniting art and religion in the sense that it seeks to convey Christian teachings in artistic forms (using the effect of art on the human spirit) and so to make them clearer to the emotional understanding than ecclesiastical dogma can make them – in short, it seeks to improve mankind through art, that is, works of art with ethical tendency (in our language, you understand me!) This is something which has always proved to be a Utopia, a very attractive Utopia – but alas, a Utopia (our friend Schopenhauer also takes this view in volume 3 of *The World as Will and Idea*); will it ever be different, will the Almighty Will, with its unchanging intelligible character, ever really allow itself to be captured by the 'illusory image'?

According to Schopenhauer the artistic contemplation and representation of ideas are independent in themselves of all ethics; and even though Wagner succeeded in the case of *Parsifal*, that does not mean to say that every other artistic undertaking which intends too strong an ethical tendency from the first does not already, insofar as it is art (Schopenhauer, Vol. 1, pp. 294ff.), contain the seeds of death in itself. Be that as it may – at all events, in an artist whose works have this strong ethical or religious tendency the religious emotion always outweighs the artistic emotion. So it is with my brotherhood: the men who had those ambitions were better Christians than artists. Perhaps you will object that the two cannot be separated; but I believe that they are separate, in principle! . . .

You say that he blasphemes the Faith? But where? His actions are pure Christianity, which in its essence has nothing to do with the 'communion of saints' and the Catholic Church. 'In the end he loves only himself', you write! NO! He *hates* or *recoils from* himself. He has recognized his true self; naturally he can only do that *completely alone*. But there is nothing un-Christian or immoral about that. In the last resort each one of us is the only person who knows *what* he is. But what he does with himself after he has recognized himself is his business! So whose business? Here too, please do not confuse me with my dramatic figure! *I* am not giving up art; and I'm not Guntram either! . . .

4 February

I can forgive you your charge of one-sidedness, but not your criticisms of my *Guntram*. You wish that Guntram was something other than what he is, and therefore you simply ignore the very elements which determine his character. For instance your allegation of the absence of tragedy! You foster an extraordinary little private hatred of sexual love these days and now you refuse to look on Guntram's voluntary renunciation of Freihild as a tragic motive. The deuce: I'm sure that *I* wouldn't have renounced the beautiful Freihild . . .

One other point: you describe Freihild's enamouredness as farcical! Leaving aside the fact that you, my very dear friend, as I have mentioned, would gladly consign all sexual love to farce, an opinion that I do not begin to share – Guntram tears himself away from Freihild without giving a reason, before Friedhold enters. The poor woman has absolutely no means of knowing why! She knows he loves her, really loves her, and so at first she supposes that there is a solely exterior reason forcing him to act as he does, for example a vow made to the brotherhood. Guntram's behaviour towards Friedhold reinforces her supposition, until finally, after Friedhold has taken his leave, she learns from Guntram the true reason for his renunciation.

8 February 1893 (Luxor)
I have written a gigantic letter, twelve pages, to Ritter, and would be very curious to know what he has said about it. Has he understood what I am trying to do in *Guntram*, or have I now given him an even greater shock? I would be very sorry if that is the case, because his various charges are based for the most part on misunderstandings, and I feel truly innocent of all of them. Do find out! Writing letters is such an unsatisfactory business and Uncle Ritter seems to me to be very much inclined to misunderstand, and it may well be that I have really put my foot in it this time with my letter, and perhaps my references to Schopenhauer do not suit him in the least!

13 February 1893 (Luxor)
I am being so diligent that I expect to finish the first act of *Guntram* in the next fortnight; eighty-eight fully scored pages lie completed in front of me, although I usually manage only three pages a day, but many of them are double size. You need not worry, dear Papa, about the large string quartet I want; I do not demand that *Guntram* should be performed at Bayreuth, but one must have a specific size of orchestra in mind in order to be able to score at all, and then the only correct size is the one I specify. This is what comes of having so great an artist on the horn for a

father. As for the four bassoons, they are almost the rule in all French scores, and I need them like my daily bread!

13 February 1893 (Luxor), to Ludwig Thuille

In Marquartstein I shall work on the notorious third act (I assume you are going to Marquartst., I would be delighted, at least, to spend some time with you there again) . . .

The row royal over my third act, which I beg you to read (my sister has it), is amusing me hugely. Uncle Ritter wrote me an imploring letter, which really touched me deeply by its good intentions, but I think I must refuse to do him the favour of changing things; because *Guntram* is now exactly what I have been trying to make it for the past four years, and from the very first Ritter has obviously read something quite different into G.'s character from what I have put there; and with the vagueness that has been typical of the poem until now, Ritter's misunderstanding was only too easy.

I have now read Schopenhauer's *World as Will* with the greatest interest (though also with a few modest reservations) and urgently recommend it to you for it is a great work of art, and I've found a lot of corroboration for my third act in it – *à propos*, see that Uncle Ritter lets you read the letter I sent him, especially as I have now found even more corroboration for Act III. Well, that will keep until we meet!

I found Rösch's letter very interesting, he has understood me on the whole, but his criticism goes too far in the other direction: Guntram cannot be a completely enlightened philosopher in the third act either. He is and he remains a warrior of love (according to his disposition and his training), but one who has recognized that his will, for which he alone bears responsibility, is unalterable. Therefore the bombastic bits must remain; in any case, right at the very end, in spite of all his 'recognition' and in spite of his religious mania having triumphed over his artisthood, Guntram still proves himself, towards Freihild, a true 'warrior of love'. With that he comes full circle.

It's precisely on the subject of 'artisthood' and pure perception that I've found some wonderful ideas in Schopenhauer and at present I'm purifying myself in a quite unusual fashion. Well, you shall all see: at all events I am becoming more and more of an artist, just as Schopenhauer is, for all his solemn protestations, as if he for instance recommended the acceptance or denial of the will: *he simply represents it.* That's all – but that's also – *all.* It's what Goethe did, it's what Wagner did, and we little chaps should follow their example and not preach a moral *sermon*. Well – etc. etc. But do read Schopenhauer! The old boy is magnificent and sharpens one's few wits quite hellishly!

13 February 1893 [in the original 1892], Franz Strauss to R.S.
Ritter has told me that he has written to you about the last act of *Guntram*. I think it better if you wait until your return before you discuss it with him.

15 February 1893 (Luxor)
I spend five or six hours a day working on *Guntram*, the first act (100 pages already) will be finished before the end of February.

24 February 1893 (Luxor)
Before this letter reaches you Act I will be finished; it has been scored very carefully and not too thickly or heavily (130 pages).

1 March 1893 (Luxor)
Two days ago, 27 February, I finished Act I, which I will send to you from Cairo . . . I shall make a gigantic cut in the prelude to Act II, as the existing symphonic poem takes up too much room there. As a result of this planned curtailment of my labours I am already looking forward to beginning to score the second act in a few days time, and I hope to have got up to the Peace Narration before leaving Cairo; then I shall set out to sea and gather new impressions in Sicily, and then in Taormina . . . I shall fall to with renewed vigour on the tasty instrumentational dish of the Peace Narration.

The first act has turned out very refined, one day in two it seems to me to be over-refined; at all events it requires very subtle performance, even if it doesn't contain any very great technical difficulties. On the alternate days I think it is just right; while I am working on it I have always had the feeling that the whole thing may be too simple and ingenuous; afterwards it seems almost too complex – it's a blessing that it can only turn out the way it wants to be. Otherwise one would never be able to set it right.

[Strauss cut 107 bars from the sketch of the orchestral interlude 'The Celebration of Victory at the Ducal Court', before the entry of D minor.]

5 March 1893 (Luxor)
Today I began Act II.

18 March 1893 (Cairo)
I shall be despatching the first act forthwith; Papa is asked not to take too much umbrage at the horn parts; apart from that, he will be pleased to observe the absence of 'pots and pans' in the first act, except in the finale.

25 March 1893 (Cairo)
The second act of *Guntram* has put on weight, fifty pages of it up to the Peace Narration; but I shall save that subtle task for Sicily . . . and enjoy myself idling until then.

4 April 1893 (Taormina)
Tomorrow or the day after I hope to move to the Hotel Timeo . . . to spend four peaceful weeks there with my second act, in sight of Etna, which will probably sing a few volcanic sounds into the second act.

10 April 1893 (Taormina)
I'm hard at work, the Peace Narration is finished, and the second act may be finished within another month, as I have now settled into the work and do four or five pages a day.

14 April 1893 (Taormina)
You find it [Act I] thickly scored? And I have been patting myself on the back over its thinness, I didn't expect that heavy sigh over the horns nearly as much as a shudder at the muted trumpets in the second scene. If things were done as my dear good Papa thinks they should be, the horns would rest throughout the whole opera except perhaps in the finale, where they might blow a few sustained notes as in *Don Giovanni* or *Zauberflöte*; I'm inclined to think that the bassoons are a little overburdened, but that doesn't worry Papchen, he's delighted if his neighbours have plenty to do. Am I right? The scoring will be rather thicker in the second act, I've just finished the War Narration and that's turned into a real *pitched* battle!* I've done a hundred pages (half) of the second act, I shall go on with it here as far as the catastrophe and then stop . . . The last two scenes will be done in Palermo . . . I'm now working quite fast, often five or six pages a day in a relatively short time.

15 April 1893 (Taormina)
I suppose I have experimented somewhat with the bass trumpet;

* '*ein richtiger Strauss*': 'der Strauss', in addition to designating, as it does here, a male person with that surname, means 'bouquet', 'ostrich' and (as it does here too, presumably) 'combat'. *Tr.*

I can always make some changes in rehearsal if need be. The only things that interest me at present are the second act, which is already 132 pages thick, and Sicily.

20 April 1893, Friedrich Rösch to R.S.

. . . the abundant, in some places almost over-abundant polyphony of your orchestral accompaniment, against which it will undoubtedly be difficult for the vocal part to assert itself, as it is not always exactly 'melodious' and for that very reason not very dominant . . .

You may yet end up a thoroughly enlightened (even clarified), tame, peaceable, blue-eyed composer – at least so far as orchestration is concerned . . . Are not the muted trumpets just a little too much in evidence? Is the bass trumpet not to let fly properly a few times? Will the poor, ever-faithful trinity of bassoons [*Fa-Götter*], with their human, all too human lungs, be equal to their task?

21 April 1893 (Taormina), to Eugen Spitzweg

Act II is already two-thirds scored and will be finished in Palermo. You can get a copy of the revised Act III from my parents, nothing has been changed in the first two . . . The score is turning out so beautiful and mouth-watering that it absolutely must be engraved, my dear, poor friend!

6 May 1893 (Taormina), to Alexander Ritter

I'm working frantically on *Guntram* (Act II).

10 May 1893 (Palermo)

Before the end of the month, within the next twelve days, if all goes well I shall have finished Act II. It's going along quickly now, but it's getting rather wild and weighty! Deuce take it – I can't get rid of a certain nervosity in the orchestra, there seems to be nothing I can do about the 'unshorn beats'! There's a restlessness in the rhythms and the colouration, and a nervosity in the figuration – but I cannot do it any other way and those who don't like it will have to fend for themselves! At the present moment I'm writing some beautiful passages for the double basses; the orchestra will have a marvellous time! And it is all the fault of the fated (but still alive to be fêted) Wagner, who fired *Tristan* into our bones, so that we shall never be rid of it again.

I wonder if you would be so kind as to make enquiries as to how to write for tenor horns, what key they should be in and what their range is: 1. the utmost possible, 2. the highest and lowest they can play *comfortably*? I need them for the on-stage music at the end of the second act, where I shall have them instead of the French horns.

14 May 1893, Alexander Ritter to R.S.
. . . regrettable poetic misadventure . . .

(?) May 1893, Ludwig Thuille to R.S.
I showed [your letter] to Uncle Ritter in all innocence, and it seems that later he launched into a furious diatribe, saying that the letter made it perfectly clear that after all you've gone and written the third act entirely according *to your own fancy*. But I think his rage has long 'evaporated', at least he shows no sign of it to me.

(?) May 1893, Ludwig Thuille to R.S.
I'm agog to see how you've set about firing off a third [act] to follow this heaven-storming second! It'll be a glorious moment, chum, when you come galloping up on *this* mount!

15 May 1893 (Palermo)
. . . sit working hard and shall finish the second act by the end of this week. It's Freihild's turn now, who will be very delicate and tidy and a beautiful contrast to the heavy artillery that went before her!

16 May 1893 (Palermo), to Ludwig Thuille
I heartily wish you congenial ideas, joy in creation and the greatest of endurance, for – the deuce – that's a dashed important part of it: I'm only too conscious of it, now that I'm almost at the end of Act II! In full score it comes to 200 pages, plus 132 pages of Act I, that makes 332; and there's still the third little chum to follow, it's beyond a joke! When all that's been done, there'll be the vocal score, but I'm in no condition to do that myself!

17 May 1893 (Palermo), to Alexander Ritter
The third act shall stay as it is until I have played it to you; I still nourish the secret hope that the music will reconcile you to it.

23 May 1893 (Palermo)
Today I played Act III of my *Guntram* to myself on the piano and in my opinion, although it's admittedly hyper-Tristan-ish, it's the most advanced in the precision of expression, the richest and most impressive in the melodic invention, and altogether by far the best thing I've ever written. Of course there'll be a dashed lot of head-shaking, but I'm really quite exceptionally pleased with Act III, and that's very nearly the most important

thing. But it will not be exactly easy to make the orchestration 'transparent and Mozartian'. Hold tight to your seats, my friends! The motivelets come so fast and furious, your heads will spin! Metaphorically speaking!

29 May 1893 (Ramacca)
I am playing a lot of music: the Countess [Blandine von Gravina, née von Bülow] is kind enough to think that my *Guntram* is very fine . . . and in the meantime I dawdle my second act *ben a ben* to its end.

4 June 1893 (Ramacca), to Hans von Bülow
I can prove that I haven't been a complete lazy-bones musically, however, if I tell you that I have orchestrated the first two acts of my opera *Guntram* in full and sketched the third. It's quite a heady piece of music.

5 June 1893, Marie Ritter to R.S. [writing about her uncle, Alexander Ritter]
His family deeply regret that his relationship with you is now other than it was, and they thank you from their hearts for your unremitting efforts to placate him!

7 June 1893
The second act of Guntram was finished on 4 June in Ramacca.

15 June 1893 (Florence) [after sending the score of Act II to Munich]
. . . in the meantime Papa shall feast his eyes on the horn parts in Act II!

[5 September 1893: full score of Act III completed in Marquartstein.]

11 October 1893 (Weimar), to Engelbert Humperdinck
The full score of my *Guntram* is completely finished and ought to be in Munich by the beginning of February! I orchestrated three acts (500 pages) in six months! I think you will like my little score! It is not without interest, very neat and polyphonic!

10 January 1894
What alterations need to be made to *Guntram* will emerge when it goes into production, until then I won't change anything, since everything is performable and in its proper place.

1 February 1894, to a Herr Baron [Bronsart?]
Please accept my heartiest thanks for your kind letter and the friendly interest you have taken in my operatic first-born. Your criticisms coincide exactly with what I myself recognize to be

> weaknesses in it, and I am very conscious that, particularly in Act III, the conceptual outweighs the 'contentual' (if you will permit the expression) and I shall take pains to overcome this weakness in future works, insofar as it can be mastered by diligence and study and is not an inherent failing in my dramatic talent. I myself have the feeling that I have poured out into *Guntram* everything that I have so far learned and only partly experienced, and thus *Guntram* really represents the end of my apprenticeship, and now I must make my way in the wide world . . . With regard to the weakness of the motivation in Act II of *Guntram*, I am convinced that, on the contrary, the music is quite plastic enough, especially in conjunction with the leitmotive, to achieve, hand in hand with solicitous acting, what I decided it would be partly too difficult, partly superfluous to try to achieve by further working on the text alone.

The ending of *Guntram*

The '*Guntram* Chronicle' has shown that Strauss worked on the text of his opera from the summer of 1887 to November 1892, and that he wrote three versions (not counting incidental changes), which he outlined in the long letter he wrote to Alexander Ritter (3–4 February 1893). In 1942, in a piece recalling the first performances of his operas, he had this to say about the final version of the third act:

> Ritter, who had given me sympathy and encouragement, unfortunately took against *Guntram* when I changed the third act to suit my own ideas and, instead of sending Guntram back to be tried by the brotherhood, as Ritter wanted, allowed him to be his own judge, which was contrary to Ritter's philosophy.[4]

Elsewhere he went into greater detail:

> It was Ritter who encouraged me to write the text of *Guntram* which became, however, the reason for the inner estrangement between us. In Egypt I got to know Nietzsche's work, whose polemics against the Christian religion in particular struck a chord in me, and reading him strengthened and corroborated the antipathy which I had unconsciously felt since my fifteenth year for this religion which frees its believers of responsibility for their own actions (through confession). Ritter never completely forgave me for the scene between Guntram and Friedhold in Act III, where Guntram turns his back on the community, passes judgment on himself and denies the brotherhood's right to punish him.[5]

Although Strauss, in that late memoir, associates his reading of Nietzsche in Egypt with the ending that he gave to *Guntram*, he in fact finished revising the text on 23 November 1892, when he was still in Athens. In the letter he sent his father from Luxor on 1 February 1893, he expressly says that he was reading only Wagner, Schopenhauer and Goethe: it is possible that he would in any case not have told his father that he was reading the 'suspect' Nietzsche. It is on record that in the autumn of 1893, in Weimar, Strauss read and discussed with Arthur Seidl, who left a personal reminiscence of the occasion, 'some passages from [Nietzsche's] principal works'. Guntram's decision to sit in judgment on himself is no justification for regarding him as a spokesman of Nietzsche's theory of the superman. Even Eugen Schmitz, one of the proponents of that view, admitted that the ascetic and Christian goal that Guntram sets himself, of immersing his soul 'in eternal, solitary contemplation of the divine' in order to draw near to 'the Saviour's Grace', was 'in strange contrast'.[6] Strauss's own, more general remarks are a more accurate reflection of the facts than the exegesis attempted by his commentators.

Strauss expressly described his religious views, in the second of the two passages quoted above and in a note on the *Alpensinfonie*, as anti-Christian. Only ten months before his death he wrote to Siegfried Trebitsch, the writer and translator of Bernard Shaw: 'Even though the time is near when they will ring the church bell for me for the third time, I shall never be converted and I will remain true to my old religion of the classics until my life's end!' (Montreux, 18 November 1948; the 'religion of the classics' was a concept minted by the philosopher Leopold Ziegler in his book *Das heilige Reich der Deutschen*, 1925.)

The argument about the ending of *Guntram* continued in Strauss's correspondence with Friedrich Rösch in March and April 1893. Rösch wrote him a thirty-page letter about 'Schopenhauer's will' (15 March), tearing the outcome of Strauss's 'independent thought' to shreds and denying Guntram any humanity. When Strauss told him not to teach him things he already knew, but to help him instead, Rösch, an anti-Nietzschean, replied: 'I'm to help you, am I? O thou Jeremiah in need of help!! What would your beloved Nietzsche have to say to that!?!' (9 April) Strauss ignored the criticisms Rösch had already made in his letter of 27 December 1892.

Strauss also referred to the subject of the ending of *Guntram* in the letter he wrote to Joseph Gregor in 1945:

> After the renunciation of tradition:
>
> mein Leben bestimmt
> meines Geistes Gesetz;
> mein Gott spricht
> durch mich selbst zu mir!
>
> [The law of my spirit governs my life; my god speaks through myself to me.]
> – which alienated even my loyal friend (Friedhold) Alexander Ritter from the work he had so long encouraged and welcomed, my path was clear at last for uninhibitedly independent creation. And this untrammeled subjectivity impressed its stamp already on the following work of opposition, *Feuersnot*, a stamp which, except in that great monument of our culture, *Meistersinger*, was completely unknown in operatic literature up to that date.[7]

All the later utterances about the ending of *Guntram* show how conscious Strauss was of its decisive significance for his personal and artistic development. The express identification of Friedhold with Alexander Ritter in the letter to Joseph Gregor needs some qualification: the growth in self-knowledge which led Strauss to make Guntram his own judge was an inner process in which Ritter played virtually no part at all, even if one surmises that Strauss may have foreseen Ritter's opposition to the new ending. It was only the vehemence of Ritter's reaction which allowed him to recognize that his old friend was using the same arguments that he had placed in the mouth of Friedhold to remind Guntram of his duty to submit himself to the laws of the brotherhood. Even if the identification of Ritter with Friedhold may be permissible, very broadly speaking, it is not so with Strauss and Guntram. The idea of personal responsibility expressed in the often-quoted (by Strauss as well as others) lines of Guntram certainly rests on the opinion Strauss had formed for himself – corroboration of which he believed he had found in Schopenhauer – but for all the fundamental significance of the idea, Strauss cannot be identified with the figure of Guntram. He himself vigorously denied any such interpretation in his letter of 13 February 1893 to Ludwig Thuille, quoted above in the '*Guntram* Chronicle'.

In his review of the première of *Guntram* in the *Neue Deutsche Rundschau* and an article 'Richard Strauss, eine Charakterskizze'

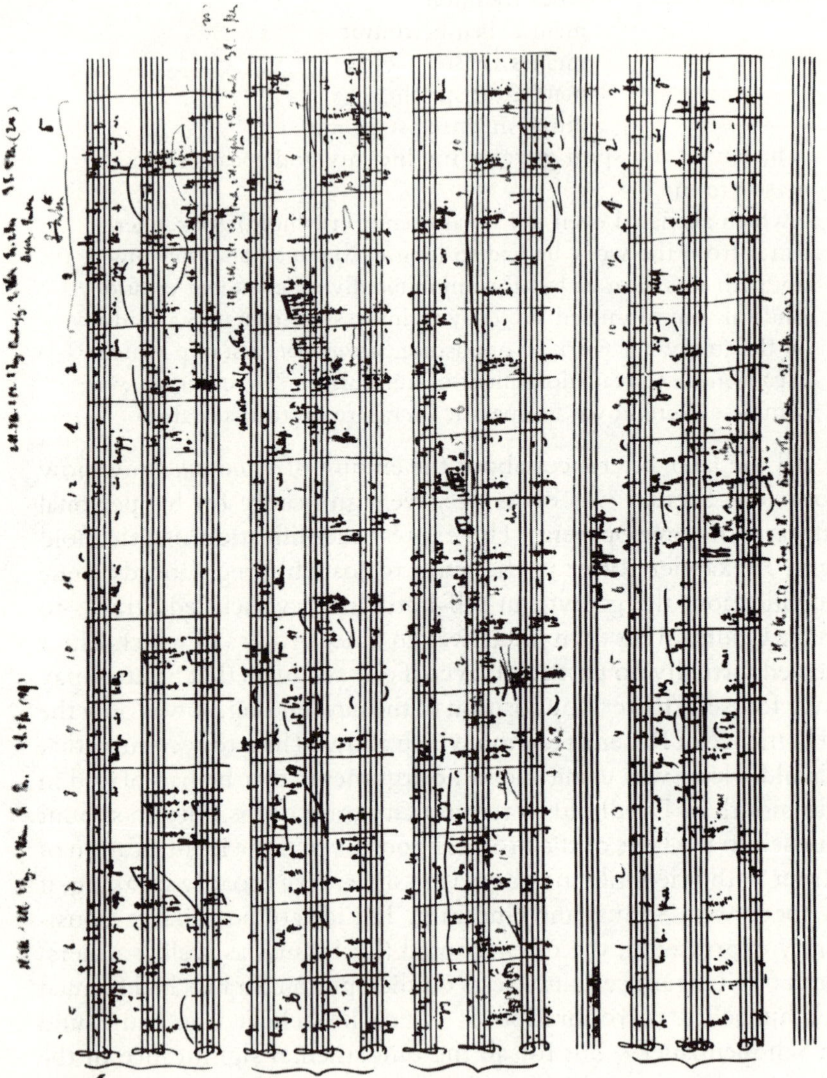

Final scene of *Guntram*, from the particello

(1896; reprinted in *Straussiana*, 1913), Arthur Seidl undoubtedly went too far in claiming that 'the mysterious brotherhood is probably to be interpreted, in the final analysis, as the *Bayreuth Grail Fellowship*, to which his mentor Friedhold (Alexander Ritter) wishes to persuade the "non-conformist" (Guntram-*Strauss*) to return, abandoning *Stirner-Nietzsche*'. The chronology of the events alone casts doubt on it: the controversial new ending had already been written – in 1892 – before Ritter knew anything about it. Strauss evidently expressly contradicted Seidl's interpretation, as emerges from a letter Seidl wrote to him: 'Remember that you rejected it, when I identified you with Guntram, Friedhold with Ritter and the brotherhood with Bayreuth in the *Rundschau*.' (15 January 1896) Seidl's interpretation anticipated a grouping of which Strauss was as yet completely unaware, one which was only beginning to shape itself at the time when he revised the ending of *Guntram*. In his review in the *Neue Deutsche Rundschau* in 1894 (signed D.A.S.), Seidl wrote:

> Guntram, however, is Strauss; the brotherhood is the Wagnerian Grail Fellowship and community of ideas; Friedhold, the emissary from the order, none other than Alexander Ritter, the young composer's friend and guide of many years standing! On this occasion it all ends in solemn and sacred renunciation – an expansive, radiant, hallowed ending, which deeply moved the entire audience and proved once and for all the theatrical effectiveness of this magnificent and incomparable work – but one does not know what may come of it. Will events prove that 'the strongest man upon earth is he who stands most alone' or that 'two heads are better than one' – 'Zwei-einig geht der Mensch am best'?

There can be no doubt that in Bayreuth *Guntram* was understood as a gesture of repudiation, or at least of distancing, but it was not until 1895 that Strauss's personal relationship with Wahnfried entered a critical phase.

Greece

Strauss's long-awaited journey to the south began on 4 November 1892. The travel diary that he started – though it peters out after the middle of December – and the long letters he wrote home are packed with information about the impressions his travels made on him, as well as about his progress on *Guntram*. The diary opens with a reference inspired by his reading of Goethe's *Wilhelm Meister*: '1892, the Wanderjahre begin!' In Brindisi he took ship on the *Mediterraneo*, spent five days in quarantine for cholera on the little island of Vido – he called it a miniature Capri – just off Corfu, and there, inspired by reading Wagner, he drafted a new drama, *Das erhabene Leid der Könige*. On Corfu he visited 'the beautiful, poetic villa of Empress Elisabeth [of Austria], whose unhappy notion, born of misguided, feminine, emotional silliness, to erect a monument to Heine introduces an ugly discord into the whole'. Once again the anti-semitism fired by Ritter reveals itself.

On the way from Corfu to Athens he called at Olympia on 15 November. The site made a deep impression on him and led to the following reflections in his travel diary:

> Uplifted by the heavenly, divinely-inspired peace of this hallowed spot, I praise the good spirit who has led me hither . . . What harmony of nature and art: the greatest contrast to our Christian-German development which finally, in the greatest inward assumption of the religious idea, brought forth the music of the nineteenth century.
>
> Bayreuth – Olympia! There, a great genius rising far above his race, who creates from his own innermost strength the loftiest monument yet erected in the cultural development of all races; *a lone genius!*
>
> Here, a whole race, so receptive to pure visual perception that, for the intrinsically trivial cause of running and wrestling contests, it creates the ideal of beauty represented by the Hermes of Praxiteles, expressing external visible form in its highest perfection. The free sense of beauty, the religion of nature, pure visual perception – Olympia!
>
> Philosophical, world-transcending sublimity, profoundest inwardness – Bayreuth!
>
> *A great race!*
>
> *A great genius!*
>
> What harmony at Olympia, nature, the gentle hills, the smiling heavens, the blissful solitude and the temples and the statuary etc.
>
> Bayreuth – a lonely colossus, raised by *one alone*, looking down upon factories, prisons, asylums!
>
> At Olympia now even the general public and the critics (transformed into chattering magpies and greedy vultures) fit within the framework.

At Bayreuth they will always be a distraction! (12 [*sic*] November 1892)[8]

The validity or otherwise of this bold antithesis is beside the point. The important thing about it is that it shows Strauss confronting – perhaps for the first time – the need to clarify and order his ideas and feelings. The outcome is to be found, on the one hand, in his diary and in other notes made over the same period, and, on the other hand, in the new ending that he gave *Guntram*, after his prolonged struggle with the material.

He arrived in Athens on 16 November, and remained there until 25 November. He described his impressions in long letters to his family. A few passages from them, referring to Greek art, will augment what has already been quoted from his diary. When the present author published Strauss's correspondence with his parents in 1954, the letters he wrote from Athens were not yet available, but there were three replies from his father. Franz Strauss declared his great joy that his son had been so profoundly impressed by the 'sublime, magnificent, divine simplicity and truth to nature of Greek art'. (25 November 1892) Of course, he did not fail to add that he prayed to God the impression would make its mark on Strauss's music. 'You have no need, my dear Richard, to confine yourself to dazzling, external artistic means, God gave you abundant powers of perception, only you must not shut them off and you must not think that simplicity is trivial.' (28 November 1892)

Strauss repeated in his letters some of the ideas he noted in his diary. He referred to the 'most hallowed mood' that had come over him at Olympia.

> I thought of Bayreuth a great deal, and pursued the most beautiful reflections on the Hellenic and the German ideals. I have been enabled to translate all my theories directly into the life of the emotions now, for these temples belong only in this landscape, beneath this sky and to a race which was able to raise the beauty of outward form to the final perfection of a Hermes of Praxiteles.

The 'gigantic force and recklessness of expression' which he encountered in the friezes of the Temple of Zeus (especially the Centauromachy) made the strongest impression of all. (17 November 1892) He also told Hans von Bülow that he had 'brought away an ineffaceable impression' from Olympia. After his first visit to the

Parthenon he told his parents: 'My eyes filled with tears, I was so moved by the powerful beauty of this building. I never thought that architecture could work on the feelings in this way!' (21 November 1892) And in the same letter – in which he also mentions the painting of the statuary – he summed up his feelings: 'A person who has never been to Athens, simply does not know what Greek art is.'

He wrote to Cosima Wagner, too, from Cairo, about the experience of Greece, enlarging on some of the ideas he had already explored in his diary:

> Yes, at this stage of my life the only sensible thing I could have done was to make this journey, I am so glad that I decided on it; for everything that I experienced in Greece, admiration for the glory of Hellenic art on the soil whence it sprang, astonishment at the magnificent buildings in the landscape for which and in which alone it was fitting they should be erected, beneath the sky that needs *must* shine above them – these are impressions that will shape my whole life.
>
> Until now I did not know that a building can move a person to tears, and I learned what sculpture is when I saw the Parthenon.
>
> One does not fully grasp the Hermes of Praxiteles, the original of which (at Olympia) far surpasses all conceivable and possible ideas of beauty (those which one might form with the aid of an audacious imagination from all its reproductions), until one has also seen the Nike of Phidias. This is the more especially so when, in a rich collection like that in Athens, one is able for the first time to survey the whole course of the development of Greek plastic art, its origins in Egyptian art, how the Greeks gradually bring those rigid forms to life, how the expression of the heads steadily becomes more characteristic, how joy in developing technical mastery leads to the 'exaggeration' of expression (in the archaic Centauromachy in the frieze on the Temple of Zeus at Olympia) and is then gradually adapted to the attainment of the highest form of beauty –
>
> *from sculpture to music*
> from the Hellenic joy of life to Christianity,
> from the outward to the inward human existence,
> *from Olympia to Bayreuth*,
>
> that I have now taken up into myself through the eye and heart, that I now know, because I have experienced it.
>
> When I stood, in Olympia, on the site of the Olympic truce, on a spot so exquisitely holy, completely encircled by gentle

green and brown hills, the sacred temple precincts between two rivers still so well preserved, I was so much put in mind of Bayreuth. Here at Olympia a race, in the closest harmony with nature, creates from within itself festivals, which are essentially trivial in content but nevertheless ultimately bring forth an ideal of exterior beauty of form like the Praxitelean Hermes. Race, art, nature, religion unite in a harmony of optimism which, through the perfection of its representation, exercises a truly fascinating effect on the spectator, and to which one must surrender, whether one will or not! Bayreuth, on the other hand, represents the utmost isolation of the Christian genius, hovering inaccessibly on the wings of music above a race which is no longer capable of following it, no longer has anything in common with it. The definition of 'race' as those who share a common need applies, in my view, only to the Greeks; now there is no longer a 'race', now there are only lonely geniuses.

I don't know if I express myself clearly enough, esteemed lady; I put it so briefly, the ideas themselves are old and long familiar to me, but as actual experiences I find them so new and wonderful.

In Egypt, as yet, interesting as the country is, wonderful as the sun, light and colour are, bustling and amusing as the life of the people is, the only impression I have received that is comparable in magnificence to anything I experienced in Greece has been from the Pyramids. For the effect they make is almost a truly artistic one; a pyramid means little enough in itself, but set in that natural landscape, against the soft lines of the sand dunes, it is the only thing that belongs fittingly to the setting and the beholder has to admire the skill with which the naivety of the ancients always unconsciously did the right thing. One draws near, as it were, to the original state of artistic feeling and refreshes oneself at this monumental naivety, like Antaeus from contact with the earth. (9 December 1892)

Before travelling on to Egypt, let us pause with Strauss in Athens. His visits to the theatre – where he heard an operetta, *Joséfine vendue par ses soeurs*, in as miserable a performance as if the Wilde Gung'l had tried to sight-read *Götterdämmerung*, and Ambroise Thomas's *Hamlet*, which he described as the acme of stupidity – disappointed him as much as the 'Greeks of today', whom he comprehensively condemned, without any real knowledge of them, in superficial and disparaging terms. While he was still in Athens he wrote down some exploratory comparisons of

Greek art and music in his diary. It is thoroughly characteristic of his interpretation of Beethoven, and also of Wagner and Liszt, in those days, that he came to the conclusion that in performing

> the masterworks of a Beethoven, a Wagner, exaggeration of expression unfortunately [seems] almost necessary, in order to rescue any part of the content, which has almost always been totally expunged by incompetents, especially at a time when a large number of guild members [i.e. professional musicians] deny that music has any poetic content at all.

And he believed that later ages would regard Wagner as the 'true classicist'. (Diary, 22 November 1892)

The Egyptian winter

On 24 November, the day on which he at last wrote out the final version of Act III of *Guntram*, Strauss took his leave of the Acropolis, and the next day, after climbing the Lykabettos for one last time in the early morning, he took ship for Egypt, where he remained a full four months, until the end of March 1893, staying at first in Cairo and spending most of the rest of his time in Luxor. While he filled his letters with accounts of external events and impressions – sightseeing, the voyage along the Nile, the exotic life of the ordinary Egyptians and the contrast it afforded to the luxury of life in Shepheard's Hotel in Cairo, the plan to sail up the Nile in a houseboat with a German couple on honeymoon and its cancellation when the young wife fell ill – in his travel diary he attempted to formulate experiences and insights as well. After visiting some mosques he noted:

> Large dimensions and remarkable, but lacking any real artistic effect after the Greek temples. I feel as if I already know Egypt and a sense of surfeit creeps over me as I recognize how transient is the hold exerted by anything which one takes in like this, from outside, without any *artistic* effect.
>
> The effect of nature is more enduring, because she is more various of course. But in the long run the only things that hold man are what he himself has produced and placed in nature: artistic work or the reception of the artistic work of others, the work of our great geniuses.
>
> The highest thing is to be alone with the great spirits, to be immersed in them. To be alone with oneself.

> Between 'nature' and 'art' (in the above sense) stands love, as that which is governed by the strongest drive (of human life) and belonging really, as the necessary extension of one's own ego, to 'being alone with oneself'. (Diary, 29 November 1892)

The day after writing that he pursued the same idea in a letter to Alexander Ritter:

> I keep myself busy, work hard, and it is very necessary that I should, because – I have to confess it – I am beginning to feel a little surfeited with all this sight-seeing. The following opinion has now taken firm root in me: everything that a man takes in from the outside – the greatest natural beauties, the most colourful bustle of everyday life, the most novel and the most curious of sights – when sheer variety in itself ceases to attract, then it all loses its effect, if its effect is not *artistic*. I could look at the Acropolis and the Hermes of Praxiteles at Olympia every day, and every day I would be amazed and deeply moved . . .
>
> The world has so little to offer; but art is eternally new, eternally beautiful; the true Eldorado is, first, the great lens through which the great spirits have looked at the world and *what* they saw, second, making one's own lens and using it, as a 'great spirit', to view the world within oneself (however small); speaking seriously: one's own artistic creations . . .
>
> *Classical* Greece filled me with the highest exaltation. One must have visited Athens to be able to understand Greek art to the full . . . I have been reading Aeschylus, Sophocles, Plato, and now luxuriate in *Wilhelm Meister*; dear God, there's so much in that book – and here I am, snuffling warm air, swallowing dust incessantly and growing into a giant. (30 November 1892)

All this is in tune with notes Strauss also made in connection with his reading of Schopenhauer at this time, to which we shall return. He found much that pleased and interested him in Egypt. The temple of Isis on the island of Philae made him think of Sarastro's 'holy halls', and in Edfu, where he visited the temple of Horus, he was greatly impressed by the gigantic dimensions of the imposing, wonderfully well preserved temples, but although they were far larger than anything Greece had to offer they could not compare with the grace and beauty of Greek temples. 'They bear the same relationship to them as Bach's B minor Mass to a Mozart G minor symphony!' Over and over again his letters refer to the sense of well-being he enjoyed at having escaped from the stresses and the burdens of his conducting career, which he pursued with such a combination of crusading zeal and distaste:

> Every day I feel this heavenly calm and tranquillity doing me more good, oh, it's wonderful not to have to wear oneself out in a miserable theatre, which is no fit place for a really serious artist but just a sty for the place-hunters. I'm so grateful to our good, kind uncle for making it possible for me to enjoy this happiness . . . Truly, it moves me so much that tears come to my eyes! (To Hanna, Luxor, 17 January 1893)

In a letter to Humperdinck, too, he waxes lyrical about the cloudless skies of Egypt, where he was living in the lap of luxury. 'The climate with its wonderfully dry, light air' suited him magnificently. (27 January 1893) Writing to his father on 25 January, he said 'I'm very well indeed, while my nerves gradually relax, my noddle is improving itself, studying and thinking up all sorts of curious things', which was a reference to his reading of Schopenhauer and his new ideas for operas. On 1 March he told his parents:

> November and December were still 'rest'; now it's time to put on weight and from now to the end of August [when he was due to return to Weimar] will probably serve my turn! I realize more and more in every respect that taking this long rest was the right and only thing for me to do at this juncture.

In February, in Luxor, he met the blind Landgrave of Hessen, with whom he had played Bach in Weimar, and the young English composer and poet, Clement Harris. Harris (1871–97), the son of a wealthy ship-owner, studied with Clara Schumann, became an intimate of Wahnfried and later of Stefan George and his circle. He travelled to the Far East in 1892 with Siegfried Wagner. He took part in the Greek rising and fell in Turkey. His death was commemorated by Stefan George in his collection *Der siebente Ring* by a poem, *Pente Pigadia*, which has the sub-title 'to Clement, fallen 23 April 1897'.[9] In his diary Harris mentioned meeting Strauss in Luxor; they had already become well acquainted in Wahnfried, so it was a pleasant surprise. They were to meet again in Karlsruhe in January 1894.

Strauss went to the opera in Cairo too, seeing *Rigoletto* and Meyerbeer's *Dinorah* among other things. With the burden, as it had become, of his work in the theatre and the concert-hall removed, his pent-up urge to create music of his own, on the foundations of the 'music of expression' which he had laid in *Don Juan*, *Tod und Verklärung* and *Macbeth*, could at last burst forth in its full strength. He wrote to Arthur Seidl: 'Best of all, I would like to stay here in the solitude of the glorious desert, quite alone with the Christian God, who is paid so little attention in Germany now, and I would compose one opera after another, quite unconcerned about what people in Europe were doing.' (19 December 1892)

He had begun to compose the music of *Guntram* while he was still in Weimar, but it was only now that it got fully under way. There are frequent references in his letters to the speed of his progress, in both sketching and orchestration. By February he was working five or six hours a day at it, so that, having completed the composition in short score in Cairo on Christmas Eve, he finished the full score of Act I on 27 February 1893 and went straight on to start Act II. When he left Luxor in the middle of March he had got as far as the beginning of Guntram's Peace Narration.

The decision to make Guntram his own judge represented – as Strauss himself was conscious – the recognition and the clearing of the artistic path along which he was determined to go from that time forward. Time and again he stressed how well and how easily he was working, left to himself. 'The more I am alone, the better I amuse myself; I only get bored when I find myself in incompatible company; when I'm alone I look at things in tranquillity and I think that's always so satisfying.' (To his father, Luxor, 24 February 1893)

His friends had noticed, too, how much he needed this rest and solitude. Alexander Ritter, for instance, had written to the singer Rosa von Milde (to whom he had dedicated several of his songs and who was a colleague of Strauss in the Grand Ducal service in Weimar) that a rest of some length was vitally important for the good of Strauss's physical and spiritual condition:

> His intention was to throw himself into his usual frenzy of work this winter. I think I may take credit for getting him to change his mind and go on holiday. I was really most concerned about him, as I had heard from his doctor that his lungs – for hereditary reasons – were not strong; that the most important thing was to get him through from his twenty-eighth to his thirty-second year in good health and that above all he should not be exposed to any kind of emotional disturbances. The public in Weimar and the Grand Duke and Duchess have of

> course always recognized and welcomed all that Strauss has done, with his heroic efforts, for the Weimar theatre. But unfortunately the extraordinary attitude of his superior [Bronsart] has caused him some very unnecessary emotional disturbances on a number of occasions. Now Strauss is in Cairo, writes some very contented letters and seems to be well. (3 December 1892)

Das erhabene Leid der Könige

In November 1892, as has already been mentioned, Strauss passed the five days of quarantine he had to spend on the island of Vido by sketching a scenario for an opera about the ancient Germans, inspired by his reading of Wagner's *Opera and Drama* and *State and Religion*. He called it *Das erhabene Leid der Könige* (The Sublime Suffering of Kings), and the principal character was to be Arminius (Hermann), the leader of German resistance to Roman rule in the age of Augustus. In Luxor he resumed work on it, producing drafts which are so voluminous that it is really only possible to give excerpts here, to illustrate the '*Ur*-Germanic cravings' – as Friedrich Rösch teasingly called them – which Strauss continued to nurture even after his return to Weimar by further reading in ancient and medieval German history. In fact this reading may have been in connection with a second operatic plan which also engaged his attention in Luxor, with the title *Der Reichstag zu Mainz* (The Imperial Diet at Mainz). Most of the sketches for *Das erhabene Leid der Könige* are to be found in one of the notebooks in which he kept his diary, immediately following sketches for *Der Reichstag zu Mainz*, but a sample of the first draft of the former is given here because it dates from as early as November 1892:

> Hermann: sanguine, moral, far-sighted, ready to sacrifice all personal interests to the good of his people, in part such as he recognizes it, in part such as the people believes it to be. In spite of the contrast between them, H. feels the warmest friendship for Marbod, as well as recognizing that political alliance with him is the sole possible means of keeping the Roman invaders at bay. Hermann has been married for three years to Th.[usnelda], a woman who loves a man to be strong! They have a two-year-old son. Marbod has fallen passionately in love with Th. and, betraying his friend, tries to seduce her. Although Th. recognizes the stronger man in M. (unconsciously still resists

[him]), she tells H. of Marbod's betrayal, demanding redress and a declaration of war against Marbod!

H. acknowledges Marbod's breach of faith, but also the political inexpediency of having him as an enemy (because of the Roman threat). Th., as a woman, for whom this is no argument against her desire for revenge, condemns H. as a weakling, believes, in her wounded honour, that she is in love with Marbod, leaves H., and, declaring herself wholly for Marbod, goes to him, taking her child and surrendering herself to him.

Thus H. has sacrificed his life's happiness to his people, as he believes. Marbod, in the possession of Thusnelda and taking advantage of a period of truce arranged with the Romans, now comes out openly against Hermann, who is still confident of the support of his people.

Act II. Heath, storm, the Bohemians draw near; Hermann, torn by doubt, finally abides by his decision to remain at peace with Marbod, at all costs. Marbod egotistical, of his nature a believer in the rule of *force*, absolute despot, who regards the good of his people as guiding them by a strong hand (whither is of secondary importance), if necessary driving them with a whip towards their prosperity. Devoid of finer feelings, in order to attain his personal ends he sets himself above all moral constraints.

The Romans are at the gate; a Roman praetor demands that the allies H. and M. should cede their land. 'The Germani have no right to the land!'

H. 'The right of the labour expended on the land!'

Pr. 'We Romans do not recognize that.'

H. 'But it is right in *German* law' and wants to dismiss the Roman claims out of hand. His Cheruscans are with him (only Arbogast warns of the danger of resisting the all-powerful Romans).

But H. feels strong enough in his alliance with Marbod to defy the Romans. Marbod, whose ambition is to be sole ruler of both Bohemians and Cheruscans, betraying Hermann, tries to mediate, asks for time to consider; his intention is to use the Romans against Hermann during the interval, believing that if he dethrones Hermann he will still be able to defeat the Romans with the combined Bohemians and Cheruscans.

Arbogast, who as a Cheruscan has the same plan (using the Romans against Marbod), warns Hermann of Marbod's treachery, but fails to shake Hermann's faith in Marbod's friendship and the national ideal. (The Romans will be defeated by the *united* Germans.) Arbogast in turn sees in H.'s blind faith in Marbod the end of the Cheruscans' *independence*, as a Cheruscan particularist he does not comprehend [?] H.'s great ideas of national unity, he now makes a secret alliance with the Romans, with Cheruscan *independence* as a condition, with the object of overthrowing Hermann and placing himself at the head of the Cheruscans to defeat Marbod.

Arbogast – – Marbod; between them the representative of the national ideal, Hermann.

A. tells Hermann that Marbod wants to overthrow him and place the Cheruscans under his own rule! Hermann does not believe it, and even if it were true: 'what matter if I rule, I am ready to renounce the throne, as long as national unity is preserved.'

Contrast with Arbogast the *particularist*:
'For every man who does not know how to rule his own inner self would be only too content to rule the will of his neighbour, according to his own proud wishes.' Faust, Part II.

Schopenhauer: reading and reservations

In Luxor Strauss once again began to read Schopenhauer with intense interest, filling the pages of his diary with numerous excerpts and page references to the edition of *The World as Will and Idea* published in Leipzig in 1888 by F. A. Brockhaus. He also noted down 'some modest reservations', many of them relating to the matter of sexual love, which appears to have concerned him particularly at that time, but there are also some comments on the question of artistic creativity, which doubtless have some association with his new dramatic plans. He had first read Schopenhauer, at Alexander Ritter's instigation, in Meiningen in May 1886, while he was working on the unfinished Rhapsody for piano and orchestra. For a time he was weary of the philosopher – admittedly during a period of exhaustion brought on by his illness in the summer of 1892: he wrote to his sister that he had been reduced to holding a conversation about gun-dogs with Ludwig Thuille, 'for no better reason than that I wanted to get Schopenhauer out of my head, as I am thoroughly sick of him'. (8 June 1892) On the other hand, in an undated letter from Egypt, he told his father that he was reading *The World as Will and Idea* and feeling greatly refreshed by 'the wonderful structure of this gigantic edifice of speculative thought'. He entrusted his reservations to his diary.

They are the only reflections of their kind that Strauss left, and for that reason the most important of them, revealing the subjective limitations of his view of Schopenhauer, are reproduced here. The following comes in the diary immediately after the second draft scenario for an opera about Don Juan:

> What a peaceful, rapt expression the moon has, on whose face the sun, the abettor of all generation, beams its light throughout the sweetness of the night.
>
> The moon here is like woman, who long continues raptly to experience not merely ideally but physically the enjoyment [she receives] in the happy hour of love from the man, whose ecstasies in the union of the two sexes are much more transient, while on her face the happy smile of rapture continues to shine long after.
>
> That smile – I have never seen such or a similar expression of the true sensation of happiness! Is not the way to the redemption of the will to be sought here (in the condition of the receiving woman)! Not in the denial of the will, but in the '*consciousness*' of affirmation?
>
> 'The ecstasy of the act of generation is the delusion practised by the species on the individual; after the act the delusion vanishes!' Yes, for the beast, or for those humans who are only beasts and make no use of their gift of human reason. But for the human being who loves with full consciousness, this consciousness is so overpowering and lasting that the consciousness of the enjoyment, the physical *as well as the psychic*, endures (in the man as well).
>
> Can love be so intensified in the male that the moment when the delusion is effaced is not experienced at all? That would be the triumph of the consciousness of the affirmation of the will (not affirmation of the body, but actually *complete consciousness of desire*; thus!)
>
> Did the will perhaps finally ultimately (?) create consciousness – for this purpose? Who knows?
>
> Will is desire: the desire for eternal being in continual renewal.
>
> The consciousness of *eternal being* in the eternally new, never-ending *becoming*; the consciousness of eternal generation (each individual does as much as he can) and, through that, of eternal being [is] the sublime happiness ensured by the enjoyment of the act of generation.

Richard Strauss in Egypt, 1893

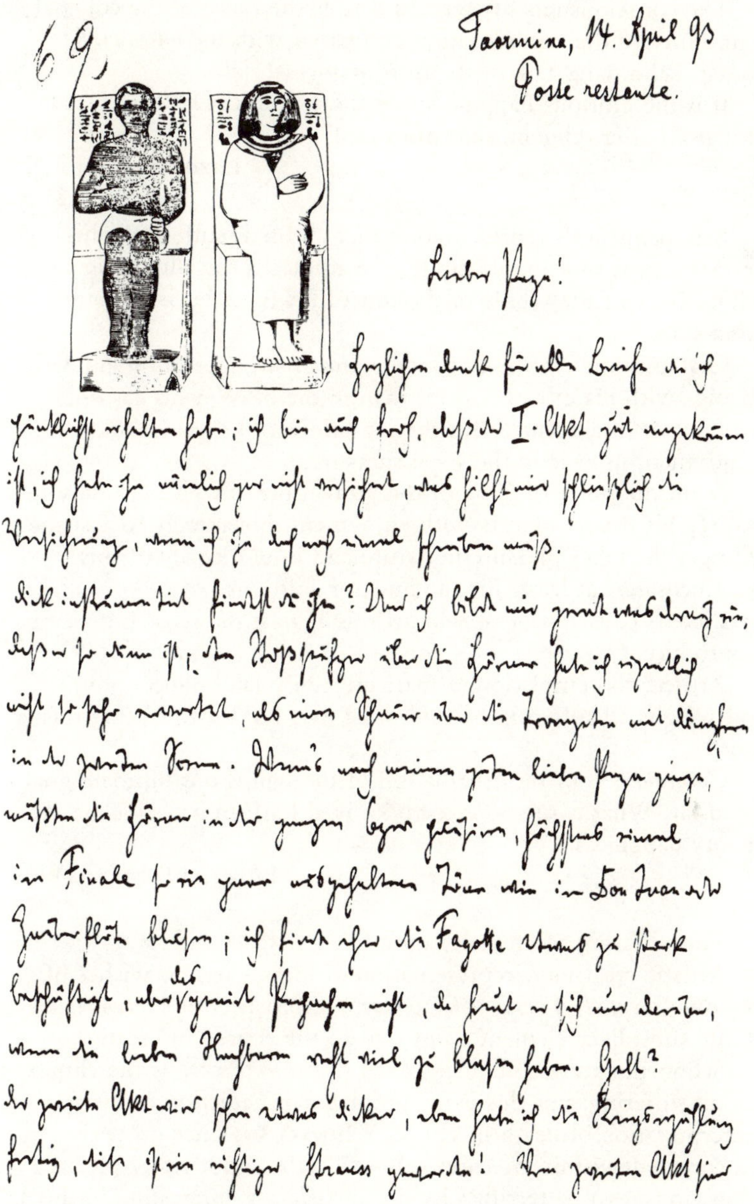
69

Taormina, 14. April 93
Poste restante.

Lieber Papa!

Letter to his father from Taormina, 14 April 1893

The consciousness of eternal being is the cause of the colossal sublimity of the said sensation compared with the *unreasoning* beast! Who dares talk of the *curse of original sin*!

It is the glorious happiness that the will has at last produced for itself after diligent objectification!

Luxor, January 1893

Schopenhauer's representation that all life is suffering – his pessimism is thoroughly subjective and lacks the admirable objectivity of the whole of the rest of his thought; is therefore one-sided.

Certainly the emotion of love is much stronger in the human being, with his gift of reason, than in the beast, who has only the gift of intelligence. But the sensations of happiness and enjoyment in exactly the same measure.

From the point of view of the human being who lives only to satisfy his desire: he eats with enjoyment, not merely to assuage hunger; he takes pleasure in nature and in works of art; this compensates, at least, for the intenser suffering.

Love is consciousness, what is this against the sensual urge to reproduce.

Artistic contemplation, artistic creativity (and philosophy) outweighs all suffering tenfold in its joy. I at least feel that this is so.

Consciousness of the affirmation of the will is our ultimate goal – so far. What is to come, who knows! I affirm consciously, that is my happiness!

Luxor, 4 February 1893

The suffering of eternally unfulfilled wishes?

Artistic creativity, representation of ideas – has no wishes of its own; *in itself it bestows happiness*; the prospect of success is a quite subsidiary element compared to the ecstasy of creation.

Schopenhauer so often speaks of death as terror, as the climax of all suffering; but this is in complete contradiction to his interpretation of death in vol. 2. Whoever has once properly acknowledged this interpretation of death cannot really (in his consciousness) be terrified by death. (Islam is interesting in this.)

Magnificent corroborative evidence is *Tristan*; since the third act of *Tristan, death as a truly tragic ending is hardly possible any more*!

Affirmation of the will must properly (p. 385) be called

affirmation of the body; for the will as such can really neither affirm nor deny but only *desire* itself.

Goal of the will – Consciousness of desire!

A woman, who has had an intimate relationship with a man for years, but who refuses when he declares that he actually wishes to marry her, because she is too proud to be married only 'for that reason'!

This last idea is taken up again in the sketches for *Der Reichstag zu Mainz*, which follow the criticisms of Schopenhauer in the diary.

Strauss's distancing of himself from Schopenhauer and the degree of self-knowledge to which he had attained are encapsulated in the words: 'I affirm consciously, that is my happiness.' Denial of the self is swept aside by affirmation of the self.

Der Reichstag zu Mainz

The fragmentary sketches for *Der Reichstag zu Mainz*, which follow the notes on Schopenhauer in Strauss's diary, are concerned essentially with the same range of ideas as those attempts to understand himself better. They are important for the confirmation of the philosophy of life which he now adopted at the relatively late age of twenty-eight, during this journey undertaken to restore his health, and they are equally important for the tendency, which is even more marked in them than in *Guntram*, to draw inspiration for his artistic creation from his personal experiences. Before reproducing the scenario and other more fragmentary drafts, it is necessary to make certain observations. First, it should be noted that initial letters are used inconsistently, that is, they change several times in the course of the notes: the man with whom Strauss identifies to a certain extent is known as both A. and P., the woman is sometimes called B. and sometimes P., and ends up with the name Magda. B. is also used for the 'artist striving for ethical goals', who is undoubtedly inspired by Alexander Ritter. The following excursus, relating to Ritter's personal life, is also necessary to explain S. and her relationship with A. and the male B.

S. stands for the Russian pianist Sonja von Schéhafzoff, whom we have already encountered as the pupil of Bülow and a friend of Marie Ritter and Friedrich Rösch. Strauss too had been on a friendly footing with her since Meiningen. Thuille, in one of his letters to Strauss, informed him that Sonja had asked after him very pressingly. At the age of fifty-nine Ritter had fallen head over heels in love with the 'heavenly child', to whom he dedicated his two Lenau settings Op. 17, *Heimatklang* and *Mahnung*. Franz Strauss frequently mentioned Ritter's infatuation in the letters he wrote to Richard between the autumn of 1892 and the autumn of 1893:

> Yesterday, for the first time since you left, I met Ritter at Leibenfrost's. Frau Ritter was with him and of course Fräulein von Schéhafzoff . . . The worthy Ritter must be dreadfully in love with that young woman. By translating his operas into French she has thrown him yet another bait. How long will it go on, I wonder? May it end soon and well! (5 October 1892)

A few weeks later:

> I very rarely see the good Ritter, who seems to be completely monopolized by the Russian girl . . . He now goes to Leibenfrost's as early as 5 o'clock and has an arrangement, as I observed on one occasion, to meet the lady there. (16 November 1892)

Once his comment is particularly severe:

> Just look at your friend Ritter; he has allowed a woman to get such a hold over him that he no longer has any interest in your affairs. In my eyes they are no friends of yours.

Franz Strauss's lack of sympathy may have derived in part from his fundamental differences with Ritter over artistic matters, but that his representation of the facts was objectively correct is confirmed by the letters Richard received from Friedrich Rösch, Ludwig Thuille and Marie Ritter. Rösch, for instance, wrote from Munich: 'Fräulein von Schéhafzoff was here for ten days, reason enough in itself to keep our good uncle in Munich by enchantment. (From 15 September Sonja is settling here permanently!!!)' (28 August 1892) Ludwig Thuille wrote: 'Ritter is still occupied with the "heavenly child" and fairly unendurable.' (30 January 1893) But a letter from Marie Ritter is particularly informative:

> I cannot express adequately my regret that my uncle has turned against [*Guntram*], after praising it so highly last summer. But the presence of Asia in Munich means that I am not so close to my uncle, since I cannot join in the unstinting glorification [of Sonja] that he demands. His family deeply regret that his relationship with you is now other than it was and they thank

> you from their hearts for your unremitting efforts to placate him! It's simply a bad time for all who were normally close to him and worst of all for his family. Let's hope that it will pass and the old circle will join up again! Till then we must be patient. You must be too, and don't come home expecting too much! (Bad Reichenhall, 5 June 1893)

Strauss will probably have received this letter just before leaving Ramacca.

It is understandable that the biography of Ritter by his son-in-law Siegmund von Hausegger makes no reference to the episode, but it has to be mentioned here, because the sketches for *Der Reichstag zu Mainz* leave no doubt that the affair gave Strauss the idea for the interplay between some of his characters, and that they represent, to some extent, himself, Ritter and Sonja. If he had written the opera, no doubt this would have been veiled in some way; perhaps the personal relevance was actually the reason for abandoning the plan. There is no way of knowing now whether in real life Sonja had a penchant for Strauss, as is suggested in the triangle formed by A. (Strauss), S. (Sonja) and B. (Ritter) in the scenario. The few letters from Sonja to Strauss provide no evidence in support of the notion, and Thuille's allusion to her, quoted above, can hardly be taken as proof.

> What is the psychological and emotional effect of vision on a blind man who has regained his sight? Three artists discuss the question:
>
> A., the truest artist, whose chief element is conscious seeing (I myself), praises the sun, the most gladdening of things, and its correlative, the eye, which grants the sight of the glories of nature, the sight of his beloved to the man formerly blind, and lets him for the first time aspire to the highest goal of the will, full consciousness of affirmation or denial.
>
> B., the artist striving for ethical goals (old): what glories will the blind man not have seen in his imagination, colours used to be far brighter to him, half the 'suffering of the world' remained invisible to his perception. He is disappointed, he had imagined the sun far more beautiful; now he can actually see all the misery which was previously only a distant, inchoate murmur, barely reaching to his ears, barely disturbing the purity of his emotional existence from afar. His emotional existence was a nocturnal vision which has now vanished; in his disappointment he

succumbs to the sin which the eye first brought into the world. If the human race was blind, sin would be impossible.

A.: And art too!

B.: We would not need art then, in order to restore the lost purity of art to mankind.

B. [*sic*, should be A.]: That is not the purpose of art at all.

In spite of that, A. achieves this goal by his art, when his singing has such an effect on Duke Heinrich that at the Imperial Diet in Mainz Heinrich voluntarily confesses to his brother Otto I [Holy Roman Emperor, 936–73] that he himself was the instigator of an attempt to assassinate him. As a reward, Otto raises the strolling players to a guild and grants them standing before the law.

The above discussion is made dramatic by the presence of a woman, S., who loves A. without being loved by him in return: she has attached herself to B., aware of his strong tutelary influence on A. B. is himself in love with her, really, while believing that what he feels for her is only heavenly love. S., who actually shares B.'s opinion, professes agreement with A., in order to find favour with him: but the more she draws close to him, the less attractive he finds her.

C., a foolish singer, butts into the conversation and agrees with B., who thereupon contradicts him and suddenly declares that A. is right, for B. is so personally subjective that he will not allow C., whom he detests, to be right even when he shares his opinion.

Duke Heinrich pursues P., a true woman (!), loved by A. and loves him in return. In his love for her, the first passionate woman without [illegible], without intellect by comparison with S., whose bluestocking wisdom, religious hysteria, repels A. as unfeminine, A. recognizes the purity of love and knows a moment of true and most profound happiness, which outweighs qualitatively so much suffering.

In a very stirring scene P. wrests Heinrich's secret from him, and reveals it to A., who decides to unmask the duke by his art, and succeeds in doing so.

(Cf. Grillparzer's self-revelations as character traits for B.)

A. argues and glorifies the beauty of true sexual love, the quite unique and ideal extension of the male and female element in nature, which Schopenhauer takes so little account of and therefore misunderstands so gravely as the mere act of physical reproduction; it is so with the beast but not with – the artist!

R. Louis, *Der Widerspruch in der Musik*, p. 31, pp. 50ff.[10]

Act I. P. conceals her love for A. (while S. makes a sentimental display of it); flirts with Duke H., recites a poem by him (or acts in a play by him), which appears to give her such delight that A. rushes off in despair. S. follows him, tries to exploit the opportunity, but A. corrects her and explains the true nature of love (perhaps B. can intervene too). In Act II H. confesses; he seeks to quiet his gnawing conscience by making love to P., as she will not listen to him, he grows frenzied, tries to force her (at this moment my brother is being killed at my behest, do you think I shall not have my way with a woman?). Thus P. learns his secret. Then A. comes to her, through the excitement of the scene her virgin modesty, which has held her back from A., is overcome, she tells him what has happened to her and at the same time confesses her love to him. (In this love scene the above ideas: happiness shining in the eyes of the loving woman, the moon etc. – p. 14 [of Strauss's diary; cf. p. 309 above].)

In the first act, in the play scene, C. plays the part of the artist whose technical ability is too slight to present in a beautiful form all the fantasies that buzz about in his head. He disgusts B., amuses everyone else!
N.B. p. 5, beginning of Act I, with reference to P. and A.

P. is a feckless youth, fritters away his genius on trifles, songs to love and springtime. Magda loves him, but will not admit it as she fears his frivolity and would rather go without love than be abandoned later. Marriage is forbidden to the strollers.

After the scene with Heinrich, however, she breaks out, take me, do not ask questions! Magda betrays to him what Heinrich let slip; he at once wants to disclose it – at first she does not want him to, in order not to have her virtue sullied (although she resisted H.). It occurs to him: What value has our word against the duke, who only needs to lie. P. then gets his idea for Act III etc. etc.

At the end of the scene he urges her to give herself to him entirely – she is weak, begins to weep, hurries into the next room. He sits silent, in muted expectation.

Without his hearing her she enters softly, puts his [*sic*] arm round him and whispers only: P. He cries aloud: Magda – they fall into each other's arms, curtain!

Next a crowd scene: the attempt to assassinate the emperor has become known. Wild confusion until a herald proclaims that the assassins have fled, but the emperor is unharmed and will hold the Diet the next day in spite of what has happened. Service of thanksgiving. Resumption of the festivities, at which the strolling minstrels are to perform etc.

The old minstrel sings an improvised hymn of thanks for the emperor's escape, in which the crowd joins in enthusiastically.

C. the poetaster, his heart full of feeling for the true and the beautiful, without the ability to create, has faith in P., and affection for him (perhaps he warns the lovers in Act II!)

P., the true poet, ability and gifts first-class, but still a trifler and not fully devoted to the service of the true Muse, true art.

B., the poet purely in the service of theories, old, finally in his religious zeal turns away from P. altogether.

C. sings a song in the first act, perhaps as a riposte to the old poet, in defence of P., who perhaps is hindered by modesty and the most delicate shame from profaning the holiest things in his heart by giving them public utterance. Only P. hears the song sympathetically, its confused form makes the other singers laugh.

Magda at the beginning of Act II (before Heinrich enters) in loving mood, thinking of P.: If he came in now, would I be able to resist him?

Final scene of the last act: the emperor raises the strollers to the status of a guild, grants them rights before the law, the wedding, M. and P. the first married couple among the strollers. P. their leader. B. bows to him, whose genius proved itself in the hour of need.

There are further notes, supplementing the scenario of *Der Reichstag zu Mainz*, in another place in the diary:

The scene with Heinrich breaks down B.'s resolve towards A., when he appears she falls into his arms weeping and confesses her love. He is astonished, overjoyed; asks, how can it be? She tells him about the scene with H., the plot to assassinate the emperor, they debate what to do (they can't simply make it known, as no one would believe strolling players), then A. thinks of the festival, his artistic mission and grows reflective.

She shakes him: 'So that's what you look like when a girl tells you she loves you.'

A. O forgive me!

Then a transition, he talks of how badly she treated him.

Exchange

A. So I'm not a windbag.

B. No (she kisses him) smiling through tears etc.

A. And will you be mine now?

B. Yes, but for ever?

A. Of course for ever, but at any rate today.

(He becomes more tender, her maidenly modesty stirs again, he grows more pressing and demands immediate acquiescence; she bursts into tears and rushes away without answering.)

He remains, seated, head propped on his hands, gloomy but tense (no musical intensification), she returns (he still in the same position), falls on his neck and kisses him tenderly, he falls at her feet, throws his arms round her and calls her name over and over. (Curtain)

A. and P. only know that he is a leader, against whom a stroller cannot bring a charge.

Transformation to crowd scene; 'someone tried to kill the emperor' ('the assassins have escaped')

A. and P. enter too and to their terror identify the incident as what P. had found out!

In Act II, *at the Diet*, they are sure of the facts. Heinrich sits beside his brother (confident that the strollers will not be able to prove anything against him).

Then A. begins his song and succeeds in so moving H.'s heart that he voluntarily confesses. Etc.

First scene: Apostle game: P., S. and other girls.

When P. draws the Apostle A., A. enters, S. at once goes into raptures over him, but she is mocked by P. and the others.

Old B. intervenes – scene between B., A. and S. then Duke H. – P. becomes lively, flirts with him – the other singers gradually join them, song contest develops etc.

P. refuses A., she loves him to much to listen to him, believes him a windbag and frivolously involved with S. (marriage is impossible for the strollers), and she will possess him only if it is to be for ever.

A. You know – let us ask the emperor for legal standing, for marriage etc., then I will marry you.

P. Oh, what a favour! You will actually marry me! Thank you very much! I will not be married 'for that reason'!

A. But you love me?

P. How do you know?

The scenario for *Der Reichstag zu Mainz* can be regarded as symptomatic of the relationship between life and fiction, the intermingling of which was to be a significant factor in Strauss's work in the future: in symphonic poems (*Ein Heldenleben*, *Symphonia Domestica*) and some of his operas (notably *Feuersnot*, *Die Frau ohne Schatten*, *Intermezzo* and *Die Liebe der Danae*). Even more significant than the triangular A.–S.–B. relationship in the *Reichstag* scenario are the self-portrait (though it is not carried through consistently) and the introduction of the initial P., which obviously refers to Pauline de Ahna. (That P. is used for the lover in one set of notes, while elsewhere a name is given to the character originally called P., was perhaps an attempt at camouflage, or it may simply have been a mistake.) It is interesting that Strauss reveals his plans for an opera on the subject of *Das erhabene Leid der Könige* in his letters, but does not once mention *Der Reichstag zu Mainz*, in which he makes the less promising attempt to mingle personal experience with a historical subject. As evidence of the human and artistic problems that preoccupied him, the sketches for *Der Reichstag* are far more informative than those for *Das erhabene Leid*, with their glorification of a Germanic Utopia, and their dramatic constructivism. When Strauss returned to Weimar, both plans were overtaken by his idea for a 'folk' opera about Till Eulenspiegel, for which numerous fragments of text exist, although Strauss eventually abandoned that plan too. The need to vary the subject from one work to the next, which dominated his opera writing in later life, is already becoming apparent. After the weighty matters dealt with in *Guntram* Strauss was drawn to the idea of something lighter, but a number of years were to pass before his wish was fulfilled in *Feuersnot*. It was not a libretto written by himself but one to which he contributed some of the essential ideas that at length enabled him to reach the goal which he had long striven in vain to find.

Prospects

His work on *Guntram* did not cause Strauss to lose sight of his plans for the future, which of course included the hope of getting his opera staged. In Frankfurt, where his partisan Wagnerianism gave rise to some justified reservations, Engelbert Humperdinck tried to smooth his path, and Franz Strauss and Thuille were asked to take soundings in Munich. Strauss's first preference at that date would have been to exchange Weimar for Karlsruhe, where Felix Mottl had raised the opera to a very high standard.

When Strauss got back to Cairo from Luxor in the middle of March he was astonished by a letter from his father, telling him about a conversation he had had with Hermann Levi, at Levi's request. The conductor had enquired of Franz Strauss whether Richard would be able to free himself of his Weimar contract in order to take up an appointment as Hofkapellmeister in Munich, on a completely equal footing with Levi himself, and superior in both rank and salary to Franz Fischer. What he required from Strauss at all costs would be a friendly attitude towards himself. It is not surprising that Levi stressed this point, because Strauss had held a grudge against him ever since his father had been so abruptly pensioned off, and the exception taken in Bayreuth, where he conducted *Parsifal*, to his Jewish origins was another reason for his wish to be assured that the younger man would work with him in a friendly spirit. In the course of his conversation with Franz Strauss, Levi declared that there were only three people who could be considered for the Munich appointment: Mottl, Weingartner and Strauss. He was already under 'a slight obligation' to Mottl, whose marriage appeared to be endangering his position in Karlsruhe, but Weingartner's contract held him in Berlin until 1896. (The fact that three names were under consideration was, in the event, the cause of ever renewed deferment of the appointment, which put an especial strain on Strauss, since the first performance of *Guntram* was bound up with the question of his engagement in Munich.)

Strauss told his father in reply to this report that he would prefer to go to Karlsruhe, and asked him, justifiably, why Levi had drawn up that particular shortlist, if he already had a provisional arrangement with Mottl. At the same time he wrote to Mottl, asking if the rumours that he was to leave Karlsruhe for Munich were true. Mottl replied on 28 March 1893:

> My dear friend,
>
> Nothing is to come of Munich, I am to stay on here

> peacefully, with my wife, and enjoy life. If I had left, I would have thought of no one but you! It gives me boundless delight to hear that you are well and that your dramatic opus is waxing and flourishing. I hope that you will give me the honour of performing it, even if I am only in little Karlsruhe!

Above all, Strauss wanted to know the views of Bronsart, his intendant in Weimar, on the whole affair (including the question of what his field of competence would be, if he was to be Levi's equal). He was reluctant to accept Levi's invitation to conduct *Die Meistersinger* in Munich that summer; he would have preferred *Tristan* or *Lohengrin*. In fact, in the following summer (1894), with his appointment due to take effect in the autumn, Strauss conducted three performances of *Tristan* (29 June, 22 August and 5 September) and one of *Die Meistersinger* (2 September) in Munich. It was a year before the matter of the appointment was settled. The negotiations can be followed in the correspondence of all parties concerned, but they make exhausting if instructive reading.[11] The decisive stage in the tale was not reached until the spring of 1894, so the telling can be deferred for a while.

In Sicily

Strauss's original itinerary had included Jerusalem, but he changed his mind about that. Early in April he travelled via Cairo and Alexandria to Taormina, where he went on working at the second act of *Guntram*, writing four or five pages a day in full score. Letters to his parents describe the progress of his work as well as the impressions he was receiving from his travels through Sicily, with Goethe's *Italian Journey* as his reading matter. There are frequent references to the question of Levi's offer, but the opera remained in the forefront of his concern. 'The only true pleasure is one's own work,' he wrote to his sister, 'of that one never tires.' (10 April 1893) It was a creed in which he never faltered throughout his life. The good his months in the south had done him is acknowledged in a letter to Alexander Ritter:

> I have been completely restored to health, of body and of soul, on this wonderful journey. I almost rejoice in myself, for I am now fit to return to the world with a resumption of vigour and warm attachment such as were strangers to me during these last years of nervosity and illness. (Palermo, 6 May 1893)

From time to time he was overcome by the longing to hear a good orchestra again, to conduct, or

> to hear a Beethoven quartet again. I shall even be capable of listening to Papa Haydn again with complete freshness of sensation, and I shall be able to take sincere pleasure again in all sorts of things which the pressure of development has made me lay aside until now. (To his father, 6 May 1893)

A few days later, referring to the prospect of negotiating with Munich, he stated 'I do not know the meaning of nerves any more'. He was confident of returning calmer and uplifted 'to a more than all too human degree'. These claims are in curious contrast to another remark he made to his father, however, about Act II of *Guntram*: 'Deuce take it – I can't get rid of a certain nervosity in the orchestra.' (Palermo, 12 May 1893) The fact is that his nerves were not really up to the strain put upon them by the prolonged uncertainties surrounding the vacancy at the Munich opera.

While he was in Sicily, Strauss visited Syracuse, Castrogiovanni, Palermo and Agrigento. His regular letters home kept not only his parents but also his sister up-to-date with his travels. From Palermo he wrote to Hanna:

> Yesterday the vocal score of *Pagliacci* [by Leoncavallo] came into my hands. What a paltry, botched thing it is! Yet another work worthy of the German public! And that's the crew for which Wagner worked and suffered for fifty years! If work itself was not so enjoyable for its own sake, it would really be best to pack it in altogether! And yet one is supposed to write 'lightly and agreeably' so that, as dear Papa maintains, it will be performed at lots of theatres. But by whom and for whom? For that miserable crew in the audience? Certainly not! One composes for oneself and for a few friends, for the rest – I couldn't care less! (19 May 1893)

In the second half of May Strauss accepted an invitation from Count and Countess Gravina, the son-in-law and daughter of Cosima Wagner and Hans von Bülow, to spend two weeks with them at Ramacca, where he arrived on 25 May. 'The house is an old monastery, extremely charming and idyllic, magnificent, bracing air.' (To his father, 26 May) He played duets with the countess who 'as Bülow's daughter is a very rhythmical pianist'; among the works they played was Thuille's arrangement for four hands of

Macbeth, which the countess had been sent by her father with the inscription '*very significant*'. Strauss ventured on horseback a few times while he was at Ramacca and felt as if he was 'half in Bayreuth, with the added blessing of the Italian sky in the glorious *campagna*'. On 4 June, three days before his departure, he finished the score of his Act II, a milestone he at once communicated to Bülow, not without adding that 'in the glorious clear air of Egypt soul and body were invigorated, the former acquired a plenitude of hitherto unsuspected new perceptions, the latter a strength which I hope will stand up to the divers storms of the north'. The same letter to Bülow reveals that his interest had been attracted on this one occasion to things that were otherwise completely foreign to him: he had been studying agriculture on the count's estates:

> That isn't just a joke, rather I count it a great gain to have learned on these travels to direct my gaze away from the single track of the German musician towards everything there is in the world, wherein I have been significantly encouraged by zealous study of Goethe and Goethe's maxim: 'Find nothing uninteresting, or not worth the trouble of looking at closely.'

On 7 June Strauss began his homeward journey, on which he took his time. Making a halt in Florence, he wrote to his parents: 'On the boat [from Naples to Leghorn] I did some more work on my plan for the new opera, I'm very pleased with it, and curious to know what you will have to say about it.' (10 June 1893) Four days later: 'Yesterday evening I drafted the plot of a highly original one-act opera!' It is not certain whether he was referring to the same thing in both letters. The expression 'my plan for the new opera' in the first letter suggests a project that had been with him for some time – perhaps *Das erhabene Leid der Könige*; but that was intended to be in more than one act, so it is more likely that in the second letter he was already referring to his idea for an opera about Till Eulenspiegel, which appears to have been planned as a one-acter originally.

While still in Florence Strauss met Hermann Levi, with whom he was able to discuss the Munich appointment 'very pleasantly, frankly and amiably', so that they parted on good terms. After a further halt of two days in Stresa, he crossed the Simplon Pass into Switzerland on 20 June. He made another detour, to Zermatt where he paused to go up the Gornergrat. The excursion to the 3156-metre-high peak and back took him seven and a half hours, and he wrote home after it that he was 'rather tired, but cheerful and in good spirits: I climbed up very slowly, my heart and my little lungs behaved capitally; with this quittance I can face the German winter with confidence'. (22 June 1893) On 15 July 1893 he arrived back in Munich, at the end of an interval which, though its primary purpose had been to allow him to recover his health, had also been of decisive importance in his personal and artistic development.

8

The last year in Weimar, 1893–4

After spending a few weeks of the summer and early autumn in Marquartstein, where he finished scoring *Guntram* on 5 September, Strauss returned to Weimar in time for the opening of the winter season. If the negotiations with Munich had not been continually beset with new delays, it would have been easier for him to endure the 'philistine atmosphere of Weimar, where all seemed 'oed' und leer'. At first he felt thoroughly bored and spoke of his

> very placid frame of mind: the whole ménage here is too trifling to get myself excited about, it's a relief to be past that stage. Cool and indifferent is my motto, and it really seems quite easy to live up to it . . . Everything here is as it was a hundred years ago, except that a certain Goethe is no longer on the scene. (19 September 1893)

This 'mournful letter' elicited a bracing reply from his father:

> Fancy giving way to depression like that! Think what a wonderful year you have experienced and enjoy it again in your memory, without the discomforts of the actual travel. Content yourself with your lot, my son, and don't forget how few people could compare themselves with you for fortunate experiences, and comfort yourself with the thought that after grey days there always come sunny ones, of which you have marked up a very large number in your life. I readily admit that your living in Weimar cannot be very agreeable for you now, but there's this to be said for it: you can devote yourself to improving your health, to strengthening and preparing yourself for renewed artistic activity, after the necessary rest. And there are books as well, which will help you to fill your free time. If I were in your shoes now I would make a serious study of history

and literary history, which would be extraordinarily useful to you, and not read so such Schopenhauer or other philosophical works!

Don't upset yourself by unnecessary anger. In particular, let me ask you not to forget what you said here at home one evening to Thuille: that even if the conditions in Weimar are unsympathetic to you you will apply all your best endeavours in your artistic activity.

He further reminded him that he had promised to write some music for his uncle Georg Pschorr:

Give some thought to eight-bar melodies which you can then use in a piece, or pieces, for your uncle. Your travels gave you a lot of pleasure, and your compositions will give your uncle a lot of pleasure too. (24 September 1893)

Siegfried Wagner also wrote to his 'liebes Sträussle' in a tone of friendly concern at this time:

Your mood has made me feel extraordinarily downcast. I can well understand that the dear old *Freischütz* is your only comfort . . . I hope I shall see you soon. We friends should meet often. I at least feel at ease only when the air breathes the spirit of our glorious Bayreuth.

Listen, O Expression, what about a symphonic poem *The Merchant of Venice*; four strands: melancholy Antonio, dissolute Venice, captivating Portia and (!) Shylock (e.g. six bassoons, muted trumpets and horns and humming basses); that would be something for you! (Karlsruhe, 9 October 1893)

It was a suggestion Strauss did not take up. Probably on the same day on which Siegfried Wagner's letter reached him he wrote despondently to Humperdinck:

Now equipped with splendid health, I am pining away, sick at heart and sick in mind, in dreary little Weimar and in the miserable state of art that prevails here in Germany and seems doubly grey and foggy to me now, after the splendours of Egypt. I am utterly dissatisfied with my present job and yet I'm almost afraid that if I leave it I shall find it even worse elsewhere. (11 October 1893)

He went on to describe the latest development, a turn for the worse, in the matter of the Munich post and enquired whether there was any possibility of an engagement as a principal conductor in Frankfurt. He was growing increasingly out of sympathy with Fritz Brandt, who seemed to Strauss to believe he was the king-pin of the Weimar theatre; on the other hand he continued to draw comfort from the sincere attachment shown him by 'de Ahnchen' and 'Zellerlein'. Pauline was being charming to him, and he regularly made music with her and Zeller – the two were his only consolation. Arthur Seidl, who had afforded him some intellectual stimulus in the past, left Weimar during this autumn. The 'damned void' began to weigh on him before the end of September: 'As I do not even get angry any more, I am stuck in a general depression, plus the miserable place, and the bleak delights of nature.' He had held a rehearsal for *Der Freischütz* with only four second violins, which he understandably described as 'pitiful', and Bronsart's well-meant suggestion that he should start rehearsing *Siegfried* struck him as absurd, given the deficiencies of the orchestra. He no longer had any social contacts with Lassen and only looked forward 'every day to the [binding] offer from Munich, so as to get away from this dashed place at last' (to his father, 22 September 1893). If he did not soon get away from Weimar, 'I shall simply fall into a doze, drift slowly into Philistia and compose fugues for organ and male-voice quartets', he wrote home in a mood of bitter irony (22 October 1893). On the same day he wrote to a conductor whose name cannot be identified: 'Nothing pleases me in Germany any more. The climate and the state of art alike are too miserable. In Egypt the sun shone all the time and of the theatre and its Beckmesserish concerns there was "not one single trace".'[1] His most devout wish was that his uncle would send him south again and release him from the forced labour which his day-to-day work in Weimar represented to him. In fact Georg Pschorr had not long to live: he died in June 1894.

The decision about the Munich appointment continued to be delayed, which gave Strauss understandable cause for concern, after the oral and to a certain extent written assurances he had had from Levi and Possart, and led him to suspect some kind of underhand manoeuvre. Although Levi's letters to Possart show that both were completely in earnest in wanting to offer Strauss a job, yet they still hankered after Mottl or Weingartner and repeatedly postponed a definite decision; there was always some question to be cleared up first, such as the new conductor's position and rank (as

Levi's successor-designate), his field of competence in regard not only to the sharing of works between the different conductors but also to rehearsals, casting, additions to the repertory and so on. Remembering the frustrations of his earlier term at the Munich opera and Levi's unpredictability in the matter of surrendering certain operas to another conductor, Strauss had good reason to insist on definite assurances more vehemently than might otherwise have been necessary; there was also the question of the first performance of *Guntram*, for which he wanted a date fixed. The situation was further complicated by the question as to what part Strauss should take in the Musical Academy subscription concerts, and on this point it was impossible to pin Levi down. One reason will have been the fluctuations of his state of health, but the fear that Strauss might usurp his position may have been another. Another factor which created yet more delay when the negotiations were at an advanced stage and conclusion was near was Strauss's request for contractual assurance of the leave that would be necessary for him to carry out his commitments as director of the concerts of the Berlin Philharmonic Orchestra, for he had in the meantime succeeded Bülow in that function.

But the fact that the names of Mottl and Weingartner were never fully withdrawn from consideration was a stumbling-block from the start. Long after the first overtures had been made to Strauss, the parties in Munich continued to hope for one or the other, who would then be placed on an equal footing with Strauss or even above him. If this hope came to nothing, then they wanted to have made sure of Strauss as a substitute. There was nothing out of the way or reprehensible about this in itself, since both names had been freely mentioned ever since Levi's initial offer. At that date Weingartner's reputation as a conductor was vastly superior to Strauss's, and this would have caused the latter either to accept a subordinate position or to refuse the post altogether. If Weingartner went to Munich, Strauss had hopes of taking his place in Berlin, but that was of course a very uncertain prospect. Although he was prepared to 'muck out Munich's Augean stables', he would still have preferred to go to Karlsruhe in Mottl's place, but he had had Mottl's definite assurance that he intended to stay where he was. Levi and Possart continued to try to win Strauss for Munich, but at the same time they did not give up the hope that Weingartner might be able to terminate his Berlin contract before it was due to expire in 1896.

Cosima Wagner advised Strauss to accept a post in Munich and simultaneously sound out the General Intendant of the Royal Theatres in Berlin, Count Bolko von Hochberg, on the matter of succeeding Weingartner in 1896. Strauss had already informed Levi, while he was still in Taormina, that he was ready in principle to go to Munich, but he had also made the proviso that he would want to thrash out the necessary guarantees face to face with him. Levi offered him the chance to conduct *Tannhäuser* and *Lohengrin* at Munich's 'so-called festival', but he turned it down at the request of Frau Wagner, to whom the Munich rivalry was a thorn in the flesh. When they met in Florence, in June 1893, he and Levi discussed the salary and his share of the repertory. The prospect Levi held out of his being able to conduct all Wagner's works except *Tristan*, and half the Musical Academy subscription concerts as well, made it an extremely tempting offer indeed, even if his own appointment failed to make that of Weingartner superfluous. But by the middle of July Levi began to vacillate: forceful arguments presented by friends, Conrad and Mary Fiedler, he wrote to Strauss, had made him change his mind about retiring in the immediate future, since he himself had prepared the undertaking in partnership with Possart, and therefore he could not leave it in the lurch at the eleventh hour. At all events he wanted to adjourn the question to the end of the summer. It would be better for Strauss, too, to work at his side for a time; once Strauss had settled in, he would be able to retire with his mind at rest. If he did so now it would look as if anger and spite had influenced him to do it, in order to damage the intendant and the Munich opera itself. (14 July 1893)

A *new* arrangement, this time between Strauss and Possart and again not held to, was that if Weingartner was not in a position to free himself by 1 October 1893, Strauss should go to Munich on 1 January 1894. Since the original date proposed for him had been 1 October 1893, but no decision had been made by the end of July, Strauss understandably became anxious and mistrustful. He rightly assumed that the people in Munich were still hoping to get Weingartner or Mottl. His annoyance is the more understandable, since it was Munich who had started the ball rolling. On 25 July 1893 he wrote from Bad Reichenhall to Hermann Levi to tell him that in no circumstances would he be able to take up an appointment in Munich on 1 October, because with everything still so uncertain, and especially now that Possart had asked him to wait until 1

October before any further move, it would be impossible for him to give notice in Weimar. Levi's reply was not calculated to raise his spirits:

> Your dissatisfaction is only too well justified, but I hope you will not unload so much as a shadow of it on to my poor head. What powers held sway during my absence from Munich in June I do not know. The fact remains that on my return I found the circumstances completely altered. Possart was cool to his very marrow, and when I called him to account we clashed so violently that for a time it was impossible for me to have anything to do with him. I have the impression that he wants to be rid of me, and he shall have his wish. Now the Fiedlers (they worked on me for two whole days, I only gave way on the third) think that if I want to go I must do so without creating a stir and that I must on no account abandon the summer performances which were undertaken with my agreement. They also put it to me – and I was especially impressed by this argument – that I ought first to induct you in your office, work side by side with you for a while, and not take my leave until you are firmly in the saddle. And I do not give up the hope that this last will be possible. Perhaps Weingartner will bring his decision with him on 10 August, the day he is due to arrive in Munich. In any case I beseech you sincerely and urgently to do nothing – in respect of Weimar – before the end of August! I have heard from another quarter that Weingartner's hopes of getting away from Berlin are completely in vain. (29 July 1893)

He had already mentioned that likelihood in an earlier letter to Strauss and it proved correct in the end, but at such a late date that Strauss had to stick it out in Weimar for another year. His reply to this letter of Levi's is lost, but it appears to have been conciliatory, since Levi's next letter expressed his pleasure at it. (1 August 1893) The first of October came and went without Strauss receiving a binding offer. During the course of the month the matter came to boiling point again, when Possart sent him a telegram: 'Contractual arrangements not yet agreed between us', which led Strauss to observe indignantly to his father:

> There it is then! Oral and written agreements have no validity for Herr Possart!! . . . Perhaps he's still thinking things over! If not, what am I to do? I can't start proceedings against Possart,

> after all I would like the thing to reach a satisfactory conclusion – I suppose I shall just have to go on waiting, until in a few weeks' time – it all comes to nothing! But no one in Munich is worried! By Jove! It takes patience to be a German musician!!! Yes, I foresee that I shall go on sitting in Weimar! (10 October 1893)

Strauss had every reason for complaint: terms had already been settled in writing on 19 June giving him a salary of 7000 marks, three years' tenure from 1 October 1893 [!], power to revise the repertory, half the Academy Concerts, and two months' annual leave. Levi, who seems to have reminded Possart of this provisional contract in October, added the following comments to it: when he had spoken to Strauss in Florence he had received an

> extraordinarily favourable impression. At all events, he is a 'personality', original and interesting. But for that very reason he will not find things easy and he will not make them easy for us. He is moreover little inclined to compromise, seems an unbending character. Has definite artistic goals and has yet to learn the lessons of experience: that it isn't always possible to have one's own way in the world or in an official position. His health seems perfectly good now. He is fundamentally honest, at all events. And all in all, I think we shall not find a better.

There can be no doubt of Levi's good will to gain Strauss for Munich, but he had to make allowances for Possart's hopes for Weingartner or Mottl. One month after the original deadline of 1 October had passed, on 1 November Strauss received a communication to the effect that an 'over-hasty settlement' would have resulted in untenable conditions. In October, too, Levi had intervened with Possart on Strauss's behalf:

> But if nothing comes of Mottl, take *Strauss* and have done with it! I can think of no other move, and besides we have already committed ourselves with Strauss so far that we have hardly any way of retreating, unless we get Mottl (in which case Strauss would be very happy to go to Karlsruhe). (6 October 1893)

It was, however, by no means certain that Karlsruhe would have taken Strauss. Levi went on in the same letter to repeat his opinion that Strauss was 'a personality', even if a rather volatile one, and there was no knowing to what heights he might not yet rise.

Moreover, he had also shown that he would listen to reason and knew how to profit from past unhappy experiences.

While the advice his parents urged upon Strauss to exercise patience and to accept the inevitable did not go entirely unheeded, nevertheless the continual postponement of a definite decision was the more irksome to him because of his longing to spread his wings far wider than was possible in the confines of Weimar, where more or less the only bright spots for him were occasional evenings playing with the violinist Carl Halir and the encouraging way his relationship with Pauline de Ahna was developing. He had the good sense not to take Cosima Wagner's advice to make the whole business public in the press, if he wanted nothing more of Munich, his principal consideration being that this would put at risk the Munich production of *Guntram* – which was planned to be its world première. The original date that had been mentioned as a possibility for this event had been March 1894; on 6 October (1893) he had been informed laconically that 1 October 1894 would be the earliest possible date 'on account of [unspecified] contractual commitments'. By November he had still heard nothing more definite than that. It was in fact to be November 1895, eighteen months after the original date, before *Guntram* was seen in Munich and by then it was the second production of the work, since Strauss had eventually had to content himself with a première in Weimar. It was good news to learn from Felix Mottl in the middle of December that Karlsruhe intended to stage *Guntram* at the end of March (the date was later fixed for 15 April), for Strauss was not to know at that point that in the end the Karlsruhe production would have to be abandoned altogether, because of the inadequacy of the tenor Emil Gerhäuser.

The title role in *Guntram* is an exceedingly demanding one, and Gerhäuser was simply not up to it. He sang the Peace Narration in Heidelberg in January 1894, to the composer's complete satisfaction, but Strauss's expectations of him were too great. He wrote to his parents: '. . . rehearsal in the afternoon with Gerhäuser, who's highly intelligent, beautiful voice, will make a splendid Guntram . . . the Peace Narration sounds magical, oozes mellifluousness'. (15 January 1894) And after the concert: 'Gerhäuser brought off the Peace Narration with great success yesterday evening, it sounded really enchanting and was greatly liked; I'm very pleased with myself, it's going to be all right!' (18 January 1894) Gustav Mahler, to whom Strauss had played excerpts from the work and sent a copy of the short score, did his best to arrange for it to be performed in Hamburg, but to no avail. It seems as though Mahler was unable to form a very clear idea of the opera from the short score, which was in any case not complete. He wrote to Strauss:

> I am very desirous of sampling your *Guntram* once more. Do please bring it with you. This time, too, I will pay attention to it with my conductor's hat on, although I'd like to bet that I shall perform your works in your spirit even without collusion. All the same, it affords a feeling of greater security to know the author's wishes. Do you know, by the way, that your motives are pursuing me in my dreams? They have made a very enduring impression on me, as I realize only now that I've had time to reflect on them. I'm looking forward enormously to the time when we shall produce it here. (2 February 1894)

But in Hamburg, too, there was to be no performance. In the first few weeks of the year Strauss still had the prospect of performance in Karlsruhe to look forward to, because Gerhäuser had sung the Peace Narration there, too, and again with great success. However, he was to prove unequal to the demands of the entire role.

Strauss wrote to Possart in October, asking for a new date by which he could expect the conclusion of a binding contract, but for a long time he received no answer. His letters to Hermann Levi keep us abreast of the situation: ass that he was, he wrote, he was gradually coming to the conclusion that he would never reach an agreement with Munich, whatever he did. Possart had failed to answer two letters making perfectly justified requests. 'I am coming to the conclusion that they don't want me at all in Munich, the only thing that puzzles me is why they made me an offer in the first place.' And he followed this only too reasonable speculation with the news that he had still been given no definite commitment with regard to *Guntram*. (29 October 1893) Levi replied in confidence that Possart was said to have 'forgotten' that he had arranged to put on a revival of Max Zenger's *Wieland* at the end of February.

Strauss poured out his indignation at the news of this excuse of Possart's to his father:

> So I've got to look out for myself over the opera as well, have I? It's getting richer all the time. Possart asked me if the second week in February would suit me for *Guntram*, I said yes, now is that, or isn't it, a definite commitment? The way those people in

> Munich think fit to treat me trumps everything. Herr Zumpe can insist on his piece of paper, Herr Weingartner and a thousand others – but for me there's no contract, no word of honour – not even an answer to my last letter. (1 November 1893)

He wrote to Possart again, telling him that he could give Munich the rights to the world première of *Guntram* only if he received a contractual assurance that it would be performed early in March, and to Hermann Levi he wrote: '. . . am very agreeable to *Guntram* piano rehearsals from 22 to 26 November . . . Whether *Guntram* is to be performed in January or February makes no difference to me whatever, but I wouldn't like to wait any longer than the end of February.' (6 November 1893) The next day Levi wrote to tell him that Zenger's *Wieland* had been chosen for performance neither by Possart nor by himself, but Possart had received a request for it from the Cabinet Secretariat – in effect, a royal command.[2] In the end Strauss agreed to let his work be postponed until 1 May 1894 after a pressing request from Levi, who assured him that no new offence was intended, and that Possart himself would have been glad to postpone an opera by Hermann Zumpe, only the composer was not prepared to wait.[3] (15 November 1893) After a reply by return from Strauss, signifying his acquiescence, Levi wrote again: 'I'm delighted by your decision. Your letter is altogether more reasonable than I had expected from such a veritable volcano as you.' (17 November 1893) Although Levi declared himself in agreement with Strauss's demand for a contractual assurance of the performance date, and there is no reason to doubt his sincerity, the fact remains that none was forthcoming, and the date of 1 May was not kept to. Meanwhile Strauss sustained another disappointment: 1 January 1894, the prospective date for him to take up the conducting appointment in Munich after 1 October 1893 had fallen through, arrived without anything having been settled, apparently because Munich still hoped (in vain) to get Weingartner instead.

It is necessary to write at such length about the wearisome to-ing and fro-ing that delayed Strauss's engagement and the performance of *Guntram* in Munich for so long, because it explains the suspicion with which Strauss regarded both Possart and Levi when he returned to his home town on 1 October 1894. His distrust of Levi, encouraged by Wahnfried, continued to seethe below the surface, not least because of Levi's evasive attitude in the matter of handing over half the Academy Concerts to Strauss.

Throughout March 1894 letters continued to pass between Weimar and Munich. Strauss was making new conditions, which it would be hard for the intendency to fulfil, Levi wrote; the salary of 9000 marks that Strauss now requested was too high; it was all he himself drew after twenty-one years at the Munich opera. He was understandably concerned, too, at the leave of absence Strauss wanted for ten Philharmonic Concerts in Berlin each year: if Strauss was to conduct eight Academy Concerts in Munich on top of that, he could hardly be counted on for any work in the theatre at all. 'I long for you or for someone as the hart desireth the water brooks', but if Possart agreed to the leave of absence, then it would be best if Strauss gave up the other conditions. Levi would let him conduct *Tannhäuser*, but he would have to wait until 1895 for the *Ring*, because it had to be given for the subscribers before then, without new rehearsals. It was therefore out of the question for Strauss to conduct the *Ring* as soon as he took up his appointment. Levi went on:

> Then the concerts: it is not for Possart, or Perfall or me to transfer them to you, as the orchestra itself elects its conductor. *The minute your contract has been ratified here, I shall resign as conductor of the Academy and recommend you as my successor.* There is not the least doubt that the orchestra will elect you, but you cannot be given a contractual assurance of the concerts. If I was in your position, I would sum things up as follows:
> 1. I want to perform my opera in Munich.
> 2. Levi is old and devoid of (theatrical) ambition, he means well by me, and I can be confident that the two of us will get on well together.
> 3. If Possart agrees to my leave of absence, I will let everything else take its natural course and not insist on having things in writing.

It would be a good thing, Levi went on, if Strauss told the Oberregisseur in Munich, Anton von Fuchs, that he was committed to Berlin and had to insist on his leave of absence; apart from that, everything should be left according to the old agreement made orally in Munich. The question of the leave of absence was a hard nut, but he (Levi) hoped to crack it. If everything turned out as it should, however, Strauss must not produce *Guntram* in Weimar first. (12 March 1894)

Having received this from Levi, Strauss allowed it to slip into his letter to the Oberregisseur (the senior civil servant with overall responsibility for the court theatres) that Levi was piling up new difficulties. Levi was wounded, justifiably, and he wrote to express his consternation: Strauss's distrust alarmed him and opened up a sorry prospect; Possart would not be able to give Strauss the *Ring*, *Tristan* or *Die Meistersinger* without his, Levi's, consent. Nevertheless, he confirmed that he agreed with every arrangement made between Possart and Strauss, and would keep only *Tristan* for himself for the time being. (17 March 1894)

Levi also wrote to Possart, bitterly lamenting Strauss's distrust of himself:

> When I was conducting the negotiations with him last year, I wrote that our collaboration would only work if he had faith in the possibility of not merely a superficial relationship with me but a genuine friendship as between colleagues . . . Now I realize, however, from his present attitude towards me, that he is as distrustful as ever, for he has written to Fuchs: 'The matter will only be settled if L. does not cause any confusion and does not pile up new difficulties.' That's the *comble* of injustice. You yourself know better than anyone that *I* bear not a shadow of blame for the failure of those first negotiations, that on the contrary I have not ceased to reiterate the possibility of getting him. I've done everything in my power to smooth his path, have made every possible sacrifice, and yet I now have to discover that he scorns even to establish any kind of rapport with me. This opens up such a sorry prospect of our future collaboration that I now almost regret having made so many concessions to him, although that does not prevent me from keeping my word in respect of what I have already agreed to. The only thing I want is a binding declaration that he intends in future to work *with* me and not against me, and that he will drop this really totally unjustified distrust towards me. Please talk this over with him thoroughly.

Levi went on to the question of the Academy Concerts. He had promised Strauss to resign and would keep that promise:

> But what happens then is beyond my ken. What if the Academy will not accept my resignation? In that case I shall insist on it and repeat my recommendation of Strauss. But then, what if, as is very possible, the Academy elects Fischer and not Strauss?

> Because they will have to alter the statutes before Strauss can take over the concerts, for at present only the incumbent *Hof*kapellmeister can be conductor of the Academy. I've explained to Strauss yet again that I can't simply hand the concerts on to him . . . I'm very annoyed by the course things are taking. If Strauss had simply written to Fuchs from Weimar accepting the conditions we had all agreed to, everything would be all right. But now he is making the difficulties, not *I*! (19 March 1894)

But at last on 20 March Strauss's contract with the Munich opera was concluded.[4] Levi received a conciliatory letter from him: Strauss was looking forward to his new post:

> I hope you will all be satisfied with me, too, and we shall be good neighbours. I am a hot-head, I admit, and a bit peppery too, but I don't think you will have any reason to complain about me. I keep my promises – and that includes what I said to you in Florence. I gratefully accept your offer regarding the Academy Concerts, and I think the orchestra will also be satisfied with me. Here's to a new life and a good friendship! (23 March 1894)

Before long, however, the question of the Academy Concerts caused renewed tensions. At first Strauss trusted Levi's assurances:

> As for the question of the concerts, I leave the decision entirely to the orchestra, and as a matter of course, my dear colleague, I relieve you of the promise you made me to offer your resignation to the Academy immediately following my engagement. The orchestra may do what it thinks best for its concerts; I will not force myself upon it. (10 May 1894)

Levi replied:

> Let us talk about concerts etc. when we meet. Only you are mistaken, if you believe that I would be glad to be relieved of the promise I made you! You know how unwillingly I have allowed myself to be persuaded to conduct any more concerts in the Odeon at all. On every occasion I have to overcome a (purely physical) disquiet, and would be very glad if I never had to enter the place (as conductor) again. But in *your* interest, I think a transitional stage is advisable. More when we meet and can talk about it. (30 May 1894)

This not very convincing letter strengthened rather than allayed

Strauss's suspicions. He had been only too well acquainted with Levi's vacillation for a long time. The wish, engendered by his precarious state of health, to be relieved of some of the burden of his work, was hardly reconcilable with his obstinate clinging to a position of artistic power, and the conflict between the two demands made it hard for him to make decisions and actually to carry out those he did make. All the same, Strauss does not seem to have grasped that one of the 'difficulties' made by Levi was a matter of fact: before he could take over the Academy Concerts the members of the orchestra would have to vote a change in their statutes, which would then have to be approved by the Prince Regent. Strauss was not going to be given the title of *Hof*kapellmeister, and only someone who bore that title – as Levi had made perfectly clear – could become the Academy's musical director. On the other hand, Levi could perhaps have done something about the regulation. But at this stage he tried to justify himself to Strauss, and said he felt rather nervous at the thought of discussing the matter with the orchestra and uncertain as to the outcome. 'Don't you think it would be wise if you took on only half the concerts to begin with? I am sure that I would be able to get the orchestra to agree to that without any difficulty or debate; moreover it could be settled *at once*.' (8 June 1894) The matter was still not settled by the end of August, when Strauss asked Levi rather brusquely whether it was or not. 'If it hasn't been done, I assume you do not wish me to join the Academy.' He asked for a speedy decision about the programme and added: 'If the repeated delays in the matter give rise to any consequences on my part, I would have to hold you alone responsible for them.' (29 August 1894) Eventually, but not before 30 October, Perfall confirmed that Strauss was to conduct eight of the subscription concerts in the 1894–5 season.

Meanwhile no date had been set for the Munich première of *Guntram*. After postponing it from March to May, Munich again reneged and gave 1 October as the first possible date. Much against Strauss's wishes he had to content himself with a world première in Weimar. An additional reason why this embarrassed and annoyed Strauss was that in mid-September 1893 he had rather coolly informed Bronsart, who would gladly have had the première in Weimar, that the Weimar orchestra was too small and he had for that reason entrusted the première to Munich. He had written to his father on 18 September: 'That *Guntram* is to be put on in

Munich first has aroused a general "Halloh!" and Schadenfreude here.'

The 1893–4 season in Weimar brought Strauss at least a little satisfaction in the theatre: he was able to put on the premières of Humperdinck's *Hänsel und Gretel* (23 December) and Mottl's one-acter *Fürst und Sänger* (9 March). The subscription concerts, which again featured Pauline de Ahna as a soloist, presented him with several stimulating challenges, above all in Beethoven's symphonies. He was particularly proud of his performances of the *Eroica* and of the last movement of the Seventh Symphony, which he 'rehearsed very meticulously' and 'didn't take too fast (because the intoxication doesn't come until towards the end)'; for him it was 'among the most magnificent music Beethoven ever wrote'. He wrote this description of his performance to satisfy his father, who had implored him to treat the Seventh 'humanely': 'Remember that the beauty of these great masterworks does not lie in their externals but in the spirit that dwells within them and must be presented to the listener only through great understanding, not through arbitrary caprices alien to the work.' (27 October 1893)

Hänsel und Gretel in Weimar

By far the most important encounter Strauss made with the work of a contemporary in the field of German opera that year was with Engelbert Humperdinck's fairy-tale opera *Hänsel und Gretel*. The world première had been planned to take place in Munich under Levi, but the illness of one of the principal singers caused the first performance in Munich to be postponed to 30 December, and so the Weimar première on 23 December 1893, conducted by Strauss, was the first performance ever. Strauss and Humperdinck had known each other for years, ever since the early 1880s, when they had met to play chamber music in a private house in Munich. It was Strauss and Wüllner who had procured Humperdinck the post of a 'musical companion' in the household of the industrialist Alfred Krupp in 1885. Since 1890 Humperdinck had been teaching at the Frankfurt Conservatory and he was also the opera critic of the *Frankfurter Zeitung*. Over the years his acquaintance with Strauss had ripened into a friendship, encouraged by Alexander Ritter. Strauss performed Humperdinck's ballad *Die Wallfahrt nach Kevlaar* (The Pilgrimage to Kevlaar, on a text by Heine, for soprano and tenor soloists, mixed chorus and orchestra) in Weimar on 30 January 1892; when Strauss first heard this work as a schoolboy he had not thought much of it, but Humperdinck had subsequently revised it and the second version was first performed in Cologne in 1887 under Franz Wüllner.

Strauss succeeded in winning Bronsart's approval for a production of *Hänsel und Gretel* in Weimar before he even knew the work. He eventually read the score in October 1893, after his return from Egypt, and wrote to tell his friend how delighted he was with it:

> Truly, it's a masterpiece of the highest quality, and I lay at your feet my fullest admiration and my sincerest congratulations on its happy conclusion; it's the first work that has impressed me for a very long time. Such heart-refreshing humour, such deliciously naive melodies, such art and refinement in the orchestration, such perfectionism in the overall shaping of the work, such vital invention, such resplendent polyphony – and all of it original, new and so authentically German.
>
> My dear friend, you are a great master, and have given the Germans a work they hardly deserve, but let us hope all the same that they will very soon learn how to appreciate it fully. (Weimar, 30 October 1893)

He made a point of asking Humperdinck to insist that he, and not 'that old simpleton Lassen', should conduct it. The day after the first performance he reported on it to Humperdinck, who had not been able to be present:

> After a truly dreadful dress rehearsal, yesterday's performance of *Hänsel und Gretel* went relatively well, and was generally enjoyed. Our coloratura soprano Fräulein Schubert (who was originally cast as Gretel) had learnt the part of Hänsel in three days, since Fräulein de Ahna had hurt her foot and was in bed, and although the part was far too low for her she did all that was humanly possible, and was especially good dramatically. Brandt provided exceptionally beautiful décor, given our slender resources, while I find very little to approve of in the rest of his dramaturgical directions. You too, probably. [To his father, Strauss said that Brandt lacked poetry.]
>
> Fräulein Kayser was very good as Gretel, as far as her little voice allowed; Wiedey excellent as the Father, ditto Fräulein Fink [the future wife of Eugen d'Albert] as the Witch. The orchestra also did better than at the dress rehearsal; eight of them were down with flu, the first wind players for instance. Well, we had

> to do our best for the Christmas production, and the shifts we made went well enough, although I personally am very unhappy about this kind of improvisation. That's what the theatre is like, everlasting imperfection, everlasting compromises for the sake of the wallet.

On New Year's Eve, he went on, the performance was to be repeated in exactly the same form, but the intendant had approved two more rehearsals, with Fräulein de Ahna, for early in January. After telling Humperdinck that there had been applause at the end of the little duet in E major and of the Witch's Song, Strauss also expressed a criticism which has been generally shared ever since:

> However, the orchestration is always a little thick, the thematic writing is a little too rich, which always overpowers the singers a little, especially in the third act, and I shall sit down now and alter the parts a little, in order to muffle the wind even more; may I perhaps cut a little from the score if it seems to serve the clarity?

He quoted his experience dealing with the same problem in *Tristan*. The final sentence of this letter is characteristic of the German chauvinism which Strauss espoused in those days: 'Your work still enchants me now as much as it did from the first and [I] congratulate you once again on this beautiful, authentically German deed!' (24 December 1893)

After the third performance, on 7 January 1894, when it was done in a double bill with Mozart's *Bastien und Bastienne*, Strauss was better satisfied and wrote home: 'On Sunday we at last had an excellent performance of *Hänsel und Gretel*, in which Fräulein de Ahna in particular distinguished herself by high spirits and humour.' (9 January 1894) Twelve years later, on 14 April 1905, Strauss gave at the Berlin Court Opera the first performance of another work by his friend, the three-act comic opera *Die Heirat wider Willen*, with a libretto Humperdinck wrote himself after Alexandre Dumas's *Les demoiselles de Saint-Cyr*.

After several reminders from his mother, Strauss sat down at the end of October 1893 to write two pieces for piano quartet (AV 182), intended for amateur performance and dedicated to his uncle Georg Pschorr in gratitude for his holiday in the south, which had been made possible by Pschorr's generosity. He finished the first, *Arabian Dance* in D minor, which employs original Arab melodies, on

7 December, and the second, *Little Love Song* in G major, only on 23 December. 'I sent off the pieces for Uncle Georg yesterday, I really had to cheese-pare the time for them, for I've not had a free moment in the last fortnight.' (To his father, 24 December 1893)

Certainly he must have been very pressed for time during the last few days before the première of *Hänsel und Gretel*, what with trying to finish the quartets for his uncle – it was the day of the performance itself before he finished and posted the fair copies – and with the extra rehearsals for the substitute Hänsel after Pauline de Ahna had sprained her foot. He was going to spend the evening of Christmas Eve with Pauline 'so that the poor soul is not left all alone and sad', he told his father in the same letter, drawing a veil over his motives. A few days later, after reporting that his new libretto (*Till Eulenspiegel in Schilda*) was advancing slowly and promised to be quite jolly, he complained 'but otherwise the winter is a barren time for me, the cold and the dark and being cooped up indoors all the time leave me absolutely unproductive and without any desire to work'. Every winter for the last ten years, except the one in Egypt, had had exactly the same effect on him. Throughout his life the summer was the time when he did his creative work; the winter, when he was in any case kept busy with his conducting engagements, was generally given over to orchestration.

While the negotiations with Munich seemed to be stalemated, Strauss kept his eyes open for other possibilities: for instance, Hamburg, where he conducted a symphony concert at the request of Hermann Wolff; the intendant Bernhard Pollini (1838–97) seemed well-disposed towards him, and Gustav Mahler, who eventually found that he did not like *Guntram*, offered nevertheless to give the first performance of it in Hamburg to help Strauss out of his difficulties. 'Whether I have the trouble and labour here [in Weimar] or in Hamburg is all one; what is not all one is whether I get a salary of 12,000 marks in Hamburg or 3000 in Weimar.' (To his father, 2 January 1894) At the beginning of February Pollini actually offered him 15,000 marks, but Strauss postponed a decision until the end of the month – he was due to conduct there again on the 26th – because he suspected that something was up behind Mahler's back, and sent a friendly warning to his colleague. He looked on Hamburg as a possible halfway station, where he could bide his time for a year or two until, as seemed the likely course of events, Weingartner moved to Munich and Berlin, he hoped, would have a place for him. Even at this stage he made a tentative approach to Count von Hochberg, the intendant of the Berlin opera. That Hermann Wolff, during the same month of February, invited him to succeed Bülow as the conductor of the Berlin Philharmonic Orchestra's symphony concerts gave him a solid foothold in Berlin already.

Meanwhile he kept things humming in Weimar: 'either things go according to *my* ideas, or I go', he wrote home on 9 January. His immediate ambition was to get Pauline de Ahna cast as Isolde, in which he met with no opposition, since Bronsart, as Strauss himself had to admit, was 'in a very good mood'. She made her début in the role on 13 January. 'Too early, of course', as Strauss admitted many years later, 'but in many respects particularly charming because of her youthfulness and her great acting talent.'[5] Invitations to conduct his own works in other towns continued to arrive, as they had before his Egyptian holiday; for example, he gave the two performances of *Tod und Verklärung* in Würzburg on 13 and 14 March which gave rise to the comments by Cosima Wagner which have already been mentioned.

The Bülow memorial concerts

Hans von Bülow died in Cairo on 12 February 1894. On 14 February Strauss, who was scheduled to conduct a concert in Hamburg on the 26th, was asked by the chairman of the Hamburg Philharmonia, Dr Hermann Behn, to alter the programme in order 'to take account of the profoundly sad news of Bülow's death'. In his reply Strauss insisted on Wagner and Liszt:

> One of the best of us has been taken from us and the only consolation is that he has passed from a painful existence into everlasting redemption.
>
> My programme for Hamburg is a purely symphonic funeral celebration. *Héroïde funèbre* or *Orpheus* (by Liszt), *Nirwana*, the *Eroica* – *Tristan* and *Meistersinger* preludes. *Mahler* can perhaps follow with the Funeral March from *Götterdämmerung*.[6]

This programme was turned down – not least, probably, because Dr Behn was away from Hamburg – and as a result Strauss refused to conduct the concert. Behn wrote to him after it had taken place:

> I perfectly understand your ideas for the ceremony and agree that they were the only right ones from your and my standpoint.

> You wanted to commemorate the great Bülow and his life's work *quasi* chronologically. (Though you could not really have omitted Brahms on such an occasion.) A possible alternative would have been to choose funereal music as such and conclude with the *Eroica* as the keystone. However, the situation here – outside *our* sphere of influence – is such that the so-called 'Bülovians', in the master's interests, out of a petty regard for personal relationships which should certainly cease to be of any account after death, thought fit to exclude Richard Wagner and Liszt. If the ceremony had taken place with your programme, those who are regarded here as Bülow loyalists par excellence would ostentatiously have absented themselves and attended a Spengelian secessionist ceremony which was also planned. If the true Bülovians here had failed to assemble his so-called congregation under our banner, the Bülow cult here would have become a laughing-stock and we had to avoid that at all costs. We could not tolerate a separatist ceremony beside our own, and therefore decided it would be better to allow a united front to be presented. Thus it was our intention that you – or Mahler, since to my sincere regret you refused to take part – should at least conduct the *Eroica*. The ceremony took place in a worthy manner on 26 February with strong public support, and I had the privilege of speaking the last words in commemoration of Hans von Bülow. (2 March 1894)

Marie von Bülow was bringing her husband's body back from Egypt to be buried in Hamburg, and a musical tribute was planned as part of the funeral ceremony, which was to take place towards Easter. The impression seems to have gained ground that it was at the funeral that Strauss was refusing to conduct, rather than at the concert on 26 February. Cosima Wagner wrote Strauss a diplomatic letter:

> The thought will not leave me that you are not to conduct the memorial concert in Hamburg. Would you not write to them again, to say that on such occasions one does not celebrate the changing opinions and views but the *merits* of a person. And those merits undoubtedly include the championing of an art, at a time when it had enemies, which now has friends and many important ones to boot. If [Bülow's] opinion with regard to my father was able to change so radically, who will maintain that it would not have changed with regard to Brahms? What does not change and what we celebrate is the outlook, the courage, the

self-sacrifice which remained constant in all circumstances. And *Tristan* may not be omitted, if for no other reason than that its performance and the piano arrangement of the score are among the brightest jewels in Bülow's crown.

A second consideration is that Bülow was never able to allow the gratitude he owed my father for the impressions and advice he had received to dry up, as this is impossible to a noble nature. You can therefore claim, from your own knowledge of his nature, that you insisted on your programme in the name of that nature!

Please write a very wonderful letter, my dear Expression. Perhaps it will work, if not, at least the right words will have been offered to his memory. People are *lamentable*! If they want to celebrate someone, they have to drag him down first!

C. W.

[PS.] I would have nothing against your conducting something by Brahms as well. It's a concession you could well make and there must be some piece or other. *Do* try to mend matters. (23 February 1894)

Bülow's daughter Daniela Thode and her husband had gone to meet Frau von Bülow on her way through Italy, and Henry Thode wrote from Verona:

When we met Frau von Bülow I pleaded the cause of your programme for the ceremony. She seemed favourably inclined, indeed the inclusion of *Tristan* and even *Meistersinger* met her own wishes, in order to celebrate the significance of the work of the dear departed in that direction. On the other hand she believes it would be against his own wishes to include Liszt in the programme. I have been forced to accept that there is hardly any hope of carrying that proposal through. On the other hand her most deeply felt wish is to see the ceremonial directed by *no one* but yourself.

It is now my opinion – after repeated consultation with my wife – that it would be advisable not absolutely to insist on it, in order to achieve a thoroughly worthy musical celebration. Perhaps you can bring yourself to let the Liszt drop, in return for your insistence that Brahms in turn be abandoned. In that way we should arrive at a programme consisting solely of the three great ones: Bach, Beethoven and Wagner. And that would be wonderful! (5 March 1894)

Daniela Thode also wrote to beg Strauss

> with all my heart, *not* to refuse to conduct the ceremony in memory of my glorious father! He loved you, you were his pupil, one of the last beings he saw in whom he took any pleasure. Do it for the love of him, and for my sake, who knew him, for the sake of my boundless grief. Insist on your programme, which alone is worthy of the occasion. Perhaps it would help if you mention my name to Hermann Wolff and tell him that I concur in your artistic suggestions – in the presence of death hurts and errors vanish, what was imperishable, what belonged and will belong to eternity, has only more validity, and those are the ideals which were a beacon to us. An easily moved temperament, an over-exalted spirit, a deeply wounded heart, they could appear to strike out along paths which deceived only those whose regard was superficial or heartless – they who loved him looked more deeply and knew that the stars which once shone on his youthful enthusiasm, for which he later fought with all his might and main, that they were never extinguished for him. Let the sounds of that time resound at his grave-side! Frau von Bülow comes here in a few days' time – she cannot be indifferent to my point of view and a wish expressed by her – whose word is final – will teach our friends in Hamburg what is best.
>
> Oh be firm in your resolution to conduct the ceremony according to your own wishes, according to *our* wishes, so that my deep sorrow shall not be increased by the painful thought that 'I hear no sounds of true lamentation to mourn this hero's death.'* Go with me to accompany my dearly beloved father on his last journey. [Undated]

Then Henry Thode wrote again:

> From your letter . . . I see that I have confused two different musical occasions, and that your dispute concerned an earlier concert, while I assumed it was a matter of the ceremony planned for the interment. This will take place shortly before or after Easter, and Frau von Bülow's hope that you will direct the musical ceremonial referred to this event which is still to come. (14 March 1894)

These imploring letters are some measure of the importance attached to the occasion, but they also demonstrate the divergence of opinions on the subject of Bülow's artistic convictions. That

* 'Doch nicht erklang mir würd'ge Klage des ersten [hehrsten?] Helden werth' (*Götterdämmerung*, final scene).

Daniela Thode's view of the matter had a kernel of truth in it is borne out by other testimonies, such as a letter Friedrich Rösch sent to Strauss, recalling a meeting with Bülow two years previously: 'And then he began to talk about Wagner in a wonderful way; perhaps he was overcome by a melancholy reminiscence!' (28 January 1892)

Strauss had also been invited to conduct Brahms's German Requiem in Hamburg, in Bülow's memory. A letter from Joseph Joachim to his fellow-violinist Carl Halir in Weimar runs: '[Strauss] is said to have rejected the suggestion that he should conduct the Brahms Requiem with the words "I don't conduct music for dilettantes"!' (14 July 1894) Halir was to ask Strauss if it was true. As Strauss was in Bayreuth at the time, Halir wrote to him, and so Strauss set his evasive answer down in writing: 'With reference to the Hamburg business, the misunderstanding is immediately revealed as such if I tell you that the programme I suggested and that dilettantes wanted to change . . . still included, apart from the Brahms Requiem, a certain *Eroica* Symphony.'[7] (18 July 1894) This was the message that Halir passed on to Joachim.

Strauss's engagement to Pauline de Ahna

Strauss's Munich appointment was finally confirmed on 20 March 1894, on terms that included a guarantee that he would conduct all Wagner's dramas except *Tristan* (this clause was composed by Strauss himself and did not prevent his conducting some extra-contractual performances). Cosima Wagner interpreted this as having a connection with his engagement to conduct at the Bayreuth Festival that summer: 'Hardly had we written to Strauss', she wrote to Prince Ernst zu Hohenlohe-Langenburg, 'when [Possart] sent his stage director to Weimar to engage him as Kapellmeister.' This places far too simplified a construction on the events. The new position in Munich and the appointment to conduct the Berlin Philharmonic concerts (on 20 March he conducted Liszt's *Les préludes* and Beethoven's Ninth Symphony, both with great success, in Berlin) meant that Strauss's financial position was now stable, and he could at last speak to Pauline de Ahna of the love that had grown out of their long friendship. An incident during a rehearsal of *Guntram* has – as we shall see – often been interpreted as the critical moment, but it should probably not be taken so seriously.

Strauss's own version of the story comes from his memoirs of the first performances of his operas and does not mention the engagement:

> At one of the last rehearsals, during which I had to rap with my baton to stop Zeller [who was singing Guntram] countless times, we at last came to Pauline's scene in Act III which she knew perfectly well. All the same she felt unsure of herself and apparently envied Zeller because of his frequent 'repeats'. Suddenly she stopped singing and asked me: 'Why don't you stop me?' I: 'Because you know your part.' With the words 'I want to be stopped', she threw the vocal score which was in her hands at that moment, aiming it at my head, but to general hilarity it landed on the desk of the second violin Gutheil (later the husband of the celebrated Gutheil-Schoder, who made her début with me that year as Pamina and Hänsel).[8]

If this incident really took place during one of the 'last' rehearsals for *Guntram*, then it was some time after the couple had become secretly engaged, for Strauss's parents and sister were informed of it before the end of March, whereas the première of *Guntram* was not until 10 May. Hanna wrote sadly on 1 April: 'Now I have lost the first right to you.' On 5 April she wrote again to say that it was impossible to keep the engagement a secret, and the news was arousing astonishment everywhere. Strauss had called on Pauline's parents before Easter, on 22 March, to ask for her hand, which they were delighted to bestow on him. The correspondence between the various members of the de Ahna family reveals that Pauline herself remained doubtful for the first few weeks of the engagement and must have quarrelled with Strauss. The principal reason was almost certainly her growing confidence in her own gifts, which was being bolstered at precisely this time by her successes in Weimar, by a recommendation from Bronsart to Hochberg in Berlin, and by offers of guest appearances in Munich; a subsidiary reason is perhaps to be found in a lack of confidence in her ability to meet the demands of matrimony.

A different version of the score-throwing incident should be included here, although it is less credible than Strauss's account and seems to be exaggerated to make a better anecdote. It is told in the memoirs of the daughter of the Berlin concert agent Hermann Wolff, Edith Stargardt-Wolff, who was a schoolgirl at the time and visiting Weimar with her parents. (When her father died in 1902 Edith took over the agency and ran it until 1935.)

In the afternoon, following the dress rehearsal, we were sitting peacefully round the coffee table in the house of my uncle Franz Schwarz [the baritone who was singing the part of the young duke], when the singer [Hans] Giessen was announced. 'Show him in', said my uncle. However his colleague would not come in but waited outside in the anteroom, very stiff and formal in a black suit and with a top hat. 'Whatever's the matter with you?' asked my uncle in astonishment [calling him 'Du' as they were close friends]. 'Herr Schwarz, I come as the bearer of a letter from Herr Kapellmeister Richard Strauss, challenging you to a duel with pistols', Giessen said formally [calling him 'Sie']. 'You have insulted his fiancée.' My uncle stared open-mouthed at this address. 'His fiancée? I'm not aware that he's engaged. I don't even know who his fiancée is.' Giessen answered: 'It's Fräulein de Ahna. You have insulted her.' What had happened? During the rehearsal the young singer Pauline de Ahna, who was singing Freihild, the principal female part in *Guntram*, had got so angry over certain remarks of the conductor, Strauss, that at the end of a short argument with him in the presence of my uncle, the violinist Halir and other witnesses she had thrown the music from the stage into the pit where it landed at his feet. Schwarz, who was a Strauss enthusiast from the very first, was made indignant by this treatment of the young master he revered, and reproached her for behaving so disrespectfully towards the musical genius, who had only just returned to his post in Weimar after convalescence from an illness. They came to verbal blows, and then Pauline de Ahna had complained to Strauss about my uncle's rebuke, and the outcome of that – a 'Happy End' – was her engagement to the conductor. Strauss, who had at first declined to be involved in the quarrel, had now taken his fiancée's part and despatched Giessen with this challenge to a duel. My uncle had to laugh heartily at his inadvertent matchmaking and after the intervention of Hans von Bronsart . . . the matter was speedily settled and Strauss and Schwarz shook hands amicably.

A letter, still in my possession, from my uncle Franz to my father, describes the whole incident humorously and reassures him as to the duel with the words 'I won't shoot your conductor.' He also writes prophetically: 'You shall have your conductor without a scratch – from me, that is; I'm afraid his

> fiancée, or wife, will not treat him so considerately.' Events were to prove him right.[9]

The claim that Pauline lost her temper because Strauss corrected her is false. Nevertheless, the kernel of the story is not likely to be a complete fabrication, although it is hard to imagine Strauss calling anyone out – unless Pauline, who always liked to remind people that her father was a general, forced him to do it, so that satisfaction for the 'insult' could be obtained according to the military practice of the time. But it is not inconceivable that in the course of several decades the affair grew in the telling to a size rather larger than it had originally been. There is no way of knowing now whether Schwarz was not merely asked to apologize.

Lotte Lehmann had another version, purportedly given her by Strauss himself. It is not completely free from discrepancies, but it has the ring of truth in its essentials:

> The story of how they became engaged is very amusing and quite typical of their relationship . . . She sang Elisabeth in *Tannhäuser* under his baton, and in a rehearsal made some mistake, or dragged or hurried the tempo (the latter seems more probable to me in view of her temperament!). In any case an argument arose between her and the young conductor, which finally reached its climax when she threw the piano score from the stage on to his head, shrieked some frightful insults, and leaving the rehearsal, rushed to her dressing-room.
>
> Strauss, terribly annoyed, laid down his baton, interrupted the rehearsal which had been so violently disturbed, and without knocking entered Pauline's artist's room. Those waiting outside heard through the closed door wild shrieks of rage and fragmentary insults – then all was quiet. Turning pale each looked at the other; who had killed whom? A shy knocking . . . Strauss opened the door and stood in the doorway beaming radiantly. The representative of the orchestra stammered his speech: 'The orchestra is so horrified by the incredibly shocking behaviour of Fräulein Pauline de Ahna, that they feel they owe it to their honoured conductor to refuse in the future to play in any opera in which she might have a part . . .' With this boycott they wanted to prove to Strauss how eager they were to take his side and to what extent they condemned Pauline de Ahna's unheard-of behaviour . . .
>
> Strauss regarded the musicians smilingly. Then he said: 'That

hurts me very much, for I have just become engaged to Fräulein de Ahna.'[10]

There is no question of anybody being challenged to a duel in this version, richly embellished though it is. Shorn of its corroborative detail, it is probably more accurate than Edith Stargardt-Wolff's account. That the shocking occurrence took place during a rehearsal of *Guntram*, rather than of *Tannhäuser*, and that it was sparked off by something completely the reverse of what Lotte Lehmann surmised, is of no great moment – though one should always be cautious in assessing the reliability of tales like this when told at second hand. Neither version offers any real evidence that the couple became engaged on the spur of the moment as a result of the contretemps during the rehearsal; at most it suggests that so public a quarrel gave rise to the public announcement of the engagement. And the incident may also explain why cards were sent out announcing the engagement on the day of the *Guntram* première (10 May), although originally this form of official notification was not planned (as a letter dated 10 April from General de Ahna to his prospective son-in-law shows).

The turbulence of the first few weeks of the engagement and the powers of persuasion needed by Pauline's relatives to overcome her lingering doubts have to be documented here in some detail, not only because Richard Strauss emerges as calm and confident by contrast with Pauline, but also because a number of accounts exist in print which diverge crassly from the facts. To mention only one example, in his memoirs Otto Strasser, a distinguished member of the Vienna Philharmonic Orchestra (he was on the orchestra's committee of management for a time and was also a member of the celebrated Vienna Philharmonic Quartet), relates a conversation he had with Pauline Strauss in Garmisch in April 1941: 'She told me that her parents were very much opposed to her marriage, as she, the daughter of a Marshal of the Court [!] and a General, wanted to marry a man whose father blew the horn in an orchestra!'[11] There is no doubting the truth of what Strasser says, because others, including the present writer, heard similar utterances. Forty-seven years after the events of 1894, Pauline's memory of them may have become distorted, or perhaps it was simply that her capricious spirit took pleasure in turning things upside down. It was not Pauline's parents who had misgivings but she herself. She wrote to Richard

Strauss on 24 March, using a mode of address ('Mein lieber Herr Strauss') which is distinctly formal for the man one is soon to marry:

> My dear Herr Strauss,
>
> It's all suddenly descending on me like a shower bath; I beg you for God's sake not to rejoice so excessively, you know better than anyone how many faults I have, and I tell you in all honesty that in spite of the happiness I feel, I am sometimes terribly afraid. Will I be capable of being what you want and what you deserve? May I not first fulfil my guest engagement in Hamburg, so that I shall at least have a triumph to show off proudly to my respected teacher? Unfortunately nothing is to come of the Monday Elisabeth. You should not overestimate me, and your parents and Hanna know my moods too; O God, and now I am suddenly supposed to turn into a model housewife, so that you do not feel disappointed. Dear friend, I am afraid that it will fail, and the more everyone else rejoices the more oppressed I feel. It's not nice of Papa to say he has been worried about me and my theatrical career; I don't understand him; up till now everything has gone smoothly and would continue to do so.
>
> Won't all the conducting you will be doing this summer be too much of a strain for you? O God, I am so worried and concerned. Will your parents like me, and Hanna, if she only knew how I have tried to dissuade you from everything. My dear friend, we really don't need to marry so soon; if each of us could first get accustomed to finding all the happiness we can in our careers; you in M[unich] and I in Hamburg; please bring my contract with you; forgive this letter but the two feelings – my happiness and my fear of a new life – weigh on me so that I am only half capable of reasoning. Please allow me at least to sing a lot more parts here; that will help me to get over some of my difficulties. I am being uncommonly diligent studying Freihild with Klatte and Gutheil; the greatest happiness is our art, dear friend, do not forget that. I can't write any more today. Please do not hold any of it against me.
>
> My most sincere greetings to your dear family; I kiss the hand of your honoured Maman and ask them all to have patience with me.
>
> Farewell and be as happy as you deserve to be.
>
> Sincerely yours, Pauline de Ahna.
>
> Please permit a postscript, since it is about Freihild. In Act II: '(Rising to her full height) "Entweiche Tod vor Freihilds Jubel" '

lies very, very high; could it be pointed [to make it easier to deliver]; then I would certainly be better able to bring off the great vocal effect that is intended; I spend almost the whole day working on it, *difficult* but beautiful!!!

This letter crossed with one of the same date from her parents. Their volatile and temperamental daughter had often caused them concern, not only for her future, and they had often expressed their complete confidence in Strauss's good influence on her and her development. Now her father wrote about his proposal:

> So the good loyal friend has been here to ask for your hand and we answered that if you and he were of one mind about your wishes and desires then we could only say 'yes' and give 'our blessing', for we know of nothing in the whole business that does not give us cause for joy . . . I am unshakeably convinced that now your happiness and contentment all depend on you alone, for Strauss has a noble mind and so warm an affection for you that it will not be hard for you to live so as to please him and to manage things so that he is never disappointed in his *firm* belief that he possesses in you a loving and loyal partner in life. Papa and Mother Strauss and Fräulein Johanna have assured us with touching sincerity how pleased they are by Richard's decision and how they will never forget how good you were to him when he was so ill!
>
> When I reflect on the uncertain, worrying future that you will now escape, by marrying a husband of good artistic repute, an interesting man and one devoted to you, I can only rejoice yet again with my whole heart that your destiny has taken this turn; the more so as the feelings you experienced in Reichenhall and Marquartstein were not entirely concealed from us. Picture yourself, on the one hand as an artist more or less at the mercy of the directorial whims and tyranny of Pollini, and on the other as the wife of a respected man who, although he has known all your good and your less good aspects for years, nonetheless loves you with his whole heart and is devoted to you, living in Munich and no longer far from home, and perhaps even you yourself also admired and respected as an artist etc., etc. – then you will understand the relief and joy felt by me and Mama and your loving Mädi. (24 March 1894)

Pauline must have written to her parents about her misgivings on the same day. She appears to have become obsessed with the prospect of the Hamburg engagement, and her parents and Mädi, her sister, worked hard to overcome her hesitation. Her sister in particular assured her that Strauss had expressly said that she could do exactly what she wanted, remain an opera singer or give up her career; it was crazy to believe that she would have to give it up because of her marriage. One interesting passage refers to Pauline's belief that she was too great an egoist to make a loyal wife for the rest of her life. Mädi wrote that she was by no means such an enormous egoist, since she had travelled with Strauss to Munich when he was ill in the summer of 1892 in spite of wagging tongues, and in Reichenhall and Marquartstein the fact that she was in love was written all over her face; let her remember how often she changed her clothes, the flowers and all the little signs! As Pauline had actually proposed to write to Strauss's parents to say that their son would not suit her, her sister's tone became even sterner:

> Everyone's patience gradually wears out in the end, and it might happen with Strauss too if you keep [him] in suspense for eternity, people get tired of that sort of thing, my dear Pauline, you love him, so don't go on playing this purely superficial role, and don't go on putting yourself in the foreground all the time, because by degrees that could make the greatest love falter.

Father de Ahna took a realistic line when he wrote:

> If you really might – as you say you may – turn Strauss down, it would be impossible for him to enter your house again because of the mortification, he certainly wouldn't do so and you would be unable to ask him or expect him to teach you and help you from that moment on. Your relationship, which up till now has simply been friendly, would have to be confined to the purely professional association that is all that is possible in rehearsal rooms and in the theatre itself! Try to picture it, and think of the social and professional harm it would do you. In any case, no one would believe that you had turned him down, it would generally be assumed that Str. had not wished to keep up his friendship with you after leaving Weimar.
>
> If you want to reflect maturely on so serious a step, which will affect your whole life, no one will hold it against you, including the Str. family. (25 March 1894)

He continued on the same tack rather more calmly the next day, describing a visit from Richard and Hanna: Richard had read a few sentences from a telegram Pauline had sent him, which was 'very sensibly and sincerely expressed'; her father indicated his appreciation of it and applauded her decision not to be over-hasty. Strauss had once again said that Pauline was entirely free to remain an opera singer if she wanted to, and he had told the general that

> if you come under an unfamiliar direction in Hamburg it will make you properly appreciate being conducted by [him] at last . . . Also I haven't quite given up hope of Bayreuth yet and I'm glad that you have proposed yourself to Frau W[agner] in a nice letter. From your letter I told Strauss that you have great misgivings about taking on the responsibility for such a serious matter. He said he thought he would help to bear the responsibility! So now I hope that everything will turn out for your happiness and satisfaction.

The general's sense of relief was short-lived. Early in April he forcefully reminded Pauline once again what an exceptionally upright and distinguished husband she was getting, and one who loved her, 'even if you are no angel in your own eyes'. The uncertainty as to whether Pauline would also be engaged at the Munich Opera contributed to the new crisis. After receiving another letter full of doubts from her sister, Mädi wrote: 'Papa was really annoyed and not in a fit state or mood to write to you, and told me to tell you that he wishes you would spare him enquiries about his health!' She referred to Pauline's 'crazy' letters and reminded her of Strauss's saying that 'what *must* happen will happen of its own accord'. Strauss did not want to insist on the Munich Opera engaging Pauline, it would not improve his position; it would do her reputation far more good if she should become not just a housewife in the autumn after making a success of her guest engagements:

> Give up this eternal struggling with your fiancé, in the long run it's bound to annoy him seriously, if he sees that all the love and respect he has for you never gets any other response than your *rather dull* refrain: Being an opera singer is the most important thing for me! You can combine the two so easily, so enjoy the period of your betrothal whole-heartedly, and be a little 'incarnate poetry' (as Count Wedell called your Isolde) off-stage as well. Then Strauss will at last get the peace he needs for his health and you will be able to make things so much easier for him (who really is so infinitely fond of you) here in the place where he is going to work, if you behave in a charming and *equable* manner. All it needs from you is a little more self-control – for when the boorish words are out you always regret them at

> once – and the two of you will make a very happy and contented musical couple. It will be all right if you have a little row now and again – I think Strauss quite enjoys *some* variety – as long as you don't do it in front of a third person . . . I'm sure he will have only beautiful and honourable things to say about you and your future, so follow his example, he is a *good, upright character*, and if Johanna comes, promise us that you will be calm and equable, of course it wouldn't do if you exaggerate things, don't ever let her hear of a serious disagreement with Strauss, his family think the world of him, quite rightly, and from other quarters too we hear nothing but praise for his talent and for his artistic reputation in the world at large. You know all this yourself, I don't need to say anything more about it, and you're proud of him, infinitely fond of him, and would be unhappy if it hadn't turned out the way it has!

The reflection of Pauline's character in this shrewd letter is undoubtedly true to life. In the end her father mastered himself sufficiently to add a few lines to it:

> . . . reinforce your good intent. And take heed that I am tired of having my old age soured by you. At your age [she was thirty-one] and when one has been making one's way in the world for some years, one ought to know what one wants and not promise *today* to be a good and loyal wife and suddenly declare tomorrow that one has changed one's mind . . . I have written and spoken more than enough about this business of yours; if you want to make yourself unhappy and cast a shadow over whole families, then do so, but thereafter I wash my hands of you. (9 April 1894)

The Weimar première of *Guntram*

It was during this critical period in his private life that Strauss had news of the cancellation of the plans to produce *Guntram* in Karlsruhe. The announcement in the *Münchner Neueste Nachrichten* of 4 April 1894 that his appointment at the Munich Opera had received royal approval will have been no consolation for this disappointment, since it was only the official confirmation of what was already settled. He received the grand ducal leave to resign from his post in Weimar on 13 April.

Now, against his wishes, he had to prepare to give *Guntram* its première in Weimar after all. Earlier, when his father had objected

Weimar.

Großherzogl. Hof-Theater.

Donnerstag den 10. Mai 1894.

Mit aufgehobenem Abonnement,
zum Vortheil des Chorpensionsfonds:

Zum ersten Mal:

Guntram.

In drei Aufzügen.

Dichtung und Musik von Richard Strauß.

In Scene gesetzt von Herrn Regisseur F. Wiedey.

Personen:

Der alte Herzog		Hr. Karl Bucha.
Freihild, seine Tochter		Frl. de Ahna.
Herzog Robert, ihr Gemahl		Hr. Schwarz.
Guntram	Sänger	Hr. Zeller.
Friedhold		Hr. Wiedey.
Der Narr des Herzogs		Hr. Gießen.
Eine alte Frau	arme Leute	Frl. Tibelti.
Ein alter Mann		Hr. Lutz.
Zwei jüngere Männer		Hr. Barth.
		Hr. Hermann Bucha.
Drei Vasallen		Hr. Fischer.
		Hr. Schustherr.
		Hr. Hennig.
Ein Bote		Hr. Hermann Bucha.
Vier Minnesänger		Hr. v. Szpinger.
		Hr. Knösler.
		Hr. Glitsch.
		Hr. Weyrauch.

Vasallen des Herzogs, Minnesänger, Mönche, Knechte und Reisige.

Die Handlung spielt in Deutschland um die Mitte des dreizehnten Jahrhunderts.

Textbücher sind an der Kasse für 80 Pfg. zu haben.

Preise der Plätze wie gewöhnlich.

Billetverkauf und Abgabe bestellter Billets vormittags von 11–12 und nachmittags von 3–4 Uhr.

Die Kasse wird **6½** Uhr geöffnet.

Anfang 7 Uhr, Ende nach 10 Uhr.

Der freie Eintritt ist ohne Ausnahme nicht gestattet.

Beurlaubt: Frl. Schmittlein, Hr. Oberregisseur Professor Brandt.

Sonnabend den 12. (**B. 67.**) **Krieg im Frieden**, Lustspiel in fünf Aufzügen von G. v. Moser und Fr. v. Schönthan. (Reif-Reiflingen — Hr. Bertram vom Stadttheater zu Stettin als Gast.) (Anfang **7** Uhr.)

166. Weimar. — G. Uschmann.

Theatre-bill advertising the first performance of *Guntram*, Weimar, 1894

First performance of *Guntram*, Act I, scene 1

to some ticklish passages for the horns and trumpets, and to the high registers in which the cellos were required to play, Strauss had retorted that everything was as it was intended to be, and that only performance would show if any changes were needed. (See above, the '*Guntram* Chronicle'.) Now, when rehearsals started, he wrote: 'Yesterday eight [!] hours sectional rehearsals for Act III of *Guntram*; sounds capital but difficult, the horns are grumbling but they enjoy it really!' (3 April) A few days later:

> The string quartet is the most difficult part, even I have begun to get cold feet, the wind parts are not so difficult, but the strings – nothing but viola, cello and double bass concertos. Very strange! But new and magnificent! But it's performable only by a very large string contingent, am curious to see it I can put it across. (11 April 1894)

The preparations and rehearsals transformed him into a general factotum, combining all the activities of 'conductor, repetiteur, set-painter, stage manager and theatrical costumier'. (To Alexander Ritter, 19 May 1894) The score asks for a very large orchestra: 3 flutes (3rd doubling piccolo), 3 oboes (3rd doubling cor anglais), 3 clarinets (3rd doubling bass clarinet), 3 bassoons, double bassoon; 4 horns, 3 trumpets, bass trumpet, 2 tenor trombones, bass trombone, bass tuba; 4 timpani (2 players), tambourine, triangle, 1 pair small cymbals, 1 pair large cymbals, bass drum, tenor drum; lute; 2 harps; 16 first and 16 second violins, 12 violas, 10 cellos, 8 double basses (a total of 62 string players); further, a stage band of 4 horns, 4 tenor horns, 4 trumpets, 3 trombones and 4 military side drums. In Weimar Strauss had to make substantial reductions in these numbers, using no more than twenty-one string players and recruiting the third player in each of the wind sections from the local military band, whose instruments were tuned only approximately to the same pitches as those of the court orchestra.

> Nevertheless *Guntram*, the score of which was not in any way suitable for the existing circumstances and bears witness to my hair-raising naivety in those days, was studied and put into rehearsal, my poor, valiant pupil Heinrich Zeller went through agonies with his insanely demanding role – at the time somebody calculated that the part had so-and-so-many more bars than that of Tristan – each rehearsal made him hoarser and hoarser and at the first performance he had a struggle to last out

> to the end. My fiancée knew her part faultlessly and her performance was vocally and dramatically outstanding. The audience applauded her tumultuously after the second act in Weimar, and it was the same story at the much later, disastrous performance in Munich . . .
>
> *Guntram* had a *succès d'estime* when it was new, but after some vain attempts to revive it with enormous cuts in Frankfurt [1900] and Prague [1910], it disappeared altogether from the stage and with it went my courage to write for the theatre for another six years.[12]

On the occasion of Strauss's seventieth birthday, a much-cut performance under Hans Rosbaud was broadcast on the radio; this encouraged Strauss to make his own cuts, and the revised version was performed in Weimar in 1940 under Paul Sixt, and in Berlin in 1942 under Robert Heger.

Although Strauss made an official announcement of his engagement to Pauline de Ahna on the day of the *Guntram* première, he was already sure of a happy outcome to her hesitations before the end of April, or he would not have committed himself to renting the flat that his parents and the de Ahna family had found for the newly-weds in Munich, at Hildegardstrasse 2/I.[13] Numerous friends and colleagues came to Weimar for the première on 10 May 1894 (Ritter, Sommer, Weingartner and others – Ludwig Thuille was kept away by shortage of money), as well as his and Pauline's relatives.

The première was given in the Grand Ducal Court Theatre. The normal subscription scheme did not apply to this performance and tickets were sold to benefit the chorus pension fund. In accordance with the custom of the time the conductor (Strauss) was not named on the programme, though of course his name appeared as composer and librettist. The production was directed by Ferdinand Wiedey, and the principal singers included Karl Bucha (the Old Duke), Pauline de Ahna (Freihild), Franz Schwarz (Duke Robert, her husband), Heinrich Zeller (Guntram), Wiedey (Friedhold), Hans Giessen (the Duke's Fool) and Louise Tibelti (an old peasant woman). The first desks in the string section were occupied by players of the first rank: Carl Halir, August Roesel and Leopold Grützmacher.

The press was divided in its response, but less than enthusiastic for the most part. The *Münchner Neueste Nachrichten* printed one of the more favourable notices, which was encouraging with the prospect of a production in Munich:

> With today's performance of *Guntram* Hofkapellmeister Strauss has scored a highly significant success. The work stands on the same ground as Wagner's music drama, but does not owe anything at all to Wagnerian rhythmic or melodic style, is consequently completely individual. At the end of the last act the composer received a tumultuous ovation.

This review was still distinctly noncommittal, and the paper followed it with a more penetrating consideration by Max Hasse, who paid more attention to the idea behind the work than to its music. The drama, which bears some resemblance in its material to *Tannhäuser* and *Lohengrin*, is in a certain sense an allegory, Hasse wrote perceptively, and the historical garb in which the librettist dresses his personages is a purely external factor.

> Only one thing can expiate the guilt of existence: renunciation. [Guntram] enjoins compassion on the duke, while himself in the grip of self-seeking. He sang for enslaved freedom and was yet the slave of his own desires, he wanted to save an oppressed people and slew the husband of the woman he loved . . .
>
> Does the librettist intend him to do penance for the sin in his heart, by leading from henceforth a life of Christian asceticism, or does he subscribe to the Schopenhauerian theory of the denial of the will to life and send the hero to a life of 'renunciation in compassion'? The text gives no certain indication. The music transfigures this last scene of decision to such a pitch that at the moment of listening to it one simply believes and only later turns to these critical deliberations. The musical language of Richard Strauss speaks altogether with a convincing power . . .
>
> Of Fräulein de Ahna one can say that she simply created Freihild. In particular the scene of frenzy in the first act and the farewell scene in the third were completely successful.

As Strauss told Ritter, the impression the work made on the composer himself in performance was exactly what he had imagined it would be; his sole cause for regret was the lack of a covered orchestra pit. (In later life, Strauss preferred the covered pit only for the performance of the *Ring*.) 'I myself am curious to see where the little ship will make to, for one is only being rowed while one supposes one is rowing.' (To Alexander Ritter, 19 May 1894) *Guntram* was given only four performances in Weimar.

Although the protracted negotiations with Munich had at last come to a positive conclusion – at the time of the *Guntram* première the only outstanding matter was the question whether Strauss was to conduct any of the Academy Concerts, which was not confirmed until 30 October – Strauss did not abandon his hope that he might be able to move to Berlin without spending an interval of years in Munich; this hope had been strengthened by his appointment to conduct the Berlin Philharmonic Concerts. He sent a copy of his Munich contract to Georg Henry Pierson in Berlin, asking him to investigate the possibility of his extricating himself from it before its term expired. In a confidential reply (in which he also promised to come to a performance of *Guntram* in Weimar on 1 June) Pierson told him:

> Alas, alas, you are bound fast. However much I think it over, weighing this possibility and that, I always have to tell myself finally that there is not one loose end. We must discuss it in detail, perhaps you will find an escape-route. In my opinion you are the only person who can have a shot at extricating yourself in an amicable fashion, whether you would succeed is an open question . . . Think over what might be done. (15 May 1894)

It is not known whether, as the outcome of his conversations with Pierson in Weimar on that occasion, Strauss ever made the attempt adumbrated in the letter, but it is not very likely, if for no other reason than that it would have put the Munich production of *Guntram* at risk. It fell out in the end that Strauss had no alternative but to go to Munich, because Weingartner's contract held him in Berlin until 1896.

The last months in Weimar

When Strauss was made director of the Berlin Philharmonic Concerts, following his conducting successes in Hamburg in January and in Berlin in March, it gave him hope for a time that, although the Grand Duke would not immediately release him, he could at least exploit his position to obtain changes in Weimar which would enable him to turn down the Munich appointment. By that time, in the early months of 1894, the Munich post was virtually assured – and the grand ducal decree releasing him from his Weimar contract was issued on 13 April – but he continued to regard the prospect with some suspicion. Bronsart refused, however, to go along with his wishes. Since Strauss could now hardly withdraw from playing a part in the 'model' performances of Wagner that were to be staged in Munich during the summer season and were regarded in Bayreuth as competition to the festival there, he loyally proposed in his correspondence with Frau Wagner to turn down Munich if she did not approve of his participation. However she had the wisdom to allow so eminent a champion of Wagner a free hand.

Strauss's provisional arrangement with Possart was for two years. When it became known in Weimar that he was leaving, rumours began to circulate that his relationship with Eduard Lassen was a primary cause. When these reached the newspapers, Strauss wrote to the Weimar paper *Deutschland* in an endeavour to deny them:

> In order to clear up an error that I think I have encountered in your columns several times, and in order to counter the manifold rumours that seem to be swarming throughout Weimar at present, from Belvederer Allee to Kaiserin-Augusta-Strasse and from Liszt-Strasse out to Tiefurt, I will be obliged if you will publish the declaration that not only does Herr Hofkapellmeister Eduard Lassen have no connection with my departure from Weimar, but that on the contrary I gladly seize this opportunity to confirm that during the five years I have spent here engaged in artistic activity Dr Lassen has always shown me the greatest possible cooperation, not merely as far as his own artistic views permitted but often much further, and has afforded to my artistic endeavours the same support which he has extended to so many aspiring young talents during his meritorious career.

The first three of the Four Songs Op. 27 which Strauss gave to his beloved Pauline on their wedding day were composed in May: *Ruhe, meine Seele* (words by Karl Henckell) on the 17th, *Morgen!* (John Henry Mackay) on the 21st and *Heimliche Aufforderung* (Mackay) on the 22nd; the fourth, *Cäcilie* (Julius Hart), was written on 9 September, the day before the wedding. In this collection, which quickly became famous, Strauss for the first time set words by poets of his own generation. He orchestrated *Morgen!* and *Cäcilie* in 1897, and fifty-four years after its composition he returned to the first of these 'bridal songs' two days before his eighty-fourth birthday; in Montreux on 9 June 1948 he wrote a new orchestral version of *Ruhe, meine Seele*.

Early in June 1894 the Allgemeiner Deutscher Musikverein held its congress in Weimar, which meant more work for Strauss. In the second concert, on 3 June, Gustav Mahler conducted his First Symphony for the first time in front of an audience consisting largely of professional musicians (it had previously had two performances before the general public, in Prague in 1889 and in Hamburg in October 1893). On this third occasion it was 'half-failure [and] half-success'; a review in the *Neue Zeitschrift für Musik* objected to the 'hotch-potch of real and transcendental concepts', which can only be a reference to the work's 'programme'.[14] This is not the place for a consideration of the relationship between Mahler and Strauss, but it began auspiciously. Before the congress Mahler wrote a long letter to Strauss which includes a reference to *Guntram*:

> I can't tell you how greatly I long to hear it. More and more I regret having only this incomplete short score here, which lacks even the orchestral interludes and linking passages, and makes the true understanding of such an original work impossible. I can only be glad to have been initiated by you yourself – and I have been drawing on that memory these last few days. (15 May 1894)

However, when Mahler had a closer look at the score two months before the Munich production, he wrote to an unidentified correspondent: 'I have never set eyes on such a mixture of childish immaturity and presumptuousness at one and the same time as *Guntram*.'[15] At an 'Authors' Concert' in Vienna on 19 February 1899, when Siegfried Wagner, Engelbert Humperdinck and Wilhelm Kienzl conducted works of their own, Mahler stood in for Strauss to conduct two preludes from *Guntram*.

Mahler's letter to Strauss of 15 May 1894 is mainly concerned with the preparation for the performance of the First Symphony: there were discrepancies between the manuscript copy of the score which Strauss was conducting from at rehearsals with the Weimar orchestra and the orchestral parts (especially the strings), since Mahler had revised the work considerably since the first performance in 1889.[16] In an undated letter to Eugen Lindner, Mahler mentions 'a little tension between me and Str.', which may have arisen in connection with Strauss's preparation of the First Symphony on this occasion. At the end of May Mahler wrote again to Lindner, announcing the date of his arrival in Weimar; he hoped that the parts of his symphony had arrived safely and added: 'One can get nothing out of Strauss, of course, since at the moment he is in a state of genuine "withdrawal from the world"' – an allusion to Strauss's engagement to Pauline.[17]

Strauss must have written to Mahler suggesting a change (or perhaps a cut) in the symphony – the letter is not available – for Mahler wrote to him:

> How can you even ask if I am offended by your candour? Believe me, I would not be even if you dressed your criticism in far less flattering garb. In the matter in question I cannot share your view, the fact that you want the resolution and as it were the summation of the whole at the place you designate only demonstrates to me that I have not expressed myself clearly enough at all, and that would be bad enough. If it does not bore you, I will come back to the subject and argue my case with you in Bayreuth. For today just one thing: at the passage marked 'bewegt' the resolution is only an apparent one (the whole a 'false close' in the true sense of the word), and it requires a new change of direction and refraction of the whole essence before a true 'victory' is achieved after such a battle. I intended to depict a battle in which victory is always furthest from the warrior at the moment when he thinks it is closest. This is the essential nature of every spiritual warrior. For it is not so simple then to become or to be a hero.
>
> Even if at some future time (when I myself may be above the battle) I come to the conclusion that I did not express my truest intention, I still shall not alter it any more. Do you know why? You will know the answer at once, if you ask yourself what you would do in such a case: *write something new* and all of it better! We agree on that, don't we?! (Steinbach am Attersee, 19 July 1894)

Guntram (on 1 June) and *Hänsel und Gretel* (on 3 June) were also heard in Weimar during the congress, both conducted by Strauss. In his report in the Leipzig *Musikalisches Wochenblatt* (14 June) Max Hasse wrote:

> A large number of German composers are building in a very serious fashion on the foundations laid by Wagner: Cyrill Kistler and Hans Sommer, Weingartner and others. But none of them has been so successful in breaking through the spell which Wagner has laid on all the works to have appeared since *Parsifal* as this South German composer [Strauss].

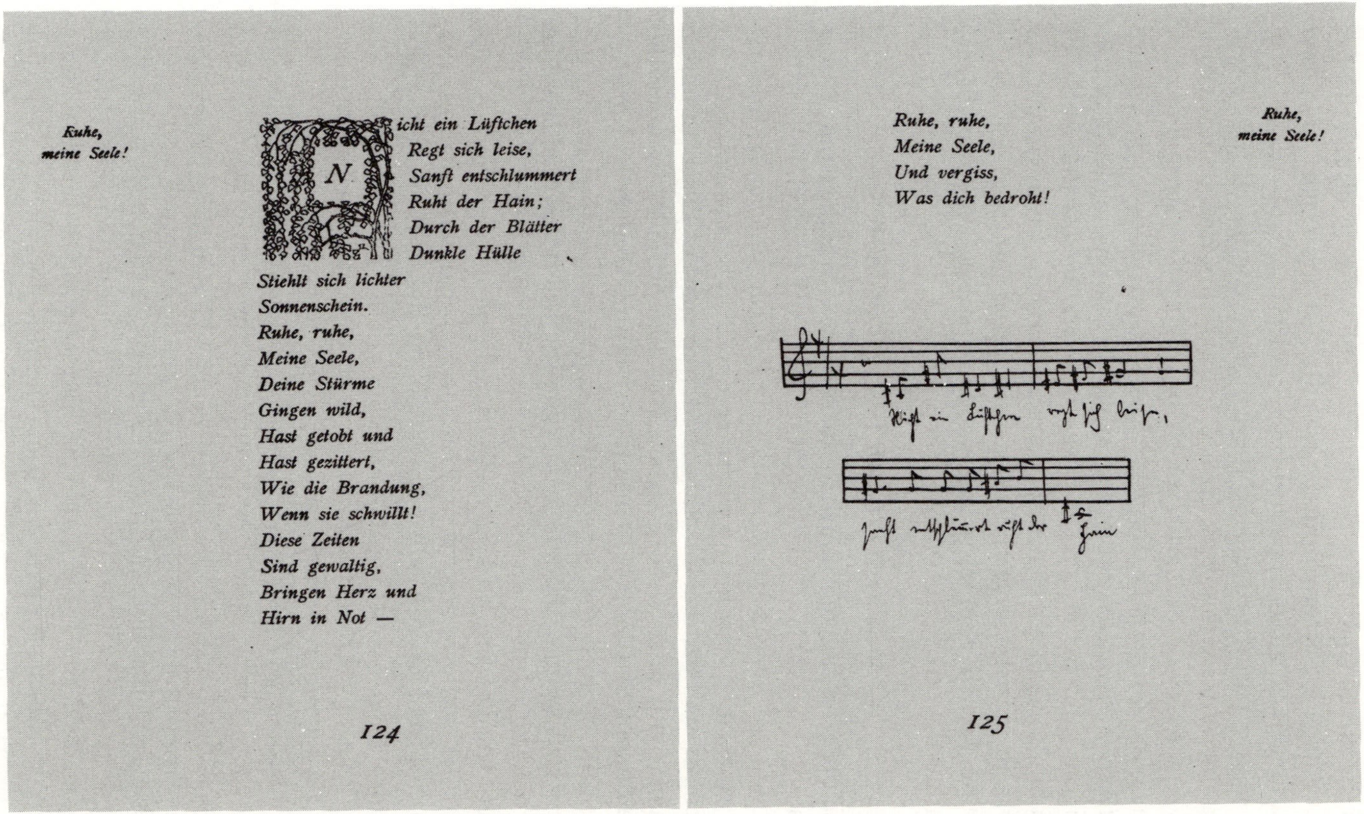

Ruhe,
meine Seele!

Nicht ein Lüftchen
Regt sich leise,
Sanft entschlummert
Ruht der Hain;
Durch der Blätter
Dunkle Hülle
Stiehlt sich lichter
Sonnenschein.
Ruhe, ruhe,
Meine Seele,
Deine Stürme
Gingen wild,
Hast getobt und
Hast gezittert,
Wie die Brandung,
Wenn sie schwillt!
Diese Zeiten
Sind gewaltig,
Bringen Herz und
Hirn in Not —

124

Ruhe, ruhe,
Meine Seele,
Und vergiss,
Was dich bedroht!

Ruhe,
meine Seele!

125

From Karl Henckell's *Mein Lied* (1905): *Ruhe, meine Seele*, with a facsimile of the first four bars of the song in Strauss's autograph

He described *Guntram* as 'the most difficult score, probably, that has ever been set before an orchestra'. Both it and *Hänsel und Gretel* had received 'a model performance' under Strauss. Verdi's *Falstaff* was also performed during the congress, conducted by Lassen. Strauss admired this work greatly, from the first time he heard it, in Weimar a few weeks earlier, on 8 April. When the correspondent of the *Neue Zeitschrift für Musik* (13 June 1894) described *Guntram* and *Hänsel und Gretel* as providing 'new, magnificent evidence of . . . vigour' and fit 'to erect a strong bulwark against the works of dubious worth which have penetrated Germany from without', he was presumably referring to *verismo* opera and to the work of some French composers (Gounod, Massenet and Saint-Saëns) rather than to Verdi's masterpiece.

The Bayreuth Festival of 1894

Before returning to Munich for his second term at the Court Opera there, Strauss at last conducted at the Bayreuth Festival. Felix Mottl conducted *Lohengrin*, Hermann Levi *Parsifal. Tannhäuser*, the first performance of which took place on 22 July, was entrusted to Strauss, and that Pauline alternated in the part of Elisabeth in this opera with Elisa Wiborg (as she had done in 1891) signified the fulfilment of a long-held ambition. Cosima Wagner had made a definite promise that he should conduct at the festival during the previous winter, though at the time she had not settled what he would be asked to do. (7 November 1893) But it was not until a very late juncture, on 3 June 1894, that she wrote to ask Strauss if his fiancée would be able to sing Elisabeth in two performances, and one of the Flower Maidens in *Parsifal* (as always this group of six soloists was cast from strength).

'It's always a marvellous feeling to enter the Festival Theatre once again and see art treated really seriously', he wrote home on 2 July. He had already taken one *Tannhäuser* rehearsal the day before in sweltering heat; Pauline had sung 'her Elisabeth so capitally' that she had given delight to Wahnfried, and Frau Wagner had at once decreed that she should sing the *first* Elisabeth. A week later he told his parents that his last *Tannhäuser* rehearsal had gone 'so capitally, so well, that Frau W. [had] cancelled the next complete rehearsal altogether' and there would be only one more, the final dress rehearsal itself. 'Pauline is well and cheerful, does all that is asked of her very well indeed and is received in Wahnfried, as I am, very kindly.' (10 July 1894) Apart from the rehearsals and performances of *Tannhäuser*, Strauss also conducted some rehearsals of the other works. According to Steinitzer, Cosima Wagner greeted Strauss after one of the first rehearsals with the words '*Ei, ei*, such a modernist and yet conducts *Tannhäuser* so well'. This dig at his composing is not likely to have escaped Strauss.

During this summer in Bayreuth he made the acquaintance of Ludwig Karpath, whom he got to know better in his years in Berlin and who, as legal adviser to the Department of Federal Theatres in the Austrian Ministry of Education, was very active as an intermediary during the crises of Strauss's period as director of the Vienna State Opera and the difficult situation following his resignation in 1924.

The end of the 1893–4 season at the Weimar opera was also the end of Strauss's five years in the Grand Duchy. Although he had hurled himself upon the tasks that awaited him with true zeal, he was incapable of enduring the restrictions of musical life in Weimar indefinitely, of exercising any moderation in his determination to put through his own ideas about repertory and interpretation, or even of accepting compromise in such matters. In old age he admitted that his attitude had alienated the sympathies of some, and people had not been sorry to see him go.

Marie Gutheil-Schoder (1874–1935), later one of the most distinguished interpreters of Straussian roles – the composer especially admired her overwhelming Elektra – was a witness of Strauss's years in Weimar, at first as a pupil of a singer under contract to the Court Theatre, Virginia Naumann-Gungl, and then, from October 1892, as a member of the permanent company herself, after Strauss had noted her promise. She made her début as First Lady in *Die Zauberflöte*. Recalling those days in her memoirs, she wrote:

> The twenty-five-year-old Richard Strauss kept intellectual and musical Weimar on tenterhooks with the inspiring achievements of his fiery genius. He put on unparalleled performances of the works of Gluck, Mozart and Wagner, and presented a magnificent production of *Tristan*, the first time it had been seen in Weimar, using exclusively the resident forces, which was an incredible achievement for the little Court Theatre.[18]

Some years before the publication of her memoirs she had published an article with the title 'Richard Strauss in Weimar': 'My artistic existence began under his banner . . .' Strauss had fired all musical hearts and minds with enthusiasm and excitement by his new and revolutionary ideas:

> My God, what evenings those were in the opera house in our beloved Weimar. Of course Strauss dominated the whole musical life of the town, and even though I was only a slip of a girl my sensitive heart warmed to that fiery spirit which kindled my own ardour too in many an hour of the most intensive study.[19]

The theatre in Weimar, his conducting engagements in other towns and his work on *Guntram* made so many demands on Strauss that he had little time for reading. To concern himself with the social and political questions of the time was completely foreign to him; in the abundance of correspondence which survives from those years he writes exclusively of music, of performances, his conducting dates and his personal affairs (travel, family news, his search for another post) and occasionally of his reading. Besides Schopenhauer and Wagner and the books he read in association with his operatic projects, Goethe was already in those days his favourite author. It was only in the following period in Munich that he gradually began to pay attention to questions of his profession and its standing.

Before going to Bayreuth that year, Strauss had already taken a first step in his work in Munich when he conducted *Tristan* (on 29 June 1894) in the summer season of Wagner performances which eventually developed into the annual Munich Festival. Two more performances under his direction took place on 22 August and 5 September, and he also conducted *Meistersinger* in Munich on 2 September. Cosima Wagner warned him of her suspicion that he had only been invited to conduct these performances in order to cause 'confusion between Munich and Bayreuth (especially in the minds of strangers)'. Possart had cynically admitted as much to Levi. (To Strauss, 9 March 1894)

The process of getting *Guntram* into print began in the late summer of 1894. Spitzweg undertook its publication, but asked Strauss to omit the designation 'action' (*Handlung*) from the title. The sub-title was originally 'in three acts'; the second version 'action in three acts'. Max Hasse's suggestions ('Drama in three actions' and '*Guntram*, in three actions') did not meet with approval, and finally Strauss and Spitzweg agreed on the first formula, '*Guntram*, in three acts'. A preface written by Strauss was also omitted and has been lost. The contract was not concluded until 8 October. The score and vocal score bear the dedication 'To my beloved parents'.

On 10 September, four months after the official announcement of their engagement, the marriage of Strauss and Pauline de Ahna took place in Marquartstein. It was celebrated in the parish office of Grassau according to the Catholic rite. After the ceremony the couple went to Italy; finding it unpleasantly cold in Bellagio, they went on to Pegli and then, after the return of summer warmth, to Venice. They returned to Munich on 6 October and moved into their first marital home at Hildegardstrasse 2/I where they remained until March 1896, when they moved into a pleasanter and roomier apartment at Herzog-Rudolf-Strasse 8/III.

9

The second term in Munich, 1894–8

Changes had taken place in Munich – at that date a city of fewer than half a million inhabitants – during the years that Strauss had spent in Weimar. The visual arts, in particular, were growing in importance and influence, though this made less impression on the native population than on the relatively large numbers of artists attracted to the city from outside. In the field of literature new forces began to stir in the middle of the last decade of the nineteenth century, and within little more than a year of Strauss's return to Munich the musical life of the city took on a new impetus with the opening of a new concert hall, named the Kaim-Saal after its founder Franz Kaim, which was inaugurated on 19 October 1895 by a performance of *Messiah* under Hermann Zumpe, followed on the very next day by a concert conducted by Felix Mottl. The orchestra founded by Kaim earned a considerable reputation within a very short time. When Gustav Mahler conducted a programme that included Berlioz's *Symphonie fantastique* as well as Beethoven's Fifth, he wrote to his sister an hour before the concert began that the final rehearsal had gone brilliantly and that he had been thunderously applauded by the players. 'The orchestra is *capital*, entirely made up of young people capable of great enthusiasm with *good* instruments. I would very much like to have this job.' (24 March 1897)[1] But by June of the same year Mahler had been appointed deputy director of the Vienna Court Opera.

Strauss, however, had to wait until 1903 before celebrating his first notable triumph in the Kaim-Saal with *Tod und Verklärung*; for the time being his conducting in Munich was confined to the two houses used by the Court Opera, the Court Theatre and the small Residenztheater, and to the Odeonssaal, built for King Ludwig I by Leo von Klenze in 1828.

The first work that fell to him to conduct after taking up his new post was Lortzing's *Der Waffenschmied* on 20 October 1894. This must have been something of a disappointment to him, but as he had been able to pay homage to his master during the summer with *Tristan* and *Meistersinger*, and had the opportunity to conduct them both again in November, followed in December by Liszt's *Saint Elisabeth*, he was not unduly downcast by this unexciting official début. The other operas he conducted before Christmas 1894 were *Oberon*, *Die Zauberflöte* and Ignaz Brüll's *Das goldene Kreuz*. In the second half of the season, after the New Year, he conducted twenty-nine performances altogether, including, in addition to the works already listed, Maillart's *Les dragons de Villars*, Flotow's *Martha*, Humperdinck's *Hänsel und Gretel*, Bizet's *Carmen*, Nicolai's *Die lustigen Weiber*, Wagner's *Tannhäuser*, Verdi's *Il trovatore*, Kreutzer's *Das Nachtlager von Granada* and a new production of *Rienzi*. It was a comprehensive and varied repertory, and he had not conducted the majority of the works before. The *Rienzi*, which had its first performance on 22 May 1895, was the outstanding item for him. He had conducted the work in Weimar, but in Munich, as he took charge of the rehearsals, he wrote regularly and at length to Cosima Wagner to discover her wishes as to its performance, which he observed to the letter, although not always completely agreeing with her. Pauline made a guest appearance at the Munich Court Theatre on 23 June 1895, as Elisabeth in *Tannhäuser* under his direction. He conducted twelve times during the Munich Wagner Festival in August 1895, three performances each of *Rienzi*, *Tannhäuser*, *Tristan* and *Meistersinger*.

In October 1894 Levi and Strauss finally came to an agreement about the Musical Academy Concerts which satisfied Strauss. In addition to the traditional repertory, with Haydn and Beethoven in the forefront, he naturally made a point of championing Liszt, and also Smetana, of whom he conducted three of the numbers from *Má Vlast: Tábor*, *Vltava* and *Šárka*. When the astronomer Egon von Oppolzer proposed that he should include Bruckner in his programmes, Strauss recalled that Levi had made a considerable impression on the Munich public with the Seventh Symphony in the past and declared his own readiness to perform another 'if circumstances permit'.[2] However, no Bruckner was performed in any of the small number of concerts directed by him.

For the first of the subscription concerts, on 16 November 1894, he chose a work particularly dear to him, Beethoven's Seventh Symphony, his interpretation of which made a good impression, according to a report in the press:

As a conductor, as an interpreter of the works of others, Strauss displayed individual and original powers of the highest quality at this concert. The promise of new impulses which will bear fruit in the practice of the arts in Munich is all the more hopeful inasmuch as the young artist has already made great progress in curbing his all too ardent musician's temperament, in sloughing the most pardonable errors of youth. His deportment and exterior mannerisms when conducting are wellbred; he is conscious of the high position to which he has been called . . . In his direction of Beethoven's Symphony No. 7 in A major, Herr Strauss confirmed in the most brilliant fashion all those conductor's virtues that have been rehearsed above. The clarity and certitude of his execution were astonishing, the phrasing and dynamics always apt, reinforcing the impact of this wonderful work.[3]

It is probable that the change in Strauss's conducting style and technique was due not only to the experience he had gained in Weimar but also, in equal measure, to the growth in inner self-confidence and the natural process of maturing; another factor is that in Munich he was at the head of an orchestra far superior to that of the court of Weimar. At his second concert, on 30 November 1894, he conducted Liszt's *Faust* Symphony – the work's première in Munich! He made a few cuts in the first movement, which he also recommended to Franz Wüllner:

As an introduction I would advise doing the first movement with the cuts; when once Liszt has the recognition he deserves, then I would perform the first movement with all its longueurs, which I myself, great as is my admiration, recognize to be longueurs – but for the time being a few cuts, especially the double repeat of the introduction, reduced in the middle, will do no harm – I can't call Bülow's cuts to mind at present, but they also affected the repeats in the first movement! (28 December 1894)

One of the reviews of this concert illustrates the reserve with which Liszt was still regarded:

Herr Strauss again revealed himself to be a musician to his finger-tips at this concert, and although we cannot disguise the

> fact that we do not understand his liking for the newest trends in music [the *Faust* Symphony was already forty years old!], it nevertheless behoves us to acknowledge, with all the greater pleasure, that he performed Haydn with the same understanding, with the same true musician's heart, as Liszt . . . The performance of the *Faust* Symphony had been prepared with conscientious exactitude and was so successful in every respect that the most fanatical Lisztians had to declare themselves delighted. There can be no doubt that the performance was the principal object of the tumultuous applause which broke out after the final bar.[4]

After the Christmas concert, which brought the first half of the winter season to an end, Strauss wrote to the orchestra to thank them for the 'model' performance of the *Faust* Symphony and also for their rendering of the two *Guntram* preludes. A review of the latter states:

> The prelude to the first act, which, in its expansive, inordinately long introduction, recalls the ecstatic violin raptures of *Lohengrin* and *Parsifal*, was received with tempestuous approval, notably by the younger admirers, and even more rapturous applause greeted the prelude to the second act, which is supposed to illustrate the celebration of victory at the ducal court; with a brief interruption by a lamenting middle section, it performs that task with overwhelming passion.[5]

Since *Guntram*'s success in the theatre was so limited, Strauss often included these two preludes in the programmes of his concerts, and also encouraged their performance by other conductors. They were published under Eugen Spitzweg's Joseph Aibl imprint as early as 1894, in full score and in the orchestral parts, with concert endings by the composer. When Franz Wüllner conducted a performance in Cologne on 22 January 1895, Strauss provided a note illuminating the programmatic aspects of the preludes, which was printed in the concert programme.

> Introductory remarks:
> a. Prelude to Act I: the gospel of divine love and sublime compassion, sealed by the act of redemption at Golgotha, has, in the thirteenth century, inspired a body of pious singers to found a brotherhood of 'warriors of love'. The ideal towards which they strive is to use the power of song to put the divine doctrine of salvation into action.

'Holiest need in the hearts of the best, that is the bond that unites us in brotherhood!'

'The yearning desire of pious singers has dedicated to the cross the wonders of art.'

Guntram is one such 'warrior of love'.

b. Prelude to Act II: Victory celebrations at the ducal court.[6]

In the belief that *Guntram* was his most important work to date, Strauss sent a copy of the score to Giuseppe Verdi with a covering letter:

> Although I know from my own experience how troublesome dedications can be, I nevertheless venture to ask you to be so kind as to accept a copy of *Guntram*, my first essay in the genre, as a token of my respect and admiration for the undoubted master of Italian opera.
>
> As I can find no words to describe the deep impression made upon me by the extraordinary beauty of *Falstaff*, and have no other means of expressing my gratitude for the enjoyment it has brought me, I beg you to accept this score, at the very least.
>
> I should count myself happy indeed, if I ever had the occasion to talk with you about the divine art, music, in order to receive new stimuli for my inspiration and my artistic creation. My friend and patron Hans von Bülow was unhappily denied the privilege. (18 January 1895)

Verdi, who was then in his eighty-second year, sent the following reply to his young colleague:

> I received a few days ago the work you so kindly sent me, and which has had such success.
>
> I leave today for Milan, where I shall spend several weeks, and so I have not had the time to read your score; but from dipping into it here and there I have seen that *Guntram* is the work of a very expert hand.
>
> It is a shame that I do not understand the language of its text, not with an eye to pronouncing judgment on it (which would ill become me, and which I would never venture to do), but so that I could admire it and share in your joy. (Genoa, 27 January 1895)

Before conducting his first Musical Academy concert in Munich, Strauss had inaugurated his first cycle of ten concerts with the Berlin Philharmonic, which must have strengthened the Munich orchestra's confidence in him. The first item in his first concert in

Berlin, on 15 October 1894, was Wagner's *Faust* Overture – a declaration of faith, although it was followed by Brahms's Violin Concerto (with Hugo Hermann as the soloist). Even in this his first programme, he was bold enough to include a new work, the prelude to the second act of Max Schillings's opera *Ingwelde*, a month before the work's première in the theatre, in Karlsruhe on 13 November. Liszt's *Mephisto* Waltz followed, and Strauss ended the concert with the same work that he chose for his first Munich concert, Beethoven's Seventh Symphony.

The ten Berlin concerts of the 1894–5 season included seven works by Beethoven, five by Liszt, three each by Anton Rubinstein and Wagner, two each by Brahms, Chopin, Haydn, Rameau, Saint-Saëns, Schubert and Richard Strauss, and one work each by d'Albert, Arensky, Berlioz, Bülow, Bruch, Dvořák, Frederick the Great, Gernsheim, Glazunov, Mahler (the first three movements of the Second Symphony), Mendelssohn, Mozart, Paganini, Popper, Ritter, Sauret, Schillings, Schumann, Smetana, Spohr, Stavenhagen, Johann Strauss, Tchaikovsky, Weber and Widor.

In his second Berlin concert, on 29 October, Strauss took quite a risk for the time and the place in performing a piece announced in the programme as a 'Musical Jest'. This was *Perpetuum mobile* by Johann Strauss, to whom the conductor wrote for help in acquiring a copy.

> Would you have the extraordinary kindness to tell me whether a charming *Perpetuum mobile* by you, which I heard in Reichenhall two years ago and like so much that I want to include it in one of my Berlin concerts, has been published and if so by whom? If the score of the work is not available in print, would you be so good as to allow me to have a copy of it and to send it please as quickly as possible, as I would like to do it in October.
>
> Forgive me for troubling you and be assured in advance of my cordial thanks! (5 September 1894)

Strauss had heard waltzes by his namesake played by Bülow in Meiningen and as late as 1925 he paid tribute to the 'natural talent' of Johann Strauss, who, in an age 'where all about him had already turned towards the complex and the premeditated', was 'one of the last to have primary inspirations'.[7] On another occasion he referred to him as a composer of genius, and in his first season at the Berlin Court Opera he gave the first performance there of *Die Fledermaus* (on 8 May 1899).

The most important première Strauss gave in his first season with the Berlin Philharmonic was unquestionably that of three movements from Mahler's Symphony No. 2 (omitting the vocal fourth movement). Otto Lessmann, in the *Allgemeine Musikzeitung*, expressed one view of the occasion with the words 'the altar consecrated by Bülow has now been defiled by pygmies'. Other first performances included Widor's A major Symphony Op. 5, Glazunov's tone poem *Spring*, the prelude of Eugen d'Albert's fairy-tale opera *Der Rubin*, Smetana's *Šárka*, and Tchaikovsky's Orchestral Suite Op. 55. He paid tribute to Bülow with the 'orchestral fantasy in the form of an overture' *Nirwana*, which he held particularly high, and to Alexander Ritter with *Olafs Hochzeitsreigen* (which he felt, however, did not give sufficient definition to the demonic element). He did not perform any of his own works until the last concert of the season, when he included four excerpts from *Guntram* in the programme (15 March 1895). He accompanied the orchestra to Vienna in April 1895, to take part in a short season of guest concerts. His programme there consisted of Beethoven's Seventh Symphony, the *Meistersinger* prelude, Liszt's *Mephisto* Waltz and Grieg's Piano Concerto (with Teresa Carreño). However, he was somewhat put in the shade by the other two guest conductors, Felix Mottl and Felix Weingartner. He had only this one season as conductor of the Berlin Philharmonic Concerts; the appointment was in the gift of the agent Hermann Wolff, who decided not to offer him a second season.[8] Late in life Strauss took the objective view that, precocious as he was, he had matured late as a conductor as in other ways, and had not proved himself worthy to follow the great Bülow. In 1895 Wolff offered the next season of concerts to 'the magnificent Nikisch' and he, Strauss, had to manage as best he could with his 7000 marks in Munich. A similar disappointment was in store for him there, as conductor of the Musical Academy: he was replaced after two seasons by Max Erdmannsdörfer.

It was already early in October 1896 when the Prince Regent decided not to renew Strauss's contract for the new season. On 22 December Strauss noted in the diary-cum-almanac that he kept in those years: '11.15, audience with the Prince Regent, who asked me *inter alia* whether and in what way I am related to the Viennese Strauss!!! The Father of my Country!' On this occasion Strauss could not console himself with the thought that he had been replaced, as in Berlin, by a better conductor, for Erdmannsdörfer was a mediocrity. Heinrich Bihrle, in the Festschrift published to celebrate the centenary of the Musical Academy in 1911, quoted an anonymous newspaper comment on Strauss, 'who at first made some bold efforts in Levi's place, but was not given the time to develop and who probably also had to struggle with divers personal problems'.[9] Whether that last phrase refers to the difficulties outstanding from the struggle Strauss had with the leader, Benno Walter, and other members of the Court Orchestra during the rehearsals for *Guntram* must now remain uncertain, but is likely.

It was not primarily Strauss's subjective, and what were felt to be 'modern', interpretations of the classics which were unacceptable to the conservative majority in the orchestra and the public at large, but rather the programmes in which he obstinately persisted along the path he had set out upon in Weimar. His own new tone poem, *Till Eulenspiegels lustige Streiche*, the eventual product of his plans for an opera on the subject, was more favourably received than two 'marine pictures' by Max Schillings; an irritated entry in his diary runs: 'Failure of Schillings's tone fantasy, demonstrative success for the 17th century. [*Sic*; in fact, some Rameau.] That's the level on which Munich stands in 1896.' He warned Franz Wüllner, who had expressed an interest in the two pieces: 'I liked the Schillings, but the public did not very much and the press even less! I would recommend *Seemorgen* as an introduction to him, as the more neatly and concisely constructed of the two, rather than *Meergruss*, which has the more significant content but is somewhat diffuse in form.' (Late January 1896)

Alexander Ritter's *Sursum corda!*, 'a Sturm-und-Drang fantasy for large orchestra' (Op. 23), which he performed at the seventh Musical Academy Concert on 6 January 1896, was also hardly the kind of piece to win support for his programme-making, though considerably less 'advanced' than Schillings's seascapes. Even two numbers from Emil Nikolaus von Rezniček's *Donna Diana*, performed on 20 March 1896, failed to please many listeners. (History has failed to uphold Strauss's high opinion of Ritter and Schillings.)

These disappointments in the concert hall, which could not fail to have some effect on his standing in the opera house as well, were to some extent compensated for by the increasing number of invitations to conduct not only his own works but those of others in towns large and small all over Germany (for example, at the Lower

Rhineland Music Festival in Düsseldorf in May 1896 he conducted *Don Juan*, *Wandrers Sturmlied* and *Till Eulenspiegel*), and on these occasions his success seemed to be greater than in Munich or Berlin. Invitations to conduct abroad became more frequent too. (A separate section of this chapter is devoted to his conducting engagements outside Munich; see below, pp. 424ff.) The controversy – sometimes going as far as open hostility – with which his new compositions were greeted, especially from *Zarathustra* onwards, did little to detract from the reputation he was forging for himself as an orchestral conductor; all the time his exciting interpretations were being steadily reinforced by a growing technical expertise and discipline. He continued to bring especial dedication to the concerts of the Liszt-Verein in Leipzig, at which he introduced soloists such as Heinrich Zeller and Pauline, and was able to perform not only his own and Liszt's works but also compositions by Ritter, Schillings and others of a similar persuasion. He conducted concerts for the Wagner-Verein of Berlin; the programme for the first, on 2 November 1896, included works by Wagner, Liszt and Hugo Wolf (prelude and interlude from *Der Corregidor*) as well as two songs with orchestral accompaniment by himself: *Verführung* and *Gesang der Apollopriesterin* (Op. 33, nos 1 and 2). Two days after this concert Strauss wrote to Oscar Grohe, a member of the board of the Mannheim Theatre:

> May I keep the *Corregidor* piano score? I have a quite extraordinary liking for the work as the expression of a great and abundant musical personality; a pity that the two orchestral numbers which I performed in Berlin do not give the slightest notion of the stature of the vocal portions of the work. At all events I am pleased if a performance can do something to bring the name of so outstanding a musician as Wolf before the public. (4 November 1896)

The concerts of new works which Strauss gave with the Berlin Tonkünstler-Orchester in the 1901–2 and 1902–3 seasons included another composition by Wolf; his Mörike setting *Anakreons Grab* shared a programme in January 1903 with songs by Strauss and Klaus Pringsheim. In later life Strauss showed himself indifferent to Wolf's lieder output, and seems not to have been very well acquainted with it. He even described Wolf as a 'pure amateur' in a letter to Max Schillings. Wolf, for his part, expressed his opinion of *Don Juan* and *Also sprach Zarathustra* in characteristically acid terms.

Pauline Strauss-de Ahna, Munich, 1895

Richard Strauss, Munich, 1895

In the first half of the opera season of 1895–6, after doing his duty by Heinrich Zöllner's opera *Der Überfall*, Strauss was at last able to present *Guntram* to the Munich public on 16 November, in the theatre where he had originally hoped it would have its world première. The effort he expended in rehearsal was wasted, as he himself related in his recollections of the first performances of his operas:

> A single, ill-starred performance took place in Munich. The two principal singers there, Madame Ternina and Heinrich Vogl, had refused the roles, the orchestra, with my own cousin and violin teacher Benno Walter at their head, went on strike and a deputation asked Intendant Perfall to relieve the orchestra of this 'scourge of God'. The tenor Mikorey, who suffered some lapses of memory even at the première, declared afterwards that he would sing at further performances only if his pension was raised. And so that performance remained the only one![10]

As in Weimar, the one cheering aspect of the evening was Pauline's outstanding performance as Freihild. *Guntram*'s failure, of which the press in particular made much, was the heaviest blow Strauss had yet experienced, not least because the work which had cost him such a struggle attracted not merely indifference but open hostility. 'The local press, the *Wagnerians* in the van, have come down fearfully hard upon the work; the public has expressed wholehearted agreement', he wrote to a colleague in Breslau. (25 November 1895) (Again, in his memoirs Strauss recalled that it was 'the Wagnerians in the *Münchner Neueste Nachrichten* and the old guard in *Der Sammler*' who found the most fault with his conducting.)[11] The composer Cyrill Kistler published a lengthy verse lampoon after the Munich performance of *Guntram*, parodying Schiller's well-known poem *Die Bürgschaft*.[12]

The review of *Guntram* which appeared in the *Münchner Neueste Nachrichten* on 18 November includes somes mention of the events surrounding the performance. The bulk of the article is quoted here, because it helps to explain the discontent and disquiet that took hold of Strauss over the next few years. The *Guntram* débâcle threw a long shadow over his second term as a conductor in Munich.

> *GUNTRAM.* Libretto and music by *Richard Strauss.* First performance at the Court Theatre, Munich, 16 November 1895.

Richard Strauss does not add the word 'opera' to the title of his stage work; his intention, no doubt, is to signal at once that his standpoint is, even outwardly, no conventional one. The 'work', then, was given its first performance in May 1894 in the Court Theatre in Weimar, where Strauss was then Hofkapellmeister. Since then he has come to our theatre and with him he has brought his first operatic essay. It has not been performed anywhere else in the interval, for which there may be a variety of reasons. One of the chief ones is undoubtedly to be found in the quite enormous demands which any more or less authentic performance of the score will make on orchestra and singers, in short, on the entire musical apparatus of any operatic institution, even one of the first rank, in terms of time and effort. For some considerable time, moreover, in musical circles where the more naive modes of expression are employed, it has been avowed by all that is holy that compared to this score the music of Wagner, Berlioz and Liszt is – pure Mozart, Haydn and Schubert. Such diagnoses may be passed over with a smile, but more serious attention should be paid to the report which has been simultaneously circulating, that the leading forces of our opera house, Vogl, Brucks and Fräulein Ternina, 'sent back' the parts, that is, they informed the management that they did not wish to undertake the roles in question; but as this is a procedure which is permitted only when there is a good reason for it, report adds that while Vogl and Fräulein Ternina furnished such reason on their own authority, Brucks even indicated that he was prepared to summon the celebrated theorist Professor Rheinberger to pass judgment on whether or not *Guntram* is music at all, and so on and so forth. We can see that the soil in which Strauss's 'work' was to be planted had been lovingly prepared: the very announcement that it was to be performed, and the study and rehearsals for it, had caused a stir similar to that which – fifty years ago – greeted the advent of the shocking 'music of the future'; in this we see 'there is nothing new under the sun'.

Now it would give us the greatest joy if we were to see the dawn and spread of another such significant and promising age. To arms! we cry, when bold spirits are stirring – 'wo kühn Kräfte sich regen, da rath' ich offen zum Krieg'. But it would be utterly perverse to wish to draw conclusions of such moment from a certain similarity in the external circumstances accompanying the event. For in the present case what we behold is by no means a new departure in the history of art, but merely the luxuriant product of a strongly and deeply *empathetic*, richly endowed nature, that of a musician who has turned to the theatre and now lays about him impudently in the realm of musical sounds, acting according to his own desires, owing responsibility only to his own whims – and completely unconcerned by the thought that even the proponents of continuous advance in 'music as the expression of sensibility', that is, the adherents of the so-called 'new direction', are obliged to shake their heads soberly over this kind of ill-proportioned squandering of harmonic, rhythmic and instrumental means, while the loyalists of the 'old school', hearing such music, feel their flesh crawl and regard it, we dare say, as the work of a musical agent of Old Nick himself.

Let there be no misunderstanding as to the undoubted nobility and purity of the artistic intentions of the young poet and composer who tests himself here in this, his first work for the stage: it testifies repeatedly to an idealistic cast of mind, a high moral earnestness and a noble and poetic sensibility. But enjoyment of the truly beautiful theatrical images created incidentally by this lofty aspiration is greatly curtailed by the directly opposite impression invoked by the unevenness in the treatment of the subject, by the lack of an ability to shape the material dramatically, even, surprisingly, in the very way the text is laid out. Even so, from time to time a dramatically promising situation is adumbrated, yet at its side, clear to see, are arrayed all the signs of what we can only call clumsiness in respect of scenic dispositions. The words of the text contain frequent reminiscences of the poems of Wagner's last period, and indeed the tendency of this piece as a whole is directed towards a reworking of the theme of the 'conquest of the tragedy of existence' by renunciation which is so wonderfully represented in *Parsifal*. Characteristics such as these have given rise to a prevalent inclination to designate all works of art of a similar nature as the products of a fictive 'school of Wagner': this is fundamentally wrong, and does great injustice to the immortal master. The fundamental requirement of a work of art belonging to a 'school of Wagner' would be that the poet should be a *dramatist*. To judge by *Guntram*, Strauss is not. From the dramatic point of view, *Guntram* might perhaps be described as 'a psychological event in one act, with two preceding acts'. It is appropriate here to recall Liszt's famous remark, when a patron and lover of music asked him, in some surprise, why the trombones always sounded so effective in Wagner; Liszt replied:

'Because Wagner only writes for the trombones when an idea for the trombones occurs to him.' The same could be said of the whole of Wagner's writing for the stage! But nowadays our young musicians cheerfully and unconcernedly write for the *stage* the ideas that have occurred to them for the *concert hall.* Virtually the only parts of *Guntram* that convey the least sense of musico-dramatic excitement are the finales of the second and third acts, and perhaps also the 'hero's' dreams of peace; the prelude, too, conveys an atmosphere.

Individual parts of Strauss's opera might be effective in the concert hall, for his score is something very like a miracle born of a gift for orchestration. On the other hand one must marvel at how it was possible, when employing such colossal orchestral resources and such a highly developed instrumental technique, to produce so little in the way of euphony and melody. The composer's instinct for beauty in sound seems to be far weaker than his gift for orchestration and his delight in counterpoint. As a result the primary impression *Guntram* makes on the listener is of an uncommonly complex *orchestral work.* Even in his writing for the voices the composer often behaves with the same sovereign unconcern that he displays in the demands he makes of his instrumentalists. But in the theatre the *singing* is still the most important thing – that must never be forgotten. For a time, as a result of *bad* performances of Wagner's works, the idea was mooted and gained credence that, thanks to Wagner (!), that fundamental principle no longer held good; that time is past to all intents and purposes, thank goodness; but it must never be allowed to return. With that proviso clearly understood, it can then be said that, as *Guntram* undeniably demonstrates, Strauss possesses a quite outstanding technique for writing for the orchestra. Whether, when he has improved his understanding of the essence and requirements of opera and has exercised some calm self-criticism, when he is more prepared to limit himself and has a better knowledge of the precise nature of his artistry and so is able to avoid excess, he will then at some future date use that technique rightly in the service of the theatre, should heaven send him a good operatic subject in an apt form, is in the lap of the gods.

Lack of space prevents us from discussing the text or the music in detail. It would in any case lead to only minor modifications of the overall verdict on the work. For today, therefore, we will confine ourselves to the observation that, in spite of everything that has already been said, the work would in all probability have made a far better impression and had a far more genuine success than can be recorded today, if all the roles had been filled as suitably and poetically as the only substantial female part in the opera, that of Freihild, was by the composer's wife, Frau Strauss-de Ahna. Building on the experience of the role gained from performing it in Weimar, she accomplished a truly brilliant rendering, which allowed her scenes to stand out with much greater musical and dramatic clarity than those of the rest of the cast. Bertram as the Old Duke, Knote as the Jester, Bauberger as Robert and Fuchs as Friedhold should also be singled out, while Mikorey in the title role confined himself to singing the notes as correctly as possible. This was all that could have been expected when he was cast in this gigantic part, which (according to a particularly conscientious statistician) amounts – if sung in its entirety – to 160 bars more than the role of Tristan. Mikorey sang a cut version. The composer conducted with circumspection and enthusiasm. Oberregisseur Fuchs directed the production with great skill – no easy task. The design is entirely appropriate to the work. The orchestra, in the execution of an exceptionally difficult task, performed miracles, even though not everything 'worked'.

The applause, which was rather restrained after the first act, reached a climax after the second. After the second and third acts the composer and the singers took repeated curtain calls.

Oskar Merz

The failure of the Munich production was too great to be offset by the rescue attempts that were made by publicists such as Strauss's former pupil and friend Hermann Bischoff, who published a detailed analysis of *Guntram* in seven instalments of the widely read *Allgemeine Musikzeitung* (Volume 23, 1896). The day after the performance Strauss had at least the satisfaction of a rise in his salary to 12,000 marks. That same evening – probably in search of relaxation after all the excitement – Strauss set out by bicycle for Bolzano. On 4 December he went to Pest to conduct a concert, although, to his regret, this engagement meant that he had to turn down an invitation from the Wagner-Verein in Berlin.[13]

An entry in his diary for 8 February 1896 illustrates the disappointment to which Strauss was prey in the following months:

Possart's knavery grows more and more blatant. After promising to put on *Guntram* once a month, whatever the circumstances, he has not scheduled the work in spite of Mikorey having declared

> himself ready to sing G. five weeks ago. He promised my wife a guest contract from 1 January 1896 (6000 marks, 40 appearances). He doesn't make a move. Offensively ignores my wife and sets the press on her and me, to make us compliant. The alternative is Perfall. Munich, good night!

Pauline had her contract in the end, but it was not used to the full.

Other events of the 1895–6 opera season went better for Strauss. There were new productions of Gluck's *Iphigenia in Aulis*. Peter Cornelius's *Der Barbier von Bagdad* and Adolphe Adam's *La poupée de Nuremberg*. Theatre history was made by Possart's new production of Mozart's *Don Giovanni* in the Residenztheater, the first occasion on which the new revolving stage installed in this theatre by Carl Lautenschläger was used (29 May 1896). The production had been preceded by one of *Le nozze di Figaro*, conducted by Levi and produced by Possart, which broke new ground in the performance of Mozart; that too was put on in the Residenztheater, on 15 February 1895. The two productions inaugurated the Mozart renaissance which led eventually to the establishment of Mozart and Wagner festivals as institutions in Munich. Strauss devoted an unusually high number of rehearsals to the preparation of this new *Don Giovanni*. After some twenty rehearsals with the piano, the first *Sitzprobe* took place on 15 May, followed by daily rehearsals from 18 to 23 May. Mozart was now assured of a permanent place alongside Wagner in the summer festivals. *Don Giovanni* was given alone in 1896, but in 1897, after Possart and Strauss had mounted new productions of *Die Entführung aus dem Serail* and *Così fan tutte* during the main season (3 February and 25 June 1897 respectively, the latter again using the revolve in the Residenztheater), all three of these works were repeated in the summer festival. *Die Zauberflöte* entered the Munich repertory on 1 May 1898.

Strauss's inspired improvisation of the *secco* recitatives in *Don Giovanni* and *Così* formed an especial attraction of his performances. He embraced *Così* with particular warmth at a time when it did not enjoy the regard it does today. His performances played an important part in promoting recognition of the work's worthiness to stand alongside Mozart's three popular masterpieces. He expressed his affection for the 'superior ironies' of *Così fan tutte* in a frequently cited essay which he wrote in 1910, on the occasion of a new production of the work in its original form, in which he also compared Eduard Devrient's German translation of the text unfavourably to Hermann Levi's 'meticulously correct' model version.[14] The intense preoccupation with Mozart's operas at this time proved to be of decisive importance for Strauss. While it in no way diminished his enthusiasm for Wagner, it provided a counterweight, the full effect of which was felt only in his later operas, in conjunction with the influence of Hugo von Hofmannsthal. From the time when he began the rehearsals for *Don Giovanni* in the spring of 1896, Mozart and Wagner became the twin fixed stars of his work at the Munich Opera. Before leaving Munich in October 1898 he conducted seventy-five performances of Mozart (*Die Entführung, Don Giovanni* and *Così*) and forty-six of Wagner (*Rienzi, Tannhäuser, Tristan* and *Meistersinger*). In 1928, in a reminiscence of these years in Munich, after touching on his disappointments, Strauss wrote:

> By contrast, *Tristan* and *Meistersinger*, which . . . I was able to conduct for the first time in the hallowed place where they first saw the light, and the Mozart Festivals, which I inaugurated together with Possart (*Figaro* was the only one taken by Levi), stand out among the truly wonderful memories of my life.[15]

This total of 121 performances of Mozart and Wagner is to be compared with a mere twenty-four of works by other composers, including *Fidelio* and Liszt's *Saint Elisabeth* (with Pauline). Besides *Figaro*, Hermann Levi reserved the *Ring* for himself. Strauss did his best to promote new operas by German composers during this term in Munich, though the management saw fit to exercise restraint. After Cornelius's *Der Barbier von Bagdad* and Zöllner's *Der Überfall*, he conducted the first performance of Ludwig Thuille's *Theuerdank* (with a libretto by Alexander Ritter under the pseudonym of W. Ehm), staged to celebrate the birthday of the Prince Regent, Prince Luitpold, on 12 March 1897. *Theuerdank* was one of three operas awarded the Luitpold Prize, the others being Alexander Zemlinsky's *Zarema* and Arthur Könnemann's *Der tolle Eberstein*. On Strauss's advice, Thuille wrote an additional overture for his opera, which was also heard in concerts with the title Romantic Overture. *Theuerdank* was no more successful than Max Schillings's *Ingwelde*, performed in Munich only a few weeks later, on 8 May, two and a half years after its première in Karlsruhe. The text of *Ingwelde* was by Ferdinand von Sporck, who also tried to write a libretto (*Schilda*) for Strauss around the subject of Till Eulenspiegel. Siegmund von

Hausegger's *Zinnober* (first performed on 19 June 1898) fared even worse than *Theuerdank* (which was given four performances) and *Ingwelde* (three), and was withdrawn after two. The lack of success Strauss had in his championing of new German operas, not excluding his own *Guntram*, was not his fault but that of the works themselves. Indeed, he was far from uncritical: he was aware from the very first that *Theuerdank*, prize or no prize, was unviable. His friendship with Thuille and Ritter did not close his eyes to the work's weaknesses. 'On Tuesday [I] conveyed Thuille's Theuerdank to the churchyard, where he will probably be interred for good tomorrow evening.' (To his parents, Friday 26 March 1897) On the day of the first performance of Arthur Könnemann's 'tone play' *Der tolle Eberstein*, which was rehearsed and conducted by Franz Fischer, he noted in his diary:

> Freshness and vigour, but deficient structure. No one can write a three-act homophonic opera nowadays (the thread of invention necessarily runs out in the third act, unless there is either polyphonic psychology or psychological polyphony). No one can go on inventing new fanfares and new violin figurations for three whole acts, and the tonic, the dominant and the dominant seventh exhaust the resources of the diatonic scale. (29 March 1898)

Humperdinck's *Hänsel und Gretel*, which Strauss had conducted during his first season in Munich, in March 1895, was the only modern German work to enjoy a happier fate. It is to some extent understandable that Strauss should have grown embittered with the Munich Opera and with the Munich audiences, whom he accused of philistinism.

Strauss's brief survey of this period in his late memoir of his early life begins: 'My second Munich engagement came to grief, before all else, on the dissension between Possart ([intendant of] the Court Theatre), who was well disposed towards me, and Perfall (intendant of court music), whose hostility towards me increased with each new work (*Eulenspiegel*, *Zarathustra*) that I produced.'[16] This statement requires some qualification. As the bitter remarks in his diaries at the time show, Strauss's relationship with Possart was by no means very good to begin with. It improved when, doubtless in an effort to please Possart, Strauss provided the music to make a melodrama out of Tennyson's *Enoch Arden*, in a translation by

Adolph Strodtmann, which Possart, versatile, ambitious and vain, then performed at countless recitals, with Strauss at the piano, an unwilling accompanist but determined to improve his position. Again his diary, on the day he finished writing the piece, records his dissatisfaction with the melodrama (the genre, as well as this particular example): 'Finished *Enoch Arden* (melodrama) for Possart. Remark expressly that I do not wish it ever to be counted among my works, as it is a worthless occasional piece (in the worst sense of the word).' (26 February 1897)

There can be no doubt that *Enoch Arden* represents a concession on the composer's part, though less to public taste – the music is thoroughly Straussian and nowhere sinks below the level of some of his more obviously pleasing songs of this period – than to its dedicatee, Possart. Strauss told Arthur Seidl that he only wrote the melodrama in order to persuade Possart to put on Schillings's *Ingwelde*. It is characteristic of the contradictions in Strauss that he nonetheless allowed the work to be published (by Robert Forberg, for a fee of 1000 marks), and even gave it an opus number (38), in spite of his earlier declaration, and in Berlin, on 8 March 1899, when he was no longer under Possart's sway, he composed a second melodrama, *Das Schloss am Meere*, on a poem by Uhland. That too was published, though without an opus number, which suggests that the publisher pressed him for another work in this popular genre. As with *Enoch Arden*, Strauss was at the piano when Possart gave the first performance of *Das Schloss am Meere*, and on later occasions when they went on tour together. Performing together in this way, they necessarily became more intimate, though tensions still arose from time to time. At all events, after the first performance of *Enoch Arden* (24 March 1897), at which Strauss 'unleashed with Possart whole rivers of feminine admiration', they were 'one heart and one soul'. (To his father, 26 March 1897) In time the pair built up a repertory of melodramas, including, besides the two by Strauss, Schumann's *Die Flüchtlinge* (after Shelley), Liszt's version of Felix Draeseke's *König Helges Treue* (poem by Strachwitz), Max Schillings's *Das eleusische Fest* (Schiller), and Alexander Ritter's ballad *Graf Walther und die Waldfrau* (Felix Dahn), which was later arranged for full orchestra by Siegmund von Hausegger and published by Max Brockhaus in Leipzig as Ritter's Op. 24. The tours with Possart represented a relatively easy source of additional income for Strauss, with which he hoped to earn more time for composition. Much has been said about his mercenariness: there was a further reason for it, namely a lifelong anxiety about the material well-being of his family, fed not least by an ever recurring scepticism as to how long his works would maintain their popularity.

Perfall, who was responsible for the running of the Court Orchestra, viewed Strauss's own new compositions, and the new works by others which he championed, with ever growing disapproval. In 1898 he offered Strauss a contract for life, but attempted to reduce his salary at the same time, with the result that Strauss left Munich.

Strauss never entirely lost his mistrust of Possart. Max Steinitzer recalled the evenings they used to spend at Leibenfrost's wine bar:

> Franz and Richard Strauss were regulars here, for their evening glass. His personal esteem for Ritter keeps Strauss listening respectfully even to the purely negative pronouncements which, coming from one whose attitude is that of complete resignation, can really do little to inspire one who yearns ardently to move forwards . . . As I proceed down Maximilianstrasse, Strauss is just coming out of the Court Theatre . . . 'The intendant Herr von Possart has just been kind enough to speak of putting Weingartner over me as the principal attraction. I've had enough of here now. And I'd like a change in any case, not the same old place for ever!'

As early as February 1896 Strauss made a move to escape from Munich again. He made an approach to Oscar Grohe in Mannheim, asking for the rank of director of the opera but offering to accept a smaller salary than the one he was already getting in Munich.[17] The negotiations did not lead to the desired end, however. In December of the same year he again made enquiries about replacing Mottl in Karlsruhe, but once more without success.

His work in the opera house, together with his regular concerts in Munich and Berlin during the first two years and the increasing number of other conducting engagements elsewhere, provided him with enough work for any musician. The paragraph in his memoirs, quoted above, which begins with his complaint about the dissension between Possart and Perfall, ends with the statement that the hours he valued most were those passed in the company of Friedrich Rösch and Alexander Ritter, in Leibenfrost's wine bar between six and seven of an evening, and occasionally in Ritter's house. This was a pleasure of no very long duration, for Alexander Ritter died on 12 April 1896, not long after Strauss had given his *Sursum corda!* at the seventh Academy Concert of the season, on 6 March, while Friedrich Rösch spent much of the period working in St Petersburg (where he performed *Till Eulenspiegel* on 18 March 1896) and Berlin. The memoir thus refers primarily to the first year and a half. Strauss gave another performance of *Sursum corda!* on 19 February 1900 at the second subscription concert of the Wagner-Verein in Berlin. An obituary for Ritter by Max Schillings, published in the periodical *Redende Künste*, earned Strauss's admiration:

> It is only today that I have had the pleasure of reading your fine obituary of Alexander Ritter. You have such a beautiful, elegant manner of literary expression that I always regret that you do not do more of this kind of thing. The calm and assurance with which you write is a blessing for the reader who likes to see his own convictions set down in black and white by another hand, *ergo* your articles, which are alas too short, always give me particular enjoyment. (3 May 1896)

Till Eulenspiegel

If the composer had to give way to the busy conductor in Weimar, especially in the first few years – it was not until April 1892 that Strauss got down to any serious composition, with the starting of *Guntram* – in Munich he found again the time and the energy for creation. He was already considering several ideas for operas when he returned from the south in the late summer of 1893. A few weeks after arriving back in Weimar he told his father he was reading up subjects for new librettos. (22 October 1893) No doubt he considered more than one subject at once, but a plan for a 'folk opera' about the adventures of Till Eulenspiegel among the citizens of Schilda* came to hold the foreground. On 4 November he told his father: 'I am pondering new librettos a great deal, but as yet nothing that's quite right is taking shape. Ah well! All in good time!' Then shortly afterwards: 'I'm already working hard on a new libretto in my head, *Till Eulenspiegel and the Burghers of Schilda*. I think it'll come to something.' (16 November 1893) In the end he decided in

* Schilda is a legendary town in the tradition of German folk lore, populated with wise fools in the mould of Thracian Abderites and English Gothamites. *Tr.*

Till Eulenspiegels lustige Streiche. First page of an autograph copy of the score, made 'for Till's 50th birthday' (1 October 1944)

favour of the Eulenspiegel plan, and could tell his father in the new year: 'My new libretto, *Till Eulenspiegel in Schilda*, is slowly advancing and promises to be quite jolly.' (2 January 1894) At the beginning of the following month he reported on his progress in a letter, the recipient of which is unknown:

> At present I'm mapping out a *Till Eulenspiegel and the Burghers of Schilda*. I've already assembled a very nice plot, only I haven't yet formed a completely clear picture of the character of Herr Till Eulenspiegel; the folk tale offers only a joker, who is too shallow for the stage – on the other hand, giving the character more depth and making him more misanthropic creates problems of its own. Should the draft ever reach a presentable form, may I perhaps take the liberty of sending it to you? (1 February 1894)

The confrontation of the quickwitted, resourceful loner Till, the 'world-despiser, who scorns mankind because at bottom he loves it', with blinkered, philistine grotesques must have been particularly appealing to Strauss at that time, when he was finding the (real or imagined) limitations of Weimar intolerable. He appears to have planned a long one-acter, with an elaborate plot laden with an excess of psychological motivation, interwoven with a love story (Hanne and the young councillor). Kurt Wilhelm published an excellent summary of Strauss's plot, with a commentary, in the *Richard-Strauss-Jahrbuch* 1954 (pp. 102–9), and the reader will find it in Appendix 2 of this book. Wilhelm is probably right in his supposition that the plan became bogged down in the quantity of philosophizing that Strauss worked into the draft libretto. From time to time he must have considered reshaping it in more than one act. A letter from Arthur Seidl includes an enquiry as to what had happened to the draft for Act I, which Wilhelm Klatte had told him was already finished (18 June 1895). (Klatte refers to this draft in an article in *Die Musik*, June 1924.)

Creating a clear and sensible relationship between Till and the people of Schilda seems to have given Strauss great difficulty, and realization of the limitations set him by his own literary talent finally led him to abandon the plan, but not until he had spent a considerable amount of time on it. In its place came the idea for a new symphonic work centring on the figure of Till alone. Although the people of Schilda were to have no part in the new piece it appears that Strauss had every intention of returning to them in a further work, without Till. In 1897, with the help of Ferdinand von Sporck, he spent some time on plans for an opera about Schilda, but nothing came of it. In the end the constellation of ideas which occupied Strauss in his draft of *Till Eulenspiegel bei den Schildbürgern* appeared in a new and original form in *Feuersnot*, where Kunrad makes a stand against Munich philistinism 'in legendary times'.

The history of the genesis of *Till Eulenspiegels lustige Streiche, nach alter Schelmenweise in Rondeauform für grosses Orchester gesetzt* ('Till Eulenspiegel's gleeful exploits, after an old rogue's tale, set in rondo form for large orchestra'), to give Strauss's Op. 28 its full title, is obscure. When and exactly why Strauss decided to make Till the hero of a symphonic poem rather than an opera is unknown. No indication is given either in his letters to his father or in any other documents. The only known fact is the date at the end of the score: Munich, 6 May 1895. In a sketchbook containing a number of sketches for *Till*, there is a remark in Pauline's handwriting, 'horrid composing', and beside it Strauss wrote 'observation by my lady wife'. He probably began the composition in 1894 before leaving Weimar. A month after finishing the full score he wrote to Franz Wüllner: 'I have finished the score of a new symphonic poem, *Till Eulenspiegel* – very funny and high-spirited.' (9 June 1895) Only ten days later he told Wüllner that he had sent it off to the printer. He had offered it together with three new songs to Eugen Spitzweg for a total of 1500 marks, hoping that this would compensate the publisher in some measure for his 'sacrificial' outlay in publishing *Guntram*; but in the end he accepted 1000 marks for *Till*.

In his plan for an opera on the subject, Strauss had moved some distance away from the 'folk book' of Till Eulenspiegel, which he got to know in Carl Simrock's version in modern German, published in 1878; for his symphonic work he adhered to it much more closely. The first performance of it was given in Cologne on 5 November 1895, at the second of the season's subscription concerts in the Gürzenichsaal, under Franz Wüllner. Strauss was prevented from conducting it himself by Levi's recurring illness and the rehearsals for *Guntram*. Wüllner had asked Strauss for some elucidation of the 'programme' underlying the work, but Strauss refused, at first by telegram: 'Analysis impossible for me. All wit spent in notes.' This was followed by a letter, which is more informative:

It's impossible for me to give *Eulenspiegel* a programme; clad in words, what I was thinking of in the individual parts would often sound damned funny and arouse a lot of objections. For once, let us leave folk to crack for themselves the nuts the scallywag is handing them. Perhaps all that is necessary to allow understanding is to quote the two Eulenspiegel themes:

*

and

which run through the whole piece in the most varied disguises and moods, and situations, until the catastrophe, where he's strung up, after the death sentence:

has been spoken over him.

The A minor episode is his graduation before the philistrious professors, in Prague I think, where Till sets off a thorough-going Babylonian linguistic confusion (the so-called Fugato) by his monstrous theses, and, after royally indulging his amusement, makes off highly *frivolously* (A♭ major, 2/4).

But please regard this as a private explanation. Remarks in the score such as 'on fire with love' etc. will certainly complete the immediate understanding of the content of the individual episodes, ditto 'lamentably': his confession, etc. etc.

My most cordial greetings, and this time let the jolly Cologners guess what kind of musical hoax a scallywag has played them. (20 October 1895)[18]

Wüllner published the last part of this letter in the programme and himself provided a brief note on the content of the work, derived from what Strauss had told him in the rest of the letter:

Undoubtedly anyone who remembers from his childhood one of the famous 'folk books' about Till Eulenspiegel . . . will pick out something of what the composer relates to us in his music, at once with the utmost temerity and with formal and orchestral mastery: Eulenspiegel's first wild japes, the practical joke he plays on the scolding market-women, his amorous adventures,

* Strauss scribbled down the phrase in haste, and the fifth note is missing, a C♯ before the F.

his graduation in Prague, where he sets off a truly Babylonian linguistic confusion among the philistine professors by his monstrous theses, the craziest exuberance suddenly cut short by his trial, the sentence, the execution . . . till at the end a charmingly reassuring 'epilogue' concludes this humorous work.

Eventually Strauss did provide a more precise key to the motives and episodes, for use in Wilhelm Mauke's 'guide' to *Till*. He wrote the following notes in Mauke's copy of the score:

Bar 1: Once upon a time there was a knavish fool
Bar 7: – named Till Eulenspiegel.
5 bars before fig. 3: He was a wicked goblin
6 bars before fig. 6: – up to new tricks.
2 bars before fig. 8: Just wait, you faint-hearts!
7 bars after fig. 9: Hop! on horseback through the market-women.
4 bars before fig. 11: He runs away in seven-league boots.
4 bars after fig. 11: Hidden in a mouse's hole.
8 bars before fig. 13: Disguised as a parson, he oozes unction and morality
5 bars after fig. 13: – but the knave peeps out at his big toe.
Fig. 14: But, because of his mockery of religion, he feels a sudden horror of his end.
10 bars before fig. 15: Till as gallant, exchanging dainty courtesies with pretty girls.
3 bars before fig. 16: He woos them.
1 bar before fig. 17: However fine, a basket still signifies refusal.
7 bars after fig. 18: Vows revenge on the whole human race.
Fig. 20: Philistines' motive.
5 bars before fig. 22: After imposing a few whopping theses on the Philistines, he abandons them, baffled, to their fate.
Fig. 24: Grimace from a distance.
1 bar before fig. 26: Till's street ditty.
Fig. 38: The trial.
5 bars after fig. 38: He whistles nonchalantly.
Fig. 40: Up the ladder! There he swings, the air is squeezed out of him, a last jerk. Till's mortal part has come to an end.[19]

Oddly enough, there is no note on the epilogue, which asserts Till's immortality.

Only two months after the première, Wüllner conducted a second performance, again in the Gürzenichsaal, on 7 January 1896. In spite of its daring and unfamiliar language, *Till Eulenspiegel* was given a far more enthusiastic reception than the previous symphonic poems, with only a few dissenting voices. One of these was heard after the first performance in Vienna, given under Hans Richter on 5 January 1896, when Eduard Hanslick wrote: 'How many charming, witty ideas spring up in the work, but not a single one that does not instantly have its neck broken by the speed with which the next one lands on its head.' Hanslick's exhaustive review is summarized by Roland Tenschert as follows: 'After comparing Strauss's roguish tricks to the Jameson Raid or the Italian war in Massawa, he concluded that the composer was nothing more than a "dazzling technical virtuoso", and his *Till Eulenspiegel* nothing more than a "product of the most refined *décadence*".'[20] Anton Bruckner, however, by then seventy-two years old, heard the piece twice, because, as he told Theodor Helm, he did not fully understand it the first time, although he had found it uncommonly interesting.

Even six years after the première, *Till* provoked Claude Debussy to an amusing review in the *Revue Blanche* (1 June 1901), following a performance given in Paris under Nikisch:

> It might be called 'An hour of the new music played to lunatics'. The clarinets form frenzied designs, the trumpets are continuously muted and the horns, awaiting a sneeze from the trumpets, retort 'God bless you!' while a big drum goes boom! boom! apparently in imitation of a kick in the pants from a clown. One wants either to scream with laughter or shriek in pain, and the amazing thing is that when the work is over all the members of the orchestra are in their right places. In the meantime if the double basses had blown down their bows, if the trombonists had drawn an imaginary bow across their brass tubes, or if Nikisch had perched himself on the knee of a programme-seller nothing here would have been in the least surprising. There is no denying that there is genius in this work, particularly in the amazing assurance of the orchestral writing and in the wild sense of movement that sweeps us along from beginning to end, compelling us to share in each of the hero's merry pranks. Monsieur Nikisch directed their tumultuous progress with admirable *sangfroid* and the ovation that greeted him and his orchestra was deserved to the highest degree.[21]

In 1944 Strauss made an autograph copy of the score of *Till* for his grandchildren, in celebration of 'Till's 50th birthday', in which he added some optional ornamentation in the 'street ditty' (Gassenhauer) passage, accompanied by the note: 'The curlicues are a witty improvisation by the clarinets in my beloved Berlin Staatskapelle!'[22]

Before 1895 was out *Till* had been heard in Mannheim, Berlin, Munich, Dresden and Elberfeld. The number of performances continued to mount rapidly in the years that followed. A statement in the programme book (simultaneously a Festschrift) published on the occasion of the Richard Strauss festival held in Munich in 1910 summed up the work's significance in the composer's career: 'This delicious, witty, orchestral humoresque silenced the opposition completely for the first time, all opinions were unanimous for the first time, and if Strauss's symphonic music can be called popular, then its popularity begins with this rogue's game.' Strauss himself conducted *Till Eulenspiegel* for the first time in the Odeon in Munich on 29 November 1895, at the second Musical Academy subscription concert. The normally rather peevish press found itself with no option but to capitulate, if somewhat grudgingly:

> *Till Eulenspiegels lustige Streiche* made, if to begin with only superficially, an imposing impression overall, leaving it impossible for anyone to resist the effect of the uncommonly vivid and colourful orchestration, which is of the highest subtlety and was deployed with wonderful bravura by the full forces of our Court Orchestra. The orchestra has never been called upon to display virtuosity of anything approaching this order before; Strauss has treated each separate instrument – violin, flute, horn etc. – as a concerto soloist. The technical foundation of the whole style of the composition is an audacious chromaticism that goes far beyond Berlioz, Liszt or Wagner. The piece won great applause, some of it sincere.

Till Eulenspiegel, which forms the greatest imaginable contrast to *Guntram* – both in choice of subject and in style and compositional technique – confirms what Strauss suggested in his observations, in 1945, on Joseph Gregor's history of the theatre: that after he had renounced tradition in the controversial conclusion of *Guntram*, his way was clear for 'uninhibitedly independent creation'; this 'untrammeled subjectivity' had already made its mark on his next opera, *Feuersnot*. It is characteristic that at the age of eighty-one Strauss thought first and foremost of his operas in this connection: he could with equal truth have mentioned *Till Eulenspiegel* instead of *Feuersnot*, for Till was the prototype of the anti-philistine. 'The man [i.e. Strauss himself] visibly plays a part in the work', as the composer wrote in 1949 in his very last, brief essay.[23] But the part he plays is only a 'guest appearance', the musical form, a complex, teasing intermingling of rondo and sonata forms, is autonomous. In another note Strauss wrote of *Till*: 'Extension of rondo form by poetic content, after the model of the finale of Beethoven's Eighth, where a tragicomic carnival procession suddenly strikes up in D minor. It was Bülow who first interpreted all these ideas in Beethoven correctly' – that is, 'programmatically', in the spirit taken to extremes long after Bülow by Arnold Schering in his book *Beethoven und die Dichtung* (Berlin, 1936), which is dedicated to Strauss.

The programme of *Till*, betraying a loose association with the folk book and with the composer's own personality in about equal measure, is also no more than a motivation for the music 'which develops logically out of itself' (Strauss). This is the only thing that explains *Till*'s enduring success, with friends of Strauss like Humperdinck as with others. More strongly than *Don Juan*, *Macbeth* or *Tod und Verklärung*, the new work throws into relief the contradictions of the greatest complexity and of simplicity; the interplay of an artistic intelligence which had now reached its prime and of a spontaneity stamped with the traits of naivety.

Some of Strauss's friends felt the inclination to place a philosophical interpretation on his works, which Strauss himself at least made no move to prevent. The nature of the trend is well illustrated by the biographical sketch of the composer written in 1896 by Arthur Seidl, who – to Strauss's growing disquiet – was particularly active at that date as a kind of 'ideologue in chief' to the New German movement.

> *Epater le bourgeois!* War against all the apostles of moderation, against the old guild of the merely virtuous and comfortable, all good philistines and the safe schools of restraint! – that could well be the motto of the whole shoot. As we approach the end perhaps it will come in reality to a graphic execution and the lamentable 'death' of Eulenspiegel on the gallows, which it is of course well-known did not happen (moreover, a Till never needs to 'fib'). Rather, the meaning, the import of it is this: though you deprive genius of light and air, though you trip him up at step after step, even though you 'lay a snare' for him and use the

> exterior force which regrettably is the source of your power to threaten him with death – you still *can't* kill him, he mocks even your summary courts; his wit soars above you, *he* remains the 'snare' and finally *his* spirit lives on in the consciousness of ordinary people, far longer and far more enduring than all your simple-minded Schilda citizenry![24]

That Seidl sometimes went too far in his speculation has already been demonstrated in the case of his interpretation of *Guntram*. He was also mistaken in his assertion that Munich could claim the doubtful honour of having planted *Till* in its composer's imagination, 'as a response to [Munich's] quite incredible reception of *Guntram*': *Till* was finished six months before the Munich performance of *Guntram* took place.

Strauss's writings in the latter part of his life refer more than once to his having lost the courage to write for the theatre after the failure of *Guntram*. The failure may have played its part in his decision to write a symphonic rather than an operatic *Till*, but he did not immediately drop the operatic plan altogether. He did abandon his own scenario and draft text, but he soon returned to the subject of Schilda, perhaps encouraged by the immediate success of the symphonic poem. The recognition that he was not cut out to be a librettist and that the earlier draft was not viable persuaded him to make other experiments in which the figure Till no longer played a part. He made his first manuscript notes for *Die Schildbürger* (The Burghers of Schilda) – the working title he used in his diary – on 10 November 1896. The idea for an opera on the subject of Till had occupied him since the autumn of 1893, as we have seen. The attempt to create an association between the figure of Till and the conclusions to which he had come as a result of his reading of Schopenhauer had failed; at all events, it did not succeed in giving the figure dramatic life. Now Strauss tried to make something of the subject of Schilda, without Till, but again without success. A few of his disconnected notes on the subject of Till can be quoted here:

> Till: despises mankind, deifies nature, has *not yet* worked his way through *to reason*, an idler, a lazy-bones, who does not cheat the good Lord of His time by spending it in useless work, who makes a fool of the men and plays tricks on them, despises the women because he thinks the love of every one of them is easily obtained! He loves heathland, because it does not serve mankind,

> [it is] his counterpart in dumb nature, which leads him astray by *fata Morgana*; which is sufficient unto itself in its own beauty, with its glorious blossoms which pay homage to the sun alone, with its swarm of attendant bees, sheltering only the thistle, which feeds his [Till's] friend the donkey, who hates domestic animals, the slaves of man; he wants to go to Krebsheim, *riding* on his donkey, comes to Schilda, whose inhabitants he knows to be complete fools, not suspecting that they believe they only play the fool.
>
> Till ugly – misanthropic – loves nature 'without human beings' who were the first to bring stupidity into the world – he has given himself up to mockery, because he takes life too seriously.
>
> Till, despiser of the world, fruitless sceptic and laughing philosopher.

These three specimens give some idea of the difficulties facing Strauss in turning this Till into a dramatic figure. In the middle of these notes he suddenly wrote down the following:

> While I write a text for *Till*, they bring two murder victims to the hospital across the road! All at once misanthropy seems a very poor thing, and I am stricken with profound pity for the wretches for whom 'passions' are the source of their suffering as well as of their highest joys.

In the following year, evidently having tired of his own efforts, Strauss turned for help to Count Ferdinand von Sporck, who had already written the librettos for Cyrill Kistler's *Kunihild* and Max Schillings's *Ingwelde*, and would write more in the future: for Eugen d'Albert's *Die Abreise*, Schillings's *Der Pfeifertag*, Hans Sommer's *Münchhausen* and others. He and Strauss at first contemplated a work in five acts, using some of the plot material and motivation from Strauss's original draft, but they did not get beyond a preliminary stage, although Strauss noted down some musical ideas, as was his custom. Even after finishing the score of *Zarathustra*, which was 'a great joy and torment', Strauss wrote that he was going to return to his opera: 'Sporck's excellent book is gradually beginning to awaken responses and new ideas in my head and my heart, and "perhaps" will come to life.' (7 September 1896) The hope was never fulfilled, however.

The process of creation

While on holiday in Cortina d'Ampezzo in the summer of 1895, Strauss took the time to answer a questionnaire which Friedrich von Hausegger, the author of *Musik als Ausdruck* (1885) and *Das Jenseits des Künstlers* (1893), had sent to him and to a number of other artists, including other musicians (such as Hans Sommer, Felix Weingartner, Rezniček and Humperdinck), writers and painters. The primary goal of Hausegger's detailed questioning was to uncover the influences which determine artistic creation. Part of Strauss's answer, relating to *Tod und Verklärung*, has already been quoted (page 180 above), and what he had to say about his song-writing will be referred to later. What he wrote about his productivity in general is of great interest and importance:

> Complete isolation is the best thing, for my production at all events.
>
> The 'ideas', the musical thoughts that suddenly come to me from out of the blue – these I usually get in the afternoon – two hours after luncheon or later – at the start of a walk, or following a long walk in the beauties of nature, perhaps after I have rested for half an hour.
>
> Dreams play no part at all in my 'invention', at least not any dreams that I am conscious of when I wake up. But I have no doubt at all that an 'inner' working of the imagination, of which I am not conscious, makes the principal contribution to my creativity. That a motive or a longer melody, which comes to me unexpectedly in this way, which I at once recognize as being of a particular expressive kind, e.g. of a comic-grotesque or religious-inspirational or some other distinct character, and which I then, having recognized so much, *consciously* try to work out further in the appropriate spirit – that that motive or melody is the outcome of an inner process which has already gone on for a long time is brought home to me by the fact that I – [here Strauss loses the thread of his involved syntax and starts again. *Tr.*] – for example: four bars of a beautiful melody come to me suddenly, let's say of a religious-inspirational character – these four bars are a bolt from the blue, I've no notion of how or whence they have come to me all of a sudden, I sit down at the piano and try to work them out further according to their thematic character and whatever else their development seems to require – in a short time these four bars evolve into an 18-bar melody, which seems to match my expressive need well and

> happily, and which I estimate will make a 32-bar period in order to be fully evolved and complete. After I have got the first eighteen bars relatively quickly, with only short stops and small alterations, all of a sudden the eighteenth bar won't go on as I want, I try three, four, five ways to develop it – it's no use – I sense that the natural production, if I may call it that, is over. As soon as I realize that, I don't attempt to go on, but I keep good hold of what I have and impress it on my mind.

A few days later, Strauss went on, just as the first idea came to him, so all of a sudden what seemed to be the right continuation of it presented itself. Therefore his imagination must have been working on it inwardly, and he was in no doubt that the initial, unexpected idea was similarly only a continuation of an inner process.

With reference to his earliest compositions, he said, *inter alia*, that he had heard a lot of music from the day of his birth, as his father had played much at home. 'When my father blew his horn, I laughed, when he played the violin, I cried. And so my imagination was absorbing musical sounds from my birth onwards; after my sixth year it brought forth its first original product from its "reminiscences" [the Schneider-Polka].' As his faculties developed and his intellect was trained, so his imagination was able to take in ever richer nourishment and produce ever more 'unexpected' ideas. He had composed most, he said, between his eighth and his eighteenth years, that is 1872–82 approximately (which is only the case if one tots up the number of his works rather than their dimensions). 'The fact that I am now getting slower and slower is due to my growing self-criticism, which has been sharpened by my cultural betterment in general and keeps an ever closer watch to ensure that I produce only what I must and not what I could.'

It was hard to decide how far to separate what was known as technique and what was known as inspiration. In artistic production technique could perhaps be defined as the ability to bring out into the light of day all that the artist concealed within himself of emotion and imagination; the highest degree of technique was the most abundant, the most highly developed linguistic ability, but that in turn was only the outcome of an exceptional expressive need. To write a good five-part fugue was no evidence of great 'technique' but belonged rather under the rubric of good craftsmanship, unless the fugue expressed something which was more than the mere ability to write well in five parts:

> My professional colleagues often accuse me of displaying a colossally well-developed orchestral technique, sumptuous polyphony, skilful new forms in my works, while there is something seriously wrong with my musical 'invention'. But if I have discovered all these new colours in the orchestra, then that must have been preceded, in an 'artist of our sort', by the need to express something with these 'new colours' that could not be said in the old colours – if that is not the case, then one simply does not come upon these new colours. 'He who does not seek, shall find.'

The Kyrie of Bach's B minor Mass, for example, was generally categorized as 'artistic technique', while an eight-bar waltz tune by Schubert was 'pure invention', 'inspiration'. What the general public found easy to understand, it lauded with expressions like 'inspired', 'work of genius'; what it did not understand was 'artistic work'. If a person did not see that Bach's Kyrie contained a thousand times more 'invention', that only a very much fuller expressive need called for forms so much more complex than a waltz form, then there was no way of explaining it to that person.

> So if I'm always accused of being too difficult, too complicated – the deuce! – I can't express it any more simply, and I struggle for the greatest simplicity possible; there's no struggle for originality in a real artist. What makes my style of musical expression often appear over-refined, rhythmically over-subtle, rich, is probably a taste that has been refined by my abundant knowledge of the entire literature and my great experience of everything to do with the orchestra; this makes me prone to regard as trivial, commonplace, over-familiar and therefore not needing to be trotted out again, things which still appear to others, not merely the lay public, as highly 'modern' and belonging to the twentieth century.

Strauss had something further to say about his creative processes: he would be reading Schopenhauer or Nietzsche or some history book, when he would get an uncontrollable urge to go to the piano; before long a quite distinct melody would appear, that is, a quite distinct 'form' would shape itself under his fingers. The precondition for this was neither a particular mood, melancholy, yearning, love etc. (inner preconditions) nor exterior impressions, such as the sight of a thunder-storm, a peaceful evening high up in the mountains, an isolated stretch of sea-coast (or anything else generally supposed to inspire the 'artist'). The intellect alone was engaged, in the effort to cut Nietzsche down to a manageable size, or drum up some admiration for the 'denial of the will'.

(This offhand attitude towards Schopenhauer and Nietzsche is of particular significance, after *Guntram* and the remarks on Schopenhauer which Strauss noted in his diary when he was composing it, and in view of the fact that at the time when he was writing to Hausegger he was just beginning to work on *Zarathustra*.)

Strauss then took as an example a tune of a comic-grotesque character. It was not to be defined in terms either of his mood or of stimulation received from reading about abstractions (unless perhaps, at most, from the need for contrast). 'So the melody has shaped itself according to inner laws I cannot discern and for which I am often unable to discover the stimulus however carefully I search my memory.' On the other hand, some ideas had come to him when he was out for walks in beautiful scenery (leisure and solitude were almost always essential as well); it had often been his experience that the lines of a landscape had been turned into the lines of a melody with the same basic mood as the landscape. He cited one particular instance, when he was in Egypt and had seen an oddly shaped mountain ridge.

More than forty years after making these observations to Hausegger, towards 1940, Strauss supplemented them: melodic ideas often came to him when he woke up in the morning, 'at the very moment, that is, when the brain, drained of blood during the night, refills with fresh blood', which led him to suppose that the blood had a greater role to play 'in the activity of the imagination' than limited effort on the part of the brain. He also set down his own experience: 'If I get stuck at a particular point when I am composing in the evening, and no profitable further working seems possible, rack my brains as I may, I close my piano or my sketchbook, go to bed and the next morning when I wake up *the continuation is there*.'[25]

Lila

During the summer of 1895 Strauss started work on a new project, the setting of Goethe's *Lila*, and he sketched two acts during the holiday he and Pauline spent in Cortina d'Ampezzo. The entry in his diary (9 July 1895) mentioning this work goes on, using the word 'and' to link the two, to record the following plan as well:

Thought about a new tone poem:

Contemplation	Worship
Experience	Doubting
Recognition	Despair

These are key words in the conception of *Also sprach Zarathustra.*

We can only speculate as to why, at this particular stage in his life, Strauss thought of writing an opera based on Goethe's text. *Lila*, written in 1776–7 and revised first in 1778 and again in 1788, was conceived as a Singspiel, that is, a play combining spoken dialogue and musical numbers in relatively simple song forms; Goethe calls for several ballets as well. We know that Strauss had known and loved the work since boyhood, for he had set some of its numbers by the time he was fourteen. The only one of these early settings to survive complete is 'Auf aus der Ruh' for tenor, mixed chorus and orchestra (o. Op. 45); his orchestral score for Almaide's aria from the second act, 'Sei nicht beklommen', is incomplete, though the piano score survives (o. Op. 44; probably January 1878). He also told Thuille that he had composed a 'chorus for my drama *Lila* by Goethe'; the expression 'my drama' indicates that he planned, even then, to set the whole work, that is, all the vocal and balletic numbers. It is not likely to have been the Singspiel form itself that attracted him to *Lila* again after *Till Eulenspiegel*, but rather a psychological interest in its theme, the therapeutic effect of music.* It is probably safe to reject the notion that Strauss was suddenly smitten with the thought that he had been following a false trail with *Guntram* and wanted to strike off in a new direction. It was, however, characteristic of him to follow a work with something of a quite different nature, and that trait may well have been a factor on this occasion.

Many years later Cosima Wagner wrote to Prince Ernst zu Hohenlohe-Langenburg: 'Wanting to read some poetry, I took up Goethe's *Lila* again, and was greatly impressed by this wonderful, delicate work, but at the same time I had to smile at myself for

* Lila becomes so melancholic when her husband is reported dead that she does not even recognize him when he comes safe home; her friends cure her by helping her to act out her fantasies of imprisonment and rescue in a kind of masque, under the direction of a doctor, the Magus (who is more successful than Mangus in Tippett's *The Knot Garden*). *Tr.*

having once advised Richard Strauss to compose the music it needs.' (12 May 1914) Her memory was at fault, for when Strauss told her of his plan he had already sketched the first three acts, and only then asked for her advice. Their exchanges about *Lila* form one of the most interesting sections of their correspondence, and deserve to be quoted here at some length. After telling Frau Wagner about his recent holiday in Cortina, Strauss wrote:

> While we were there I began a curious labour. Do you know Goethe's play *Lila*, a subtle, gossamer piece? Well, I have composed 'modern' music for the items that need setting in three of the acts; but now I'm stuck, and Regisseur Savits in Munich with me, at the fourth act, because neither of us knows how to set about this fourth act. Goethe doesn't seem to have been very sure what to do with it either, because after the great Spinning Choruses (why are they spinning, all of a sudden?) he writes '(Above tutti . . . etc. etc.; the ballet master in the form of the Demon – the whole direction of the fourth act is left entirely to his taste)'.
>
> Who this tasteful ballet master is, I do not know – now, this is my big request: revered lady, if you would spare half an hour to read this little play, I have a secret hope that the idea that does not come to Goethe or to me will come to you quite by chance. (3 September 1895)

Cosima's advice was as follows:

> I would order the Demon's scene so that it contains the peripeteia of the drama. The Demon would turn out to be Lila's husband and the recognition scene (pantomimic on his part, sung on hers) would be acted out to the accompaniment of the final chorus. I believe that thus we follow Goethe's original ideas most closely.
>
> But since something like that must belong in its context, I have also thought out the scene with the monster (preferably not '*ogre*'), further marked what is to be spoken, what to be sung and what to be danced, made some cuts, in short tried to imagine the work as a whole.
>
> [Cosima added a parenthesis, to follow the words 'what is to be spoken': (The whole of the first act would be spoken, but Lila sings throughout until she hears her husband's call, with which she sinks into his arms and neither speaks nor sings another word. The scenes *with* her are all sung, while the scenes of the others are spoken, with the exception of Friedrich's little song.)]

A friend of my youth who is here writes under the name of Günther von Freiberg. Since execution is everything in such a case, I have asked her to do it. In order that her work shall not be in vain, I ask you, my dear friend, to let me know by telegraph whether you agree with my sketchy outline or not. (Lucerne, 26 September 1895)

The fourteen-page-long 'sketchy outline' drawn up by Cosima's friend (Ada Pinelli) is in the Strauss archives in Garmisch and bears the following inscription in Strauss's hand (probably not added until the late 1930s or early 1940s): 'Adaptation of Goethe's *Lila* for Dr Richard Strauss by Cosima Wagner.' It contains some small changes to Acts I and III, while Act II remains unchanged, and some more substantial alterations to Act IV, intended to clarify the proceedings. A remark in Cosima's letter to Strauss of 3 November 1895 – 'I will pass on the thing for *Lila* to you in Munich' – presumably refers to this document, but Strauss had written to express his thanks before he even received it.

Many thanks for the kind attention you are giving to my 'violet' problem.

Your idea of identifying the 'ogre' with Lila's husband is marvellous, positively 'goethly'.* I'm very much looking forward to the promised sketchy outline.

There is only one thing, as I ventured to say in my telegram, where I do not agree with you, if you will excuse my objection, namely that *all* the scenes with Lila should be sung. Nothing about the piece must be at all operatic, the music should be confined to the bare essentials and be extremely discreet, and one great attraction of the whole thing is: solving the problem of effecting skilful transitions from dialogue to music and back, but solving it in a way as if 'the works' [of Wagner] had not been written. If we take away from *Lila* the 'old-fashioned, modish, rococo' elements . . . we take from it the aura of moonshine, which we murder with twentieth-century electricity.

What attracts me to the work is that the two kinds of music which exist today are brought together in it in a highly drastic confrontation; do you understand exactly what I mean? Music as the expression of the human psyche (of Lila's hallucination, in our case) and music as the play of notes (which is what all the old pros and chamber-music-playing dilettantes, who abuse Liszt

* '*göthlich*': a pun on 'Goethe' and 'göttlich' (divine, god-like). *Tr.*

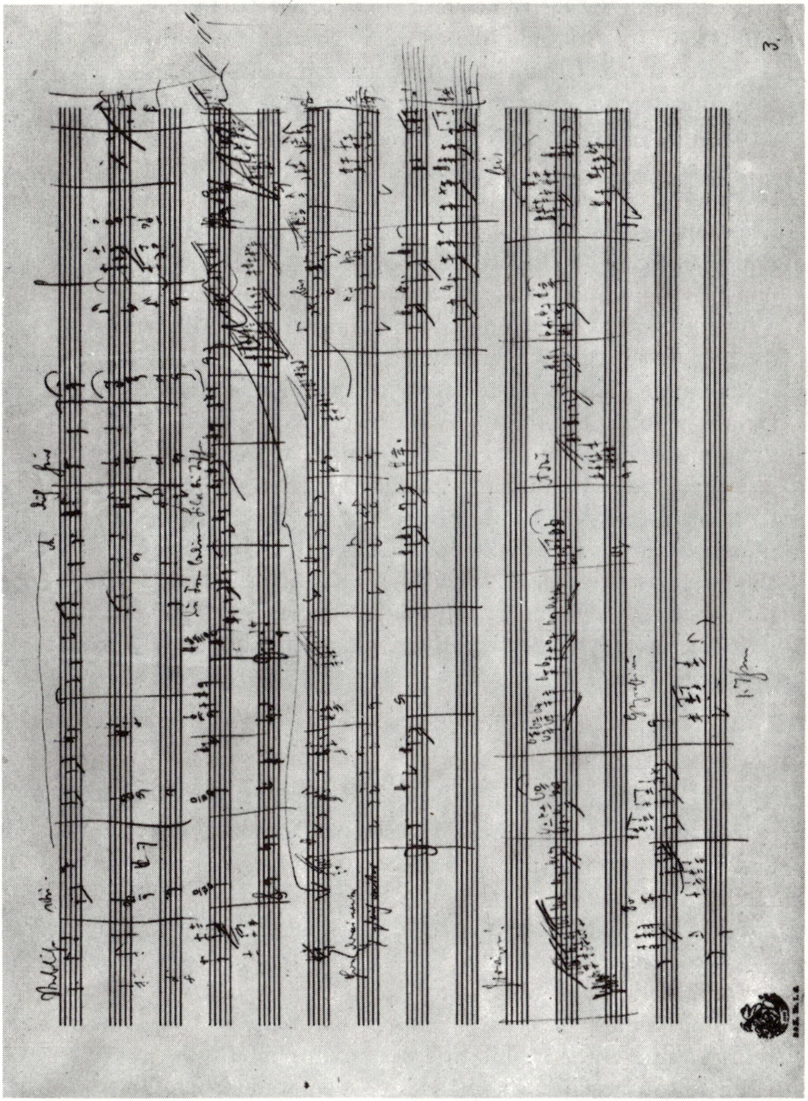

A page of the composition sketch for Act II of Goethe's *Lila*

etc. etc. on the strength of following Hanslick and attending Academy Concerts, take it for, and what it is as a therapeutic medium in the hands of the doctor and his companions).

But all that must only be hinted at, like a pen-and-ink sketch.

Concerning the distribution of singing and dialogue, if you will permit me, I would like to leave the second and third acts as far as possible as Goethe set them out, the more so because I have already composed music for all the passages that Goethe wrote in verse in the two acts.

On the other hand I am in complete agreement with a major alteration to the scene with the Demon in Act III and to the whole of Act IV, none of which I have yet set. Perhaps an important scene for Lila could be added to Act IV, at the spring which is mentioned, where the chains fall from her arms.

The motive of gardening and spinning probably derives from the idea that such peaceful activity protects people from madness, just as it helps to rescue the prisoners from the Demon's power. Could the two dancers who have to dance with the monster be given allegorical costumes appropriate to that interpretation? The very first passage for Lila (beginning of Act II) is characteristic, I think, of the way in which Goethe wants music and prose to be juxtaposed. Lila is not completely mad, she only has fixed ideas. When she is rational she speaks. 'But then a sleep, a swooning, comes upon me again.' Then the *idée fixe* ('the melody of death') enters, creeps up unnoticed: music!! (30 September 1895)

Cosima's reply to this letter bears the same date, so either she or Strauss was one day out. She wrote:

My deep violet Expression,

Certainly, Lila is not mad, but she has withdrawn from reality and in doing so has lost the sensible use of language, which she recovers only when she recognizes her husband and calls out his name.

There is no means for the shading of music into words, even if you have a solo violin fading down to *pianissimo* and then stopping. You know as well as I do that these are two contrary worlds represented by Lila and her environment.

Prose composed in the manner of melodrama could be shaded into the verse songs. Bold strokes cannot be advised, however, but only accomplished, and I could convince you (as with *Rienzi*, Act III) only by realization, and that is your affair.

She went on to indicate the drift of her adaptation, which affected primarily the fourth act, and to justify her earlier suggestion about the distribution of scenes spoken and set to music.

But her suggestions seem if anything to have inhibited rather than helped Strauss, who put the project on one side for a while. His growing inner alienation from Bayreuth may well have made him regret his impulse to consult Frau Wagner about Lila and view her contributions as an incubus. She referred to *Lila* once more in her letter of 3 November 1895, but by then he had already for several months been thinking about a symphonic poem 'freely after Nietzsche', that is, *Also sprach Zarathustra*, the sketch of which he began on 7 December 1895. At the same time he was drawn once more to song composition, spurred on by the happiness he experienced in his marriage; most of the songs of this period have associations with Pauline Strauss. Only when *Zarathustra* had long been finished (on 24 August 1896) and the early notes for the Schilda opera were already on his desk, did Strauss return fleetingly to *Lila* and compose some ballet music for it on 15 November 1896. It seems probable that this return to the Singspiel was connected with a visit he had paid to Frau Wagner in Marienbad three days previously. After this the plan was never mentioned again.

At some time during 1895 or early 1896 Strauss fell out with Siegfried Wagner. Nothing definite is known of the immediate cause of their disagreement, but its underlying reasons are probably to be sought in the reserve and mistrust with which Wahnfried greeted successively the *Guntram* prelude ('empty'), the opera as a whole (there is some justice in the criticism of the 'abstract brotherhood'), and in particular *Till Eulenspiegel*. A further ground was perhaps the failure to invite Strauss back to participate in the Bayreuth festival. Siegfried conducted at the festival for the first time in 1896. The commitments that Strauss now had in Munich perhaps constituted one reason for his not being invited back to Bayreuth: he had three of Wagner's works to conduct in the summer of 1895 alone. The very fact that the Munich Opera dared to stage these 'model performances' of Wagner was unwelcome in Wahnfried, and it cannot be ruled out that some difference of opinion arose with Strauss on that point. Envy of Strauss's artistic and material success as a composer may have contributed its mite too, as appears from an allusive remark in a letter Strauss wrote to Max Schillings from Cortina d'Ampezzo: 'The mountains here rise even higher than Humperdinck's royalties (without envy: Master

Siegfried!) and are even stranger in "form" than the songs of Richard Strauss.' (12 July 1895)

In spite of everything, a friendly tone was maintained in the correspondence between Strauss and the Wagner family. That Strauss had expressed himself in forthright terms about Bayreuth and Frau Wagner even while he was still in Weimar emerges from one of her letters to him at the time: 'I have been told that you once again uttered the craziest things about Bayreuth and my person on the occasion of the performance in Munich. God forgive the sorry creatures!' (21 October 1893) It would appear that Strauss had given vent to his disappointment at Frau Wagner's attitude during his negotiations with the Munich Court Opera that year, and that some characteristically frank, unguarded remarks had been exaggerated before reaching her ears.

Strauss's fanatical adherence to the Bayreuth 'cause' during the years in Weimar and his unconditional submission to Cosima's will, in which even the disagreement of 1892 ended (though it left a residue of inner reservations), were bound to continue to influence his relationship with Bayreuth, although his trip to Egypt had increased his self-knowledge and his return to composition with *Guntram* had strengthened his self-confidence. But the following entry appears in his diary, dated 11 January 1896: 'Momentous conversation with Siegfried Wagner, unspoken but nonetheless irrevocable separation from Wahnfried-Bayreuth. Only indirectly my fault.'

The question that springs to mind is whether any part, direct or indirect, was played in the argument with Siegfried by the fact that Strauss had started a symphonic poem on a Nietzschean subject just five weeks before, but it must remain unanswered in the absence of any evidence. Wahnfried's attitude to *Zarathustra* is revealed in a letter Cosima sent to Houston Stewart Chamberlain, two and a half months after Strauss's 'conversation' with Siegfried: 'They say that Strauss is composing *So sprach Zarathustra* [*sic*]; all that sort of thing is "trend", splendidly dealt with [by Richard Wagner] under the heading "Kunstlehre".' (26 March 1896)

Cosima referred to the disagreement with Siegfried in a letter to Strauss, in which, among other things, she enquired about *Lila*:

> Siegfried has told me about his argument with you and even though I was very sorry to learn that you had been disturbed in that way, yet I was pleased to think that you had had that

> opportunity to learn to know him in all his frankness, simplicity and friendship for you. *Auf Wiedersehen*, to a right good, expressive *Wiedersehen*, my dear friend! God be with you!
>
> Give your dear, excellent wife the most cordial greetings from us all, and receive the warm sympathy and most cordial wishes yourself from everyone in Bayreuth. (8 March 1896)

The façade was maintained, the tone of friendship preserved. Cosima Wagner was only too well aware of Strauss's importance to the Wagnerian cause.

Strauss did not reply to her letter until 12 April, as he had been to Moscow in the meantime, and then spent twelve days in bed with influenza immediately after the move into their new apartment on Herzog-Rudolf-Strasse on 26 March. He too made an effort to write in a tone of friendship, but a hint of his bitterness is still discernible:

> Far from not being sincerely grateful to you, respected and gracious lady, for your advice and the insight it displays, I shall follow it to the best of my ability; but while it contains a host of golden verities, just recently I have had to expend a great deal of self-conscious effort, in order to disregard all the fantastic rumours and gossip which have swarmed thickly about my ears, and to toss them calmly to the four winds, without first even examining them to discover whether there is any truth in them.

He further confirmed – what her letter to Chamberlain shows she already knew – that he was 'working on a symphonic poem, the title of which will actually be *Also sprach Zarathustra*: it takes up so much of my energies that for the time being I have to put *Lila* on one side, without giving it up altogether'.

In Wahnfried this information will have been interpreted as the covert declaration of war that it was intended to be. Nevertheless the personal relationship continued to be upheld. Strauss went to Bayreuth again in the middle of August, to hear Siegfried conduct a *Ring* cycle. He wrote home to tell his wife that he had met Frau Wagner, 'who was very amiable and took me and Vogl and Chamberlain to Fantaisie [a country park]. In the evening to a soirée in Wahnfried, everyone, Siegfried included, very amiable, I ditto, we behave as if nothing had happened.' (16 August 1896) The following day he wrote to her about the performance of *Das Rheingold*, which he had greatly enjoyed, as something 'that can be done only in Bayreuth. After the performance I went to supper in Wahnfried, where everyone is enormously amiable towards me; I have been invited to [second] breakfast there at noon today.' After *Die Walküre* he wrote: 'Brünnhilde [Lilli Lehmann] atrocious, an old Jewish grandmother without acting talent and without trace of feeling. But Rosa Sucher [as Sieglinde] quite extraordinary, magnificent, a dramatic achievement of the very first rank.' (18 August)

But betweenwhiles his anger broke out again, and in his next letter to Pauline he exclaimed: 'O Bayreuth, pigsty to beat all pigsties', presumably a comment on Siegfried's 'miserable' direction of the *Ring*; the circle of Bayreuth acolytes must have got on his nerves as well. He wrote to Max Schillings a few weeks later that everything seemed to him to have gone appallingly badly under Siegfried, 'but in Wahnfried they nevertheless agreed, with Chamberlain and all the other literary lackeys, that only now has the *Ring* been "established", the individual works have been made clearer in their distinctiveness etc. etc.' (7 September 1896)

In January 1897 Cosima Wagner attended a rehearsal of Mozart's *Die Entführung* in Munich and Siegfried paid a visit to the Strausses on 25 February. Cosima saw Strauss again in Wiesbaden on 24 April. When Mahler replaced Wilhelm Jahn at the Court Opera in Vienna, Strauss was convinced that Mottl's move to Munich was now only a matter of time, and so he wrote to Cosima asking her to support his bid to move to Karlsruhe in Mottl's place. (9 April 1897)

Pauline Strauss went to Bayreuth the following January to sing Saint Elisabeth in a performance of Liszt's oratorio, following which Cosima wrote to Richard: 'We were delighted to have your dear wife here, her voice sounded soft and beautiful and her deeply felt and simple delivery made a great impression on everyone.' (30 January 1898) This letter was promptly followed by another, in which she thanked her 'dear Expression' for his reply to the first:

> When one goes for a long time without meeting or communicating in writing, a cordial word, such as you speak to me, has twofold strength.
>
> What you say about your composing is what I have always felt about it, and particularly where others find you 'complex and tendentious', to me you seem naive and spontaneous. It is your strength and may God preserve it in you through all the vexatiousness of life.

Her closing paragraph conveys a sincere goodwill:

> May you experience only what is good, my dear Expression! Continue to think kindly of us, and may you and your dear wife rest assured of my warm regard and the sincere affection of my children. (4 February 1898)

In April Frau Wagner had dinner with the Strausses during a visit to Munich. The outward forms of friendship were preserved for a long time to come.

A letter which Arthur Seidl wrote to Strauss only four days after the latter's argument with Siegfried Wagner gives an indication of the reasons for the inner estrangement from Wahnfried:

> I hear that you are now talking of a period in your life, called 'Wahnfried', as being closed for good, and it grieves me in the depths of my soul that I have been proved right. I will only remind you of our long and animated conversation about Frau Wagner and the Wagner Societies the first time you came to see us, and of your denial when I identified you with Guntram, Friedhold with Ritter and Bayreuth with the Brotherhood in the *Rundschau.* I was quite sure about it even then and I foresaw all of this – you yourself will have to admit now that I was right, and I'm truly sorry that you could not be spared such unhappy experiences. Imagine, if you had married Eva Wahnfried! These strict Wahnfriedists around the Meisterin, on the conservative right wing, who always have to run to her for all their answers and offer up one *sacrificium intellectus* after another to their own convictions, are – this has been my view for a very long time, ever since the one occasion on which I met the lady in person at the Glasenapps' in Villa Feustel [in Bayreuth] – pitiful milksops, sad marionettes, inferior intellectual slaves and furtive pussy-footers without the guts to live their own lives; in other respects many of them are highly gifted, noble minds, refined natures and admirable characters, but an empty nothing when Cosima hath spoken and brandishes her terrorism over their heads . . .
>
> As for the worthless, dandified shows of that itinerant conducting fop Siegfried! I had a real heart-to-heart with uncle Ritter on that subject in Munich last summer. (15 January 1896)

The conducting engagement which took Strauss to Moscow in 1896 was a concert on 16 March. Nikisch had conducted there only a short time before, which put Strauss at something of a disadvantage. His programme consisted of *Tod und Verklärung, Till Eulenspiegel* and Beethoven's Fourth Symphony. The press was divided on the merits of his own works, but the audience in the hall received them well. In an interview the Russian critic A. Koptyeyev laid particular emphasis on Strauss's interest in Russian music, especially Tchaikovsky, Glazunov, Cui, Rimsky-Korsakov and Balakirev, though in fact his acquaintance with those composers must have been restricted to a very small number of their works. A review by Arsemii Korechenko praised Strauss's outstanding technique and 'command of the most varied orchestral effects'. *Till Eulenspiegel* made the strongest impression. Strauss wrote to his parents to describe his journey through Poland and White Russia ('white with snow') to Moscow, where he had been packed into an open sledge, to his horror,

> but there is nothing else here, not even for ladies in décolleté ball gowns. Asia is very interesting, the Kremlin as tasteless as it is magnificent, hundreds of churches, painted all the colours of the rainbow (green, blue, red etc.). But the people are very lively, remind me a little of the Arabs, immense streets, crazy sledge drivers; today dreadful flurrying snow. (1 March 1896 [Old Style; 13 March New Style])

Also sprach Zarathustra

Strauss had already begun to take a deep interest in Nietzsche before he set off for Greece and Egypt, as we have seen, and it persisted after his return to Weimar, while the move to Munich may even have intensified it, since discussion of Nietzsche was in full flood there at the time. For Strauss there was a direct association between his ending for *Guntram* and the type of human being represented by the Nietzschean Superman, actively creative, free of all ties and fashioning new values. At the side of Till, the anti-philistine, he set the free artist, driven by the longing for something higher to aspire beyond the self-satisfied normality of the society of his day. Arrogance, the will to power, the spirit of the Wilhelmine age have been read into Strauss's *Zarathustra*, ever since the time of its first appearance to the present day. Romain Rolland, for instance, following the performance in Paris in 1899, placed just such an interpretation on the work in his *Journal*.

The new tone poem signified an artistic act of self-liberation which had been pre-figured in the ending of *Guntram*. Originally Strauss had planned to give it the sub-title 'Symphonic optimism in fin-de-siècle form, dedicated to the twentieth century', a light-hearted formulation with a hint of mockery, which nevertheless betrays his consciousness of having reached a turning-point, and above all reinforces the insight recorded in his Egyptian diary in association with his reading of Schopenhauer: 'I affirm consciously, that is my happiness!' There is not the least trace of decadence in the work.

Strauss's first sketches for *Zarathustra* dated from February 1894 in Weimar, but – as we have seen – it was not until the holiday in Cortina d'Ampezzo in July 1895 that he really 'thought about' it, and he began the planned, systematic composition on 7 December of that year. His most intensive periods of work on it were 31 March to 4 April, 7–11 April and 13–18 April 1896 (Alexander Ritter died on 12 April, probably without knowing anything about the new work). The particello or short score (Strauss himself always used the term 'sketch') was finished on 17 July 1896, but the autograph of the full score is headed 'Begun 4 February 1896, my beloved Paula's birthday', and it was finished on 24 August 1896, in Munich. 'Zarathustra's Prologue', from Nietzsche, with which Strauss introduces the score, is no more to be understood as a 'programme' than Ritter's poem inspired by *Tod und Verklärung*; its purpose is to attune the listener, to prepare him for the conceptual world of the symphonic poem. The sub-headings, also from Nietzsche, given to the separate sections of the work really correspond to the musical development only in the first few sections; in the later sections Strauss no longer keeps very strictly to the kind of content indicated by the sub-headings but adapts his musical material quite freely. The work bears the sub-title 'Tone poem (freely after Nietzsche)'. There are eight sub-headings, the first not coming until bar 22: 'Of the Backworldsmen', 'Of the great longing', 'Of joys and passions', 'The Song of the Grave', 'Of Science', 'The Convalescent', 'Dance Song', and 'Song of the Night Wanderer'. The 'Science' (or 'Knowledge': Wissenschaft) section contains the celebrated twelve-note theme, which proceeds out of the two principal keys (C and B) and comes in the third bar to a confrontation of

major triads on the tritonally related E♭ and A; this confrontation of polar opposites was to be a hallmark of Strauss's later harmonic style. The comparable confrontation, or overlapping, of the two principal keys of the whole work, B and C, in the finale has, of course, a symbolic significance. A philosophy of life, a Weltanschauung, takes concrete form in musical terms. What Strauss intended was the objective establishment and recognition of two underlying forces which determine human fate: nature and the human being (yearning) confront each other. The twelve-note 'Science' theme places the two keys, the symbols of nature and the human being, in direct confrontation with each other at its start. Strauss himself confirmed that he thought of the keys in these terms when he wrote: 'Taken musically, *Zarathustra* is laid out as an alternation between the two remotest keys (the second).' The 'remotest keys' are in fact, of course, those separated not by the interval of the second but by the tritone, which Strauss later employed as the basis of his *Symphonia Domestica*. At all events, while *Zarathustra* is the product of Strauss's reading of Nietzsche, it does not amount to a confession of allegiance to his philosophy. In 1946, in a letter to Martin Hürlimann which refers to Nietzsche's critique of Wagner, Strauss speaks of 'a sick philosopher's head running against the Himalayas', something not to be taken seriously; at the same time, however, he acknowledges that the poetic visions of Nietzsche's *Zarathustra* offer 'much aesthetic enjoyment'.[26] Taken together, the two comments demonstrate clearly enough that it is mistaken to assume that Strauss identified with the Superman.

Notes jotted in one of his sketchbooks give a fragmentary indication of what was in Strauss's mind when he conceived *Zarathustra*: he gives the heading 'universe' to the initial phrase C, G, C, then: 'The sun rises. The individual enters the world or the world enters the individual.' Beside the theme C, E, G, he notes:

> Remains immobile, rigid, unchanged to the end. Worship – Doubting/Doubt/Recognition – Despair – /reviving again in the red light of dawn/then 'Freedom' has made it its own. The priests are on the increase. Large diminuendo and extinction up to the beginning of the fugue, large build-up until all the Life themes come together! Their combination ends with Despair D minor, out of which finally Yearning B minor gently spreads its wings out over the one exhausted by the struggle with the ghosts of 'Life'. Leads B major and him to 'Freedom'. C major 3/4.

He goes on to remark:

> What is known as 'working-out' or 'development' is something that is in opposition to the possibility of the existence of today's 'absolute' music. Let the form tell us clearly what it is, then the hearer has something to latch on to, let its conflict with the other forms of the small, purely human drama be limited to the briefest intimations, which will be understood by the listener who really hears the music, even if his nose hasn't been rubbed in it seven times, while the layman can use them as a source of information until, within a short time, a new 'form' offers itself to him. The excessive length of the development is something which Wagner rightly found to be a failing in the Lisztian symphonic poem.

This is followed by another note which illustrates Strauss's conception of colour in music: 'Passion theme in A♭ major (brass, dark blue).'

Strauss conducted the first performance of *Also sprach Zarathustra* for which Spitzweg had paid him 3000 marks, in Frankfurt on 27 November 1896, at the fourth Museum Concert of the season, four days after conducting a Liszt-Verein concert in Leipzig. In accordance with his express wish, the programme contained neither the words of Zarathustra which preface the printed score, nor any of the 'sub-headings'.

Strauss was apt to vary in his attitude to the 'music guides' common in his day and to the inclusion in programme notes of the poetic 'programme' underlying his symphonic works. At all events, the well-known guides to the orchestral works, compiled by Herwarth Walden, and to the music dramas, compiled by Georg Göhler,[27] which are still referred to today, were compiled with his collaboration, or at the very least with his consent. On 14 February 1898 he wrote to Arthur Seidl, who was writing an introduction to *Zarathustra*: 'An analysis of this kind must be detailed and complete, otherwise there's no point in it'; and he even threatened: 'If Dr Bechhold won't give way, I will forbid the analysis and we'll easily find another publisher. My last word!'[28] On this occasion, in fact, he appears to have been referring to the question of ample musical examples. In a letter to Romain Rolland about *Ein Heldenleben*, as in the letter about *Till* which he sent to Franz Wüllner, Strauss took a rather different line. Gustav Mahler's attitude was equally inconsistent; like Strauss, as he accumulated more experience, he increasingly resisted the exposure of the inner drives behind his compositions.

The other works performed in the concert at which *Zarathustra* had its première included Liszt's *Prometheus* and Gustav Brecher's symphonic poem *Rosmersholm*, which Strauss pronounced 'glorious' in a letter to Pauline, and several other of his own works: the Peace Narration from *Guntram*, *Aus Italien*, and three songs sung by Heinrich Zeller (*Heimliche Aufforderung*, *Allerseelen* and *Ständchen*). Strauss was well satisfied, both with the piece and with its performance by the Frankfurt City Orchestra. After the general rehearsal, at which the work was warmly received, he wrote to Pauline in a tone of unusual enthusiasm:

> *Zarathustra* is glorious – by far the most important of all my pieces, the most perfect in form, the richest in content and the most individual in character. The beginning is glorious, all the many passages for the string quartet have come off capitally; the Passion theme is overwhelming, the Fugue spine-chilling, the Dance Song simply delightful, I'm enormously happy and very sorry that you can't hear it. The climaxes are immense and scored!!! Faultlessly scored – and the beautiful concert hall helps. Orchestra is excellent – in short, I'm a fine fellow, after all, and feel just a little pleased with myself, and I shan't allow the population of Munich to spoil the feeling. (26 November 1896)

Numerous friends and acquaintances were present for the big occasion (Strauss premières were now regarded as nothing less): Friedrich Hegar, Hans Huber and Robert Freund from Switzerland, Friedrich Rösch and the entire Ritter family, Philipp Wolfrum, Humperdinck and many others. On the following day Strauss went to Cologne to play the work through to Franz Wüllner, one of his most energetic champions. Three days later, after Nikisch had given the work in Berlin on 30 November with a 'sensational success', he himself conducted the third performance of the work in Cologne on 1 December, at the fourth in that season's series of subscription concerts. Dr Victor Schnitzler, the distinguished lawyer who was made an honorary doctor of the University of Cologne in 1925 for his services to the Conservatory, recalled the occasion in his memoirs:

> My father, who was rigidly conservative in every other respect, was greatly interested in Strauss and admired his wide reading and his profound understanding of philosophy. One evening before the general rehearsal of his *Zarathustra*, Strauss came to tea

> . . . and the two men became so engrossed in a conversation about the philosophy of Nietzsche that they lost all notion of place and time, and Strauss was late for the rehearsal.[29]

The reference to the people of Munich in the letter to Pauline quoted above betrays Strauss's dissatisfaction with the circumstances in which he now found himself in the city of his birth. In September he had had a violent quarrel with Possart on the subject of Hermann Levi's retirement. The scene was described as follows in his diary:

> Possart served me a shabby turn today. Taking advantage of my difficult position over my appointment for 1 October, on which no definite decision has been taken yet, he expects me to annul the contract for my wife to make twenty guest appearances, which is supposed to be valid from 1 March to 30 September, by making the options which have already passed without being taken up by Possart available for him to use later as he chooses. When I wouldn't agree to that, he threatens, on the grounds of being my only friend here, which I utterly deny, not to take my part at Friday's meeting. Ugly scenes over *Guntram* etc. In short – dirty, rotten trickery. (24 September 1896)

The incident illustrates how precarious Strauss's position still was. Two days later, however, on 26 September, Perfall offered him a two-year contract as Hofkapellmeister in succession to Levi and at Levi's salary; Strauss's rank and title had previously been that of Royal Kapellmeister. The appointment came into force on 1 October, but since Possart first had to report to the Prince Regent on 3 October, it was not officially confirmed until 6 October. The position was still not very satisfactory for Strauss, who had counted on a contract of longer duration and a higher salary.

Strauss spent his summer break in 1896 in Marquartstein, where Pauline's parents had a villa. The relationship between Strauss's parents and Pauline became very tense in the September of this year, but reconciliation soon followed, with Pauline taking the initiative. It was in all probability at this time that Strauss wrote the letter dated only 'Tuesday evening', in which he reproaches his parents with having too little consideration for, or understanding of, 'the idiosyncrasies' of Pauline's nature, and for that reason proposes, as delicately as he can, that they should cease to consort with each other altogether, for the sake of everyone's peace of mind.[30]

On 29 September Strauss received the score of Alexander Ritter's *Sursum corda!* as a gift from Ritter's daughters, in gratitude for the performance of it which he had conducted on 6 March. In the following year he eagerly recommended *Sursum corda!* and Max Schillings's *Zwiegespräch* (Duologue, for violin, cello and small orchestra, Op. 8) to Gustav Kogel, the conductor of the Frankfurt Museum Concerts (20 April 1897). He was very angry when Weingartner dropped *Zwiegespräch* from a concert programme at the last minute in November 1898, because it had been a flop at the public rehearsal. 'Men of their word!'

On 3 October 1896 Pauline and Richard Strauss set off for a holiday in Italy. They made Florence their base for several weeks, studiously visiting everything that should be seen there, and making excursions to Perugia and Assisi. While they were in Florence, Strauss received the news that the Munich Academy Concerts were to be conducted by Mottl and Erdmannsdörfer that year. His comment was one that Alexander Ritter was accustomed to use on similar occasions: 'Auch gut', an expression of dignified but rather tight-lipped acceptance. He called on the painter Arnold Böcklin in Fiesole on 8 October, and played *Till Eulenspiegel* to him on the piano, as well as a Beethoven Adagio, and Pauline sang five Strauss songs. They called on Böcklin again on 10 October. The following day, when they had made their way up the Via dei Colli to San Miniato, Strauss noted in his diary: 'First idea for an orchestral piece: Don Quichote, mad, free variations on a knightly theme.' (11 October 1896) They paid a third visit to Arnold Böcklin on 21 October, when Strauss played more Beethoven at their host's express wish.

Conducting tours

Immediately after the return to Munich Strauss set off again, this time for Berlin to conduct, of his own works, *Till Eulenspiegel* and two new songs for solo voice and orchestra (Op. 33, 1 and 2), which satisfied him even at the rehearsal. He met numerous old acquaintances – Oscar Bie, Mackay, Halir, Heinrich Welti, Wilhelm Klatte, Friedrich Rösch and others – and made a new one, Arthur Schnitzler, when he went to call on his new publisher Adolph Fürstner. To maintain his contacts with the Berlin Opera he called on Count Bolko von Hochberg, the general intendant of the Prussian Royal Theatres, and on Georg Henry Pierson, the artistic director. On 2

November he conducted a concert of the Berlin and Potsdam Wagner-Vereine in Berlin, at which the programme consisted of Liszt's *Mazeppa*, the prelude and interlude of Wolf's *Der Corregidor*, his own two new orchestral songs, *Apollopriesterin* and *Verführung*, sung by Rosa Sucher, and his *Till Eulenspiegel*, and, by Wagner, the *Faust* Overture and the prelude and 'Liebestod' from *Tristan*. In his diary he wrote: 'Have never conducted *so* well.' He was still in Berlin when he heard the news of the award given to Thuille's *Theuerdank*, the première of which he conducted in Munich the following March.

Back in Munich he made his first notes for his new operatic project, *Die Schildbürger*, on 10 November, and five days later, after seeing Cosima Wagner in Marienbad, he wrote the ballet music for *Lila*, as already mentioned. On 20 November he was off again, this time to conduct a concert of the Liszt-Verein in Leipzig, and by 27 November he was in Frankfurt, to give the first performance of *Zarathustra*. The new work was heard in several other German cities within a matter of weeks, and it was not long before performances took place in London, Vienna, Brussels and New York. When he went to Brussels to conduct in the first week in December, the orchestra received him with an ovation. He in turn was delighted with them: 'Splendid string players with a magnificent, ardent cantilena, wonderful woodwind; the brass is good, but not as polished a sound as ours.' (To his parents, 3 December 1896) To his wife he wrote: 'I've never heard the B major business in *Tod und Verklärung* played so thrillingly.' Joseph Dupont (1838–99), conductor at the Théâtre de la Monnaie and of the series of popular concerts given in Brussels, had told him that he was the only composer since Wagner with anything significant to say, and had said a lot of other things which, although they were of course examples of French amiability and politeness, did not fall the less pleasantly or agreeably on his ears for that. There appear to have been no objections to paying the fee of 1000 marks Strauss had requested. Originally he had suggested to Dupont a concert consisting entirely of his own works: *Aus Italien*, *Don Juan* or *Macbeth*, and *Till*; but he declared himself willing to conduct a symphony by Berlioz or Beethoven or something by Liszt or Wagner in the first half instead of *Aus Italien*. The concert, on 6 December, eventually included *Tod und Verklärung*, *Macbeth* and *Till*, as well as the two orchestral songs he had conducted in Berlin five weeks before, this time sung by Milka Ternina, who also sang two arias from *Tannhäuser*. The evening was a great success with public and press alike: Strauss was particularly pleased with a review in the *Etoile belge*. Strauss had a very good relationship with Joseph Dupont, who gave him a warm welcome and engaged him again in 1897,[31] but he found Sylvain Dupuis, the Liègeois conductor of the Brussels Symphony concerts, more trustworthy; Dupont was 'a bit of a *faiseur*'. He nonetheless expressed his gratitude to Dupont in the dedication of *Don Quixote*. Strauss met other musicians in Brussels and held conversations with Vincent d'Indy and Eugène Ysaÿe among others, as well as with the music historian and critic Maurice Kufferath, and at the house of an admirer, Georges Khnopff, he met the sculptor Constantin Meunier. He went on to Antwerp, where he met Paul Gilson, the Belgian composer of a symphonic poem called *La mer* (1890). From Antwerp he sent his wife an amusing account of one of the evenings he had spent in Brussels:

> On Sunday Dupont invited me to a slap-up dinner, attended by three other of his friends, two of whom had brought their ladies along, feather-brained coquettes, the genuine article, one of them reeking horribly of patchouli, the other blond but a thoroughly nice, jolly little creature, on whom I practised my grisly French, but was as good as gold. I'll tell you all about it when I see you. As the lion of the hour, without so much as a with your leave or a by your leave I was apportioned a smacking kiss by each of them, at which, in all probability, I think, I pulled a frightfully silly face and, 'oh, comme il est timide' – I was laughed out of court, the evening was thoroughly frivolous and ended in two Théatres [*sic*] variétés. (8 December 1896)

In Liège Strauss conducted the *Eroica* and his own *Don Juan* and *Zarathustra*, the first performance of the latter outside Germany. Here too he made many new acquaintances. He travelled home via Düsseldorf, where he conducted *Zarathustra*, the two *Guntram* preludes and *Wandrers Sturmlied*.

Pauline appears to have taken umbrage at one of her husband's letters – it can hardly have been the one describing his evening on the town in Brussels, in view of the dates – for he wrote to her again from Liège on 9 December.

> Dearest paddy-muffin!* Have just received your wrathful missive – ah, that's my old, cutting little woman again, signed

* '*Zornbrötlein*'.

> 'Bi' this time too, that always portends something of a tempest! It doesn't matter, my dear Bauxerl, I've had so many dulcet letters by now that I can perfectly well sustain the occasional one that modulates into the minor.

This was his customary, good-humoured manner of responding to his wife's explosions.

The steadily growing number of engagements to conduct in towns and cities all over Germany and abroad as well made great demands on Strauss's energies. His duties in Munich meant that as a rule he travelled overnight. Hardly had he arrived at his destination than it was time for rehearsals, and generally he set out again immediately after a concert, either to go back to Munich or to travel on to another town where he was to give another concert. The programmes always included something by himself, often songs both with orchestral accompaniment (Op. 33) and with piano in the same programme, as well as a symphonic poem: *Tod und Verklärung*, *Till Eulenspiegel* and, from the end of 1896 onwards, *Zarathustra* were played more often than *Don Juan*; the preludes from *Guntram* and, of his earlier works, *Wandrers Sturmlied* were also often performed. In addition his programmes would usually include a symphony by Beethoven, a symphonic poem by Liszt or, occasionally, an overture by Berlioz. Among contemporary works, apart from his own, he gave several performances of the prelude of Max Schillings's opera *Ingwelde*. Schillings and his wife were particularly close friends of Richard and Pauline Strauss during those years in Munich. Although Strauss did not receive the complete score of *Ingwelde* until 24 December 1896, and did not conduct the work in the theatre until May 1897, in Munich, he conducted the prelude for the first time at a concert in Budapest on 4 December 1895. On that occasion the other works performed were Beethoven's Pastoral Symphony, *Tod und Verklärung* and Liszt's *Festklänge*. At one of the concerts of the Leipzig Liszt-Verein, he conducted the *Ingwelde* prelude in the company of Liszt's *Hamlet*, the two *Guntram* preludes, his Violin Concerto (with Alfred Krasselt as soloist) and Alexander Ritter's *Olafs Hochzeitsreigen*.

The most important of the concerts he gave as a guest conductor during the period of his second term at the Munich Opera were at the Lower Rhineland Music Festival in Düsseldorf in May 1896 (*Don Juan*, *Till*, *Wandrers Sturmlied*) – immediately prior to beginning rehearsals for the new production of *Don Giovanni* in the Munich

Residenztheater; the return to Düsseldorf on 17 December of the same year (the two *Guntram* preludes, *Sturmlied* and *Zarathustra*); in Heidelberg on 15 February 1897 (*Zarathustra*, given for once with the full orchestral forces required in the score); two concerts with the Concertgebouw Orchestra in Amsterdam (7 and 11 October 1897). In the first of the Amsterdam concerts he conducted Beethoven's Seventh Symphony, Wagner's *Faust* Overture and *Siegfried Idyll*, Berlioz's *Lear* Overture, and *Tod und Verklärung*; in the second, Mozart's *Eine kleine Nachtmusik*, Beethoven's *Eroica*, his own *Don Juan* and a second performance of *Tod und Verklärung*, which the audience received more warmly than had been the case at the first performance, which was poorly attended. The Dutch press was rather reserved, except for the composer Alphons Diepenbrock, [32] who wrote in the avant-garde weekly *De Kroniek*: 'It happens so rarely in this day and age that one does not have to seek one's musical enjoyment among the dead, that it was a pleasure that continues to vibrate in us to see Richard Strauss in our midst, to hear his works and to see him conduct them.' (No. 147, 17 October 1897) Diepenbrock called on Strauss in his hotel and accompanied him on a visit to the Rijksmuseum. He wrote to his friend, the pianist and composer Carl Smulders:

> I took a very particular liking to Strauss as a person . . . I found him modest and unaffected. But I was alone with him, and his success on the first evening was only middling . . . Strauss has not put on the virtuoso here, at least not nearly enough. The orchestra's opinion is that he 'can't conduct'.

Strauss wrote to Pauline from Amsterdam: 'Whenever one is abroad, one realizes how provincial Munich is, and what boorish fools its inhabitants are, and so one has to take the opportunity to refresh oneself away from home.' (8 October 1897) In a second letter to her, written on the same day, he added:

> The orchestra is really splendid, full of youthful vigour and enthusiasm, excellently pre-rehearsed, so that it's a real pleasure to conduct it. *Tod und Verklärung* was a gigantic success. I have just seen Sarah Bernhardt drive off; she also played here last night and has been staying at my hotel. A great crowd of people gathered, she is still handsome, but the whole hotel has reeked of her perfume since yesterday. As she doesn't play again until next Monday, to my regret I shan't see her act. In the Museum I've seen glorious Rembrandts, Frans Hals and Ruisdaels, these

Dutchmen are fresh, healthy fellows, full of life. (8 October 1897)

In a third letter from Amsterdam he reported that the second concert, attended by 2000 people, was a brilliant success and that his desk was wreathed in laurel. He sent his father a keg of oysters. The orchestra must have been well pleased with his performance in the end, since it accompanied him to the railway station *en masse* when he left.

A letter from Frankfurt in the same month shows Strauss's steady refusal to be ruffled by Pauline's temperamental outbursts, which normally gave way very quickly to remorse:

Dearest Wife! Your two letters and telegrams were waiting for me! Thank you once again for your adorable contrition: but you really ought not to make so much of these things. Since I know you so very well, and also know for certain that you are very fond of me, 'scenes' like this are never going to be able to shake my trust in you. The only thing is that I'm often distressed for you, because your nerves are not strong enough to help you stand up to these bursts of feeling as you should, though they're small enough in themselves and often partly justified. So calm down, my sweet darling, because all the dear, good things I have from you, not least our splendid, glorious Baby, always make me forget these little 'incidents' very quickly, and my love for you is always the same. So there's nothing to forgive, and the only advice I have for you is to take very good care of your health and your nerves. (28 October 1897)

On 4 November Strauss conducted in Hamburg (Mozart's Jupiter Symphony, the *Tristan* prelude and 'Liebestod', Liszt's *Mephisto* Waltz, Strauss's *Don Juan*) and a few days later he was in Barcelona, where he gave two concerts (11 and 14 November): in the first he conducted Beethoven's *Eroica*, Wagner's *Meistersinger* prelude, the *Mephisto* Waltz and *Don Juan* again; in the second, the programme consisted of Beethoven's *Leonore* Overture No. 3, *Eine kleine Nachtmusik*, the overture to *Tannhäuser* and the prelude and 'Liebestod' from *Tristan*, the prelude to Act II of *Guntram*, and *Tod und Verklärung*. The two symphonic poems, *Don Juan* and *Tod und Verklärung* were encored. As he wrote to Pauline, the journey south did him good: 'I thawed out like a frozen plum and naturally, as is my wont, I at once began to compose.' (11 November 1897) To his parents he wrote:

I had a gigantic success yesterday evening; the kind of applause

> that was quite new to me – the bullfights have made these people used to a different kind of tempo . . . after *Don Juan* such a tumult broke out that after taking five bows I had to play the whole piece again. The orchestra is very good (apart from the solo violin and cello), it's been capitally drilled in serious music by the excellent [Antonio] Nicolau [the conductor of the Catalan Concert Society]. I was amazed by how well the *Eroica* and *Don Juan* went. The brass is a bit rough, in the Italian manner, takes a swing at the F, without then being able to sustain the note beautifully; woodwind, especially the oboe, very good! All enormously willing and very easy to guide, they follow capitally. Rehearsals here are held from 1.30 to 4.30, and in the evening from 9 to nearly midnight, the concert yesterday lasted from 9.15 to 12.15! (12 November 1897)

Before the end of the same month Strauss was back in Brussels, where he conducted at a popular concert, consisting entirely of his own compositions: *Don Juan*, four songs with orchestra and three with piano (with Pauline as soloist), *Till Eulenspiegel*, the Piano Quartet and the Violin Sonata (21 November 1897). On the following evening the poet Georges Khnopff had arranged a *cercle artistique*, at which Pauline again sang songs by Strauss. Georges Khnopff was the brother of the celebrated Belgian Symbolist – painter, draughtsman, sculptor and stage-designer – Fernand Khnopff. The admiration of Georges for Strauss was so great that when his son was born in April of the following year he christened him Richard Till. After he had sent Strauss this news, Khnopff received a reply in which the composer wrote that he was busy with rehearsals for Siegmund von Hausegger's 'excellent' *Zinnober*, had written about fifteen new songs and was 'working diligently on the sketch for a new tone poem: *Eroica*'. (14 June 1898)[33] To the delight of his admirer he appended a little musical joke on the text 'Richard Till Khnopff: long may he live!'

Even this, scribbled in an idle moment, bears Strauss's harmonic signature. The four bars of music travel from a chord of G♭ major to a chord of C major, the distance of a tritone, via triads on F and E, with chromatically descending parallel fifths in the two lower parts. Strauss's use of the tritone is one of his most characteristic hallmarks, from *Symphonia Domestica* to his very last song, *Malven* (23 November 1948), in which an E♭ major cadence is followed by the chord of A major (*quasi* plagal) before resolving on to the final chord, an E♭ major triad.

Strauss still had another engagement before November 1897 was out: on the 28th of the month he conducted in Paris for the first time. He and Pauline arrived there on 24 November; his first impression of the city was of 'a great deal of old junk and a great deal of tradition and just a little bit of the present day'. (To his father, 25 November 1897) On his very first day he called on Alfred Bruneau, Ernest Reyer, Victorin de Joncières, Edouard Colonne and François Servais; and on Théodore Dubois, Camille Chevillard, Charles Lamoureux, Claude Paul Taffanel, Vincent d'Indy and Louis de Fourcaud in the following days; and he received calls at his hotel from Charles-Marie Widor, Bruneau, Servais and the publisher Jacques Durand. Strauss had approached Durand in August 1897 on the possibility of producing d'Indy's opera *Fervaal* in Munich. Nothing came of the plan, perhaps because of Strauss's departure from Munich at the end of the 1897–8 season. D'Indy wrote to Strauss about the matter on 20 August 1897 and he also referred to *Zarathustra*, which he may have heard in Brussels, or perhaps knew only from the score: '*Zarathustra* has made a lofty and enduring impression on me – it is really a masterpiece!' He also asked if there was a version without the organ part.

Strauss was in Paris to conduct the orchestra founded by the music publisher Georges Hartmann and Edouard Colonne. He told his father that it was 'an outstanding orchestra: *Eulenspiegel*, *Tod und Verklärung* will go splendidly'. (25 November 1897) After the concert he wrote:

> A colossal success, for Paris sensational. Pauline made a great impression and had to repeat *Morgen* in the middle of the sequence, in response to tempestuous demand. After the two songs [on this, as on other occasions, there were two groups, one with piano and one with orchestral accompaniment] we were called back three times, ditto *Tod und Verklärung*

> (performance wonderful). The brass hasn't the sonority of ours, but the whole orchestra has a technical perfection, precision and clarity which is quite exceptional. (30 November 1897)

Strauss went to the theatre several times: to the Théâtre Renaissance, where he now at last got to see Sarah Bernhardt, but also to the variétés and vaudeville. He saw *Don Giovanni* at the Opéra Comique; in his diary he wrote the one word 'unbelievable'.

From Paris, Strauss went straight to London, where, at a concert in the Queen's Hall on 7 December, he followed *Eine kleine Nachtmusik*, the *Meistersinger* prelude, the *Tannhäuser* overture, the prelude and 'Liebestod' from *Tristan* and the Good Friday music from *Parsifal* with the English première of *Tod und Verklärung*. During his stay in London, for which he had prepared himself by taking English lessons in the previous March, he visited the painters Sir Edward Burne-Jones and Sir Lawrence Alma Tadema, who were then all the rage.

His friendship with Friedrich Hegar led to a concert in the Tonhalle in Zürich on 25 January 1898, where Pauline, with seven songs, and he himself, with *Wandrers Sturmlied* and *Zarathustra*, had a 'colossal success', as he told Franz Wüllner. In addition to his own works he performed the overture to *Der Freischütz*. Her husband was among those highly satisfied with Pauline's performance in Zürich; writing to her four days later he described himself as 'the proud husband of his sweet singer'. She had gone to Bayreuth, to sing Saint Elisabeth in Liszt's oratorio, under Julius Kneise, on 29 January. It was her favourite part and she had already been acclaimed for her performances of it in Weimar, Munich and Dresden. Strauss was unable to go with her to Bayreuth, and wrote:

> I hope everything goes equally well in Bayreuth, of which I do not have the least doubt, if you are in as good voice as you were in Zürich. After all, the part of Elisabeth is tailor-made to your sweet little shape, and if you supply the necessary incorporeality (not of voice but of 'damned, sinful' flesh), you will certainly receive a sanctifying kiss from Frau Kniese. So, best of luck, my dear comrade in life and art!! (29 January 1898)

Cosima Wagner's praise of this performance has already been mentioned in another context. Strauss himself recorded an anecdote from this stay of Pauline's in Bayreuth:

> Pauline, on the occasion when she sang Liszt's Elisabeth at Bayreuth under Kniese, was invited to Wahnfried several times. At one tea-time she came out with: 'Oh, my Richard is just too bourgeois for words', whereat the worldly-wise Wala Cosima promptly replied: 'Be glad of it, dear girl!'

In January 1898 Strauss received an offer to conduct performances of Wagner in St Petersburg, which he declined. In February he travelled to Spain again. Passing through Paris he and Pauline happened to see Emile Zola drive up to the Palais de Justice, where he was on trial on charges arising from his famous 'J'accuse' letter. 'A lot of policemen, but of the crowds they were there to control not a sign. The Parisians have given up interest in the trial after a week.' (To Franz Strauss, 24 February 1898) It is not inconceivable that the Strausses passed the young Marcel Proust and his friend Reynaldo Hahn, who attended the hearings every day. Strauss conducted three highly successful concerts in Madrid, with the following programmes. On 27 February 1898: Beethoven's Fifth Symphony, four orchestral songs and three piano songs by Strauss, two Wagner preludes (*Lohengrin* and *Meistersinger*), and Strauss's *Don Juan*. On 6 March: by Wagner, the *Tannhäuser* overture (replacing Elisabeth's Prayer, as Pauline was unwell), the *Meistersinger* prelude, the Good Friday music, and the overture to *Der fliegende Holländer*, and by Strauss, *Till Eulenspiegel*. On 13 March: by Beethoven, *Leonore* No. 3 and the *Eroica*, by Wagner, Elisabeth's Prayer and the *Tristan* prelude and 'Liebestod' (with Pauline Strauss as soloist), and by Strauss, *Tod und Verklärung*. Strauss noted of this last concert: 'colossal success'.

The Infanta Isabella invited the Strausses to see over the Royal Palace, where Strauss particularly admired the Tiepolos, and they were received by the Queen and the Infanta. Strauss was awarded the Order of Carlos III and Pauline was given a valuable bracelet. The Prado museum made a particularly strong impression on Strauss; within a few days of their arrival in Madrid he wrote to his parents: 'I've already been to the museum today, and saw some glorious Velazquez, of which we have absolutely no conception at home.' And, as usual, he described the orchestra for his father's benefit: 'Orchestra, like all those in the south, is pretty good, better than in Barcelona. Quartet very good, woodwind decent, brass very middling, horns quite bad.' After rehearsing the *Meistersinger* prelude, 'great rejoicing' had broken out in the orchestra.

Strauss also went to a performance of *Il barbiere di Seviglia* in Madrid, but left no record of what he thought of it. The three concerts in Madrid meant that he could not be present at the first performance of his *Don Quixote*, which was conducted by Franz Wüllner in Cologne on 8 March. However, he conducted the second performance of it himself at a Museum Concert in Frankfurt on 18 March. The baritone Anton von Rooy sang two songs, Op. 33 nos 3 and 4, in the same concert, and the cello soloist in *Don Quixote* was Hugo Becker; Strauss praised both as 'masters of the art of declamation'.

In April Strauss returned to Weimar, where he conducted a concert in aid of the Widows' and Orphans' Fund, with a programme consisting exclusively of his own works: *Don Juan*, four orchestral and three piano songs (with Pauline) and *Tod und Verklärung* (4 April 1898). The next day he played the piano in a performance of *Enoch Arden* for the Wagner-Verein, and then attended a Ladies' Evening at the Künstlerverein. Bronsart had invited him back to Weimar to conduct *Don Juan* as early as August 1896, but it had been impossible to fix a date at that time. As he assured Bronsart, the work was 'in the best of hands with Weingartner'.

The daily round in Munich

The foregoing survey of Strauss's activities as a guest conductor has hurried us forward almost to the end of his second term as a resident conductor at the Bavarian Court Opera. It was on the whole a period which afforded him little joy professionally, but the concerts away from home represented its brighter moments. The failure of *Guntram* at its only performance in Munich was a bitter experience which cast its shadow over his position in the opera house from the first, and the failure to achieve outstanding success in the concert hall in the two crucial engagements as conductor of the Philharmonic Concerts in Berlin and of the Academy Concerts in Munich, while it did not shake the self-confidence that accrued to Strauss from his successes as composer and conductor elsewhere, remained nonetheless a disappointment which it was not easy for him to surmount. The hope that Pauline would be engaged at the Munich Opera was also only partly fulfilled, in the form of a limited guest contract, which was already a cause of bitter dissension between Strauss and Possart in the autumn of 1896. The contract was concluded on 6 March 1896, and made provision for twenty appearances by Pauline at the Court Opera, although previously the figure of forty had been promised. Strauss was not a comfortable colleague and was unable to conceal his mistrust of Possart and Perfall from them, and these facts were a continual underlying cause of new friction, which served only to strengthen the reserve with which his superiors met each new artistic and financial demand. In his hometown Strauss felt constricted and he could breathe more freely elsewhere. Thus he wrote to his parents from Barcelona: 'I live like a reigning prince in a luxury hotel, and, as always when I am away, I am blissfully contented.' (12 November 1897) Only a few days after Strauss had enjoyed a marked success at the Lower Rhineland Festival in Düsseldorf in May 1896, and had returned to Munich to conduct the rehearsals for the epoch-making new production of *Don Giovanni*, Hermann Levi accused him of paying too much attention to the orchestra; that was not the way to conduct for the theatre. (29 May 1896)

Compared with the interest shown in Strauss's works as both composer and conductor in other cities in Germany and abroad, the impression he made on the general public and the press in Munich could not be called spectacular, but there were a few cheering exceptions among residents of Munich who overcame their innate resistance to all things new and emerged from their reserve – or what Strauss was accustomed to think of as their stolidity. He drew especial comfort from his friendships with certain musicians: Max Schillings, Ludwig Thuille, Felix von Rath, Hermann Bischoff, Siegmund von Hausegger and – up to the time of his death – Alexander Ritter, with whose family Strauss continued to maintain close ties. Alexander's niece Marie, in particular, and her and Strauss's friend, later her husband, Friedrich Rösch, were two of his most intimate friends in this period in Munich and later in life. Occasionally Strauss mixed with members of Munich's literary circles as well, but formed no real friendships with any of them.

The poets of Strauss's songs*

The lyric poets of Strauss's own generation, whose work expressed a new outlook and new responses to life and society, had begun to arouse the composer's interest while he was still in Weimar. The poets he set in his Op. 27 songs, his wedding gift to Pauline, were

* See Appendix 3 for a list of the songs composed in Munich between 1895 and 1898, with a note on those written in the following few years in Berlin.

John Henry Mackay (two poems), Karl Henckell and Julius Hart. In the following years in Munich he had some contact with Otto Julius Bierbaum, the founder, and for a time the editor, of *Pan*, a progressive journal of literature and the arts with a certain bibliophile emphasis, which ran from 1894 to 1900. As the editor for two years, furthermore, of the *Moderner Musenalmanach* – in which Hofmannsthal's *Der Tor und der Tod* was first published – Bierbaum had gathered about himself a large circle of contemporary writers and artists. While in Munich Strauss set several of his poems, including *Traum durch die Dämmerung*, which became one of his best-known songs. In May 1895 Bierbaum entertained the hope that Strauss would compose the music for his ballet scenario *Pan im Busch*, but in vain.[34] The ballet was composed by Felix Mottl, in fact, and performed in Karlsruhe. After setting another of Bierbaum's poems in October 1900, Strauss wrote to the poet: 'Yesterday I composed your delightful poem . . . *Freundliche Vision*. I hope it will match the already incredibly popular *Traum d. d. Dämmerung*.' Bierbaum was delighted by this news and in his reply also referred to his ballet: 'I'm very pleased with Mottl's *Pan im Busch*; I've offered to direct it myself.' In this same year Strauss and Bierbaum (who had in the meantime founded another short-lived bibliophile monthly, *Die Insel*) discussed a plan for another ballet, *Der rote Stern*, which got no further off the ground than *Der Kometentanz*, a ballet scenario by Paul Scheerbart, in which Strauss expressed an interest at about the same time, but which, as he told Bierbaum, he found extremely entertaining to read but believed would be absolutely impossible to stage. In spite of that *Der Kometentanz* preoccupied him for some time; he had already recounted the plot to Romain Rolland in the preceding March.[35] Other ballet scenarios considered but not composed were Hugo von Hofmannsthal's *Der Triumph der Zeit* and one by Richard Beer-Hofmann. Finally he drafted his own scenario, *Kythere*, and sketched a considerable amount of music for it, but he did not complete it.[36]

Frank Wedekind, whom Strauss had not met personally at that date, was another writer who approached him with the idea for a ballet in 1896. He proposed 'a great spectacular',

> a ballet in seven tableaux, with the most splendid conceivable visual effects, with plenty of chances for music of every kind, from the sublimely lyrical to the magnificently elemental, and

> with incessantly compelling reasons for dances to unfold, each of which will surpass its predecessor in taste and effectiveness, and all of which will display a great variety of character arising out of the action. (11 February 1896)

By the same post Wedekind sent Strauss two of his scenarios, with the request that Strauss would give him his opinion as to their suitability for the stage, and he also promised to send *Der Erdgeist*, written the previous year. Strauss liked the scenario *Die Flöhe oder der Schmerzenstanz*, and began to sketch some music for it, but once again he abandoned the project. Wedekind's scenario was published first in 1897, in his *Die Fürstin Russalka*, and subsequently in 1914, in volume 6 of his collected works, and in both of these editions the action is arranged in three, not seven, tableaux or acts, sub-divided into three, five and six scenes respectively.

Between *Die Flöhe* and the ballet scenarios which he contemplated in 1900, Strauss was also offered a 'dance-play', *Lucifer*, by Richard Dehmel, several of whose poems he had already set and with whom he carried on a correspondence from December 1895 onwards.[37] In March 1898 Dehmel sent Strauss the first third of the work (which was eventually published in his collected works), saying that he believed he had overcome the 'awkward inartistic elements of the old mystery play and the modern ballet alike':

> The whole thing cries out for music and in my opinion you are the only person who can compose it. Of course you would have to make allowances for dance and march rhythms throughout, or the choreographer will go on strike; but I think that even within those limitations an elevated style is possible in all moods, grave and gay. I have also kept the staging in the forefront of my mind; even the colour and lighting effects are all perfectly feasible on the stage. I have made careful enquiries among the specialists.
>
> The drama is meant to be full-length. There are three parts, each in two acts. It leads so to speak from the ancient earth, through the medieval hell to the modern heaven. It's finished in draft. If the enclosed Part One (Antiquity) tempts you to composition, you can have the other two, which I've still to write out in fair copy, in at most six weeks. If you are not taken with the idea, please be so kind as to send the manuscript back to me as soon as possible.

The letter ended with Dehmel's sincere good wishes and a message of greetings from Detlev von Liliencron, who was his guest at the time. (27 March 1898)

Strauss appears to have expressed interest when he replied, but also some doubts as to whether the piece was really practicable. Dehmel answered:

> I suppose I am correct in assuming, from your letter about *Lucifer*, that you are not altogether uninterested in composing the dance-play. Reservations about the feasibility of performance have always been voiced whenever anything new has been put forward; let me remind you only of Richard Wagner's triumphs of staging. In my opinion *Lucifer* does not present half as many technical problems as, for example, the *Ring*.

But as Strauss was not prepared to make up his mind at once, Dehmel had to accept things.

> So that's all right, I'll wait for the moment, until we are able to thrash out the subject of *Lucifer* face to face. It's precisely the extra psychological depth of ballet that attracted me to write the poem in this form, and all the figurative elements in the first act (the mother and child, Saturn and Thanatos, the angels, Cupid and the little cupids, the fauns, apes, bats etc.) are only there to allow a psychological drama to develop in the second and third acts between Lucifer and Venus on the one hand, and between the pair of them and mankind on the other hand. As in all my poetry, the decorative, visual element is only a means to the end; just like the luxuriant orchestration in your own work. You see, I do have some knowledge of your music, although from the technical point of view I am a musical Boeotian. (22 April 1898)

That so many plans for ballets came to nothing is explained in part by a consideration which Strauss aired to Max Steinitzer, that the composer could not guarantee the exact matching of motive and gesture entirely on his own; satisfactory results could be brought about only through a gradual process of trial and error, but that was directly contrary to his way of making musical decisions instantly. But another factor, which Strauss himself perhaps did not take into account, may have been the absence of dramatic conflict from all these scenarios, with the result that his imagination soon faltered.

Dehmel first sent Strauss one of his poems, *Stiller Gang*, on 20 December 1895. Strauss set it to music on 30 December; it is the only one of his songs with an optional part for another instrument,

Traum durch die *Dämmerung*, Munich, 1895 (publisher's autograph copy)

the viola, in addition to the piano accompaniment. Dehmel was very upset later, when Strauss told him that he had set one of his early poems, *Mein Auge*:

> I am sending you under open cover the new edition of my *Erlösungen. Please, please, throw the first edition on the fire*, so that you are not led again into the temptation to set poems like *Mein Auge*; my innards are churning at the very thought of it. The hazardous distortions of syntax, the far-fetched images and the unimportant things worked to death in them!
>
> Please, will you do me the favour of sending me a copy of your composition as quickly as possible? Then I will try to shape the text a bit more tolerably, in accordance with your music. Since we are both past the age for youthful asininities, I don't suppose I need to excuse myself for wanting to do this; you were probably touched by the sincere emotion of the little thing, but that alone is not enough before the tribunal of beauty. (24 April 1898)

In spite of Strauss's assurances that he had set the poem 'really very beautifully', Dehmel still kept up his plea (in vain):

> And the song – why, it's precisely because I took it for granted that you had set it 'really very beautifully' that I was in such anguish about my text. For that really is *not* very beautiful (as you will see from [the new edition of] *Die Erlösungen*, *Mein Auge* is one of the poems I've dropped) and it's not at all pleasant for me to think that my immature words are now to go out into the world on the wings of your mature art. So if it's at all possible to send me the proofs, I would really be eternally grateful to you (for once the expression is justified), and naturally I shall allow myself to be governed in my alterations entirely by your rhythm, just as I shall not of course make any 'improvements' that will spoil the naive emotional tone of the poem. All I want to do is eliminate, as far as possible, the crass technical ineptitudes (which have a rather different significance in poetry from what they have in music).
>
> (PS. My wife is musically thoroughly well educated.) (26 April 1898)

The first edition of the book of verse which Dehmel published under the title *Die Erlösungen*, where Strauss found *Mein Auge*, had been published in 1891. In the copy of the newly published, much altered, second edition which Dehmel sent him in April 1898, the poet wrote a dedicatory verse:

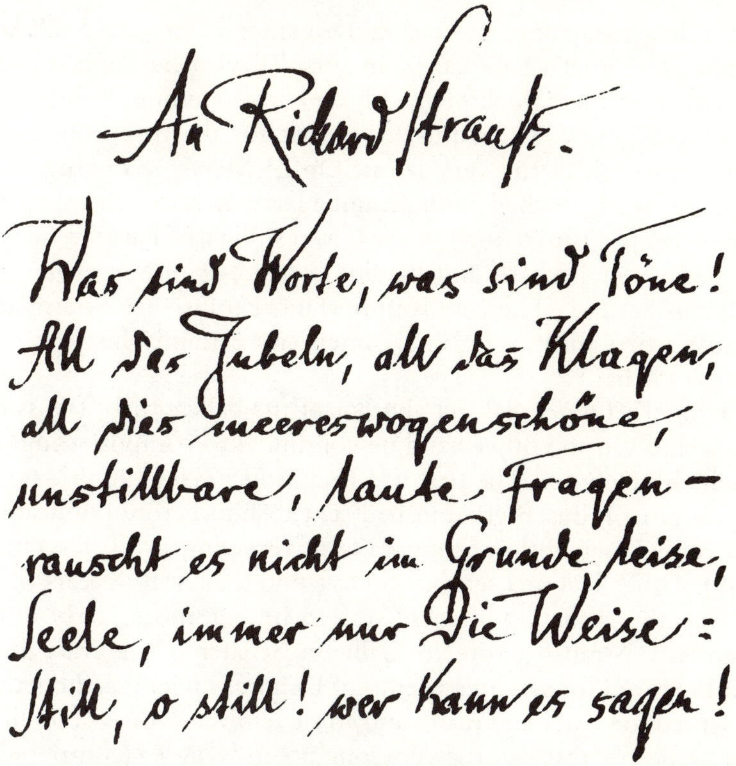
An Richard Strauß.

Was sind Worte, was sind Töne!
All das Jubeln, all das Klagen,
all dies meereswogenschöne,
unstillbare, laute Fragen –
rauscht es nicht im Grunde leise,
Seele, immer nur die Weise:
Still, o still! wer kann es sagen!

(What are words, what is music! / All jubilation, all lamentation, / all this sea-wave-beautiful, / unquenchable, loud questioning – / does it not whisper softly in the depths, / Soul, ever the only wise one – / Hush, o hush! Who can say it!)

Two days later Dehmel sent the poem to the young writer Alfred Mombert, explaining that he had written it for 'a total stranger, the composer Richard Strauss, who has "composed" one of the most maladroit products of my green youth'.

Mein Auge was one of a set of six songs, Op. 37, which Strauss dedicated to his wife. Dehmel, who was liable to keep on tinkering with his verses, made a few changes in 'Was sind Worte . . .', and included it in later editions of *Die Erlösungen.* Two editions of his collected works appeared in his lifetime: in the first, ten-volume edition of 1906–9, the little poem has the title *Das Eine* (The One), in the second, three-volume edition of 1913, it is called *Sprachgeheimnis* (Secret of Language). In the selected edition of poems, letters and documents compiled by Johannes Schmidler and published to celebrate the poet's centenary in 1963, it appears as the second in a group of poems brought together under the title *Dichtersprache* (The Poet's Language). In spite of what he implied in his letter to Mombert, Dehmel had been corresponding with Strauss for several years. They must have met for the first time in the following year, at the very latest. On 23 March 1899 Hugo von Hofmannsthal lunched with Count Harry Kessler, and then the two drove to visit Dehmel in the Berlin suburb of Pankow, where they also met Richard and Pauline Strauss, Paul Scheerbart and Wilhelm Schäfer. The date is important, because it was probably Strauss's first meeting with Dehmel, and certainly his first with Hofmannsthal.

Dehmel's *Lucifer* was yet another of the ballets that Strauss did not write. On the other hand he continued to compose songs on poems by Dehmel. The first had been *Stiller Gang* Op. 31, no. 4, which Otto Julius Bierbaum had sent to him before publication, and Strauss set within a few days of receiving it (30 December 1895). Other Dehmel settings followed in the last five years of the nineteenth century, and there was to be one more, early in the twentieth. Strauss wrote to Wilhelm Schäfer on 10 May 1897, thanking him for sending twenty of Dehmel's poems. Altogether, he set ten for voice and piano and an eleventh for voice, solo violin and orchestra; this was the very long poem *Notturno* (composed 11 June 1899), originally published in *Die Erlösungen*, and referred to by Dehmel, in a letter to Strauss, as a 'Romance "Apparition" '. Dehmel sent Strauss his *Ballade von der schönen wilden Welt* when it was in proof in 1910, adding some indications of how he envisaged its composition, but Strauss did not set it. A copy of the score of *Notturno* was sent to Dehmel by Strauss's publishers Bote & Bock, and Strauss himself sent the two Dehmel settings from his Op. 41, *Wiegenlied* and *Am Ufer*. Dehmel wrote in acknowledgment:

> *Your* missive has just arrived, too. And now here I stand like Buridan's famous ass, but I shall solve the problem somehow. Isn't Van Rooy to sing the *Notturno* in Mannheim? If so, please tell me more, so that I can go to hear it. I'm used to head-shaking, from myself. Extra thanks for *Am Ufer*. It's one of my favourites.

To one correspondent, Dehmel said he thought that Strauss's setting of his poem *Befreit* was 'a little too soft for the poem' (to Elise Naegele, 20 March 1902); he repeated this opinion in very similar words in public, in the periodical *Die Musik* (vol. 3, pp. 1461f.). To his first wife Paula he wrote: 'Of Strauss's compositions on texts of mine, I like best *Lied an meinen Sohn* and *Notturno* (this last with a large orchestra). I find he simply hasn't got the measure of *Der Arbeitsmann*; too convulsive.' (26 February 1902) More than a year earlier he had said to another correspondent: 'The others (except Ansorge)[38] are eclectics to one degree or another, and the only one except Ansorge who isn't [i.e. Strauss] strikes me as basically a disguised naturalist with romantic impulses. That last is no commendation in my view; romanticism is *behind* us.' (To Willy Seibert, 11 December 1900)

The eleven Dehmel settings were spread out over six years, from the end of 1895 to 1902, in the period of Strauss's greatest productivity in song-writing. During those years he turned from the older poets, principally those of the immediately previous generation, whom he had chosen to set hitherto (Hermann von Gilm, Adolf von Schack, Felix Dahn), and towards his own contemporaries: John Henry Mackay, Detlev von Liliencron, Karl Henckell, Dehmel, Otto Julius Bierbaum, Emanuel von Bodmann and Carl Busse. The sense of a new age dawning that inspired the Jugendstil movement, the pervasive spirit of change and optimism for the future, could not help but touch Strauss and the combative streak in his nature for a time – however transient the contact proved to be. The hostility and opposition which Dehmel, in particular, had to fight against, were the very things to strengthen Strauss's interest in the poet. The fact that he was drawn on a few occasions to poems reflecting social problems – Dehmel's *Der Arbeitsmann* (The Worker), Henckell's *Lied des Steinklopfers* (Song of the Stone-knapper) – can be more readily explained in terms of a spirit of opposition to prevailing received opinion than of profound sympathy with Socialism. Similarly, his setting of Dehmel's agitated *Lied an meinen Sohn* must be seen in association with an inclination to rebel against established conventions. Otherwise, Strauss was more attracted by Dehmel's more contemplative, purely lyrical poems; it is no accident that he composed two groups of them during summer holidays at the house of his parents-in-law in Marquartstein, in the countryside of Upper Bavaria. Five of the songs are settings of depictions of peaceful atmospheres, which Strauss found in the published volumes of Dehmel's verse: *Stiller Gang* (Op. 31, no. 4), *Mein Auge* (Op. 37, no. 4), *Leises Lied* (Op.

39, no. 1), *Am Ufer* (Op. 41, no. 3) and *Waldseligkeit* (Op. 49, no. 1) all reflect this lyrical strain, and the two lullabies (Op. 41, no. 1 and Op. 49, no. 3) can be added to them. But since contrast is one of the dominant characteristics of Strauss's oeuvre, it can cause no surprise to find these tender poems from one border area of Dehmel's output confronted by a piece depicting sterner realities (*Der Arbeitsmann*, Op. 39, no. 3) and another highly emotional, dramatic piece, the 'rearing and plunging' *Lied an meinen Sohn* (Op. 39, no. 5). In spite of the degree of softness to which Dehmel objected in the setting of *Befreit* (Op. 39, no. 4) with its broad, sweeping flow and saturated harmonies, this once much-performed song is one of the most important of Strauss's lyrical products, inasmuch as it anticipates some of the lyrical elements to be found in the operas. Strauss himself had a very high opinion of the song; he wrote in his diary on 1 June 1898: 'Composed song *Befreit* by Dehmel very beautifully.' He wrote out the fair copy of the song the next day, 2 June. For performance by Pauline he transposed it from the original key of E major to 'our key', D major. Sending her a copy of the transposed version during a temporary separation, he wrote the following letter on the manuscript:

> So, my dear Bauxerl, now it's 10 o'clock in the evening. I took a bath at 7.30, then consumed a small pike; now I intend to read a little Treitschke and then crawl into bed around 10.30. It's nice when things are different! Good night, my dear, dear Bauxerl. Baby has long been sleeping the sleep of the – little egoist! God, how much longer am I to be without the two of you! I don't miss Frieda so much! Are you singing a lot? And properly – for a long time and with *full* voice? Write me a long letter soon!! (20 September 1899)

The little-known *Notturno* for baritone and orchestra, with solo violin (Op. 44, no. 1), does not include the first seven or the last one of Dehmel's verses. The painful sweetness of the melodic writing and harmonies that look forward to *Salome* blend with the ghostly, uncanny timbres of the orchestral sound to create what is perhaps the most successful marriage of Strauss's music with Dehmel's poetic vision. Dehmel's poetry did not have for Strauss the importance that it did for Arnold Schoenberg, the first of whose many settings of Dehmel dates from 1897, and who wrote to the poet on the occasion of his fiftieth birthday in 1913 that one of his poems played some part or other at almost every turning-point of his own development. But we nevertheless owe some of the best of Strauss's songs to the attraction Dehmel's poetry exercised on him for several years. Some years later Strauss wrote orchestral versions of four of the ten that originally had a piano accompaniment: *Wiegenlied* in 1916, *Waldseligkeit* in 1918 and *Mein Auge* and *Befreit* in 1933. The personal relationship between the poet and the composer can be traced up to the end of 1910. Dehmel wrote to his second wife Isi from Danzig, where he had seen Hans Memling's *Last Judgment*:

> At my recital last night I kept feeling as if I was in the middle of that picture, with the crowd of the Resurrected all round me. It was so full that they had even put chairs on the platform; incidentally Richard Strauss was in the audience, standing at the side against a pillar, and so I got him a seat. (18 October 1910)

Two months later he sent Strauss his *Ballade von der schönen wilden Welt* and in the accompanying letter asked for two seats for the première of *Rosenkavalier*, due to take place in January 1911, for himself and his 'signora'. The fact that Dehmel and Strauss were joint editors of the weekly *Morgen*, launched by the publishers Marquart & Co in Berlin in 1907 (Strauss wrote an article for the first number, on 17 June, entitled 'Is there a progressive party in Music?'),[39] will not have given rise to more than occasional contacts between them; there were four other editors, including Hofmannsthal.

Strauss's closest association with the Jugendstil movement – which it is far easier to define in the visual, and especially the applied, arts than in literature or music[40] – is to be found in his settings of poems by Otto Julius Bierbaum. Bierbaum was a very prolific writer, and Strauss in fact composed only six of his poems between 1895 and the end of 1900, although he was to mark quite a large number of the poems in his copy of the collection *Irrgarten der Liebe* (1901) as possible candidates for setting. He made the personal acquaintance of Bierbaum by October 1895 at the latest, for he wrote to Max Schillings on 31 October: 'To Herr und Frau Maxi the news that the wordsmith Bierbaum drinks tea with us tomorrow, Friday at 4 (3.30 Seestrasse time). Herr and Frau Guntram beseech your punctual arrival.'

Three of the Bierbaum settings – *Traum durch die Dämmerung* (4 May 1895, Op. 29, no. 1), *Nachtgang* (7 June 1895, Op. 29, no. 3) and *Freundliche Vision* (5 October 1900, Op. 48, no. 1) – are in a mood similar to that of the one group of Dehmel songs, striking 'notes of peace, transfigured happiness, smiling rapture', as Hans Bethge said. The others – *Schlagende Herzen* (7 June 1895, Op. 29, no. 2), *Wir beide wollen springen* (7 June 1896, o. Op. 90) and Pauline's favourite, *Jung Hexenlied* (31 May 1898, Op. 39, no. 2) – belong at the very heart of Jugendstil song. It was a sphere which Strauss was to leave before very long. He chose poems to set that suited his mood of the moment; when his mood changed, so his choice of poems changed, and he would turn once more, perhaps, to *Des Knaben Wunderhorn* or to older poets like Rückert, for whom he retained a lifelong affection (as in the Op. 36 settings). Bierbaum made repeated attempts in later years to persuade Strauss to set his poems, Singspiel texts and ballets, but the composer resisted them all, except for the one occasion in October 1900, when *Freundliche Vision* took his fancy. In October 1899 Bierbaum made a quite extraordinary approach to him:

> I am sending you two poems of my own, which may tempt you to compose. The circumstances are exceptional. That infamous scoundrel Fried,[41] who used the hospitality which he received at Engklar during my absence so to bamboozle my wife with his outrageous lies and shabby behaviour that she has run off with him, set these songs from the manuscript (without my knowledge) and it is no longer possible for me to publish them *without music*, since if I did the law would give him the right to have them printed with his music. If you like them, I am prepared to give you the sole right to publish them, and then the songs could be printed with the note: The text is printed after the manuscript, every reproduction, including reproduction with music, is expressly forbidden.

Not surprisingly, Strauss did not take up the offer.

It was not long after taking up residence in Munich again in 1894 that Strauss became acquainted with the editors of the 'illustrated weekly for art and life' founded in Munich by the liberal, progressive publisher Georg Hirth. The title of this magazine, *Jugend* (Youth), gave its name to the movement that extended its reach to all areas of life and art. It was still in the planning stage when Strauss was invited to contribute. *Jugend* was intended to 'discuss and illustrate everything of interest, everything that moves minds and spirits', everything that was 'beautiful, good, characterful, stylish and – genuinely artistic'; 'no area of public interest shall be excluded, but neither shall any one area occupy the foreground'. The new weekly would give space to high, higher and the highest art, interior decoration, ornament, fashion, sport, politics, music and literature, taking a grave view one day and a humorous or satirical one the next, according to the nature of the subject and the circumstances.

An enterprise which shared the eclecticism of the nineteenth century but at the same time took such an optimistic line in contrast to the mood of decline and fall that beset the fin-de-siècle years, and raised the banner of vitality, joie de vivre and confidence, could not help but strike a chord of sympathy in Strauss. He should have contributed to the first number of *Jugend*, which was originally due to appear in the autumn of 1895, but delays arose which made it seem likely that the first issue would not be published until Christmas, and so it was decided to make it expressly a 'Christmas' number. The editor Fritz von Ostini wrote to Strauss:

> Lack of space makes it impossible for us to print two songs in the first issue of *Jugend*. It happens that the other song that we are thinking of is a Christmas song and therefore we ought to print it first, as we're dressing the number up as a kind of Christmas number. So please be kind enough to forgive us, if your song is held over until the second number, for which we have also kept back some very beautiful artistic contributions. (25 November 1895)

The Christmas song to which Ostini referred was August Bungert's *Frau Maria an der Wiege*, a setting of an old anonymous poem. Around the turn of the century Bungert earned vociferous but short-lived fame with his tetralogy *Homerische Welt*, a Greek counterpart to Wagner's *Ring* based on the *Odyssey*. His cradle-song was printed in the first number of *Jugend*, a double issue which eventually appeared on 1 January 1896. Strauss's reply to Ostini's letter was as follows:

> It is contrary to our agreement, if a song expressly requested and delivered for publication in the first number of *Jugend* is now to appear in the second number. If you are so set on making it a *Christmas* number, however, since the publication of the first issue has been so delayed, then I agree to the proposed postponement, but expressly remark that *if printing a composition*

> *by Richard Strauss* – after recent events – could be harmful to the success of the first or second or whatever issue of *Jugend*, or might cause any embarrassment of any kind to you, honoured Herr von Ostini – I will, if you so wish, gladly release you from the undertaking to print my song in *Jugend*.[42]

By 'recent events' Strauss meant the flop of *Guntram* in Munich a week or so before. The song he wrote for *Jugend*, *Wenn . . .* to words by Carl Busse, was finally published in the fourth issue, on 25 January 1896. (The death of Paul Verlaine on 8 January occasioned the dedication of almost an entire issue of *Jugend* to his memory, which probably explains the further postponement.) The song, composed 15 June 1895, begins in D♭ major but ends in D major; at the point where the key changes, seven bars before the end, Strauss caused a jocular footnote to be inserted: 'The composer advises singers who intend to perform this work in public before the end of the nineteenth century to sing it transposed down by one note [that is, in D♭] from this point onwards, so that the piece concludes in the key in which it began!' He recalled later: 'The story of my joke in *Jugend* – the song that ended a semitone higher than it began – was for ever after retailed by [Perfall] in high dudgeon.'[43]

When *Wenn . . .* was published later in 1896 as one of the Op. 31 set, it and the two other Busse songs in the set bore the dedication 'To my dear sister Johanna, 8 July 1895'. That was the date of Johanna's wedding to Otto Rauchenberger, at the time a lieutenant in the King's Own Infantry Regiment in Munich, who eventually rose to the rank of lieutenant-general and was ennobled; he died in 1943. The couple had a son, Wolfgang, who was born 29 June 1901 and died 28 April 1974, leaving two sons, Dietrich and Bernhard. The footnote was also included in this edition; only in later printings, in the twentieth century, was it omitted, logically enough. The editors of *Jugend* appear to have attached great value to Strauss's contributions; another of his songs was published in issue no. 42, on 17 October 1896, immediately following a poem by Rainer Maria Rilke (only one of the many leading younger poets of the age whose work appeared in *Jugend* during its first year). This time the song was *Wir beide wollen springen*, one of the Bierbaum settings, which Strauss had sketched on 4 January and finished on 7 June; it was reprinted at the end of 1896 in *Der bunte Vogel von 1897*, a so-called 'calendar-book' compiled by Bierbaum, illustrated with nearly two hundred drawings by Felix Valloton and E. R. Weiss, which is now a collectors' piece and regarded as a superb example of Jugendstil book production. One of the poems in it is Bierbaum's *Lied der jungen Hexe*, which Strauss was to set as *Jung Hexenlied*. The setting of *Wir beide wollen springen* appears in *Der bunte Vogel* in facsimile, within an allegorical border drawn by the Munich painter, illustrator and designer Julius Diez, then twenty-six years old. Strauss never included the song in any of his published collections, and appears to have forgotten all about it.[44]

In spite of his relationship with Bierbaum Strauss decided not to set either his Singspiel *Lobetanz* or his five-act drama *Gugeline*. The published edition of the text of the latter, illustrated with vignettes and other decorations by Thomas Theodor Heine and E. R. Weiss, is an example of Jugendstil book production at its purest. These verse dramas were too trifling for Strauss's taste. Bierbaum had already offered *Lobetanz* to Hugo Wolf in 1895. Strauss passed it on to Max Schillings and, when he too declined it, to Ludwig Thuille. After overcoming 'certain reservations that you too will already have had yourself', Thuille composed *Lobetanz*, which turned out to be his greatest success. It was first performed in Karlsruhe on 6 February 1898, and was given only four days later in Berlin, where Strauss revived it on 25 September 1913. Further productions were staged before the outbreak of the First World War, in Zürich, Vienna, Strassburg, Sopot, New York, Philadelphia and Riga. Thuille also composed *Gugeline*, but the work was quietly forgotten after its première in Bremen on 4 March 1901. Strauss did his best to get it put on at the Court Opera in Berlin, but without success, so he included a performance of the third act in a concert of the Berlin Tonkünstler-Orchester on 21 January 1902, with Emmy Destinn and Kurt Sommer in the leading roles. Strauss's relations with Bierbaum were severed in 1903, when the latter published a sarcastic review in the *Allgemeine Zeitung* of *Taillefer*, Strauss's setting of a ballad by Ludwig Uhland for mixed chorus, soloists and orchestra, Op. 52, which was first heard in Munich in the Kaim-Saal on 13 November 1903 under Bernhard Stavenhagen. Strauss asked his parents:

> Have you read Bierbaum's shabby attack on *Taillefer*? What does he know about setting Uhland? Can I help it if the piece is performed with too small a choir, which was inaudible, in too small a room, where it made a gigantic noise? It expressly states

in the score that the piece is intended only for large halls and a big choir, could none of my 'friends' in Munich take the trouble to explain this to that amateur Bierbaum?

Or — wouldn't they? Well, well!!

Life is very interesting, if one views it from on high.

(26 November 1903)

Another of the poets to whom Strauss was drawn during this period in Munich and his first years in Berlin was Detlev von Liliencron, four of whose poems he set. The first was *Sehnsucht* Op. 32, no. 2, composed on 24 January 1896, then *Glückes genug*, of which he wrote a first and a second version on 2 and 3 February 1898, and the final version on 8 February, and *Ich liebe dich*, sketched on 3 February and finished on 7 February (Op. 37, nos 1 and 2), and finally *Bruder Liederlich*, written in Charlottenburg on 16 August 1899 (Op. 41, no. 4). More than two years later, Liliencron was to write to a friend: 'Richard Strauss has not composed *Bruder Liederlich*, at least it doesn't seem so to me, but according to others he has composed it (divinely!).' (To Else Kössler, 19 October 1901)[45] Strauss also composed two more songs to poems by John Henry Mackay: *Verführung*, one of the orchestral songs of Op. 33, of which he wrote the short score on 6 June 1896 and finished the full score on 5 July, and *In der Campagna* (24 August 1899, Op. 41, no. 2). Other poets whose work attracted him briefly included Gustav Falke (*Meinem Kinde* Op. 37, no. 3), Emanuel von Bodmann (*Gesang der Apollopriesterin* for soprano and orchestra, 7 July to the end of September 1896, Op. 33, no. 2; *Herr Lenz*, 9 June 1896, Op. 37, no. 5), Julius Hart and Anton Lindner, who in 1902 suggested Salome to Strauss as a subject for an opera and actually started to draft a libretto for it.

The poetry of the Socialist Karl Henckell meant more to Strauss than any of the above. Between 1894 and 1901 he set nine of his poems (the first was *Ruhe, meine Seele*, one of the Op. 27 songs given to Pauline on their wedding day), almost all of them purely lyrical except for *Das Lied des Steinklopfers* (24 September 1901), one of the poems of social protest that represent an important part of Henckell's output. It was also in 1901 that Henckell proposed a series of 'music and poetry evenings' to Strauss, but although Strauss was at first interested in the idea the plan for a tour came to nothing, as the number of engagements was too small. Henckell attached great importance to the association with Strauss. It began in December 1895, when the composer sent him a copy of *Ruhe, meine Seele.* Henckell wrote to thank him:

> I first got to know your work about six months ago, I was moved to hear these verses of my tempestuous early youth (I wrote them when I was nineteen or twenty, if I am not mistaken) interpreted in music that shivers so lightly, with hardly a wave breaking – I wanted to write to you there and then, but what are words of thanks?
>
> But now that you yourself send me the song with words of such warmth, I must extend my hand to you. Will you permit me? Especially in the passage 'Stiehlt sich lichter Sonnenschein' and 'wie die Brandung, wenn sie schwillt' with its emotional content, it seems to me that you have transcribed the verse, or absorbed it, or whatever the correct expression is, quite magnificently.
>
> May I take the liberty of having my publisher send you some of my volumes? I do not in the least seek to commit you by doing so – perhaps you will leaf through one or other of them at some time, and if then a stanza should once again strike your ear and stimulate you to musical creativity, I shall regard it as an outstanding piece of luck. (Zürich, 12 December 1895)

After Strauss had moved to Berlin, Henckell sent him another, 'definitive' edition of his poetry, with illustrations by Fidus (Hugo Höppener), published under his own imprint in Zürich in 1898 (some of his earlier work had been banned in Germany for its political inflammatoriness), with a warmly worded inscription. In a later volume (*Mein Lied*, 1905), in addition to ornaments by Fidus (the device on the binding, end-papers, *ex libris*, frontispiece, title page, borders for the initial letters), each of the poems that had been set by Strauss was illustrated by a facsimile of the opening of the setting, in the composer's autograph, and the song *Kling!* . . . (Op. 48, no. 3) was in addition printed (engraved, not in facsimile) in full. Strauss did not merely leaf through the volumes Henckell sent him, he put crosses in the margin against a large number of the poems, and in some cases noted down keys in the margin beside individual verses or lines, even though he did not subsequently set them. Many other books of poetry in his possession were treated in the same way: the second edition of Carl Busse's verse, and volumes of Conrad Ferdinand Meyer, Mackay, Dehmel, Hermann Hesse and others. After *Ruhe, meine Seele* in 1894, Strauss returned to Henckell to set *Ich trage meine Minne, Liebeshymnus* ('Heil jenem Tag') and *O süsser Mai*, all in the first three months of 1896 (Op. 32, nos 1, 3 and 4); in September and October of 1900 he wrote four more, *Ich schwebe, Kling! . . ., Winterweihe* and *Winterliebe* (Op. 48, nos 2–5); a year later, on 24 September 1901, he set *Das Lied des Steinklopfers* ('Ich bin kein Minister'; Op. 49, no. 4); and he went back to Henckell one last time to write *Die Blindenklage* (no. 2 in the Op. 56 set, 1903–6), one of the most powerful of all of his songs. No other poet among his contemporaries occupied Strauss for such a long time – twelve years altogether.

Strauss enjoyed reading the early poems of Christian Morgenstern, but did not think them suitable for composing, although he does appear to have contemplated composing one called *Sonnenaufgang*, to judge by a delighted letter he received from the then twenty-four-year-old Morgenstern (12 June 1895). In fact, Strauss did not then set it, but four years later he set Morgenstern's *Leise Lieder* (Op. 41, no. 5; 4 April 1899).

Writing the songs

The years from 1894 to about 1902 were the most prolific period in Strauss's song-writing, if one discounts the very large number he wrote in boyhood, between 1870 and 1883. In this period, in his thirties, he wrote sixty-three solo songs (Opp. 27, 29, 31, 32, 36, 37, 39, 41, 43, 46–9), compared with thirty-six in the previous eight or nine years (Opp. 10, 15, 17, 19, 21, 22, 26). As well as all the songs for solo voice with piano accompaniment, he also wrote six songs with orchestral accompaniment in 1896–7 and 1899 (Opp. 33 and 44), which were followed by two more in 1902 and 1906 (Op. 51, nos 1 and 2). Although the composition of songs never ceased to be a welcome diversion for him, thereafter, in the forty-seven years from 1902 to his death he wrote no more than slightly over fifty more songs with piano accompaniment, and in the great majority of these he did not set poems by contemporaries. The exceptions were *Die Blindenklage*, the twelve songs in *Der Krämerspiegel* (1918), the two songs to poems by Josef Weinheber (o. Op. 129 and 130; 1942) and his very last song, *Malven*, on a text by the Swiss poet Betty Knobel, written in the last year of his life, while three of the Four Last Songs, with orchestral accompaniment, written just a year before his death, are settings of poems by Hermann Hesse, a somewhat younger contemporary. Even in the most prolific period

Strauss sometimes chose older poets (Klopstock, Goethe, Schiller, Rückert, Bürger, Uhland, Heine, as well as folk songs from Alsace and out of *Des Knaben Wunderhorn*), but texts by poets of his own generation were in the majority during these years.

The four songs of Op. 27, written for Pauline, were followed by others in which a positive stimulus was provided by his married happiness and the birth of their son. The eleven songs of Op. 32 and Op. 37 are again dedicated to Pauline, the inscription in the latter collection making specific mention of Franz's birthday, 12 April. The prospect and the experience of fatherhood produced *Meinem Kinde* (Op. 37, no. 3), written on 7–8 February 1897, a few weeks before the birth, and the two Dehmel settings, *Lied an meinen Sohn* and *Wiegenlied*, as well as *Muttertändelei* (on a poem by Gottfried August Bürger). Pauline Strauss was particularly successful as a performer of her husband's songs, both in recitals where he accompanied her and in the context of orchestral concerts, where she would sing not only two or three of the songs with orchestral accompaniment but also some with piano accompaniment. There were so many songs to choose from that the couple were able to compile different programmes for every city they visited.

On 7 January 1897 Strauss orchestrated Schubert's *Ganymed* for a centenary concert in Munich (31 January). The arrangement has unfortunately been lost. The soloist was Pauline who sang four songs by Liszt and *Allmacht* as well as *Ganymed*, while the programme also included Schubert's B minor Symphony, conducted by Strauss. Her husband also orchestrated two of Beethoven's songs for Pauline in January 1898: *Ich liebe dich* (12 January, not in AV) and *Wonne der Wehmut* (14 January, AV 189).

Pauline did not confine herself to lieder-singing in these years. As we have seen, one of her favourite roles remained Liszt's Saint Elisabeth. In spite of the six-month guest contract she concluded with the Munich Opera, to run from 1 March 1896, she did not appear there very often, as she had a run of illness. However, she was heard as Ada in Wagner's *Die Feen*, as St Elisabeth, as Marzelline in *Fidelio*, as Wellgunde in *Das Rheingold* and as Elisabeth in *Tannhäuser*. It was only after her son's birth that she retired from the operatic stage, but she still continued to sing in concerts. Strauss himself wrote on 7 May 1910:

> After her marriage . . . she devoted herself more and more to concert work and earned . . . the reputation of the model

> [altered from 'most significant'] interpreter of Strauss's songs. Her performance is distinguished in equal measure by the most subtle penetration of the poetic content, impeccable taste in shaping the melody, refinement and grace.[46]

When she sang in Vienna for the first time in January 1900, at a concert where *Ein Heldenleben* had its first performance in the Austrian capital, Eduard Hanslick, after savaging the tone poem, wrote:

> The singing of Frau Strauss-de Ahna, Richard's graceful wife, shone out like a ray of bright, warm sunlight over this battle-field . . . Frau de Ahna's excellently trained, rich, sweet soprano voice did our hearts good! Richard Strauss proved an incomparable accompanist, and his wife's performance earned enthusiastic applause. We may surely call her his better and more beautiful half.

And in the 'little memorial' that Strauss dedicated to her in Lugano on 22 May 1947 (the 124th anniversary of Wagner's birth), he praised, not for the first time, her

> thoroughly poetic interpretation, which . . . earned her great applause in the performance of my songs, especially in America [in 1904]. A critic there wrote: 'Frau Strauss performed her husband's songs so vitally that one could believe *she* had composed them herself, while *he* sat somewhat over-bored at the piano.' Her excellent breathing technique stood her in good stead, particularly, in Pamina's aria, Agathe's A♭ major cavatina and in Elisabeth's Prayer (at Bayreuth), which I have never since heard sung with such poetry as by Pauline. Similarly *Traum durch die Dämmerung, Morgen, Freundliche Vision*, with a completely even tone and poetic interpretation. She had to sing *Jung Hexenlied da capo*, as well as many others which were having their first American performances . . . On my concert tours [in Europe] the songs I had orchestrated for her (*Cäcilie, Rosenband, Liebeshymnus, Morgen, Wiegenlied, Freundliche Vision*) [were always sung] *da capo*. What a shame that she turned too early to the wonderful career of an excellent, model housewife and mother![47]

Strauss often spoke of the genesis of his songs. For example, in his reply to the questionnaire from Friedrich von Hausegger in the summer of 1895 which has been quoted already, he wrote:

> I will have had no desire to compose for months; suddenly one evening I will pick up a volume of poetry, leaf through it carelessly; then a poem will jolt me, and a musical idea for it will come to me, often before I've finished reading it properly: I sit down; the whole song is finished in ten minutes . . . If I should happen, at a time when the vessel is full to the brim, so to speak, on a poem whose content is even only roughly appropriate, the opus is there in a jiffy. If the poem – all too often, alas – does not present itself, then the urge to produce something is still satisfied, and any poem that strikes me as in the least suitable gets set to music – but then it's slow work, a lot of artifice goes into it, the melody flows dourly, I have to summon up all my technical skill in order to produce something which will stand up to my own strict self-criticism. And all because at the decisive moment I didn't have the two right flints to strike together, because the musical idea which – God knows why – had prepared itself inwardly did not find the completely appropriate poetic vessel, and now must be remodelled, reinterpreted, in order to take shape at all. Why don't I write my own poem, in that case? That would be the best thing to do. But the composer and the poet do not correspond in me at a moment's notice, inasmuch as the composer in me is far superior or far more practised in the techniques of self-expression, compared to the poet.

His experiences with *Guntram* were fresh in his mind when he wrote that. The two different manners of composition – the spontaneous and the slow – account for the unevenness in his output of songs, but the former manner predominated, as even the entries in his diary show: the songs were nearly always composed in a single day, though they were occasionally interrupted – probably by some external factor in most cases – and the fair copy was then not executed until a day or two later.

In reply to an enquiry from Julius Bahle, Strauss described how he came to write one of his most famous songs, *Traum durch die Dämmerung*, on 4 May 1895:

> I was going to go out for a walk with my wife one evening, and already had my hat in my hand. As my wife wasn't ready, I went back into my room again briefly, and Bierbaum's poem just happened to be lying open on the desk; I read it through and as I did so I heard, keeping pace with its walking rhythm, the melody of the voice part, which yielded itself out of the words.

> I wrote the song down, then asked my wife if she was ready, and when she said she was, I answered, 'So am I, let's go'.[48]

Max Marschalk told a similar story of the composition of another song (Op. 69, no. 1) over twenty years later. He went to call on Strauss one day in June 1918, in Bad Ischl, and Strauss said to him:

> Just now, while I was waiting for you, I picked up [Achim von] Arnim and read the little poem *Der Stern*, and while I was reading the musical inspiration yielded itself to me. I wrote the song down at once and if you like I will play it to you.[49]

The spontaneity of the composition of so many of his songs explains Strauss's cavalier treatment of the verses in some cases: the frequent minor changes in the wording are obviously due to mistakes of memory.[50]

When accompanying his own songs at the piano Strauss often treated them very freely, as many – including the present author – have observed. In his memoirs the composer himself wrote that he had 'never attained to a clean technique' in playing the piano, but on the other hand he had 'accompanied songs well in a rather free fashion – never entirely faithful to the notes'.[51] The most circumstantial description comes from the Viennese music historian Alfred Orel, who once turned the pages for Strauss at a recital he gave with Elisabeth Schumann in Vienna in the early 1920s; Orel had the opportunity to observe his procedure at the very closest quarters:

> When I opened the music at the first song, Strauss whispered to me, 'You mustn't follow the music, because I play it quite differently.' And so I was able to enjoy from direct observation an accompanist's art such as I have . . . never again experienced. Such freedom and at the same time the highest degree of accuracy in suiting the music to the singer, and then again such guiding of her delivery, such support, in addition to knowing to a hair's breadth where she would need assistance, whether in giving her time to breathe, or in helping her to avoid straining her own breath support, in short there has probably never been so perfect a oneness between singer and accompanist.
>
> The printed notes were often admittedly no more than aids to the composer's memory, a vocal score as it were, from which the singer could rehearse with her repetiteur. Without becoming expressly 'orchestral', he went far beyond the printed

> accompaniment and exploited all the possibilities of the piano in a quite inimitable fashion. Thus I can remember that in *Heimliche Aufforderung* the rising run for piano began far lower, and therefore was played much more quickly, than it is notated, probably with the purpose of allowing the contrast with the peaceful quavers that follow to be that much more marked. Countless times Strauss doubled the bass line and enriched the chords. Yet he could also, in *Morgen* for instance, follow the written notes punctiliously. In *Cäcilie*, certainly, it was as though one was hearing the surge of a full orchestra.
>
> The most interesting thing for me that evening, however, was not so much the master's accompanying as his behaviour between the individual songs. While he left the singer to acknowledge the applause between the numbers on her own, and while I was placing the music for the next song in front of him, he fingered the keys apparently at random. Great was my amazement when I realized that it was always passages from his operas with which he made the transition to the new song, and specifically passages which were musically closely related to the song in question, but revealed that close relationship only now in the way he played them. Thus before *Du meines Herzens Krönelein* he played very softly – apparently entirely for himself – the famous closing duet from *Der Rosenkavalier.* Sometimes I could not identify the operatic passage at the moment when he was playing it, but it was an irrefutable demonstration of the great unity which encompasses Richard Strauss's total oeuvre and of which the composer himself was also deeply aware, down into the smallest details.[52]

What Orel notes in the last paragraph naturally applies only to the later years, but for the rest his manner of accompanying and of playing transitional passages developed essentially during the years he spent giving recitals with his wife.

Song-writing was often a means of respite and recreation for Strauss in the middle of composing or scoring his major works, but it sometimes served him as the opportunity for experimentation and preparation for larger works. He particularly liked to try out harmonic innovations in songs, but the smaller form also gave him the chance to tackle new ways in vocal declamation. He used the word 'experiments' of songs as early as the Op. 22 set, *Mädchenblumen* (1886–8), and it could be applied to many of the songs of his term in Munich in the 1890s; for example, to *Leises Lied*, which recurrently uses the whole-tone scale, or to the playful ending of *Für fünfzehn Pfennige*, where, through the use of the minor sixth E♭/D♯, the two arpeggiated triads moving in contrary motion (C minor and B major) present a quasi-bitonal expansion of the basic G major: a joke which had serious consequences in *Salome*:

Other songs employ chromatically altered cadences, yet others free, functionless sequences of ninths: the list could be extended. Even in the lyrical depictions of mood there are frequently turns which anticipate the psychologically motivated, displaced cadences of *Don Quixote*, while harmonic innovations in the Dehmel setting *Notturno* anticipate *Salome*.

The orchestral songs of this period, like the two Op. 51 songs for bass soloist and orchestra written later in Berlin, occupy a special place in Strauss's oeuvre, with the deeply serious mood common to them and to the two sixteen-part songs for mixed, unaccompanied choir (Op. 34) which date from the spring of 1897. The first of these was started on 2 March and finished on 16 March, the second was started on 18 March and finished on 25 April, but not written out in fair copy until 7 May. *Der Abend*, on a text by Schiller, was first performed on 2 May 1898 by the Conservatory Choir in Cologne under Franz Wüllner, but *Hymne* (Rückert) was not performed until 14 June 1903, when Hermann Suter conducted it at the congress of the Allgemeiner Deutscher Musikverein, held that year in Basel. Eugen Spitzweg paid Strauss a fee of 2000 marks for the two choruses in May 1897, which was a busy month for Strauss, as he also had to compose and rehearse a work commissioned for the opening of the Munich Secession exhibition, a setting for female chorus, brass ensemble and large orchestra of a distich by Schiller, *Licht, du ewiglich eines*, o. Op. 91. Strauss started this piece on 10 May, finished it on 14 May and conducted its first performance on 1 June.

Meanwhile an important event had taken place in his private life.

In March 1897 the doctor attending Pauline predicted that she would in fact give birth to twins, a false diagnosis probably explained by the great weight of the boy who was born on 12 April. Strauss received the news of the birth by telegram when he was in Stuttgart, touring *Enoch Arden* with Possart. Six exclamation marks follow the announcement in his diary for the day, 'Hallelujah' is written in red ink diagonally across the page, and he also pasted in the telegram itself – 'A giant boy just arrived safely. Pauline well' – and wrote underneath 'God be praised and thanked! My dear Paula in the gravest danger; but all has turned out well!' Before he was able to go home to his wife and son in Munich, he had to 'celebrate' the detested melodrama in Würzburg and Nuremberg, collecting a fee of 300 marks for each performance as 'maternity grant'. At last on 15 April he saw his son for the first time. Over the following days and weeks Strauss frequently recorded the baby's weight, and the letter he wrote to the 'parents and grandparents' on Good Friday is full of such important details:

> After the severe trial of four days' absence, I returned home yesterday earlier than expected, I've seen my splendid giant boy for the first time and embraced my beloved wife. Hanna was kind enough to meet me at the station and told me gently, so as to allay my earliest fears, of the terrible danger in which Pauline and the child were for a time, and how everything turned out happily in the end. I am happier than I can say, the baby is magnificent, more than eight [metric] pounds, a gigantic cranium measuring 39 cm. round, my big grey eyes, a head covered with brown hair, 37 cm. round the chest, nose halfway between Pschorr and de Ahna, Pauline's pretty cupid's bow mouth, huge paws, and he sleeps so peacefully and healthily. When he's awake, he looks up unwaveringly with big, serene eyes at everyone who talks to him.

The letter goes on to describe some of the complications of the birth, which was indeed a dangerous one for both mother and child. In the emergency the child had been baptized 'Richard' but, as his father went on to tell his parents, 'I shall overrule the emergency baptism and will call him *Franz* Alexander, as he was born on the anniversary of Ritter's death!' (16 April 1897)

Cosima Wagner telegraphed her congratulations: 'Hail to the Expression family, beg not Zarathustra as teacher, offer self as governess.' (17 April 1897) Strauss hastened to 'inform the greatest and most inspired of teachers that the delighted parents, with their hearts full of gratitude, accept the most kind offer of governess-ship for "Franz Alexander", in all the pertinent knowledge of the nineteenth and all preceding centuries.' (In the same letter he told her he would be visiting her while she was staying in Wiesbaden. He had written to her in the previous month, asking her to recommend him to the intendant of the Karlsruhe theatre as Mottl's successor, although Possart was ready to keep him on in Munich as well as Mottl, if Mottl took Levi's place. However, as three years before, Mottl did not want to make the move.)

On 19 June Strauss escorted his wife and son to Marquartstein, where they remained until 23 September, the very day on which the momentous invitation arrived from Edouard Colonne to conduct in Paris for the first time. During the time he spent alone in Munich he paid a visit to the Deutsches Theater, in a party that included Arnold Böcklin and the tenor Hans Giessen, to see Hermann Bahr's dialect play *Das Tschapperl*, 'an extremely interesting, excellent play, admirably done'.

Don Quixote

Several months passed between the completion of *Also sprach Zarathustra* in August 1896 and the commencement of new symphonic works. The time was filled not only with concert tours and Strauss's activities in the Munich Opera – notably the performances of Mozart and Wagner in the September, followed by more in February and March 1897, and the preparation and first performance of Ludwig Thuille's *Theuerdank* – but also with the *Enoch Arden* tours with Possart. His diary for 16 April 1897 contains the entry: 'Symphonic poem *Held und Welt* [Hero and World] begins to take shape; as satyr play to accompany it – *Don Quichote*.' The wording makes it clear that this was not the date of the first conception of the two works, but that the ideas had not previously taken any firm 'shape'. The 'first idea' for *Don Quixote* had come to Strauss in Florence on 10 October 1896 (as previously noted), but now the association between the two pieces – *Ein Heldenleben* (as *Held und Welt* was eventually to be known) and *Don Quichote* (as Strauss regularly spelt the title in the early stages) – was explicitly stated. Strauss always insisted on the complementary relationship between them, and tried to persuade other conductors to perform them in the same concert. In a note he wrote in 1941, he suggests the pairing of the two to make a complete evening's programme.[53] When the first performance of *Ein Heldenleben* was under discussion, Strauss wrote to the director of the Frankfurt Museum Concerts, Gustav Kogel:

> *Don Quixote* and *Heldenleben* are conceived so much as immediate pendants that, in particular, *Don Q.* is only fully and entirely comprehensible at the side of *Heldenleben*. Since this is also the very first (decisive) performance of *Heldenleben*, I feel it is very important. Of course it would then be an extremely progressive programme . . . But for the very first performance of *Heldenleben* I think I may be allowed a little licence.

His wish remained unfulfilled, however, until October 1900, when both works were performed at the same concert in Brussels.

He began both simultaneously, although at the time in question he was also busy with other work: the Rückert *Hymne* for sixteen-part unaccompanied choir, and *Licht, du ewiglich eines* for the opening of the Munich Secession show. In the middle of April he had begun rehearsals for Max Schillings's opera *Ingwelde*, which had its première on 6 May; on 7 May he found time to write out the fair copy of *Hymne*; meanwhile he was also conducting rehearsals for the summer festival performances of *Die Entführung aus dem Serail* and travelling to Augsburg and Cologne to perform *Enoch Arden*. On 27 May he wrote in his diary: 'Working busily on *Don Quichote*'; on both 7 and 8 June he was 'busy on *Don Quichote* and *Held und Welt*'. On 28 June he 'invented [a] D major melody in 6/8'. It is not certain which melody it was that he thought important enough to record in this way. It is possible, though – in view of his usual fixing of associations with particular keys – not very likely, that it was the closing melody of *Ein Heldenleben* (section 6, 'The Hero's retirement from the world and the fulfilment of his life'), which is in E♭ major. In his sketchbook Strauss used the expression 'solemn resignation' (the Marschallin's resignation at the end of Act I of *Der Rosenkavalier* is also in E♭ major). During his 'alas, far too short' summer holiday, begun in Sankt Wolfgang in the Salzkammergut and continued at Marquartstein, he was 'busy on *Don Quichote* and the Heroic Symphony'. (3 July 1897) He had already started the instrumentation of *Don Quixote* when he wrote to Pauline, who was still at Marquartstein with little Franz, that the piece was now getting very 'fiddly' and would wring many a sigh from him, 'although not as many as it will eventually from the critics, when they have to listen to it', a prognosis which proved correct. In the same letter he assured his wife that he was conscientiously carrying out her instructions and had interviewed several nannies ('at 20 marks and 4½ litres of beer a day'). (20 August 1897)

He finished the ending of *Don Quixote* on 22 July, but some of the variations still remained to be written at that point. Shuttling to and fro between Munich and Marquartstein, he began the scoring at noon on 12 August, and recorded its progress meticulously in his diary: he had done ten pages by 18 August, twenty-six by 3 September, thirty-nine by 15 September, fifty by 30 September, sixty by 22 October and sixty-eight by 18 December. The score was finished at 11.42 a.m. on 29 December 1897.

Already in the sketchbooks, besides motives and their working-out, Strauss noted precise descriptions of the content of individual episodes in the work; for instance, after Sancho Panza has emitted a string of adages: 'Don Q. continues to maintain his convincing calm, Sancho reluctant, wants to leave him, then Don Q. unfolds his vision of peace to him, when S. again expresses his doubts after this, Don Q. becomes enraged, whereupon S. holds his tongue and goes to bed; then cello solo, vigil, lament.' There are also notes on the disposition of the series of variations: 'Barcarole Var. 8 etc., after this nothing but fast and short D minor variations.' Or: 'Don Q. cured from madness. Death and conclusion. Seized by trembling, death approaches, last, *swift* battle, ends on pedal point [as?] memory.' In an unpublished note dating from the 1930s or later, Strauss describes *Don Quixote* as 'the battle of *one* theme against a nullity'.

The work, in which he 'took variation form *ad absurdum* and showered tragicomic persiflage upon it',[54] was given the somewhat ceremonious title *Don Quixote, introduzione, tema con variazioni, finale. Fantastic variations on a theme of knightly character, for large orchestra*, Op. 35. In the score the only themes identified by names are those of the Don and of Sancho Panza, but later the composer provided his own synopsis and advised Wüllner to circulate the 'guide' by Arthur Hahn[55] among the audience for the world première performance in Cologne. His synopsis is as follows:

> Introduction: From much reading of romances of chivalry, Don Quixote loses his wits and decides to become a knight errant himself.

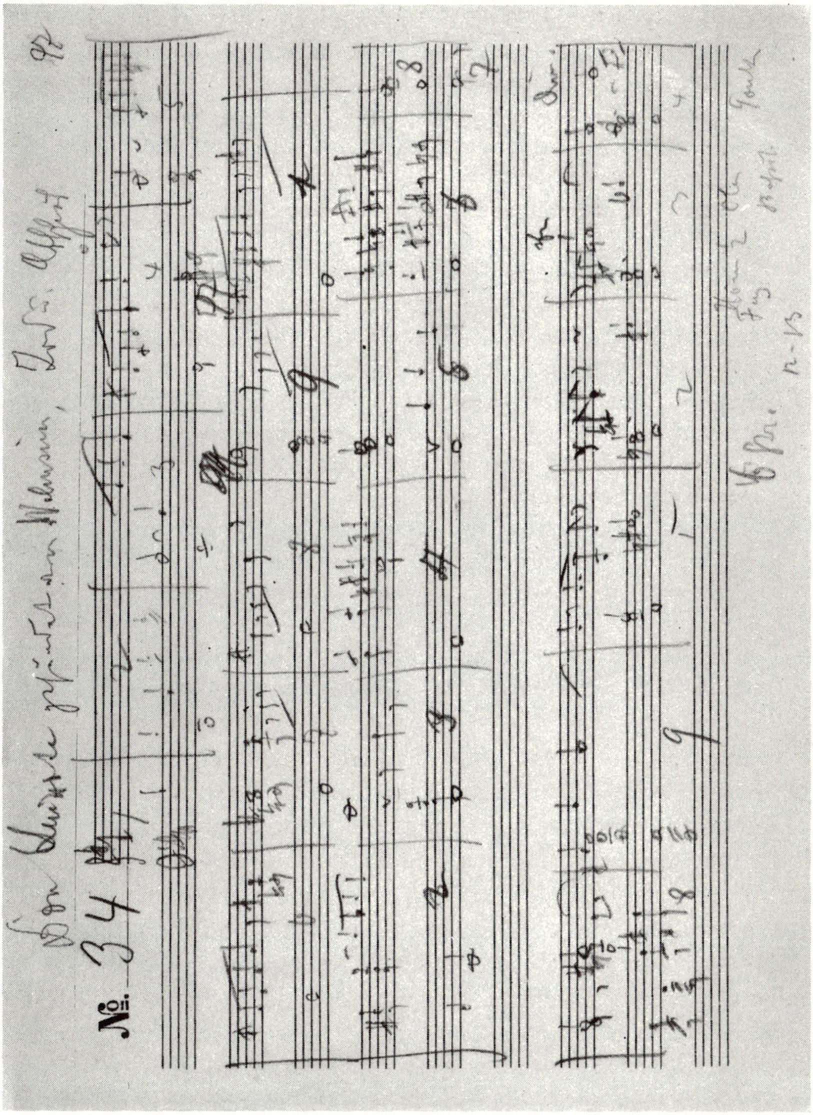

From the sketches for *Don Quixote*, start of the finale

Theme: Don Quixote, the knight of the sorrowful countenance (solo cello), Sancho Panza (bass clarinet, tenor tuba and solo viola).
Variation 1: The strange pair ride out wearing the favours of the fair Dulcinea of Toboso; adventure with the windmills.
Variation 2: Victory over the army of the great emperor Alifanfaron (battle against the herd of sheep).
Variation 3: Conversation between knight and squire: Sancho's demands, questions and adages, the knight's precepts, pacifications and promises.
Variation 4: Unfortunate adventure with a procession of penitents.
Variation 5: Don Quixote's vigil over his weapons. Pours out his heart to the distant Dulcinea.
Variation 6: Meeting with a peasant girl, who Sancho tells his master is Dulcinea under an enchanter's spell.
Variation 7: Ride through the air.
Variation 8: Ill-starred voyage on the enchanted boat (barcarole).
Variation 9: Battle against the supposed enchanters, two little priests on their mules.
Variation 10: Single combat with the knight of the shining moon. Don Quixote struck to the ground, bids farewell to his arms and returns home, with the intention of becoming a shepherd.
Finale: Having recovered his senses, he decides to spend his remaining days in meditation. Don Quixote's death.

Compared with Strauss's normal working speed, he took a relatively long time to orchestrate *Don Quixote.* He fulfilled a number of important conducting engagements abroad that autumn (Barcelona, Brussels, Paris, London), and he composed some more songs during the same period: *Für fünfzehn Pfennige* was sketched on 20 August and the fair copy written out on 2 September, an ode by Klopstock, *Das Rosenband*, was set on 10 September to celebrate his third wedding anniversary, and he started to orchestrate it on the same day that he wrote the fair copy, 22 September, having orchestrated *Morgen!* for Pauline two days before. He finished orchestrating *Liebeshymnus* on 27 September. He also met Serge Diaghilev on 14 August, in the Bayerischer Hof hotel in Munich. Thus the two had already been long acquainted at the time of Strauss's collaboration with Hugo von Hofmannsthal and Count Harry Kessler on *Die Josephslegende* for the Ballets russes.

His situation in Munich suddenly grew fraught again when he received a tempting offer from Pollini in Hamburg. He presented Possart and Perfall with an 'ultimatum' at the end of August, delivering it in writing to the latter:

> Your Excellency. Having informed Herr Hoftheaterintendant von Possart this noon that Herr Pollini in Hamburg has made me the offer of an engagement from 1 September 1898 at a salary of 15,000 marks, with three months' summer leave etc. etc., I do myself the honour, at the express desire of Herr von Possart on the one hand and, on the other, in accordance with my belief that in all matters of business the written course is the only proper one so that no kind of misunderstanding may be allowed to arise, of proposing to Your Excellency with the utmost deference, supposing that it should be Your Excellency's gratifying wish that I remain in Munich as Hofkapellmeister, the following conditions on which it would be my privilege and my pleasure to continue my artistic work in Munich as Your Excellency's executive:
>
> 1. Permanent appointment as First Hofkapellmeister from 1 November 1897, with an annual salary of 12,000 marks and the right to the customary pension, in the calculation of which I would request that the years I have already spent in the royal service should also be included;
>
> 2. Assurance of six weeks' contractual leave during the winter months.
>
> I take the liberty of requesting Your Excellency most respectfully to be kind enough to inform me, by or at the latest on 5 September, whether Your Excellency will consider me on the above conditions. Should a definitive and binding declaration on Your Excellency's part, which would already have to have the most gracious approval of HRH the Prince Regent, if Your Excellency is considering me, not have been made by next Sunday 5 September, I would come to a conclusive arrangement with Herr Pollini.
>
> With the expression of the most profound respect
> Your Excellency's most obedient and devoted,
> Richard Strauss
> Royal Hofcapellmeister (31 August 1897)[56]

He wrote to his wife in Marquartstein about the matter, saying that Possart had already refused flatly to engage her, and that he

> warns against Pollini, but I have as good as made up my mind. Pollini offers 15,000 marks and half from all the concerts for which he gives me leave! If Pollini will engage you, I shall go to him, if he won't have you any more than Possart will, then I'll stay in Munich. Oh, this eternal theatrical chicanery! How it disgusts me! (1 September 1897)

However, Pauline wrote to him on the same day, perhaps before she had received his letter:

> With reference to the question of your job, I implore you, after mature reflection and self-questioning, to give *no* consideration at all to my engagement, but if *you* will be happier and better off in Hamburg go there, and if *you* will be happier in Munich with 12,000 marks, then we'll stay in Munich, dearest!
>
> If you want to go to Hamburg because of the way they try to hold you back in Munich – darling – then go to Hamburg, *without* trying to push through my engagement immediately; I shall go with you, and if I find that the climate, the circumstances, *your* domestic comfort make it *sufficiently* possible for me to resume my artistic career, then, when we have both *settled down* there, it will be time enough to think of me. But *at the moment* please leave me out of your conditions altogether, and choose only what is the *best* in every respect for you, for us and for Baby!!!
>
> Enough of that, and my most heartfelt blessings and good wishes on you in the matter . . . You and Baby are all my happiness; may it long be mine and let us take care to earn a lot of money, so that you can soon live *your own life* . . . For now a good, good night, my Richard! I hug you with the utmost love! Paula (1 September 1897)

Richard's diary records the receipt of this 'enchanting' letter from his 'glorious' wife. He answered:

> Your letter was so enchanting and glorious that I don't know how to thank you for it. It gave me real support in the worries that I have to keep on weighing up in my mind in the present crisis, so as to work out what is the wisest and most beneficial thing for the well-being and contentment of us both. You are a dear, good, wonderful wife and the man who calls you his has a prop and a comforter for life, and has no need to fear whatever the future may hold. In the meantime the business here has made a big turnabout in the main crisis: I had an important conversation with Possart yesterday, who claims that Perfall has

as good as changed his mind and is now ready to give me a permanent appointment at 12,000 marks. If this should really come to pass, then I think the most sensible thing, even without your engagement, which Possart won't agree to, will be to accept the safe post here with the pension, which will allow us (1000 marks a month) to spend the rest of our days without a care and devote ourselves to our little boy – *the more so* because the question of engaging you has not yet been raised in the negotiations with Pollini and there will be the constant danger that Pollini will always use your engagement, your work etc., as a means of keeping me under his thumb. I know, my dear sweet wife, what a great and splendid sacrifice you offered me yesterday in your letter, when you renounced your engagement so heroically, and I am sad that I can't push it through here (I'm curious as to Pollini's attitude) – but in the last resort my own *permanent appointment*, at 12,000 marks, is something that will *take care* of us for the rest of our lives, without binding us, and then if something really prestigious for us both turns up, *I can always leave here*, whereas the Hamburg contract ties me down for three years. So I have been wavering this way and that, with a thick head and a heavy heart, and have known some relief only since receiving your adorable letter, which will always be a treasured memory, as the decision to stay here, the fear of moving and the appalling thought that after the three years are up I shall have to begin this whole dreadful engagement business again with Pollini, while, if the matter is pushed through here at last this time, I shall be at peace for ever after and no worries about our daily bread will ever be able to affect me again – the scales of my decision since yesterday have tilted heavily on the side of Munich again.

One remarkable thing is that the entire Munich press has come round to my side, even the jealous Merz, with whom I had a long and illuminating conversation yesterday.

This evening I shall allow myself a little diversion, as I have been indoors all day working, and take Hanna to the Deutsches Theater (Dumas's *Kean*) . . .

Once again a thousand thanks for your glorious letter, don't be sad any more and always think happily of your husband who hugs you with all his heart,
R. (3 September 1897)

Ten days later he was able to tell her that although Perfall and others were against him, Possart was for him. He was going to stay in Munich on the following terms: his permanent appointment would date from 1 November 1898, but it was already assured by the Prince Regent; he was to have an immediate rise in salary to 10,800 marks and four weeks' extra leave; this was not as good as Pollini's offer, but he would be better off in the long run with his Munich pension.

His new Munich contract came into force on 1 October 1897, and he took the twenty-eight days' leave it allowed him there and then, beginning on 4 October. It was just as well that he decided not to go to Hamburg, for Pollini, who engaged Karl Gille instead of him, died on 27 November 1897. The Munich truce did not last long, however, and a year later Strauss left the city in some vexation. But more of that in due course.

By and large, in spite of the tensions in his relationship with his superiors and some short-lived difficulties with his parents and his sister, who did not always get on very well with Pauline, the years 1896 and 1897 were by no means as unremittingly dismal as Strauss sometimes felt they were. He was able to look back at the end of both years with some satisfaction, as his diary reveals. At the beginning of 1896 he had noted 'the new year ushered in with the observation that the human race is an even greater crew of swine than one had supposed even at the worst', but on 31 December he wrote: 'Began the scoring of Schiller's hymn [Op. 33, no. 3] – this good year ended cheerfully for us in the company of Marie Ritter, Schillings, Rösch and Bischoff.' And on 31 December 1897 (two days after finishing the score of *Don Quixote*) he wrote 'Pauline and I spent the evening with Marie Ritter and Rösch. A really good year. May we continue thus!' This temporary sense of satisfaction was due not so much to his activities and experiences in Munich as to his success as a composer and a conductor in Germany and abroad (not to mention the improvement this brought in his financial position – on 1 February 1897, after having received 2000 marks from Bote & Bock for the Four Orchestral Songs Op. 33, which had just been published, Strauss was able to record that the sum brought his cash holdings to a round figure of 24,000 marks).

His father had retired from the Munich Academy (formerly the Royal School of Music) and from directing the Wilde Gung'l in the autumn of 1896. Strauss's portrait was painted several times during these four years in Munich, in January 1897 by Helene Raff, the daughter of Joachim Raff, and in the very next month by one of the best-known Jugendstil painters, Fritz Erler, then twenty-nine years old, who was a leading figure in the Scholle group around the turn of the century. Erler, who sometimes accompanied Strauss on his visits to the theatre, also did the title-page lithograph for Max Schillings's opera *Ingwelde*.

The compositions of the Munich period were, with a few exceptions, offered to Strauss's old friend Eugen Spitzweg, who risked a considerable outlay, in particular, on the engraving of *Guntram*, as Strauss was quick to acknowledge: 'I've been thinking – in view of the noble sacrifice you have made for *Guntram* (for which you will have your reward, let us hope), this time, as an exception, I will give you *Eulenspiegel* and the three songs that I have ready [Op. 29] for 1500 marks.' (9 June 1895) Admittedly, after the great success of *Till Eulenspiegel* he began to expect larger fees; he asked for 3000 marks for *Zarathustra*, even before he had finished it. (9 June 1896) The Op. 31 songs were taken by Adolph Fürstner, who was to become Strauss's principal publisher during his years in Berlin. Fürstner had first approached Strauss in 1890 with an offer to publish some of his songs, and in a brief reply (18 October 1890), which also contained an order for two copies of the vocal score of *Rienzi*, Strauss offered him *Mädchenblumen* (Op. 22, composed in 1888) for 800 marks, a sum which Fürstner paid without haggling. *Enoch Arden* Op. 38 and the Five Songs Op. 39, which date from the last two years in Munich, were published by Robert Forberg. It became harder for Spitzweg to keep pace with the fees that Strauss now felt he had the right to ask; nonetheless he paid 1900 marks for the ten songs published as Opp. 36 and 37, 2000 marks apiece for the two unaccompanied choral works, and 5000 marks for *Don Quixote*, the last major work by Strauss to appear under the Joseph Aibl imprint. Strauss had been contented with much smaller fees for the earlier symphonic poems and had always included his autographs in the bargain. These manuscripts passed into the ownership of Universal Edition when that firm absorbed Joseph Aibl in 1904, and were later sold to collectors (such as Louis Koch who bought the autograph of *Till Eulenspiegel* in 1923) for very considerable sums of money at a time of recession. When Spitzweg enquired about the five songs which make up Op. 39, Strauss replied:

> Dear friend, I'm afraid I've already given the five songs to Forberg; 1. Because with the last ten songs, which have only just

> appeared in print, you moaned about the large number, because you lose no opportunity of complaining about the high costs of translation etc. 2. As I knew you were ill, I wanted to spare you new offers which would make your head ache again, but at the same time I didn't want to leave the things lying about because I need quite a lot of money to pay for my move to Berlin, and Forberg will pay exceptionally well for the songs and for *Enoch Arden*, which has been ready for two years without your having asked for it. More when we can meet and talk about it! (23 July 1898)

Strauss had prepared 'the last ten songs' (Opp. 36 and 37) for the printer more than three months earlier, on 11 April. The separate printings of single songs dating from the Munich period appeared in wrappers, the design of which was often in very questionable taste.

Strauss devoted what was to be his last New Year's Day in Munich to reading the score of Thuille's *Lobetanz*, which gave him 'a few very enjoyable hours', and led him to write his old friend a letter of congratulations ending 'I predict a very great success, and let me wish you once more my most sincere and devoted wishes for a truly profitable *Lobetanz* year. With warmest greetings from our house to your house, ever your old Richard.'

Although he wrote in his diary that the new year had 'begun very well indeed with my dear Bauxerl' (1 January 1898), before the week was out he had occasion to write a letter of complaint to the editor of the *Allgemeine Musikzeitung*, Otto Lessmann, about the periodical's coverage of musical events in Munich. According to Strauss, the critic Rudolf Louis

> places performances given by our Court Orchestra at the Academy Concerts on approximately the same level as the amateurish strummings of any pair of misses of high or low degree from the remotest provincial nook – in other words, manifests himself to be so immeasurably unjust that a rebuttal is called for.

While his own official and unofficial associations with the orchestra prevented him from taking up the cudgels in print himself, Friedrich Rösch 'who is certainly no friend or supporter of the views of Herr Erdmannsdörfer [as conductor of the Academy Concerts]' was ready to do so. (4 January 1898)[57] Lessmann did not take up the proposal.

In this same month of January 1898 Strauss wrote one song, *Anbetung* to words by Rückert (Op. 36, no. 4), and scored the two songs by Beethoven for Pauline, *Ich liebe dich* and *Wonne der Wehmut*. At the end of the month he began a series of guest engagements with a concert in Zürich in aid of the Hilfskasse, the self-help charitable fund of the Zürich Tonhalle Orchestra. The Strausses' host in Zürich was Professor Bamberger, whose wife Lily (née Sertorius) had known Strauss since they were both teenagers in Munich, where they had often played chamber music together. After her first husband's death Lily married the industrialist Hermann Reiff (who was portrayed by Thomas Mann in *Doktor Faustus*). Her friendship with the Strausses continued, and whenever he visited Zürich, right into the 1930s, the composer always stayed with Frau Lily Reiff, at whose house a circle of artists used to gather every week. In 1935, in a survey of musical life in Zürich since the opening of the Tonhalle in 1895, Ernst Isler recalled the first of what were to be Strauss's many personal appearances in Zürich; the account draws on Isler's own review of the concert published at the time in the *Neue Zürcher Zeitung*, and it illustrates the kind of impression Strauss made in those days, in Zürich and elsewhere, on audiences who came to see and hear the rising star in the musical firmament. The concert began

> with a performance of *Wandrers Sturmlied* by the Zürich Mixed Chorus, its centrepiece was the first performance in Zürich of the tone poem *Also sprach Zarathustra*, and some songs with piano accompaniment were placed between the larger works and the disarming finale. Even in those days enthusiasm ran high, and differences of opinion ran even higher, over the revolutionary music of *Zarathustra*. Strauss conducted in those days with the same clear beat, given by the right hand, which still distinguishes his conducting today and made it easy for the orchestra to follow him; he did more with the left hand then than he does now, and in order to achieve a pianissimo he frequently bent so deep at the knees that his head barely rose above the top of the desk. *Wandrers Sturmlied*, which is influenced to no small extent by Brahms, went down well, the songs were received with delight, in particular the impromptu modulations with which the composer, accompanying them at the piano, linked them. But *Zarathustra* aroused as much shaking of heads among the older generations of concert-goers (the development section of the Dance Song was dubbed by fairly general consent

> a poultry-yard), as it did enthusiasm among us youngsters, armed with our scores and our music guides. (Oh! those music guides of yore!) A fascinating rendering of the *Freischütz* overture at the end served to reunite the audience in enthusiasm for the young beaming god of music. How Hegar had rehearsed *Zarathustra*, taking the strings through their parts desk by desk, punishing himself to get the beat right in the 'Science' fugue, was the talk of the town.[58]

Don Quixote had its first performance on 8 March in Cologne under Franz Wüllner. Strauss did not hear it until he conducted it himself on 18 March at a Museum Concert in Frankfurt. He wrote to his mother: 'I really enjoyed *Don Qu.* in Frankfurt; it's very original, utterly new in its colouring and a really jolly snook cocked at all the muttonheads who, however, didn't recognize as much and even laughed at it.' (30 March 1898) The passage with the baaing sheep shocked some hearers, and aroused noisy protest, not only in Frankfurt. The Leipzig weekly *Musikalisches Wochenblatt* said after the première in Cologne: 'The work . . . aroused the greatest interest in all musicians, without always gaining their sympathy at the same time' (issue no. 12, 1898), and in the following issue, after the second performance in Frankfurt: 'R. Strauss's new symphonic poem *Don Quixote* aroused the most intense interest in Frankfurt . . . and was warmly applauded, even though there was some dissent.' This is perhaps also the place to quote Romain Rolland's opinion, written while he was attending the Düsseldorf festival in May 1899:

> Humour and highly coloured psychology of *Don Quixote* – an inferior work, incidentally . . .
>
> There is remarkable intelligence in *Don Quixote*. The two figures of Don Quixote and Sancho are excellent, the one with his air of stiffness, languid, swash-buckling, the aged Spaniard, with something of the troubadour in him, always changing his ideas and always coming back to the bee in his bonnet; the other with his breeziness and his bantering proverbs. These are really sketches, scenes in miniature, rather than real descriptions. (Diary, 20 May 1899)

Rolland was also there when Strauss conducted *Don Quixote* in Paris in the following year, with the Lamoureux Orchestra.

> Indignation from one section of the public. The good old French

> public which, the less musical it is, the more it is a stickler for musical good taste, does not tolerate a joke, thinks it is being laughed at, that people are disrespectful to it. The baaing of the sheep infuriates it. At the end, applause and cat-calls: 'Bravo!' and 'It's disgraceful!' Strauss, placid and drowsy, seems indifferent to it all. (Diary, 11 March 1900)[59]

On 7 April 1898 Strauss received an invitation to conduct thirty operatic performances in London in May and June, for a fee of 15,000 marks. The exact reasons why nothing came of the proposal are unknown, but his commitments in Munich alone would have been enough to make it out of the question. He set off for Berlin on the same day, for a performance of *Enoch Arden* in the Bechstein-Saal. His future was decided while he was there. In the middle of March Carl Halir, whom he had known well in Weimar and who was now leader of the Court Orchestra in Berlin as well as a member of the Joachim Quartet, had told him that Weingartner, who was to take over the Kaim Orchestra in Munich, was going to surrender all his work in Berlin except the Philharmonic Concerts. Strauss asked Halir to take soundings on his behalf and on 18 March Halir passed on the information that Pierson, the Artistic Director of the Royal Theatres in Berlin, was not in a position to do anything unless Strauss himself made the first move and let it be known that he wished to leave Munich, in which case a contract would be offered him. By the time of Strauss's visit to Berlin three weeks later things were so well advanced that on 9 April he was able to agree the terms of his contract with the Berlin Court Opera; it was to run for ten years, from 1 November 1898 to 1 November 1908, Strauss was to draw a salary of 18,000 marks, and he was guaranteed a pension of 4200 marks, plus a pension of 2000 marks for his widow. At the same time that he was negotiating with the Berlin Opera he had received an offer from the agent Hermann Wolff to take over Anton Seidl's position at the Metropolitan Opera House in New York, which would have brought him an annual income of 42,000 marks, but he sensibly declined it in favour of the greater security of the Berlin post. He wrote to Pauline from Berlin: 'If they will meet my conditions here, Berlin is the more practical proposition for me at the moment, so that I can bruit my name abroad a bit longer in Europe and not *lose my place in the queue* too early, which would be the risk in going to America.' (8 April 1898) To his mother he wrote:

> I shall still be able to graze in American pastures ten years from now, while at the moment it's more important to make myself still better known in Europe. In the Berlin press, operatic reviewing is the province of my best friends, Dr Bie, Klatte, [Carl] Krebs, Welti etc. Pierson has taken enormous pains not to let me escape, since, if Berlin had not come to anything, I would have gone to America after all. Ah, the joy of being able at last to throw the big stick back at the feet of that crew in Munich, who have treated me really shamefully . . . Pauline and I are looking forward to Berlin very much, although we shall have the sorrow of not being so close to you, dear parents, any more – but I had to steal a march on Possart, so as not to be driven away by the advent of Mottl. I'm going now, before Mottl has finally made up his mind; I'll have twice the wage in Berlin and an extra month's holiday in the summer, which is especially important . . . I shall breathe more easily, away from the atmospheric pressure in Munich. (10 April 1898)

Strauss had never ceased to be haunted by the worry that Mottl would come to Munich, and that this would restrict his own sphere of action. After he had given notice, Munich once again tried to get Mottl, but on 12 May it was confirmed that Karlsruhe would not release Mottl, as Strauss noted in his diary, not without a touch of Schadenfreude.

Before leaving Berlin, Strauss called on the famous pianist (and sometime wife of Eugen d'Albert) Teresa Carreño in her luxurious eight-room apartment on the Kurfürstendamm. On 15 April, three days after little Franz's first birthday (he was now 81 cm. tall and weighed approximately 13 kilos), having conducted a rehearsal for *Die Zauberflöte* and entertained Frau Wagner at dinner in his home, he sent the contract back to Berlin with his signature on it. Telegrams of congratulation from Heinrich Welti and Friedrich Rösch had arrived even before the news was made public the next day. Strauss noted in his diary: 'The city of Munich calm and dignified as always on great "tragic occasions". The *Neueste Nachrichten* prints the news without a word of *comment*!' After receiving the confirmatory telegram from Berlin and writing a letter of thanks to the General Intendant of the Royal Prussian Theatres, Count Bolko von Hochberg, on 17 April, he gave notice to the intendancy of the Court Theatre in Munich that he would not be taking up the permanent appointment as Hofkapellmeister from the following November after all.[60] By 21 April a new offer arrived from Berlin,

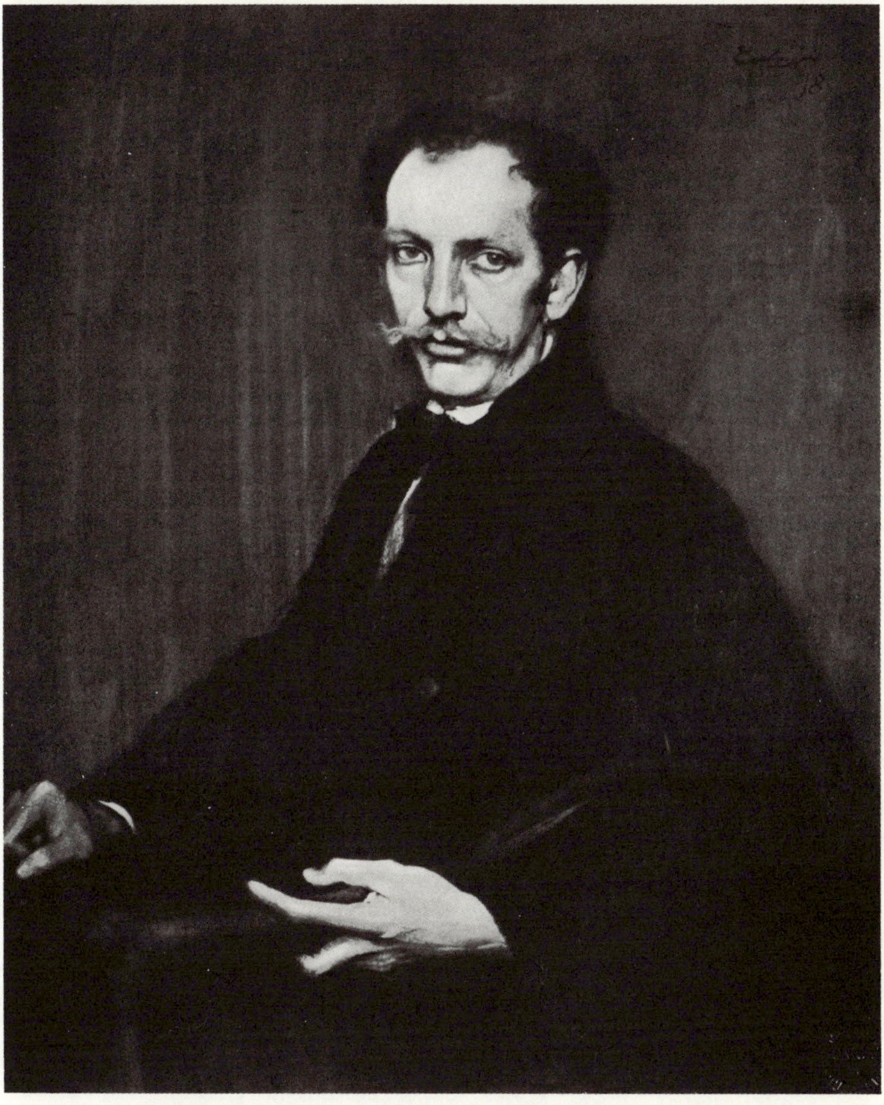

Richard Strauss, portrait by Fritz Erler, Munich, 1898

this time again from Hermann Wolff, of a teaching post at the Stern Conservatory, but this Strauss refused.

The joy the Strausses felt at being at last able to shake the dust of Munich from their feet was clouded by the severe illness of Richard's mother, who had to be readmitted to the institution where she had been a patient several times before, and where she

Pauline Strauss with her son Franz, aged one

now remained from 20 April until 6 June. In July Possart, who was still, as previously, bound to him by *Enoch Arden*, consented to his leaving Munich on 30 September, instead of 31 October, but in fact Strauss conducted three performances in the Munich Opera in October, two of *Fidelio* and one of *Tannhäuser*, and after he had started work in Berlin he allowed himself to be persuaded to do another performance of *Tannhäuser* in Munich at short notice on 11 December, when the scheduled conductor was unable to appear. He was succeeded as second conductor in Munich by Bernhard Stavenhagen, who had become Hofkapellmeister in Weimar in 1895, when Lassen retired.

Strauss's delight at the prospect of Berlin bubbled over at every opportunity. In his letter to his Belgian friend and admirer Georges Khnopff which has already been quoted, he wrote:

> On 1 October I shall be in Berlin! . . . Berlin is a delightful city; my wife has rented a wonderful flat there (Knesebeckstrasse 30 . . .): nine rooms with warm-air heating, 2800 marks . . .
>
> They've made the most marvellous attempts to keep me here, I'm beginning to be extremely popular here now – *too late* ! (14 June 1898)

Ein Heldenleben

Once the Berlin contract had been concluded Strauss felt as though a great burden had been lifted from him, with beneficial results for his composing. He wrote some songs, mainly to texts by Richard Dehmel, but it was above all the new symphonic poem that increasingly engaged him. Its 'pendant' *Don Quixote* had long been finished, while the composer had not yet settled on the final title for his new work. Another plan, for a 'Spring Symphony', had been abandoned, probably because it did not lie in the direction in which Strauss was now moving, towards drama.

The diary contains references to the progress of his work on what was to be *Ein Heldenleben*: on 29 April, on 23 May and on 14 June he recorded that he had done some work on 'Eroica'; but on 18 July 'the war in *Heldenleben*' was finished, so he had decided on the title by then. He used it again the next day in a letter to Eugen Spitzweg: 'I'm working very hard on the new symphonic poem *Heldenleben* and have written five songs for Forberg in Leipzig [Op. 39], which I'm sure you won't mind. Forberg is also going to publish *Enoch*

Arden.' (19 July 1898) Four days later he wrote to Spitzweg once more from Marquartstein, in ironic vein:

> As Beethoven's *Eroica* is so very unpopular with our conductors and therefore is seldom performed nowadays, I am now composing, in order to meet a pressing need, a great tone poem entitled *Heldenleben* (true, it has no funeral march, but it *is* in E♭ major and has lots of horns, which are of course well versed in heroism); thanks to the bracing country air, the sketch is so far advanced that I hope, if nothing in particular gets in the way, to have finished the score by the new year. (23 July 1898)

In fact he finished the sketch on 30 July, and wrote in his diary: 'Evening, 10 o'clock, the great Bismarck has been dismissed!' Then, on a new line: '*Heldenleben* finished.' It was quite exceptional for him to mention a political event; the fact that Bismarck was dismissed on the very day that the Hero withdrew into solitude is pure coincidence – no connection between the two existed in the composer's mind. He began to score the work only three days later, and again kept a record of its progress in his diary. Having started the orchestration on 2 August, he had done seventeen pages by 25 August, forty by 26 September, sixty by 11 October, seventy by 17 October, eighty by 16 November, ninety by 25 November, and the diary records the completion of the score on 1 December, in Berlin (though in fact the ending of the work was to be changed later).

Sketches and notes for *Ein Heldenleben* are scattered through Strauss's notebooks among those for other works: *Don Quixote*, songs, the orchestral *Hymnus*, the sixteen-part Rückert motet, the 'Spring Symphony', even notes about the Schilda opera. As Strauss was later to explain to Romain Rolland, the verbal captions written against individual motives were intended not merely to remind him where he had got to but as a means of fixing the idea, the 'programme', to use that term for once. It had been the same when he was working on *Don Quixote*. A note beside one of the sketches reads: 'As Adagio the longing for peace, after the battle with the world. Flight into solitude, the idyll.' The Hero theme went through a number of stages before Strauss arrived at the definitive form. In one of the sketchbooks he wrote:

> (a) after the love-scene, the envious and the critics cease to be heard. He remains immersed in D♭ major.
> (b) war-cry B♭ major; he bestirs himself and looks and sinks back

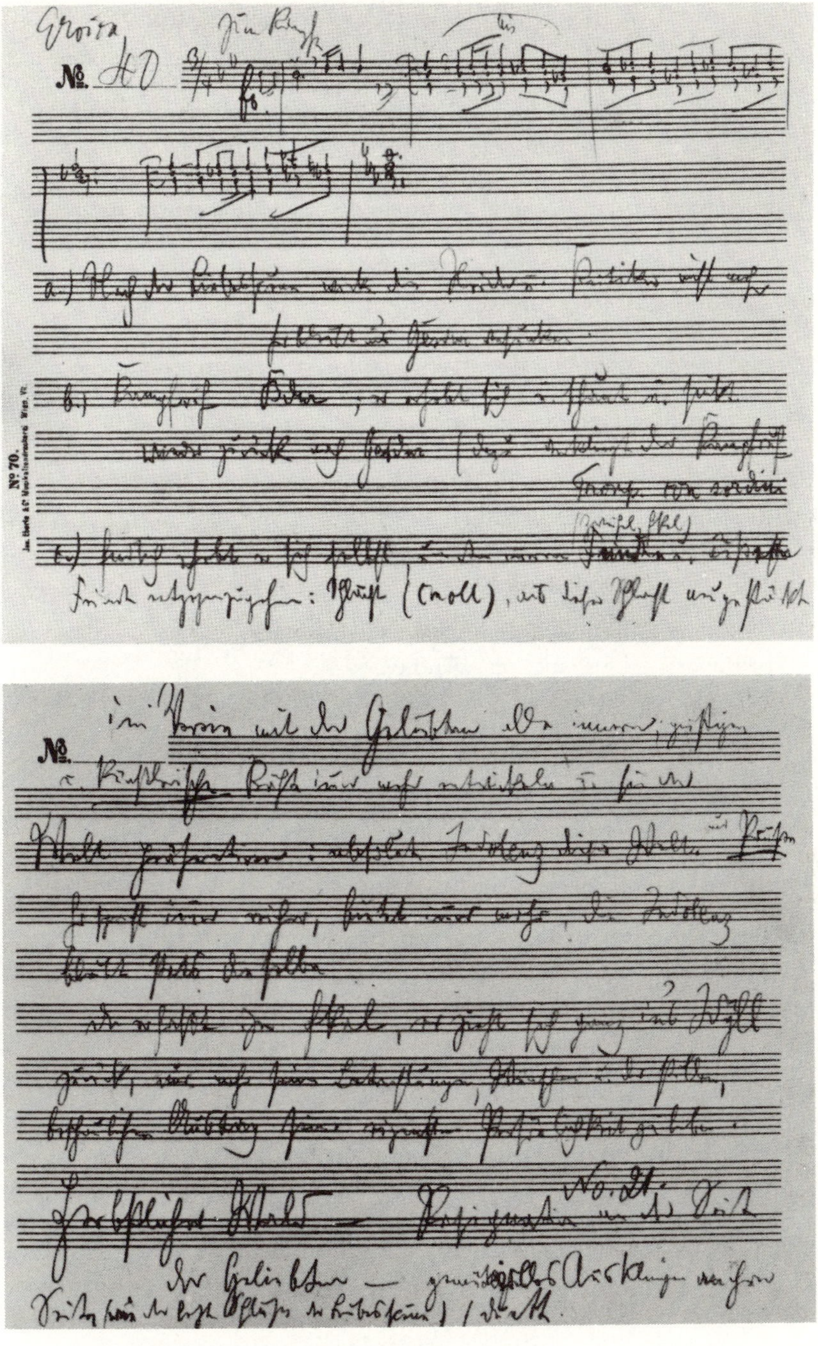

A note for *Ein Heldenleben*

again into G♭ major (accompanied by the war-cry, trumpets *con sordini* – doubt, disgust).
(c) finally he rouses himself, in order to proceed against new enemies and former friends: battle (C minor), coming from this battle now strengthened in union with the beloved [,] all inner, spiritual and *artistic* powers develop more and more and are presented to the world: absolute indolence of this world and [illegible]. He speaks ever more softly, offers ever more, the indolence remains the same. Then he is seized by disgust, withdraws entirely into the idyll, in order to live only for his thoughts, his wishes, the unfolding of his own personality in quiet and contemplation. Autumnal forest – resignation at the side of the beloved – music dies away warm-heartedly, several pages like the last close of the love-scene/duet.

This entry is followed immediately by the Disgust motive, and some musical jottings with the captions: 'Junghexenlied (Bierbaum)', 'Harrowing of Hell (theme caricaturing Handel)', 'battle', 'lark', and then:

Close battle in C major, tremolo E, then let the delicate works of the arts take shape, *pp*, all solos:

Solo string quartet } septet, nonet
Solo piano quartet }

Answer each time  18 July 1898

Intensify embrace, victorious jubilation, love theme into first theme, extend this and into B major.

The use of words to fix the 'poetic idea' in the form of a guiding 'clue' nearly always preceded the invention of the musical material. Strauss talked about this procedure to Romain Rolland in Berlin, a few days after the performance in Cologne on 18 April 1899:

He begins by mapping out for himself very precisely his literary text; and then he goes on to the music. It certainly seems . . . that the musical phrases never come at the same time as the poetical ideas, but afterwards. Nevertheless he considers it pointless for the public to follow his *Heldenleben*, for example, in a little booklet. It is sufficient, he says, to feel the two elements: the hero, and his enemies. (Rolland's diary, entry dated 'April, 1899')

As the sketchbooks show, there are in fact some exceptions to the general rule, in the form of rough sketches for individual motives and themes; in the majority of cases, however, these jottings are not developed any further, as in the plan for a 'Spring Symphony' on which he started work on 2 May 1898 but which seems to have offered too little opportunity for musical development. The 'poetic idea' had to contain some dramatic elements – like the opposition of the Hero and his adversaries in *Ein Heldenleben* – in order to retain Strauss's interest. This is undoubtedly what he was referring to when he said that the symphonic poems were only a preparation for his dramatic oeuvre.

There is no programmatic exposition in the score of *Ein Heldenleben*. 'The exact title was settled only at the time of the first performance', Strauss declared to Paul Zschörlich on 21 February 1902. However, with the help of Friedrich Rösch and Wilhelm Klatte an introduction such as was regarded as indispensable in those days, especially by the promoters of concerts, was compiled, in which six sectional headings were provided: 'The Hero – the Hero's adversaries – the Hero's companion – the Hero's deeds of war – the Hero's works of peace – the Hero's retirement from the world and the fulfilment of his life.' Rösch's explanatory booklet also includes a 'poetic paraphrase' by Eberhard König.[61]

The 'programme' of *Ein Heldenleben* is enough in itself to show that Strauss is to be identified with the Hero only under the observation of strict qualifications. The final section, the 'retirement from the world and self-fulfilment in contemplation', is so directly contrary to Strauss's own attitude to life and to his own self-image that, although personal elements undoubtedly make an important contribution, total identification of Strauss and the hero of his work – as in the case of *Guntram* – is out of the question.

After the première in Berlin on 22 March 1899, Strauss wrote to his father:

> Of the reviews so far, the *Lokalanzeiger* (Klatte) and the *Vossische Zeitung* (Urban) are very good; the rest spew gall and venom, principally because they have read the analysis (by Rösch) as meaning that the hideously portrayed 'fault-finders and adversaries' are supposed to be themselves, and the Hero me, which is only partly true. (24 March 1899)

Many years later, in a letter to the present author, referring expressly to *Ein Heldenleben*, Strauss again spoke out against the 'search by the musical theorists for "personal experiences" and "confessions"': 'Comparisons between the *Eroica* and my *Heldenleben* . . . would produce some interesting studies of experience compared with the free play of artistic imagination . . . As for my *Heldenleben*, of course I didn't engage in battles myself, but I could express the works of peace only by using themes of my own.' (30 July 1946)

In one of the sketchbooks the words 'heroic strength' are written against a sketch of the Hero's principal theme: Strauss would never have claimed that attribute for himself. On the other hand, the love-scene, the confrontation with the adversaries and, in particular, the portrayal of the Hero's companion (Gefährtin, expressly female) are based on the most personal experiences, as Strauss admitted to Romain Rolland, who wrote in his diary after a performance in Paris on 4 March 1900:

> I question him about the Hero's wife (in the symphony) which so greatly intrigued the audience – some considering her a depraved woman, others a flirt, etc. He says 'Neither the one nor the other. It's my wife that I wanted to portray. She is very complex, very much a woman, a little depraved, something of a flirt, never twice alike, every minute different from what she was the minute before. At the beginning, the Hero follows her, goes into the key in which she has just sung; but she always flies further away. Then, at the end, he says: "No, I'm staying here." He stays in his thoughts, in his own key. Then she comes to him.' In any case this very long, very developed section serves as a foil, an intermediary, between the two outbursts at the beginning and at the battle. (Diary, 9 March 1900)

As Strauss went on to say in the same conversation: 'It would be impossible to continue at such a pitch'; that is, the formal function is no less important than the psychological. The autobiographical elements are not nearly so pronounced in *Ein Heldenleben* as they are in the *Symphonia Domestica* of several years later, or even in the operas *Feuersnot* and *Intermezzo*. It cannot be denied that Strauss's attitude towards 'confessional' elements in his work was ambivalent. Only a few weeks before his death he wrote:

> Why don't people see what is new in my works, how in them, as is found otherwise only in Beethoven, the human being visibly plays a part in the work – it begins already in the third act of

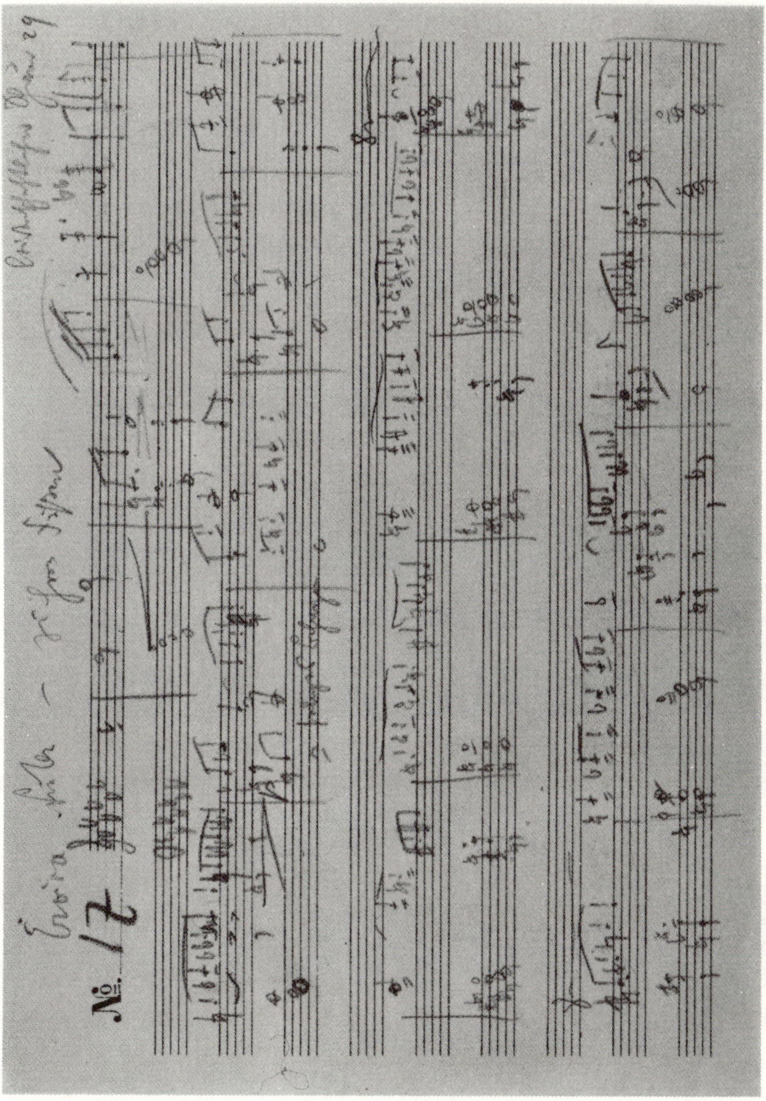

From the sketches for *Ein Heldenleben*, the love-scene

The original, quiet ending of *Ein Heldenleben*

> *Guntram* (renunciation of collectivism), *Heldenleben*, *Don Quixote*, *Domestica* – and in *Feuersnot* the tone of mockery, of irony, of protest against the conventional operatic libretto, is something that is consciously new and individual.[62]

It is significant that Strauss includes *Don Quixote* in this group, a work where heroism is refracted through irony.

According to his diary the score of *Ein Heldenleben* was completed on 1 December 1898, but in the published score, and in the autograph, the date is given as 27 December 1898. There is no contradiction here, rather, two endings exist, the earlier of which does not include the grand rising sequence of chords with which the known version of the work ends. Frau Nini Sieger reminded Strauss over forty years later of the circumstances in which the ending had been altered. (Strauss had been on friendly terms with her husband, Dr Fritz Sieger, the president of the Museums-Gesellschaft in Frankfurt, since the middle of the 1880s and dedicated the Op. 39 songs to him.)

> You had arrived with your wife from Paris at 7 o'clock in the morning, with a heavy cold and tired out. Frau Pauline was very anxious, the doctor had to be called at once but found nothing serious and advised conserving your strength as much as possible; prescribed glasses of port with egg in short pauses during the rehearsals. I chased after you in the pauses with the flask containing this mixture, you grumbled but drank it just the same. The medicine helped, the orchestra found it amusing, with the result that at my third coming I was sent away again, but that earned me the reproaches of Frau Pauline and Dr de Bary. Then we had a fright on the morning of the concert. There was a banging on our bedroom door at 7 o'clock. Frau Pauline cried out in tones of great alarm: 'The concert must be cancelled, Richard has an inflammation of the lungs, the doctor must come.' He came, declared there was no question of inflammation, it was all due to nervous excitement, and the symptoms would disappear as soon as the concert was over.
>
> The concert was an outright success. Your wife had to give encores of several of the songs, she never once confused 'Felder' and 'Wälder', the Concertgebouw Orchestra had sent a deputation with a laurel wreath of such a weight and such a size that the two gentlemen from Amsterdam could hardly carry it, in short it was a day to remember. A 'Museum Supper' to follow and instead of a lady burdened with 'charming

> limitations' the company of the Rösches over caviar and champagne.
>
> The Rösches had already been staying here since the Monday, and already at the first breakfast on the Tuesday morning Herr Rösch urged you to give *Heldenleben* a *forte* ending. 'Richard, that's another *pianissimo* close. The public simply won't believe that you can end *forte*!!' You stared at him, then [to the daughter of the house] 'Leonie, bring pen and ink', and in a few minutes you had written that wonderful sequence of chords that I love so much. (14 April 1942)

In spite of all the circumstantial detail in this letter, it presents some puzzles. The orchestral rehearsal of which Frau Sieger writes took place on 17 March 1898, when the Strausses had returned via Paris from Spain, and the concert, on the next day, was that at which Strauss conducted *Don Quixote* for the first time. This, however, was more than four months before he finished the particello of *Ein Heldenleben* (with the first version of the ending) on 30 July. The possibility suggests itself that Frau Sieger confused the circumstances of one visit with an incident that took place during another visit several months later, but no such visit is on record at an appropriate date. It seems more likely that during the visit to Frankfurt in March 1898 (the composer's diary confirms that Friedrich Rösch and Marie Ritter were staying with the Siegers at the same time) Strauss narrated the course of events in his new symphonic poem, as it is given in his sketchbooks of the same period, or he may even have played something from the as yet fragmentary particello. Certainly Rösch's comment, and the fact that it was made at the breakfast table, sort with the idea of a verbal exposition. It then seems remarkable that Strauss completed the score on 1 December in the form that he had originally planned. Perhaps it was again Rösch, whom he saw frequently in Berlin, who persuaded him to follow his earlier advice as to the nature of the ending. Strauss always resisted changes when they were suggested to him, and it would not be surprising if the first version of the ending was that which he had originally had in mind. At all events, it was towards the end of December that he went to work on changing it. On 23 December he wrote in his diary that he had 'begun to score the new ending of *Heldenleben*', and on 27 December that he had 'finished second ending of *Heldenleben*'. Until now the second version of the ending was the only one known. Wilhelm

Klatte hinted at the existence of the first in 1924, in an article in which he also interpreted the final chords of the second version as a musical symbol of a hero's grave.[63] The original ending was published for the first time in 1976, when the autograph was reproduced in facsimile in the German edition of the present book. (At the final rehearsal for a performance of *Ein Heldenleben* under the direction of Volkmar Andreae in Zürich, on 14 August 1946, Strauss turned to the present author during the closing bars, winked and murmured 'State funeral!')

The campaign for musical copyrights

During the last months in Munich Strauss began to take an interest in some of the financial problems relating to his profession. He was the moving spirit behind the establishment of a new order in the relationship of composers and publishers, but the role played by Friedrich Rösch, whose legal training stood them in good stead, must not be underestimated. Other friends and colleagues – Max Schillings, Siegmund von Hausegger and Hermann Bischoff – took a lively part in the debate. It was by no means personal disappointment which drove Strauss to participate with such energy: rather, the fact that he was already the most highly regarded and successful composer of his generation compelled him to take the initiative in getting the out-of-date copyright laws revised.

On 14 July 1898, in the middle of the most decisive phase of his work on *Ein Heldenleben*, Strauss drafted a circular letter to other German composers, which Spitzweg undertook to duplicate and distribute.

> Sir:
>
> I would like to draw your attention most urgently to a pamphlet by Professor Hans Sommer of Brunswick, published recently in Leipzig by Commissionsverlag Leede, and entitled *The Valuation of Music.* In it Professor Sommer has pointed out a cause for grave concern, namely that Imperial German law protects all intellectual property for only thirty years after the death of the author; this law, to mention only one example (for others I refer you to Sommer's pamphlet), will place *Parsifal* (*against its creator's express wishes*) at the tender mercies of publishers and theatre managements in a mere fifteen years from now. At the recent congress of the Allgemeiner Deutscher Musikverein in Mainz, Professor Sommer also proposed the

setting in train of agitation on the part of German composers with the object of proposing to the Imperial Government a revision of the copyright law of 11 June 1870, which would guarantee the protection of intellectual property beyond the period of thirty years after the author's death.

Sommer's proposals at the said congress were rejected as being

doomed to failure

and yet, as I read a few days ago in the newspapers, *the federated governments intend to present a bill to the Reichstag this very autumn, which is intended to bring about a revision of the copyright law of 11 June 1870.*

I do not need to tell you how important it is that the wishes of German composers first and foremost should be heard in the debate on this matter. However, at that same congress in Mainz, at the same time as a number of *music publishers, conductors, writers on music* and composers (there were hardly any composers present) voted in favour of new statutes for the Allgemeiner Deutscher Musikverein, they also passed some important resolutions, proposed by Dr von Hase (proprietor of the publishing firm Breitkopf & Härtel), supporting concerted action by German publishers *and* composers (*although hardly one of the latter was present*) to get a law passed to ensure that in future works of living composers intended only for the concert hall will be awarded a royalty such as at present is already enjoyed by the authors of dramatic works in their lifetime, but by their heirs for only thirty years after the authors' death.

Desirable as it is that 'non-dramatic' composers should also enjoy royalties, nevertheless – leaving aside the *injustice* of the proposal that the author and publisher of the 'concert work' in question shall receive an *equal* share of 1% of the gross proceeds of the concert, that is, ½% each – *the benefit of this law will be exactly nothing*, unless, at the same time as this 'Concert Royalty Law' comes into force, the law of 11 June 1870 is revised to make works that are already 'free' – that is, the works for *both the stage and the concert hall* of masters who have already been dead for thirty years or more – *once again liable for the payment of royalties* (in the favour either of surviving heirs or, if there are none, perhaps of a new institution to be founded for the purpose of supporting and encouraging young, impecunious talents, or of some other *enterprise furthering artistic progress* etc. etc.).

It is already the case today that, irrespective of their inherent merits, but by virtue of their age, by virtue of the popularity they enjoy with interpreters and listeners for that very reason, by virtue of the greater ease with which they may be performed (all the scores have already been acquired or are obtainable cheap from Breitkopf & Härtel Popular Editions, very few rehearsals necessary !!!) etc. etc., the works of classical masters, or let us say at least of masters who are already dead, still make it very difficult, as you all know to your cost, for the works of living composers (who, even if they make no claim to immortality, nevertheless have the right to be played and heard, and to be heard often) to be given the entrée into our concert halls. How much greater is the difficulty bound to become when, additionally, performance royalties are demanded for these works which are barely tolerated and which the majority do not want (while the works of dead masters, already available in – let us say simply – 'popular' editions, exempt from royalties, and much more popular on account of their age and familiarity to the listener, are already to hand with the scores and the parts on the shelves of every library, while the performance material for new works must first be obtained for precious money, without the applause-hungry concert-promoter knowing in advance whether the 'success' will repay the great expense).

What I outline briefly here was expounded exhaustively at the Mainz Congress by Herr Hans Sommer, Herr Friedrich Rösch and Dr Neitzel; these three gentlemen represented the rights of German authors in commendable fashion. By 17 votes to 14, their proposals were

defeated.

Herr Hans Sommer and Herr Friedrich Rösch are now prepared to set forth their proposals for the protection of the intellectual property of, especially, those living composers who were not present in Mainz in a

memorandum,

which it is intended to submit to influential figures in the Imperial Government and the Reichstag, if a number of German composers of good standing will come forward, prepared to sign a document of such very great urgency at the present time.

I am writing to request you to make available *your signature for this purpose*, and I take upon myself full responsibility that this memorandum (which is both a protest against the resolutions violating authors' rights passed by the congress of the Allgemeiner Deutscher Musikverein and at the same time a petition to the Government and the Reichstag asking for better guarantees of the rights of authors and *of their heirs by means of revision of the above-mentioned Imperial law in accordance with our*

> *wishes*) will represent the rights of living authors and of the extant heirs of the dead in a manner both worthy and gratifying.[64]

The circular letter marks the beginning of Strauss's lifelong struggle for composers' copyrights – a struggle which led to major changes in the law, from which several generations of composers have since profited. But what is taken for granted today was achieved by slow and dogged stages, accompanied by reverses, disappointments and acrimony. The fight took a considerable toll of Strauss's time and energy, but in the midst of his success he regarded it as a duty he must not shirk.

What he and his fellows wanted led to misunderstanding for the most part among publishers, who resisted every inch of the way. The situation is illustrated by a letter Strauss wrote to his old friend and publisher Eugen Spitzweg:

> Dear friend, it is with regret that I learn of your refusal to take *Heldenleben*, because, as I have said before, it is absolutely impossible for me to give the performance rights of my works to the publisher in future. This is the cardinal point in our whole movement, and as instigator I cannot set a bad example.
>
> *Publishing rights to the publisher.*
>
> Author's rights to the author.
>
> There's no other way from this day forwards.
>
> You have written a long screed about the percentages that we want to claim all for ourselves. I can assure you, not for the first time, that we composers have completely renounced all demands for percentages, and claim no percentages for ourselves at all, and we even dispute the right of publishers to claim percentages for works of which they have not expressly bought the performance rights. (22 November 1898)

The circular letter makes clear Strauss's reasons for declining nomination for election to the committee and the music sub-committee of the Allgemeiner Deutscher Musikverein at this time. The association had declared its approval of the establishment of the Anstalt für musikalisches Aufführungsrecht (Institute for musical performance rights) by the Verein der deutschen Musikalienhändler (Association of German music publishers and retailers), while Strauss and his colleagues were opposed to the Anstalt's policy on royalties for non-dramatic works. Only after some fundamental changes which led to the election of an almost entirely new committee did Strauss accept nomination as president, at the Heidelberg Festival in 1901.

The circular letter was distributed to approximately 160 addresses on 23 July. By 2 August Strauss had already had 31 affirmatory answers and 11 which either rejected his proposals or expressed some reservations. By 10 August the number of favourable replies had risen to 119. This overwhelmingly positive response was encouraging, and early in September Strauss sent out another invitation, this time to a conference, which duly took place on 30 September in the Kaufmännisches Vereinshaus in Leipzig. At it Strauss explained his ideas for clarifying and safeguarding performance rights, and a resolution was passed unanimously which led to the foundation of a composers' association, the Genossenschaft deutscher Tonsetzer.

The conference caused some stir. The Leipzig *Musikalisches Wochenblatt* published a lengthy report in its issue for 13 October (no. 42), although the proceedings had been 'conducted in the strictest confidence'.

> Fifty voices were represented at the congress; a further 150 had trustingly expressed their agreement in advance. Principal result: absolute unanimity in the world of German composers. (Ed.: *ca* 150 participants at the congress do not quite amount to the *whole* world of German composers!)
>
> It is not possible at the present time to give a full account of the decision to establish a 'Union of German Composers', to promote 'effective, comradely protection of all musical copyrights, and the professional interests associated therewith', nor do we have access at present to information about the 'memorandum' from the united German composers which is shortly to be submitted to the Imperial Government and in due course to the Reichstag; this sets forth wishes, initiatives and proposals relating both to the economic position of their profession in general and to the question of musical authors' copyrights in particular. However, we can give a fuller report on one of the other principal resolutions of the Leipzig composers' congress. The Anstalt für musikalisches Aufführungsrecht touches not only the narrower circle of composers but also to a very great degree the interest of performing artists, of musical associations of all kinds, of concert-giving institutions and thus of the music-loving public at large: after the most careful debate at the Leipzig congress, this institute, together with its tackling

of the matter of royalties for non-dramatic works exclusively by *living* composers, was unanimously *denounced*. The united German composers have deliberately set themselves up in opposition on this point to the Verein der deutschen Musikalienhändler, who called the Anstalt für musikalisches Aufführungsrecht into being, with the backing of the Allgemeiner Deutscher Musikverein. In consequence of their resolution, the Leipzig composers' congress also called for all those composers who have already announced their readiness to cooperate with one of the committees to withdraw their cooperation. We shall now have to wait and see whether the Allgemeiner Deutscher Musikverein will also withdraw its support for the Anstalt, for the vote in favour of it enjoyed only a small majority, and moreover that came about entirely by chance. This would be the only way for the association to avoid a secession which would have the most profound effects on every sector of the association's membership. It would also smooth the path for the various interests which hitherto have been in collision on the question to come to an amicable agreement by way of peaceful discussions first and foremost between the bodies representing the composer and the publishers.

The preliminary inquiry into changes in the copyright law opened on the 10th of this month at the Imperial Office of Justice; at the invitation of the said ministry to send a delegate to the inquiry, the Leipzig composers' congress voted unanimously to send Herr Friedrich Rösch.

If the membership of the Genossenschaft deutscher Tonsetzer numbered 150 to begin with, it had risen to 250 by the middle of November, while no composers of standing threw in their lot with the Anstalt. It was nonetheless a long haul before the establishment of a new 'Institute for musical performance rights' (under the same name) in Berlin in 1903, with the moral support of Strauss and above all the legal and organizational skills of Friedrich Rösch and Hans Sommer behind it. The legal foundations for it were laid by the new German copyright laws passed in 1901.

Farewell to Munich

On the day after the Leipzig conference, 1 October, Strauss conducted a concert of the Leipzig Liszt-Verein, a task he always performed with particular relish. On this occasion the programme included no works by Liszt but was given over entirely to living composers: Joseph Rheinberger's overture to *The Taming of the Shrew*, a piano concerto by Carl Reinecke, Humperdinck's overture to *Die Königskinder*, Variations by Ernst Rudorff, the overture to Eugen d'Albert's *Der Rubin* and Felix Draeseke's *Jubel* Overture, and songs by Bernhard Scholz, Herman Zumpe, Albert Fuchs, Max Schillings, Felix Weingartner, Hugo Wolf, Salomon Jadassohn, Hans Sommer and Julius Prüfer.

Although he was on the go throughout the months from August to October 1898, travelling hither and thither between Berlin, Munich, Marquartstein, Leipzig, Chemnitz, Plauen, Frankfurt, Aachen, Amsterdam and Berlin again, Strauss continued to work on the score of *Ein Heldenleben*. After the withdrawal of Siegmund von Hausegger's *Zinnober* in June, after only two performances, he conducted twenty-one performances of opera in Munich between 31 July and 18 October: *Die Entführung*, *Don Giovanni*, *Così fan tutte*, *Die Zauberflöte*, *Fidelio*, *Tannhäuser* and *Tristan*. His last performance, on 18 October, was *Fidelio*. The previous day he wrote to Pauline: 'Tomorrow, *Fidelio* for the last time! Then *finis*! Off and away – into your arms!' At last the object for which he had yearned for so long, to leave Munich, was achieved. He was acclaimed at this farewell performance and his head crowned with six laurel wreaths. He had taken his leave of the orchestra the previous evening at a party in the cellar of the Augustinerbräu, after having reached page 70 of the score of *Ein Heldenleben* on the same day. Without wasting a day, he set off on a tour of concert engagements: *Enoch Arden* in Leipzig on 19 October, Berlioz's *King Lear* Overture, the prelude to *Lohengrin*, *Till Eulenspiegel* and songs both with piano and with orchestral accompaniment sung by Pauline in Chemnitz on 22 October, and the same programme two days later in Plauen, where he was installed as an honorary member of the town's Wagner-Verein; next to Aachen, where on 27 October he conducted *Don Juan* and *Till Eulenspiegel*, and the sixteen-part chorus *Der Abend* (Op. 34, no. 1) was 'capitally sung under Schwickerath'. On 23 October *Tod und Verklärung* was performed in Innsbruck under the elder Joseph Pembaur at the funeral of the murdered Empress Elisabeth of Austria.

From Aachen Strauss went on to Amsterdam, where he heard Anton Averkamp's *a cappella* choir sing both his Op. 34 choruses, and on the following day, 30 October, he attended a concert where

Willem Mengelberg conducted *Tod und Verklärung*, and then he himself conducted *Also sprach Zarathustra*. 'Best performance the work has had yet, greatest triumph', he wrote in his diary. His reception in Amsterdam was such as he had never experienced before: even in the instrument room in the Concertgebouw he found his picture hanging on the wall, wreathed with flowers and laurel. When he went into the concert hall itself for the rehearsal, the orchestra received him with a *Tusch*, and high up on the wall he observed his own name in letters of gold beside those of Liszt and Wagner: that of Gounod had been obliterated to make room for his.

> At the concert itself the audience gave me an ovation straight after *Tod und Verklärung* (which Mengelberg conducted capitally): they rose as one and applauded me where I sat in the middle of the hall. With the applause thundering in my ears I made a slow progress up to the conductor's desk and was called back more times than I could count, and then the same again after *Zarathustra* . . . They had held sectional rehearsals for it for the past three weeks. It was wonderful!!! (To his father, 1 November 1898)

In spite of the demands of rehearsals, concerts and social obligations, he found time to visit the Rembrandt exhibition. Something more than twenty-four hours after the performance of *Zarathustra* in Amsterdam he at last arrived in his new home in Berlin, at 1.28 a.m. On 2 November he was introduced to the orchestra by the General Intendant Bolko von Hochberg, and paid formal calls on Pierson, on his new colleague, the conductor Karl Muck, and on the writer Oscar Bie, with whom he had already been on close terms since 1896 and who was to become one of his loyalest champions.[65]

Six months after the move to Berlin, Romain Rolland called on Strauss. They had been introduced as long ago as the summer of 1891, in Wahnfried, but no closer friendship had developed from that first meeting. In the absence of any comparable memoirs of Strauss in Munich in the years up to the move to Berlin, by contemporaries of Rolland's stature, the French writer's observations are a valuable substitute; although they are coloured by his memories of Strauss in later life, and include some rather critical comments, they give a picture of the man at the stage when he was adapting himself from the atmosphere of Munich to that of Berlin.

The reader should bear in mind that they are memoirs, and not notes made at the time. Moreover, in the time between the meeting in 1899 and the composition of the memoirs, Rolland had published the novel *Jean Christophe*, in which the hero encounters at one point a German composer called Hassler, to whom the author gave some isolated traits borrowed from Strauss. 'Malevolent people', Rolland wrote in his memoirs,

> have used this scene against Strauss, and however much I protest my readers refuse to understand me . . . Not for one moment while I was writing did I intend a parallel between the deceitful Hassler, ossifying in his success and sinking ever deeper into the downy cushions of blasé indifference and contempt for others, and the vital genius of a Richard Strauss. The latter had never stopped working, *nulla dies sine linea*, and always retained his respect for his noble calling. But sometimes in a flash another man would appear at his elbow, who was possessed by a demon of lassitude, limpness, irony and indifference. Strauss was on his guard, however. He knew the dangers of his own nature better than anyone, and while he would stroke the demon affectionately, he always kept it on a tight leash . . .
>
> He played the jesting cynic, in order to pull the wool over the philistines' eyes; he had an Eulenspiegel sense of humour and he was fond of paradox in remarks made for the public ear, but *tête à tête* with a friend whom he respected (*rara avis*!) he revealed his true self: very judicious and moderate. The most remarkable thing about him was an almost rhythmical psychological alternation between his two natures: one all energy and impetuosity, the other all lethargic immobility; flight feathers in the wind and feather bed . . .
>
> Strauss was grateful to the true friend who was able to read him, to recognize his weaknesses, tell him of them and to love him in spite of them.

Rolland also describes the composer's physical appearance, in a passage that closely follows the entry in his diary on 1 March 1900:

> He had a smooth and translucent skin like a child's, a high, shining forehead and a narrow nose. The lower part of his face had a twist to it; the mouth often became ugly, when he contorted it in irony or annoyance. One's eyes were drawn to his hands, which were long, delicate, well-kept, giving the impression of an invalid refinement, and did not correspond at

> all to the rest of his person. His tone and manner altered completely according to the person he was speaking to.[66]

As he left Munich, Strauss could give a deep sigh of relief. During the four years that he had stuck it out in his birth-place, he had not received, either as conductor or as composer, the amount of recognition that he thought he deserved. Nothing had ever happened to allay his suspicion that his superiors in the opera house would have preferred a conductor without personal creative ambitions, and his pronounced bias in favour of Wagner, Mozart and modern composers had never met with approval. The hopes of obtaining Mottl for Munich, which had led to the delays in confirming Strauss's appointment in the first place, and had never been abandoned since, added fuel to the fires of his mistrust, the more so because of the frequent opposition met with by his artistic and financial demands. In 1898 Perfall once again tried to reduce the agreed salary, which was all that was needed to confirm Strauss's resolve to leave.

If Strauss was not as aware as he might have been of the new artistic and intellectual forces at work in Munich during these years, it is because he had no very close relationship with the writers, painters and others who were in the vanguard of the modern movement, or, at any rate, such relationships as he had did not lead to intimate and lasting friendships. In Munich his work in the opera house, his composing, his family, and the growing number of performing engagements elsewhere in Germany and abroad left him little time for anything but a small circle of friends and acquaintances, nearly all of whom were musicians. His contacts with other social circles in Munich were isolated and peripheral to his life: though one house at which he did from time to time attend evening parties, remaining on at least one occasion until 2 a.m., according to his diary, was that of the amateur of the arts Alfred Pringsheim, professor of mathematics at Munich University; here he met the charming daughter of the house Katja and her twin brother Klaus (fifteen years old in 1898), who were both working with private tutors for their matriculation examinations. In 1905 Katja was to marry Thomas Mann, whom Strauss did not meet during the four years when they both lived in Munich. Klaus Pringsheim forged himself a sterling reputation as composer, conductor and teacher of music; Strauss, who included one of his songs in a concert programme at an early stage in his career, remained in touch with him, though they were not close friends.

Strauss enjoyed his visits to the theatre, sometimes in his sister's company, and he was an avid reader, continually widening his horizons. He was especially well-read in Dostoyevsky, Turgenev and the other great Russian novelists, but he was also well acquainted with Ibsen, and volumes of memoirs and works on cultural history remained his favourite reading throughout his life. The special and permanent exhibitions in Munich's art galleries and museums helped to broaden his interests. But it was in Berlin with its vibrant and varied cultural life that all these influences began to bear fruit in Strauss's own creative work. The discontent that had gathered in him in Munich soon found an artistic outlet in Berlin in the 'Singgedicht' ('musical' or 'lyric' epigram) *Feuersnot*, the libretto of which was written for him by Ernst von Wolzogen, whom he had first met in Munich. Inserted in the central section of this work is the burlesque sermon in which the hero Kunrad castigates the townspeople, in a tone that contrasts sharply with the rest of the work. In 1945 Strauss wrote:

> *Feuersnot* has always been criticized for mixing the style of a harmless farce with Kunrad's sermon. I admit the justice of this objection – but without it the whole thing would have been too simplistic, and Kunrad's sermon was the most important issue to me, and the rest merely a jolly background, and anyway people should at least acknowledge the courage that it took for an at that date still unsuccessful operatic composer to read his own compatriots a little lecture for their behaviour towards Richard Wagner.[67]

By that time it was Wagner's treatment at the hands of Munich rather than his own which seemed more important. Nonetheless it was high time that he left his hometown, holding as he did a view of it that was probably excessively negative and one-sided. The move signified a change of direction, the consequences of which can hardly be overestimated. He was to spend the next twenty years in Berlin, and late in life he recalled the period with especial gratitude:

> I never had cause to regret my situation in Berlin; I experienced really nothing but joy, and met with great sympathy and hospitality. The fifteen years of symphony concerts with the Royal Orchestra gave me unadulterated hours of the most

> wonderful artistic work. My good relations with the Berlin Opera persisted throughout all changes of fortune [i.e. later, when he was in Vienna].[68]

The symphony concerts he conducted began in 1908 and went on to the season of 1919–20. For another thirteen years after that he returned to conduct individual concerts. In the memoir he does not even refer to the discord which surrounded the performance of *Feuersnot* in Berlin, and also cast something of a shadow over *Salome* and *Rosenkavalier*. In Berlin, not only did the conductor, at first sharing the position of Hofkapellmeister with Karl Muck, reach the peak of his career, but the composer, too, made the decisive breakthrough to musical dramatist with the operas *Salome*, *Elektra* and *Rosenkavalier* (notwithstanding the fact that their premières were all held in Dresden).

Strauss's own contention that the symphonic poems served as a preparation for his operas, though perhaps a little exaggerated, is by and large the truth. Although he had mastered the craft of composition at a very early stage, and with youthful facility produced a large number of works at great speed, it was nonetheless necessary for him to travel a relatively long way after the crucial experience of Wagner before he could be fully aware of the nature of his own calling. The failure of *Guntram* naturally caused his self-confidence to falter for a time, and the number of ideas for operas which he considered between *Guntram* and *Feuersnot*, only to abandon them, bears witness to this; in that respect alone, *Feuersnot*, though only an occasional piece, was an important step.

In the early part of 1899, his first spring in Berlin, Strauss tried once more to write his own libretto for a work to which he gave the title *Ekke und Schnittlein*. He wrote two drafts, but then abandoned it like the others. He appears still to have occupied himself with the idea of a 'Spring Symphony', without building on the sketches that already existed, and he was no more successful with the *Künstlertragödie* (Artist's Tragedy),[69] which he began in 1900 with a passage depicting a sunrise that eventually found its way into the *Alpensinfonie*, or with the ballet *Kythere*, for which he wrote his own scenario. The *Symphonia Domestica*, the sketch of which was begun in May 1902 and finished in July 1903, and the scoring completed on 31 December 1903, was the only large-scale work executed before a new stage in his creative career was ushered in by his encounter with Oscar Wilde's *Salome* and his decision to set the text (in

Hedwig Lachmann's translation) as it was, apart from some cuts and contractions. As we have seen, in the first years in Berlin he continued to devote himself to the song with piano accompaniment, but from the moment when Pauline began to reduce her appearances in the concert hall and finally gave them up altogether, his productivity in that genre dropped.

His relations with the city of his birth were at a nadir when he left it. Past disappointments, the failure of his impulsive temperament to make any headway against real and imagined indolence, narrow-mindedness and illiberality, cast their shadow over his memories of Munich. Berlin represented a vital, pulsating present and a future rich with promise. Strauss accepted the summons to go to the capital of the German Empire with joy and the highest of expectations: he was not to be disappointed.

Appendix 1

Guntram: a synopsis

An excerpt from Wolfgang Jordan, *Guntram von Richard Strauss* (Leipzig, 1902), later incorporated in Georg Göhler's *Richard Strauss, Musikdramen*, Schlesingersche Musikbibliothek, Meisterführer 9 (Berlin and Vienna, 1909).

Strauss sets his freely invented action in the Middle Ages. The background to the drama is provided by a knightly religious brotherhood of 'good men' . . . whose purpose is to disseminate the idea of Christian love; the brothers cherish as the highest good the ideal of the fraternal union of all mankind in world peace through the working of love, and it is through the art of noble song that they seek to win the hearts of men for this doctrine of salvation. Guntram has grown to manhood in the beliefs and teachings of the brotherhood, and is filled with ardour and enthusiasm; sent out into the world to be a warrior in the cause of love, he comes upon a land sucked dry by an insatiable prince. Need and distress are rife among the people, who have attempted in vain, in a number of desperate uprisings, to break the power of the tyrant. An event destined to change his life clears his path to the prince's court and thus takes him towards the first opportunity to act for love's sake. He rescues Freihild, the bountiful wife of Duke Robert, from the death she seeks by drowning; she has sought to put an end to her loveless life because her only remaining consolation, the relief of her people's suffering, has been forbidden her by the command of her unloved husband. Guntram recognizes her as a kindred spirit, and he is seized by a deep sympathy for the noble woman. In gratitude Freihild's aged father invites his daughter's rescuer to a feast at the ducal court, in celebration of the suppression of the popular revolt.

At the feast Guntram, confident of the irresistible strength of the idea that inspires him, and inflamed by the presence of Freihild whom he sees suffering exactly as the people do in the bonds of lovelessness, sings thrillingly in praise of the blessings of peace, in the hope of winning the heart of Duke Robert for the work of peace and the renunciation of all further deeds of violence, so that people and prince may be united in love. The duke, however, who knows no power but that conferred by brute force, suspects that this champion of the people is only an ambitious rebel who has come to seize his crown; he pours scorn upon the singer, and a fight breaks out between them, in which Guntram, parrying the other's vicious attack and anticipating his blow, slays the duke.

In the cell where the old duke commands him to be thrown to await punishment, Guntram is tormented by frantic doubts as to the purity of his deed, which he had thought of as one of liberation. Friedhold, his former teacher, enters, sent by the brotherhood to call him to account for the deed which was against its laws; peaceful victories, in the spirit of the idea of love, are the only victories allowed to the brothers, and they carry swords only to defend themselves; even though the death of the tyrant means relief for the people and the prospect of freedom from oppression (the old duke has fallen in battle against insurgent vassals), the brotherhood nevertheless condemns the killing as a deed of passion and regards it as an absolute 'sin'.

Guntram has become guilty, but he does not feel himself to be guilty as the brotherhood would have it; it was love for the woman that unknowingly directed his words and actions. His blow laid low the oppressor of the people: in that sense his deed was good; but Guntram feels guilt in being the thrall of the love which lives in his will; his desire slew not the tyrant but the husband of the woman he loves. He renounces his love, in order to become once more, in solitude, the master of the strength he knows himself to possess, to become a free man himself; thanks to the love which has burned in him, thanks to its flaring up into passion, he has now learned that freedom cannot be bestowed but can only be wrought from one's own strength; thus he is able to perceive the delusion at the heart of the work and thought of the 'good' brotherhood; therefore he casts himself loose from it for ever . . .

Appendix 2

Kurt Wilhelm: Strauss's plan for a Volksoper about Till Eulenspiegel

(First published in *Richard-Strauss-Jahrbuch* 1954; in this translation the longer quotations from Strauss's verse draft are paraphrased and abridged.)

It was Max Steinitzer who first recorded that, after *Guntram*, Strauss contemplated an opera about Till Eulenspiegel, and that he actually completed a draft text for the first act while still in Weimar. This draft was found among his papers after his death. It has nothing but the name in common with the symphonic poem which was the eventual product of Strauss's plan. Above all, there is one vitally important element that is completely absent from the symphonic poem: the action takes place in Schilda.

Strauss's primary concern in this draft is obviously to represent the struggle that the exceptional person (Till) wages against the philistines, and the contempt that he feels for them. Schilda provides the context for this. The few brief notes Strauss made before working out the scenario show that he intended to present the conflict in the following terms: on the one side there were to be the philistines, the petty bourgeoisie, depicted with all the characteristics and narrow-minded stupidity associated with such people. Schilda would be the embodiment of bourgeois philistinism, exaggerated to the point of grotesque absurdity. On the other side there would be an equally overdrawn character: Till, 'who scorns mankind because at bottom he loves it', Till, 'the fruitless sceptic, the laughing philosopher'.

Thus an opposition is set up between two grotesque extremes, worlds apart. Between them stands the element that can draw them together, the normal run of humanity, represented by a pair of lovers (Hanne and the young councillor).

Something of the basic elements of this material was eventually brought to musical life under a different sign in *Feuersnot*. There, the opposition of the lightly caricatured citizenry of Munich and the Wagner-like Kunrad is nothing like as crass as the contrast in the Eulenspiegel draft, but the parallels are obvious enough.

Synopsis:
The scene is the market-place in Schilda. In the background the town hall with no windows, the door standing wide open. Downstage left, benches and tables for the council meeting.

The people of Schilda are discovered in the act of trapping the daylight, in order to carry it into their town hall, which they have forgotten to provide with windows. Some are catching it in sacks, or loading it into baskets with shovels and garden forks, others are collecting it in cooking pots, and one is even trying to snare it with a mouse-trap.

In all Schilda there is only one man who has secret misgivings about the wisdom of his fellow citizens: the 'young councillor', but he has a strong sense of duty. Since doubting Schilda's 'wisdom' in any way is a capital crime he keeps his doubts to himself. He is therefore caught in a tragic quandary, being on the one hand a thinking person, and on the other a loyal, faithful son of his hometown. There are however others who have doubts about the noble burghers: the women of Schilda, but they hold their tongues and let their menfolk do things their own way. Only one rebels: Hanne (the principal female role in the opera), a sound young woman, with heart and mouth in the right place. The young councillor loves her with all his heart but tries to resist his feelings, because in his opinion she is too outspoken. He looks on her as a heretic against the sacred laws of Schilda. She, on the other hand, tries to convert him to reason and open his eyes to the folly of his fellow citizens. Early on there are some short verbal skirmishes between the two.

The town council, led by the plump, inexpressibly stupid burgomaster, stops the collection of daylight and opens its session. There is an important topic on the agenda: the emperor has announced that he will visit Schilda, and the council discusses how to give him a suitable welcome. After much debate it is suggested that a maid of honour should be sent to meet the emperor outside the gates and greet him with a kiss. Heated arguments ensue (which would have taken the form of a turbulent musical ensemble) as to who should be chosen. They finally settle on Hanne, a choice which the young councillor passionately opposes.

At this point the session is rudely interrupted. A stranger is dragged in, who has committed the heinous crime of asking 'whether this is the town where they forgot to put any windows in the town hall because they're such wiseacres'. The stranger (it is Till) is ceremoniously condemned to death. But then Hanne leaps to her feet: 'That's the last straw! Instead of punishing him in your vanity and folly, you should make him burgomaster. He has spoken the first sensible words to be heard in this town for years!'

There is a long, astonished pause. Mumbled consultation. Automatic sentence of death spoken over Hanne, too. Then the young councillor interjects that she is needed to greet the emperor with a kiss. Thereupon she is acquitted *nem. con.* Before long the whole subject is forgotten anyway, because one of the essential characteristics of the burghers of Schilda is that they remember only the last thing they hear. Everything preceding that is quickly forgotten.

Then one of the people in the crowd suddenly recognizes in the stranger the man who shortly before failed to pay for his drink. At that a second, and then a third person recalls something put over on him by the stranger. Others join in, and a whole litany of knavery à la Eulenspiegel is recited. Till listens to it all, laughing, and then declares that he is a great sinner, there is only one verdict possible for him and he pronounces it himself: he condemns himself to death. The burghers for that reason promptly do him the greatest injury they can think of: they acquit him. If there is to be a trial, they want to hold it themselves. Once again the young councillor protests. Since no agreement can be reached they decide to cast the stranger into the town gaol. A big ensemble follows, in which opinion sways hither and thither. Everyone forgets what it is that the stranger has or has not done. He, meanwhile, pays more and more attention to Hanne, to whom he takes a great fancy, while ignoring everything else. Finally it occurs to the burgomaster to ask the stranger who he is and what his name is.

He introduces himself: 'As Eulenspiegel I am known, far and wide my fame is strown, a merry coxcomb, ready for fun . . . One who will not squander God's good time in useless toil, who roves gaily throughout the wide world, carelessly takes whatever he pleases of its joys, grabs whatever Philistia's morals forbid.

'The scourge of the Philistines, the slave of liberty, reviler of folly, adorer of nature – but stopping short of man, for nature bungled when she created reason. A prankster, morning, noon and night, Till Eulenspiegel is the wight who stands here now within your sight.'

1st burgher: 'My mind stands still.'
2nd burgher: 'So that's the notorious Till!'
Hanne: 'I'm glad to make you welcome here,
I've heard you talked of far and near.'

At that moment there is a shout from the watchman on the tower, to announce the return of the messenger sent to the emperor.

Till and Hanne are forgotten. General rejoicing, as the townspeople hurry off to meet the messenger. Till seizes his chance, quickly arranges a tryst with Hanne and is on the point of making off when the young councillor catches him and prevents his flight.

Now the messenger enters and tells of his gracious reception by the emperor, who sends his greetings to the people and lets it be known that he wishes to test their celebrated wisdom for himself.

'His words of greeting in due time
You must answer with a rhyme.'

Consternation. What is a rhyme? No one knows. Time is short. The emperor will arrive this evening, and the day is already well advanced. The burgomaster is at his wits' end, as the townspeople clamour for him to make a rhyme. Then Hanne has an idea: the first person to make a rhyme shall be elected burgomaster. Deep thought on all sides. Everyone would like to become burgomaster in this way. One makes a brave effort:

'I have it!
Now listen to me,
And see
If the wisest I be.
"My name is known unto you all,
And I lean my pike against this – fence."'

Laughter. Another tries.

'"Good gentlemen, I enter here,
And quench my thirst with a glass of – wine."'

The burgomaster quavers:

'I have the first line in my pate,
But do not know a rhyme for "state".'

An argument breaks out, which Hanne puts a stop to by pointing out that it's no use their making up any old rhyme in advance: they must wait until the emperor has spoken, and then answer with something that rhymes with his words. This leads to renewed bickering between the young councillor, Hanne and Till.

That is as far as Strauss's verse draft goes. The sequel can only be constructed out of the material of the Till legends. Probably Till will be made burgomaster, do something outrageous when the emperor arrives, and havoc will ensue.

Strauss himself was probably not very clear as to how the plot would develop, and that could have been the reason why he abandoned the work. This much is indicated in some notes: Till falls genuinely in love for the first time in his life. As he falls on his knees before Hanne to confess his love at the moment of his supposed triumph, the young councillor erupts in a whirlwind of jealousy that sweeps away all the shackles of philistinism. He sends his rival packing. From this moment on he is the man Hanne has always wanted him to be. The course of events has turned him into a person who has shed all conventions and all folly. And when Till asks what is to become of himself, Hanne throws his cynicism back in his face: 'You despise life and plague the philistines. Isn't that enough? Isn't that the whole of your life?' And Till has to accept it.

Some of Strauss's notes indicate that the work was conceived as a one-acter. There is a mention of a change of scene, from the market-place to where Hanne's cottage stands, outside the town. At the end, when the two lovers are united, they walk away over the brow of a hill. Their mingled voices gradually die away in the distance and Till is left alone. He picks up his bundle and makes off towards the sunrise, to mock alone. For good. One of Strauss's quiet endings.

The draft is written in ink, in a small, neat script on foolscap sheets. It includes a large number of alterations and emendations, not so much affecting the text itself as interpolating new material, new scenes, new psychological motivation. In the end the overall impression is that the number of philosophical elements gradually introduced in this way make the work confused and stilted. The material, which could have served for a small, satirical morality, became too extensive for the barely thirty-year-old composer to grapple with, after his experience with *Guntram* had taught him that the combination of poetic and musical gifts had not been bestowed on him as generously as on Wagner. The work needed a greater poet than he was himself, and in the end it may have been that insight which led him to abandon it . . .

There are no apparent associations between the symphonic poem *Till Eulenspiegels lustige Streiche* Op. 28 and Strauss's operatic draft. 'Schilda' became completely separated from the 'Till' theme, and continued to preoccupy Strauss as a new, independent project for some time to come. There are no surviving sketches for the 'Till' opera; there probably never were any, at that stage of working on the text. It is possible that musical ideas originally conceived in association with the opera were used in the symphonic poem, but there is no evidence one way or the other.

Two years later (1897) Strauss again worked on a plan for an opera about Schilda. A sheet of notes on the subject was found among his papers after his death; they are fragmentary in the extreme and amount to only a few suggestions for improvements to the text drafted by Count Ferdinand von Sporck. This opera was to be in five acts, and the plot, it seems, was to have some things (the emperor's visit) in common with Strauss's original 'Till' opera. Different names were to be used: the lovers were to be called Märten and Marlies, and the role played by Till appears to have been transferred to a character called the 'Jewish Pedlar'; naturally Till himself does not appear.

There is one more brief note in a sketchbook of 1897, relating to the third act of this project. The sketchbook even contains three brief musical motives: one in duple time, headed 'The deserted women of Schilda'; one headed 'The Pedlar', which changes from 3/4 to 4/4 and then to 6/8 time; and a third with no indication whatever as to its function.

There is no very clear evidence as to why this plan, too, came to nothing. Perhaps the text was unsatisfactory – besides, Strauss had other irons in the fire in 1897: the same sketchbook is filled with drafts of passages in *Don Quixote* and the first sketches for *Ein Heldenleben* . . .

Appendix 3

The songs of the Munich years, 1894–8

Op. 29: Three songs after poems by Otto Julius Bierbaum, for high voice with piano accompaniment:

Traum durch die Dämmerung	4 May 1895
Schlagende Herzen	7 June 1895
Nachtgang	7 June 1895

(Dedicated to the singer Eugen Gura)

Op. 31: Three songs (1–3) by Carl Busse for a (high) voice with piano accompaniment:

Blauer Sommer	1 January 1895
Wenn . . .	15 June 1895
Weisser Jasmin	24 June 1895

(Dedicated to Johanna Rauchenberger-Strauss on her wedding day)

Op. 31, no. 4, song by Richard Dehmel for voice and piano, with an optional part for viola:

Stiller Gang	30 December 1895

(Dedicated to Marie Ritter)

Op. 32: Five songs for voice and piano, after poems by Karl Henckell, Detlev von Liliencron, and from *Des Knaben Wunderhorn*:

Ich trage meine Minne (Henckell)	26 January 1896
Sehnsucht (Liliencron)	24 January 1896
Liebeshymnus (Henckell)	25 February 1896
O süsser Mai (Henckell)	28 March 1896
Himmelsboten an Liebchens Himmelbett (*Wunderhorn*)	3 January 1896

(Dedicated to the composer's wife)

o. Op. 90: words by Otto Julius Bierbaum:

Wir beide wollen springen	7 June 1896

Op. 33: Four songs for solo voice with orchestral accompaniment.

Verführung (Mackay)	begun 6 June 1896, finished 5 July 1896

Gesang der Apollopriesterin (Bodmann)
begun 7 July 1896, finished 1 October 1896
Hymnus (attrib. Schiller)
begun 25 December 1896, finished 5 January 1897
Pilgers Morgenlied (Goethe)
begun 21/22 December 1896, finished 25 January 1897

Op. 36: Four songs for high voice and piano:
Das Rosenband (Klopstock)
(sketched 10 September 1897) 22 September 1897
Für fünfzehn Pfennige (*Wunderhorn*)
(sketched 20 August 1897) 2 September 1897
Hat gesagt – bleibt's nicht dabei (*Wunderhorn*) 31 March 1898
Anbetung (Rückert) (sketched 8 January 1898) 24 March 1898
(No. 1 dedicated to Marie Riemerschmid-Hörburger; Nos 2–4 dedicated to the singer Raoul Walter)

Op. 37: Six songs for high voice with piano accompaniment:
Glückes genug (Liliencron) 8 February 1898
Ich liebe dich (Liliencron) 7 February 1898
Meinem Kinde (Falke) 7/8 February 1897
Mein Auge (Dehmel) (sketched 13 April 1898) 16 April 1898
Herr Lenz (Bodmann) 9 June 1896
Hochzeitlich Lied (Lindner) (sketched 1 February 1898) 30 March 1898
(Dedicated to the composer's wife on their son's birthday)

Op. 39: Five songs for voice and piano:
Leises Lied (Dehmel) (sketched 30 June/1 July 1898) 2 July 1898
Jung Hexenlied (Bierbaum) 31 May 1898
Der Arbeitsmann (Dehmel) 12 June 1898
Befreit (Dehmel) 1 June 1898
Lied an meinen Sohn (Dehmel) 8 July 1898
(Dedicated to Fritz Sieger)

During this period in Munich Strauss orchestrated five songs to which he had originally given a piano accompaniment:
Cäcilie (Op. 27, no. 2) (?)1897
Morgen! (Op. 27, no. 4) 20 September 1897
Liebeshymnus (Op. 32, no. 3) 27 September 1897
Das Rosenband (Op. 36, no. 1) 22 September 1897
Meinem Kinde (Op. 37, no. 3) (?)1897

Years later he orchestrated songs written during the Munich period:
Der Arbeitsmann (Op. 39, no. 3) 12 December 1918 (lost)
Mein Auge (Op. 37, no. 4) 5 September 1933
Befreit (Op. 39, no. 4) 10 September 1933
Ich liebe dich (Op. 37, no. 2) 3 August 1943

This period of special fecundity in Strauss's song-writing continued for several years after the move to Berlin. There, between 1899 and 1901, he wrote the Five Songs Op. 41 (texts by Dehmel, Mackay, Liliencron and Morgenstern), the Three Songs of older German poets Op. 43 (Klopstock, Bürger and Uhland), the Five Poems by Friedrich Rückert Op. 46, *Weihnachtsgefühl* o. Op. 94 (a re-working of a youthful setting of a poem by Martin Greif, published only in the magazine *Die Woche*), the Five Songs on poems by Otto Julius Bierbaum and Karl Henckell Op. 48, and the Eight Songs Op. 49 (Dehmel, Paul Remer, Henckell, Oscar Panizza, and *Des Knaben Wunderhorn* and *Elsässische Volkslieder*). After an interval of several years, Strauss published another set of songs with piano accompaniment in 1906, the Six Songs Op. 56 (poems by Goethe, Henckell, C. F. Meyer and Heine).

During the same period he wrote some more songs with orchestral accompaniment: the Two Songs for low voice and orchestra Op. 44 (*Notturno* by Dehmel and *Nächtlicher Gang* by Rückert), and Two Songs for bass voice and orchestra Op. 51 (*Das Thal* by Uhland and *Der Einsame* by Heine).

Chronological summary, 1864–98

1864	11 June: Richard Strauss is born in Munich.
1867	9 June: his sister Johanna (Hanna) is born in Munich.
1868	Begins piano lessons with August Tombo.
1870	Earliest compositions.
1872	Begins violin lessons with Benno Walter.
1874	Enters the Ludwigs-Gymnasium.
1875	Transfers to Carl Niest for his piano tuition. Begins to study composition with Friedrich Wilhelm Meyer (until 1880).
1881	First public performances: 14 March: première of the String Quartet Op. 2 (composed in 1880). 16 March: Cornelia Meysenheim includes three of his songs in a recital. 26 March: première of the D minor Symphony at a subscription concert of the Musical Academy, conducted by Hermann Levi. Festive March in E♭ major Op. 1 published.
1882	Leaves school in August. First attendance at the Bayreuth Festival, where his father is playing. 27 November: première of his Serenade for thirteen wind instruments Op. 7 in Dresden, under Franz Wüllner. 5 December: première of the Violin Concerto Op. 8 in Vienna, with Benno Walter as soloist and the composer at the piano.
1883	26 November: première of the Cello Sonata Op. 6 by Hans Wihan and Hildegard von Königsthal in Nuremberg. 26 December: première of the Suite for Wind Op. 4 by the Meiningen Court Orchestra under Hans von Bülow in Meiningen. Strauss plays in the Wilde Gung'l, the amateur orchestra conducted by his father (until 1885, with a break in the winter of 1883–4).
1883–4	Visit to Berlin (end of December to end of March).
1884	18 November: conducting début, directing his Suite for Wind Op. 4 at a matinée of the Meiningen Court Orchestra in Munich. 13 December: première of the F minor Symphony, given in New York by the New York Philharmonic Society, directed by Theodor Thomas.

1885 13 January: first German performance of the F minor Symphony, in Cologne under Franz Wüllner.

June: Strauss attends Bülow's piano course at the Raff Conservatory in Frankfurt.

8 December: première in Weimar of his prize-winning Piano Quartet Op. 13.

1885–6 On Bülow's recommendation Strauss works in Meiningen as Hofmusikdirektor (October to April). Meets Brahms and Alexander Ritter.

1886 8 March: première of the Horn Concerto Op. 11 in Meiningen.

April–May: Strauss visits Italy for the first time.

1 August: takes up appointment as third conductor (Musikdirektor) at the Court Opera in Munich.

1887 2 March: première of the symphonic fantasy *Aus Italien* Op. 16, directed by the composer at a subscription concert of the Musical Academy in Munich.

8 March: première of *Wandrers Sturmlied* Op. 14 in Cologne under the composer.

During the summer Strauss meets Pauline de Ahna in Feldafing.

8 and 11 December: first foreign conducting engagements, in Milan.

1888 May: visit to Italy.

30 September: *Don Juan* completed.

3 October: première of the Violin Sonata Op. 18 in Elberfeld, by Robert Heckmann and Julius Buths.

1889 June: Franz Strauss pensioned off from the Munich Court Orchestra.

July–August: Strauss attends the Bayreuth Festival as a musical assistant.

1 October: goes to Weimar as Kapellmeister to the Grand Duke of Saxe-Weimar-Eisenach.

11 November: première of *Don Juan* in Weimar under the composer.

18 November: *Tod und Verklärung* completed.

1890 31 January: performance of *Don Juan* in Berlin by the Philharmonic Orchestra under Hans von Bülow.

4 February: repeat performance at a 'popular' concert under Strauss.

8 June: performance of Alexander Ritter's one-act operas *Wem die Krone?* (première) and *Der faule Hans* in Weimar under Strauss.

21 June: premières of *Tod und Verklärung* and the *Burleske* (with Eugen d'Albert as soloist) under Strauss in Eisenach, at the congress of the Allgemeiner Deutscher Musikverein.

13 October: Strauss conducts *Macbeth* in Weimar.

Guest engagements to conduct in other German towns.

1891 May: serious bout of pneumonia. Convalescence in his uncle Georg Pschorr's villa in Feldafing.

August: in Bayreuth. Pauline de Ahna sings Elisabeth in *Tannhäuser*.

1892 17 January: *Tristan und Isolde* in Weimar.

29 February: Strauss conducts *Macbeth* in Berlin, with the Berlin Philharmonic Orchestra.

May: serious illness (pleurisy and bronchitis); convalescence in Munich, Feldafing and Bad Reichenhall. Returns to Weimar in late September.

November: leaves for Greece and Egypt.
24 December: finishes particello of *Guntram* in Cairo and begins scoring.

1893 In Egypt until the end of March; spends April and May in Sicily; returns to Munich at the end of July, and to Weimar in October.
5 September: finishes the score of *Guntram* in Marquartstein.
23 December: conducts the première of Humperdinck's *Hänsel und Gretel* in Weimar.

1894 20 January: sees Hans von Bülow for the last time, in Hamburg.
12 February: Bülow dies in Cairo.
10 May: première of *Guntram* in Weimar under Strauss, who makes his engagement to Pauline de Ahna public on the same day.
May–September: composes the Four Songs Op. 27 for Pauline. Conducts *Tannhäuser* at Bayreuth, with Pauline singing Elisabeth in alternate performances.
10 September: wedding takes place in Marquartstein.
1 October: Strauss takes up post of Kapellmeister in Munich.
30 October: appointed conductor of the Musical Academy subscription concerts (until 1896).

1894–5 Conducts the Berlin Philharmonic Orchestra for one season.

1895 6 May: finishes *Till Eulenspiegel*.
Summer holidays in Cortina d'Ampezzo.
5 November: première of *Till Eulenspiegel* in Cologne under Franz Wüllner.
16 November: first and only performance of *Guntram* in Munich, with Pauline Strauss-de Ahna as Freihild (as at the première in Weimar).

1896 The performance of Wagner and Mozart is Strauss's chief preoccupation at the Munich Opera; between now and 1898 he also promotes a number of premières of operas by contemporary German composers.
Numerous conducting engagements in Leipzig, Moscow, Cologne, Berlin, Brussels, Antwerp, Liège, Düsseldorf, etc.
24 August: finishes *Also sprach Zarathustra*.
September: holidays in Marquartstein.
October: visits Italy with Pauline; Hermann Levi retires and Strauss is promoted to Hofkapellmeister.
27 November: première of *Zarathustra* in Frankfurt under the composer.

1897 Concerts in Heidelberg, Amsterdam, Hamburg, Barcelona, Brussels, Paris, London.
Tours with Possart, performing *Enoch Arden*.
12 April: birth of his son, Franz Alexander.
Pauline and the child spend the summer in Marquartstein.
29 December: Strauss finishes *Don Quixote*.

1898 Concerts in Zürich, Madrid, Weimar.
8 March: première of *Don Quixote* in Cologne under Wüllner.
15 April: Strauss concludes a contract with the Berlin Court Opera, making him first Kapellmeister to the Court of Prussia from 1 October (as Karl Muck's colleague).
18 April: gives notice in Munich.

30 July: finishes short score of *Ein Heldenleben.*

Summer holidays in Marquartstein.

30 September: conference at which the Genossenschaft deutscher Tonsetzer is founded, with Strauss, Friedrich Rösch and Hans Sommer as the moving spirits.

18 October: farewell performance in Munich – *Fidelio.*

1 November: takes up Berlin appointment.

5 November: Berlin operatic début – *Tristan.*

1 December: finishes full score of *Ein Heldenleben* (first version of the ending).

27 December: finishes the second version of the ending of *Ein Heldenleben.*

List of works (up to 1898)

Works with definitive opus numbers

Op. 1	*Festmarsch* for large orchestra, E♭ major	1876
Op. 2	String Quartet, A major	1879–80
Op. 3	Five Pieces for piano solo	1880–1
Op. 4	Suite for thirteen wind instruments, B♭ major	1884
Op. 5	Piano Sonata, B minor	1880–1
Op. 6	Sonata for cello and piano, F major	1880–3
Op. 7	Serenade for thirteen wind instruments, E♭ major	1881
Op. 8	Concerto for violin and orchestra, D minor	1880–2
Op. 9	*Stimmungsbilder* for piano solo	1882–4
Op. 10	Eight Poems, from *Letzte Blätter* by Hermann von Gilm, for high voice with piano	1885
Op. 11	Concerto for horn, with orchestral or piano accompaniment, E♭ major	1882–3
Op. 12	Symphony for large orchestra, F minor	1882–4
Op. 13	Piano Quartet	1883–4
Op. 14	*Wandrers Sturmlied* (Goethe) for six-part choir and large orchestra	1884
Op. 15	Five Songs for middle and high voice with piano (Michelangelo, Schack)	1884–6
Op. 16	*Aus Italien*, symphonic fantasy for large orchestra, G major	1886
Op. 17	Six Songs (Schack) for high voice and piano	(?) 1885–7
Op. 18	Sonata for violin and piano, E♭ major	1887
Op. 19	Six Songs, from *Lotosblätter* by A. F. von Schack, for solo voice and piano	1885–8
Op. 20	*Don Juan*, tone poem (after Lenau) for large orchestra	1888
Op. 21	*Schlichte Weisen*. Five poems by Felix Dahn for high voice and piano	1887–8
Op. 22	*Mädchenblumen* (Dahn) for solo voice and piano	1886–8

Op. 23	*Macbeth*, tone poem (after Shakespeare) for large orchestra.	
	First version (unpublished)	1886–8
	Second version	1889–91
Op. 24	*Tod und Verklärung*, tone poem for large orchestra	1888–9
Op. 25	*Guntram*, in three acts (libretto by the composer)	1887–93
Op. 26	Two Songs (Lenau) for solo voice and piano	1891
Op. 27	Four Songs (Henckell, Hart, Mackay) for high voice and piano	1894
Op. 28	*Till Eulenspiegels lustige Streiche, nach alter Schelmenweise in Rondeauform für grosses Orchester gesetzt*	1894–5
Op. 29	Three Songs (Bierbaum) for high voice and piano	1895
Op. 30	*Also sprach Zarathustra*, tone poem (freely after Nietzsche) for large orchestra	1895–6
Op. 31	Four Songs (Busse, Dehmel) for (high) voice and piano (no. 4 has an optional part for viola)	1895–6
Op. 32	Five Songs (Henckell, Liliencron, *Des Knaben Wunderhorn*) for solo voice and piano	1896
Op. 33	Four Songs (Mackay, Bodmann, Schiller [attrib.], Goethe) for solo voice and orchestra	1896–7
Op. 34	Two Songs (Schiller, Rückert) for 16-part unaccompanied mixed choir	1896–7
Op. 35	*Don Quixote. Introduzione, tema con variazioni, finale.* Fantastic variations on a theme of knightly character for large orchestra	1896–7
Op. 36	Four Songs (Klopstock, *Des Knaben Wunderhorn*, Rückert) for high voice and piano	1897–8
Op. 37	Six Songs (Liliencron, Falke, Dehmel, Bodmann, Lindner) for high voice and piano	1896–8
Op. 38	*Enoch Arden* (Tennyson, *tr.* Strodtmann), melodrama with piano accompaniment	1897
Op. 39	Five Songs (Dehmel, Bierbaum) for solo voice and piano	1898
Op. 40	*Ein Heldenleben*, tone poem for large orchestra	1897–8

Works without opus numbers

The first two volumes of the thematic catalogue of Strauss's works, compiled by Erich Mueller von Asow and completed after his death by Alfons Ott and Franz Trenner (known as the Asow-Verzeichnis, AV for short), are devoted to the works with definitive opus numbers. The third volume lists all his other works, sub-divided into several categories but with one overall sequence of numbers. Within the categories the order is chronological. Surviving works without a definitive opus number (ohne Opuszahl) are numbered as o. Op. AV 1–150; the other categories (numbers AV 151ff.) include lost works, fragments, unrealized projects, arrangements of works by other composers and writings.

The following lists observe the AV numbering (except that, as in the body of the text, works with 'o. Op.' numbers are designated as, e.g., o. Op. 22 rather than o. Op. AV 22). The appearance of a work with an AV number higher than 150 in the first list indicates that the work in question has come to light since AV was completed. An asterisk indicates that the work has been published.

In the case of songs, where no details are given beyond the poet's name in parentheses, the work is for solo voice with piano accompaniment.

o. Op. 1	*Schneider-Polka* for piano	1870
*o. Op. 2	*Weihnachtslied* (Schubart)	1870
*o. Op. 3	*Einkehr* (Uhland)	1871
*o. Op. 4	*Winterreise* (Uhland)	1871
*o. Op. 5	*Waldkonzert* (Vogel)	1871?
*o. Op. 6	*Der weisse Hirsch* (Uhland) for contralto, tenor, bass and piano (voices alternating)	1871?
*o. Op. 7	*Der böhmische Musikant* (Platzsch)	1871?
o. Op. 8	*Herz, mein Herz* (Geibel)	1871
o. Op. 9	Moderato for piano, C major	1871?
o. Op. 10	*Panzenburg-Polka* for piano	1872
o. Op. 11	Slow movement for piano, G minor	1872
o. Op. 12	Two études for E♭ horn and E horn	1873?
*o. Op. 13	*Der müde Wanderer* (Hoffmann von Fallersleben)	1873?
*o. Op. 14	*Husarenlied* (Hoffmann von Fallersleben)	1873?
o. Op. 15	Overture to a Singspiel, *Hochlands Treue*, for orchestra	1872–3
o. Op. 16	Five small pieces for piano	1873?
o. Op. 17	Sonatina no. 1 for piano, C major	1874
o. Op. 18	Sonata no. 2 for piano, F major	1874
o. Op. 19	Sonata no. 3 for piano, B♭ major	1874
o. Op. 20	Composition for piano in C minor, with a section in the major	1874?
o. Op. 21	Fantasia for piano, C major	1875?
o. Op. 22	Two small pieces for piano	1875?
o. Op. 23	Movement with four-part harmony, B♭ major	1875?
o. Op. 24	Chorale movement with four-part harmony, B♭ major	1875?
AV 157	Concertante movement for piano, 2 violins and cello	1875?
o. Op. 25	Two songs (Eichendorff) for unaccompanied mixed four-part choir	1876
o. Op. 26	Four-part movement, D minor	1876
o. Op. 27	Four-part movement for piano, A♭ major	1876
o. Op. 28	Four scenes from a Singspiel for voices and piano	1876
*o. Op. 29	*Alphorn* (Kerner) for solo voice, piano and horn	1876?
o. Op. 30	Concert overture for orchestra, B minor	1876
o. Op. 31	Four liturgical movements for unaccompanied mixed choir	1877
o. Op. 32	Serenade for orchestra, G major	1877
*o. Op. 33	*Der Fischer* (Goethe)	1877

⋆o. Op. 34	*Die Drossel* (Uhland)	1877
⋆o. Op. 35	*Lass ruhn die Toten* (Chamisso)	1877
⋆o. Op. 36	*Lust und Qual* (Goethe)	1877
o. Op. 37	Piano trio no. 1, A major	1877
o. Op. 38	Sonata no. 1 for piano, E major	1877
o. Op. 39	Contrapuntal studies, 1 (exercises in imitation and canon)	1877–8?
⋆o. Op. 40	*Spielmann und Zither* (Körner)	1878
⋆o. Op. 41	*Wiegenlied* (Hoffmann von Fallersleben)	1878
⋆o. Op. 42	*Abend- und Morgenroth* (Hoffmann von Fallersleben)	1878?
⋆o. Op. 43	*Im Walde* (Geibel)	1878
o. Op. 44	Aria for Almaide, from the Singspiel *Lila* (Goethe), for soprano and orchestra	1878?
o. Op. 45	'Auf aus der Ruh', from *Lila* (Goethe), for tenor, mixed chorus and orchestra	1878
⋆o. Op. 46	*Der Spielmann und sein Kind* (Hoffmann von Fallersleben)	1878
⋆o. Op. 47	*Nebel* (Lenau)	1878?
⋆o. Op. 48	*Soldatenlied* (Hoffmann von Fallersleben)	1878
⋆o. Op. 49	*Ein Röslein zog ich mir im Garten* (Hoffmann von Fallersleben)	1878
o. Op. 50	Twelve variations for piano, D major	1878
o. Op. 51	Overture for orchestra, E major	1878
o. Op. 52	Introduction, theme and variations for horn and piano	1878
o. Op. 53	Piano trio no. 2, D major	1878
o. Op. 54	Contrapuntal studies, 2 (nine fugues)	1878–9
⋆o. Op. 55	*Waldesgesang* (Geibel)	1879
o. Op. 56	Introduction, theme and variations for flute and piano	1879
⋆o. Op. 57	*Aus alter Zeit*, small gavotte for piano	1879?
o. Op. 58	Andante for piano, C minor	1879?
o. Op. 59	*Skizzen*, five small piano pieces	1879
o. Op. 60	Grand sonata no. 2 for piano, C minor	1879
o. Op. 61	Romance for clarinet and orchestra, E♭ major	1879
o. Op. 62	Overture for large orchestra, A minor	1878–9
o. Op. 63	Scherzo for piano, B minor	1879?
⋆o. Op. 64	*In Vaters Garten heimlich steht ein Blümlein* (Heine)	1879
o. Op. 65	Contrapuntal studies, 3 (three fugues)	1879–80
⋆o. Op. 66	*Die erwachte Rose* (Sallet)	1880
o. Op. 67	Seven four-part songs for vocal quartet or unaccompanied mixed choir (Eichendorff, Gensichen, Böttger, Reinick)	1880
o. Op. 68	Two small pieces for piano	1879–80
o. Op. 69	Symphony for large orchestra, D minor	1880
o. Op. 70	Scherzando for piano, G major	1880
o. Op. 71	Fugue on four subjects for piano	1880

*o. Op. 72	*Begegnung* (Gruppe)	1880
*o. Op. 73	*John Anderson mein Lieb* (Burns)	1880
o. Op. 74	Chorus from *Elektra* (Sophocles) for male-voice choir and orchestra (only the *piano score survives)	1881
AV 168	*Ständchen* for piano quartet, G major	1881
o. Op. 75	Romance for cello and orchestra, F major	1883
*o. Op. 76	*Rote Rosen* (Stieler)	1883
o. Op. 77	Largo for piano, A minor	1883?
o. Op. 78	*Stiller Waldespfad* for piano (early version of Op. 9, no. 1)	1883
AV 174	Variations on a dance-tune by Cesare Negri for string quartet	1883
o. Op. 79	Song without words for orchestra, E♭ major	1883?
o. Op. 80	Concert overture for large orchestra, C minor	1883
o. Op. 81	Improvisations and *fugue on an original theme for piano, A minor (= AV 177)	1884
AV 178	*Festmarsch* for piano quartet, D major	1884
o. Op. 82	*Der Zweikampf*, polonaise for flute, bassoon and orchestra (probably not by Strauss)	1884?
*o. Op. 83	*Schwäbische Erbschaft* (Löwe) for unaccompanied male-voice choir	1884?
o. Op. 84	*Festmarsch* for orchestra, D major	1884–5
	Second version	1888
*o. Op. 84A	*Wer hat's gethan?* (Gilm)	1885
*o. Op. 85	*Burleske* for piano and orchestra, D minor	1885–6
*o. Op. 86	Incidental music for *Romeo and Juliet* (Shakespeare), for voices and small instrumental ensemble	1887
o. Op. 86A	Andante for horn and piano (from an unfinished sonata)	1888
o. Op. 87	*Festmarsch* for large orchestra, C major	1889
*o. Op. 88	*Ůtan svafvel och fosfor* for male-voice quartet	1889
o. Op. 88A	Fanfare for orchestra, for *Die Jäger* (Iffland)	1891
o. Op. 89	Four pieces for orchestra to accompany *tableaux vivants* (*no. 3, with the title *Kampf und Sieg*)	1892
AV 182	Two pieces for piano quartet (1. Arabischer Tanz; 2. Liebesliedchen)	1893
*o. Op. 90	*Wir beide wollen springen* (Bierbaum)	1896
o. Op. 91	*Licht, du ewiglich eines* (Schiller), for wind ensemble, large orchestra and female-voice choir	1897
–	*Richard Till Khnopff* for four-part mixed choir	1898

Lost compositions

AV 151	*Des Alpenhirten Abschied* (Schiller)	1872?
AV 152	Polka, waltz and other small piano pieces	1872?
AV 153	Sonatina no. 1 for piano, C major (probably a first version of o. Op. 17)	1873?

AV 154	Sonatina no. 2 for piano, E Major	1873?
AV 155	Sonata no. 5 for piano, E♭ major	1874
AV 156	Sonata no. 6 for piano, D major	1874
AV 158	*Für Musik* (Geibel)	1879
AV 159	*O schneller mein Ross* (Geibel)	1879
AV 160	*Die Lilien glühn in Düften* (Geibel)	1879
AV 161	*Das rote Laub* (Geibel)	1879
AV 162	*Frühlingsanfang* (Geibel)	1879
AV 163	*Hochzeitsmusik* for piano and children's band	1879
AV 164	*Die drei Lieder* (Uhland)	1879
AV 165	*Der Morgen* (Sallet)	1880
AV 166	*Immer leiser wird mein Schlummer* (Lingg)	1880
AV 167	*Mutter, o sing mich zur Ruh* (Hemans)	1880
AV 169	*Festchor*, with piano accompaniment	1881?
AV 170	*Geheiligte Stätte* (Fischer)	1881
AV 171	*Albumblatt* for piano (perhaps a study for Op. 9, no. 1)	1882
AV 172	*Waldesgang* (Stieler)	1882
AV 173	*Ballade* (Becker)	1882
AV 175	*Mein Geist ist trüb* (Byron)	1884
AV 176	*Der Dorn ist Zeichen der Verneinung* (Bodenstedt)	1884
AV 177	Improvisations, A minor (see o. Op. 81)	1884
AV 179	Cadenzas for Mozart's C minor Piano Concerto, K 491	1885
AV 180	*Rosenzeichen* (poet unknown; perhaps identical with o. Op. 76)	1885?
AV 181	*Bardengesang* (Klopstock), for male-voice choir and orchestra (first version)	1886

Unfinished compositions

AV 193	*Gute Nacht* (Geibel) (for soloist or for four-part mixed choir, and piano)	1871
AV 194	Two small pieces for violin and piano	1873
AV 195	Sonatina no. 4 for piano, E major	1873
AV 196	Counterpoint and harmony studies	1873–6
AV 197	Sonata no. 7 for piano, G minor	1873
AV 198	Sonata no. 8 for piano, G major	1873
AV 199	Sonata no. 9 for piano, C minor	1873
AV 200	Sonata for piano, E♭ major	1873
AV 201	Sonata movement for piano, D major	1873
AV 202	Sonatina for piano, E minor	1874
AV 203	Allegro assai for piano, B♭ major	1875
AV 204	String quartet movement, C minor	1875
AV 205	Four scenes from a Singspiel for voices and piano (supplementary to o. Op. 28)	1876
AV 206	*Der Kampf mit dem Drachen*, Singspiel for voices, piano and small ensemble	1876

AV 207	Overture for orchestra, E minor, for the opera *Ein Studentenstreich*	1876
AV 208	Overture for orchestra, E♭ major, for the opera *Don Sebastian*	1876
AV 209	Andante cantabile for orchestra, D major	1877
AV 210	Andante for orchestra, B♭ major	1877
AV 211	String quartet movement, E♭ major	1879
AV 213	Rhapsody for piano and orchestra, C♯ minor	1886
AV 221	*Lila*, Singspiel (Goethe)	1895

Arrangements of works by other composers

AV 183	*Franz Lachner*, Nonet for wind and string ensemble, arranged for piano duet	1880–1
*AV 184	*Joachim Raff*, two marches for orchestra from *Bernhard von Weimar*, arranged for piano duet	1885
*AV 184A	*Alexander Ritter*, overture to *Der faule Hans*, piano arrangement for the vocal score	1885
AV 185	*Richard Wagner*, additional material for *Die Feen*, Act II	1888
AV 188	*Alexander Ritter*, orchestration of *Nun hält Frau Minne Liebeswacht* (from *Liebesnächte* Op. 4, for soprano and piano)	1889
*AV 186	*Christoph Willibald von Gluck, Iphigenia in Tauris*, revision and new translation	1889–90
—	*Richard Wagner, Rienzi*, re-orchestration of introduction and trio (Act I) and finale (Act III)	1890
AV 187	*Franz Schubert*, orchestration of *Ganymed* (Goethe) (lost)	1897
—	*Ludwig van Beethoven*, orchestration of *Ich liebe dich* (Herrosee)	1898
AV 189	*Ludwig van Beethoven*, orchestration of *Wonne der Wehmut* (Goethe)	1898

Notes

1. Family background and early childhood

1 On Franz Strauss see Franz Trenner, 'Franz Strauss (1822–1905)', *Richard-Strauss-Jahrbuch* 1959/60 (Bonn, 1960).

2 Richard Strauss, 'Erinnerungen an Hans von Bülow', *Betrachtungen und Erinnerungen*, zweite, erweiterte Ausgabe (Zürich, 1957), pp. 183ff.

3 Richard Strauss, 'Erinnerungen an meinen Vater', *Betrachtungen und Erinnerungen*, pp. 194ff.

4 On Strauss's genealogy see Franz Seraph Kerschensteiner, 'Familiengeschichtliches um Richard Strauss und die Walter von Parkstein', *Zeitschrift für Musik*, 101:6 (Regensburg, June 1934); Adolf Roth, 'Wo Richard Strauss es her hat', *Der Zwiebelturm*, 4:9 (1950); Franz Trenner, 'Die Vorfahren von Richard Strauss', *Bayerland*, 56:6 (1954). Family trees in Kerschensteiner and in Franz Trenner, *Richard Strauss, Dokumente seines Lebens und Schaffens* (Munich, 1954).

5 The memoirs of Johanna von Rauchenberger-Strauss are quoted from her 'Jugenderinnerungen', *Richard-Strauss-Jahrbuch* 1959/60.

6 This information originates with the Munich genealogist Barbara Heller and was transmitted to the author by Dr Franz Trenner.

7 'Erinnerungen an meinen Vater', pp. 200–1.

8 There is a facsimile of the entry in Franz Trenner, *Richard Strauss, Dokumente seines Lebens und Schaffens*.

9 *Die Welt um Richard Strauss in Briefen* . . . ed. Franz Grasberger (Tutzing, 1967), no. 1.

10 'Aus Familiengeschichte und Jugendjahren', *Richard Strauss und seine Vaterstadt* (Munich, 1934), pp. 9–13.

11 'Aus meinen Jugend- und Lehrjahren', *Betrachtungen und Erinnerungen*, p. 203.

12 Reproduced in *Festschrift zur Jubiläumsfeier des Ludwigs-Gymnasium München* (Munich, 1949).

2. Boyhood

1 But cf. AV 3, pp. 1648–9: 'Addenda zu o. Op. 10'.

2 'Erinnerungen an meinen Vater', p. 199.

3 'Erinnerungen an meinen Vater', p. 201.

4 Max Steinitzer included some excerpts from Strauss's letters to Thuille in his biography of the composer, notably the irreverent remarks about Wagner.

Strauss's letters to Thuille appeared in full in 1969, but the complete correspondence, including Thuille's letters, appeared for the first time in 1980.

5 Alfred Steinitzer, 'Aus Familiengeschichte und Jugendjahren', p. 13.

6 On the Strausses and their involvement with the Wilde Gung'l, see *Hundert Jahre Orchesterverein 'Wilde Gung'l', Festschrift* ed. Franz Trenner (Munich, 1964, and *Münchner Orchesterverein Wilde Gungl, Festschrift* (Munich, 1974); the latter includes an extended version of Franz Trenner's article 'Richard Strauss und die "Wilde Gung'l"', first published in *Schweizerische Musikzeitung*, 90:8/9 (1950).

7 'Brief über das humanistische Gymnasium: an Professor Reisinger', *Betrachtungen und Erinnerungen*, pp. 128ff.

8 Arthur Seidl (1863–1928), writer on music, graduated from Leipzig University in 1887 with a dissertation on aesthetic theory, *On the Serene in Music*. He lived in Weimar from 1888 onwards, where he became the General Secretary of the 'Mutual Aid Society for the Mass Dissemination of Good Literature'. He published editions of some of Nietzsche's writings and letters, and it was through him that Strauss became acquainted with Nietzsche's philosophy. He was co-author, with Wilhelm Klatte, of the first independent publication about Strauss: *Richard Strauss, eine Charakterskizze* (Prague, 1896), and he published a collection of articles about Strauss as *Straussiana* (Regensburg, 1913). In 1917 he took over the editorship of the series *Die Musik* (Berlin), which Strauss founded in 1904.

9 On Hans Wihan (1855–1920), see J. B. Foerster, *Der Pilger, Erinnerungen eines Musikers* (Prague, 1955), N. B. Heran, *Hanuš Wihan* (Prague, 1947), and *Die Musik in Geschichte und Gegenwart*, 14.

10 The letter was first published by Arthur Holde. See his articles in *Neue Zeitschrift für Musik*, 119 (1958): 12, and in *Mitteilungen der Internationalen Richard-Strauss-Gesellschaft*, 19 (November 1958) and 20 (February 1959). The text of the song, by Carl Stieler, is as follows:

> Weisst Du die Rose, die Du mir gegeben?
> Der scheuen Veilchen stolze, heisse Schwester;
> von deiner Brust trug noch ihr Duft das Leben,
> und an dem Duft sog ich fest mich und fester.
>
> Ich seh Dich vor mir, Stirn und Schläfe glühend,
> den Nacken trotzig, weich und weiss die Hände,
> im Aug' noch Lenz, doch die Gestalt erblühend
> voll wie das Feld glüht um Sonnenwende
>
> Um mich weht Nacht, die kühle wolkenlose,
> doch Tag und Nacht, sie sind in eins zerronnen.
> Es träumt mein Sinn von Deiner roten Rose
> und von dem Garten drin ich sie gewonnen.

(Do you know the rose you gave me? The proud, hot sister of the shy violets? Its scent still bore life from your breast, and I breathed the scent in, hard and yet harder.

I see you before me, brow and temples glowing, neck proud, hands soft and white, spring still dwelling in the eyes, but the figure in full flower, as the meadow glows at the solstice.

Night, cool and cloudless, wafts about me, but day and night have run together in one. I dream of your red rose and of the garden where I won it.)

3. The Berlin winter, 1883–4

1 The annotations in Strauss's copies of Beethoven's symphonies were published by Franz Trenner in *Neue Zeitschrift für Musik*, 125 (1964), pp. 250–60. On Strauss's view of Bülow as a conductor of Beethoven cf. also *Briefe an die Eltern 1882–1906* (Zürich and Freiburg im Breisgau, 1954), pp. 60f.

2 On 20 July 1884 Bote & Bock courteously declined to publish the C minor Concert Overture o. Op. 80; in fact the work has never appeared in print.

3 Cf. Alfred Gotthold Meyer, *Reinhold Begas*, in the series *Künstler-Monographien*, ed. by H. Knackfuss (Bielefeld and Leipzig, 1897).

4 Cf. Alfons Ott, 'Richard Strauss und sein Verlegerfreund Eugen Spitzweg', *Musik und Verlag, Karl Vötterle zum 65. Geburtstag* . . . ed. Richard Baum and Wolfgang Rehm (Kassel, 1968).

5 'Erinnerungen an Hans von Bülow', p. 185.

4. Meiningen, 1885–6

1 Hans von Bülow, *Briefe und Schriften*, ed. Marie von Bülow, 8 vols (Leipzig, 1896–1908), 6, p. 367.

2 I am indebted to Gerhard Ohlhoff for acquainting me with the records of the duke's involvement with the orchestra.

3 *Wer hat's gethan?* was first published, with a facsimile of the autograph and a commentary by Willi Schuh, in 1974 (Tutzing).

4 J. A. Stargardt, Marburg, *Autographen-Auktionskatalog* 602 (1973).

5 Cf. the letters to his father of 19, 20 and 26 December 1885 in *Briefe an die Eltern*, and the letters exchanged between Strauss and Bülow, 19, 23 and 26 December 1885 (*Richard-Strauss-Jahrbuch* 1954).

6 The speech was later also printed in Hans von Bülow, *Briefe und Schriften*, 6, pp. 400f., and in Siegmund von Hausegger's biography of Alexander Ritter (Berlin, 1907), pp. 79f.

7 'Erinnerungen an Hans von Bülow', p. 183. See also W. Bollert, 'Hans von Bülow als Dirigent, Marginalien zur künstlerischen Laufbahn', *Melos/Neue Zeitschrift für Musik*, 1975:2.

8 The first biography of Alexander Ritter, which dwelt particularly on his early life, was by Friedrich Rösch; it appeared in twelve instalments in the Leipzig weekly *Musikalisches Wochenblatt* (30 December 1897 – 14 April 1898). In 1907 Ritter's son-in-law, the composer and conductor Siegmund von Hausegger, published another biography, in Strauss's series *Die Musik*. Cf. also Max Schillings, 'Alexander Ritter', *Redende Künste*, 2 (1896); Josef Hofmiller, 'Alexander Ritter, der Dichter und Komponist', *Die Gesellschaft*, 1894: 4; 1898:8 (both reprinted in *Versuche*, Leipzig, 1909); Hermann Teibler, 'Alexander Ritter', *Die Musik*, 1:4 (1902); Hans Joachim Moser, *Geschichte der deutschen Musik*, 3 (Stuttgart and Berlin, 1928), pp. 222ff.; idem, *Das deutsche Lied seit Mozart*, 2 (Zürich, 1927; rev. ed. Tutzing, 1968), pp. 180f.

9 Originally published by Huneker in *Overtones, a Book of Temperaments* (New York, 1904); published in German translation by H. Conrat in *Die Musik*, 4: 8 (special Strauss issue, 16 January 1905), p. 86.

10 At the time of this alleged conversation, reported by Abell in his book *Talks with Great Composers* (New York, 1955), Ritter was still alive.

5. At the Munich Opera, 1886–9

1 Franz Trenner published a survey of all the operas Strauss conducted in Munich in 'Richard Strauss und die Münchner Oper', *Blätter der Bayerischen Staatsoper*, 1963/4:3.

2 Lily Reiff-Sertorius, 'Jugenderinnerungen an Richard Strauss', *Neue Zürcher Zeitung*, 13 and 14 November 1949.

3 Richard Strauss, in a preface to *Das Bühnenwerk von Richard Strauss in den unter seiner Mitwirkung geschaffenen letzten Münchner Inszenierungen/The Stage Works of Richard Strauss produced in Munich with the assistance of the composer* (Zürich and London, 1954) [German text with an introduction in German and English by Willi Schuh].

4 *Die Welt um Richard Strauss in Briefen*, no. 33. In June 1888 Strauss composed a short passage for insertion in Act II of *Die Feen* (AV185).

5 These three letters were published for the first time in *Mitteilungen der Internationalen Richard-Strauss-Gesellschaft*, 46 (September 1965).

6 Jean Louis Nicodé (1853–1919), composer, pianist and conductor. He conducted the Philharmonic Concerts in Dresden 1885–8, as well as concerts organized by himself, with an emphasis on choral music. Cf. Alfons Ott, 'Richard Strauss und Jean Louis Nicodé im Briefwechsel', *Quellenstudien zur Musik. Wolfgang Schmieder zum 70. Geburtstag* (Frankfurt, London, New York, 1972).

7 Cf. Hermann Friess, 'Eine Bühnenmusik zu Shakespeares *Romeo und Julia*', *Richard-Strauss-Jahrbuch* 1959–60, pp. 51ff.

8 Franz Zagiba, *Johann L. Bella und das Wiener Musikleben* (Vienna, 1955).

9 'Vom melodischen Einfall', *Betrachtungen und Erinnerungen*, pp. 165f. Friedrich von Hausegger's *Die Musik als Ausdruck* (Vienna, [1]1885, [2]1887) 'is probably the most orthodox theoretical base of neo-romantic musical aesthetics, and the opposite pole to Hanslick's *Vom Musikalisch-Schönen* [Leipzig, [1]1854, [15]1922].' (*Riemann Musiklexikon*, Mainz, 1959).

10 From an article published in the *Dresdner Anzeiger* in 1934.

11 'Pauline Strauss-de Ahna', *Betrachtungen und Erinnerungen*, pp. 247–9.

12 Hans Bronsart von Schellendorff (1830–1913) was also a composer (chamber works, a piano concerto, orchestral works – some with chorus, a cantata *Christnacht*, an opera *Der Corsar*). His wife was the pianist and composer Ingeborg von Starck (1840–1913), whose opera *Hiarne* was performed in Weimar in 1891.

13 Eduard Lassen (1830–1914) was also held in esteem as a composer, especially of lieder. He held the post of Hofkapellmeister at Weimar from 1858 to 1895, as Liszt's subordinate for the first two years.

14 This letter was first published, together with five others from Strauss to Bronsart, by Gerhard Ohlhoff in an article 'Richard Strauss' Berufung nach Weimar', *Schweizerische Musikzeitung* 104:3 (1964), pp. 155ff.

15 See the section 'The campaign for musical copyrights' in the last chapter of this book. The address Strauss gave at Rösch's funeral was published in *Betrachtungen und Erinnerungen*, pp. 116–17.

16 Cf. August Göllerich, *Anton Bruckner, ein Lebens- und Schaffensbild*, ed. and completed by Max Auer, vol. 4, ii (Regensburg, 1936).

17 On Strauss's attitude to Bruckner see also 'Aus meinen Jugend- und Lehrjahren', p. 210, and Richard Strauss, *Briefwechsel mit Willi Schuh* (Zürich, 1969), pp. 47 and 49.

18 The first two verses run:

Geduld sagst du und zeigst mit weissem Finger
auf meiner Zukunft fest geschlossne Tür.
Ist die Minute, die da lebt, geringer
als jene ungebornen? Sage mir!

Kannst mit der Liebe du den Lenz verschieben,
dann borg ich dir für eine Ewigkeit,
doch mit dem Frühling endet auch das Lieben,
und keine Herzensschulden zahlt die Zeit.

19 Hans Fischer-Hohenhausen, in his 'novel from the master's youth' (*Richard Strauss, ein Tonkünstlerroman aus des Meisters Jugend*, Sontra, 1924), gives an account of Strauss's love for Dora – under the name of 'Frau Nitschak' – which is valueless as biography and a complete distortion of the truth in all essentials. Naturally the author did not know the three letters from Dora, which are published for the first time here. Cf. also the correspondence between Strauss and the present author, p. 117, where Strauss writes, after reading the book, 'the "artist's novel" is a brazen concoction, lies from beginning to end and badly invented lies at that. Biographically quite worthless! Waste-paper basket!'

6. The first years in Weimar, 1889–92

1 In his biography of Strauss, Steinitzer (p. 58) gives some examples of the conventions of the Weimar production which Strauss would no longer tolerate, such as Lohengrin's practice of taking a friendly stroll up and down the banks of the Scheldt with his young brother-in-law before stepping into his boat to leave.

2 Excerpts from Strauss's letter were published in 'Aus dem Jenseits des Künstlers', in *Gedanken eines Schauenden*, a posthumous collection of Friedrich von Hausegger's essays edited by his brother Siegmund von Hausegger (Munich, 1903).

3 See the facsimile edition of *Tod und Verklärung* published by the Wiener Philharmonischer Verlag (C. F. Peters).

4 This letter was brought to the author's attention by Dr Götz Klaus Kende of Vienna.

5 A reasonably full account of the operatic, theatrical and concert repertory in Weimar over the years is given in Adolf Bartels's *Chronik des Weimarischen Hoftheaters 1817–1907* (Weimar, 1908).

6 *Die Welt um Richard Strauss in Briefen*, no. 42.

7 Hans Sommer (1837–1922), whose real name was Friedrich August Zincken, first studied mathematics and took a doctorate at the university of Brunswick in 1858, but thereafter he worked as a conductor and composer. He worked in Weimar from 1888 to 1898, when he returned to Brunswick. Seven of his operas reached the stage, while excerpts from others were given concert performances. He also wrote works for orchestra and for male-voice choir. In 1898 he was a co-founder with Strauss, Rösch and Max Schillings of the Genossenschaft deutscher Tonsetzer. See E. Valentin, *Hans Sommer* (Brunswick, 1939).

8 K. H. Ruppel, *Grosse Stunden der Musik* (Munich, 1975), p. 214.

9 Roger Delage, 'Correspondance inédite entre Emmanuel Chabrier et Felix Mottl', *Revue de Musicologie*, 49 (Paris, July 1963).

10 Richard Strauss et Romain Rolland, *Correspondance. Fragments de Journal.* Cahiers Romain Rolland, 3 (Paris, 1951), p. 119. English translation, edited and annotated with a preface by Rollo Myers (London, 1968), p. 113.

11 Since the appearance of the German edition of the present book, the correspondence has been published in full (so far as it survives). The edition includes the correspondence between Strauss and other members of the Wagner family. Cosima Wagner – Richard Strauss, *Ein Briefwechsel*, ed. Franz Trenner, with Gabriele Strauss. Veröffentlichungen der Richard-Strauss-Gesellschaft, München, 2 (Tutzing, 1978).

12 Wilhelm Hertz (1835–1902) was a literary historian and man of letters in Munich. He wrote a number of modern versions of medieval French and German epic poems. His *Spielmannsbuch* (1886) is a collection of shorter poems and *contes* from the twelfth and thirteenth centuries.

13 'Vorwort zu *Intermezzo*', *Betrachtungen und Erinnerungen*, pp. 142–3.

14 Otto Zoff, *Great Composers through the eyes of their contemporaries* (New York, 1951), p. 424.

15 Reprinted in Alexander Berrsche, *Trösterin Musica* (Munich, 1942, [2]1949).

16 Steinitzer, *Richard Strauss*, pp. 154–5.

17 *Briefwechsel zwischen Cosima Wagner und Fürst Ernst zu Hohenlohe-Langenburg* (Stuttgart, 1937), p. 92.

18 Cf. Roland Tenschert, *Richard Strauss und Wien. Eine Wahlverwandschaft* (Vienna, 1949), p. 15.

19 'Aus meinen Jugend- und Lehrjahren', p. 214.

20 John Henry Mackay (1864–1933), though a Scot by birth, spent most of his life in Germany and wrote in German.

21 Max Stirner was the pen-name of Johann Kaspar Schmidt (1806–56). *Der Einzige und sein Eigentum* was first published in 1845 and re-issued in 1907, edited by H. G. Helms.

22 Short excerpts from this letter were published in the catalogue of a sale of autographs in 1960 (J. A. Stargardt, Marburg, *Autographen-Auktionskatalog* 549). The letter was published in full for the first time by Reinhard Gerlach, 'Richard Strauss: Prinzipien seiner Kompositionstechnik', *Archiv für Musikwissenschaft*, 23:4 (Wiesbaden, December 1966).

23 Victor Nessler's opera *Der Trompeter von Säckingen* (1884) was based on a nineteenth-century verse bestseller by J. V. von Scheffel. Mascagni's *L'amico Fritz* (1891) was first heard in Germany in 1892.

24 Reinhard Gerlach, 'Richard Strauss: Prinzipien seiner Kompositionstechnik'.

7. *Guntram* and the Egyptian winter, 1892–3

1 Wilhelm Klatte (1870–1930), a Berlin music critic and a pupil and friend of Strauss from the Weimar years onwards, wrote among other things introductions to *Ein Heldenleben* and *Symphonia Domestica*.

2 From *Die Musik*, 16:9 (June 1924). Klatte illustrated his article with a facsimile of a page from Act II, Scene I.

3 'Betrachtungen zu Joseph Gregors *Weltgeschichte des Theaters*', *Betrachtungen und Erinnerungen*, p. 178.

4 'Erinnerungen an die ersten Aufführungen meiner Opern', *Betrachtungen und Erinnerungen*, p. 220.

5 'Aus meinen Jugend- und Lehrjahren', pp. 211–12.

6 Eugen Schmitz, *Richard Strauss als Musikdramatiker, eine aesthetisch-kritische Studie* (Munich, 1907).

7 'Betrachtungen zu Joseph Gregors *Weltgeschichte des Theaters*', p. 179.
8 Strauss's travel diary was published in the *Richard-Strauss-Jahrbuch* 1954. Although the entry quoted here is dated 12 November, the sequence of entries ('Saturday 12 November . . . Sunday 13 November . . . Monday 12 [*sic*] November . . . Wednesday 16 November . . .') makes it look as if he visited Olympia on Tuesday 15 November, and wrote up his diary later. *Tr.*
9 Cf. C. V. Bock, *Pente Pigadia und die Tagebücher des Clement Harris* (Amsterdam, 1962).
10 Rudolf Louis's *Der Widerspuch in der Musik*, a dissertation for a Vienna degree, was published in Leipzig in 1892. It was substantially influenced by the ideas of Julius Bahnsen, a proponent of characterology and a philosophy derived from Schopenhauer.
11 The letters Strauss received from Levi and Ernst von Possart are in the Strauss Archives in Garmisch, while those he sent to them are in the Manuscript Department of the Bavarian State Library in Munich. Ernst von Possart (1841–1921) was appointed administrative director of the Munich Court Opera in January 1892 in succession to Karl von Perfall (who, however, remained intendant of court music); in 1895 Possart was made intendant-general of the royal theatres in Munich.

8. The last year in Weimar, 1893–4

1 J. A. Stargardt, Marburg, *Autographen-Auktionskatalog* 603 (1974).
2 Max Zenger (1837–1911), director of the Choral Society of the Musical Academy, professor of singing, music history and harmony at the Munich School of Music; historian of the Munich opera. He composed four operas; *Wieland der Schmied*, 1879, performed in Munich in 1881, was revised in 1895. There is no record of a performance in 1894.
3 Hermann Zumpe (1850–1903), Hofkapellmeister in Stuttgart from 1891, director of the Kaim Concerts in Munich from 1895, Generalmusikdirektor in Munich from 1900.
4 The document is in the archives of the Bavarian State Opera.
5 'Aus meinen Jugend- und Lehrjahren', p. 213.
6 J. A. Stargardt, Marburg, *Autographen-Auktionskatalog* 567 (1964).
7 J. A. Stargardt, Marburg, *Autographen-Auktionskatalog* 558 (1962).
8 'Erinnerungen an die ersten Aufführungen meiner Opern', p. 221.
9 *Wegbereiter grosser Künstler* (Wiesbaden, 1954).
10 *My many lives* (New York, 1948), pp. 136f.
11 *Und dafür wird man noch bezahlt. Mein Leben mit den Wiener Philharmonikern* (Vienna and Berlin, 1974).
12 'Erinnerungen an die ersten Aufführungen meiner Opern', pp. 220f.
13 Cf. Richard Strauss, *Briefe an die Eltern*, p. 197.
14 *Neue Zeitschrift für Musik*, no. 24 (13 June, 1894), p. 278. For a fuller account of the symphony's reception in Weimar see Henry Louis de la Grange, *Mahler*, Vol. 1 (New York, 1973), pp. 299–301, and Donald Mitchell, *Gustav Mahler, the Wunderhorn Years* (London, 1975), p. 201.
15 J. A. Stargardt, Marburg, *Autographen-Auktionskatalog* 580 (1967).
16 For the German text of Mahler's letter see *Die Welt um Richard Strauss in Briefen*, no. 74. Donald Mitchell gives a translation of the passages concerning the symphony (which also touch on the size of the Weimar orchestra) in *Gustav Mahler, the Wunderhorn Years*, p. 200.
17 J. A. Stargardt, Marburg, *Autographen-Auktionskatalog* 549 (1960).

18 *Erlebtes und Erstrebtes* (Vienna, 1937).
19 *Die Theater- und Musikwoche* 1:29 (Vienna, 1919), pp. 7ff.

9. The second term in Munich, 1894–8

1 Hans Schneider, Tutzing, *Katalog 199: 400 Musikerautographen* (1976).
2 J. A. Stargardt, Marburg, *Autographen-Auktionskatalog* 593 (1970).
3 Heinrich Bihrle, *Die Musikalische Akademie München 1811–1911* (Munich, 1911), p. 114.
4 Ibid., p. 144.
5 Ibid., p. 115.
6 *Richard Strauss und Franz Wüllner im Briefwechsel* (Cologne, 1963).
7 'Über Johann Strauss', *Neues Wiener Tagblatt*, 25 October 1925; *Betrachtungen und Erinnerungen*, p. 115.
8 I am indebted to Hans Schneider, Tutzing, for information about two letters Strauss wrote to Hermann Wolff, energetically resisting the latter's intention of not re-appointing him to conduct the 1895–6 season in Berlin, and referring to a telegram Wolff had sent him, confirming his engagement for two seasons (25 May and 8 June 1895). However, there was no legally binding contract.
9 Bihrle, *Die Musikalische Akademie*, p. 119.
10 'Erinnerungen an die ersten Aufführungen meiner Opern', pp. 221f.
11 'Aus meinen Jugend- und Lehrjahren', p. 215.
12 It originally appeared in the periodical *Kissinger Blätter*, which Kistler edited from his home in Kissingen, and was reprinted in Arthur Seidl's *Straussiana*, pp. 129–30. It begins 'Zu Possart, dem Tyrannen, schlich/*Richard*, den Guntram im Arme,/dass er der Musik sich erbarme . . .'.
13 J. A. Stargardt, Marburg, *Autographen-Auktionskatalog* 609 (1976), no. 753.
14 'Mozarts *Così fan tutte*', *Betrachtungen und Erinnerungen*, pp. 98–105.
15 'Die Münchener Oper', *Betrachtungen und Erinnerungen*, p. 119.
16 'Aus meinen Jugend- und Lehrjahren', pp. 214f.
17 *Die Welt um Richard Strauss in Briefen*, no. 83.
18 Strauss's telegram and this letter to Wüllner are to be found in their published correspondence, as is the programme note written by Wüllner.
19 See W. Mauke, *Till Eulenspiegels lustige Streiche Op. 28* . . ., Der Musikführer 103 (Stuttgart, 1896); this was incorporated in Herwarth Walden's *Richard Strauss, Symphonien und Tondichtungen*, Schlesingersche Musikbibliothek, Meisterführer 6 (Berlin and Vienna, 1908).
20 Tenschert, *Richard Strauss und Wien. Eine Wahlverwandschaft*, p. 17.
21 All but the last sentence is from the translation by Edward Lockspeiser in his book *Debussy, his Life and Mind* (Cambridge, 1978), vol. 2, p. 69. The whole of Debussy's review is in *Monsieur Croche et autres écrits*, ed. F. Lesure (Paris, 1971), pp. 43f.
22 A facsimile was printed in *Richard Strauss 1864–1949*, the catalogue of a commemorative exhibition mounted by the Theatermuseum, Munich, with the Bavarian State Opera (15 August – 26 September 1954), p. 11.
23 'Letzte Aufzeichnung', *Betrachtungen und Erinnerungen*, p. 182.
24 *Lebensskizze*, reprinted in *Straussiana*.
25 'Vom melodischen Einfall', pp. 163f. See also note 2 to Chapter 6.
26 Curt von Westernhagen, *Richard Wagner. Sein Werk, sein Wesen, seine Welt* (Zürich, 1956), p. 523.
27 Issued as nos 6 and 9 respectively in the series of Meisterführer published by

the Schlesingersche Buch- und Musikhandlung (Robert Lienau) in Berlin and by C. Haslinger (later Tobias) in Vienna.

28 Hans Schneider, Tutzing, *Katalog 199: 400 Musikerautographen* (1976).

29 Victor Schnitzler, *Erinnerungen aus meinem Leben* (Cologne, 1955), p. 108.

30 *Briefe an die Eltern*, p. 201.

31 Excerpts from Strauss's letters to Dupont, 1896–7, in J. A. Stargardt, Marburg, *Autographen-Auktionskatalog* 577 (1966).

32 Eduard Reeser, 'Richard Strauss und Alphons Diepenbrock. Ein Briefwechsel', *Mitteilungen der Internationalen Richard-Strauss-Gesellschaft* 32 (March 1962), pp. 5–8.

33 J. A. Stargardt, Marburg, *Autographen-Auktionskatalog* 534 (1957).

34 From Bierbaum's letter to Hermann Ubell, director of the Francisco Carolinum Museum in Linz, 14 May 1895.

35 See the excerpt from Rolland's diary, 9 March 1900 (p. 132 in Rollo Myers's translation; cf. Chapter 6, note 10).

36 Richard Strauss, '*Kythere*. Ballettentwurf', and W. Schuh, 'Das Szenarium und die musikalischen Skizzen zum Ballett *Kythere*', *Richard-Strauss-Jahrbuch* 1959/60, pp. 59–83 and 84–98.

37 Dehmel's letters to Strauss are in the Strauss Archives in Garmisch. The other letters by him quoted in the following pages were published in Richard Dehmel, *Ausgewählte Briefe aus den Jahren 1883–1902* (Berlin, 1923).

38 Conrad Ansorge (1862–1930), pianist and composer, whose settings of some of his poems Dehmel particularly liked.

39 'Gibt es in der Musik eine Fortschrittspartei?', *Betrachtungen und Erinnerungen*, pp. 14ff.

40 Cf. Jost Hermand, *Jugendstil, ein Forschungsbericht 1918–64* (Stuttgart, 1965); Hans Hollander, *Musik und Jugendstil* (Zürich, 1976); Horst Weber, 'Jugendstil und Musik in der Oper der Jahrhundertwende', *Die Musikforschung* 27:2 (1974), pp. 171ff.

41 The composer and conductor Oscar Fried, born in Berlin in 1871; a pupil of Engelbert Humperdinck, he helped prepare the vocal score of *Hänsel und Gretel* and wrote a popular orchestral fantasy on themes from that opera. Following his studies with Humperdinck, he spent three years in Munich, where he was friendly with Knut Hamsun, Frank Wedekind, the painter Thomas Theodor Heine and Bierbaum. Later he studied under Xaver Scharwenka, and held conducting posts in Berlin. In 1934 he emigrated to Tiflis, where he was musical director at the opera house, and he died in Moscow in 1942.

Fried made his name above all as a conductor of Mahler and Strauss. Among other things he conducted the world premières of Mahler's Second Symphony (though Strauss had previously conducted the instrumental movements) and Sibelius's Fourth. Of his compositions, his Nietzsche setting *Trunkenes Lied* (1904) attracted the most attention. He also set Dehmel's *Verklärte Nacht* for tenor and large orchestra, and the same poet's *Erntelied*; other works include a double fugue for large string orchestra, and an Adagio and Scherzo for thirteen wind instruments (inspired by Strauss's serenade and suite for the same forces). His portrait was painted by Max Liebermann and Lovis Corinth. Cf. Paul Stefan, *Oscar Fried* (Berlin, 1911), and the article by H. Becker in *Die Musik in Geschichte und Gegenwart*.

42 This letter is in the possession of the author.

43 'Aus meinen Jugend- und Lehrjahren', p. 215.

44 It was published in facsimile, with the Diez border, in Tutzing in 1968. This edition, which has an introduction by Alfons Ott, also includes facsimiles of the three autograph versions of the song. Cf. also Hans Hollander, *Musik und Jugendstil*, pp. 47–9.
45 J. A. Stargardt, Marburg, *Autographen-Auktionskatalog* 572 (1965).
46 J. A. Stargardt, Marburg, *Autographen-Auktionskatalog* 597 (1971).
47 'Pauline Strauss-de Ahna', pp. 248f.
48 J. Bahle, *Umgebung und Tat im musikalischen Schaffen* (Leipzig, 1939).
49 M. Marschalk, 'Gespräche mit Richard Strauss', quoted from Franz Trenner, *Richard Strauss, Dokumente seines Lebens und Schaffens.*
50 Cf. the comments by Franz Trenner in the complete edition of Strauss's songs (London, 1964).
51 'Aus meinen Jugend- und Lehrjahren', p. 203.
52 A. Orel, 'Richard Strauss als Begleiter seiner Lieder. Eine Erinnerung', *Schweizerische Musikzeitung* 92:1 (1952), pp. 12f.
53 'Meine Werke in guter Zusammenstellung', *Betrachtungen und Erinnerungen*, p. 160.
54 'Vom melodischen Einfall', p. 167.
55 A. Hahn, *Don Quixote Op. 35*, Der Musikführer 148 (Berlin, 1898); incorporated in H. Walden, *Richard Strauss.*
56 The letter is reproduced here by kind permission of Annette Zwinck-Papst, Altenau, Ober-Bayern.
57 J. A. Stargardt, Marburg, *Autographen-Auktionskatalog* 574 (1965).
58 E. Isler, 'Das Zürcherische Konzertleben seit der Eröffnung der neuen Tonhalle 1895 (1. Teil 1895–1914)', 123. *Neujahrsblatt der Allgemeinen Musikgesellschaft in Zürich auf das Jahr 1935* (Zürich, 1935), pp. 10f.
59 These passages are quoted in the translation by Rollo Myers (see above, note 10 of Chapter 6), pp. 120–1 and 136.
60 The letter to Hochberg is in *Die Welt um Richard Strauss in Briefen*, no. 104; the letter to the Munich intendancy, dated 18 April 1898, is in the archives of the Bavarian State Opera.
61 F. Rösch, *Ein Heldenleben, Tondichtung für grosses Orchester von Richard Strauss; Erläuterungsschrift, nebst einer umschreibenden Dichtung von E. König* (Leipzig, 1899). Cf. also W. Klatte, *Ein Heldenleben Op. 40*, Der Musikführer 154 (Berlin, 1899), incorporated in H. Walden, *Richard Strauss.*
62 'Letzte Aufzeichnung', p. 182.
63 W. Klatte, 'Aus Richard Strauss' Werkstatt', *Die Musik* 16:9 (1924).
64 First published, with facsimile, in *Musik und Dichtung, 50 Jahre Deutsche Urheberrechtsgesellschaft*, Gesellschaft für musikalische Aufführungs- und mechanische Vervielfältigungsrechte (Munich, 1953), pp. 14–16.
65 Oscar Bie (1864–1938), writer on music and the fine arts, editor of the monthly *Neue Deutsche Rundschau* (formerly *Freie Bühne*) and opera critic of the Berlin *Börsen-Courier.* He published the fugue of Strauss's Improvisations and Fugue on an original theme, in A minor, for piano o. Op. 81 as an appendix in his book *Das Klavier und seine Meister* (Munich, 1898, ^{2}1900). In 1906 he published *Die moderne Musik und Richard Strauss*, the third, much enlarged edition of which was issued in 1925 in the series *Die Musik*, with the title *Die neuere Musik bis Richard Strauss.* His monumental *Die Oper* (Berlin, 1913) reached its tenth edition by 1923. He wrote about Strauss's songs in *Das deutsche Lied* (1926). The correspondence between Bie and Hofmannsthal was published in the *Almanach Hugo von Hofmannsthal* (Frankfurt am Main, 1973).

66 From *Aus meinem Leben. Erinnerungen an Kindheit und Jugend.* Translated by Ré Soupault (Amsterdam, 1949), pp. 299f.
67 'Betrachtungen zu Joseph Gregors *Weltgeschichte des Theaters*', pp. 179f.
68 'Aus meinen Jugend- und Lehrjahren', p. 216.
69 The idea of *Die Künstlertragödie* owed something to a *cause célèbre* of the 1890s, the suicide for love of Karl Stauffer-Bern, painter, sculptor and engraver.

Bibliography

A short list of the principal sources of documentation drawn upon in the writing of the present book; other works are mentioned in the notes.

Bibliography

Richard Strauss-Bibliographie, Teil 1 (1882–1944): bearbeitet von Oswald Ortner, aus dem Nachlass herausgegeben von Franz Grasberger (Wien, 1964); Teil 2 (1944–64): bearbeitet von Günter Brosche (Wien, 1973) (Museion, Veröffentlichungen der Österreichischen Nationalbibliothek, N. F., 3. Reihe, 2)

Complete catalogue of works

E. H. Mueller von Asow, *Richard Strauss. Thematisches Verzeichnis.* 1 (Wien, 1955); 2 (Wien, 1959–62); 3, nach dem Tode des Verfassers vollendet und herausgegeben von Alfons Ott und Franz Trenner (Wien, München, 1966–74) (Cited as AV)

Letters

Hans von Bülow, *Briefe und Schriften*; herausgegeben von Marie von Bülow. 8 Bde (Leipzig, 1896–1908)

Hans von Bülow, Richard Strauss, *Briefwechsel*; herausgegeben von Willi Schuh und Franz Trenner. *Richard-Strauss-Jahrbuch* 1954 (Bonn, 1954). Translated into English by Anthony Gishford as *Hans von Bülow and Richard Strauss: Correspondence* (London, 1955)

Richard Strauss, *Briefe an die Eltern 1882–1906*; herausgegeben von Willi Schuh (Zürich, Freiburg i. B., 1954)

Die Welt um Richard Strauss in Briefen; in Zusammenarbeit mit Franz und Alice Strauss herausgegeben von Franz Grasberger (Tutzing, 1967)

Richard Strauss, Ludwig Thuille, *Briefe der Freundschaft 1877–1907*; herausgegeben von Alfons Ott (München, 1969)

Richard Strauss und Franz Wüllner im Briefwechsel; herausgegeben von

Dietrich Kämper (Beiträge zur Rheinischen Musikgeschichte, 51) (Köln, 1963)

Wolfgang Schneider, '57 unveröffentlichte Briefe und Karten von Richard Strauss in der Stadt- und Universitätsbibliothek Frankfurt/Main', in *Festschrift Hellmuth Osthoff zum 65. Geburtstag*; herausgegeben von Lothar Hoffmann-Erbrecht und Helmut Hucke (Tutzing, 1961)

Memoirs, documents, biographies, catalogues

Johanna von Rauchenberger-Strauss, 'Jugenderinnerungen', herausgegeben von Franz Trenner; in *Richard-Strauss-Jahrbuch 1959–60* (Bonn, 1960)

Richard Strauss, *Betrachtungen und Erinnerungen*; herausgegeben von Willi Schuh (Zürich, Freiburg i. B., 1949); 2. erweiterte Ausgabe (1957) (Cited from the second edition). Translated into English by L. J. Lawrence as *Recollections and Reflections* (London, 1953)

Max Steinitzer, *Richard Strauss* (Berlin, 1911)

Richard Strauss. Dokumente seines Lebens und Schaffens; Auswahl und verbindender Text von Franz Trenner (München, 1954)

Richard Strauss in Selbstzeugnissen und Bilddokumenten, dargestellt von Walter Deppisch (Rowohlts Monographien) (Reinbeck, 1968)

Katalog der Ausstellung Richard Strauss und seine Zeit, veranstaltet vom Freistaat Bayern und der Landeshauptstadt München. Bearbeitung des Katalogs: Signe von Scanzoni; musikwissenschaftliche Beratung: Franz Trenner (München, 1964)

Richard Strauss. Ausstellung zum 100. Geburtstag (Katalog), bearbeitet von Franz Grasberger und Franz Hadamowsky (Österreichische National-Bibliothek) (Wien, 1964)

Index

Note: RS *is used for Richard Strauss throughout*